Visual Basic 5
Development

John D. Conley III, Ashton Hobbs, Dan Horsefield,
Paul Kimmel, Anthony T. Mann, Lowell Mauer,
Mike McMillan, Mark Spenik, Rob Thayer

SAMS
PUBLISHING

201 West 103rd Street
Indianapolis, IN 46290

UNLEASHED

Copyright © 1998 by Sams Publishing

FIRST EDITION

International Standard Book Number: 0-672-31072-4

Library of Congress Catalog Card Number: 97-65470

2000   99   98   4   3   2   1

Interpretation of the printing code: the rightmost double-digit number is the year of the book's printing; the rightmost single digit, the number of the book's printing. For example, a printing code of 98-1 shows that the first printing of the book occurred in 1998.

Composed in Garamond and MCPdigital by Macmillan Computer Publishing

Printed in the United States of America

Publisher	*Joseph B. Wikert*
Executive Editor	*Christopher Denny*
Managing Editor	*Jodi Jensen*
Indexing Manager	*Johnna L. VanHoose*
Director of Software and User Services	*Cheryl Willoughby*
Director of Marketing	*Kelli S. Spencer*
Marketing Coordinator	*Linda B. Beckwith*

Acquisitions Editor
Sharon Cox

Development Editor
Fran Hatton

Software Development Specialist
John Warriner

Production Editors
Mary Ann Abramson
Susan Shaw Dunn

Copy Editors
Nancy Albright
Kimberly K. Hannel
Sean Dixon
Kate Talbot

Indexers
Greg Pearson
Kelly Talbot

Technical Reviewers
Ricardo Birmele
Vilas Ekbote

Editorial Coordinators
Mandie Rowell
Katie Wise

Technical Edit Coordinator
Lynette Quinn

Editorial Assistants
Carol Ackerman
Andi Richter
Rhonda Tinch-Mize
Karen Williams

Cover Designer
Jason Grisham

Book Designer
Gary Adair

Copy Writer
David Reichwein

Production Team Supervisor
Brad Chinn

Production
Marcia Deboy
Michael Dietsch
Cynthia Fields
Maureen West

Overview

Contents

Tell Us What You Think!

As a reader, you are the most important critic and commentator of our books. We value your opinion and want to know what we're doing right, what we could do better, what areas you'd like to see us publish in, and any other words of wisdom you're willing to pass our way. You can help us make strong books that meet your needs and give you the computer guidance you require.

Do you have access to the World Wide Web? Then check out our site at `http://www.mcp.com`.

> **NOTE**
>
> If you have a technical question about this book, call the technical support line at 317-581-3833 or send e-mail to support@mcp.com.

As the team leader of the group that created this book, I welcome your comments. You can fax, e-mail, or write me directly to let me know what you did or didn't like about this book—as well as what we can do to make our books stronger. Here's the information:

Fax: 317-581-4669

E-mail: `programming_mgr@sams.mcp.com`

Mail: Christopher Denny
         Comments Department
         Sams Publishing
         201 W. 103rd Street
         Indianapolis, IN 46290

PART

I

Object-Oriented Programming: What It Means to You

Understanding Object-Oriented Programming

by John D. Conley III

IN THIS CHAPTER

CHAPTER 1

Object-oriented programming (OOP) is the process of developing *code* (one to many lines of programming instructions) based on well-defined design models. A *design model* is a graphical illustration that represents different views of objects, their parents (from which they derive functions and property variables), and their interaction with each other. For instance, a class model would be a static design model, because it gives you a view only of relationships among classes, with no illustration of behavior. A *sequence diagram* is a dynamic model, as it shows how objects communicate with each other to carry out some system behavior expected by the user (or human actor).

With all the hoopla surrounding the emergence and increasing acceptance of object-oriented programming—in a technological world still dominated by older technologies and concepts that struggle against this emergence—you might be saying to yourself, "Oh, boy!" Every week it seems, some new technology pronounces itself the guardian of true object orientation: Java/Corba, C++/Visual Basic/ActiveX/MFC, and so on. Databases are becoming more object-relational, and even the Internet is moving away from CGI (Common Gateway Interface) services to more robust distributed object architectures that use Corba, Java Servlets, ActiveX Server Pages, and Oracle Web Application Server cartridges. Seasoned object-oriented practitioners merely fold useful technologies into their minds with little learning curve. But if you aren't accustomed to object technology (and all its children) and your skills still depend on more classical predecessor technologies, the steady rise of object-oriented programming is a frightening, unknown menace, threatening to overturn the status quo. "What does this all mean?" you might ask.

Significant shifts in technology always seem to increase fear. Yet when you stop to think about this, the fear is usually derived from not knowing the technology from the ground up. Many books explain OOP very well, but new groups of professionals aren't aware of some of these other books. Many OOP novices are trying to learn OOP through Visual Basic. The aim of this chapter is to help you, the OOP apprentice, understand Visual Basic and OOP properly. Looking at the term *properly*, you shouldn't necessarily infer that other books and periodicals have done a poor job. In fact, the idea here is that because OOP is relatively new for the Visual Basic (VB) community—OOP has been around since the 1960s—many newcomers to VB, and some seasoned VB developers, haven't had the opportunity to understand OOP and object technology in general.

Coping With Old Programming Practices

To understand how to use object-oriented programming, you need to re-evaluate past programming habits. (If you're very experienced in OOP, you should still read this section because it could give you information to pass to other programmers trying to migrate to OOP.) Without a proper object-oriented background, many novices to OOP in Visual Basic have taken their old on-the-fly, VB3-style code; wrapped them in generic, vague class modules (if class modules are used at all); and considered themselves OOP experts. When it comes time to re-use such "classes," the "expert" has to re-engineer the class code all over again from scratch. Further, other enterprise development teams usually find they can't use such classes because of poorly defined class interfaces, which are the public functions (methods) and state variables (properties) of each class. (Interfaces and protocols are discussed later in the section "Understanding How Objects Talk to Each Other.")

On-the-fly programming (OTFP) is the easiest, most popular, and worst programming style that ever mutated in the software development community. In OTFP, almost every function or sub is public and global, with hardly any concern for the arguments in the argument list. At least with structured analysis and structured design (SA/SD) methods, there's some thought in creating well-defined functions and subs (although SA/SD isn't recommended either). OTFP is a horrid mutation that evolved as a knee-jerk reaction by programmers responding to the high-pressure deadlines placed on them by sometimes unreasonable project schedules, which themselves are creatures of OTFP and chaotic project planning.

Even in small, cozy environments where everyone knows your name, OTFP tends to waste money in the long run because the resulting program depends extremely on both the original programmer and the technology it uses at a point in time. This means two things:

- If the programmer dies or quits, the often-undocumented program will have to be rewritten, and the person who rewrites it will likely use OTFP.

- If the technology becomes extinct or greatly changes (which happens very often), the programmer will have to surf through the entire code base to find every reference to members of that technology (API calls, object references, and so on).

OTFP generally leads to what's commonly referred to as *spaghetti code*. In OTFP, all code is perfect to the original programmer, but beauty is in the eyes of the beholder. Developers working in a small, informal environment can get away with OTFP because it takes far less analysis and design, and it may provide increased job security for them (but provides little benefit to their clients). But they still face the risk of changes in technology and user requirements now and in the future. In OTFP, they'll have to change every line of code (which can be hundreds or thousands of lines of code) to accommodate such changes, whereas in OOP they would simply go to the object responsible for that technology or behavior.

What's more, OTFP doesn't lend itself at all to team development. The common response to this statement is, "Well, there are only two developers: Frank and I. We know each other well, and we just get together and hammer out our differences." This seldom (if at all) works, because this represents on-the-fly design (OTFD), on which no program architecture is based. Without some organized methodology for the programming process, one person's spaghetti-code style takes precedence over that of the other programmer. This is especially damaging where that other programmer is timid and non-confrontational, which is a prevalent behavior in the programming community. More often than not, one of these programmers usually quits or in some way is removed from the project when things go wrong (and with OTFP, they very, very often do).

Going From OTFP to OOP

OOP—and the entire object-oriented process—provides much better and longer-lasting benefits to every project stakeholder (programmer, manager, end user, and so forth). Visual Basic 5.0 offers enough features to ease the implementation of object technology and formal object-oriented analysis and design methodologies. Team development is also easier in VB5, and facilitates the creation of projects that incorporate each developer's individual talents. The VB project, in any corporate enterprise, also reflects the competence of its team members. In this context, a project represents a group of people who have as a common goal the development of an application or suite of applications to carry out some business process.

OOP lends itself well to project team development because of the capability to break down a complex system into simpler *abstractions* (understandable portions). Each abstraction, then, can be more easily assigned to team members for better definition and construction (application design and programming). Without an OOP background, VB novices tend to revert to traditional waterfall techniques (if that much) as soon as the first problem comes up in the project. This chapter will help you avoid these mistakes by helping you embrace OOP.

Understanding Classes

Please read the following carefully. (You may want to read it twice if you're still grappling with some OOP terms.) Some real-world explanations follow: A *class* is an *abstract entity* (a "thing" that carries out a subset of your user's requirements) with *behavior* (a set of functions or methods) and *attributes* (variables or properties that identify the class).

You might say that a class is a template. Some people call classes *cookie cutters* because they can be *instantiated* (brought into your computer's memory) into real-world, *concrete* objects (with which you can interact in your application). Although this is true of *concrete classes*, this isn't completely true of *every* class. This might help you grasp the concept of classes: They define the behavior and identity of objects. Some classes can also define the behavior and identity of other classes. Such classes are called *base classes*. Base classes that can't be instantiated into concrete objects are called *abstract classes*. Objects implement (provide runtime code logic for) the behavior of concrete classes. Because VB isn't as object-oriented as C++ (not C) or SmallTalk, your classes will generally be concrete or *pure virtual* (its child class must implement every one of its methods).

The Visual Basic Class

The structure of a class is physically deployed differently in different programming languages, although the structure itself remains the same. For instance, in C++ the class is usually separated into a header file and an implementation file. The header file contains the definitions of the class itself, including its methods and properties (attributes). The implementation file shows how each member (method or property) of the class is used in a particular domain. In Visual Basic there's no such distinction—at least not quite (more on this in a moment).

The Visual Basic class module is virtually the same as the familiar form module, which, unfortunately, has led to some confusion over the difference between the graphical user interface form object and the class module. For example, a form module and a class module can implement the interface of another class. To *implement* an interface means that the implementing class assumes the public responsibilities of the supplier class and executes them for its clients. You can add properties and methods to both form and class modules. Both have a constructor and destructor. For the form, the constructor would be Form_Load and the destructor would be Form_Unload. For the class, the constructor would be Class_Initialize and the destructor would be Class_Terminate. As a result, many VB developers place lots of business logic code into forms that make it very difficult to try to reuse such code, much less partition the application into packages that can then be assigned to individual developers on a team.

Figure 1.1 shows what a typical class module looks like.

FIGURE 1.1.

An example of a class module in Visual Basic 5.0.

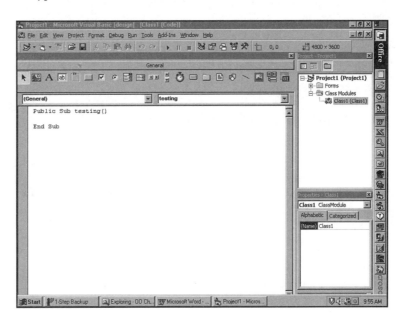

A class module consists of the definition and implementation of class members. These class members are methods (functions or subs) and properties (variables that hold information about an object whose type is defined by a class). You define the name and return type (if any) of the methods as well as the data types of the properties. The members of a class can be defined as *public*, *private*, or *friend*.

The keyword Public means that the member is accessible to all modules within the project and in external projects. If you don't want any members to be public outside the project, you can insert the following line of code in the general declarations section of the class module:

```
Option Private
```

The keyword `Private` means that the member is accessible only by other members within the class module. This doesn't mean that you can't pass the value of the private property to an external module via a public property or method, however. Suppose that you have a class called `CheckingAccount` with the members in Listing 1.1.

Listing 1.1. Class members for the class `CheckingAccount`.

```
'General Declarations
Private mvarpAccountNumber As String

Public Property Get pAccountNumber() As String
    pAccountNumber = mvarpAccountNumber
End Property

Public Property Let pAccountNumber(ByVal sNewAccountNumber As String)
    mvarpAccountNumber = sNewAccountNumber
End Property
```

Because the property `pAccountNumber` is publicly available, the value of the private module-level variable `mvarpAccountNumber` is also publicly available, even though the variable `mvarpAccountNumber` itself isn't.

An Example of Class Identities

Now for some interesting illustrations to help you remember the object-oriented concepts just discussed. The automotive industry provides one of the best analogies for understanding OOP. Think of Chrysler, for example, as a base class for the Sebring class of cars. When you go to the Chrysler dealer, you don't actually buy a Sebring; you buy an instance of a Sebring. The instance you buy is the actually Sebring object because you can interact with it by driving it. The Sebring class, then, is a concrete class, because with it, the assembly plant knows how to make real-world cars (objects) based on the Sebring class specification (behavior and attributes).

The Sebring class has methods (ways of operating), such as ignite the engine, turn the wheels, go in reverse, open doors, adjust speed, and so on. Its properties (or variables or attributes) would be color of car, current speed, maximum speed, light status (off or on), wheel base, wheel size, window tint, cabin style (sunroof, convertible, hardtop), retail price, and so on. When you instantiate a Sebring class into an actual Sebring car, these properties will be filled in by an *actor* (a human who interacts with a system, such as the automotive engineer or assembly person in this example). Thus, the color might be red, window tint might be dark smoke, wheel size might be 15 inches, price might be $25,000, and so on. These values, taken together, represent the current *state* of the object.

Did you notice something interesting about the Sebring class? Some of its methods and properties have something in common with other cars Chrysler makes. For instance, all Chrysler cars ignite engines, turn wheels, go in reverse, open doors, adjust speed...you get the idea. They also each have color, wheel size, wheel base, and so on. So rather than re-create these methods and properties for each subclassed car (*subclass* means child class), Chrysler created abstract classes such as the H-Body cars, among others.

This is a good example of what an abstract class means—that is, you can't go to the Chrysler dealer and pay for an H-Body car itself. The dealer, instead, will recommend H-Body car classes, such as the Sebring. The point is that H-Body is abstract (and actually might be pure abstract because certain behavior might be implemented at a finer level for certain subclasses). The Sebring class implements the H-Body abstract class. These entities are more important to the automotive engineer and repair technician than the buyer (end user). The actual Sebring car is the object that you, the end user, buys.

Creating VB Classes

By now, you should be fairly comfortable with the idea of classes and objects and their interrelationships. Let's revisit the Visual Basic development environment, where you'll actually create a class and observe simple class behaviors at runtime.

There are four ways (also known as *development processes*) to create classes in Visual Basic:

- Add class module
- Add class from template
- Create class in Class Builder
- Create class in modeling tool

In the Learning, Professional, and Enterprise Editions of Visual Basic, you can simply add a new class module from the standard menu or the right-click pop-up menu, or by adding a new class module based on an existing class template in the \Vb\Template folder. In the Enterprise Edition, you can use the Class Builder to create a new class, or use a modeling tool such as Rational Rose/VB or Microsoft Visual Modeler. Because these tools are principally for automating the design phase/iteration of the object-oriented software engineering life cycle, they are discussed in more detail in Chapter 3, "Implementing Object-Oriented Design in VB5." For this chapter, you'll concentrate on the first three development processes.

NOTE

In Chapter 3, you learn how to elaborate the requirements, which are embodied in use cases, into a robust set of design models. These design models will provide the foundation for your programming code.

By far the easiest way to add a new class to a Visual Basic project is simply to add a new class module from the menu. Two implementations of this process support this menu-driven approach:

■ Choose Project | Add Class Module from Visual Basic's menu bar. A dialog box like the one in Figure 1.2 appears. Double-click the Class Module icon to add a new class module with the default name `Class1` to your project.

FIGURE 1.2.

The Add Class Module dialog box lets you add a new class from scratch or create a new one based on one of the class templates shown.

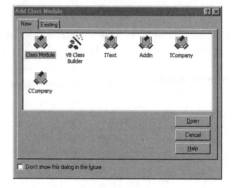

■ Right-click in the Project browser on the right side of the Visual Basic IDE. From the pop-up menu, choose Add Class Module. At this point, you'll also see the Add Class Module dialog box (refer to Figure 1.2). Double-click a Class Module icon, or double-click an existing class template icon.

Building Classes With the Class Builder

If you have the Enterprise Edition of Visual Basic 5.0, you can create classes from scratch by using the helpful Class Builder. This utility is a distant cousin of Rational Rose/VB and Microsoft Visual Modeler in that it lets you build classes automatically.

If you haven't done so already, make sure that Class Builder is available in the Add-In Manager. To make it available, choose Add-Ins | Add-In Manager from the menu. You should see the Add-In Manager dialog box (see Figure 1.3). Select the VB Class Builder Utility by clicking the checkbox associated with this item. Click OK.

FIGURE 1.3.

The Add-In Manager dialog box.

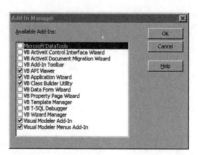

Now you're ready to work with Class Builder. To start this utility, choose Add-Ins | Class Builder from the menu. You should see the Class Builder utility applet, as illustrated in Figure 1.4.

FIGURE 1.4.

Class Builder automates the process of creating classes in Visual Basic 5.0 Enterprise Edition.

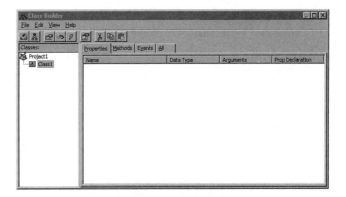

> **NOTE**
>
> If you've already added a class module to the existing project before with Class Builder, you'll get an informational dialog box telling you that the hierarchy of the classes created outside Class Builder can be incorporated into Class Builder. You also can't edit or delete members of that class; if you get this dialog box, just click OK. You can always edit existing classes manually or in design tools such as Rational Rose/VB or Microsoft Visual Modeler.

Not only does Class Builder automate the process of creating classes, it also tracks the hierarchy of all your classes and collections. Class Builder also generates the skeleton code you'll need to implement the classes and collections, including the properties, methods, and events of each class.

> **NOTE**
>
> An event is similar to a method or function but is triggered by a human actor or an external system action. VB Forms have built-in events; however, you can raise your own events as well by using the RaiseEvent keyword. Events are particularly useful in ActiveX controls, where you can allow programmers who use your controls to execute code for your control's event. Thus, when your control's event occurs, your programmer/user can insert code that handles further processing.

On examining the Class Builder utility environment, notice the Windows Explorer-style visual representation. The standard menu and toolbar reside at the top. Below these two is the Object Model pane on the left and the Properties, Methods, and Events pane on the right.

The Object Model pane visually displays the hierarchy of the classes and collections in your project. If you click a class in this pane, you make it available for editing in the Properties,

Methods, and Events pane. In turn, if you click a method, property, or event in the Properties, Methods, and Events pane, that class member becomes available for editing.

Classes and collections that existed in previous sessions of the Class Builder can't be edited or deleted in later Class Builder sessions. Therefore, you must manually edit or delete unwanted members that survived (or persisted) beyond a previous Class Builder session.

You also can modify classes by using drag-and-drop features to, for instance, copy a property from one class to another.

The Menus

The Class Builder menus are pretty standard. The File menu offers these commands:

- If you choose New, you have the option of adding a new Class, Collection, Property, Method, or Event.
- Delete deletes the currently selected class, collection, or class member.
- Rename allows you to rename the currently selected class, collection, or class member.
- Update Project immediately updates your current Visual Basic project with the new or modified class and collection information.
- Exit closes Class Builder after saving current changes not previously updated.

The Edit menus commands are as follows:

- Cut and Copy work in the same manner as in any other Windows application. You can cut or copy the currently selected item.
- Choosing Properties displays an edit dialog box for the currently selected class or class member.

The View menu seems insignificant at first:

- Choosing Toolbar toggles the display of the toolbar on (displayed) and off (not displayed). Simple enough.
- Then there's the Options command. Choosing Options brings up the unimposing, yet far-reaching, Class Builder Options dialog box (see Figure 1.5).

FIGURE 1.5.

The Class Builder Options dialog box has far-reaching implications for your Visual Basic project.

The Class Builder Options dialog box gives you two code-generation options:

- Include Debug Code in Initialize and Terminate Events
- Include Err.Raise in All Generated Methods

Because these two options are tightly coupled with development processes related to the design phase/iteration of the project life cycle, detailed discussions of them will be taken up in Chapter 3, "Implementing Object Oriented Design in VB5." For now, suffice it to say that these options let you track the creation and destruction of objects at runtime, as well as trap and raise errors in each object's methods at runtime. Keep in mind that objects are runtime copies (or instances) of classes.

The Help Menu is pretty straightforward, allowing you to access information about the Class Builder utility. The Toolbar contains shortcut buttons for operations already available in the menu.

The Properties, Methods, and Events Pane

In the Properties, Methods, and Events pane on the right, you see an index tab control with four tabs: Properties, Methods, Events, and All.

The Properties page (see Figure 1.6) shows all the properties of the currently selected class. With this page, you can add, edit, and delete properties from the currently selected class. The container area is broken into four columns: Name, Data Type, Arguments, and Prop Declaration. The Name column shows the name of a given property in the class. The Data Type column shows the data type for each property. The Arguments column lists the arguments that the property method accepts (remember that properties in VB can be implemented as property methods). Finally, the Prop Declaration column indicates what type of operation the property method performs on the property.

FIGURE 1.6.

The Properties page allows you to add, edit, and delete properties from the currently selected class.

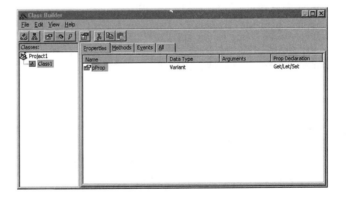

In the Prop Declaration column, the Get type allows clients (other modules needing a value or service) to access the current value or object reference of the property. The Let type allows other modules to change the value of the property. The Set type is similar to the Let type, but other modules can change only the object reference (assuming that the class property was declared as `Variant` or `Object`). If you right-click anywhere in the tab container area, a pop-up menu lets you add a new property, delete a property, perform cut and copy operations, rename the property, or display the detailed specification of each property. Figure 1.7 shows a detailed specification, which is housed in the Property Builder dialog box (double-clicking the tab container area also brings up this dialog box).

FIGURE 1.7.

The Property Builder dialog box allows you to view and modify information about each property.

By using the Property Builder, you can specify a name and data type for the property, as well as declare its scope (`Public Property`, `Friend`, or `Public Variable`). You also can specify that one of the properties is the default property of the class. This way, when you use the class variable in code like any other variable, the value of the default property is set or returned.

Similar to the Properties page is the Methods page, which displays the methods of the currently selected class or collection. You access the Method Builder the same way you access the Property Builder. By using the Method Builder (see Figure 1.8), you can perform the same maintenance operations as with the Property Builder. The key differences are these:

- You can specify a return value. The absence of a return value means that the method is a `Sub`; otherwise, it's a `Function`.
- You can specify that the method is a `Friend`, meaning that it's available to all modules in the project, but not to modules outside the project.
- You can specify whether the current method should be the default method. Therefore, if you used the class variable in code as you would a function or a sub, the VB compiler would use the default method to provide the requested service.
- There's no Prop Declaration column.

FIGURE 1.8.

The Method Builder dialog box.

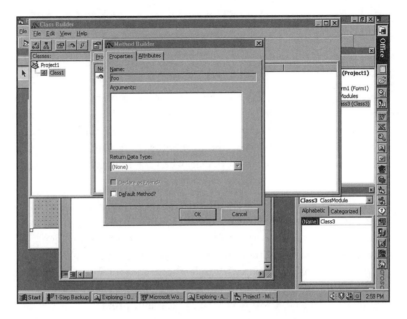

The Events page in the Class Builder shows all the events associated with the current class or collection. Because the creation and maintenance of events is the same as that of methods, double-clicking in the Events page brings up the Method Builder as well. The difference between a method and event, as far as Class Builder is concerned, is that an event doesn't require a data type.

Finally, the All page combines the specifications for every member of the current class into one convenient list.

> **TIP**
>
> To convert a class in the Object Model Pane into a collection, right-click the class and choose Set As Collection. To convert back to a class, right-click the collection and choose Set As Class.

Understanding the Difference Between Collections and Aggregations of Objects

In the earlier discussion of Class Builder, you came across the word *collection* and probably wondered what it meant. *Collection* is synonymous with the expression *object collection*, which is, well, a collection of objects. It's a list of objects, you might say. By that, you should understand that a collection is, itself, an object. This object holds references to other objects and has methods for adding, accessing, and deleting objects within it. An *aggregation* of objects is an object that contains other objects, but not in the sense of a collection. In VB, a collection is a nice object mechanism for manipulating the similarly named methods and properties of objects.

There's no sense of context (the purpose for using objects in the collection) other than for bundling them into a collection for easy access. With aggregation, though, there is a reason that the aggregate object owns other objects. That is, the subordinate object (contained object) serves the aggregate object. This means that the contained object's lifetime depends on the lifetime of the aggregate and, in particular, when the aggregate needs to use the contained object. Whew! Let's look at the Sebring example again.

On further examination, have you noticed that the Sebring is actually composed of other objects? These objects would include tires, the steering wheel, the door, the window, brakes, headlights, and so forth. You can say that the Sebring is actually an aggregate of all these objects. A collection of objects—sometimes hard to identify in the real world—might include the fuse box under the dashboard (another object) or under the hood (another object). Each fuse is an object and the fuse box is a collection of fuse objects. A key method of each fuse would be to shut down a car's electrical system to avoid major problems.

Understanding How Objects Talk to Each Other

Objects talk to each other via their *interfaces* and the *protocols* set forth by the designer for carrying out this communication. Together, the public methods and properties of an object are the object's *interface*. This interface implements the protocol of the object. A *protocol* is the way two objects communicate with each other to properly carry out some goal. One object's interface, then, dispatches a message (a value, an object, or a pointer to a method) to another object's interface. Again, the Sebring class will help you understand the interface.

In the fuse box collection, you find that the fuses all interact with the same interface to relay electrical information to the engine (another object) and, in particular, the engine's computer (another object, which means the engine is also an aggregate). The fuse box itself has an interface to each electrical component in the Sebring. The protocol—I hope I'm not stretching this one—is based on each component expecting a particular voltage of electricity from the fuse to shut itself down when a problem is encountered. (By *problem*, I mean the state of the car. The subsequent activities related to this state would be the *scenario* for defining how these objects interact.) If the voltage isn't the one the component expects, the electrical message is ignored.

In case that wasn't pretty straightforward, look at another example: the automatic transmission as an object. The usual methods for an automatic transmission are park, drive on normal roads, drive on slight incline, drive on steep incline, drive in reverse, and free the transmission (neutral). Together, these selections (which would be modeled as methods in your models) represent the interface to the transmission. The protocol (gulp!) would involve the nasty details of the stick interaction with the gears, among others.

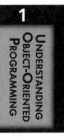

Let's try another one to be safe. The air conditioner (AC) is an object whose behavior is to supply cool air when the weather is hot. Of course, you don't simply tell the AC to turn itself on and adjust itself to your favorite temperature (but that technology isn't far off). The high-level protocol calls for you to push some buttons and slide some levers. These buttons and levers are the interface to the AC. When you push the On button, this event (pushing the button) causes the button's internal methods to send an electric message to the AC to power up. Another way of explaining this power-up process is that the AC initializes itself to default (factory) settings or your previous settings. Other real-world objects have interfaces as well, such as your thermostat in your home, your microwave, and your television, among others. In turn, these objects interface with the object that supplies electricity. Because the real world operates with classes, objects, and their interfaces, why not use the same paradigm in software development?

Understanding Subsystems

Now that you've become familiar with the nature of classes and objects, it's time to introduce another concept. In the real world—or, at least, in theory—every object is made up of smaller objects. For instance, humans are made up of organs. In turn, these organs are made up of atoms. Likewise, a well-developed object-oriented application is made up of *subsystems* (categories or packages), which are then made up of classes (or sometimes other subsystems).

Understanding Application Subsystems

A *subsystem* is a portion of the application/system that carries out a particular behavior of the entire application/system. This portion can consist of classes as well as other subsystems. For instance, you may design a portion of an application to manage all database retrieval and storage (database subsystem), another to handle the display of data in and retrieval of data from GUI objects (GUI subsystem), and yet another to handle printing and reporting (printing and reporting subsystem).

Returning to the Sebring example, the portion of the car (synonymous with application for these purposes) that handles the movement energy is the engine. The portion that handles stopping is the braking mechanism. The portion that handles air flow and temperature control is the AC. The engine *subsystem* (or portion), in turn, consists of different classes of nuts and bolts, as well as other subsystems, such as timing, cooling, starting (ignition), and so on. On another front, your house would be like an application, and it, too, has portions. Your house contains the AC subsystem (with some abstract similarities to the car's AC), the plumbing subsystem, the electrical subsystem, and so forth. Get the idea? The class, then, would be the atomic unit (assuming that it didn't contain other objects).

Understanding How Subsystems Talk to Each Other

Subsystems (or categories) communicate with each other through classes that play the role of subsystem brokers or subsystem interfaces. If you think of subsystems as themselves being big classes, a class within it would act as an agent on behalf of the subsystem. You might also view this agent class as a diplomat or an ambassador. When two subsystems need to communicate, one dispatches an ambassador's envoy (a message) to the other's ambassador. The hosting ambassador validates the message (making sure that it's not a package bomb that might blow up and crash your system). If the ambassador feels the message has come to the right place, it passes the message to the proper "authorities" (some delegated class) for further processing.

Suppose that a user of your application enters some personal information such as name, address, and the like, and clicks a button to save the data to the database. At a high level this is simple: Just save it to the database straight from the form (or dialog box, for you C++ transplants). However, in OOP, the process is more method-based and organized. The form actually sends a message (packed with the data) to the GUI subsystem, which in turn separates the data from the form objects (for example, the text box, list box, and so on) and sends it to a business layer class. This business layer class places each data value to its attributes (or properties), does some business rule processing, and, if all is okay, sends this data to the database subsystem, which then saves this data to the database. (This process of saving class property values to the database is called *persistence*, because the data persists beyond the current application session.) When you finish reading this book, you should be able to think your applications through in this manner. The idea of breaking an application down into subsystems (or packages) is the core of object-oriented methods.

Summary

In this chapter, you learned about the fundamentals of object-oriented programming. At the center of this evolving technology is the class and its runtime equivalent, the object. A class is a design-time template that determines the behavior of objects based on it. Visual Basic 5.0 lets you perform OOP with the class module and the Class Builder utility.

The fundamental idea to keep in mind in OOP is that the Visual Basic project must be viewed as a round trip (or cyclical), evolving process, meaning that the artifacts of the analysis phase need to be synchronized with the design and construction phases. Without this periodic synchronization process, you lose the ability to trace the classes you create from the analysis phase down to the construction phase. This is where novice object-oriented programmers—sometimes bent on being impatient—get confused and discouraged. When requirements need to be revisited, novice OO programmers can't tell what class corresponds to what entity in the analysis and design models. Traceability, then, is of fundamental importance to object-oriented programming.

Chapter 2, "Using Analysis to Discover Your VB5 Classes," shows how to discover and evolve class identities from user requirements (even if you'll be the primary user) into a use-case model that's the foundation for the class model. Chapter 3, "Implementing Object-Oriented Design in VB5," shows how to iterate or evolve from the analysis phase to the design phase—meaning

that you'll learn how to evolve your project from the use-case model to the class and object models. Design tools such as Class Builder, Rational Rose/VB, and Microsoft Visual Modeler are discussed. Finally, Chapter 4, "Making Classes Communicate With Each Other," teaches you how to make classes and subsystems (class packages) communicate with each other properly. This communication-building process is also associated with the software development (or construction or programming) phase of the project life cycle.

Using Analysis to Discover Your VB5 Classes

by John D. Conley III

IN THIS CHAPTER

For many, many years, programmers have gone through each project life cycle with that enduring and possibly natural enmity toward the analysis process. The standard thinking is that users don't know how to tell programmers what they want. There's some real-world precedence for this. Before business management gurus Edward Deming and Peter Drucker came on the scene, most companies tended to ignore their customers' wishes. (For that matter, monopolies have a natural tendency to ignore customers; just look at your utility monopolies' response to your billing complaints.) Then Deming and Drucker came along and led the corporate world toward more customer- and employee-oriented management styles.

Likewise, the three leading figures of the object-oriented software development paradigm shift—Jacobson, Booch, and Rumbaugh—have also led the software development community toward not just object-oriented styles of programming, but also toward user-oriented project-planning. The central idea behind object-oriented systems is that objects respond to stimuli (events or messages) from human users at some point in the execution of a business process. The response of the objects can incorporate issuing client requests to other external systems, which would make the client system an actor as well (more on actors in a moment).

The important thing to understand about the analysis process is that you must be able to effectively translate the initial set of user requirements into a model or foundation on which your design models can be implemented properly.

Realizing the Importance of Using Analysis Methods

Now that you've gone through the object-oriented programming aspects well enough (and there will be plenty more on OOP later), step back a bit and look at analysis. You might think that analysis is a waste of time. Most newcomers to OOP bring this attitude with them from the procedural, non-OOP world, where most application logic is hammered out in the isolated world of programmers. Many programmers favor this approach because they each decide for themselves how the application will work and avoid getting caught up in "analysis paralysis." If there's a team of developers, each programmer simply splits the user requirements document up, codes in isolation, and returns to the team to argue over who's wrong or right, what should be hacked out of the current release, and so on. As complex as user requirements are, such an approach is prone to errors, and users usually end up with a system they didn't really ask for or want. To get along with (or out of sympathy for) the developers—who probably stayed up all night for a whole week—users say something like, "Yeah, this looks okay. I guess I can do my work with this." Then a month later, the application is seldom used or is full of major bugs, and users return to the manual way of doing business.

The same thing applies when you try to implement OOP without doing the necessary analysis. In general, *analysis* is the process of bringing a discovered solution to a business problem from being a dream in someone's head to being a high-level, often user-friendly, model that can evolve into an application. Using a *methodology* (an organized, disciplined system for doing something) or carrying out some goal(s) to cultivate this evolutionary process is crucial. Perhaps the most widely used methodology for this process is the objectory method introduced by Ivar Jacobson. It's also generally known as object-oriented software engineering (OOSE). With it, you initiate a process of identifying what the current problem is, and then help users identify how they see themselves using the proposed application.

Building the Foundation for Object-Oriented Analysis

To effectively use OOA to create a solid, easily extensible system with Visual Basic, you should understand the overall approach to the project. This means that every activity you expect to undertake in creating a Visual Basic application really should be reasonably thought out beforehand. That is, you as a Visual Basic developer must concede that you usually (but not quite always) wear many hats on a typical development project, and these hats (or roles) should be identified and specified. Further, in performing these roles, you perform tasks related to each role. These tasks, too, must be identified and quantified. The roles you'll be concerned about in this chapter are *requirements gatherer*, *object-oriented analyst*, and *architect*.

The Requirements Gatherer

As a requirements gatherer, you typically interrogate end users, business managers (or domain experts), project managers, or anyone else who had the misfortune of getting in your way. Usually, there's no predefined method for gathering requirements; you simply draft an almost ad hoc list of questions centered around mouse clicks instead of business processes executed by users. A requirements model is never generated. However, as a requirements gatherer, that's exactly what you want to do. A requirements model captures all the ways users will use the Visual Basic system you're developing. Figure 2.1 shows what a typical requirements model might look like.

In gathering requirements, you ask yourself and users how the system will be used. Initial requirements gathering activities should shy away from inquiries such as, "When you click such and such a button onscreen, what happens next?" In this respect, you're forcing users to think like a machine rather than like a business process user. Requirements gathering centered on graphical user interface (GUI) objects tends to focus on the semantics of clicking controls and moving a mouse as opposed to the business tasks to be accomplished by users. When centered on GUI objects, requirements gathering misses the big picture, and the foundation for further analysis activities becomes inefficient as the project evolves.

FIGURE 2.1.

A requirements model (the initial use-case model) visually illustrates how end users will use your system from a business processing perspective.

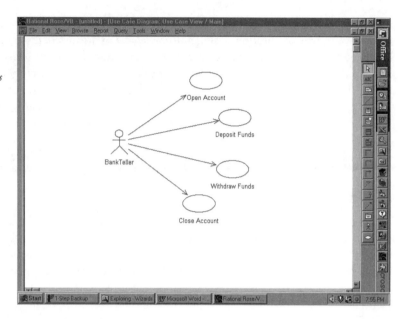

The Object-Oriented Analyst

As analysts in traditional projects, some developers are probably driven by a simplified focus of just making the gathered requirements fit into the Visual Basic project. They may have quickly come up with a list of global or form-level functions that seem to roughly provide the expected system behavior; analysis is over in a heartbeat. Analysis is really design, if that. Then, VB developers grab some programming tips and tricks books and start forcing this analysis and design model of functions to incorporate their ideas of how the system should work. This fly-by-the-seat-of-your-pants development is also known as *programming by chaos*.

Quoting noted object-oriented methodologist Jim Rumbaugh, analysis "is the careful examination of the requirements for a system with the intent of understanding them, exploring their implications, and removing inconsistencies and omissions." Effective analysis builds on the mature (or evolved) requirements model by evolving an ideal structure that endures throughout the life cycle of the proposed system under development. At this stage—which can and should be revisited throughout the project lifetime—you don't want to try to come up with a detailed list of low-level functions that you want to rush out the door without a concern for how users use the system and how the system responds to those uses. You should understand *low-level* to mean that you don't want to worry about which database you're using, which neat trick you want to incorporate to make a MAPI or Windows API call, or similar notions. This is important because changes in vendors, for instance, may necessitate changes in tools or even operating systems. Also, by avoiding the detailed design stuff early in the analysis iteration, you can better concentrate on the activities of the business process user, as the analysis model is far simpler than the design model(s).

A mature design model provides direct guidance to your programming activities, whereas an analysis model provides a solid foundation for your design model(s). Figure 2.2 gives you an example of a simple analysis model. Note how it's focused only on high-level business objects when initially created. In the User Services layer of the proposed system (on the left), a Teller Interface class encapsulates your understanding of the interaction between users and the system. Don't worry about button clicks or mouse movements. Also, there are Checking Account and Savings Account classes to encapsulate your knowledge of each account type. You could have easily had one class called Account at this stage; it just depends on your particular environment. Finally, a Persistence class is responsible for storing and retrieving information created or modified in your application, as well as getting rid of information users want destroyed. In the analysis model, it's called *persistence* rather than *database management* because you don't know whether the data repository will be a database or a flat file (regular text or binary file you store anywhere on your hard disk). That kind of detail is left to your design model.

FIGURE 2.2.
A service model.

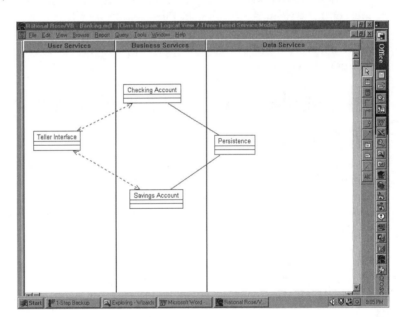

The Architect

As pseudo-architects in a traditional shop, developers actually do what you might call detailed analysis, but it's really ad hoc design. Such developers take the list of functions and manipulate each one to communicate with another. Often, the code for some functions is hidden behind GUI control events (for example, Command1_Click) for the sake of convenience (ad hoc spaghetti architecting). Such architecting makes it extremely difficult to trace application behavior back to the requirements and analysis models.

Object-oriented architects work with analysts—and sometimes are the analysts—to ensure that project team members can trace the names of business objects between the requirements and analysis models. (Architects also work with designers and developers, but your concern is analysis here.) In traditional analysis, end users and managers assumed that programmer-analysts had a near perfect understanding of the problem domain (the business functionality being addressed by the proposed system under development). This inevitably led to a decreased emphasis on analysis and more emphasis on construction activities. Because the actual gap in knowledge between the users and developers isn't adequately addressed in the beginning, all members and beneficiaries of the project teams (also known as *stakeholders*) experience higher-than-necessary levels of stress as the project approaches its deadline.

The driving assumption behind object-oriented analysis, on the other hand, is that the analyst doesn't have anywhere near a perfect knowledge of the problem domain. That is, a gap in knowledge is acknowledged between the users ordering the application being developed and the manufacturers of that system. Hence, all stakeholders in the project tend to depend on the round-trip development process offered by object-oriented technology to help bridge this gap over time. Given that, the benefits to Visual Basic developers of the object-oriented analysis approach become quite clear.

Implementing the Use-Case Methodology for Your Environment

When Microsoft released version 5 of Visual Basic Enterprise Edition, the Visual Basic language moved into the ballpark of object-oriented languages (though only as a "pinch hitter" perhaps, but close enough). The capability to create classes whose interfaces can be implemented by other classes and the capability to create complex ActiveX components have really made Visual Basic a serious commercial development tool. Added to that is the automation of the design process with the help of Microsoft Visual Modeler. However, Visual Basic doesn't help with the discovery and identification of classes, actors (human and external system), and use cases. To compound this situation, the vast majority of VB programmers don't have object-oriented backgrounds, which leaves them resorting to traditional, familiar ways of developing software.

The reality is that solid system architectures and class structures never evolve or mature properly when programmers don't know how to discover use cases and classes. As a result, Visual Basic 5.0, which is actually a very strong development tool for implementing object technology, will continue to be maligned as you try to pour new wine into old wineskins. The rest of this chapter explains how to use object-oriented analysis techniques—specifically, use-case identification and modeling—to help you successfully initiate the analysis process and give Visual Basic a better name in the development community.

The Problem Statement

Figure 2.1 showed what a simple use-case model looks like. Of course, the elements within a use-case model don't appear out of thin air. As an analyst, you would have asked users, "In what ways do you want to use the system?" Users, who are tellers within your development context, respond that they want to be able to open an account, close an account, deposit new funds, and withdraw funds. Notice how each phrase includes important verbs, such as *open, close, deposit,* and *withdraw*. These verb phrases, as I'll call them, taken together with the actor (the teller in this case) performing these verbs, provide the context for your system. When formally written down, these phrases become the core verbiage in what's called the *problem statement*. In other words, a problem statement provides the formal boundaries (or context) for the foundation of your Visual Basic application. Figure 2.3 gives you an idea of what a problem statement might resemble.

FIGURE 2.3.

By using a word processor such as Microsoft Word, you can document a plain-English, high-level description of how users will use the system you'll be developing with Visual Basic.

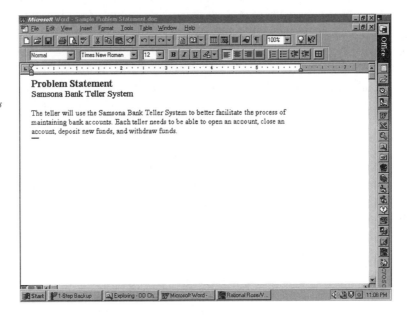

After the problem statement matures over one or more sessions with domain experts (users knowledgeable about a particular area of concern), you'll want to peruse this document to identify key nouns and verbs. The list of nouns actually becomes a list of candidate actors or classes, whereas the list of verbs (and sometimes *gerunds*—nouns that are verbs ending with *-ing*) provides a candidate list of business processes carried out by actors (human users of your system or external systems that interact with your system) or methods that are members of a candidate class. By *candidate* I mean that these nouns and verbs require further analysis to determine whether they're truly actors, classes, business processes (or use cases), or methods.

Based on your problem statement, the following list represents candidate classes and actors:

> teller
>
> Samsona Bank Teller System
>
> process
>
> bank accounts
>
> account
>
> funds

In analyzing each actor/class candidate, you or your team determine whether each item is meaningful to the context of the business processes being addressed by your system. By *meaningful*, I mean something that represents a role performed by users or external system, helps users produce a product or service that's valuable to the business, and isn't too vaguely defined within the context of your proposed system. For instance, the word *funds* is too vague for your system because the tellers don't actually create the funds or place the funds into your system. They merely accept funds from customers or give funds to them. Therefore, funds would be eliminated from your list of candidates.

If you're a beginning or intermediate object-oriented practitioner (an architect, analyst, designer, programmer, and tester), you might wonder why customers aren't mentioned in the problem statement. Answer: Customers aren't in the context of your system (your problem domain). The exchange of cash or information between tellers and customers is outside the scope of the Samsona Bank Teller System. Recall from the problem statement that your system helps tellers "better facilitate the process of maintaining bank accounts." Tellers interface with their customers in one context and then interface with your system in another. Your problem domain is concerned only with the second context. Business process engineering (designing and modeling of business tasks/responsibilities and events at the enterprise or workgroup level) would likely be concerned with the first context.

Going back to your list of candidate actors/classes, you'll notice that *teller* is obviously an important noun because this is the main actor who will use your system. Therefore, you now have your first actor. The noun *Samsona Bank Teller System* is actually the name of your system and, at this point, you assume that you don't have a compelling reason to model it as an actor or a class; therefore, it's no longer a viable candidate.

> **NOTE**
>
> In general, you wouldn't model your application as an actor or class. However, it can be modeled as a subsystem or package if it's part of a suite of applications.

The noun *process* actually describes the act of maintaining accounts and is too vague to be anything more than a description to help express the problem statement more fully for system developers. It, too, is no longer a viable candidate.

The noun *bank accounts* is a collection of accounts. Within the sentence that mentions bank accounts, you see that they're the main objects that tellers manage and, hence, as a collection, would be a strong candidate for a class (or more specifically, a collection class).

> **TIP**
>
> If you discover pluralized nouns in your problem statement that are significant to your system, make a design note to yourself that such nouns might be a collection class, which Visual Basic supports. An example of pluralized nouns are nouns with an s at the end that imply more than one of something.

Along similar lines, the noun *account* is also a strong candidate for a class. Again, the noun *funds* doesn't fit within your context, and is therefore not a viable candidate. Now you have a more streamlined, definitive list of actors and candidates that resembles Table 2.1.

Table 2.1. Strong candidate actors and classes.

Noun	Type
Teller	Actor
Bank Accounts	Class
Account	Class

You may also want to journal the reasons for rejecting a candidate. This list becomes an artifact that might help future stakeholders on this project or other enterprise projects so that even the process of analyzing requirements and use cases can be reused throughout the company.

Your candidate list of verbs and verb phrases would include

> use
>
> facilitate
>
> maintaining bank accounts
>
> needs
>
> open an account
>
> close an account
>
> deposit new funds
>
> withdraw funds

Again, you want to model only meaningful verbs that provide value to the problem domain. This list of verbs and verb phrases eventually provides the context for a use-case model (which is roughly similar to the functional model of the Object Modeling Technique, or OMT), a class model, and an object model. (The class model and sequence diagram are discussed in Chapter 3, "Implementing Object-Oriented Design in VB5," and Chapter 4, "Making Classes Communicate with Each Other.") Some verbs in your list of candidate verbs will be superfluous. Identifying such verbs might appear to be an elusive goal to beginners, but with only a few practice runs you should get a good feel for the process.

The verb *use* is too generic. It simply restates what you already know—that users will use your system. Hence, you would discard this verb from the list. The verb *facilitate* is also used merely as an expression of how users use the system; it doesn't convey any behavior that's meaningful for the actor (teller) or the system.

Maintain bank accounts sounds meaningful because, within the context of your system, tellers will do something with bank accounts, which at first glance might include some sort of management of such accounts. So let's keep it.

The verb *needs* conveys only that the following information is a requirement. Therefore, while the information that follows could very well pass from candidate to real verb, the verb *needs* by itself doesn't mean anything to the behavior of the system. So let's discard this verb.

Open an account, close an account, deposit new funds, and *withdraw funds* each sound like something tellers need to do with your system. A normal part of a teller's business processes is to open and close accounts, as well as deposit and withdraw funds. Let's keep this one.

IDENTIFYING TRUE ACTORS

Keep in mind that within the requirements context of your system, human tellers use your system, not customers. If it were customers, each teller would need to be an automated teller machine, and therefore opening and closing accounts wouldn't be meaningful to your system for logistical and legal reasons.

This is your list of verb phrases:

> maintain bank accounts
> open an account
> close an account
> deposit new funds
> withdraw funds

Now comes a gray area for most OOP novices. At this point, you could continue on to the use-case model and then on to design. However, the trained practitioner will notice that there's a potential conflict or overlapping of verbs. That is, you've just identified that your actor, the teller, can maintain accounts, as well as open and close accounts, and withdraw and deposit funds. Therefore, a question arises: Exactly what does *maintain bank accounts* mean? Is it not the operation (within your context) of opening and closing accounts and withdrawing and depositing funds? The intermediate object-oriented practitioner might say it is and proceed to eliminate the verb-like noun phrase *maintain bank accounts* from your list of system uses. However, the advanced practitioner might say that *maintain bank accounts* can be a high-level description of the grouping of operations represented as open account, close account, withdraw funds, and deposit funds. The assessment you choose is entirely up to you; however, for the sake of simplicity, discard *maintain bank accounts,* as it's a grouping of the other verbs. Now your list looks more like this:

> open an account
>
> close an account
>
> deposit new funds
>
> withdraw funds

The Use-Case Model

The use-case model captures the verbs you discovered to be meaningful, with the actor and business domain classes that support each use case. A *use case* is an identified use by the actor of the system under development. In its simplest form, a use case is a description of one of many ways users use your system. These *ways* are also called *transactions*. Users (or human actors) perform a sequence of steps (or events) from beginning to end; that is what a use case captures. A use case can be *customized* (or instantiated) to capture how users execute the use case for a given scenario.

For instance, tellers can open an account (a use case), but how do they open an account when a customer wants to open it with more than $10,000 cash? As you might know, in this situation the bank must file paperwork with the federal government to comply with laws that govern bank transactions involving cash amounts in excess of $10,000. This scenario, then, is a different instance (or customization) of the use case *open account.* It's certainly different from opening an account with less than $10,000 in cash. Use-case scenarios (and their corresponding sequence diagrams) describe each path (or instantiation) the use case can take.

Now re-examine the use-case model in Figure 2.1. This use-case model is the end result (or artifact) of your initial analysis process. At this point, you'd be proud to have your first use-case model complete. You're so proud, in fact, that you race off to display your stroke of genius with your domain experts (expert users or managers) who own the business process(es) behind this model.

At first, the experts are pleasantly surprised and impressed. They brag about you to an actual teller who will use the system being developed. The teller is pleased that progress is being made but notices something missing. He needs to be able to look up the customer's account information before closing it to make sure that the customer doesn't owe money to the bank and to make sure that the person is authorized to close the account. Also, he may just want to view the account information to answer a customer's questions.

In the traditional analysis process, you would have to restructure the data-flow diagrams in various places and redo the program code (because you probably already started coding the requirements). This rework usually involves patching in the new functionality, meaning new global functions were inserted in some module somewhere, or the code was tucked behind a button on a form. Some programmers aren't even this nice; they might growl that the requested feature wasn't in the original specs and therefore can't be incorporated.

With the object-oriented analysis approach, such crucial change requests are easily incorporated, provided they naturally fit within the context of your problem domain. Clearly, the viewing of account information is a mission-critical feature (as agreed by each stakeholder in the project) and as such needs to be added to your use-case model. Because you've done no coding, the only time needed is to insert another use case into your model and update the problem statement (another often overlooked step). Figure 2.4 shows your updated problem statement; Figure 2.5 represents the updated use-case model.

Figure 2.4.

The updated problem statement.

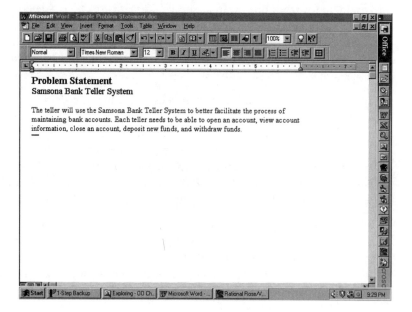

FIGURE 2.5.

The updated use-case model.

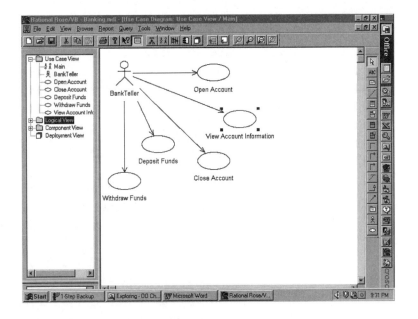

The Sequence Diagram

As alluded to earlier, a sequence diagram (also known as an *interaction diagram* or *event trace diagram*) is a diagrammatic representation of a specific instance of a use case. This specific use-case instance is called a *scenario*. There are two types of scenarios: normal and abnormal.

The *normal scenario* captures the normal interaction between the actor and the system. At the analysis level, the system is represented by the main domain object that's the object affected by the actor's activities. You don't care about forms, buttons, or interfaces at this point; these objects are exposed during the design iteration (or phase). In diagramming a normal scenario, you're asking yourself and your project stakeholders what actions the actor will normally carry out when there are no anomalies or error conditions.

A normal scenario can take alternate paths, each of which is still normal. For instance, the use case *open account* could have at least two alternate normal scenarios: *open savings account* and *open checking account.*

Abnormal scenarios capture use-case paths that take into consideration anomalies and error conditions. For instance, an abnormal path for *close account* might be this: The account being closed doesn't exist. Also, for the *withdraw funds* use case, you'll have a scenario that deals with the situation where there aren't enough funds to withdraw.

To build a list of normal and abnormal scenarios to illustrate in your sequence diagrams, you'll need to interview domain experts and end users. Assuming that this was accomplished, the current scenarios are listed in Table 2.2.

Table 2.2. Use cases and their respective scenarios.

Use Case	Scenario
Open an Account	The customer is new with no previous accounts and has the minimum required balance.
	The customer has an existing account that's active.
	The customer has an existing account that's inactive.
	The customer is new but doesn't have the minimum required balance.
	The customer is new with no previous accounts but wants to deposit more than $10,000 in cash.
Close an Account	An active account exists and the customer is authorized to close it.
	The account being closed is inactive.
	The customer isn't authorized to close the account.
	The customer is authorized to close the account, but the account is deficient or the customer owes money to the bank.
Deposit New Funds	An active account exists and the customer is authorized to deposit money in it.
	The customer isn't authorized to deposit money in the account.
	The amount being deposited exceeds $10,000 in cash.
Withdraw Funds	An active account exists and the customer is authorized to withdraw money from it.
	The customer isn't authorized to withdraw money from the account.
	The teller tries to withdraw more money at the customer's request than is available.

For simplicity's sake, you'll concentrate on the first sequence diagram for the *open an account* use case. Assume that you had a use-case meeting with the users and domain experts, who then elaborated on the steps involved.

The First Sequence Diagram

As noted in Table 2.2, the first scenario is the normal path that reads "The customer is new with no previous accounts and has the minimum required balance." Before diagramming this scenario, you should elaborate on the steps involved. A good format for proceeding would be to identify the scenario that belongs to the use case. You could assign a unique identifier to the use case as well as the scenario as follows:

Use Case 001: Open an Account

Scenario 01: The customer is new with no previous accounts and has the minimum required balance

Step 1: The Teller provides the customer information to the system

Step 2: The Teller wants to check the customer's checking history with Telecheck

Step 3: Once the Teller sees that the customer has a good checking history, the Teller provides the opening deposit balance to the system

Step 4: The Teller prints out the new account information

Notice that in elaborating on the steps involved in this use case, you've actually uncovered some more significant nouns and verbs, as follows:

Nouns	*Verbs*
customer information	provide the customer information to the system
customer	check the customer's checking history
system	provide the opening deposit balance to the system
checking history	print out the new account information
Telecheck	
opening deposit balance	
account information	

Before creating the sequence diagram, you must again determine which nouns and verbs are significant and which aren't.

The nouns *customer information* and *account information* each have a word in them that provides strong clues as to its importance in your proposed system: *information*. Words such as *customer information* or *account information* almost always imply properties (or attributes) of classes in your system. They certainly imply relational database tables. Because the words *customer* and *account* are so pivotal in your domain, the architects, analysts, and lead designers agree that these should be nominal domain classes. Let's keep them.

The noun *customer* is just another representation of *customer information*. You already decided to incorporate a nominal class named *customer*, so this is repetition. You can discard it.

The noun *system* is a more generic reference to your application name, which is Samsona Bank Teller System. If you want the analysis-view use case to remain generic enough to be reused across your enterprise, it's probably best to leave it as *system*. However, if you decide that the actual application name is more meaningful, by all means use the full system name. Because you already have identified the system as the Samsona Bank Teller System, use the full name. Thus, you've just replaced the word *system* with *Samsona Bank Teller System*.

The noun *checking history* is rather interesting. For simplicity's sake, you've left out that there's more than one kind of account in banking systems. Furthermore, in your domain (or context), the domain experts and users didn't mention any particular type of account. After a quick meeting with these stakeholders, you agreed that for this release of the system, you won't consider the various kinds of accounts. Therefore, *checking history* becomes a nominal class, but not a specialization of the Account class you already identified in your earlier analysis.

> **NOTE**
>
> Many object-oriented novices miss this very important point entirely. Don't create classes and actors simply because it seems logical. Stick to the project plan. Such deviations, although thoughtful, usually slow down the object-oriented process, which then lead many to sarcastically exaggerate the length of time object-oriented projects typically take. (In many ways, this negative impression is similar to the impression others have of VB: It's slow. However, it seems slow because of the competence level of the professionals using it.) You can speed up object-oriented projects by not adding unnecessary or uncalled-for features and objects to the project.

The noun *Telecheck* is, in the familiar English composition sense, an indirect object in that it's on the receiving end of the action initiated by the Teller. However, you don't know exactly what Telecheck means, so you ask the experts. They tell us that it's a vendor who provides research services to the bank. The Teller views the information supplied by Telecheck to determine whether the customer can establish an account. On further investigation, you discover that an electronic interface exists between the bank teller's machine and the vendor. Through this interface, the Teller sends customer information to Telecheck for verification and research. The results of the research are returned directly to the terminal screen in the current system.

Based on this behavior, you've concluded that Telecheck is an actor that you could stereotype as an *external system*. Therefore, you promote it from a noun to an actor and have to update your use-case model. Figure 2.6 shows what your new use-case model looks like.

The noun *opening deposit balance* is a monetary amount. You might be tempted to model it as a class, but does it really exhibit behavior or have attributes? If it were a candidate class, it would have only one attribute (or property): Value. Identifying classes and members of classes (properties and methods) isn't always an easy process, and even the very best object technologists admit that sometimes they don't always immediately identify classes correctly the first time. So, on further analysis, you discover that *opening deposit balance* is actually a property of your Account class. How did you gather this? The adjective *opening* provides a big clue—it implies that something other than the object *balance* is going to fluctuate at some point in time. Balances fluctuate, but so do accounts. Then you remember that when you get a monthly account statement from your bank, there's a beginning balance and an ending balance. And because the account statement is merely a snapshot (or instance) of your account information, you've finally decided that Balance is an attribute of the Account class. In general, a good rule of thumb to use (loosely) is that if a candidate class has only one property (or attribute) and no methods, it might actually be a property of a larger class.

FIGURE 2.6.

The actor Telecheck is incorporated into your use-case model.

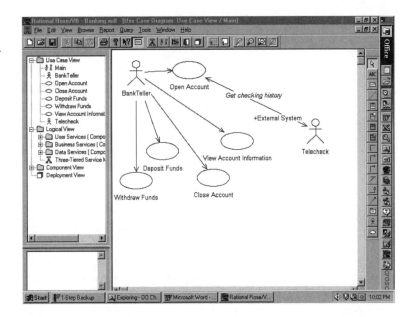

The verb phrase *provide the customer information to the system* (*system* now being *Samsona Bank Teller System*) indicates an action taken by the Teller against the system. This action is also known as an *event*. You've decided that this event is valid and, therefore, will incorporate this verb phrase into your sequence diagram.

The verb phrase *check the customer's checking history* is an action the Teller carries out by using the interface to the Telecheck system. Therefore, you should incorporate it into your sequence diagram.

The verb phrase *provide the opening deposit balance to the system* (*system* now being *Samsona Bank Teller System*) specifies information about the new account being supplied by the Teller. Thus, you should incorporate it into your sequence diagram.

The verb phrase *print out the new account information* is also an event initiated by the Teller against the system. Therefore, you should incorporate it into your sequence diagram.

NOTE

Because the Teller is specifying that account information be printed out, this suggests that *print* is a possible method for your Account class. This is true of each verb and verb phrase; they become possible methods for the class indicated in the indirect object part of the sentence or phrase.

Now you're ready to create your sequence diagram. Samsona Bank Teller System will be represented by some class that implements one of its behaviors. Your nominal nouns and verbs phrases list looks like this:

Nouns	*Verbs*
customer	provides the customer information to the Samsona Bank Teller System
Samsona Bank Teller System	
checking history	checks the customer's checking history
Telecheck	provides the opening deposit balance to the Samsona Bank Teller System
account (property: Balance)	
	prints out the new account information

Figure 2.7 shows what your sequence diagram looks like. The stick figures are the Jacobson symbols for actors. Although Telecheck is a machine-based system, you still model it as a stick-figure actor. The lines with the arrow at one end represent events and actions being carried out by actors and domain class instances (or objects). The rectangle preceding each line is called the *focus of control bar.* These bars indicate that each line protruding from it is part of the same event or action. For instance, the Teller-initiated event Provide Info is the only event in the Teller's focus of control (or duration of a single event or action). However, both Check lines, as well as the Supply History and Display History lines, are all part of the check history event initiated by the Teller.

FIGURE 2.7.

The sequence diagram shows the stimuli being sent from one object to another. The main actor, the Teller, initiates the events and is therefore the first object on the left.

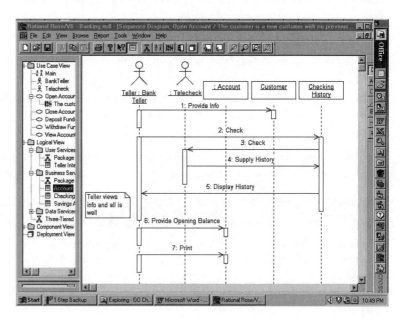

> **NOTE**
>
> Rational Rose/VB allows you to do this type of modeling automatically. Rational Rose/VB, based on the Unified Modeling Language (UML), is available for a hefty price from Rational Corporation (www.rational.com). If you don't have the resources to purchase Rational Rose, simply do it by hand. According to some rumors, Visio's latest version offers features for the Unified Modeling Language (UML).
>
> At Microsoft's Web site (www.microsoft.com), Visual Modeler is available free to owners of Visual Basic 5.0 Enterprise Edition. It doesn't incorporate use cases, however, so you can't do sequence diagrams in it.

The Analysis Class Model

By now, you've identified a collection class (BankAccounts), and several classes (Account, Customer, CheckingHistory). The initial class model will have these three classes as model items. Figure 2.8 shows what this model looks like.

FIGURE 2.8.

The initial class model.

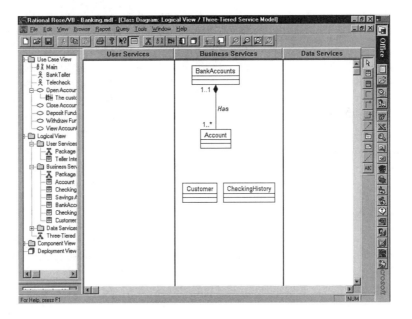

Notice that the collection class BankAccounts contains many Account class instances (or objects). The black diamond indicates this relationship, which in Visual Basic would be represented as ByVal (as opposed to just ByRef). This relationship is named *Has*, which is another way of saying that BankAccounts contains many Account objects. The notation 1..1 and 1..* together is known as the relationship's *cardinality*. Because there's only one BankAccounts object, its cardinality is 1..1; because you can have one to an unlimited number of Account objects in your collection, Account's cardinality in the relationship is 1..*. The asterisk (*) represents an unlimited number. The `Customer` and `CheckingHistory` classes are relationships that have meaning only with respect to the actors in your system. You can formalize these actors' events in your system through *control objects*, a subject you'll examine in Chapter 3, "Implementing Object-Oriented Design in VB5."

Summary

In this chapter, you should have gained not only a better understanding of the role of analysis in object-oriented system development, but a lasting appreciation of it. There can be no effective object-oriented programming in Visual Basic without a thorough and iterative analysis process. Analysis should never be confused with design or programming; doing so leads to a flawed system architecture and *hacking* (or disorganized, haphazard programming). Using a *methodology* to cultivate this evolutionary process is crucial. An analysis methodology centered on how users expect to use the proposed system is absolutely necessary. Ivar Jacobson provides perhaps the best methodology for capturing these expected uses. This methodology is part of the overall objectory method and gives birth to the use-case modeling technique.

The three primary roles usually involved in the use-case identification process are the requirements gatherer, the object-oriented analyst, and the architect. The requirements gatherer typically interrogates end users, business managers (or domain experts), and project managers to draft a problem statement and, optionally, an initial requirements model. The object-oriented analyst carefully examines the requirements model to understand the requirements and elaborates on the requirements model, assesses the implications of each requirement, and removes inconsistencies and requirements discovered to no longer be valid. Object-oriented architects work with analysts and designers to ensure that project team members can trace the names of business objects between the list of requirements, analysis models, and design models. Architects sometimes perform the roles of analyst and designer; otherwise, the architect is a mediator and final decision-maker with regard to the system architecture. With the advent of the software reuse structure of the business organization, these roles will become more specialized (partitioned into smaller roles).

The problem statement is used to capture, in plain English, how users see the system helping them complete their business processes. From this problem statement, the analyst and architect identify and list meaningful nouns and verbs, which helps technicians identify potential actors, classes, class behavior, and use cases. When a list of these objects is drafted, the superfluous or vague items are discarded in favor of those with stronger meaning to the current problem domain (or business context). The main artifacts of the analysis process are the problem statement, the use-case model, and an analysis class model.

In Chapter 3, "Implementing Object-Oriented Design in VB5," you'll learn how to take the artifacts of the analysis process and create a more refined design class model, design-view scenario diagrams, and other design artifacts.

Implementing Object-Oriented Design in VB5

by John D. Conley III

IN THIS CHAPTER

As with analysis, design is usually a whirlwind "quickie" process for many developers, where decisions about the detail architecture of the proposed system under development are made for the most part on an ad hoc basis. Such crucial decisions are usually made in isolated settings, where one individual uses his or her thought processes from a previous whirlwind design process to dictate the design process for the current domain. Typically, fellow developers, analysts (if any), and domain experts don't provide a healthy "sanity check" (or organized feedback).

This isn't entirely the programmer's fault, however. Executives and managers, accustomed to the mainframe application development processes, have seldom established their IS and IT departments as they would other business groups. There's no separation between a designer role and the programmer role. They apply pressure to programmers to double as designers (and sometimes analysts, architects, testers, documenters, and so on). Such a variety of roles, coupled with the typical unreasonable deadline, would cause anyone undue stress.

System design should be a very careful, methodical process. It's during the design phase where you want to pursue different coding strategies based on the initial architecture exposed by the analysis phase. Architectural flaws discovered during design are far less costly than architectural flaws discovered during the actual development phase, because during design, no coding is done (except for evolving a prototype as a sanity check for proof of concept). The artifacts of design are non-programming models, meaning that when logic flaws are discovered, those flaws can be corrected easily by modifying the corresponding document. Correcting these flaws while the system is still a model on paper is less costly compared to the cost of having to hunt down these same architectural flaws while you're halfway into the process of programming the system. You might even realize a tenfold development cost savings when flaws are detected and corrected on paper. When you skip or skim past design, the inevitable flaws you'll encounter during programming will cost you in terms of

- Many extra hours of overtime
- Unnecessarily increased levels of stress
- Abnormally high levels of impatience among users and managers
- Personnel turnover
- Faulty programmer assumptions about the system made in isolation
- Excessive cost overruns
- An abnormally high increase in the risk of project failure

Programmers who've never tried implementing design in their software development repertoire criticize this phase as wasteful, time-consuming, and pointless. Usually, such believers are novices or have never given thought to the historical problems of the software development process. Unfortunately, many of these programmers hail out of the Visual Basic camp, because VB makes development work seem intuitively simple and straightforward. However, it must be stressed time and time again that the design phase is absolutely critical to the development of high-quality software. Incorporating object-oriented design principles in your development efforts pays off in the long run in terms of

- Increased productivity
- Lower project costs on average
- Greater respect for your productive abilities among your peers and managers

This chapter will help you on your way toward these ends.

Understanding Object-Oriented Design

Implementing object-oriented design helps you identify classes and objects you've discovered in the analysis phase, as well as those not yet discovered. During design, you also elaborate on the architecture of the system, including the identification of possible design patterns and frameworks. Design patterns, in simple terms, are repeated ways that objects communicate with each other to carry out some system goal.

> **NOTE**
>
> Although you'll look at design patterns in the last section of this chapter, not enough space is available to discuss all the design patterns discovered thus far. You can find more information at http://st-www.cs.uiuc.edu/users/patterns/DPBook/DPBook.html (it's mainly for C++, but some patterns can be translated for VB).

When you finish with the last design iteration (there can be many iterations through the design phase, depending on the complexity of your proposed system), you'll have enough of a detailed system specification to develop the system without having to make assumptions about the system architecture or user motivations. The problems discovered during the actual development phase should be minor, and they should require minor iterations through the design phase to update the corresponding models. At the same time, minor updates in design models should lead to very minor updates in the analysis models, such as changes in the name of a class or class member or the addition of an argument to a private method.

Major changes—such as drastic changes in the way objects communicate, the addition of a new subsystem or package, changes to the graphical user interface, or changes to interfaces between systems—shouldn't occur during the development phase. If such changes weren't addressed during design before development, this might suggest inadequate skill sets among domain experts, analysts, architects, or designers. In any event, such modifications should be deferred to a future release of the system, if possible. If it's not possible, the development phase must be postponed while the design flaws are revisited.

The object-oriented community has many flavors of object-oriented design these days. The following sections briefly introduce the most pervasive ones:

- Object-oriented software engineering (Objectory)
- Object Modeling Technique (OMT)
- Booch

Object-Oriented Software Engineering (Objectory)

Noted object-oriented methodologist Ivar Jacobson is the brains behind the Objectory method. Because of its ease of use and powerful effectiveness in accurate document and model requirements (via the use-case model), it has become the foundation behind object-oriented design efforts in general. However, Jacobson also offers the object-oriented software engineering (OOSE) approach to software construction (or design and programming).

The OOSE design approach models the behavior of the system as documented by the use cases into logical parts, also known as *classes*. At the core of the design model in OOSE are three types of classes, whose instances are objects:

- Entity
- Interface
- Control

Entity Classes

Entity classes represent the type of objects whose data needs to be stored persistently beyond the lifetime of the application session. This persistent storage is usually realized in the form of a database or flat file. Because you're not always sure which storage approach a project will incorporate, you want to logically refer to these storage media as *information repositories* or *information persistence*. Thus, as storage media changes over time, your project artifacts (models and documentation) can better stand the test of time and be reusable for future projects.

An example of an entity class is in order. Suppose that a Visual Basic entity class is structured as follows:

Class:

```
SavingsAccount
```

Properties:

```
Number

CurrentBalance

DepositAmount

WithdrawalAmount

InterestRate
```

Methods:

    depositFunds

    withdrawFunds

    viewTransactionHistory

As part of your domain-specified requirements, you may need to persistently store the savings account number, current balance, deposit amount, withdrawal amount, and interest rate. Alternatively, you might feel that the current balance is a derived property value, meaning that a cumulative query of your persistent storage media would give you the current balance.

Derived properties are typically borderline issues that must be taken up on a case-by-case basis. Nevertheless, you should understand what an entity class is. Entity classes are usually the first types of classes discovered during the earliest stages of analysis. For instance, if you're developing a system for a defense contracting firm, you might discover a class called ProcurementRuleEnforcement or GovernmentCustomer. If your client is a bank, a key entity class would be Account or Customer. Many times, such entity classes become subsystems (or packages). Use cases provide the justification for entity classes. Any entity class not addressed in a use-case model should be eliminated to avoid *scope creep*, where projects get off track and behind schedule.

Interface Classes

Interface classes represent the type of objects that allow actors (humans or external systems) to interact with your proposed system. As Jacobson mentions in several books and magazine articles, object instances of interface classes convert inputs from actors into events and method invocations within your system. For instance, one of the use cases for the Samsona Bank Teller System is Open a new account. After several design reviews with users, you find that you need to have a GUI button captioned Open New Account. That button is an interface object with an associated Click event, among others. In turn, the Click event may trigger the invocation of several class methods. Because these method invocations can become quite complex, it's not unusual to have a control object handle the details of invoking the proper methods.

Control Classes

Control classes represent the type of objects that don't easily fit into entity or interface classes. More complex systems (and, hence, more complex use cases) require the inclusion of control objects in your domain. Control classes may translate user inputs into method invocations on more than one entity class. For instance, if your users need the capability of canceling an in-process request for checking account and credit history information for a particular banking customer, they would click a Cancel button. This would call a control object, possibly named CustomerVerification, that would then invoke the appropriate methods on entity objects named CheckingAccountHistoryInfo, CreditHistoryInfo, Account, and Customer (among possibly many others). Control objects control the flow of events for complex use cases.

OMT

Jim Rumbaugh developed the Object Modeling Technique (OMT) to help developers capture the design specification of a proposed system. OMT is primarily based on entity/relationship modeling (Rumbaugh has a database design background) with emphasis on modeling classes, inheritance, and encapsulated behavior. The cornerstone of the OMT process includes the following:

- Analysis
- System design
- Object design
- Coding
- Testing

The analysis phase is pretty much similar to what you learned in Chapter 2, "Using Analysis to Discover Your VB5 Classes." System design is concerned with the initial versions of the Object model, the Dynamic model, and the Functional model. The *Object model* shows the relationships (or links) between classes. The *Dynamic model* elaborates on states of objects and events that are associated with changes in state. The *Functional model* shows how the invoking of methods (or class operations) generate resulting values from a set of input values. The object design phase is an elaboration of the system design phase. Coding and testing aren't unlike what you'll learn about in Chapter 4, "Making Classes Communicate With Each Other." Much of OMT's notation has been captured in the Unified Modeling Language, which you explore later in this chapter.

Booch

The Booch method, fathered by Grady Booch, poses questions for designers to use in the elaboration of class structures and relationships. The questions follow the following formats:

- Candidate Class A "is a" type of Class B
- Candidate Class A "has a" Class B type of object
- Candidate Class A "uses" Class B

The "is a" relationship suggests that A is everything that B represents (and possibly more). This is called *inheritance* (albeit, implementation inheritance is restricted in Visual Basic 5.0). For instance, a checking account *is a* type of account.

The "has a" relationship suggests that A owns B for its own purpose, meaning that the lifetime of B depends on the lifetime of A. There has been much heated discussion on this topic in the OOP community. Essentially, the idea is that, for instance, a bank customer *has* several accounts with the bank. When the customer stops being a customer of the bank, these accounts also cease as the customer closes them (at least, in most cases).

The "uses" relationship suggests that A uses B for a particular task or activity but doesn't own B. For instance, in the Samsona Bank Teller System, the `Account` class might use the `CheckingAccountHistoryInfo` class to verify the customer's checking account history before opening a new account. The `Account` class doesn't own `CheckingAccountHistoryInfo`; `Account` just uses it for this verification process. In Visual Basic, a uses relationship might look like the following:

```
cmdVerifyCheckAccountHistory_Click()
     theAcount.verifyCheckAccountHistory(SomeCustomerSSN)
End Sub
```

In the `Account` class, this method call would then have the following uses relationship:

```
Public Sub verifyCheckAccountHistory(SomeCustomerSSN)
     theCheckingAccountHistoryInfo.verify(SomeCustomerSSN)
End Sub
```

In most cases, the uses relationship resembles delegation, where an object delegates one or all of its responsibilities to another object.

The Booch method is primarily concerned with discovering the chief *abstractions* (areas of specialized focus) of classes and objects as parts of the overall system in your problem domain. The identification process looks at the vocabulary of the business domain, much the way OOSE does. Booch also looks at the contextual meaning of these classes and objects and how they're used by others. Grasping the meaning of classes and objects is by no means an easy process and involves many iterations through design and analysis to fully realize. Thus, domain experts become critical stakeholders in the producing of analysis and design models and other artifacts.

Finally, Booch breaks the system down into several views and models. Among the views are the Logical View and the Physical View, the basis of Microsoft's Visual Modeler. The Logical View encompasses the structure of and relationships between classes and objects. The Physical View encompasses the actual file location of the classes in the Logical View.

UML

UML (Unified Modeling Language) represents the combination of the most important object-oriented methodologies in the software development community today. The three top methodologists—Ivar Jacobson, Jim Rumbaugh, and Grady Booch—are the chief architects behind UML. The UML creation process began in late 1994 when Booch and Rumbaugh collaborated to unify their respective methodologies. Jacobson joined them shortly thereafter.

The UML doesn't really represent an elimination of OOSE, the OMT, or the Booch method, as some have suggested. Instead, it represents a unified way of modeling elements in each. Of course, the UML creation process has led to some version upgrades in the top three methodologies, but the UML represents only a standard way to express each one.

The UML is wholly encapsulated within the Rational Rose automation tool. This shouldn't be surprising, because Jacobson, Booch, and Rumbaugh are the joint chiefs of Rational Corporation. Because UML and Rational Rose 4.0 are so tightly intertwined, you'll learn more details of the UML in the section on Rational Rose later. For now, remember that the UML incorporates four views of the system:

- The Use Case View encompasses all the use-case models, including the actors.
- The Logical View encompasses the classes and objects needed to support the use-case models.
- The Component View, like Booch's Physical View, shows the actual location of the files for each class and component (that is, ActiveX controls and other third-party tools).
- The Deployment View encompasses the physical locations of key processors and hardware devices in your system domain.

You'll see examples of these later in this chapter.

Using Rational Rose/VB and Microsoft Visual Modeler

As seasoned software developers will tell you (if you don't know already), having automation tools that help ease the process of developing sophisticated software is a must in today's technology-intensive environment. Two tools stand out in this arena: Rational Rose/VB and Microsoft Visual Modeler.

Similarities and Differences

Some of you may be saying, "Hey, these tools look alike." This is because Microsoft, the masters of the graphical user interface, and Rational, the rulers of automated object-oriented software development, joined forces to provide a much-needed facelift to Rational Rose. (If you remember the previous versions of Rose, you're probably pretty glad the GUI was brought up to speed.)

Although a number of similarities exist between Visual Modeler and Rose/VB, using both will quickly bring to light the obvious differences. The following are the obvious similarities:

- Both tools support Microsoft's three-tier (or partition) approach to application architecture. The three tiers are User Services (GUI-centered objects), Business Services (rules and entity objects), and Data Services (database objects, recordset objects, flat-file interfaces, and so forth).
- Both tools support the Logical and Physical Views of the application.

The key difference is that Rose/VB supports the Use Case View, whereas Visual Modeler doesn't, possibly due to licensing restrictions negotiated by Rational. Whatever the reason, the lack of the Use Case View in Visual Modeler makes it more difficult to enforce traceability from the use cases to the detail design class models. Thus, project risks must be assessed appropriately and allocated to this situation.

Common Activities

The most important project activity you engage in with Rose/VB or Visual Modeler is the creation of architecture models, diagrams, and documentation. You also can create the necessary class modules and class utilities (or general code modules) to support the evolving system architecture as you iterate and increment through the various project phases. With either tool, you can also reverse-engineer an existing Visual Basic project, thereby creating a model automatically.

The Importance of Traceability

Traceability is that attribute of a project artifact wherein business-related entity classes can be followed from the actual code to the lowest class models, up to the high analysis models, and to the project documentation itself. Master test cases and test scripts also refer to the same class, object, and actor names as other artifacts of the project life cycle.

Unfortunately, too many projects give little attention to the necessity of traceability. It might seem like extra work, but be sure to keep all artifacts (documents, models, diagrams, and code files) in sync when it comes to business domain terminology. Failing to do so very often results in unnecessary confusion and stress down the road.

The Design-View Class Model

When you get into modeling your classes in the design phase, the resulting models become more detailed with each iteration. Figure 3.1 shows what the class model from the analysis phase now looks like. Notice that traceability is still evident.

As you can see, two more classes have been added to the class model: CheckingAccountHistoryInfo and CreditHistoryInfo. For the sake of simplicity, these classes each have a method called verify to handle customer information processing. That both classes can have a method with the same name but different implementations is an example of a form of polymorphism.

POLYMORPHOSIS

Polymorphism literally means "many forms." In languages that support full interface and implementation inheritance, such as Java, many different subclasses that inherit from a single common base class can customize the abstract class methods for specialized

continues

continued

purposes. The language compiler resolves which method between the parent class and child class is invoked. VB now supports only interface inheritance, and even then true inheritance polymorphism can't be implemented because the class that implements an interface class must implement every public method and property. But classes in a collection that have methods with the same name can contribute to that collection exhibiting polymorphic behavior.

Consider a collection class named `colAccountHistoryInfo`. It has two objects: `CheckingAccountHistoryInfo` and `CreditHistoryInfo`. The following code would use this collection's implied polymorphic behavior:

```
For Each AccountHistoryObject In colAccountHistoryInfo
    AccountHistoryObject.verify
Next
```

The method name `verify` is the same for both objects in the collection, but the respective classes of each object do different things when their `verify` methods are invoked.

Some would argue that this still doesn't qualify as polymorphism, and given the mix of existing definitions, this argument may have some merits. Generally speaking, polymorphism was mainly aimed at getting rid of large, complex `If...Then` statements and other condition-branching mechanisms. The common understanding in the object-oriented community is that if your code has an `If...Then` or `Select` statement whose processing is based on an object type, it's a red flag that polymorphic behavior wasn't a factor in your design. Late binding of object types, where the type of the object isn't known until the object is needed at runtime, is crucial ingredient for implementing polymorphism.

FIGURE 3.1.

The updated class model has two more classes due to new discoveries about the domain.

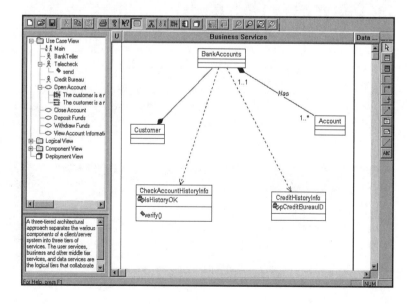

The modeling tools (Visual Modeler and Rational Rose/VB) let you show the methods for each class. Figure 3.2 shows each class with its methods and properties displayed. Note that in most cases, you don't want to show more class members than necessary to explain a particular scenario. Otherwise, the models become cluttered with model elements and become almost unreadable.

FIGURE 3.2.

Now the class diagram has more expressive classes with properties and methods.

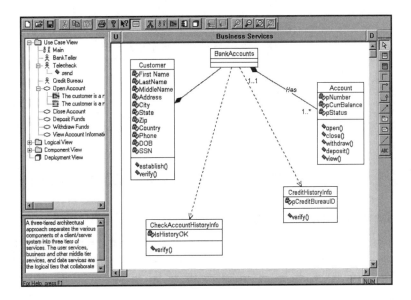

The lack of clutter in models is important because readability is one of the obvious benefits of object-oriented models. Certain scenarios call for different views of the class model. Breaking a complex model into simpler models with different views is ideal. For instance, if you have a scenario that deals with the opening of an account where the customer has a valid Social Security number and has a good credit and checking account history, your class model view would show only the members of the `Account` and `Customer` classes. All other classes would display only a name and possibly a single method that's meaningful to the context (if at all).

Sequence Diagrams

Sequence diagrams literally show a sequence of interactions between actors and objects in your system. In the analysis phase in Chapter 2, you saw an illustration of such a diagram. Many novices to OOP immediately associate sequence diagrams to data flow diagrams (DFDs). They aren't the same. DFDs show only dimly defined paths of function calls. Sequence diagrams show the interaction between actors and objects for a given scenario, with focus on state changes and timing issues.

Figure 3.3 shows the sequence diagram from Chapter 2 updated to include the two new classes (`CheckingAccountHistoryInfo` and `CreditHistoryInfo`). If you don't have Rational Rose/VB, you can just as easily create sequence diagrams by hand.

FIGURE 3.3.

The sequence diagram has been updated to incorporate the new classes.

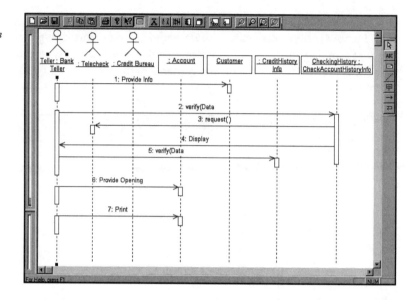

Collaboration Diagrams

Collaboration diagrams are similar to sequence diagrams, except they don't look as sequential and structured. Figure 3.4 shows what the sequence diagram would look like as a collaboration diagram.

FIGURE 3.4.

The sequence diagram as a collaboration diagram.

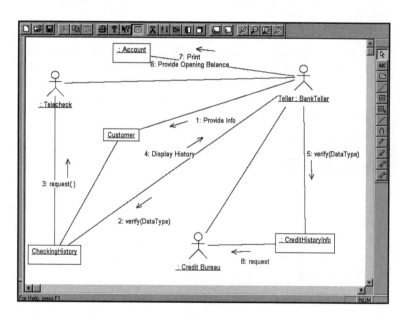

Collaboration diagrams aren't as popular with some OOP camps as the sequence diagram. Nevertheless, in some situations, the collaboration diagram captures views of the system that better show method invocations on objects. Generally speaking, the choice is really more a matter of taste than science.

Breaking a Proposed VB Application into Subsystem Packages

As if the concept of classes and objects wasn't already difficult enough, you must also become familiar with the idea of breaking your applications into logical subapplications or subsystems. A *subsystem* consists of one-to-many classes whose object instances interact with each other to carry out a common application behavior. Groupings of classes are also called *packages*. For example, you have a subsystem that handles communications between the data repository (database, flat file, and so forth) and the application.

There's no sense in having every form need to communicate directly with the data repository, as has become the idiom in the Visual Basic development community. This leads to flattening the system architecture and graying the lines between the User, Business, and Data Services layers, and thus can cause spaghetti code. What's more, it's next to impossible to hope for code reuse when all the layers of the application code are embedded within forms. Delegating key functionality to subsystems not only helps avoid spaghetti code, but greatly increases the code's readability and the capability of assigning parts of the application to each member of a team of developers.

> **WHAT ABOUT DATA CONTROLS?**
>
> It's okay to have data controls (although not advisable in most cases), as long as you have a central subsystem that handles the actual communication with the database. This is done by passing the data control to the database subsystem, which then "dresses up" the control, as required, to display and save data. For advanced OOP experts, the idea of dressing up the data control is similar to the Visitor design pattern.

Naming Subsystem Packages, Classes, and Objects

Naming and coding standards aren't very pervasive among newcomers to programming (and sometimes among seasoned developers who have managed to skirt the issue of implementing such standards). Microsoft's naming suggestions, of course, are fine, but I'll mention the ones that apply to classes and objects:

- Class names might start with a capital c (CAccount), as is the case with Microsoft Visual C++. Or you can opt to capitalize the first letter of the class, as in Account. Class names should be in the form of a noun, and they should adequately and briefly describe the types of functionality and attributes the class will encapsulate. The same naming convention holds true for subsystems (or packages), which also are classes that are aggregates of one-to-many classes.

- Object names start with cls (clsAccount). Or you might choose to prefix object names with the or rep—for example, theAccount or repAccount.

- Methods start with lowercase verbs (openAccount). Avoid using nouns as the name of a method, because you might confuse it with a property. Method names with verb forms also accurately convey that an action will be carried out by the class (which is a noun).

- Class properties start with lowercase p (pName), unless you can differentiate between methods and properties (which is possible with the suggestion on naming methods).

- Implementation variables at the module level start with a lowercase m or m_. Class Builder prefixes implementation property variables with mvar. Implementation variables are just variables used internally within a class.

As far as coding standards are concerned, whole books have been written on this (including those by Jacobson, Booch, and Rumbaugh). At a high level, you'll use a mix of limited inheritance and delegation to express "is a," "has a," and "uses" relationships (discussed earlier in the section "Booch"), where delegation would be the default in your Visual Basic design models. You'll want to develop your interfaces (or protocols) so that they don't change; only the implementation changes.

You can have newer versions of an interface, which means that during some overlapping period, you'll support the old and new interfaces for compatibility (but compatibility isn't your immediate concern). You'll want to break your application model into nice categories (or subsystems) so that each developer has an island of classes with which to work. The idea here is that while these categories are being worked on, no two developers need to try to develop together. Only when the interfaces of each category are developed well will the two come together for integration (which shouldn't take too much time, depending on the complexity of the behavior being carried out). If one finishes before the other, the slower developer (for lack of a better term) could check out the category with which to work.

Understanding Advanced Design Issues: Design Patterns

Although identifying patterns isn't a new science, the concept of design patterns has been gaining rapid popularity in the object-oriented software development community over the last several years. The purpose of design patterns within the object-oriented community is to make available a repository of problems and solutions to help software overcome common issues that repeat themselves. Identifying design patterns facilitates the communication of in-depth knowledge and experience about these recurring problems and points out how best to implement solutions. Having this at the disposal of developers, especially VB developers, helps them evolve well-structured system architectures that provide rapid reuse for the client and understandability among fellow developers.

The idea of object-oriented design patterns is very complex and is for intermediate-to-advanced object technologists. The premier book on design patterns is *Design Patterns: Elements of Reusable Object-Oriented Software* by Erich Gamma, Richard Helm, Ralph Johnson, and John Vlissides. Several others exist. It's advisable that you acquire such books to familiarize yourself with the idea of design patterns. Be forewarned, however, that current design pattern books are written with C++ in mind, because many design patterns deal with inheritance, an area in which VB isn't yet capable.

Christopher Alexander, a noted scientist and building architect/theorist, describes a *pattern* as

> …a three-part rule, which expresses a relation between a certain context, a problem, and a solution. The pattern is, in short, at the same time a thing, which happens in the world, and the rule which tells us how to create that thing, and when we must create it. It's both a process and a thing; both a description of a thing which is alive, and a description of the process which will generate that thing.

> **NOTE**
>
> Because the term *design pattern* has become immensely popular to the point of being a buzzword, too many vanity patterns have entered the community that really aren't solutions, but merely vain attempts at seeking glory by the pattern author/discoverer.

When to Use Design Patterns in Your Project

Because design patterns are a somewhat advanced topic, you might not want to delve into them until at least one of the following is true:

- You have access to an OOP mentor or architect who is knowledgeable about implementing design patterns.
- Time is allocated toward the end of the first release of the project—or sometime thereafter—to examine the need and implementation of design patterns.

Attempting to learn both OOP and design patterns can be overwhelming, so pace yourself. Meanwhile, the next two sections provide examples of design patterns that you can use in your Visual Basic code.

The Singleton Pattern Example

If you've had any experience with Visual Basic 3.0 programming, you probably remember how difficult it was to allow users to start only one instance of your application. Or if you've been doing a little object-oriented programming, you may have come to the point where you needed to make sure that only one instance of a particular object was in memory. The Singleton design pattern is quite analogous to the first situation, and it's a solution to the second one.

The Singleton pattern makes sure that only one instance of an object is available to prospective client objects. The enforcement of one object instance can be quite important if that object is global within your application, and even more so if that object is global to other applications within an enterprise or across several enterprises. An example of a Singleton object would be a reporting object that resides on a server and is the broker for all requests for reporting services. Another example in the Samsona Bank Teller System might be the Customer class, because the teller user (for simplicity's sake) can handle account transactions for only one customer at a time.

Assuming that the Customer class needs to make sure that only one instance of it can be in memory, the Singleton class would look like Listing 3.1.

Listing 3.1. The Singleton Customer class.

```
VERSION 1.0 CLASS
BEGIN
  MultiUse = -1  'True
END
Attribute VB_Name = "Customer"
Attribute VB_GlobalNameSpace = False
Attribute VB_Creatable = True
Attribute VB_PredeclaredId = False
Attribute VB_Exposed = False
Attribute VB_Ext_KEY = "SavedWithClassBuilder" ,"Yes"
Attribute VB_Ext_KEY = "Top_Level" ,"Yes"
'local variable(s) to hold property value(s)
'Private mvarpSoleInstance As Customer  'local copy
Private mvarpSoleInstance As Object   'local copy

Friend Property Set pSoleInstance(ByVal vData As Object)
'used when assigning an Object to the property, on the left side of a Set
statement.
'Syntax: Set x.pSoleInstance = Form1
    Set mvarpSoleInstance = vData
End Property

Friend Property Get pSoleInstance() As Object
'used when retrieving value of a property, on the right side of an assignment.
'Syntax: Debug.Print X.pSoleInstance
    Set pSoleInstance = mvarpSoleInstance
End Property
```

```
Public Static Function createSoleInstance() As Customer
Attribute createSoleInstance.VB_UserMemId = 0
If TypeName(mvarpSoleInstance) = "Customer" Then
        MsgBox "Only one instance allowed"
        Exit Function
    End If

    Set mvarpSoleInstance = New Customer
    MsgBox "New Customer object created"
End Function

Private Sub Class_Initialize()

End Sub
```

The property pSoleInstance was declared as Friend so that only those objects within the project can access the Customer class instance. The createSoleInstance method is the key enforcer in the class. In it, you allow only one instance of the Customer class via the Set...New syntax. Of course, you can create more than one instance of Customer outside the class, which means that the one instance that's created (in this case, theCustomer) must be mutually agreed to be the only broker for creating instances of the Customer class. Nevertheless, you could have designed this method as in Listing 3.2.

Listing 3.2. The modified createSoleInstance method.

```
Public Static Function createSoleInstance() As Customer
Attribute createSoleInstance.VB_UserMemId = 0
    Dim m_InstanceCount As Byte  'local copy
    If m_InstanceCount = 1 Then
        MsgBox "Only one instance allowed"
        Exit Function
    End If

    Set mvarpSoleInstance = New Customer
    MsgBox "New Customer object created"
    m_InstanceCount = 1
End Function
```

In the createSoleInstance method in Listing 3.1, the TypeName method is used to test whether the late-bound object is of the type Customer. When the class is first initialized, it's of the type Object. Thus, the check for the TypeName method is False on the first invocation of createSoleInstance. However, because it's the first time, the object will be set to something other than Object—namely, Customer. Thus, when a second Set...New Customer is encountered, the TypeName test becomes True, meaning that additional instances can't be allowed. In Listing 3.2, on the other hand, a Static instance counter is used to limit the instance count to 1. Either pattern is effective for ensuring that only one instance exists.

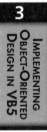

Gearing Up for Code Implementation

The main complaint about the entire object-oriented development process is that it takes too long to move a project from inception to production. Critics also ignore that most projects end disastrously or achieve hardly any of their initial goals, for numerous reasons. No doubt, your first object-oriented project will be slow because you're actually forced to think about the proposed system from the user's point of view.

In traditional environments, programmers placed themselves on the same pedestal as users (sometimes higher than that!). This often led to products that had to satisfy user and programmer equally, and compromises left users dissatisfied. If a programmer's attitude was boisterous enough, users were bullied into accepting the application, and then a month or two later, abandoned its use. Because programmers typically aren't around to see this long-term end result, they're left with the erroneous perception that the project was successful.

With true object-oriented development, the foundation of the system is constructed with only user needs in mind. Note the word *true* in the previous sentence. Many newcomers to OOP bring their previous traditions with them into the process. This untrue OOP process leads to faulty use cases and, thus, foundations that have cracks everywhere. Only the end users and domain experts can provide the concrete for the foundation. It's your job to fashion and mold it into a stable, long-lasting slab. Just as with building a real house, laying a solid foundation consumes the bulk of the time it takes to develop the entire system. If you try to take shortcuts to produce a foundation in record time, your foundation will inevitably crack and, just as with building contractors, you may be held liable for the damages. If you're an independent consultant, you'll want to take your time to develop the system's foundation properly.

When the foundation is nicely laid, the rest of the process becomes quicker than you ever expected. Future projects that overlap with the first object-oriented project become that much faster because you can reuse code and documentation. With each successive project with similar requirements, the project deadlines become easily met, with time to spare. Time-to-market is thus minimal. But be patient! It may take up to three years before you reach the point where a project benefits from full reuse, much shorter if you hire a consultant with reusable class libraries and libraries of standard use cases. Because software is a capital asset of a company, it's wise to consider the three years or less as the initial investment period of the asset.

Summary

In this chapter, you gained a better understanding of the object-oriented design process. You became familiar with the Objectory design process introduced by Ivar Jacobson, the Object Modeling Technique by Jim Rumbaugh, and the Booch method by Grady Booch. You learned about the importance of traceability from one model and diagram to another, as well as the design-view class model.

You were introduced to two software development automation tools: Rational Rose/VB and Microsoft Visual Modeler. You learned some reasons you might want to use them and explored the differences and similarities between them. You also learned how to break a proposed Visual Basic application into subsystem packages and how to name subsystem packages, classes, and objects.

Finally, you became familiar with an advanced issue in object-oriented design—design patterns. Examples of the Singleton and Adapter patterns were provided in the form of Customer class. Chapter 4, "Making Classes Communicate With Each Other," rounds out the fundamental concepts of OOP with lots of example code and explanations following the Samsona Bank Teller System example.

Making Classes Communicate With Each Other

by John D. Conley III

IN THIS CHAPTER

CHAPTER 4

In Chapter 1, "Understanding Object-Oriented Programming," you learned about the fundamentals of object-oriented programming and what OOP pillars Visual Basic supports. In this chapter, you take your learning a step further. You learn how to construct actual Visual Basic code from the simple Rational Rose/VB sequence diagrams you created in the previous chapter. You could have also created these diagrams by hand.

Identifying Technical Constraints of the Implementation Environment

Because Visual Basic 5.0 still doesn't allow you to fully implement every pillar of object-oriented programming, you need to keep some notions in mind. Along with these notions, this chapter offers some solutions.

Visual Basic doesn't support *implementation inheritance*, which means that the private members of class A can't be inherited by class B. However, Visual Basic does support *limited interface inheritance,* which means that class B can inherit the public members of class A. It's *limited* because class B can't inherit the public members that class A inherits from another class.

The inheritance of public members in Visual Basic is done via the `Implements` keyword. The keyword `Implements` doesn't imply implementation inheritance, however—it facilitates interface inheritance. *Interface inheritance* is when a subclass inherits the public methods and attributes of a superclass. *Implementation inheritance* is when a subclass inherits both the public and private methods and attributes of a superclass.

In any event, you can replace the use of implementation inheritance in most cases with *delegation.* Whole books have been written about delegation, but the idea (as explained briefly in Chapter 1) is that object A delegates some or all of its behavior to object B. Although you may not have noticed it, delegation was also used in Chapter 3, "Implementing Object-Oriented Design in VB5." The `Account` class used the `CheckingAccountHistoryInfo` class to verify a customer's checking account history. Hence, the `Account` class instance (`theAccount`) used the `CheckingAccountHistoryInfo` class instance (`theCheckingAccountHistoryInfo`) as follows:

```
Public Sub verifyCheckAccountHistory(SomeCustomerSSN)
    theCheckingAccountHistoryInfo.verify(SomeCustomerSSN)
End Sub
```

The concept of delegation is synonymous with the uses relationship defined in the Unified Modeling Language.

Visual Basic also doesn't support the kind of polymorphism associated with inheritance lattices. In other words, assume the following: a superclass named `theSuperClass` has a method called `print`; a subclass of `theSuperClass`, `theSubclass`, also has a specialized (or customized) method called `print`; and a subclass of the `theSubclass` has a specialized method named `print`. The compiler would use the specialized method of the class instance being used for a given context (or section of code).

With the absence of implementation and full interface inheritance, this kind of polymorphism is practically nonexistent. (Of course, a class's interface can be inherited one level down as though it were a pure virtual base class, but Visual Basic expects the public methods and properties to be implemented by the client class.)

Visual Basic supports the other kind of polymorphism, where a collection of objects with one or more methods of the same name will have varying behaviors when iterated. In the Samsona Bank Teller System example, you have a collection of history verification objects: `theCheckingAccountHistoryInfo` and `theCreditHistoryInfo`. As you saw in Chapter 3, each of these objects has a method called `verify`. To create a collection object called `HistoryVerifiers`, follow these steps:

1. Start a new project in Visual Basic.

2. Create a class called `CheckingAccountHistoryInfo` and one called `CreditHistoryInfo`. If you're using Rational Rose/VB or Visual Modeler, you can generate by choosing Tools | Code Generation Wizard from either application's menu.

Working With Design Models

To fully benefit from the object-oriented features in Visual Basic 5.0, you need some effective way to capture the attributes and behaviors of classes, as well as how they interact with one another at runtime as objects. Toward this end, the class diagram and scenario diagrams provide you with the capability of modeling these elements.

A class diagram shows the unique identity of one or more classes and their behaviors, as well as any inheritance, delegation, or aggregation relationships. Scenario diagrams (along with collaboration diagrams) capture how the instances of these classes interact at runtime to carry out some system behavior. Because of the easy-to-follow nature of these model types, you can break down complex systems into simpler abstractions. Together, they provide the architectural expression of the proposed system.

The Importance of Not Deviating From the Architecture

The requirements for the proposed system expressed by end users and domain experts to project technicians must be directly translated into a use-case model, which then must be translated into the architecture of the system. Requirements not adequately expressed by users before the evolution of the system's architecture winds down will lead to a very lopsided architecture that will crack at the foundation during system construction. The causes of inadequate expression of user requirements—and, thus, architecture deviation—can be many, but the most common appear to be the following:

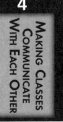

- Lack of executive sponsorship of a project
- Inexperienced system architects or business analysts
- Impatient software developers/programmers
- Uncooperative users

Lack of Executive Sponsorship of a Project

Lack of executive sponsorship is the single biggest risk to any Visual Basic project. It's usually the result of competition between executives for a particular fiefdom in an aging, antiquated corporate environment. During the inception phase of the project (the one that rarely involves any technical experts), many managers and executives seem to make big political promises to employees and shareholders with such sloganeering as "Change is constant" and "The new system will satisfy all your needs." However, when the project moves past the inception phase into the iterative elaboration phase—after they seal the campaign victory—these same managers and executives disappear, vanishing into the political black holes found in most companies.

Executives seldom want to sponsor fledgling software projects because if one fails (and a high probability of failure exists), they'll look bad or—worse—be demoted or fired. Thus, the reality is that many executives make big promises and then quickly back out of the limelight, secretly hoping against hope that the project will somehow succeed.

Other executives take more drastic measures by hiring a scapegoat project manager to hold the sole responsibility for a project. In some cases, these project managers don't have the right skill sets to ensure the project's success. For instance, the typical characteristics of project managers for object-oriented client/server projects is that they be middle-aged, have a long background exclusively in mainframe software development (without a clear development methodology), and secretly prefer the security of the mainframe versus the rapidly evolving technology of object-oriented client/server projects. Project managers typically are non-combative, meaning that whatever executives want them to do, that's what they'll do.

How does this relate to architecture deviation? It's the most prevalent cause of failed projects that no one wants to discuss. Experienced architects, in giving architectural advisories to project managers and executives, typically run into subtle hostility, jealousy, and brick walls. That is, project managers are prone to treat the object-oriented project much the way they treated legacy software development: minimize the analysis and maximize the programming, at any cost, with little or no attention paid to methodology. This leads to architectural foundations built on sand, where new requirements that lie outside the scope of the project are added with reckless abandon to satisfy demanding users. Because the core of the system was never designed in a methodical way, these additions almost always put undo stress on the project and the system architecture (if you can call it that).

Executive sponsorship is to the project what the use-case model is to the system architecture: the absolute foundation that determines the success or failure of the project. Lack of executive sponsorship can lead to inadequate use cases, which then leads to inadequate system architectures.

Inexperienced System Architects or Business Analysts

Inexperience among the top echelon of a project's technical staff can have a devastating effect on the project's outcome and use cases. Proper executive sponsorship of a project can increase the chance of finding and hiring the right technical architects and business analysts, but it can't give 100 percent assurance of this. Inexperienced technical leaders may not know how to adjust a given object-oriented methodology to the dynamics of user and executive behavior. This alone leads to inadequate use cases (if any) and faulty system architectures. Other factors include inability to make a transition of a project from one iteration to another, to give technical advisories to less-experienced stakeholders in the project, and to manage the artifacts of the project.

Impatient Software Developers/Programmers

Assume that you have reasonably proper executive sponsorship, knowledgeable project managers, and proactive user involvement in conveying use cases, and thus could develop a sound architecture for the system. Because many VB programmers haven't embraced object-oriented programming, the chances of hiring impatient developers is high. This is important because many programmers believe that OOP minimizes individualistic efforts, a threat to programmer creativity. Many others feel that reading project artifacts and spending time to follow design models are useless activities. Of course, such sentiments couldn't be further from the truth, yet they persist.

Impatient developers have a tendency to take shortcuts, resorting to the disorganized spaghetti-style coding prevalent among many developers. User input is minimized in order to maximize programmer satisfaction. Such developers frown on anything resembling a use case, thus increasing the risk of the system's architecture being faulty, to say the least.

Uncooperative Users

To put it bluntly, the more your users are uncooperative, the greater the risk of project failure. Non-participation by users is usually a symptom of the existence of one or more of three problems listed previously, but not always. If users don't actively participate in the early architectural design of the system, you may as well update your résumé. Not only will the architecture of the system be completely faulty, division and strife will creep up over time among the project stakeholders, programmers will have to work around the clock to attempt a miracle cure to help the project manager save face, and everyone will experience unnecessarily high levels of stress.

Programming solutions just seem to appear out of thin air. Users determine the system behavior, and without their participation, there is no architecture and thus no scope, which leads to architecture deviation.

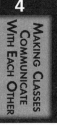

4

MAKING CLASSES COMMUNICATE WITH EACH OTHER

Code Generation in Rational Rose/VB and Visual Modeler

Automating the process of creating object-oriented programming code considerably reduces the normal risks associated with software development projects. Such risks include the obvious human error factor in coding, the risk of not making a proper transition from a model to the actual code base, the risk of not properly documenting code, and so on. Rational Rose/VB 4.0 and Microsoft Visual Modeler offer automated code engineering and reverse code engineering to drastically reduce these risks. Because Rational Rose/VB is used for the use cases in Chapter

2, "Using Analysis to Discover Your VB5 Classes," and class modeling in Chapter 3, "Implementing Object-Oriented Design in VB5," this chapter uses Microsoft Visual Modeler.

> **NOTE**
>
> The process of creating code from models and reverse-engineering existing code are exactly the same in both products, so you can use the following steps in either tool.

If you own Visual Basic 5.0 Professional or Enterprise Edition, you can go to www.microsoft.com/vbasic, register in the Owners' Area as a licensed user, and download Visual Modeler free. Otherwise, you need to go to www.rational.com and make arrangements to pay for Rational Rose/VB.

Generating Code for the Samsona Bank Teller System Example

You create the code for the ongoing Samsona Bank Teller System example in this chapter. To do so, you need to launch Visual Basic 5.0, if you haven't already done so.

> **CAUTION**
>
> Make sure that you have plenty of hardware capacity when running VB 5.0 and Visual Modeler simultaneously. I work with these tools on a P133 with 32M of RAM and 5G of disk space (with the maximum recommended virtual memory setting). Otherwise, these tools may suffer serious performance degradation and could crash your machine.

With VB running, follow these steps:

1. Start Visual Modeler.
2. In the browser window, right-click the package folder named Logical and choose New Class. A class icon appears in the browser window.
3. With the default class NewClass highlighted, enter **Customer**.
4. Double-click the Customer class icon you just created. The Class Specification for Customer dialog box appears.
5. Notice the Methods and Properties tabbed pages. On each page is a big white box. Right-click this box and choose Insert to add the methods and properties for the Customer class.

Repeat these steps for the other classes except for the BankAccounts collection. Instructions for creating this collection class follow the class listings.

Class:

Customer

Properties:

FirstName

LastName

MiddleName

Address

City

State

Zip

Country

Phone

DOB

SSN

Methods:

establish

verify

Class:

BankAccounts (Collection class)

Class:

Account

Properties:

Number

CurrBalance

Status

Methods:

open

close

withdraw

deposit

view

Class:

CreditHistoryInfo

Properties:

```
CreditBureauID
```

Methods:

```
verify
```

Class:

```
CheckingAccountHistoryInfo
```

Properties:

```
IsHistoryOK
```

Methods:

verify

Class:

```
Teller_Interface
```

Methods:

```
closeAccount(argAcctNum As String)

depositFunds(argAmount As Currency)

openAccount(argSSN As String)

queryCheckingHistory(argSSN As String)

queryCreditHistory(argSSN As String)

Private: verifyExistingAccount(Optional argSSN,
  Optional argAcctNum)

withdrawFunds(argAmount As Currency)
```

Notice that BankAccounts is a collection class that you'll implement in Visual Basic. You can manually put in the standard methods and properties that collections typically have. Or you can automate the process of creating collection classes by following these steps:

1. Choose Tools | Class Builder Utility from the menu. If you've used VB5 before reading this chapter or read Chapter 1, "Understanding Object-Oriented Programming," you'll recognize the familiar Class Builder window.

2. Choose File | New Collection from the Class Builder's menu. The Collection Builder dialog appears.

3. By default, the name suggested for the new collection is Collection1; change this to BankAccounts. (Delete the BankAccounts class from the model if you're going to continue with this process; otherwise, add the typical collection properties and methods to the existing BankAccounts class in the model and don't proceed with the remaining steps.)

Leave the Based On: drop-down list box alone because you're creating a new collection.

4. In the Collection Of section, choose New Class to trick the utility into letting you proceed (you won't need the class it creates). Click OK.

5. Choose File | Update Project from Class Builder's menu (VB needs to be running).

6. Exit Class Builder.

7. The Reverse Engineering Wizard welcome dialog box appears. Because you're creating the BankAccounts collection class first with the Class Builder utility within Visual Modeler, you must reverse-engineer it into your current model. Click the Next button.

8. You don't need to select a component, so click Next again.

9. Assign the new collection class to a Logical View Package. The standard packages are User, Business, and Data Services:

   ■ User Services includes the class associated with graphical user interface processes.

   ■ Business Services has those classes associated with real-world entities in the client's environment.

   ■ Data Services houses the classes that facilitate saving precious business information from an application session to a persistent information repository, such as a database or a flat file.

   The BankAccounts collection class is a business domain class, so it belongs in the Business Services package. Drag it to the Business Services package folder and click the Next button.

10. The Wizard copies the collection class to your current model. Click the Finish button.

11. Click the Close button.

Now to generate the code, choose Tools | Code Generation Wizard from Visual Modeler's menu. The Code Generation Wizard dialog box appears. For this simple exercise, click the Next button in each dialog box that displays until you see the Finish button. Then click the Finish button.

NOTE

Although this example exercise made navigating through the code-generation steps easy, in the real world, you should give serious thought to the decisions in each step, such as error-raising options and debug information insertion. Failure to properly consider these decisions might result in improperly developed code.

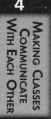

4

MAKING CLASSES
COMMUNICATE
WITH EACH OTHER

> **NOTE**
>
> If you didn't have VB running during the code-generation process, Visual Modeler would have notified you that VB must be running to generate code.

To see your newly generated code, switch to your current Visual Basic session. You should see several cascaded code windows for each class created.

Putting On the Finishing Touches

Although Visual Modeler is a pretty smart tool, it's still not smart enough to provide all the logic necessary to make your code work the way your client wants the system to work. If it did, you would probably be out of a job!

For your newly generated code to work, you have to re-examine the use cases to further determine what users want. This activity may prompt several more use-case iterations with the users to ensure that every requirement for the current release of the system is in place and that there are no discrepancies. It's far cheaper in terms of time and money to verify use cases before coding than afterward, so be patient with this process. The use cases will also guide you in developing the components of the graphical user interface, because they generally tell you how users will use the proposed system.

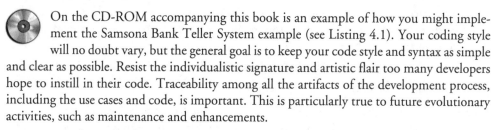 On the CD-ROM accompanying this book is an example of how you might implement the Samsona Bank Teller System example (see Listing 4.1). Your coding style will no doubt vary, but the general goal is to keep your code style and syntax as simple and clear as possible. Resist the individualistic signature and artistic flair too many developers hope to instill in their code. Traceability among all the artifacts of the development process, including the use cases and code, is important. This is particularly true to future evolutionary activities, such as maintenance and enhancements.

Listing 4.1. An example of the Samsona Bank Teller System.

```
VERSION 1.0 CLASS
BEGIN
  MultiUse = -1  'True
END
Attribute VB_Name = "BankAccounts"
Attribute VB_GlobalNameSpace = False
Attribute VB_Creatable = True
Attribute VB_PredeclaredId = False
Attribute VB_Exposed = False
Attribute VB_Ext_KEY = "ClassBuilderProperty" ,""
Attribute VB_Ext_KEY = "SavedWithClassBuilder" ,"Yes"
Attribute VB_Ext_KEY = "Collection" ,"Class1"
Attribute VB_Ext_KEY = "Member0" ,"Class1"
Attribute VB_Ext_KEY = "Top_Level" ,"Yes"
Attribute VB_Ext_KEY = "RVB_UniqueId" ,"340AE45103CA"
'
```

```
Option Base 0

'local variable to hold collection
'##ModelId=340AE4540186
Private mCol As Collection

'##ModelId=340AE5030142
Public theCustomer As Customer

'##ModelId=340AE50403CC
Public theAccount As Collection
'##ModelId=340AE45402D0
Public Function Add(Key As String, Optional sKey As String) As Class1
    'create a new object
    Dim objNewMember As Class1
    Set objNewMember = New Class1

    'set the properties passed into the method
    objNewMember.Key = Key

    If Len(sKey) = 0 Then
        mCol.Add objNewMember
    Else
        mCol.Add objNewMember, sKey
    End If

    'return the object created
    Set Add = objNewMember
    Set objNewMember = Nothing

End Function

'##ModelId=340AE4560136
Public Property Get Item(vntIndexKey As Variant) As Class1
Attribute Item.VB_UserMemId = 0
    'used when referencing an element in the collection
    'vntIndexKey contains either the Index or Key to the collection,
    'this is why it is declared as a Variant
    'Syntax: Set foo = x.Item(xyz) or Set foo = x.Item(5)
  Set Item = mCol(vntIndexKey)
End Property

'##ModelId=340AE4570208
Public Property Get Count() As Long
    'used when retrieving the number of elements in the
    'collection. Syntax: Debug.Print x.Count
    Count = mCol.Count
End Property

'##ModelId=340AE45800E6
Public Sub Remove(vntIndexKey As Variant)
    'used when removing an element from the collection
    'vntIndexKey contains either the Index or Key, which is why
    'it is declared as a Variant
    'Syntax: x.Remove(xyz)

    mCol.Remove vntIndexKey
End Sub
```

4

MAKING CLASSES
COMMUNICATE
WITH EACH OTHER

continues

Listing 4.1. continued

```
'##ModelId=340AE459010E
Public Property Get NewEnum() As IUnknown
Attribute NewEnum.VB_UserMemId = -4
    'this property allows you to enumerate
    'this collection with the For...Each syntax
    Set NewEnum = mCol.[_NewEnum]
End Property

'##ModelId=340AE45903A2
Private Sub Class_Initialize()
    'creates the collection when this class is created
    Set mCol = New Collection
End Sub

'##ModelId=340AE45A024E
Private Sub Class_Terminate()
    'destroys collection when this class is terminated
    Set mCol = Nothing
End Sub

VERSION 1.0 CLASS
BEGIN
  MultiUse = -1  'True
END
Attribute VB_Name = "Account"
Attribute VB_GlobalNameSpace = False
Attribute VB_Creatable = True
Attribute VB_PredeclaredId = False
Attribute VB_Exposed = False
Attribute VB_Ext_KEY = "RVB_UniqueId" ,"33D412D90352"
Attribute VB_Ext_KEY = "SavedWithClassBuilder" ,"Yes"
Attribute VB_Ext_KEY = "Top_Level" ,"Yes"
'
Option Base 0

'set this to 0 to disable debug code in this class
#Const DebugMode = 1
#If DebugMode Then
    'local variable to hold the serialized class ID that
    'was created in Class_Initialize
    '##ModelId=340B72E600A0
    Private mmlClassDebugID As Long
#End If

'##ModelId=33E6AE1D02BC
Public pNumber As Variant

'##ModelId=33E6AE2302E4
Public pCurrBalance As Variant

'##ModelId=33E6AE2E0186
Public pStatus As Variant

'##ModelId=33D8246C00FA
Public theVariant As Variant

'##ModelId=340AE50403CB
```

```
Public theBankAccounts As BankAccounts

'##ModelId=33E6AE060276
Public Sub closeAccount()
    On Error GoTo closeErr

    'your code goes here...
    MsgBox "Account will be closed..."
    Exit Sub
closeErr:
    Call RaiseError(MyUnhandledError, "Account:close Method")
End Sub

'##ModelId=33E6AE00035C
Public Sub openAccount()
    On Error GoTo openErr

    'your code goes here...
    If theCustomer.establish Then
        pNumber = "0001" 'example purpose only
        MsgBox "Account Established"
    End If
    Exit Sub
openErr:
    Call RaiseError(MyUnhandledError, "Account:open Method")
End Sub

'##ModelId=33E6AE060276
Public Sub close()
    On Error GoTo closeErr

    'your code goes here...

    Exit Sub
closeErr:
    Call RaiseError(MyUnhandledError, "Account:close Method")
End Sub

'##ModelId=33E6AE00035C
Public Sub open()
    On Error GoTo openErr

    'your code goes here...

    Exit Sub
openErr:
    Call RaiseError(MyUnhandledError, "Account:open Method")
End Sub

'##ModelId=33E6AE060276
Public Sub close()
    On Error GoTo closeErr

    'your code goes here...

    Exit Sub
closeErr:
    Call RaiseError(MyUnhandledError, "Account:close Method")
```

4

MAKING CLASSES
COMMUNICATE
WITH EACH OTHER

continues

Listing 4.1. continued

```
End Sub

'##ModelId=33E6AE00035C
Public Sub open()
    On Error GoTo openErr

    'your code goes here...

    Exit Sub
openErr:
    Call RaiseError(MyUnhandledError, "Account:open Method")
End Sub

'##ModelId=340B89570168
Public Property Get mlClassDebugID() As Long
   Let mlClassDebugID = mmlClassDebugID
End Property

'##ModelId=340B89550226
Public Property Let mlClassDebugID(Value As Long)
   Let mmlClassDebugID = Value
End Property

'##ModelId=340B72E90190
Private Sub Class_Terminate()
    #If DebugMode Then
    'the class is being destroyed
        Debug.Print "'" & TypeName(Me) & "' instance " & CStr(mlClassDebugID) _
           & " is terminating"
    #End If
End Sub

'##ModelId=340B72E802E4
Private Sub Class_Initialize()
    #If DebugMode Then
        'get the next available class ID, and print out
        'that the class was created successfully
        mlClassDebugID = GetNextClassDebugID()
        Debug.Print "'" & TypeName(Me) & "' instance " & CStr(mlClassDebugID) _
           & " created"
    #End If
End Sub

'##ModelId=33E6AE0A03CA
Public Sub withdraw(argTransAmt As Currency, _
argOptionCtrl As OptionButton)
    On Error GoTo withdrawErr

    'your code goes here...
    'pCurrBalance>0 assumes no overdraft protection, otherwise
    'insert a variable for overdraft in place of 0, thus giving
    'pCurrBalance > pCurrBalance - mc_OverdraftAmt
    If argOptionCtrl(eTransOption.withdraw) And pCurrBalance > 0 Then
        pCurrBalance = pCurrBalance - argTransAmt
    End If
```

```
    Exit Sub
withdrawErr:
    Call RaiseError(MyUnhandledError, "Account:withdraw Method")
End Sub

'##ModelId=33E6AE100050
Public Sub deposit(argTransAmt As Currency, _
argOptionCtrl As OptionButton)
    On Error GoTo depositErr

    'your code goes here...
    If argOptionCtrl(eTransOption.deposit) Then
        pCurrBalance = pCurrBalance + argTransAmt
    End If
    Exit Sub
depositErr:
    Call RaiseError(MyUnhandledError, "Account:deposit Method")
End Sub

'##ModelId=33E6AE170032
Public Sub view()
    On Error GoTo viewErr

    'your code goes here...

    Exit Sub
viewErr:
    Call RaiseError(MyUnhandledError, "Account:view Method")
End Sub

#If DebugMode Then
    '##ModelId=340B72E6028A
    Public Property Get ClassDebugID() As Long
        'if we are in debug mode, surface this property that consumers can query
        ClassDebugID = mlClassDebugID
    End Property
#End If

Public Sub processTrans(argTransAmt As Currency, _
argOptionCtrl As OptionButton)
    If TypeOf argOptionCtrl Is OptionButton Then
        'Only one method invocation will work
        deposit argTransAmt, argOptionCtrl
        withdraw argTransAmt, argOptionCtrl
    End If
End Sub

VERSION 1.0 CLASS
BEGIN
  MultiUse = -1  'True
END
Attribute VB_Name = "CheckingAccountHistoryInfo"
Attribute VB_GlobalNameSpace = False
Attribute VB_Creatable = True
Attribute VB_PredeclaredId = False
Attribute VB_Exposed = False
Attribute VB_Ext_KEY = "RVB_UniqueId" ,"33E6A47F01F4"
Attribute VB_Ext_KEY = "SavedWithClassBuilder" ,"Yes"
```

4

MAKING CLASSES
COMMUNICATE
WITH EACH OTHER

continues

Listing 4.1. continued

```
Attribute VB_Ext_KEY = "Top_Level" ,"Yes"
'
Option Base 0

'set this to 0 to disable debug code in this class
#Const DebugMode = 1
#If DebugMode Then
    'local variable to hold the serialized class ID that
    'was created in Class_Initialize
    '##ModelId=340B72FD003C
    Public mlClassDebugID As Long
#End If

'##ModelId=33E6AD6B00F0
Private mIsHistoryOK As Variant

'##ModelId=33E6A50C03A2
Public theVariant As Variant

'##ModelId=340B89600398
Public Property Get IsHistoryOK() As Variant
    If IsObject(mIsHistoryOK) Then
        Set IsHistoryOK = mIsHistoryOK
    Else
        Let IsHistoryOK = mIsHistoryOK
    End If
End Property

'##ModelId=340B895F01B8
Public Property Let IsHistoryOK(Value As Variant)
    Let mIsHistoryOK = Value
End Property

'##ModelId=340B72FF00C8
Private Sub Class_Terminate()
    #If DebugMode Then
    'the class is being destroyed
        Debug.Print "'" & TypeName(Me) & "' instance " & CStr(mlClassDebugID) _
            & " is terminating"
    #End If
End Sub

'##ModelId=340B72FE0258
Private Sub Class_Initialize()
    #If DebugMode Then
        'get the next available class ID, and print out
        'that the class was created successfully
        mlClassDebugID = GetNextClassDebugID()
        Debug.Print "'" & TypeName(Me) & "' instance " & CStr(mlClassDebugID) _
            & " created"
    #End If
End Sub

'##ModelId=33E6AD9A03CA
Public Sub verify(argCustomerSSN As DataType)
'History of customer is returned
```

```
End Sub

#If DebugMode Then
    '##ModelId=340B72FD0186
    Public Property Get ClassDebugID() As Long
        'if we are in debug mode, surface this property that consumers can query
        ClassDebugID = mlClassDebugID
    End Property
#End If
VERSION 1.0 CLASS
BEGIN
  MultiUse = -1  'True
END
Attribute VB_Name = "CreditHistoryInfo"
Attribute VB_GlobalNameSpace = False
Attribute VB_Creatable = True
Attribute VB_PredeclaredId = False
Attribute VB_Exposed = False
Attribute VB_Ext_KEY = "RVB_UniqueId" ,"33E6A495019A"
Attribute VB_Ext_KEY = "SavedWithClassBuilder" ,"Yes"
Attribute VB_Ext_KEY = "Top_Level" ,"Yes"
'
Option Base 0

'set this to 0 to disable debug code in this class
#Const DebugMode = 1
#If DebugMode Then
    'local variable to hold the serialized class ID that
    'was created in Class_Initialize
    '##ModelId=340B73000352
    Public mlClassDebugID As Long
#End If

'##ModelId=33E6ACEE00E6
Private mpCreditBureauID As Variant

'##ModelId=340B8994003C
Public Property Get pCreditBureauID() As Variant
    If IsObject(mpCreditBureauID) Then
        Set pCreditBureauID = mpCreditBureauID
    Else
        Let pCreditBureauID = mpCreditBureauID
    End If
End Property

'##ModelId=340B89920316
Public Property Let pCreditBureauID(Value As Variant)
    Let mpCreditBureauID = Value
End Property

'##ModelId=340B73020226
Private Sub Class_Terminate()
    #If DebugMode Then
    'the class is being destroyed
        Debug.Print "'" & TypeName(Me) & "' instance " & CStr(mlClassDebugID) _
            & " is terminating"
    #End If
End Sub
```

continues

Listing 4.1. continued

```vb
'##ModelId=340B730103B6
Private Sub Class_Initialize()
    #If DebugMode Then
        'get the next available class ID, and print out
        'that the class was created successfully
        mlClassDebugID = GetNextClassDebugID()
        Debug.Print "'" & TypeName(Me) & "' instance " & CStr(mlClassDebugID) _
            & " created"
    #End If
End Sub

'##ModelId=33E6ACAB014A
Public Sub verify(argCustomerSSN As DataType)
'History of customer is returned

End Sub

#If DebugMode Then
    '##ModelId=340B73010046
    Public Property Get ClassDebugID() As Long
        'if we are in debug mode, surface this property that consumers can query
        ClassDebugID = mlClassDebugID
    End Property
#End If
VERSION 1.0 CLASS
BEGIN
  MultiUse = -1  'True
END
Attribute VB_Name = "Customer"
Attribute VB_GlobalNameSpace = False
Attribute VB_Creatable = True
Attribute VB_PredeclaredId = False
Attribute VB_Exposed = False
Attribute VB_Ext_KEY = "RVB_UniqueId" ,"33D825080316"
Attribute VB_Ext_KEY = "SavedWithClassBuilder" ,"Yes"
Attribute VB_Ext_KEY = "Top_Level" ,"Yes"
'
Option Base 0

'set this to 0 to disable debug code in this class
#Const DebugMode = 1
#If DebugMode Then
    'local variable to hold the serialized class ID that
    'was created in Class_Initialize
    '##ModelId=340B72F7023A
    Private mlClassDebugID As Long
#End If

'##ModelId=33E6AEB601F4
Private mFirst_Name As Variant

'##ModelId=33E6AEBF01FE
Private mLastName As Variant

'##ModelId=33E6AEC300F0
Private mMiddleName As Variant
Public Function attributesHaveValues()
```

```
        attributesHaveValues = (First_Name <> "")
        attributesHaveValues = (LastName <> "")
        attributesHaveValues = (Address <> "")
        attributesHaveValues = (City <> "")
        attributesHaveValues = (Country <> "")
        attributesHaveValues = (DOB <> "")
        attributesHaveValues = (MiddleName <> "")
        attributesHaveValues = (State <> "")
        attributesHaveValues = (Phone <> "")
        attributesHaveValues = (Zip <> "")
        attributesHaveValues = (SSN <> "")
End Function

'##ModelId=33E6AECC01D6
Private mAddress As Variant

'##ModelId=33E6AED00140
Private mCity As Variant

'##ModelId=33E6AED40140
Private mState As Variant

'##ModelId=33E6AED90032
Private mZip As Variant

'##ModelId=33E6AEDC037A
Private mCountry As Variant

'##ModelId=33E6AEE00384
Private mPhone As Variant

'##ModelId=33E6AEE6037A
Private mDOB As Variant

'##ModelId=33E6AEEA023A
Private mSSN As Variant

'##ModelId=33E6A4E003AC
Public theVariant As Variant

'##ModelId=340AE5030141
Public theBankAccounts As BankAccounts

'##ModelId=340B89850154
Public Property Get SSN() As Variant
    If IsObject(mSSN) Then
        Set SSN = mSSN
    Else
        Let SSN = mSSN
    End If
End Property

'##ModelId=340B8983019A
Public Property Let SSN(Value As Variant)
    Let mSSN = Value
End Property

'##ModelId=340B898200D2
```

continues

4

MAKING CLASSES
COMMUNICATE
WITH EACH OTHER

Listing 4.1. continued

```
Public Property Get DOB() As Variant
    If IsObject(mDOB) Then
        Set DOB = mDOB
    Else
        Let DOB = mDOB
    End If
End Property

'##ModelId=340B89800118
Public Property Let DOB(Value As Variant)
    Let mDOB = Value
End Property

'##ModelId=340B897F0082
Public Property Get Phone() As Variant
    If IsObject(mPhone) Then
        Set Phone = mPhone
    Else
        Let Phone = mPhone
    End If
End Property

'##ModelId=340B897D0140
Public Property Let Phone(Value As Variant)
    Let mPhone = Value
End Property

'##ModelId=340B897C0032
Public Property Get Country() As Variant
    If IsObject(mCountry) Then
        Set Country = mCountry
    Else
        Let Country = mCountry
    End If
End Property

'##ModelId=340B897A00F0
Public Property Let Country(Value As Variant)
    Let mCountry = Value
End Property

'##ModelId=340B897900FA
Public Property Get Zip() As Variant
    If IsObject(mZip) Then
        Set Zip = mZip
    Else
        Let Zip = mZip
    End If
End Property

'##ModelId=340B897701EA
Public Property Let Zip(Value As Variant)
    Let mZip = Value
End Property

'##ModelId=340B89760190
```

```
Public Property Get State() As Variant
    If IsObject(mState) Then
        Set State = mState
    Else
        Let State = mState
    End If
End Property

'##ModelId=340B89740280
Public Property Let State(Value As Variant)
    Let mState = Value
End Property

'##ModelId=340B8973024E
Public Property Get City() As Variant
    If IsObject(mCity) Then
        Set City = mCity
    Else
        Let City = mCity
    End If
End Property

'##ModelId=340B8971037A
Public Property Let City(Value As Variant)
    Let mCity = Value
End Property

'##ModelId=340B89700384
Public Property Get Address() As Variant
    If IsObject(mAddress) Then
        Set Address = mAddress
    Else
        Let Address = mAddress
    End If
End Property

'##ModelId=340B896F0136
Public Property Let Address(Value As Variant)
    Let mAddress = Value
End Property

'##ModelId=340B896E0140
Public Property Get MiddleName() As Variant
    If IsObject(mMiddleName) Then
        Set MiddleName = mMiddleName
    Else
        Let MiddleName = mMiddleName
    End If
End Property

'##ModelId=340B896C02DA
Public Property Let MiddleName(Value As Variant)
    Let mMiddleName = Value
End Property

'##ModelId=340B896B0320
Public Property Get LastName() As Variant
    If IsObject(mLastName) Then
```

continues

Listing 4.1. continued

```
      Set LastName = mLastName
   Else
      Let LastName = mLastName
   End If
End Property

'##ModelId=340B896A0136
Public Property Let LastName(Value As Variant)
   Let mLastName = Value
End Property

'##ModelId=340B896901AE
Public Property Get First_Name() As Variant
   If IsObject(mFirst_Name) Then
      Set First_Name = mFirst_Name
   Else
      Let First_Name = mFirst_Name
   End If
End Property

'##ModelId=340B89670384
Public Property Let First_Name(Value As Variant)
   Let mFirst_Name = Value
End Property

'##ModelId=340B72FA03CA
Private Sub Class_Terminate()
   #If DebugMode Then
   'the class is being destroyed
      Debug.Print "'" & TypeName(Me) & "' instance " & CStr(mlClassDebugID) _
         & " is terminating"
   #End If
End Sub

'##ModelId=340B72FA0172
Private Sub Class_Initialize()
   #If DebugMode Then
      'get the next available class ID, and print out
      'that the class was created successfully
      mlClassDebugID = GetNextClassDebugID()
      Debug.Print "'" & TypeName(Me) & "' instance " & CStr(mlClassDebugID) _
         & " created"
   #End If
End Sub

'##ModelId=33E6AE4C0294
Public Function establish()
   On Error GoTo establishErr

   'your code goes here...
   If attributesHaveValues Then
      establish = True
   End If
   Exit Function
establishErr:
   Call RaiseError(MyUnhandledError, "Customer:establish Method")
End Function
```

```
'##ModelId=33E6AE68030C
Public Sub verify()
    On Error GoTo verifyErr

    'your code goes here...

    Exit Sub
verifyErr:
    Call RaiseError(MyUnhandledError, "Customer:verify Method")
End Sub

#If DebugMode Then
    '##ModelId=340B72F703B6
    Public Property Get ClassDebugID() As Long
        'if we are in debug mode, surface this property that consumers can query
        ClassDebugID = mlClassDebugID
    End Property
#End If
VERSION 5.00
Begin VB.Form frmTellerSystem
    BorderStyle     =   3   'Fixed Dialog
    Caption         =   "Samsona Bank Teller System"
    ClientHeight    =   5670
    ClientLeft      =   45
    ClientTop       =   330
    ClientWidth     =   9300
    LinkTopic       =   "Form1"
    MaxButton       =   0   'False
    MinButton       =   0   'False
    ScaleHeight     =   5670
    ScaleWidth      =   9300
    ShowInTaskbar   =   0   'False
    StartUpPosition =   3   'Windows Default
    Begin VB.CommandButton cmdClose
        Caption     =   "Close Account"
        Height      =   375
        Left        =   2400
        TabIndex    =   36
        Top         =   5040
        Width       =   1215
    End
    Begin VB.CommandButton cmdOpen
        Caption     =   "Open Account"
        Height      =   375
        Left        =   120
        TabIndex    =   35
        Top         =   5040
        Width       =   1215
    End
    Begin VB.CommandButton cmdProcessTrans
        Caption     =   "Do Transaction"
        Height      =   375
        Left        =   5040
        TabIndex    =   34
        Top         =   5040
        Width       =   1215
    End
```

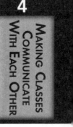

4

MAKING CLASSES
COMMUNICATE
WITH EACH OTHER

continues

Listing 4.1. continued

```
Begin VB.CommandButton cmdDone
   Caption         =   "Done"
   Height          =   375
   Left            =   7560
   TabIndex        =   33
   Top             =   5040
   Width           =   1215
End
Begin VB.Frame Frame1
   Caption         =   "Account Information"
   Height          =   1215
   Index           =   1
   Left            =   120
   TabIndex        =   21
   Top             =   3720
   Width           =   8655
   Begin VB.Frame Frame2
      Height          =   975
      Left            =   5280
      TabIndex        =   28
      Top             =   120
      Width           =   3135
      Begin VB.OptionButton optTransactionType
         Caption         =   "Deposit"
         Height          =   255
         Index           =   1
         Left            =   1680
         TabIndex        =   32
         Top             =   630
         Width           =   1215
      End
      Begin VB.OptionButton optTransactionType
         Caption         =   "Withdrawal"
         Height          =   255
         Index           =   0
         Left            =   1680
         TabIndex        =   31
         Top             =   360
         Width           =   1335
      End
      Begin VB.TextBox txtNewAccount
         Height          =   375
         Index           =   14
         Left            =   120
         TabIndex        =   29
         Top             =   480
         Width           =   1455
      End
      Begin VB.Label lblNewAccount
         Caption         =   "Transaction Amount"
         Height          =   255
         Index           =   16
         Left            =   120
         TabIndex        =   30
         Top             =   240
         Width           =   1455
      End
```

```
         End
         Begin VB.TextBox txtNewAccount
            Height          =   375
            Index           =   11
            Left            =   240
            TabIndex        =   24
            Top             =   600
            Width           =   1815
         End
         Begin VB.TextBox txtNewAccount
            Height          =   375
            Index           =   12
            Left            =   2160
            TabIndex        =   23
            Top             =   600
            Width           =   1455
         End
         Begin VB.TextBox txtNewAccount
            Height          =   375
            Index           =   13
            Left            =   3840
            TabIndex        =   22
            Top             =   600
            Width           =   1335
         End
         Begin VB.Label lblNewAccount
            Caption         =   "Account Number"
            Height          =   255
            Index           =   19
            Left            =   240
            TabIndex        =   27
            Top             =   360
            Width           =   1815
         End
         Begin VB.Label lblNewAccount
            Caption         =   "Account Status"
            Height          =   255
            Index           =   18
            Left            =   2280
            TabIndex        =   26
            Top             =   360
            Width           =   1215
         End
         Begin VB.Label lblNewAccount
            Caption         =   "Current Balance"
            Height          =   255
            Index           =   17
            Left            =   3840
            TabIndex        =   25
            Top             =   360
            Width           =   1215
         End
      End
      Begin VB.Frame Frame1
         Caption         =   "Customer Information"
         Height          =   3495
         Index           =   0
         Left            =   120
```

continues

Listing 4.1. continued

```
TabIndex        =    0
Top             =    120
Width           =    8655
Begin VB.TextBox txtNewAccount
   Height       =    375
   Index        =    10
   Left         =    5880
   TabIndex     =    37
   Top          =    1440
   Width        =    2295
End
Begin VB.TextBox txtNewAccount
   Height       =    375
   Index        =    9
   Left         =    3600
   TabIndex     =    19
   Top          =    2880
   Width        =    3135
End
Begin VB.TextBox txtNewAccount
   Height       =    375
   Index        =    8
   Left         =    240
   TabIndex     =    9
   Top          =    2880
   Width        =    3135
End
Begin VB.TextBox txtNewAccount
   Height       =    375
   Index        =    7
   Left         =    4800
   TabIndex     =    8
   Top          =    2160
   Width        =    975
End
Begin VB.TextBox txtNewAccount
   Height       =    375
   Index        =    6
   Left         =    3600
   TabIndex     =    7
   Top          =    2160
   Width        =    975
End
Begin VB.TextBox txtNewAccount
   Height       =    375
   Index        =    5
   Left         =    240
   TabIndex     =    6
   Top          =    2160
   Width        =    3135
End
Begin VB.TextBox txtNewAccount
   Height       =    375
   Index        =    4
   Left         =    240
   TabIndex     =    5
```

```
         Top             =       1440
         Width           =       4935
      End
      Begin VB.TextBox txtNewAccount
         Height          =       375
         Index           =       3
         Left            =       6720
         TabIndex        =       4
         Top             =       600
         Width           =       1455
      End
      Begin VB.TextBox txtNewAccount
         Height          =       375
         Index           =       2
         Left            =       4080
         TabIndex        =       3
         Top             =       600
         Width           =       2535
      End
      Begin VB.TextBox txtNewAccount
         Height          =       375
         Index           =       1
         Left            =       2160
         TabIndex        =       2
         Top             =       600
         Width           =       1815
      End
      Begin VB.TextBox txtNewAccount
         Height          =       375
         Index           =       0
         Left            =       240
         TabIndex        =       1
         Top             =       600
         Width           =       1815
      End
      Begin VB.Label lblNewAccount
         Caption         =       "Social Security Number"
         Height          =       255
         Index           =       10
         Left            =       5880
         TabIndex        =       38
         Top             =       1200
         Width           =       2295
      End
      Begin VB.Label lblNewAccount
         Caption         =       "Phone"
         Height          =       255
         Index           =       9
         Left            =       3600
         TabIndex        =       20
         Top             =       2640
         Width           =       1095
      End
      Begin VB.Label lblNewAccount
         Caption         =       "Country"
         Height          =       255
         Index           =       8
         Left            =       240
```

continues

Listing 4.1. continued

```
        TabIndex        =    18
        Top             =    2640
        Width           =    1095
     End
     Begin VB.Label lblNewAccount
        Caption         =    "Zip Code"
        Height          =    255
        Index           =    7
        Left            =    4800
        TabIndex        =    17
        Top             =    1920
        Width           =    975
     End
     Begin VB.Label lblNewAccount
        Caption         =    "State"
        Height          =    255
        Index           =    6
        Left            =    3600
        TabIndex        =    16
        Top             =    1920
        Width           =    855
     End
     Begin VB.Label lblNewAccount
        Caption         =    "City"
        Height          =    255
        Index           =    5
        Left            =    240
        TabIndex        =    15
        Top             =    1920
        Width           =    1095
     End
     Begin VB.Label lblNewAccount
        Caption         =    "Address"
        Height          =    255
        Index           =    4
        Left            =    240
        TabIndex        =    14
        Top             =    1200
        Width           =    1095
     End
     Begin VB.Label lblNewAccount
        Caption         =    "Date of Birth"
        Height          =    255
        Index           =    3
        Left            =    6720
        TabIndex        =    13
        Top             =    360
        Width           =    1455
     End
     Begin VB.Label lblNewAccount
        Caption         =    "Last Name"
        Height          =    255
        Index           =    2
        Left            =    4080
        TabIndex        =    12
        Top             =    360
        Width           =    1215
```

```
      End
      Begin VB.Label lblNewAccount
         Caption        =     "Middle Name"
         Height         =     255
         Index          =     1
         Left           =     2160
         TabIndex       =     11
         Top            =     360
         Width          =     1215
      End
      Begin VB.Label lblNewAccount
         Caption        =     "First Name"
         Height         =     255
         Index          =     0
         Left           =     240
         TabIndex       =     10
         Top            =     360
         Width          =     1095
      End
   End
End
Attribute VB_Name = "frmTellerSystem"
Attribute VB_GlobalNameSpace = False
Attribute VB_Creatable = False
Attribute VB_PredeclaredId = True
Attribute VB_Exposed = False
Private Sub cmdClose_Click()
    theAccount.closeAccount
End Sub

Private Sub cmdDone_Click()
    End
End Sub

Private Sub cmdOpen_Click()
    theAccount.openAccount
End Sub

Private Sub cmdProcessTrans_Click()
    theAccount.processTrans txtNewAccount(14), optTransactionType
End Sub

Private Sub Command1_Click()

End Sub

Private Sub lblNewAccount_Click(Index As Integer)

End Sub

Private Sub txtNewAccount_Change(Index As Integer)
    theCustomer.First_Name = txtNewAccount(0)
    theCustomer.MiddleName = txtNewAccount(1)
    theCustomer.LastName = txtNewAccount(2)
    theCustomer.DOB = txtNewAccount(3)
    theCustomer.Address = txtNewAccount(4)
    theCustomer.SSN = txtNewAccount(10)
    theCustomer.City = txtNewAccount(5)
```

continues

Listing 4.1. continued

```
    theCustomer.State = txtNewAccount(6)
    theCustomer.Zip = txtNewAccount(7)
    theCustomer.Country = txtNewAccount(8)
    theCustomer.Phone = txtNewAccount(9)

    theAccount.pNumber = txtNewAccount(11)
    theAccount.pStatus = txtNewAccount(12)
    theAccount.pCurrBalance = txtNewAccount(13)
    theAccount = txtNewAccount(14)
End Sub

Attribute VB_Name = "modClasses"
Global theAccount As Account
Global allBankAccounts As BankAccounts
Global theCheckingAccountHistoryInfo As CheckingAccountHistoryInfo
Global theCreditHistoryInfo As CreditHistoryInfo
Global theCustomer As Customer
Global theTellerInterface As Teller_Interface

Public Enum eTransOption
    deposit
    withdrawal
End Enum
```

As you may have noticed, more code is added to the example than previously anticipated. That's normal. When you're elaborating on the body of code, you'll add code to make the system work smoothly. The idea is to add the code in an object-oriented way: methods belong to classes that make sense; there is very little use of global variables (preferably none at all); there are edit checks for required fields and sanity checks for significant business processes (such as closing accounts); and so on.

> **CAUTION**
>
> The references to model numbers are for Visual Modeler. Don't mess with these values; otherwise, your model won't work properly.

Summary

In this chapter, you learned the essence of object-oriented programming in Visual Basic 5.0. In other words, you learned how to make classes communicate with each other to carry out a behavior or set of behaviors for a proposed system. You also became familiar with design models and the importance of not deviating from the architecture of the system. You received some background on generating code in Rational Rose and Visual Modeler and on identifying the known technical constraints of Visual Basic. After you generated some example code, you got an idea of how to put the finishing touches on the application and saw a sample listing.

II

PART

Energizing Your Applications With ActiveX

Working With ActiveX and DCOM

by Dan Horsefield

IN THIS CHAPTER

CHAPTER 5

In Redmond, Washington, on July 26, 1996, Microsoft Corporation announced a lofty plan to fulfill its vision of open channels for ActiveX. To achieve this vision, Microsoft executives announced that they would transition the ActiveX specifications and the underlying technology to an industry-standards body. To do this, they selected an independent group to assist with establishing a meeting where interested industry spokespeople would gather and determine how the transition would take place.

Understanding ActiveX's Independence

To the uninitiated, Microsoft's announcement was another boring press release, but it inspired Internet service providers, information technology professionals, server system vendors, desktop operating system vendors, computer manufacturers, and many program developers interested in the new technology. They saw an opportunity to jump on a successful bandwagon with a booming growth market. This announcement meant that major corporations could embrace the new technology, knowing it would be supported by a cross-segment of interested vendors of software and hardware technology and tools.

If this cross-segment of vendors of hardware and software could work out the details, new standards would provide a solution to many compatibility and efficiency problems plaguing their industries. Many barriers would fall by the wayside. A group consisting of customers, independent software vendors (ISVs), and operating system vendors would convene to determine the process for transitioning ActiveX technology to an independent organization. The group of professionals, referred to as the Working Group, later appointed a smaller group of professionals, the Open Group, to work out the details.

The Working Group, led by Microsoft and other customer-driven companies, would develop a way for everyone to share the benefits of interactive content. ActiveX would become an open, cross-platform set of technologies used to integrate distributed computing with components over all networks, including the Internet. Microsoft's contribution to the process of inspiring the formation of an independent ActiveX Group would be three-fold. Microsoft announced commitment to the following:

- Providing source-code reference implementations on multiple platforms including UNIX, Macintosh, and Windows. Key implementations of ActiveX, by using COM (Component Object Model) and DCOM (Distributed Component Object Model), would be included to help vendors create their own solutions incorporating the new technology.

- Unveiling the technology and specifications behind COM, which had become a popular and widely used technology. COM would assist in the implementation of a language that would allow various components to work together in one application. Now the requirement for licensing COM would become more relaxed.

- Exposing DCOM, the key new technology that made ActiveX so attractive. DCOM would assist in the implementation of a language that would allow the various components to work together over networks, especially the Internet. DCOM implementation would "bind" objects (application components and applications) residing on different platforms at various locations.

- Providing the necessary specifications used in the technology.
- Granting appropriate rights to ActiveX trademarks.

Looking at Cross-Platform Vendor-Neutral Standards

Microsoft took another step toward transforming ActiveX component architecture from a proprietary specification to an industry standard. A large task group met and voted to name the Open Group as an outside arbiter to head up the effort of transitioning ActiveX to an independent body. A majority of representatives from more than 100 companies voted at the task group's first meeting on Oct. 1, 1996, to turn over licensing, branding, and management of the ActiveX specification to the Open Group.

The Open Group is an industry consortium experienced in promoting other cross-platform technologies. The meeting brought together a cross-section of the industry to form a group that Microsoft referred to as *ActiveX stakeholders*. At the meeting, 63 votes were cast in support of handing over ActiveX to the Open Group, which would, in turn, organize a subgroup called the Active Group. The Active Group would handle licensing, branding, and validation of ActiveX technologies.

At that October meeting, Microsoft identified the following items that the company would turn over to the Open Group for use by the Active Group. These topics comprise the ActiveX technologies, according to Microsoft:

- Reference implementations of ActiveX on Windows (Win32), Macintosh, and UNIX platforms
- Specifications for ActiveX core technologies:
  - *Component Object Model (COM)*.
  - *Distributed Component Object Model (DCOM)*. Microsoft indicated that COM and DCOM are the underlying architecture "object models" for ActiveX. See "Learning How ActiveX Works" later in this chapter for details about COM and DCOM and how they enable ActiveX computing.
  - *Microsoft Remote Procedure Call (MS-RPC)*. This compatible implementation of DCE RPC is also known as *Object Remote Procedure Call (ORPC)*. It provides scalability, marshaling, and privacy support. DCE (Distributed Computing Environment) is an older cross-platform architecture already supported by multiple vendors. DCE is managed and promoted by the Open Group.

5

WORKING WITH
ACTIVEX AND
DCOM

- *Standard Security Provider Interface (SSPI)*. NT LAN Manager (NTLM) SSPI allows secure invocation of components. NTLM is the security protocol of Windows NT.

- *Structured Storage of COM components*, a rich, transaction-based hierarchical file format. The hierarchical file format allows applications to share files across application and platforms.

- *The COM registry*. Similar to the Windows 95 Registry, this provides a database of COM components and their configuration information.

- *Monikers*. Monikers provide for persistent, intelligent names.

- *Automation*. OLE Automation allows objects to expose functionality to high-level programming languages and scripting environments.

In summary, ActiveX is a relatively new set of client/server technologies that represent a major rework of earlier technologies. The new technology initially was created and controlled exclusively by Microsoft. The cross-platform set of technologies was widely adopted by information technology professionals, managers of information systems, technical directors, communications architects, network architecture professionals, corporate solutions providers, and information services groups.

Exploring System Interoperability

Interoperability became a buzzword in 1996. All Microsoft executives used the word to describe a new way of computing with distributed components over the Internet. The term might best be defined as the means by which different computer applications, various computer languages, and various operating system platforms could share *common threads* over a diverse network. The threads they would share have come to be known as ActiveX controls and the underlying code that makes them work. *ActiveX controls* are computer components (objects) enabled for use on the Internet.

All computer users can share ActiveX controls residing on Internet sites only if interoperability is in place. Interoperability requires the incorporation of a few groups of technologies being used by Microsoft and others for distributed computing. These technologies, including COM and OLE, are the basic building blocks making interoperability a reality over all networks, including the Internet. DCOM is Microsoft's *definition* (suggested standard or specification) regarding how this interoperability should be implemented on various platforms. A standard is necessary so that ActiveX controls will be accessible and functional for all users.

Understanding DCOM and Platform Compatibility

The popularity and flexibility of the Java programming language has helped inspire rapid growth on the Internet. Java lets you launch independent applets within other programs over a network. The vision of DCOM and its primary benefits are explained in the following text. Some of the information is condensed from *DCOM: A Business Overview* (`dcombiz.exe`), which you can download from `http://www.asia.microsoft.com/ntserver/info/dcom.htm`.

Information technology managers consider the ramifications of Java technology and its evolving impact on the Internet to be of critical importance to the future of computing as we know it today. One key technology in this evolution is distributed component computing over a network. The basis of this technology includes DCE (Distributed Computing Environment) and DCOM (Distributed Component Object Model).

DCE, an older architecture already supported by some vendors, enables cross-platform computing. DCOM is Microsoft's new specification for a cross-platform, client/server computing environment. It supports the use of components (applets) over existing networks.

> **NOTE**
>
> Think of *components* as ActiveX controls containing useful visual objects such as command buttons, input boxes, checkboxes, marquees, animated objects, image controls, and the like.

DCOM is paving the way for widespread use of component software technology over networks. With this technology, you can break large, complex software applications into a series of flexible, prefabricated software modules. One logical conclusion to be drawn from this new technology's popularity is that prefabricated ActiveX controls will affect the computing industry just as prefabricated home components did in the residential and commercial construction industries almost a decade ago.

Similar to the modules found in the COM (Component Object Model) technology, the controls can be easily developed, understood, and modified. These applets (including ActiveX controls) are the means of delivering software solutions more quickly and at a lower cost. The goal of the new technology is to achieve economies of scale for software deployment across multiple platforms and networks. (*Economies of scale* means that programs of widely varied sizes, purposes, and complexities can be written and deployed to various systems and still take advantage of the same core benefits.) This new component architecture for building software applications promotes fast, affordable, and flexible applications because of the following benefits:

- *Faster development.* As a programmer, you can build solutions more quickly and create software by assembling prebuilt parts.

- *Lower integration costs.* You can create a common set of interfaces (Netscape Navigator and Internet Explorer, for example) for software programs from specialized software vendors. The interfaces reduce the custom work required to integrate components into complete solutions.

5

WORKING WITH
ACTIVEX AND
DCOM

- *Programming flexibility.* Many of the new DCOM interfaces are programmable, as are almost all third-party ActiveX components based on DCOM. They feature built-in support for plug-ins, or the distributors of the software offer the source code for modification and reuse.

- *Deployment flexibility.* COM makes it easier to customize a specific software solution for different divisions of a company by simply changing *some* of the components in the overall application.

- *Lower maintenance costs.* Software functions are isolated into discreet components, providing a low-cost, more efficient mechanism to upgrade a component. This eliminates the necessity of retrofitting an entire application.

DCOM Architecture

A distributed component architecture provides unique benefits for multiuser, multiplatform applications:

- *COM support.* DCOM is based on the most widely used component technology today: COM. DCOM has been characterized very simply as "COM with a longer wire"—a low-level extension of the Component Object Model, which is the core object technology within Microsoft ActiveX.

- *Ready-made tools.* Major development tools vendors—including Microsoft, Borland, Sybase/Powersoft, Symantec, ORACLE, IBM, and Micro Focus—already sell software-development tools that produce ActiveX components. These tools and the applications they produce automatically support DCOM, providing the broadest possible industry support.

- *Native to the Internet.* DCOM is an ActiveX technology that works natively with Internet technologies such as TCP/IP protocol, the Java language, and the HTTP network protocol. It's the key link that allows business applications to work on the Internet.

Businesses can realize the benefits of a modern component application architecture without having to replace investments in existing systems, staff, and infrastructure. Why? Consider these three factors: the largest installed base, native support for Internet protocols, and open support for multiple platforms.

DCOM enables distributed Java today without requiring any communications-specific code or add-on schemes such as remote classes. DCOM is an open technology that runs on several popular platforms. The ActiveX Working Group (the Active Group) is openly licensing DCOM technology to software companies to run on all the major operating systems, including multiple implementations of UNIX-based systems.

Software AG has DCOM running on the Solaris-based operating system today. Also, Microsoft broke ground in 1996 by working with the Internet standards bodies, including the Internet Engineering Task Force (IETF) and the World Wide Web Consortium (W3C), to promote DCOM as a public Internet technology.

> **NOTE**
>
> A technical publication that contains a publicly available description of the DCOM network protocol can be found at `http://www.microsoft.com/oledev/olecom/draft-brown-dcom-v1-spec-01.txt`.

Object Technology

Component-based development is established today as a mainstream business technology on the desktop. DCOM has its roots in Microsoft's object technology. Let's briefly look at the evolution of this technology:

- The first big evolutionary step the past decade was from DDE (dynamic data exchange) to OLE (object linking and embedding). DDE is a form of messaging between Windows-based programs. OLE provides a means for embedding visual links between programs within an application.

- OLE then evolved into COM, which is used as the basis for all object binding. By opening, binding to, and later closing objects, remote calls to these objects can add functionality to a client application.

- The latest step in the evolutionary chain is ActiveX (COM enabled for the Internet). ActiveX gets its power from DCOM, which uses an enhancement to the network protocol DCE RPC.

The evolution of this technology shares a common theme: Each iteration reduces the complexity of building large applications while allowing the delivery of progressively improved functionality for end users.

This process lowers application development costs because you can *leverage* prebuilt components and their interfaces without having to spend as much time testing and integrating the work of many people. It is common knowledge that applications built from components are simply easier to generate and debug than large, monolithic applications.

Examples of Present and Future Benefits

Many of you have read and reviewed the problems regarding the year 2000 and its impact on legacy-based applications. Almost all large organizations, including financial institutions, are scrambling to resolve this potential fiasco. In two years, when computer clocks begin using the year 2000 with data and applications that don't support numbers beyond 1999 (or, in some cases, 99), the predicted outcome is data integrity failure. To avoid failure when the date changes to the new millennium requires an application design solution. This isn't simply a date problem—it's a problem brought by a lack of foresight in the design of many software programs. Databases and production systems are very vulnerable to potential disaster.

If legacy applications were written with a common date component, the fix would be easy to isolate and inexpensive to repair. That's what DCOM is bringing to the future of computing. An accurate time control source is now available on the Internet, courtesy of the National Institute of Standards and Technology.

Suppose that everyone used a common dataset for their date information. A standards body maintains redundant sites with this dataset and computers automatically synchronize with the dataset at regular intervals—minutes, days, weeks or years. Because everyone synchronizes with the single dataset, when the year 2000 arrives, all clients of the dataset would face the same problem and the same patch would work for everybody.

This would be a single date component or mini-application. A relatively simple upgrade to this single theoretical Internet-based component would be all that's necessary to avoid pending catastrophe for thousands of companies.

If this dataset had been designed 100 years ago and the technology was available then, we wouldn't be facing the Year 2000 problem. Most Windows developers understand DCOM's benefits and are already using the ActiveX component architecture, even if they don't call it ActiveX. Remember, this is just the next step in an evolution of Microsoft's object technology. Because DCOM is included as part of Microsoft's most recent operating systems, it has eliminated the need to acquire third-party Object Request Broker (ORB) software.

Another appropriate example of how this new technology makes programs easier to generate and debug is a modern stock ticker running in a Web browser window. You can use a single database to run all the tickers used on numerous Web pages across the Internet. With DCOM, all the individual desktop applications update their respective ticker like this:

1. A single query to a database of ticker information runs on the server.
2. A new current dataset is created with the latest figures for the ticker.
3. The individual desktop PCs linked to the Internet would run a "personalized" query against that single dataset when they update their ticker.

You can see how much computing work this would eliminate. It also permits customization because the desktop query can request only information needed from the dataset.

Widespread Acceptance of DCOM

That the DCOM technology has been turned over to a vendor-neutral standards body for distribution and standardization doesn't mean every computer program developer will embrace and use it. According to Microsoft, however, more than 3 million programmers are trained on ActiveX and its technologies—OLE, COM, and DCOM. Hundreds of independent software companies are shipping thousands of prebuilt software components.

You can use Microsoft Visual Basic, PowerBuilder, Micro Focus Visual Object, COBOL, and other popular tools to manipulate these commercial software controls, utilities, interfaces, and full-featured applications. The key business benefits of ActiveX on the desktop extend to DCOM across the network: Because ActiveX is language-neutral, you can build ActiveX components from any language. ActiveX components built in COBOL can work with components built in Java, Visual Basic, VBScript, and so on.

The logical boundary for component applications is no longer on a single platform, such as a Windows-based IBM-compatible PC. Shared applications on multiple machines are now available because of ActiveX and related technologies. These programs are referred to as *n-tier applications*, because *tiers* of application logic, presentation services, business services, information retrieval and management services are broken into different components that can communicate directly with each other across a network.

Each tier of service would reside on a computer system other than the system where users interact with the program. A three-tier application, for example, may be a very basic PC application that features extensive functionality, because it draws on resources from three tiers available on three sophisticated computer systems.

To end users, these applications appear as a seamless extension of their existing desktop or mainframe environment. For the information technology or information systems manager, these applications represent the opportunity to apply the economics and flexibility of desktop development across a broader set of challenges. For example, a business can deploy a new personnel management system based on a multitier application design by using components. The application includes different data-entry components, each designed for a separate department or division.

These components all use a common, single payroll income tax calculation component that runs on a server. As income-tax laws change, the company must change only the tax component located on the server, without retrofitting the components for each department or division. ActiveX technology, when used to save money, permits downsizing of computer software.

DCOM is an ideal technology solution for three-tier applications because it allows ActiveX components to work across networks. You can easily build complex systems that escape single-machine boundaries. For example, you can achieve number crunching on a large mainframe server and use the resulting data on a PC with more limited processing capability. This way, you can integrate the components without having to worry about network programming, system compatibility, and integration of various components that were built with different languages.

DCOM is popular because it allows the millions of existing ActiveX programmers to build server components that interoperate with desktop counterparts, thereby broadening the target audience and user base for the application. Companies can assign the same developers to client and server applications, therefore reducing training costs, the number of tools purchased, and support costs. DCOM was designed initially to run on Windows 95 and Windows NT, but also works on Macintosh, UNIX, and legacy operating systems. This way, platform designers have a basis for a *common application infrastructure*, which can broaden the entire computing environment, thus lowering integration costs while reducing integration complexities.

Complying With Earlier Technologies

DCOM is layered on the Open Group's Distributed Computing Environment Remote Procedure Call mechanism (DCE RPC), a network communications protocol developed and endorsed by IBM, Sun Microsystems, Hewlett-Packard, and DEC.

Because a source code implementation of DCOM is available free from the Open Group, additional computer vendors will be incorporating it. Examples of the additional object-related extensions to the DCE RPC required by DCOM are contained within a text file available at http://www.microsoft.com/oledev/olecom/draft-brown-dcom-v1-spec-01.txt.

Businesses will use the new Internet protocols and ActiveX technology to link component-based applications across public and private networks, projecting a presence of their business systems onto the World Wide Web. The simplicity, ubiquity, and industry momentum of standard Internet protocols such as HTTP make DCOM an ideal technology for linking components together in applications that require more than just a desktop PC to function.

HTTP is easy to use, is inherently cross-platform, and supports an accessible, universal naming service. Much of the excitement generated by the Java language derives from its potential as a mechanism to build distributed component applications on the Internet. For example, many companies have built investment portfolio management systems that rely on Internet-based data streams, such as PointCast, for stock information. PCQuote is enlisting programmers to develop spreadsheet-based stock analysis data streams. Many others are developing these kinds of Internet services and capabilities, using ActiveX, DCOM, and related technologies.

Using DCOM and ActiveX Development

Integrating existing services and applications into in-house solutions by using browsers and Web technology is the new norm. You can simply plug in the services of a remote server component that's already communicating with many clients over the Internet to provide a low-cost—sometimes free—way to enhance the functionality of an in-house software offering.

DCOM is ideally positioned to become a mainstream Internet technology for business applications because it's considered *transport neutral.* This means that it doesn't matter what protocols the client and server are using to communicate. DCOM supports connection-oriented (analog, satellite, and the like) and "connectionless" transport (cabled or wired LAN) including TCP/IP, UDP/IP, IPX/SPX, AppleTalk, and HTTP protocols.

Because you can embed ActiveX components into browser-based applications, DCOM allows a rich application infrastructure for distributed Internet applications that leverage the latest browser technology. Today's browsers use DCOM's efficiency, network recovery, and security offerings. DCOM supports security by integrating Internet certificate-based security with an even richer level of Windows NT-based security, combining the best of both worlds.

As distributed applications built from simple components and Internet protocols emerge, a new set of enterprise platform services for component applications will be required. Some are already emerging. Likewise, computer users can benefit from new advances in technology through HTML (Hypertext Markup Language) anchors that point to sources of upgrades and allow users to automatically upgrade their systems with ActiveX components. These components can be in the form of .cab files that automatically update the operating system registry as the browser downloads the software.

A key goal of any component software architecture is to separate business logic (how a tax component calculates tax rates, for example) from execution logic (whether the tax component runs in a browser or on a multiprocessor server). DCOM extends the separation of business logic and execution logic even further because the same components can communicate with each other across processes in a single machine or across the Internet via HTTP. Components by themselves don't solve all the issues of enterprise application complexity, such as exception handling, system failures, network outages, and performance load peaks.

To address the enterprise requirements for a distributed component architecture without sacrificing rapid development and cost effectiveness, Microsoft is integrating DCOM into the ActiveX Server Framework, a series of technology services that speed deployment of componentbased applications across the Internet and corporate intranets. Some of the ActiveX Server Framework services include

- Transactions, a term that describes rollback and recovery for component-based applications in the event of system failure.
- Queuing, which represents the integration of component communication with reliable store-and-then-forward spooling queues. These queues allow component applications to operate on occasionally or frequently unavailable networks.
- Server scripting, which refers to the easy integration of components by using a programming language within HTML files. Scripting works with browser pages and browser-compatible application interfaces referred to as *active documents*.
- The integration of component applications with legacy production systems, including mainframe systems running CICS and IMS.

The ActiveX Server Framework technologies were built with publicly available Internet protocols and began to appear in 1996. DCOM first shipped with Windows NT Server 4.0 and Windows NT Workstation 4.0 in mid-1996. On Sept. 18, 1996, Microsoft released the DCOM for Windows 95 Developer Beta at no charge to Windows developers and Windows 95 customers.

DCOM for the Macintosh was offered on the Internet at the beginning of 1997. DCOM for Solaris was available for download on the Internet in late 1996. Additional implementations of DCOM on other Internet and enterprise platforms are emerging now. For the latest information on Windows NT Server, go to http://www.microsoft.com/backoffice.

Working With Third-Party Controls

The emergence of controls other than those packaged with ActiveX Control Pad and offered at no charge by Microsoft quickly gained popularity among developers in the third quarter of 1996. The list of available controls is expanding at a rapid pace.

Some of the popular new controls are offered at no charge or for less than $20, but others sell for $1,000 or more. You can add some controls to the ActiveX Control Pad toolbox utility, whereas some have limited functionality in Control Pad. More than 1,000 of these independent controls—some of them merely variations of the existing controls—were being offered by dozens of software vendors by the first quarter of 1997. Some appeared to have some significant sophistication and usefulness for developers. Some even required monthly fees to acquire.

Dozens of small, medium, and large software companies are creating the controls, including Borland, Oracle, and Sybase/Powersoft. Some of these companies also offer development tools to build ActiveX controls. Fourteen companies that create Web design and development tools have built ActiveX support into their products, allowing their customers to create and use the controls in their programs.

When this book was written, Metrowerks was working with Microsoft to build support for ActiveX into the Macintosh computer platform. Bristol and Mainsoft were working to develop support on UNIX platforms. Because of these efforts, ActiveX controls will have one of the broadest computer markets of any software being distributed. This move to ActiveX cross-platform compatibility could inspire a seriously radical trend in software marketing. If ActiveX is supported universally, the controls will obviously have more appeal with a wider customer base.

It's important to remember that ActiveX involves both client and server technologies. Its elements include

- *The ActiveX controls*, interactive objects in a Web page or application that provide interactive and user-controllable functions
- *ActiveX documents*, technology that lets users view non-HTML documents such as Microsoft Excel or Word files in a Web browser window
- *Active Scripting*, a language used to control the integrated behavior of several ActiveX controls or Java applets from the browser or server
- *Java Virtual Machine*, the code that allows the browser to run Java applets and integrate applets with ActiveX controls
- *ActiveX Server Framework*, a framework that provides a number of Web server-based functions, such as security, database access, and others

You can find an ActiveX Web site at `http://www.microsoft.com/activex/gallery/`. This commercial Web site promotes the sale and use of free and proprietary ActiveX controls (and interfaces). Full-featured programming environments used to build specific types of controls, such as interactive animated movies, are also offered.

Learning How ActiveX Works

At the heart of ActiveX technology is a method for allowing an object, otherwise known as a *component* or *control*, to dynamically call on external resources to carry out its intended function. Most of you are familiar with dynamic links of this nature. DDE is a phenomenon of significant importance in distributed computing. It allows an object to remain small while the functionality of the object is less restrained. How these objects bind to the code segments they depend on is what sets ActiveX technology ahead. The reliable binding of objects over a very diverse network is what makes ActiveX unique.

Most of you understand how DLLs and OLE work. DLLs are organized code segments or code snippets used by an application. More than one part of the program can call on different parts of the DLL to carry out a function. OLE files are linked or embedded and act as visual placeholders in a document or program. They help keep the code small by not duplicating each instance of the file.

COM is a first cousin to DLLs and OLE files. COM distributes computing that uses computer program components. These components, to put it simply, are prebuilt code shells that serve specific purposes. A text box, for example, is a COM object shell for ASCII data. By using this COM object, you can assign certain properties, methods, and events to the COM object to determine how users can use the shell and generate an action.

Each COM component has something in common with all the other COM components: They rely on the same underlying code to function. The underlying code is a sort of a common headquarters or base of operations. With ActiveX, the common headquarters scenario is more complex. The base of the code can be local or remote. Ordinary COM objects rely on this base of operations to function. Each COM object in a program *seems* to be an independent program module, but really the COM objects are very dependent. Their illusion of independence is necessary to make the COM objects simple to build, change, deploy, organize, and launch.

COM allows you to build complex applications faster and at a lower cost because the "common" code that the objects rely on doesn't have to be duplicated for each object. You can think of COM objects as prefabricated walls. The walls have different shapes, thickness, and colors, but each has common features including the lumber, drywall, nails, and paint. You take the basic shell of a wall and fabricate it to specification without having to know much about the rest of the building. You don't have to know details about the rooms in the building that your wall will eventually become a part of.

DCOM is a closely related technology with additional features. It takes care of the task of conforming to network and platform differences. DCOM's purpose is less specific than COM. DCOM uses a fairly complex networking technology that takes into account variances in protocols and operating systems. It's technically a sophisticated network protocol. A basic introduction to how DCOM and distributed computing works is a prerequisite for learning how ActiveX works.

To get a basic understanding of DCOM without studying DCOM specifications and network architectures in detail, let's try to draw on some simple analogies. Think of DCOM as the electrical current in a network of independent appliances in a laundry business. This laundry is an unmanned store where people go to wash and dry their clothes. Picture the laundry as the Internet. Without DCOM (the electricity), the laundry can't carry out its function. The laundry depends on DCOM.

To illustrate how ActiveX controls work, I'll refer to ActiveX controls as COM objects. The COM objects in the laundry are the individual appliances—the washers and dryers. Each COM object has a function. The appliances in this laundry come in different colors, sizes, and shapes. That's the nature of the Internet—diversity. Each COM object is like a washer or dryer because each has different capacities, cycles, timers, pumps, heating elements, and the like. These differences—including the COM object's visual representation, its purpose, its properties, events, and methods—are what make the controls unique. On the other hand, they're similar enough to each other to be programmed by using a single programming interface such as Visual Basic.

All the COM objects have a common purpose. The purpose of each control isn't much different from the purpose of programs two decades ago—to allow a user to create an input and then generate an output. The actual inputs and outputs are much different, however, than what was seen in those early days of computing. The appliances in the laundry analogy, like COM objects, must work together reliably to consistently get the clothes from their dirty state to a clean state.

The washers come in different brands and configurations. Think of an Apple Macintosh COM object as one brand, a UNIX workstation COM object as another brand, and an IBM-compatible PC COM object as a third brand. DCOM must conform to each platform's needs so that everything will work together. It does this behind the scenes by using "transformers" that allow the electrical current to be conditioned for each unique platform. The development of these transformers is considered "work in progress" for some computer platform manufacturers.

In 1996, Microsoft released code source implementations of DCOM on various platforms. DCOM was already running on the Solaris platform in addition to 32-bit Windows platforms. In 1997, some new DCOM-compatible platforms and operating systems emerged. Perhaps in the future almost all platforms will feature interoperability using DCOM.

To understand ActiveX a little better, consider that each appliance has its own configuration. The Java applet appliance, for example, works differently from the Brand X ActiveX control appliance. The two appliances are related, however, because they're both objects that rely on DCOM and DCOM's underlying technologies for interoperability. They can work together in the same application just as the washers and dryers work together in the laundry.

DCOM allows distributed Java without requiring any communications-specific code or add-ins. Remote classes aren't required for Java to work under DCOM. This may be one reason Microsoft has embraced Java and made significant efforts to incorporate Java's functionality into its own technology fold. Whether DCOM or Java arrived on the scene first is a moot point; the important point from your perspective is that they can coexist.

COM, a scaled-down version of DCOM, was originally intended for DDE in desktop applications. In some cases, a network that uses a particular protocol to sustain the dynamic links is used with COM. For example, in a peer-to-peer local area network (LAN), a drive mapping would allow COM to work over the network. If the network fails, the COM link typically fails and the program can crash. DCOM is a technology that allows this dynamic link to be stronger and more versatile by standardizing the method of binding and sustaining the link. The intent is to make the link more reliable when differences are encountered or when the network fails.

COM and DCOM support the use of components. The most commonly used components of this nature today are COM objects. Think of COM objects as *common* objects—they're common in use and have common functionality. When you consider the analogy of COM objects to appliances, picture these appliances with a model number (class ID) and a serial number (filename). Each appliance has an ID and serial number so that the platform can interpret the code to generate the desired results. Each COM object has a unique function but belongs to a class of similar objects.

Microsoft, Borland, Sybase/Powersoft, Symantec, ORACLE, IBM, and Micro Focus already sell software-development tools used to produce ActiveX components. This broad industry support is what has made DCOM the distributed computing technology of choice. Because a few thousand ActiveX controls are already built with these tools, the use of DCOM in the marketplace is becoming prevalent. This is true despite some developers not really understanding the details of how DCOM works.

Since Microsoft openly licensed DCOM in 1996 and then agreed to transition the technology to a third-party task force to make the technology independent, the implementation of DCOM on various platforms continues to expand. In 1996, DCOM was running on a Solaris-based system, and other implementations were on a number of UNIX systems. By the end of 1996, Macintosh was offering DCOM functionality. Some platform vendors complained that DCOM was a technology better suited for a Windows environment than for their platform, but DCOM really is just an application of existing Internet technologies that were founded on network protocols, programming languages, and platforms from various vendors, including Microsoft.

DCOM protocol works hand in hand with TCP/IP and HTTP, the primary protocols used for Internet traffic. In technical terms, DCOM is *layered* on—and therefore compatible with—the Distributed Computing Environment. It's also layered on TCP/IP and HTTP. You could see this phenomenon as technology borrowing from other technologies, because it's not to anyone's advantage to rewrite standards that already have been proven to work.

Compatibility and multiplatform usefulness means that companies can build applications by using existing investments in networks, programs, objects, databases, and platforms. One major benefit of interoperability and the way ActiveX works is the availability of remote components for use in local applications. For example, a company selling financial services can use Object Remote Procedure Calls built into DCOM (based on RPC and borrowed from DCE) to acquire data from a database that contains stock data. In this way, each company can create its own unique stock ticker while using a common data source, dramatically decreasing the cost of providing timely stock data to users.

Interoperability will continue to boost the use of browsers in the future because ActiveX components can be embedded into browser-based applications. DCOM provides an application infrastructure for distributed Internet applications that make efficient use of the latest browser technology.

Some organizations with Internet Web sites are tackling the issues of standardizing this interoperability. You can find one such organization, Object Management Group, at `http://www.omg.org`. This group became involved with ActiveX when Microsoft decided to expose how it was using ActiveX and revealed the core technologies it was using.

You can find another standards group, the ECTF (Enterprise Computer Telephony Forum), at `http://www.ectf.org/ectf_about.html`. This group has a more specialized interest in standardizing the interoperability of a particular computing environment. If you're interested in the standards associated with interoperability in general or for specific types of computing, search the Internet with the keyword `interoperability`.

Handling Necessary Network Tasks

DCOM helps you handle the authentication, authorization, and message integrity capabilities of DCE's Remote Procedure Call. A DCOM implementation may support any level of DCE RPC security. You can make any connection or call as secure or as insecure as the client application dictates. The client and the server negotiate this level of security. Developers commonly make the mistake of getting the proverbial cart before the horse when trying to use this authentication and authorization process for the first time. The key to avoiding this pitfall is to make sure that the first step (authentication) is completed before attempting the second step (authorization). Servers don't always respond quickly enough with these calls to permit you to attempt this with two lines of code. There has to be code between the authentication and authorization calls that checks to see whether the processing of the first call is complete before proceeding with another call.

DCOM uses universally unique identification (UUID) to determine and handle different interface versions. During remote procedure calls by objects (ORPC), the object's ID field (contained in the invocation header) sends an IPID to the server being called. (An IPID, or *interface pointer identifier*, is a 128-bit identifier.) The IPID specifies a particular interface on a particular object in a particular server. The IPID is located in the object ID fields of a remote procedure call. The static type of IPID is really a UUID, but you have to make a distinction between the two; IPIDs and UUIDs are different birds.

IPIDs are relative to the server process that originally allocated them. In other words, they aren't global or universal in scope. IPIDs don't necessarily use the standard UUID allocation algorithm. They may use a machine-specific algorithm that organizes how the data is dispatched. This is one key to successful interoperability. To put it another way, the identifier is "machine-dependent." When it comes time to process the object, the server determines how the data is dispatched.

The interface ID field of the RPC header specifies the identification of the object and the arguments found in the body of the object. RPC normally works this way. When viewed from the DCOM perspective, however, an additional first argument is always present that isn't part of the COM interface specification. It's placed as the first identifier in the body of the request Protocol Data Unit (PDU, a packet of data that's passed across a network). This special type of argument, known technically as ORPCTHIS, assists the machine in generating an 8-byte alignment of arguments. The ORPCTHIS is padded with bytes of zeros, if necessary, to achieve this alignment for the remaining arguments.

The replies to the ORPC—output or feedback to the client—have a corresponding additional return value, not found in COM. This value, is technically known as ORPCTHAT, is also placed in the body of the PDU (in this case, the response PDU) before the normal return values.

ORPC calls might summon a method on an interface that isn't supported by that interface. The method number is, in technical terms, beyond the number of methods the server recognizes for that interface. In DCOM, this generates a fault. When a fault is encountered, the ORPCTHAT is placed in specific locations in the response packet. The locations depend on whether the call was connectionless (non-network) or connection-oriented (network). This form of error-trapping, unique to DCOM, prevents crashes. The client can handle the fault PDU with an error message such as Method Not Supported. ORPCTHIS and ORPCTHAT are necessary to retain the 8-byte alignment necessary for evaluation by the client and server on all platforms.

When ActiveX uses remote objects and procedures, the DCOM protocol or DCE RPC is used to control the traffic. This traffic control relies on OXID resolvers (formerly referred to as IObjectExporter) on the client and server. In the earlier laundry analogy, a transformer is needed to make sure that the appliances will work together despite their differences. These transformers are the OXID resolvers.

Transforming Information and Binding

Here is how the transformation of information works: An OXID resolver on the server receives a call from an object. Packaged with the object's call arguments and other identification, described previously, is a packet of information that informs the server regarding the type of binding being requested. This information doesn't contain any data regarding how to bind to the desired objects or dispatch the data. If it did, the code would be bulky and would have to take into account too many variations in operating systems. Instead, this data, known as an *identifier*, defines the type of binding being sought by the client. This information is carried in a 64-bit value called an *object exporter identifier*. The object exporter identifier has recently been renamed OXID.

The server evaluates the OXID to create the necessary binding work on the server's end. To evaluate the OXID requires the OXID resolver that was referred to previously as a transformer. This resolver (one per machine, per protocol) is located at specific ports on the server's network, depending on the type of protocol being used for communication. These ports are known in DCOM terminology as *endpoints*.

The important thing about OXID resolvers is that they work strategically to keep the binding active and carry out the actual invocation of the binding. This work opens the door for two-way communication with objects and keeps the objects "alive," so to speak. The resolver also keeps the client and server in constant communication despite any inactivity on either end while the interaction work is under way. In this way, the binding exchanges can be frequent or infrequent, and bulky processing work can take place on the server or the client without losing the link.

An OXID resolver is on the client as well. This OXID resolver can cache information about the response OXIDs so that repeated calls to the server for this information aren't needed.

To draw on another analogy, think of this two-way communication as a telephone call to Japan. Japanese and U.S. citizens in a room in America are on a conference call with Japanese and U.S. citizens in a room in Japan. Interpreters are in both rooms. Sometimes, during the interpretation work, one interpreter might have to explain that he's still listening to a lengthy explanation and isn't ready to give the translation yet. Another interpreter might have to indicate that he's still waiting for a response or reaction from the other room. In DCOM and other network protocols, this communication negotiation is achieved with *pings*, simply bursts of data between the client and server that inform each other they're standing by, waiting for the other party to send. The OXID resolvers are the translators in this analogy, and they ping each other to keep the communication alive during periods of inactivity.

You can think of an OXID as the *scope of implementation* sought by the object. This is the general description of the assignment that the object carries to the server for processing. It can refer to a given process, a thread within a process, or a whole machine. The scope of implementation doesn't affect the protocol itself. DCOM's resolvers take the scope of the task into account and react accordingly. Meanwhile, the data structure of the program that exported the object's call or response keeps track of the IPIDs (128-bit interface pointer identifiers).

The actual OXID resolver is a DCE RPC interface. One OXID service on a given machine keeps track of all the OXIDs, and there may be several at any given moment. The OXID resolver does its work by caching the mapping information used to create and maintain the bindings for dynamic exchange of data. When a destination application receives an object reference (an OXID), it checks to see whether it recognizes it. If it doesn't, the OXID resolver is queried for the translation, and the resolver saves the resulting set of string bindings in a local table that maps OXIDs to string bindings.

Each OXID is associated with an OXID COM object that depends on a COM interface (IRemUnknown) to manage reference counts and requests. Interface references are a new data type that can be marshaled. DCOM extends the Network Data Representation (NDR) by defining these interface references to an object. This is the only extension to NDR made by the DCOM protocol. In technical terms, an OBJREF is the data type used to represent an actual marshaled object reference. This OBJREF can be empty (Null) or assume one of three variations (Standard, Custom, or Handler). Which variation the OBJREF assumes depends on the degree to which the object being marshaled uses the hook architecture in the marshaling infrastructure.

OBJREF contains a *switch flag* (determines type) and then the appropriate data. The OBJREF variations are as follows:

- *Null* points out that there's no object.
- *Standard* contains one interface of an object marshaled in standard form. This means it contains a standard reference and a set of protocol sequences and network addresses that can be used to bind to an OXID resolver. The standard variation contains several items:
    - An IPID (interface pointer) that uniquely specifies the interface and object.
    - An object ID (OID), which uniquely specifies the unique object on which the IPID is found (depending on the OXID with which the object is associated).
    - An OXID.
    - A reference count, indicating the number of references to this IPID being conveyed. This count, typically a value of 1, can be 0, 1, or more.
    - Any pertinent flags useful for identification of state.

  The OXID resolver can translate the OXID in the STDOBJREF. This is useful when using (marshaling) a proxy (go-between) to give to another machine. The first machine (marshaling machine) identifies the saResAddr for the OXID resolver on the server machine. This eliminates a need for the "unmarshaler" to call the go-between back to get this information. The first machine doesn't need to keep the OXID in its cache to satisfy requests from clients that it just gave the OBJREF to. Table 5.1 lists the members of the OBJREF standard variation.
- *Custom* contains a class ID (CLSID) and class-specific information. The custom variation gives an object control over references to itself. For example, an immutable object might be passed by value, in which case the class-specific information would contain the object's immutable data. Table 5.2 lists the members of the custom variation.
- *Handler* specifies that the object requires handler marshaling. For example, an object is to be represented in client address spaces by a proxy object that caches state. The class-specific information in this variation is a standard reference to an interface pointer that the proxy object (handler) uses to communicate with the original object. Table 5.3 lists members of the OBJREF handler variation.

Table 5.1. The OBJREF standard variation members.

Member	Data Type	Semantic Description
signature	unsigned long	Must be OBJREF_SIGNATURE
flags	unsigned long	OBJREF flags
GUID	iid	Interface identifier
std	STDOBJREF	A standard object reference used to connect to the source object
SaResAddr	STRINGARRAY	The resolver address

Table 5.2. The OBJREF custom variation members.

Member	Data Type	Semantic Description
signature	unsigned long	Must be OBJREF_SIGNATURE.
flags	unsigned long	OBJREF flags.
GUID	iid	Interface identifier.
clsid	CLSID	The CLSID of the object to create in the destination client.
cbExtension	unsigned long	The size of the extension data.
size	unsigned long	The size of the marshaled data provided by the source object, plus the size of the extension data, and passed in pData.
pData	byte	The data bytes that should be passed to IMarshal::UnmarshalInterface on encountering a new instance of class clsid to initialize it and complete the unmarshal process (class-specific data). The first cbExtension bytes are reserved for future extensions to the DCOM protocol and shouldn't be passed into the custom unmarshaler.

Table 5.3. The OBJREF handler variation members.

Member	Data Type	Semantic Description
signature	unsigned long	Must be OBJREF_SIGNATURE
flags	unsigned long	OBJREF flags

Member	Data Type	Semantic Description
GUID	iid	Interface identifier
std	STDOBJREF	A standard object reference used to connect to the source object
clsid	CLSID	The CLSID of handler to create in the destination client
SaResAddr	STRINGARRAY	The resolver address

Developing Network Architectures

A key part of keeping networked computing intact on such a diverse hierarchy of clients and servers requires some creative thinking with respect to network architectures and how to make protocols work with these architectures. In response to this challenge, DCOM's authors arrived at some network architecture conclusions that led to some unique thinking.

For example, in the DCOM protocol, remote reference counting is conducted and each interface pointer represents a count of 1. The actual increment and decrement calls are carried out by using RemAddRef and RemRelease. These methods are part of a COM interface known as IRemUnknown found on the OXID object associated with each OXID. The interface pointer for the OXID is returned by the function IOXIDResolver::ResolveOxid.

What's important about DCOM's handling of the resolver is that a single call can increment or decrement numerous interface pointers, improving network efficiency. Also, on the client, the actual remote release of all interfaces on an object is typically deferred until all local references to all interfaces on that object are released.

DCOM allows for secure releases and secure transmission of data to avoid snooping and to keep virus programs from maliciously trashing a program by disrupting the bindings being used. This is achieved only when a client or host application requests secure references. This method isn't as efficient and requires additional communication. It works like this:

1. The application must call RemAddRef (and later RemRelease) securely and request private references. Private references are stored by client identity, so one client can't release another client's references.

2. DCOM requires that each client make a call to get its own secure references. The clients can't receive a secure reference transmission belonging to another client.

DCOM shines when you consider the thought behind the creation of a new way of keeping object bindings alive without cluttering bandwidth with redundant pings. Abnormal termination of a program can disrupt the reference-counting scheme; telephone transmission interference, a system malfunction, or an electrical outage breaks the connection between the client and server. Periodic pings have always been used to detect abnormal termination in all the primary protocols used on the Internet and on connection-oriented networks.

The older DCE RPC architecture used context handles to deal with abnormal program termination. Context handles aren't incorporated into DCOM, however, because of the expense of redundant pings. DCOM's authors believed that naïve use of RPC context handles would result in per-object per-client process pings being sent to the server, resulting in an overtaxed communication bandwidth. The DCOM protocol uses a pinging infrastructure that significantly reduces network traffic by relying on the client's OXID resolver (the OXID implementation) to conduct local management of this phenomenon.

The pings are sent only on a machine-to-machine basis, are used on a per-object level (per OID), and aren't associated with the individual interface pointers. Each exported object (exported OID) gets a `pingPeriod` time value assignment on the server. An additional counter value, `numPingsToTimeOut`, works with the `pingPeriod` value to determine the overall amount of time that must elapse before expiration of the remote references (the *ping period*). If the ping period expires before receiving a ping on that OID, all the remote references to IPIDs associated with that OID expire.

After the remote references expire, the interfaces can be reclaimed on the basis of "local knowledge." The time to reclaim the interface is implementation-specific and depends on the server. If the server's COM infrastructure delegates what's commonly called *garbage collection* tasks in this situation (perhaps because it has local references keeping the interface pointer alive) and it later receives a ping, it can recover based on the indication that a network partition recovered. This recovery is known in network architecture terms as a *partition healing*. Now the resolver can consider the remote references to be reactivated and can continue remote operations.

When interface pointers are conveyed from one client to another (incoming or outgoing parameters to a call), the interface pointer is marshaled in one client and unmarshaled in the other. This is done by incrementing one reference count and decrementing another reference count. To successfully unmarshal the interface, the destination client must obtain at least one reference count on the interface, which is usually accomplished by passing in the marshaled interface `STDOBJREF` a `cPublicRefs` of one or more. The destination client then takes ownership of that many (more) reference counts to the indicated IPID, and the source client then owns that many fewer reference counts on the IPID.

If the destination client is also the object's server (local processing on the client), special processing is required by the destination client. This is necessary because the remote references have to be removed as the references are converted to local references. The reference counts present in the `STDOBJREF` are decremented from the remote reference count for the IPID in question.

Because of the manner in which some objects are used, some instances don't require any pings at all. These objects are identified by the presence of a flag in a standard `STDOBJREF` to an interface on the object. Objects that aren't pinged don't need reference counts. For all other objects, assuming that the ping period is a positive number, it's the responsibility of the holder of an interface reference on some object to assure that pings reach the server frequently enough to prevent expiration of the object.

Increasing Networking Efficiency

There's a method to customize the manner in which the pings are handled so that clients and servers can be more compatible and more efficient in terms of communication. The frequency used by a client depends on the ping period, the reliability of the channel between the client and the server, and the probability of failure on the network. If no pings get through, the client may not tolerate the disruption and may not recover. The ping packet or its reply may request changes to the ping period. Through this mechanism, network traffic can actually be reduced. With slow links to busy servers, the pings can be infrequent and the ping periods high without losing the link.

DCOM uses something called the *Delta Mechanism* to further reduce ping traffic. In some scenarios, ping messages can be unwieldy. For example, if a desktop PC held 1,024 remote object references (OIDs) on a server in an adjoining state, the client would send about 16K of byte ping messages. This could be annoying and not very efficient if the set of remote objects was relatively stable and the ping messages were identical from ping to ping. The Delta Mechanism reduces the size of ping messages, using a ping-set interface that allows the pinging of a single set to replace the pinging of multiple OIDs. Rather than ping each OID, the client defines a set. Then each ping contains only the set ID and a list of additions and subtractions to be made to the set.

DCOM uses the IRemUnknown interface to handle more than one task. The interface, as well as conduct the reference-counting activity, handles QueryInterface calls for remote clients for interface pointers managed by that object exporter. In other words, the IRemUnknown interface is optimized for network access by being able to retrieve multiple interfaces at once.

DCOM goes beyond the older DCE RPC technology in several areas. For example, DCOM requires the object ID field of the header to contain the IPID (interface pointer ID). Because Object RPC sits on top of DCE RPC, this kind of variation is necessary. Also, the interface ID of the RPC header must contain the IID, even though it's not needed because there's an IPID. This is what permits ORPC to sit on top of DCE RPC.

When the DCE packet header is formatted this way, an unmodified DCE RPC implementation will still correctly dispatch data based on IID and IPID. An optimized RPC may dispatch data based solely on the IPID. An IPID uniquely identifies a particular interface on a particular object on a machine. The opposite is not true—a particular interface on a particular object may be represented by *multiple* IPIDs. IPIDs are unique on their OXID; they may be reused, but this reuse of IPIDs is discouraged. Datagram broadcasts aren't allowed in ORPC.

Avoiding Network Failures

Some other requirements of DCOM that go beyond the DCE RPC standards include the requirement that faults are returned in the stub fault field of the DCE RPC fault packet. Any 32-bit value may be returned. Only `RPC_E_VERSION_MISMATCH` is prespecified. DCE RPC cancel is supported. All interface version numbers must be 0.0.

The COM network protocol is built on several fundamental data types and structures. These types are illustrated in the DCOM specification that can be found at `http://www.microsoft.com/oledev/olecom/draft-brown-dcom-v1-spec-01.txt`.

DCOM uses ORPC flags referred to as `ORPCINFOFLAGS`, which Table 5.4 describes.

Table 5.4. Various `ORPCINFOFLAGS` in the DCOM specification.

Flag	Meaning
ORPCF_NUL	This isn't a real flag; it's really just a defined constant that acts as a placeholder indicating the absence of any flag values.
ORPCF_LOCAL	The destination of this call is on the same machine on which it originates. This value cannot be specified in remote calls. This flag indicates that network protocol work isn't necessary.
ORPCF_RESERVED1	If ORPCF_LOCAL is set, this flag indicates that it's reserved for local use (locked). Otherwise, it's reserved for future use.
ORPCF_RESERVED2	If ORPCF_LOCAL is set, this flag indicates that it's reserved for local use. Otherwise, it's reserved for future use.
ORPCF_RESERVED3	If ORPCF_LOCAL is set, this flag indicates that it's reserved for local use. Otherwise, it's reserved for future use.
ORPCF_RESERVED4	If ORPCF_LOCAL is set, this flag indicates that it's reserved for local use. Otherwise, it's reserved for future use.

DCOM implementations may use the local and reserved flags to indicate any extra information needed for local calls. The inclusion of the last four flags in the DCOM protocol gives developers flexibility to set flags for specific uses of the DCOM protocol that they define.

> **NOTE**
>
> If the ORPCF_LOCAL bit isn't set and any of the other bits are set, the receiver should return a fault.

The keyword comversion is used to set the version number of the COM protocol used to make the particular ORPC. The initial value will be 5.1. Each packet contains the sender's major and minor ORPC version numbers. The client's and server's major version numbers must be equivalent. Backwardly compatible changes in the protocol are, of course, indicated by higher minor version numbers. Therefore, a server's minor version must be greater than or equal to the client's.

On the other hand, if the server's minor version exceeds the client's minor version, it must return the client's minor version and restrict its use of the protocol to the minor version specified by the client. Protocol version mismatches cause the RPC_E_VERSION_MISMATCH ORPC.

DCOM uses *body extensions* to convey additional information regarding invocations. These extensions are UUID-tagged blocks of data useful for conveying out-of-band information on incoming invocations (within ORPCTHIS) and in replies (within ORPCTHAT).

Any implementations of the DCOM protocol may define its own extensions with their own UUIDs. Implementations should skip over extensions that they don't recognize or don't want to support. Body extensions are marshaled as an array of bytes with initial 8-byte alignment. There are several existing body extensions, including the Debugging Extension and the Extended Error Extension. You can find details regarding these extensions with error-description tables in the DCOM specification found at http://www.microsoft.com/oledev/olecom/draft-brown-dcom-v1-spec-01.txt. Generally, the errors are very semantically intuitive. An invalid argument will generate an error with the words Invalid and Argument.

Another DCOM improvement over DCE RPC conserves resources when numerous protocols are used. In a homogeneous network, all machines communicate via the same protocol sequence. In a heterogeneous network, machines may support multiple protocol sequences. Because it's often expensive in terms of resources to allocate endpoints (RpcServerUseProtseq) for all available protocols, ORPC provides a mechanism where they can be allocated on demand. To implement this extension, changes in the server are needed. If these optional changes aren't made, ORPC will still work, but not as efficiently on a heterogeneous network.

In DCOM, the server may or may not implement *lazy protocol registration*, where the implementation of ResolveOxid is modified slightly. When the client OXID resolver calls the server OXID resolver, it passes the requested protocol's *sequence vector*. If none of the requested protocol sequences have endpoints allocated in the server, the server OXID resolver allocates them according to its own endpoint allocation mechanisms.

If the server doesn't use lazy protocol registration, all protocol sequences are registered by the server at server initialization time. When registering protocol sequences, the server registers endpoints and its string bindings will contain the complete endpoints. If the server doesn't register endpoints when it registers protocol sequences, a mapping process is used to forward the call to the server.

Summary

ActiveX was solely controlled by Microsoft until July 1996, when Microsoft announced plans to transition the technology to an independent standards body. In October 1996, a group voted to move the technology into the hands of the Open Group, an experienced organization with roots in distributed computing.

Vendor-neutral standards and their impact opened up ActiveX so that rapid improvements in various lucrative fields could be made without having to pay Microsoft to use the technology each time.

Enhancing and enabling system interoperability was the goal of creating the DCOM protocol. ActiveX uses the protocol to allow COM objects to run and interact on different types of computers.

ActiveX objects (COM objects) use DCOM as an Object Request Broker (ORB) to control the traffic between client and server portions of an application.

Third-party controls quickly gained popularity even before Microsoft released all the technology, and the new independent standards helped boost the technology for several reasons, including that Microsoft won't require any major fees to use it.

Creating and Using ActiveX Controls

by Dan Horsefield

IN THIS CHAPTER

Creating and using ActiveX controls isn't difficult when you use the development tools offered in Visual Basic and by Microsoft on its Sitebuilder Network Web site (`http://www.microsoft.com/sbnmember/download/download.asp`). One of the most versatile tools for generating and programming these controls is ActiveX Control Pad (free download with guest membership), which includes a very useful HTML layout interface for creating customized sections of a window filled with various controls. Control Pad gives HTML layout files the `.alx` extension, to identify each file as a control containing a group of one or more controls. Files with the `.ocx` extension are installed on the client computer and contain the code that makes the interactive controls functional.

In this chapter you'll explore a real-life example of using the controls with a fill-out form designed for an Internet Web site. You'll use an HTML layout to build the ActiveX page in ActiveX Control Pad.

Building a Control With ActiveX Control Pad

Imagine this assignment: You're told by your supervisor that you need to create a Web page that must include an interactive form. The form should contain input text fields and buttons that visitors to your company's Web site will activate by clicking. They click the buttons to indicate what types of materials they want your company to send.

These visitors use the online form to request company-specific information. The information entered in the form is forwarded automatically to the sales manager's electronic mailbox at your company when visitors click a Submit button. The information referenced on this form should include

- A product catalog
- A distributor's information packet
- A company prospectus
- A business profile for the company

The form also can be used by an existing customer to request a call from a customer service representative, or by a new customer to request a call from a sales representative. Above the form, you need to include a simple scrolling marquee showing your company's 800 telephone number on the Web page. You won't use Control Pad to create the marquee because you can create the marquee with a simple line of HTML text.

The order form also must include textbox areas for your visitors to fill in information regarding where the materials they request can be sent.

The CEO of your company wants to review the fill-out form on the company's Web site tomorrow. It's a good thing for you that you have a few basic Web-building tools installed on your computer.

What the boss and your supervisor don't realize is that it will take about an hour to create the form, integrate ActiveX controls with it, and deploy it at the Web site. Now for the crash course on how to pull it off. Here is a list of tools you've loaded on your computer:

■ ActiveX Control Pad.

■ An HTML editor such as Microsoft Front Page (optional).

■ Internet Explorer 3.01 (or newer).

■ WS_FTP_LE(3).EXE. Also known as WS_FTP, this program uploads and downloads Web files to and from an FTP site. It's freeware that you can download from http://www.sharepaper.com/apps/reviews/ws_ftp.html and from various other Internet sources.

To set up the Control Pad interface so that it resembles the Visual Basic interface you're familiar with, follow these steps:

1. Launch ActiveX Control Pad; a page of commands for a blank HTML Web page appears. The HTML commands are simple to learn, but you don't need to do anything to this template yet.

2. Maximize your window so that you'll have some work space onscreen.

3. Choose File | New HTML Layout from the menu to open a window called Layout1. This HTML Layout control is a child window that you can simply think of as the *control window.* Technically, this is the HTML Layout Editor window.

   You'll also see a toolbox with a few tools in it. Don't worry how many tools appear; you can customize the toolbox and add tools as you go.

   Figure 6.1 shows how your screen should appear at this point.

FIGURE 6.1

Launching ActiveX Control Pad opens a default window called Page1 (representing the HTML Web page) and a window representing the HTML Layout control you're planning to construct.

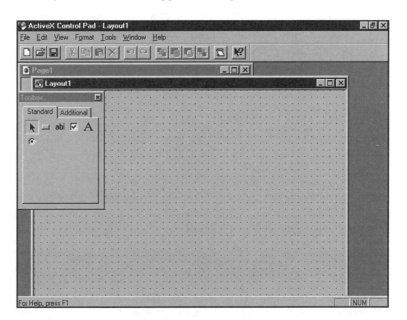

4. Maximize the HTML layout window so that it fits the screen rather than extend beyond the bottom of the window.

5. Drag the toolbox as far to the right and to the bottom of the window as it will go.

TIP

As you add controls, you can view their properties in an associated Properties window. Double-click a control to view its properties. Drag the window containing the table of properties to the far right and above the toolbox. When using the Properties window, you may find it to your advantage to stretch the box as tall as possible so that you can see as many properties as possible without having to scroll.

NOTE

This interface is very familiar to Visual Basic programmers. The HTML Layout Editor uses a WYSIWYG (What You See Is What You Get) window that acts as a container for all controls placed in it. When you complete an HTML layout, it's saved as a text document with an .alx extension. This file is associated with your Web page and run by the browser when the Web page is loaded.

6. To decrease the height of the Layout1 window, right-click it and choose Properties. Click the word Height. The value for Height may be 293 or 300. This number now also appears in the text box at the top of your layout properties chart. Highlight the number 300 in the text box to the right of the Apply button. Overwrite the value with the value 175. Press Enter or click Apply. You now have a long horizontal window.

Drawing Your Controls

You will place all your ActiveX controls in the HTML Layout Editor window. To create a small ActiveX control in which users can click a button to request an item of information, follow these steps:

1. To add a new tool to the toolbox, right-click an empty area in the toolbox and choose Additional Controls. Scroll down to the Microsoft Forms 2.0 OptionButton selection and mark its checkbox. Click OK.

TIP

Placing your mouse pointer over the radio button in the toolbox displays a text description of the tool (OptionButton). This way, you can verify that you've placed the correct tool you were seeking in the toolbox.

2. Click the new OptionButton tool. In the upper-left corner of the window, click and drag a long horizontal rectangle down two grid marks and to the right far enough so that the box can contain a long sentence. (In Control Pad, the corner of your rectangle will snap to the grid dots unless you turn the Snap option off.)

TIP

Always make the rectangle wider than needed so that browsers with larger fonts can still display the entire text. A text line generally appears to be longer in the browser window than in Control Pad.

A radio button automatically appears on the left, and the default text OptionButton1 appears on the right. The text represents the Caption property of the OptionButton control you just created. OptionButton1 also is the control's default ID property—that is, the object's name—and doesn't need to be modified unless you want to rename the object.

If the rectangle isn't large enough for the text, click it and drag one of its handles to reshape it. If you move the mouse pointer over the edge of the highlight, you can click and drag the whole rectangle to reposition it when the pointer changes to an arrow shape.

3. Save the project under the filename rfinfo.alx (your request for info control).

4. Right-click OptionButton1 and choose Properties to display the Properties window. You'll see the default properties for this object, including Caption, ID, GroupName, and Value.

5. In the Properties window, select the Caption property and then type **PLEASE SEND A PRODUCT CATALOG** in the input box at the top to the right of the Apply button. Then click Apply to set the value.

TIP

You also can change the Caption property by typing directly over the default text in the OptionButton1 control. Click the text to highlight it, overwrite it with the new text, and then click outside the control.

6. Select OptionButton1. In the Properties window, select GroupName. Set this property to Group1.

You won't assign this group name to any other objects you might place in the request for info control. That means Group1 will be "independent" of any other object in the control and can be turned on or off without having any effect on the other option buttons.

At runtime, users can select only one option button in each group. If you don't understand how these groups work, you will by the time you've created the rest of your control and tested it.

7. In the Properties window, scroll to the `Value` property and select it. Type **False** in the text box at the top and click the Apply button. This setting deselects the radio button control to the left of your text line.

Figure 6.2 shows how the control should appear at this time.

FIGURE 6.2.

Notice in the Properties window the text box that you use to revise properties.

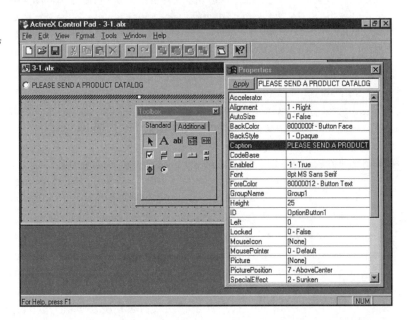

8. Click the `OptionButton1` object, press Ctrl+C to copy it, and then press Ctrl+V to paste it. Drag the pasted control so that it's immediately below the first. Continue copying and pasting until you have six controls stacked vertically. (Don't worry about the captions; you'll change those soon.)

You now should have six identical rectangles with radio buttons on the left and text to the right. Now would be a good time to resave the project.

Altering Properties Quickly

Copying the control copied all the property settings assigned to it except for the `ID` setting; each pasted object received a new default `ID` (`OptionButton2`, `OptionButton3`, and so on).

To modify these properties, click the second OptionButton from the top. Its property settings appear in the Properties window. Change the caption to read `Please Send Distributor Materials` and then click the Apply button. In the same manner, change the `GroupName`

Creating and Using ActiveX Controls

CHAPTER 6

125

6

CREATING AND
USING ACTIVEX
CONTROLS

property to Group2. For OptionButton3, change the caption to read PLEASE SEND INVESTOR'S PROSPECTUS and change GroupName to Group3. OptionButton4 gets a caption that reads PLEASE SEND A BUSINESS PROFILE and change GroupName to be Group4. OptionButton5 gets a caption reading HAVE A CUSTOMER SVC. REP. CALL, and the GroupName property is changed to Group5.

On the sixth option button, change the caption to read HAVE A SALES REPRESENTATIVE CALL. But rather than change the GroupName property to Group6, you will join this control's interactivity with the OptionButton5 radio button by changing OptionButton6's GroupName property to Group5. Now if a user clicks OptionButton5 at runtime, the OptionButton5 radio button turns black (and the corresponding value for the button changes from False to True).

Now, when users click OptionButton6, OptionButton6 is selected (True is assigned to the Value property) and OptionButton5 is deselected (assigned False). The way the buttons work in Group5 is inherent to these intrinsic ActiveX controls. You don't have to add code to make them act as a group; simply give them the same GroupName property. If users again click OptionButton5, OptionButton5 is selected again and OptionButton6 is deselected. Because these two objects have the same GroupName property, they function as a group, and only one in the group can be selected at any time. Therefore, users can select any or all of the first four buttons, but only one of the last two buttons in the HTML layout. Save your file again.

> **TIP**
>
> The value property for all the controls should already be set to False. To change a property for several controls at once, drag a window around the controls to select them and then change the property in the Properties window.

Adding Functionality to Your Control

Now you have a slight problem to overcome. The controls you created are still bare; they require functionality. At runtime, users can click the first four buttons to select them. If users make a mistake and select one but then try to deselect it by clicking again, the button remains selected.

Perhaps the easiest way to program a workaround is to use ActiveX Control Pad's CommandButton tool to create another button, and then insert a few simple lines of code in the Script Wizard. Click the CommandButton tool (it looks like a rectangle in the toolbox) and place a button immediately to the right of your OptionButtons, slightly overlapping them. Center the button vertically between OptionButton3 and OptionButton4 (vertical center of the control). Change CommandButton1's Caption property to read Clear Buttons At Left, and then save your file again.

The HTML Layout Editor window is larger than you need it to be because you maximized it before creating the HTML layout control. You can resize the window by dragging the edges until your controls fit loosely in the window.

Save your file. Figure 6.3 shows how your finished controls should look in ActiveX Control Pad.

FIGURE 6.3.

The HTML Layout control rfinfo.alx, *after adjusting the height and width of the control.*

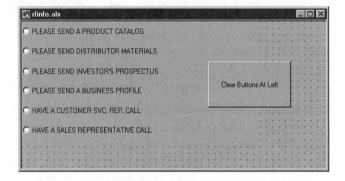

Open the rfinfo.alx file in a text editor and scroll through the code lines to get a feel for the syntax associated with these objects' properties. The object descriptions appear in the same order as you placed the controls on the page. At the top of the code window, you'll add a few code lines to add functionality to your command button to solve the problem with the radio buttons.

At runtime you want users to click the command button object to deselect all six radio buttons at left and return their values to False. To program this functionality, right-click OptionButton1 and choose Script Wizard (or click the toolbar icon that looks like a scroll). You now see an event pane on the left, an action pane on the right, and a script pane with two different view options at the bottom. In the left event pane, click the plus sign near CommandButton1 to view the available events that can be programmed. Find and highlight the Click event.

Click the Code View selection button in the script pane at the bottom of the window. In the action pane on the right, click the plus sign near OptionButton1 and double-click the action item Alignment to paste a code line in the code view at the bottom. Overwrite the code line with OptionButton1.Value=False. Copy and paste this code line in the code view window for each option button. Remember to change the OptionButton *names* in the code view to 1–6. (You don't need to end your subroutine with an End Sub because the Script Wizard is going to add this for you.)

Click OK. You can open the file in a text editor again and view the code lines. The VB Scripting Edition code lines will appear at the top of the file. Your HTML layout control file rfinfo.alx is complete and should resemble the lines that appear in Listing 6.1.

Listing 6.1. The minimal code generated when you created the HTML layout file.

```
<SCRIPT LANGUAGE="VBScript">
<!--
Sub CommandButton1_Click()
OptionButton1.Value=False
```

```
OptionButton2.Value=False
OptionButton3.Value=False
OptionButton4.Value=False
OptionButton5.Value=False
OptionButton6.Value=False
end sub
-->
</SCRIPT>
<DIV ID="Layout1" STYLE="LAYOUT:FIXED;WIDTH:390pt;HEIGHT:184pt;">
<OBJECT ID="OptionButton1"
CLASSID="CLSID:8BD21D50-EC42-11CE-9E0D-00AA006002F3"
STYLE="TOP:0pt;LEFT:0pt;WIDTH:305pt;HEIGHT:25pt;TABINDEX:0;ZINDEX:0;">
<PARAM NAME="BackColor" VALUE="2147483663">
<PARAM NAME="ForeColor" VALUE="2147483666">
<PARAM NAME="DisplayStyle" VALUE="5">
<PARAM NAME="Size" VALUE="10760;882">
<PARAM NAME="Value" VALUE="False">
<PARAM NAME="Caption" VALUE="PLEASE SEND A PRODUCT CATALOG">
<PARAM NAME="GroupName" VALUE="Group1">
<PARAM NAME="FontCharSet" VALUE="0">
<PARAM NAME="FontPitchAndFamily" VALUE="2">
<PARAM NAME="FontWeight" VALUE="0">
</OBJECT>
<OBJECT ID="OptionButton2"
CLASSID="CLSID:8BD21D50-EC42-11CE-9E0D-00AA006002F3"
STYLE="TOP:25pt;LEFT:0pt;WIDTH:305pt;HEIGHT:25pt;TABINDEX:1;ZINDEX:1;">
<PARAM NAME="BackColor" VALUE="2147483663">
<PARAM NAME="ForeColor" VALUE="2147483666">
<PARAM NAME="DisplayStyle" VALUE="5">
<PARAM NAME="Size" VALUE="10760;882">
<PARAM NAME="Value" VALUE="False">
<PARAM NAME="Caption" VALUE="PLEASE SEND DISTRIBUTOR MATERIALS">
<PARAM NAME="GroupName" VALUE="Group2">
<PARAM NAME="FontCharSet" VALUE="0">
<PARAM NAME="FontPitchAndFamily" VALUE="2">
<PARAM NAME="FontWeight" VALUE="0">
</OBJECT>
<OBJECT ID="OptionButton3"
CLASSID="CLSID:8BD21D50-EC42-11CE-9E0D-00AA006002F3"
STYLE="TOP:50pt;LEFT:0pt;WIDTH:305pt;HEIGHT:25pt;TABINDEX:2;ZINDEX:2;">
<PARAM NAME="BackColor" VALUE="2147483663">
<PARAM NAME="ForeColor" VALUE="2147483666">
<PARAM NAME="DisplayStyle" VALUE="5">
<PARAM NAME="Size" VALUE="10760;882">
<PARAM NAME="Value" VALUE="False">
<PARAM NAME="Caption" VALUE="PLEASE SEND INVESTOR'S PROSPECTUS">
<PARAM NAME="GroupName" VALUE="Group3">
<PARAM NAME="FontCharSet" VALUE="0">
<PARAM NAME="FontPitchAndFamily" VALUE="2">
<PARAM NAME="FontWeight" VALUE="0">
</OBJECT>
<OBJECT ID="OptionButton4"
CLASSID="CLSID:8BD21D50-EC42-11CE-9E0D-00AA006002F3"
STYLE="TOP:74pt;LEFT:0pt;WIDTH:305pt;HEIGHT:25pt;TABINDEX:3;ZINDEX:3;">
<PARAM NAME="BackColor" VALUE="2147483663">
<PARAM NAME="ForeColor" VALUE="2147483666">
<PARAM NAME="DisplayStyle" VALUE="5">
```

continues

Listing 6.1. continued

```
<PARAM NAME="Size" VALUE="10760;882">
<PARAM NAME="Value" VALUE="False">
<PARAM NAME="Caption" VALUE="PLEASE SEND A BUSINESS PROFILE">
<PARAM NAME="GroupName" VALUE="Group4">
<PARAM NAME="FontCharSet" VALUE="0">
<PARAM NAME="FontPitchAndFamily" VALUE="2">
<PARAM NAME="FontWeight" VALUE="0">
</OBJECT>
<OBJECT ID="OptionButton5"
CLASSID="CLSID:8BD21D50-EC42-11CE-9E0D-00AA006002F3"
STYLE="TOP:99pt;LEFT:0pt;WIDTH:305pt;HEIGHT:25pt;TABINDEX:4;ZINDEX:4;">
<PARAM NAME="BackColor" VALUE="2147483663">
<PARAM NAME="ForeColor" VALUE="2147483666">
<PARAM NAME="DisplayStyle" VALUE="5">
<PARAM NAME="Size" VALUE="10760;882">
<PARAM NAME="Value" VALUE="False">
<PARAM NAME="Caption" VALUE="HAVE A CUSTOMER SVC. REP. CALL">
<PARAM NAME="GroupName" VALUE="Group5">
<PARAM NAME="FontCharSet" VALUE="0">
<PARAM NAME="FontPitchAndFamily" VALUE="2">
<PARAM NAME="FontWeight" VALUE="0">
</OBJECT>
<OBJECT ID="OptionButton6"
CLASSID="CLSID:8BD21D50-EC42-11CE-9E0D-00AA006002F3"
STYLE="TOP:124pt;LEFT:0pt;WIDTH:305pt;HEIGHT:25pt;TABINDEX:5;ZINDEX:5;">
<PARAM NAME="BackColor" VALUE="2147483663">
<PARAM NAME="ForeColor" VALUE="2147483666">
<PARAM NAME="DisplayStyle" VALUE="5">
<PARAM NAME="Size" VALUE="10760;882">
<PARAM NAME="Value" VALUE="False">
<PARAM NAME="Caption" VALUE="HAVE A SALES REPRESENTATIVE CALL">
<PARAM NAME="GroupName" VALUE="Group5">
<PARAM NAME="FontCharSet" VALUE="0">
<PARAM NAME="FontPitchAndFamily" VALUE="2">
<PARAM NAME="FontWeight" VALUE="0">
</OBJECT>
<OBJECT ID="CommandButton1"
CLASSID="CLSID:D7053240-CE69-11CD-A777-00DD01143C57"
STYLE="TOP:50pt;LEFT:239pt;WIDTH:107pt;HEIGHT:58pt;TABINDEX:6;ZINDEX:6;">
<PARAM NAME="Caption" VALUE="Clear Buttons At Left">
<PARAM NAME="Size" VALUE="3784;2046">
<PARAM NAME="FontCharSet" VALUE="0">
<PARAM NAME="FontPitchAndFamily" VALUE="2">
<PARAM NAME="ParagraphAlign" VALUE="3">
<PARAM NAME="FontWeight" VALUE="0">
</OBJECT>
</DIV>
```

Now save the file one last time and test your code. To test the code, you need to create a fairly simple HTML file—a simple Web page—and add the control to it. Then you add a few code lines to make the form on the Web page communicate its data to an e-mail mailbox.

Creating and Using ActiveX Controls

CHAPTER 6

129

6

CREATING AND
USING ACTIVEX
CONTROLS

Creating a Simple Web Page

Create a very simple HTML file with your HTML editor or a text editor. ActiveX Control Pad is great for editing Web pages when you're inserting or programming controls, but it's not intended to be used as a full-featured HTML editor. If you have an HTML editor such as Microsoft FrontPage 2.0, most of the code lines you'll be adding don't need to be typed; you can pick a tool from the toolbar, click the page, view the code to see the properties for the HTML tags, and so on.

In the FrontPage editor, open a new file, choose Insert | Marquee from the menu, and type **Call 1-800-*YOUR NUMBER GOES HERE*** in the dialog box. If you view the source code for the HTML page, you will see a simple line of code. In a text editor you can add `<marquee>Call 1-800-`*YOUR NUMBER GOES HERE*`</marquee>` to your HTML file for the same effect. Now create an HTML form and assign the form the action URL `http://www.myWebsite.com/cgi-bin/mailit.cgi`. In this form, create a simple two-column table, and then insert the `rfinfo.alx` file object as shown in Figure 6.4.

FIGURE 6.4.

This shows where you'll place the `rfinfo.alx` *file in the table in FrontPage Editor.*

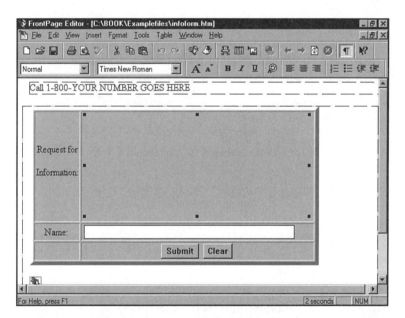

CAUTION

Open and save the file in the same directory. If you save to a remote directory, your reference to objects, such as the control `rfinfo.alx`, will be assigned a full pathname to the file. You want the reference to be to a local file.

The control file here is being placed in the second column of the first row. Place the text line `Request for Information` in the first cell of the first row. Then add a form element—a text input box (`<input type ="text" name="FirstName">`)—in the second column of the second row and enter **Name:** in the first cell of the row. (If you are using a text editor and aren't familiar with using HTML to place an input box, refer to the code example in Listing 6.2.) Now add a Submit button and a Clear button below the table. Give the HTML file the title `Request for Information Form`.

Now the code for your HTML file should look something like Listing 6.2. You're getting close to having a working form. Save your file as `infoform.htm`. This code is generated by your HTML editor. It isn't the finished file; the file will be complete after you add the script to bind data from the control to the form.

Listing 6.2. The code for infoform.htm.

```
<!DOCTYPE HTML PUBLIC "-//IETF//DTD HTML//EN">
<html>
<head>
<meta http-equiv="Content-Type"
content="text/html; charset=iso-8859-1">
<meta name="GENERATOR" content="Microsoft FrontPage 2.0">
<title>REQUEST FOR INFORMATION FORM</title>
</head>
<body bgcolor="#FFFFFF" text="#000000" link="#663333"
vlink="#000000" topmargin="6" leftmargin="20" language="VBSCRIPT">
<p align="center"><marquee bgcolor="#FFFFFF">Call 1-800-YOUR
NUMBER GOES HERE</marquee></p>
<form action="http://www.myWebsite.com/cgi-bin/mailit.cgi"
method="POST" name="MainForm">
<div align="left"><table border="6" cellpadding="2"
bgcolor="#C0C0C0">
<tr>
  <td align="center">Request for<p>Information:</p>
</td>
<td><object id="rfinfo_alx"
classid="clsid:812AE312-8B8E-11CF-93C8-00AA00C08FDF"
align="baseline" border="0" vspace="12" width="390"
height="151"><param name="ALXPATH" value="rfinfo.alx"></object>
            </td>
</tr>
<tr>
<td align="center">Name: </td>
<td valign="top"><input type="text" size="40"
name="FirstName"> </td>
</tr>
<tr>
<td align="center"> </td>
<td align="center"><input type="submit" name="Send"
value="Submit"> <input type="reset" name="Clear"
value="Clear"> </td>
</tr>
</table>
</form>
</body>
</html>
```

Creating and Using ActiveX Controls

CHAPTER 6

131

6

CREATING AND
USING ACTIVEX
CONTROLS

Open the new HTML file in your ActiveX-enabled browser. Make sure that the `rfinfo.alx` file is in the same directory as `infoform.htm`. Experiment with the control buttons. You'll get an error or no response if you try using the submit button because you haven't finished adding functionality to it. You may have noticed that you placed the ActiveX control in the right-hand cell of a two-column table within `infoform.htm`. You can add the rest of the form fields for text input to the simple HTML file now.

The first input box code (FirstName) is shown in Listing 6.2. The others will be similar. You'll merely substitute LastName for FirstName, and so on, as you add these input boxes. You'll want to add input boxes for Address1, Address2, City, State, Zipcode, Email, and Phone, and you may want to add another large text box for anything not listed on the form that users may want to request.

 You'll add validation to your file later to make sure that the correct boxes contain input. You can validate by ensuring that numbers (as opposed to alpha characters) appear in the Zip Code or Phone Number textbox. A functioning `infoform.htm` is on the disk accompanying the book. The file must be modified to reflect the correct URL path to the CGI script it calls. Also, you can find a similar HTML file with validation code at `http://www.laserusa.com/rfq.htm`.

Adding the Form Submission Script

Now you need a custom script to *bind* (append) the data from the ActiveX HTML Layout control `rfinfo.alx` to the form data generated by the text input boxes. Then you submit the whole data package by using the `mailit.cgi` script referred to by the `Action` property when you created the form.

 To add your custom script, open the `infoform.htm` file on the CD-ROM and paste the code lines shown in Listing 6.3. These lines should follow the last form tag, `</form>`, and be above the `</body>` and `</HTML>` tag to maintain integrity of the form and the file.

Listing 6.3. The code to bind data from the OptionButtons to the data from one of the form's input boxes.

```
</div>
<script language="VBScript">
<!--
Function MainForm_OnSubmit()
Title="Request for Information"
Set TheForm=MainForm
dim x()
x1=TheForm.rfinfo_alx.optionbutton1.value
x2=TheForm.rfinfo_alx.optionbutton2.value
x3=TheForm.rfinfo_alx.optionbutton3.value
x4=TheForm.rfinfo_alx.optionbutton4.value
```

continues

Listing 6.3. continued

```
TheForm.FirstName.Value=TheForm.FirstName.Value & "Catalog=" & x1
 & " DistributorInfo=" & x2 & " Prospectus=" & x3 & " Profile=" & x4
 & " Cust Svc Call=" & x5 & " Sales Rep Call=" & x6
End Function
-->
</script><p align="left"> </p>
```

Make sure that the last few tags, `</body>` and `</html>`, are in your file and save the `infoform.htm` file again.

Writing a Simple CGI Script

The following simple CGI script is compatible with many commercial Web servers. The Internet service provider (ISP) that maintains the Web server you'll be using can suggest changes to the lines in this simple script that might point to an incorrect path for the SendMail program.

Remember, this script is being called by the following HTML code in your `infoform.htm` file:

```
<form action="http://www.myWebsite.com/cgi-bin/mailit.cgi"
method="POST" name="MainForm">
```

You need to modify this line to point to the actual URL where this CGI script resides on the server. This URL can be relative, as in `mailit.cgi`, if the CGI file resides in the same directory as the Web page.

> **TIP**
>
> Your Internet service provider may suggest where the CGI script file should reside. It's a good idea to talk to your ISP because location of this file may help prevent anyone from tampering with the script, depending on the server security used by your ISP.

You can temporarily place the file in the same directory as the `infoform.htm` file for testing purposes. Make sure that the HTML tag points to the file in the same directory (`action="mailit.cgi"`). This script invokes a SendMail program on the server, assigns all the name-value pairs from the form to a simple e-mail message area, and submits the mail message to the specified e-mail address.

This script was derived from a similar script made public on the Web. You can search for other similar shared public CGI script files on the Web by using `CGI` and `MAILTO` as keywords. At the end of the file are a few simple HTML lines that generate confirmation text in a simple HTML window so that users know the form has been submitted correctly.

Confirming the Submission

This confirmation should contain a hyperlink back to the form or to the URL where the company's Web site home page resides. Use a full-path URL—`http://www.myWebsite.com/`

Creating and Using ActiveX Controls

CHAPTER 6

133

6

CREATING AND
USING ACTIVEX
CONTROLS

index.html—where *myWebsite* is your company's domain and *index.html* is the home page filename. You don't have to use a CGI script like the simple one in Listing 6.4 to send the e-mail, but this simple method gets the data forwarded automatically as soon as the form is submitted.

Listing 6.4. The simple CGI script that launches a SendMail program to forward the Web form's data to a specified e-mail address.

```
#!/usr/bin/perl
# Down and dirty Web form processing script.  Emails the data
# to the recipient.
$mailprog = '/usr/sbin/sendmail';
$recipient = 'yourpobox@yourdomain.com';
# Print out a content-type for HTTP/1.0 compatibility
print "Content-type:text/html\n\n";
# Get the input and shape it into something legible
read(STDIN, $buffer, $ENV{'CONTENT_LENGTH'});
$postinput = $buffer;
$postinput =~ s/&/\n/g;
$postinput =~ s/\+/ /g;
$postinput =~ s/%([\da-f]{1,2})/pack(C,hex($1))/eig;
# Now send mail to $recipient
open (MAIL, "|$mailprog $recipient") || die "Sorry, can't open $mailprog!\n";
print MAIL "Subject: Request for Information Form Data\n\n";
print MAIL $postinput;
print MAIL "\n\n";
print MAIL "Server protocol: $ENV{'SERVER_PROTOCOL'}\n";
print MAIL "HTTP From: $ENV{'HTTP_FROM'}\n";
print MAIL "Remote host: $ENV{'REMOTE_HOST'}\n";
print MAIL "Remote IP address: $ENV{'REMOTE_ADDR'}\n";
close (MAIL);
# Print a thank-you page
print <<EndHTML;
print "
<html>
<head>
<Title>THANKS</Title>
</Head>
<body>
<H2>Thank you for this opportunity to provide you with more information!</H2>
Return to our <a href="http://www.myWebsite.com/index.htm">home page</a>.<p>
</body>
</html>
EndHTML
;
# the end
```

Uploading the Files to Your Web Site

Assuming that you have a functioning Web site that's maintained offsite with a dial-up connection to an FTP server, this procedure uploads your files after you test everything but the e-mail submit function. Open WS_FTP_LE.EXE and configure the login and password for your

Web site. Make sure that your dial-up connection logs you in with the correct login and password. If your server requires Passive Transfer Mode, set it under the options in `WS_FTP_LE.EXE` if you aren't having any luck.

Work with your ISP until you get the login to open automatically to the remote directory you'll be loading your files into. Click the Connect button. When you see a directory listing in the host window, click the ASCII selection button. Change your local directory window to show the contents of the directory where your `rfinfo.alx`, `infoform.htm`, and `mailit.cgi` files reside.

Ctrl+click each file to select them, and then click the Transfer button. Your status window indicates the status of each transfer. You can scroll this window back or simply view the updated directory listing in the host window. You may need to refresh the host window manually to see your files.

When the files are there, you can minimize WS_FTP and launch Internet Explorer. Navigate to the Web site and add the filename `infoform.htm` at the end of the Web site URL. The HTML file and the form should load first. The status window in IE 3.01 indicates `Done`, the `rfinfo.alx` file loads into the browser, and your ActiveX controls are visible.

TIP

If the HTML file loads but the `.alx` file doesn't, check the HTML source code by choosing View | Source from Internet Explorer's menu. Make sure that the path points to the file. If you change the path in Notepad or a similar editor, be sure to resave the file to your local directory to overwrite the old file, and then maximize WS_FTP and retransfer the file to the Web site.

You can continue to work in ActiveX Control Pad, FrontPage Editor, and WS_FTP until everything is working correctly.

Assuming that you have access and authority to modify the Web site's home page (or other page where a link would be appropriate), you can now add a simple anchor (hyperlink) on the page. The hyperlink will point to the new `infoform.htm` file that you created. When users click the hyperlink, your form and the controls load.

Suppose that your company's home page is at `http://www.pencapital.com/index.htm`. Open a copy of `index.htm` in FrontPage Editor or similar HTML editor window. Go to where you want the link and place a line of text that reads,

> If you would like more information or specific company materials available, visit our Request For Information page.

Now select the `Request For Information` text and choose Insert | Hyperlink from the menu. In the dialog box, place the local path to the `infoform.htm` file.

Creating and Using ActiveX Controls

CHAPTER 6

135

6

CREATING AND
USING ACTIVEX
CONTROLS

You can also do this by adding a similar code to your Web's home page HTML file:

```
Click here to see our <font color="#FF0000">[</font>
<a href=" http://www.pencapital.com/infoform.htm">
<font color="#FF0000" size="3">Request For Information Form</font></a>
<font color="#FF0000" size="3">]
```

You can add this code to your existing `infoform.htm` file and substitute the word `infoform.htm` after `href=` to reload the page when you click the link.

Figure 6.5 shows how your finished Web page should look in Internet Explorer 3.01. The `rfinfo.alx` file must reside in the same directory.

FIGURE 6.5.

This is how the finished Web page looks in Internet Explorer 3.01.

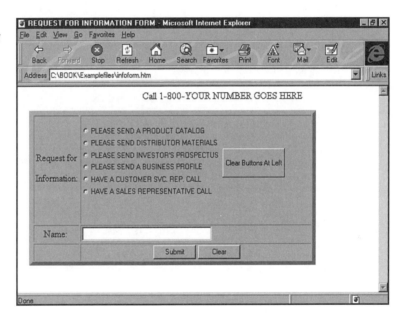

Summary

Creating HTML pages, HTML layout controls, and other ActiveX controls is fairly simple. You can create these items by using available free tools.

In this chapter, you learned how to create a simple Web page, create and insert a simple control, add functionality to an object in the control with a script, create a form, and create a way for the form's information to be submitted to an e-mail address. You also explored a method to move these files onto a remote Web site.

The process has numerous steps, but you can complete the work very quickly with the tools used for the examples.

Manipulating ActiveX Controls

by Dan Horsefield

IN THIS CHAPTER

CHAPTER 7

In the examples in this chapter, the basic differences between intrinsic and common ActiveX controls are explored. The chapter uses ActiveX scripting and gives some examples of VBScript and brief references to JavaScript.

The scripting emphasis is on VBScript, which uses a more familiar subset of Visual Basic commands. You can find information regarding JavaScript in documents available on the Internet (search on the words JavaScript and Scripting). For more on VBScript and ActiveX scripting, see Chapter 9, "Creating ActiveX Scripts With VBScript."

Working With Intrinsic and Common ActiveX Controls

Microsoft engineered Internet Explorer to include built-in support for several ActiveX controls. When ActiveX Control Pad is running, it can access several OCX and DLL files placed in the C:\Windows\System subdirectory: isctrls.ocx, intrinsc.ocx, plugin.ocx, marquee.ocx, shdocvw.dll, and raocx32.dll. Internet Explorer uses the objects defined in these files when the controls are identified and loaded in the browser. They're all automatically accessible by users.

Internet Explorer's installation executable file is very large. Although the program file installed on your system is big, it relieves the server of most of the processing and communicating of data that would be required if it weren't for these intrinsic controls. IE's handling of intrinsic controls has made processing the active content featured in the controls very convenient. As new releases of Internet Explorer become available, the number of intrinsic controls packaged with the installation will likely increase. For example, the HTML Layout control wasn't included in the initial release of IE 3.0.

The other controls, referred to here as *common controls*, are ones that may depend on the installation of additional necessary system files on users' computers to run properly. This installation may not even be required to run the controls if the Codebase property in your design-time control points to an appropriate URL where the ActiveX code file resides. I'll refer to some of these remote URL files as *third-party ActiveX controls*.

Distinguishing between intrinsic controls and common controls is important, especially when execution speed or size of the files being processed is important to the overall impact of the control. To distinguish between these controls, I'll define *intrinsic controls* as all the controls in ActiveX Control Pad that rely on the dynamic link library FM20.DLL. These controls are the basic building blocks immediately available to most programmers. Most intermediate and advanced VB developers are very familiar with many of these controls. The intrinsic controls include CheckBox, ComboBox, CommandButton, Frame, Image, Label, ListBox, MultiPage, OptionButton, ScrollBar, SpinButton, TabStrip, TextBox, and ToggleButton.

> **NOTE**
>
> Other books on this topic will refer to *intrinsic control objects* as a defined set of controls with different names. They may have different names, but they have similar functionality to those described here. They may also require you to enter HTML (Hypertext Markup Language) tags manually or use other HTML editors to program them.

The named objects used here are identified by the same names in the Control Pad toolbox's standard and additional control options on a PC with the Control Pad 1.0, IE 3.01, and Microsoft Word installed on it.

Choosing Edit | Insert ActiveX Document in Control Pad lists *all* objects installed on a user's system, but some of these objects may have unpredictable results in Control Pad. Control Pad 1.0 handles the intrinsic controls listed in this chapter with no problems.

Common controls immediately available to programmers with these basic programs installed include the MarqueeCtl object (MARQUEE.OCX), the Microsoft ActiveX HotSpot Control 1.0 (ISCTRLS.OCX), the Microsoft ActiveX Image control (ISCTRLS.OCX), the Microsoft Web Browser control (SHDOCVW.DLL), the RealAudio ActiveX 32-bit object (RAOCX32.DLL), the ActiveX Plug-In object (PLUGIN.OCX), and the Active Movie Control object (AMOVIE.OCX, installed with IE3.01 and run with AMOVIE.EXE). More specific intrinsic controls include the Chart control, the Preloader, the Animation Button, the Stock Ticker, and the New Item control.

You may need to manually download and install software to program some of these ActiveX controls and many others available today. Some common controls not immediately available in Control Pad can be run with the Codebase property set to Microsoft's ActiveX Gallery at http://www.microsoft.com/workshop/.

> **TIP**
>
> Because servers on the Internet aren't always available when users need access to a control, it's advisable to limit the use of common controls to non-critical parts of an application or Web page unless users are known to have the software loaded in their systems to support the controls. Some people won't have the patience to install components or to use controls that rely on remote links to unreliable servers, unless they want to add functionality to their system.

Intermediate and advanced developers may also want to download the latest ActiveX SDK installation files, which range in size from 9M to 11M. Be sure to extract the SDK executable ACTIVEX.EXE by typing **activex.exe -d** at a DOS prompt after downloading the file. Go to http://www.microsoft.com/msdownload/activex/03000.htm. If you don't use the -d switch, the SDK source files will extract into a flat file structure rather than into their proper subdirectories.

ActiveX scripting, described in more detail in Chapter 9, "Creating ActiveX Scripts With VBScript," must be used to bind and manipulate the common controls. Some intrinsic controls don't require any scripting to be functional. The same is true of some common controls.

A marquee control object, for example, is technically a common ActiveX control processed by IE. You can create a simple marquee in an HTML file by enclosing the text string that will scroll across the screen within `<MARQUEE>` and `</MARQUEE>` tags. That's the way marquees were first used, and some developers still use this method to program marquees. On the other hand, the common Control Pad's Marquee control object, which doesn't rely solely on HTML tags to define it, relies on the `MARQUEE.OCX` file in the `C:\Windows\System` subdirectory. Parameter tags are used to define the properties.

You can program many of the common and intrinsic controls without Control Pad if you have a good working knowledge of HTML options and ActiveX scripting. This chapter focuses on efficiently generating the majority of the code lines, including scripting, by using the visual interface provided in ActiveX Control Pad.

Each control, intrinsic or otherwise, has default properties assigned to it. With common controls, these default properties are specified in the code lines with parameter tags that define them. With some intrinsic controls, all the properties may not be visible, especially if they were programmed by manually entering the HTML code.

Using a Control Pad Control

To use a control in ActiveX Control Pad, first check to see whether it appears in the HTML Layout Editor's toolbox. If the tool isn't available, right-click the toolbox and select Additional Controls. Make sure that the Insertable Objects and Insertable Controls checkboxes are marked.

On the left is a list of the controls that you can add to the toolbox. Each tool is associated with an OCX or DLL file, many of which are located in the `\Windows\System` subdirectory. Click the appropriate box next to the control name. The tool is selected and the code file to which it's linked is listed in the bottom of the window. Now click OK.

Refer to the section "Building a Control With ActiveX Control Pad" in Chapter 6, "Creating and Using ActiveX Controls," if you encounter difficulty.

> **NOTE**
>
> If you've recently accessed an Internet site and downloaded and installed software on your system, you may see some new controls that weren't there previously.

To access controls not available in the window or toolbox, visit `http://www.microsoft.com/workshop`. Click the link to ActiveX controls. Most of the commonly used free controls are located here. If you have a control that doesn't run properly and are concerned that the necessary control isn't supported by your or your user's system, use the Codebase property and reference this same URL. Then test to see whether the control runs while connected to the Internet.

Creating Intrinsic Controls

The following sections list capabilities for Internet Explorer's intrinsic controls and exercises to create them. You can become familiar with control design and scripting through the brief descriptions of each control, the properties and events supported, and code examples. You can test each sample exercise by following the brief instructions, inserting the HTML layout into an HTML file as outlined in Chapter 9, opening the HTML file in IE, and testing the event interaction programmed.

 Following some of the exercises are code listings of the HTML file and the various controls programmed. You can find the complete files on the CD-ROM accompanying this book.

7

MANIPULATING
ACTIVEX
CONTROLS

> **NOTE**
>
> Some of IE 3.0's older intrinsic controls, such as RadioButton, don't even appear in Control Pad but can be programmed with HTML tags. Some controls addressed here, such as the OptionButton control, are reworks of earlier controls and are considered *form controls* in Internet Explorer 3.01. IE treats HTML Layouts as form objects. ActiveX Control Pad's toolbox dialog box lists all the intrinsic controls addressed here, with the words Microsoft Forms 2.0 in front of them.

The Label Control

The Label control is a simple rectangular box to which you can attach text in the form of a caption or an image. Its properties include Accelerator, AutoSize, BackColor, BackStyle, BorderColor, BorderStyle, Caption, Codebase, Enabled, Font, ForeColor, Height, ID, Left, MouseIcon, MousePointer, Picture, PicturePosition, SpecialEffect, TabIndex, TabStop, TextAlign, Top, Visible, Width, and WordWrap. The Label control's events include AfterUpdate, BeforeDragOver, BeforeDropOrPaste, BeforeUpdate, Click, DblClick, Enter, Error, Exit, MouseDown, MouseMove, and MouseUp.

In Control Pad, choose File | New HTML Layout. The Label control is a standard tool indicated by a large letter A. Click it once and then click your page.

Double-click the control to view its properties. One property listed is Caption, and the value for the property is set to Label1 by default. Change the property to I'm a label and click Apply.

Click the BackColor property. From the drop-down list to the right, select the last selection, Info Background. Right-click the control and select Script Wizard. Click the plus sign near the Label1 icon in the events pane and click the Click event.

In the action pane click the plus sign near the Label1 icon and click the Caption property. Click the Insert Action button at the bottom of the window. To replace the existing Caption property value, at the prompt enter **Now I'm a clicked label**.

In the action pane, select BackColor and click the Insert Action button. In the dialog box that appears, click the color red and click the OK button directly below the color boxes. Then click OK in the bottom of the Script Wizard window.

Save your HTML layout file as testpad.alx. Then choose File | New HTML to open a blank page of code for an HTML file. Now choose Edit | Insert HTML Layout. Select the testpad.alx file and save your HTML file in the same directory. Open the file in Internet Explorer and click Label1. The text should change from I'm a label to Now I'm a clicked label, and the background color should change from a light tan to red.

The CheckBox Control

The CheckBox control is a simple box with a text caption to the right. The caption text should be replaced with text to describe an option. If users select that option (therefore placing a checkmark in the box), the value property of the CheckBox control changes from False (unchecked box) to True (checked).

Properties for the CheckBox control include Accelerator, Alignment, Autosize, BackColor, BackStyle, Caption, Codebase, Enabled, Font, ForeColor, GroupName, Height, ID, Left, MouseIcon, MousePointer, Picture, PicturePosition, SpecialEffect, TabIndex, TabStop, Top, TripleState, Value, Visible, Width, and WordWrap. Events for the control include AfterUpdate, BeforeDragOver, BeforeDropOrPaste, BeforeUpdate, Change, Click, DblClick, Enter, Error, Exit, KeyDown, KeyPress, KeyUp, MouseDown, MouseMove, and MouseUp.

Open the testpad.alx file and click the CheckBox tool in the toolbox (a standard tool with an arrow icon). With the crosshair mouse pointer, move to just below the existing Label1 control and click once. The default CheckBox control rectangle appears. Click the area where the text appears. Type over the existing text with **Click in the box to select option**. Now drag to the right the control's right handle, stretching the control horizontally until all your text and some space is visible in the rectangle.

To view your control in Internet Explorer, you must insert your saved HTML layout in a new HTML page. In Control Pad, choose File | New HTML. An HTML code window appears. Choose Edit | Insert HTML Layout, select the testpad.alx file, and save your HTML page under the filename intrinsc.htm.

Launch the browser. Under File | Open click the Browse button and select the intrinsc.htm file. In Control Pad, double-click your CheckBox control's border. The properties window will appear. Figure 7.1 shows how your controls will appear in Control Pad at this point.

FIGURE 7.1.

An illustration of your control in Internet Explorer after adding a CheckBox.

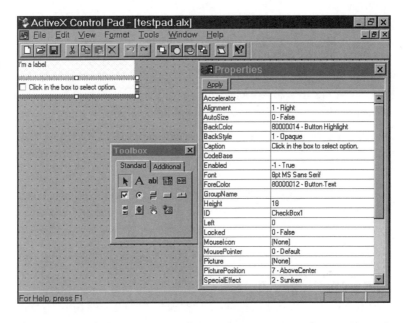

Change the CheckBox1 properties as follows:

- Change BackColor to Button Highlight.
- Change Value from blank to False, to change the checkbox from gray to white.
- Right-click the control and select Script Wizard. Select the Click event for CheckBox1. Select the Caption property in the action pane and click the Insert Action button (visible in List View, which is turned on with the button at the bottom of the Script Wizard window). Type **Your option is selected**.
- Click BackStyle and then the Insert Action button again. Select 0 - Transparent.

To program interaction between the two controls, click the Label1 control in the action pane and click Insert Action. Type **You selected CheckBox1**, select Label1's BackColor property, and click Insert Action. Select a blue color and click OK to close the dialog box. Click OK again to close the Script Wizard. Then save the file and preview it in IE.

Now when you click Label1, the text changes and the background changes to red. When you click the checkbox, the text near the checkbox changes and the background changes from white to gray. The background for the label changes to light blue and the text in the label changes.

The TextBox Control

The TextBox control is a simple rectangular box in which you can input text. Its properties include AutoSize, AutoTab, AutoWordSelect, BackColor, BackStyle, BorderColor, BorderStyle, Codebase, DragBehavior, Enabled, EnterFieldBehavior, EnterKeyBehavior, Font, ForeColor, Height, HideSelection, ID, IMEMode, IntegralHeight, Left, Locked, MaxLength, MouseIcon, MousePointer, MultiLine, PasswordChar, Scrollbars, SelectionMargin, SpecialEffect, TabIndex,

TabKeyBehavior, TabStop, Text, TextAlign, Top, Value, Visible, Width, and WordWrap. The control's events include AfterUpdate, BeforeDragOver, BeforeDropOrPaste, BeforeUpdate, Change, DblClick, DropButtonClick, Enter, Error, Exit, Keydown, Keypress, KeyUp, MouseDown, MouseMove, and MouseUp.

Add a text box to your HTML layout and change the Text property to Password. Change the PasswordChar to * and change the background color to orange.

In the Script Wizard event pane, select AfterUpdate. In the action pane, select Hide Control and click Insert Action, and then select Layout1's BackColor property and click Insert Action. Select a pink color.

Test the control. If you tab from control to control, the text characters appear as a string of highlighted asterisks. If you change the text in TextBox1 and leave the box, the control disappears and the background of the rest of the controls changes to pink.

You can already see that you can use this as a password box when validation code is attached.

The ComboBox Control

The ComboBox allows users to enter data or select from a drop-down list. It's similar to a list box except that it must be clicked to make the list contents appear. Change the ComboBox's Style property from 0 to 2 to make it appear like a list box in which users can select only from the list.

Properties for the ComboBox control include AutoSize, AutoTab, AutoWordSelect, BackColor, BackStyle, BorderColor, BorderStyle, BoundColumn, Codebase, ColumnCount, ColumnHeads, ColumnWidths, DragBehavior, DropButtonStyle, Enabled, EnterFieldBehavior, Font, ForeColor, Height, HideSelection, ID, IMEMode, ListRows, ListStyle, ListWidth, Locked, MatchEntry, MatchRequired, MaxLength, MouseIcon, MousePointer, SelectionMargin, ShowDropButtonWhen, SpecialEffect, Style, TabIndex, TabStop, Text, TextAlign, TextColumn, Top, TopIndex, Value, Visible, and Width. Of the 17 programmable events, the primary one is Change. The events also include AfterUpdate, BeforeDragOver, BeforeDropOrPaste, BeforeUpdate, Click, DblClick, DropButtonClick, Enter, Error, Exit, Keydown, Keypress, KeyUp, MouseDown, MouseMove, and MouseUp.

To program a combo box, use the Script Wizard and some VB background basics to create a list of options in the box. First, place a long combo box in the HTML Layout Editor window. Now display the properties for the control. Change Style to 2 - DropDownlList.

Now you'll use the rest of the default properties and another feature of scripting with the Script Wizard to manipulate the box. Right-click in the window and select Script Wizard. In the event pane, select Layout1, which refers to your HTML layout window. Select the OnLoad event, and then select Code View in the view pane. Now the default EnterFieldBehavior property for ComboBox1 is set to 0 - SelectAll. Change it to 1 - RecallSelection so that when users re-enter the field, the last selected item in the list appears.

In the action pane, select ComboBox1, scroll down to the `EnterFieldBehavior` property, and double-click to place this code line in the code view:

```
ComboBox1.EnterFieldBehavior=1
```

Use the `additem` method to propagate the list box in four lines of code. The last line adds a blank so that users will quickly recognize the end of the list.

```
for x = 1 to 10
ComboBox1.additem " This is Item " & x
next
ComboBox1.additem
```

Review your work by saving the changes and previewing the `intrinsic.htm` file in Internet Explorer.

Suppose that you later want to add an item called This is Item 4.1 to your ComboBox. You can do so without breaking up the `For` loop by inserting this code line in your on-load routine:

```
ComboBox1.additem " This is Item 4.1", 4
```

This code uses the index value 4 as a pointer after which the line will be added.

Now you can refresh IE and see the new item.

If you want to run conditional actions based on user selection, use the `Click` event. This event is activated when users select an item from the drop-down box or enters an item and leaves the box.

In the Script Wizard, select ComboBox1's `Click` event, and then select Code View in the code pane. Now enter the following code lines, or use the action pane to add the ones already available:

```
If ComboBox1.value=" This is Item " & 1 then
TextBox1.Visible = True
TextBox1.BackColor = &H00FF0000
end if
If ComboBox1.value=" This is Item " & 2 then
TextBox1.Visible = True
TextBox1.BackColor = &H00FFFF00
```

> **TIP**
>
> In Control Pad, custom actions interfere with the generation of code lines for other properties. To get the hexadecimal color equivalent in the preceding example, use the event pane and select the `DblClick` event. Then select TextBox1 in the action pane, and double-click the `BackColor` property to launch the color selector. After you select the color, view the code line, cut it from the `DblClick` routine, and paste it in the code view for your action.

The CommandButton

The CommandButton is a scalable rectangular button. Its properties include `Accelerator`, `AutoSize`, `BackColor`, `BackStyle`, `Caption`, `Codebase`, `Enabled`, `Font`, `ForeColor`, `Height`, `ID`, `Left`, `Locked`, `MousePointer`, `Picture`, `PicturePosition`, `TabIndex`, `TabStop`, `TakeFocusOnClick`, `Top`, `Visible`, `Width`, and `WordWrap`. It also features 15 Windows programmable events: `AfterUpdate`, `BeforeDragOver`, `BeforeDropOrPaste`, `BeforeUpdate`, `Click`, `DblClick`, `Enter`, `Error`, `Exit`, `KeyDown`, `KeyPress`, `KeyUp`, `MouseDown`, `MouseMove`, and `MouseUp`.

After placing the CommandButton in your HTML layout, view its properties and change `Caption` to `DblClick` to change `CheckBox` colors.

In the Script Wizard, click the CommandButton1 `DblClick` event. In the view pane select List View, and in the action pane double-click CheckBox1's `BackColor` property. Select the color black and click OK. Select Code View in the view pane. You should see this:

```
CheckBox1.BackColor = &H00004000
```

Many programmers use the CommandButton control's `Click` event and invoke custom functions in VBScript or JavaScript. The CommandButton supports the `Picture` and `PicturePosition` properties, so you can place a bitmap in the button and make it look like a picture rather than a button.

For this control's example, you'll use a bitmap file that also resides on the user's platform. Place another command button in the layout window and click and drag the lower-right handle to make the button appear as a square box.

Now click the control and view the properties. Change `BackStyle` to `Transparent`. Remove the CommandButton2 name from the `Caption` property and click Apply. Click Picture, and the input box will show (None).

Click the three dots to the right to get a dialog box that permits navigation to the Windows directory. In the Windows directory, select `256color.bmp` and click OK. Change the `PicturePosition` property to `12 - Center`.

In the Script Wizard, select the CommandButton2 `Click` event in the event pane; in the action pane, select CommandButton1's `HideControl` action. Save the file and refresh the view in Internet Explorer. Interact with each control. Remember to double-click the first command button and single-click the button with the `256color.bmp` picture.

When you click CommandButton2 (the picture), CommandButton1 is hidden from view and thus disabled. Refresh your view in Internet Explorer. Your control appears similar to Figure 7.2.

FIGURE 7.2.

Your control should appear similar to this. Here, the user selected Item3 in the ComboBox while interacting with the controls.

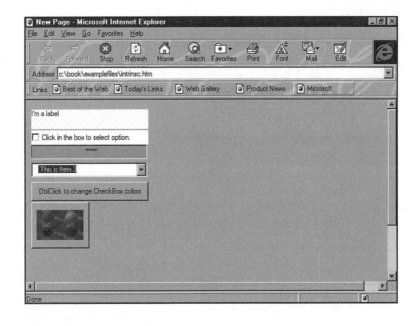

You've just explored placing a few controls on the page and doing some simple programming. You may not have had to type many code lines, but as you can see in Listing 7.1, your HTML Layout control contains many lines of script and parameter tags identifying the properties.

Listing 7.1. The code lines generated in `testpad.alx`.

```
<SCRIPT LANGUAGE="VBScript">
<!--
Sub Label1_Click()
Label1.BackColor = &H000000FF
Label1.Caption = "Now I'm a clicked label"
end sub
-->
</SCRIPT>
<SCRIPT LANGUAGE="VBScript">
<!--
Sub CheckBox1_Click()
CheckBox1.Caption = "Your option is selected."
CheckBox1.BackStyle = 0
Label1.Caption = "You selected Checkbox1."
Label1.BackColor = &H00FFFF80
end sub
-->
</SCRIPT>
<SCRIPT LANGUAGE="VBScript">
<!--
Sub TextBox1_AfterUpdate()
TextBox1.Visible = False
Layout1.BackColor = &H00C080FF
```

continues

Listing 7.1. continued

```
end sub
-->
</SCRIPT>
<SCRIPT LANGUAGE="VBScript">
<!--
Sub Layout1_OnLoad()
ComboBox1.EnterFieldBehavior=1
for x = 1 to 10
ComboBox1.additem " This is Item " & x
next
ComboBox1.additem
ComboBox1.additem " This is Item 4.1", 4
end sub
-->
</SCRIPT>
<SCRIPT LANGUAGE="VBScript">
<!--
Sub ComboBox1_DblClick(Cancel)
end sub
Sub ComboBox1_Click()
If ComboBox1.value=" This is Item " & 1 then
TextBox1.Visible = True
TextBox1.BackColor = &H00FF0000
end if
If ComboBox1.value=" This is Item " & 2 then
TextBox1.Visible = True
TextBox1.BackColor = &H00FFFF00
end if
end sub
-->
</SCRIPT>
<SCRIPT LANGUAGE="VBScript">
<!--
Sub CommandButton1_DblClick(Cancel)
CheckBox1.BackColor = &H00004000
end sub
-->
</SCRIPT>
<SCRIPT LANGUAGE="VBScript">
<!--
Sub CommandButton2_Click()
CommandButton1.Visible = False
end sub
-->
</SCRIPT>
<DIV ID="Layout1" STYLE="LAYOUT:FIXED;WIDTH:477pt;HEIGHT:293pt;">
<OBJECT ID="Label1" CLASSID="CLSID:978C9E23-D4B0-11CE-BF2D-00AA003F40D0"
 STYLE="TOP:0pt;LEFT:0pt;WIDTH:149pt;HEIGHT:25pt;ZINDEX:0;">
<PARAM NAME="BackColor" VALUE="2147483672">
<PARAM NAME="Caption" VALUE="I'm a label">
<PARAM NAME="Size" VALUE="5256;882">
<PARAM NAME="FontCharSet" VALUE="0">
<PARAM NAME="FontPitchAndFamily" VALUE="2">
<PARAM NAME="FontWeight" VALUE="0">
</OBJECT>
<OBJECT ID="CheckBox1" CLASSID="CLSID:8BD21D40-EC42-11CE-9E0D-00AA006002F3"
 STYLE="TOP:26pt;LEFT:0pt;WIDTH:149pt;HEIGHT:18pt;TABINDEX:1;ZINDEX:1;">
<PARAM NAME="BackColor" VALUE="2147483668">
```

```
<PARAM NAME="ForeColor" VALUE="2147483666">
<PARAM NAME="DisplayStyle" VALUE="4">
<PARAM NAME="Size" VALUE="5256;635">
<PARAM NAME="Value" VALUE="False">
<PARAM NAME="Caption" VALUE="Click in the box to select option.">
<PARAM NAME="FontCharSet" VALUE="0">
<PARAM NAME="FontPitchAndFamily" VALUE="2">
<PARAM NAME="FontWeight" VALUE="0">
</OBJECT>
<OBJECT ID="TextBox1" CLASSID="CLSID:8BD21D10-EC42-11CE-9E0D-00AA006002F3"
 STYLE="TOP:44pt;LEFT:-1pt;WIDTH:149pt;HEIGHT:18pt;TABINDEX:2;ZINDEX:2;">
<PARAM NAME="VariousPropertyBits" VALUE="209733659">
<PARAM NAME="BackColor" VALUE="33023">
<PARAM NAME="Size" VALUE="5256;635">
<PARAM NAME="PasswordChar" VALUE="42">
<PARAM NAME="Value" VALUE="Howdy">
<PARAM NAME="FontCharSet" VALUE="0">
<PARAM NAME="FontPitchAndFamily" VALUE="2">
<PARAM NAME="ParagraphAlign" VALUE="3">
<PARAM NAME="FontWeight" VALUE="0">
</OBJECT>
<OBJECT ID="ComboBox1" CLASSID="CLSID:8BD21D30-EC42-11CE-9E0D-00AA006002F3"
 STYLE="TOP:67pt;LEFT:0pt;WIDTH:148pt;HEIGHT:18pt;TABINDEX:3;ZINDEX:3;">
<PARAM NAME="VariousPropertyBits" VALUE="748701723">
<PARAM NAME="DisplayStyle" VALUE="7">
<PARAM NAME="Size" VALUE="5221;635">
<PARAM NAME="MatchEntry" VALUE="1">
<PARAM NAME="ShowDropButtonWhen" VALUE="2">
<PARAM NAME="FontCharSet" VALUE="0">
<PARAM NAME="FontPitchAndFamily" VALUE="2">
<PARAM NAME="FontWeight" VALUE="0">
</OBJECT>
<OBJECT ID="CommandButton1" CLASSID="CLSID:D7053240-CE69-11CD-A777-00DD01143C57"
 STYLE="TOP:91pt;LEFT:0pt;WIDTH:149pt;HEIGHT:24pt;TABINDEX:4;ZINDEX:4;">
<PARAM NAME="Caption" VALUE="DblClick to change CheckBox colors">
<PARAM NAME="Size" VALUE="5239;846">
<PARAM NAME="FontCharSet" VALUE="0">
<PARAM NAME="FontPitchAndFamily" VALUE="2">
<PARAM NAME="ParagraphAlign" VALUE="3">
<PARAM NAME="FontWeight" VALUE="0">
</OBJECT>
<OBJECT ID="CommandButton2"
CLASSID="CLSID:D7053240-CE69-11CD-A777-00DD01143C57"
DATA="DATA:application/x-oleobject;BASE64,
...
(reference to bitmap description omitted due to length)
...
AA==
"
 STYLE="TOP:116pt;LEFT:0pt;WIDTH:74pt;HEIGHT:58pt;TABINDEX:5;ZINDEX:5;">
</OBJECT>
</DIV>
```

The Frame Control

The Frame control is a scalable rectangular control that supports images. You can use it to segment a page with various oversize windows fitting within the framed window.

Its properties include `BackColor`, `BorderColor`, `BorderStyle`, `Caption`, `Codebase`, `Cycle`, `Enabled`, `Font`, `ForeColor`, `Height`, `ID`, `KeepScrollBarsVisible`, `Left`, `MouseIcon`, `MousePointer`, `Picture`, `PictureAlignment`, `PictureSizeMode`, `PictureTiling`, `ScrollBars`, `ScrollHeight`, `ScrollLeft`, `ScrollTop`, `ScrollWidth`, `SpecialEffect`, `TabIndex`, `TabStop`, `Top`, `VerticalScrollBarSide`, `Visible`, `Width`, and `Zoom`. Its events include `AddControl`, `AfterUpdate`, `BeforeDragOver`, `BeforeDropOrPaste`, `BeforeUpdate`, `Click`, `DblClick`, `DropButtonClick`, `Enter`, `Error`, `Exit`, `KeyDown`, `Keypress`, `KeyUp`, `Layout`, `MouseDown`, `MouseMove`, `MouseUp`, `RemoveControl`, `Scroll`, and `Zoom`.

The Image Control: Button, CheckBox, and Combo

The Forms Image Control enables viewing of a bitmap or similar image. It's an object with a rectangular frame. The image is imported at original size.

Properties of the Image control include `AutoSize`, `BackColor`, `BackStyle`, `BorderColor`, `BorderStyle`, `Codebase`, `Enabled`, `Height`, `ID`, `Left`, `MouseIcon`, `MousePointer`, `Picture`, `PictureAlignment`, `PictureSizeMode`, `PictureTiling`, `SpecialEffect`, `Top`, `Visible`, and `Width`. Its programmable events are `AfterUpdate`, `BeforeDragOver`, `BeforeDropOrPaste`, `BeforeUpdate`, `Click`, `DblClick`, `Enter`, `Error`, `Exit`, `MouseDown`, `MouseMove`, and `MouseUp`.

Add the Forms Image Control to the toolbox in the HTML Layout Editor in Control Pad and draw a rectangular box about 1 1/2 inches square. Double-click the control to see the properties sheet. Change the following properties:

- `Picture`. Select `C:\windows\Straw Mat.bmp` from your directory listing.
- `PictureSizeMode`. Select `1 - Stretch`.
- `MousePointer`. Select `11 - Hourglass`.
- `SpecialEffect`. Select `2 - Sunken`.

Now draw a text box directly below the Image control and change the following properties:

- `Text`. Eliminate the caption for this property.
- `Font`. Click the ... button and select 12-point type from the dialog box.
- `Visible`. Select `0 - False`.

The text box remains hidden until user interaction changes the `Visible` property to `True`.

Now place a CommandButton below the text box. Type `Click Me` for the `Caption` property.

Place another text box above the Image control. Set the caption property to read `Enter the secret phrase in the box below....` Set the `Visible` property to `0 - False` to hide the control until there is user action.

Launch the Script Wizard after saving your changes. Click the TextBox1 `Exit` event. Add the following conditional lines of code to test the value in TextBox1:

```
Sub TextBox1_Exit(Cancel)
If TextBox1.value="Get Out of Jail Free" then
msgbox "You Win.", 16, "ActiveX Test Message"
exit sub
end if
msgbox "Try Again. Hint: Think of Monopoly.", 16, "ActiveX Test Message"
```

Notice that the exit sub statement prevents you from having to use the else statement. The subroutine immediately exits if users type the correct data; otherwise, the second message appears instead of the first.

For CommandButton1, click the Click event. In the action pane select TextBox1 and double-click the Show Control action. In the action pane, double-click the TextBox2 control's Show Control action. The code view should show these lines:

```
Sub CommandButton1_Click()
TextBox1.Visible = True
TextBox2.Visible = True
```

Save your changes. Name the file Image1.alx. Now open a new HTML page (not a Layout) and click the lines of HTML between the body tags. Choose Edit | Insert HTML Layout. Navigate to the Image1.alx file, select it, and click OK.

You now have an HTML file. Save it as Image1.htm. If you open the file in your browser, you should see a picture, two textboxes, and a command button that reads Click Me (see Figure 7.3).

FIGURE 7.3.

The control in the browser window after you click the Click Me CommandButton and before you exit the lower text box.

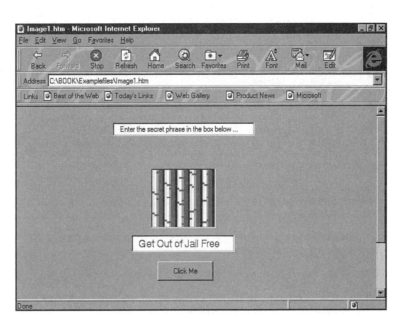

Click the button and the CommandButton's click event displays TextBox2 above the image and TextBox2 below the image. The text in the top box tells users to enter text in the lower text box. If users enter **Get Out of Jail Free**, the You Win message box should appear. If users enter anything else or otherwise exit TextBox1, the Try Again message box appears.

Listing 7.2 shows the complete code for the image1.alx file.

Listing 7.2. The complete code generated in the example for the image1.alx HTML Layout file.

```
<SCRIPT LANGUAGE="VBScript">
<!--
Sub CommandButton1_Click()
TextBox1.Visible = True
TextBox2.Visible = True
end sub
-->
</SCRIPT>
<SCRIPT LANGUAGE="VBScript">
<!--
Sub TextBox1_Exit(Cancel)
If TextBox1.value="Get Out of Jail Free" then
msgbox "You Win.", 16, "ActiveX Test Message"
exit sub
end if
msgbox "Try Again. Hint: Think of Monopoly.", 16, "ActiveX Test Message"
end sub
-->
</SCRIPT>
<DIV ID="Layout1" STYLE="LAYOUT:FIXED;WIDTH:400pt;HEIGHT:300pt;">
<OBJECT ID="Image1"
 CLASSID="CLSID:4C599241-6926-101B-9992-00000B65C6F9"
 DATA="DATA:application/x-oleobject;BASE64,
QZJZTCZpGxCZkgAAC2XG+QACFADgBwAAAAsBAv
 //AABeCwAAPAoAALCBZ9pK
ws8RtYQAqgCnHRpsdAAATgIAAEJNTgIAAAAAAABOAAAAKAAAAB4AAAAgAAAA
AQAEAAAAAAAgAAEwsAABMLAAAGAAAABgAAAAAAAAgIAAgICAAMDAwAAAA
//8A////AEUyEEUyEEUyEEUyEEUyEABFMhBFMhBFEhBFMhBFMhAHRTIQQRIQ
RTIQRTIQETIQ/0UyEBUyEEUyEEUyEEUREABFMhBFMhBFMhAVMhBFMhAHRTIQ
RTIQRRIQRTIQRTIQ/0ESEEUyEEUyEEUyEEUyEAAVMhBFMhBFMhBFMhAH
RTIQRTIQRTIQETIQRTIQ/0UyEEUxEEUyEEUREEUyEABFMhBFMhBFMhBFMhBF
MhAHRTIQRTIQRTIQRTIQ/0UyEEUyEEEREEUyEEUyEABFMhBFMhAVMhBF
MhBFMhAHRTIQRTIQRRIQRTIQETIQ/0UREEUyEEUyEEUyEEUyEABFMhBBEhBF
MhBFMhBFEhAHRTIQRTIQRTIQRTIQ/0ESEEUyEEUyEEUyEAAVMhBF
MhBFMhBFMhAHRTIQRTIQQRIQRTIQRTIQ/0UyEEUSEBUyEEUyEEUyEABF
MhBFMhBFMhBBMhBFMhAHRTIQQRIQRTIQFTIQQRIQ/0UyEBUyEEUyEEUyEBUy
EABFMhBFMhBFMhBFMhAHRTIQRTIQRTIQRTIQ/0UyEEUyEEESEEUy
EEUyEABFMhBFMhBFMhBFMhBFMhAHRTIQRTIQRTIQQRIQRRIQ/0UREEUyEEUy
EBUyEEUyEAhFMhBFMhBFMhBFMhADAAA=
"
 STYLE="TOP:66pt;LEFT:165pt;WIDTH:83pt;HEIGHT:74pt;ZINDEX:0;">
</OBJECT>
<OBJECT ID="TextBox1" CLASSID="CLSID:8BD21D10-EC42-11CE-9E0D-00AA006002F3"
 STYLE="TOP:149pt;LEFT:140pt;WIDTH:132pt;
```

```
  HEIGHT:21pt;TABINDEX:0;DISPLAY:NONE;ZINDEX:1;">
<PARAM NAME="VariousPropertyBits" VALUE="746604571">
<PARAM NAME="Size" VALUE="4656;741">
<PARAM NAME="FontHeight" VALUE="240">
<PARAM NAME="FontCharSet" VALUE="0">
<PARAM NAME="FontPitchAndFamily" VALUE="2">
<PARAM NAME="FontWeight" VALUE="0">
</OBJECT>
<OBJECT ID="CommandButton1" CLASSID="CLSID:D7053240-CE69-11CD-A777-00DD01143C57"
 STYLE="TOP:182pt;LEFT:173pt;WIDTH:72pt;
 HEIGHT:24pt;TABINDEX:1;ZINDEX:2;">
<PARAM NAME="Caption" VALUE="Click Me">
<PARAM NAME="Size" VALUE="2540;846">
<PARAM NAME="FontCharSet" VALUE="0">
<PARAM NAME="FontPitchAndFamily" VALUE="2">
<PARAM NAME="ParagraphAlign" VALUE="3">
<PARAM NAME="FontWeight" VALUE="0">
</OBJECT>
<OBJECT ID="TextBox2" CLASSID="CLSID:8BD21D10-EC42-11CE-9E0D-00AA006002F3"
 STYLE="TOP:8pt;LEFT:116pt;WIDTH:182pt;
 HEIGHT:17pt;TABINDEX:2;DISPLAY:NONE;ZINDEX:3;">
<PARAM NAME="VariousPropertyBits" VALUE="746604571">
<PARAM NAME="Size" VALUE="6403;582">
<PARAM NAME="Value" VALUE="Enter the secret phrase in the box below ...">
<PARAM NAME="FontCharSet" VALUE="0">
<PARAM NAME="FontPitchAndFamily" VALUE="2">
<PARAM NAME="FontWeight" VALUE="0">
</OBJECT>
</DIV>
```

The ListBox Control

A ListBox control is similar to the ComboBox control, with two differences:

- The list in a ListBox is visible at runtime. Any items in the list that don't fit within the control's boundaries are made visible with an automatic scroll bar.

- A ListBox allows user entry without having to change any default properties. With the ComboBox, the Style property is changed to create this effect.

The properties of the ListBox control include BackColor, BackStyle, BorderColor, BorderStyle, BoundColumn, Codebase, ColumnCount, ColumnHeads, ColumnWidths, Enabled, Font, ForeColor, Height, ID, IMEMode, IntegralHeight, Left, List, ListIndex, ListStyle, Locked, MatchEntry, MouseIcon, MousePointer, Multiselect, Selected, SpecialEffect, TabIndex, TabStop, Text, TextColumn, Top, TopIndex, Value, Visible, and Width. The numerous events for the control include AfterUpdate, BeforeDragOver, BeforeDropOrPaste, BeforeUpdate, Change, Click, DblClick, Enter, Error, Exit, KeyDown, Keypress, KeyUp, MouseDown, MouseMove, and MouseUp.

Open a new HTML Layout in Control Pad and draw a tall list box about 2 inches across. Change the properties as follows:

7

MANIPULATING ACTIVEX CONTROLS

- ■ MatchEntry. Select 1 - Complete.
- ■ BackColor. Click the … button and select a dark blue color from the color palette.
- ■ ForeColor. For the ForeColor (text), select a white color.
- ■ Font. Click the … button and select bold and 10-point type.

Now open the Script Wizard and propagate the list. Choose the layout OnLoad event and enter the following lines of code:

```
dim m(13)
m(1)="January"
m(2)="February"
m(3)="March"
m(4)="April"
m(5)="May"
m(6)="June"
m(7)="July"
m(8)="August"
m(9)="September"
m(10)="October"
m(11)="November"
m(12)="December"
for i = 1 to 12
ListBox1.additem "Month of " & m(i)
next
ListBox1.additem
```

By simply adding a command button and programming a Click event, you can perform a query against the value of the selection to determine whether it matches the validation criteria. Draw a CommandButton on the HTML layout left of the ListBox. Change the CommandButton Caption property, and then type **Check for December**.

In the Script Wizard, select the CommandButton Click event and enter the following criteria to test to see whether the selection is valid:

```
If ListBox1="Month of December" then
msgbox "Insert your conditional code here.", 16, "ActiveX Testing"
exit sub
end if
msgbox "Your selection does not match the criteria.", 16, "ActiveX Testing"
```

Now save your file and insert it into an HTML file. Name the HTML file testlist.htm. Listing 7.3 shows the code you generated. Test your file by clicking various selections and then clicking the CommandButton. Figure 7.4 shows the results of this example.

Listing 7.3. The code generated for the HTML layout testlist.alx.

```
<SCRIPT LANGUAGE="VBScript">
<!--
Sub Layout2_OnLoad()
dim m(13)
m(1)="January"
```

```
m(2)="February"
m(3)="March"
m(4)="April"
m(5)="May"
m(6)="June"
m(7)="July"
m(8)="August"
m(9)="September"
m(10)="October"
m(11)="November"
m(12)="December"
for i = 1 to 12
ListBox1.additem "Month of " & m(i)
next
ListBox1.additem
end sub
-->
</SCRIPT>
<SCRIPT LANGUAGE="VBScript">
<!--
Sub CommandButton1_Click()
If ListBox1="Month of December" then
msgbox "Insert your conditional code here.", 16, "ActiveX Testing"
exit sub
end if
msgbox "Your selection does not match the criteria.", 16, "ActiveX Testing"
end sub
-->
</SCRIPT>
<DIV ID="Layout2" STYLE="LAYOUT:FIXED;WIDTH:400pt;HEIGHT:200pt;">
<OBJECT ID="ListBox1" CLASSID="CLSID:8BD21D20-EC42-11CE-9E0D-00AA006002F3"
 STYLE="TOP:8pt;LEFT:107pt;WIDTH:132pt;
 HEIGHT:159pt;TABINDEX:0;ZINDEX:0;">
<PARAM NAME="BackColor" VALUE="12615680">
<PARAM NAME="ForeColor" VALUE="16777215">
<PARAM NAME="ScrollBars" VALUE="3">
<PARAM NAME="DisplayStyle" VALUE="2">
<PARAM NAME="Size" VALUE="4656;5603">
<PARAM NAME="MatchEntry" VALUE="1">
<PARAM NAME="FontEffects" VALUE="1073741825">
<PARAM NAME="FontHeight" VALUE="200">
<PARAM NAME="FontCharSet" VALUE="0">
<PARAM NAME="FontPitchAndFamily" VALUE="2">
<PARAM NAME="FontWeight" VALUE="700">
</OBJECT>
<OBJECT ID="CommandButton1" CLASSID="CLSID:D7053240-CE69-11CD-A777-00DD01143C57"
 STYLE="TOP:66pt;LEFT:8pt;WIDTH:91pt;
 HEIGHT:33pt;TABINDEX:1;ZINDEX:1;">
<PARAM NAME="Caption" VALUE="Check for December">
<PARAM NAME="Size" VALUE="3202;1165">
<PARAM NAME="FontCharSet" VALUE="0">
<PARAM NAME="FontPitchAndFamily" VALUE="2">
<PARAM NAME="ParagraphAlign" VALUE="3">
<PARAM NAME="FontWeight" VALUE="0">
</OBJECT>
</DIV>
```

7

MANIPULATING
ACTIVEX
CONTROLS

FIGURE 7.4.

The testlist.htm *file with the* testlist.alx *HTML layout should appear like this in Internet Explorer.*

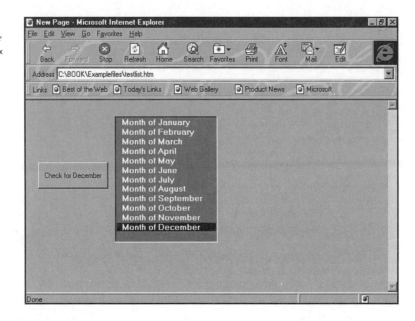

The MultiPage Control

The MultiPage control is similar to the TabStrip control. Each page has a tab at the top which, when clicked, allows the contents of the page to be viewed. The properties and effects are slightly different. Use the MultiPage control if you want to use a horizontal or vertical scroll bar or if you want to use the TransitionEffect and TransitionPeriod properties.

The properties of the MultiPage control include Accelerator, Caption, ControlTip, Cycle, Enabled, Index, KeepScrollBarsVisible, Name, Picture, PictureAlignment, PictureSizeMode, PictureTiling, ScrollBars, ScrollHeight, ScrollLeft, ScrollTop, ScrollWidth, Tag, TransitionEffect, TransitionPeriod, VerticalScrollBarSide, Visible, and Zoom. The control's events include AddControl, AfterUpdate, BeforeDragOver, BeforeDropOrPaste, BeforeUpdate, Change, Click, DblClick, Enter, Error, Exit, KeyDown, Keypress, KeyUp, Layout, MouseDown, MouseMove, MouseUp, RemoveControl, Scroll, and Zoom.

For this example, place the MultiPage control in your toolbox in the HTML Layout Editor and click the tool. Click the page to place the control. Now place a CommandButton to the left of the MultiPage control, and change its Caption property to Add A Page.

With a simple line of script attached to the Click event for CommandButton1, you can add a page to the control on the fly. Save the file with the filename multest.alx. Launch the Script

Wizard. Click the event pane on CommandButton1's `Click` event. Add the following line of code to define the object you're adding a button to and adding it at the same time:

```
Set MultiPage1.Pages = MultiPage1.Add
```

Save your changes. Insert your HTML layout into an HTML page and assign it the filename `multest.htm`. Test your code by opening `multest.htm` in Internet Explorer.

Now suppose that you need to remove pages. Open your layout in the editor window and launch the Script Wizard. In the event pane, select CommandButton1's `KeyUp` event.

> **NOTE**
>
> The `KeyUp` event is activated by pressing the up-arrow key. Using `KeyDown` in this example would scroll the page down and initiate any other action code attached to the `KeyDown` event.

Insert the following code lines. When the `KeyUp` event is initiated, this code removes the last page in the collection.

```
n = MultiPage1.Pages.Count - 1
MultiPage1.Remove(n)
```

Save the file, refresh the `multest.htm` file in Internet Explorer, and click the CommandButton. Each `Click` event adds a page to the control. Now press the up-arrow key to remove a page from the control. Each time the key is pressed, a page disappears from the control.

Figure 7.5 shows what the control looks like after you click the CommandButton a few times. Listing 7.4 provides a look at the complete HTML Layout code.

Listing 7.4. The code for `multest.alx`, the HTML Layout control created in the exercise.

```
<SCRIPT LANGUAGE="VBScript">
<!--
Sub CommandButton1_KeyUp(KeyCode, Shift)
n = MultiPage1.Pages.Count - 1
MultiPage1.Remove(n)
end sub
Sub CommandButton1_Click()
Set MultiPage1.Pages = MultiPage1.Add
end sub
-->
</SCRIPT>
<DIV ID="Layout1" STYLE="LAYOUT:FIXED;WIDTH:477pt;HEIGHT:293pt;">
<OBJECT ID="MultiPage1" CLASSID="CLSID:46E31370-3F7A-11CE-BED6-00AA00611080"
 STYLE="TOP:17pt;LEFT:107pt;WIDTH:231pt; HEIGHT:91pt;TABINDEX:0;ZINDEX:0;">
```

continues

Listing 7.4. continued

```
</OBJECT>
<OBJECT ID="CommandButton1" CLASSID="CLSID:D7053240-CE69-11CD-A777-00DD01143C57"
 STYLE="TOP:50pt;LEFT:8pt;WIDTH:83pt; HEIGHT:25pt;TABINDEX:1;ZINDEX:1;">
<PARAM NAME="Caption" VALUE="Add A Page">
<PARAM NAME="Size" VALUE="2910;873">
<PARAM NAME="FontCharSet" VALUE="0">
<PARAM NAME="FontPitchAndFamily" VALUE="2">
<PARAM NAME="ParagraphAlign" VALUE="3">
<PARAM NAME="FontWeight" VALUE="0">
</OBJECT>
</DIV>
```

FIGURE 7.5.

This is the multest.alx *HTML layout created in the example.*

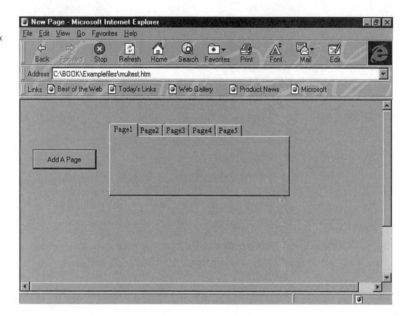

The OptionButton Control

The OptionButton control is a programmable true/false button that can interact with other OptionButtons in a group. OptionButtons are helpful when users need to select a single option from a list of options.

The properties for OptionButton are Accelerator, Alignment, AutoSize, BackColor, BackStyle, Caption, Codebase, Enabled, Font, ForeColor, GroupName, Height, ID, Left, Locked, MouseIcon, MousePointer, Picture, PicturePosition, SpecialEffect, TabIndex, TabStop, Top, TripleState, Value, Visible, Width, and WordWrap. Its events are AfterUpdate, BeforeDragOver, BeforeDropOrPaste, BeforeUpdate, Change, DblClick, Enter, Error, Exit, KeyDown, Keypress, KeyUp, MouseDown, MouseMove, and MouseUp.

> **CAUTION**
>
> One drawback of the OptionButton control is that if an OptionButton is used in a group by itself and is selected, users can't deselect the button by clicking it. Attempts to program the button to automatically deselect itself when clicked again could drive one to madness. A workaround involves using another control's event to set the value of the selected OptionButton back to `False`. Perhaps a future version of the control will toggle on and off if it remains in a group as a sole entity. Use CheckBox controls if you want a single control that can be toggled between `True` and `False`.

This exercise gives you a real-life example of an order form control, in which customers use OptionButton controls to submit information regarding the product or products they select. In this example, T-shirts are offered in three sizes and three colors. Assume that a form above your HTML Layout with controls contains specific information about a customer and payment information. Your OptionButton control focuses on product selection and quantity.

You'll place three OptionButtons groups on the page. Three OptionButtons will be in the first and second groups; the third group will contain only two OptionButtons. You'll also place eight Label controls on the page, two TextBoxes, and two CommandButtons. The example also will show you some shortcuts so that you can design the page very quickly.

Before you begin your design, look at Figure 7.6 to see where on the page the controls should appear. Notice that the text box at the far right is visible for now. When you're designing the page, leave that text box's `Visible` property set to `True`; after you complete the design work, set the `Visible` property for the text box to `False`.

FIGURE 7.6.

Design your control to resemble this layout in the exercise. Prevent users from having to scroll the page to see the layout.

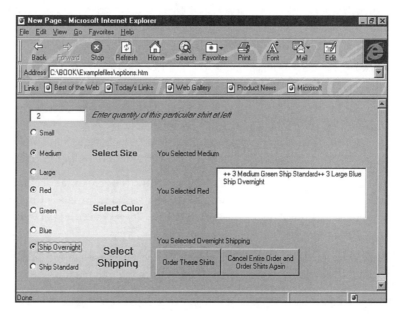

> **NOTE**
>
> In this example, the word *button* indicates an OptionButton control.

To begin, start about 1/2 inch down and 1/4 inch to the right of the upper-left edge on the layout window. Place your eight buttons on the page by selecting the appropriate tool in the toolbox, placing the first button on the page, stretching it horizontally, and then copying and pasting seven more.

Setting the Properties

Activate the Properties window. Select all eight controls by drawing a large rectangle around them. Change the Value property to False for all eight buttons.

Now select the bottom two buttons by using the shortcut method you probably are familiar with—Ctrl+clicking. Click the eighth button, and then Ctrl+click the seventh button. Both buttons are selected, and the properties sheet shows the combined properties of both buttons.

Change the selected buttons' BackColor property to a light green (clicking the ... button and select a color from the palette). Click Apply. Change the buttons' GroupName property to Group3 in the same manner. Click the eighth button and change its caption to Ship Standard. Click the seventh button and change its caption to Ship Overnight.

Ctrl+click the fourth, fifth, and sixth buttons. Change their GroupName property to Group2 and their BackColor to yellow. Select the sixth button and change its Caption to Blue. Select the fifth button and change its Caption to Green. The fourth gets Red as its caption.

Now select the first three buttons and change GroupName to Group1 and BackColor to a light blue-green. Select the buttons individually and change their captions to read Small, Medium, and Large, respectively.

Click the Label tool. Place one to the right of the first button control. Change the Label's Caption property to You Selected Small and change the Visible property to False.

Copy and paste the Label control to the right of the second button control in line vertically with the first label. Change the second label's Caption property to You Selected Medium. Make sure that the label is properly aligned horizontally with the second button. To place the other six labels, copy and paste the first two, and then place them in line under the first two.

You now have a group of four labels. Copy those four and paste again, dragging the last four labels in line under the first four. Change the captions for labels three through eight to You Selected Large, You Selected Red, You Selected Green, You Selected Blue, Ship Overnight, and Ship Standard.

Place a text box to the right of the labels; it doesn't matter where. Make it as long as you can without coming closer than about 1/4 inch from the right edge of the layout window. Change the `MultiLine` and `WordWrap` properties to `True`. Don't change `WordWrap` property first; the control will ignore the `WordWrap` property if `MultiLine` isn't changed to `True` first.

> **TIP**
>
> Don't let any controls touch any boundaries of your window. In your HTML file, the HTML Layout controls that touch the right boundary will require scrolling in Internet Explorer.

Now place a second text box above your buttons and to the left. Use the default properties. Place another Label (Label9) to the right of the new text box and change the `Caption` property to `Enter quantity of this particular shirt at left`.

Enter three more labels on top of the three groups and assign them the captions `Select Size`, `Select Color`, and `Select Shipping`. Select all three and change the property for `BackStyle` to `Transparent`. Change the `Default Font` properties to `12-point` and `Bold`.

Now create two CommandButtons at the bottom of the page to the right of the buttons. Change the first CommandButton caption to `Order These Shirts` and the second CommandButton caption to `Cancel Entire Order and Order Shirts Again`.

You've already programmed some functionality into the OptionButton groups by assigning `GroupName` properties to them. Now users can select only one button in each group at a time.

Adding Some Script

To program more functionality into the control, launch the Script Wizard. Program the OptionButton `Click` event for the first button so that when it's selected, the label for that button becomes visible and the labels for the other two buttons in the group are hidden. Use the following code snippet to program the first one, or use the Label1 `ShowControl`, Label2 `HideControl`, and Label3 `HideControl` actions in the action pane:

```
Sub OptionButton1_Click()
Label1.Visible = True
Label2.Visible = False
Label3.Visible = False
```

Do the same for all the buttons in each group, hiding the labels for the options not selected and showing the label for the button selected.

Next, you need to make sure that the top text box acquires focus not only on loading, but when users refresh the screen in the browser. Click Layout1 (or Layout2 if this is the default assigned to your HTML Layout control) and click the `OnLoad` event. In the action pane, double-click the TextBox2 SetFocus action. In the code view, the action will appear like this:

```
Sub Layout1_OnLoad()
call TextBox2.SetFocus()
```

7

MANIPULATING
ACTIVEX
CONTROLS

While still in the Script Wizard, program the CommandButtons. First, you may want to make sure that users have entered the quantity of shirts desired. This simple validation snippet will work:

```
If TextBox2.Value="" then
msgbox "You must Enter a Quantity", 16, "TO RESUME ORDERING"
exit sub
End If
```

Then you need to program the Click event further so that its action will append all the data collected by the eight option buttons to a single text box, which later will be transmitted with other order information. To do this, perform simple conditional tests on the Value property of each button. If any are True (selected), append a text string indicating what users selected to the first text box (right side of screen). Remember first to append the quantity from TextBox2 to the value in TextBox1. Immediately after appending the quantity, clear TextBox2 of its former value because it's no longer needed for this event.

The following code snippet for CommandButton1 was used to make the sample layout control. It should follow the preceding code snippet.

```
TextBox1.Value= TextBox1.Value & "++ " &  TextBox2.Value
TextBox2.Value=""
If OptionButton1.Value=True Then
TextBox1.Value=TextBox1.Value & " Small"
End If
If OptionButton2.Value=True Then
TextBox1.Value=TextBox1.Value & " Medium"
End If
If OptionButton3.Value=True Then
TextBox1.Value=TextBox1.Value & " Large"
End If
If OptionButton4.Value=True Then
TextBox1.Value=TextBox1.Value & " Red"
End If
If OptionButton5.Value=True Then
TextBox1.Value=TextBox1.Value & " Green"
End If
If OptionButton6.Value=True Then
TextBox1.Value=TextBox1.Value & " Blue"
End If
If OptionButton7.Value=True Then
TextBox1.Value=TextBox1.Value & " Ship Overnight"
End If
If OptionButton8.Value=True Then
TextBox1.Value=TextBox1.Value & " Ship Standard"
End If
```

Before proceeding, you need to clear the values stored in the OptionButtons and return their state to False (unchecked). You also need to hide the Label controls next to the buttons:

```
OptionButton1.Value=False
OptionButton2.Value=False
OptionButton3.Value=False
OptionButton4.Value=False
OptionButton5.Value=False
```

```
OptionButton6.Value=False
OptionButton7.Value=False
OptionButton8.Value=False
Label1.Visible = False
Label2.Visible = False
Label3.Visible = False
Label4.Visible = False
Label5.Visible = False
Label6.Visible = False
Label7.Visible = False
Label8.Visible = False
```

CAUTION

It's not practical to write four or five lines of code with array variables to hold the place for the OptionButton identifications. For example, the following snippet would generate a script error in IE, indicating a type mismatch:

```
For i = 1 to 8
OptionButton(i).Value=False
Next
OR
For I = 1 to 8
OptionButton(Cstr(i)).Value=False
Next
```

Enabling Cancellations

Now programming CommandButton2 is simple. If users want to cancel the various shirt orders appended by using CommandButton1, simply wipe the contents of TextBox1. Don't forget to reset the control's values to the defaults with the following code for CommandButton2:

```
TextBox1.Value=""
TextBox2.Value=""
OptionButton1.Value=False
OptionButton2.Value=False
OptionButton3.Value=False
OptionButton4.Value=False
OptionButton5.Value=False
OptionButton6.Value=False
OptionButton7.Value=False
OptionButton8.Value=False
Label1.Visible = False
Label2.Visible = False
Label3.Visible = False
Label4.Visible = False
Label5.Visible = False
Label6.Visible = False
Label7.Visible = False
Label8.Visible = False
```

Now test the control in Internet Explorer after inserting your HTML Layout file options.alx into an HTML file options.htm. You should be able to select only one option in each of the three groups. A label should appear each time you select an OptionButton. If you leave the quantity box (TextBox2) blank and click CommandButton1, you should get a message box that prompts users to include a quantity.

Each time CommandButton1 is clicked, the values of the buttons and the quantity text box string should be appended to the text box at the right, and the controls are reset to default values except for TextBox1, which now contains a string of text. Each time CommandButton2 is clicked, Value properties for all controls including TextBox2 are cleared.

After carefully checking your work, get back into Control Pad. Change the TextBox2 default Visible property to 0 - False. Save your work.

 You can dress up your HTML Layout by importing illustrations into image controls instead of using labels for the options. You can change the background color for the entire layout control, or use the SpecialEffect property and frame controls to change the appearance of the HTML Layout control. You can view the code for options.alx by opening the file from the accompanying CD-ROM in a text editor.

The ScrollBar Control

The ScrollBar control is a simple scroll bar that acts as an independent control manipulated by interaction with other controls, such as text boxes, that contain a Value property.

ScrollBars have the following properties: BackColor, Codebase, Delay, Enabled, ForeColor, Height, Width, ID, LargeChange, Left, Top, Max, Min, MouseIcon, MousePointer, Orientation, ProportionalThumb, SmallChange, TabIndex, TabStop, Value, and Visible. The ScrollBar's default event is Change. Its other events are AfterUpdate, BeforeDragOver, BeforeDropOrPaste, BeforeUpdate, Change, Enter, Error, Exit, KeyDown, Keypress, KeyUp, Scroll, Layout, MouseDown, MouseMove, MouseUp, RemoveControl, Scroll, and Zoom.

To program the ScrollBar control, you must first understand a little about how it works. A ScrollBar can be horizontal or vertical.

The Max property refers to the integer value assigned to the rightmost position of the horizontal ScrollBar. The Min property refers to the value assigned to the leftmost position of the horizontal scrollbar in units. If the scrollbar is vertical, Min would refer to the value at the top and Max would refer to the value at the bottom. The exception is if you want values to decrease as the scrollbar moves to the right, you could swap Min and Max. The same goes for the vertical scrollbar: Scrolling down decreases value if Max refers to the value at the top.

Scroll bars can be activated by users clicking and dragging the indicator, by clicking the bar on either side of the indicator, or through user action on another control.

To program interaction, place two ScrollBars on a new HTML Layout control. Stretch the first ScrollBar horizontally across the page and make it about 1/4 inch high. Place a second ScrollBar below the first, stretch it vertically, and compress the width to about 1/4 inch.

Draw a series of five text boxes horizontally under the first ScrollBar and make them evenly spaced. Click ScrollBar 1 and change its Max property to 5 and Min property to 1.

Now, with the Value property selected, you can click the scroll bar at various locations to see what the value will be for any particular position. Center TextBox1 under the Value 1 position and TextBox2 under the Value 2 position, and so on. Do the same with the vertical scroll bar. Draw a thin horizontal textbox and copy and paste seven more. These will be assigned TextBox7 through TextBox14 identifications. Change the Max property to 8 and the Min property to 1.

TIP

To make the textboxes line up properly, choose Format | Snap to Grid. Drag each textbox down and slightly to the left until it snaps into place. Drag each one individually until they're all aligned on the same row of grid markers. Then deselect Snap to Grid to align the ScrollBars with the textboxes. Shrink the ScrollBars so the edges of the textboxes are aligned with the edges of the pointer in the scrollbar.

Select the eight textboxes by drawing a window that crosses all eight boxes and no other controls. In the properties window, change the Font to 10-point type, the TextAlign property to 2 (Center), and the Visible property to 0 (False).

Select the five textboxes under the horizontal scroll bar, and change the Font property to 12-point boldface type, the TextAlign property to 2 (Center), and the Visible property to False.

Now you need to assign captions to the boxes. TextBox1's caption should be Black, TextBox2's White, TextBox3's Red, TextBox4's Green, TextBox5's Blue, and TextBox6's Yellow.

Change the Caption property for the rest of the boxes. TextBox7 will be Black, TextBox8 White, TextBox9 Red, TextBox10 Green, TextBox11 Blue, TextBox12 Yellow, TextBox13 Orange, and TextBox14 Magenta.

Assign a background color to each text box by clicking the control, selecting the BackColor property in the property sheet, and then clicking the … button to access the color palette. Click OK.

Figure 7.7 shows how your finished control layout, lacking any real functionality until the scripting is added, appears in Control Pad. The color captions reveal the background color of each box.

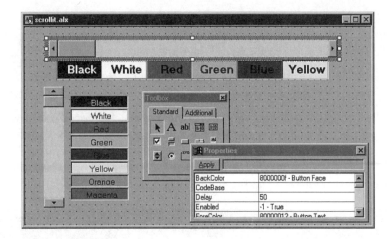

FIGURE 7.7.

This is how the layout for scrollit.alx *should appear in this exercise.*

Creating an Interactive Control

Now you need to add functionality. Events associated with scrolling the bar need to trigger noticeable actions in the window. To do this, launch the Script Wizard. In the event pane, select ScrollBar1's Change event; in the action pane, double-click TextBox1's Hide Control action. Double-click the Show Control action to place two lines of code in the code view of the view pane. You'll be selecting each line to copy and paste:

```
TextBox11.Visible = True
TextBox11.Visible = False
```

You need to determine what you want the ScrollBar to show or hide. For the example, program ScrollBar1 to show nothing until scrolled, and then to display each colored text box as the scroll pointer is moved.

You'll also program a surprise. When the scroll pointer is dragged over one of the colored text boxes hidden from view, the background color of the entire layout changes and remains that color until it's changed by the user's next scroll action. Because ScrollBar1's Value property is the default property in this subroutine, you merely type the line

```
If ScrollBar1=1 then
```

This line evaluates the location of the pointer by checking its Value property to determine whether it's in position over the black text box. If it is, the following line of code is processed to change the BackColor of the control:

```
Layout1.BackColor=0
```

> **NOTE**
>
> The hexadecimal `BackColor` property values, as identified in the properties sheet for the textbox background colors you selected, won't work at runtime if pasted into the code for the other controls. Instead, open your `.alx` file after creating the textboxes and view the code lines that define the background color of the textboxes. Copy and paste the background color value into the subroutine where you want to change the background color.

Pasting Your Code

Now you need to program the individual boxes to appear if the value of the pointer matches the test (Value 1) and program the others to be hidden when the ScrollBar control's pointer is moved:

```
TextBox1.Visible=True
TextBox2.Visible=False
TextBox3.Visible=False
TextBox4.Visible=False
TextBox5.Visible=False
TextBox6.Visible=False
end if
```

Cut and paste eight of the nine lines listed here into the window below the first nine lines. Remember that the second line (which changes the background color to black) will be omitted for the remaining five boxes. Program ScrollBar2 in a similar manner for the remaining eight textboxes by copying and pasting.

Save your code, and then save the HTML Layout as `scrollit.alx`. In Control Pad, insert the HTML layout into a new HTML file and open the file in IE 3.01. When you begin scrolling, the textboxes should appear below or to the right of the two ScrollBar controls. As you scroll, the background color changes to the appropriate color.

 Open `scrollit.alx` from the CD-ROM accompanying this book in a text editor to compare your code generated for the Layout Control. Figure 7.8 shows how the control appears in IE after you scroll to the yellow textbox.

The SpinButton Control

The SpinButton control is somewhat similar to a scroll bar in that its default property is `Value`. The SpinButton, however, is primarily used to increment and decrement another control's value. It can be programmed to generate many other actions, as indicated by the long list of events associated with the control. You can place SpinButtons, like ScrollBars, horizontally or vertically.

FIGURE 7.8.

The file scrollit.htm
*as it appears in IE
3.01.*

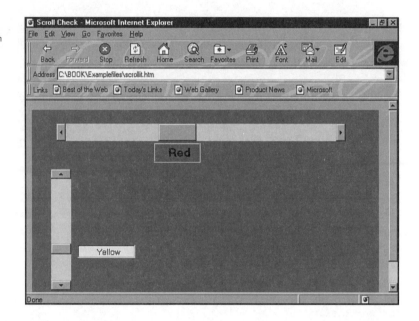

The SpinButton control is supported by numerous properties: BackColor, Codebase, Delay, Enabled, ForeColor, Height, ID, Left, Max, Min, MouseIcon, MousePointer, Orientation, SmallChange, TabIndex, TabStop, Value, and Visible. Its default event is Change. Its other events include AfterUpdate, BeforeDragOver, BeforeDropOrPaste, BeforeUpdate, Change, Enter, Error, Exit, KeyDown, Keypress, SpinDown, and SpinUp. SpinDown occurs when users click the lower or left SpinButton arrow. SpinUp occurs when users click the upper or right SpinButton arrow.

Try this: Place three ComboBoxes on your page and propagate them with months January–December, days 1–31, and years 1990–2008. Then place three spin buttons on top of the down arrows attached to your ComboBoxes. Place a label around the six controls and change the background color to Red. Now you have a Layout control containing spin buttons.

To program the controls, first use the ListIndex property to manipulate the ComboBoxes. The ListIndex property contains an index of the selected row in a list. Values of ListIndex range from –1 to one less than the total number of rows in a list. When no rows are selected, ListIndex returns –1. You'll set your ComboBox values to show something other than a blank, so set the default ListIndex property to 1 with the OnLoad event of the Layout1 control.

Set up the spin buttons so that they react to the SpinUp and SpinDown events. You need to test to see whether you've reached the top of your list with the SpinUp subroutine and test for the bottom of your list with the SpinDown event. If you reached a boundary, set the ListIndex property back to the other end of the scale.

Listing 7.5 shows the code used for propagating the ComboBoxes with the AddItem method (Sub Layout1-OnLoad). Note that an extra blank item was added at the end of each ComboBox, so that if you picked the wrong `ListIndex` number before debugging, you would get another blank rather than a scripting error. Also observe the testing and incrementation syntax in Listing 7.5 for programming each `SpinUp` and `SpinDown` subroutine for the three SpinButtons.

Listing 7.5. The code for the `spinit.alx` file you created in this example.

```
<SCRIPT LANGUAGE="VBScript">
<!--
Sub Layout1_OnLoad()
ComboBox1.additem "January"
ComboBox1.additem "February"
ComboBox1.additem "March"
ComboBox1.additem "April"
ComboBox1.additem "May"
ComboBox1.additem "June"
ComboBox1.additem "July"
ComboBox1.additem "August"
ComboBox1.additem "September"
ComboBox1.additem "October"
ComboBox1.additem "November"
ComboBox1.additem "December"
ComboBox1.additem
ComboBox1.ListIndex=0
for x = 1 to 31
ComboBox2.additem x
next
ComboBox2.additem
ComboBox2.ListIndex=0
for y = 1990 to 2008
ComboBox3.additem y
next
ComboBox3.additem
ComboBox3.ListIndex=0
end sub
-->
</SCRIPT>
<SCRIPT LANGUAGE="VBScript">
<!--
Sub SpinButton1_SpinDown()
If ComboBox1.ListIndex=0 then
ComboBox1.ListIndex=11
end if
ComboBox1.ListIndex=ComboBox1.ListIndex - 1
end sub
Sub SpinButton1_SpinUp()
If ComboBox1.ListIndex=11 then
ComboBox1.ListIndex=-1
end if
ComboBox1.ListIndex=ComboBox1.ListIndex + 1
end sub
-->
</SCRIPT>
<SCRIPT LANGUAGE="VBScript">
<!--
Sub SpinButton2_SpinUp()
```

7

MANIPULATING
ACTIVEX
CONTROLS

continues

Listing 7.5. continued

```
If ComboBox2.ListIndex=30 then
ComboBox2.ListIndex=-1
end if
ComboBox2.ListIndex=ComboBox2.ListIndex + 1
end sub
Sub SpinButton2_SpinDown()
If ComboBox2.ListIndex=0 then
ComboBox2.ListIndex=31
end if
ComboBox2.ListIndex=ComboBox2.ListIndex - 1
end sub
-->
</SCRIPT>
<SCRIPT LANGUAGE="VBScript">
<!--
Sub SpinButton3_SpinDown()
If ComboBox3.ListIndex=0 then
ComboBox3.ListIndex=19
end if
ComboBox3.ListIndex=ComboBox3.ListIndex - 1
end sub
Sub SpinButton3_SpinUp()
If ComboBox3.ListIndex=18 then
ComboBox3.ListIndex=-1
end if
ComboBox3.ListIndex=ComboBox3.ListIndex + 1
end sub
-->
</SCRIPT>
<DIV ID="Layout1" STYLE="LAYOUT:FIXED;WIDTH:477pt;HEIGHT:293pt;">
<OBJECT ID="Label1" CLASSID="CLSID:978C9E23-D4B0-11CE-BF2D-00AA003F40D0"
 STYLE="TOP:17pt;LEFT:11pt;WIDTH:182pt; HEIGHT:66pt;ZINDEX:0;">
<PARAM NAME="BackColor" VALUE="255">
<PARAM NAME="Size" VALUE="6403;2329">
<PARAM NAME="FontCharSet" VALUE="0">
<PARAM NAME="FontPitchAndFamily" VALUE="2">
<PARAM NAME="FontWeight" VALUE="0">
</OBJECT>
<OBJECT ID="ComboBox3" CLASSID="CLSID:8BD21D30-EC42-11CE-9E0D-00AA006002F3"
 STYLE="TOP:41pt;LEFT:138pt;WIDTH:47pt; HEIGHT:15pt;TABINDEX:3;ZINDEX:1;">
<PARAM NAME="VariousPropertyBits" VALUE="746604571">
<PARAM NAME="DisplayStyle" VALUE="3">
<PARAM NAME="Size" VALUE="1632;529">
<PARAM NAME="MatchEntry" VALUE="1">
<PARAM NAME="ShowDropButtonWhen" VALUE="2">
<PARAM NAME="DropButtonStyle" VALUE="3">
<PARAM NAME="FontCharSet" VALUE="0">
<PARAM NAME="FontPitchAndFamily" VALUE="2">
<PARAM NAME="FontWeight" VALUE="0">
</OBJECT>
<OBJECT ID="ComboBox2" CLASSID="CLSID:8BD21D30-EC42-11CE-9E0D-00AA006002F3"
 STYLE="TOP:41pt;LEFT:94pt;WIDTH:41pt; HEIGHT:15pt;TABINDEX:2;ZINDEX:2;">
<PARAM NAME="VariousPropertyBits" VALUE="746604571">
```

```
<PARAM NAME="DisplayStyle" VALUE="3">
<PARAM NAME="Size" VALUE="1446;529">
<PARAM NAME="MatchEntry" VALUE="1">
<PARAM NAME="ShowDropButtonWhen" VALUE="2">
<PARAM NAME="DropButtonStyle" VALUE="3">
<PARAM NAME="FontCharSet" VALUE="0">
<PARAM NAME="FontPitchAndFamily" VALUE="2">
<PARAM NAME="ParagraphAlign" VALUE="3">
<PARAM NAME="FontWeight" VALUE="0">
</OBJECT>
<OBJECT ID="ComboBox1" CLASSID="CLSID:8BD21D30-EC42-11CE-9E0D-00AA006002F3"
 STYLE="TOP:41pt;LEFT:21pt;WIDTH:66pt; HEIGHT:15pt;TABINDEX:1;ZINDEX:3;">
<PARAM NAME="VariousPropertyBits" VALUE="746604571">
<PARAM NAME="DisplayStyle" VALUE="3">
<PARAM NAME="Size" VALUE="2328;529">
<PARAM NAME="ColumnCount" VALUE="2">
<PARAM NAME="cColumnInfo" VALUE="2">
<PARAM NAME="MatchEntry" VALUE="1">
<PARAM NAME="ShowDropButtonWhen" VALUE="2">
<PARAM NAME="DropButtonStyle" VALUE="3">
<PARAM NAME="FontCharSet" VALUE="0">
<PARAM NAME="FontPitchAndFamily" VALUE="2">
<PARAM NAME="ParagraphAlign" VALUE="3">
<PARAM NAME="FontWeight" VALUE="0">
<PARAM NAME="Width" VALUE="70;211">
</OBJECT>
<OBJECT ID="SpinButton1" CLASSID="CLSID:79176FB0-B7F2-11CE-97EF-00AA006D2776"
 STYLE="TOP:34pt;LEFT:73pt;WIDTH:17pt; HEIGHT:25pt;TABINDEX:0;ZINDEX:4;">
<PARAM NAME="Size" VALUE="600;873">
<PARAM NAME="Max" VALUE="20">
</OBJECT>
<OBJECT ID="SpinButton2" CLASSID="CLSID:79176FB0-B7F2-11CE-97EF-00AA006D2776"
 STYLE="TOP:34pt;LEFT:121pt;WIDTH:17pt; HEIGHT:23pt;TABINDEX:4;ZINDEX:5;">
<PARAM NAME="Size" VALUE="582;820">
<PARAM NAME="Max" VALUE="10000">
</OBJECT>
<OBJECT ID="SpinButton3" CLASSID="CLSID:79176FB0-B7F2-11CE-97EF-00AA006D2776"
 STYLE="TOP:34pt;LEFT:170pt;WIDTH:17pt; HEIGHT:23pt;TABINDEX:5;ZINDEX:6;">
<PARAM NAME="Size" VALUE="600;820">
<PARAM NAME="Max" VALUE="20">
</OBJECT>
</DIV>
```

In the example, you placed the SpinButton controls over the down arrows attached to the ComboBoxes. If you want, you can change the ComboBox ShowDropDownWhen property to 0 - Never. Also, if you place the Label last in your sequence of drawing controls, you can choose Format | Send to Back to move the red object behind the other controls.

Figure 7.9 shows how the control looks in Internet Explorer.

FIGURE 7.9.

*The SpinButton
controls pasted over
ComboBoxes in
Internet Explorer. The
controls are positioned
over another control,
a Label with its
BackColor property
set to red.*

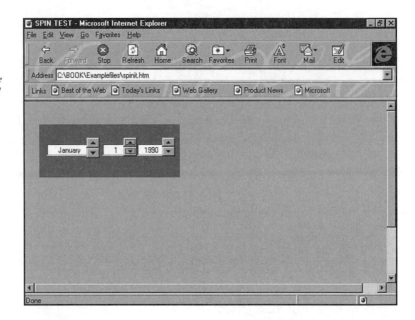

The TabStrip Control

The TabStrip control is similar to the MultiPage control. Each page has a tab at the top which, when clicked, allows the contents of the page to be viewed. Each tab is numbered automatically.

The TabStrip properties are Accelerator, BackColor, CodeBase, Enabled, Font, Object, ForeColor, Height, ID, Left, Top, MouseIcon, MousePointer, MultiRow, SelectedItem, Style, TabFixedHeight, TabFixedWidth, TabIndex, TabOrientation, TabStop, Value, and Visible. Its events include BeforeDragOver, BeforeDropOrPaste, Change, Click, DblClick, Enter, Error, Exit, KeyDown, Keypress, KeyUp, Layout, MouseDown, MouseMove, and MouseUp.

To place items in the TabStrip, stack controls on top of it. Then show the items only when a Click event changes the TabStrip's Value property (clicking a tab changes the value).

For this example, place a TabStrip on the page. Then change the first tab's title to Abbot by clicking the control and then clicking the title (Tab1). Right-click in the same place. A dialog box allows you to set the title, accelerator key ("A" for Abbot), and control tip text (type **Click Me For Abbot's Info**).

Now place a large text box over the lower part of the TabStrip. In the text box, type **This is information about Costello. He likes to eat ... His phone number is 555-555-5555.** Change the Font property to 14 point.

> **NOTE**
>
> The text lines up as though there were paragraph returns. To achieve this effect, add spaces after the text, until the next sentence wraps to the next line.

Click the first tab and view the Value property; it should be set to zero (default for first tab). The second tab, Costello, should have a 1 in the Value box in the properties list. Save your changes in a file called `stripit.alx`. Figure 7.10 shows how the control now appears in Control Pad.

FIGURE 7.10.

This is how your control appears for `stripit.alx` *in Control Pad.*

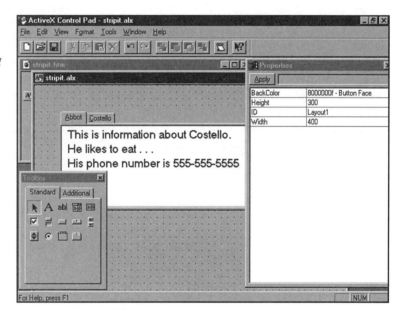

Now program the control with the Script Wizard. In the event pane, select the TabStrip's Change event. In the view pane, place the following code lines in code view:

```
If TabStrip1.Value=0 then
Layout1.BackColor=0
TextBox1.Visible = False
end if
If TabStrip1.Value=1 then
Layout1.BackColor=255
TextBox1.Visible = True
end if
```

You've programmed two actions for each tab on the TabStrip. Save your file again and open a new HTML file in Control Pad. Insert the HTML Layout `stripit.alx` and save your file as `stripit.htm`.

View the control in Internet Explorer. When you click Abbot first, nothing changes because you are only testing for the value if the tab value changes. Now click Costello's tab. The Layout control's background color should change to Red and the text box should appear.

Listing 7.6 shows the complete code for the file.

Listing 7.6. The complete code for the TabStrip HTML Layout exercise.

```
<SCRIPT LANGUAGE="VBScript">
<!--
Sub TabStrip1_Change()
If TabStrip1.Value=0 then
Layout1.BackColor=0
TextBox1.Visible = False
end if
If TabStrip1.Value=1 then
Layout1.BackColor=255
TextBox1.Visible = True
end if
end sub
-->
</SCRIPT>
<DIV ID="Layout1" STYLE="LAYOUT:FIXED;WIDTH:400pt;HEIGHT:300pt;">
<OBJECT ID="TabStrip1" CLASSID="CLSID:EAE50EB0-4A62-11CE-BED6-00AA00611080"
 STYLE="TOP:33pt;LEFT:33pt;WIDTH:256pt; HEIGHT:124pt;TABINDEX:1;ZINDEX:0;">
<PARAM NAME="ListIndex" VALUE="0">
<PARAM NAME="Size" VALUE="9022;4366">
<PARAM NAME="Items" VALUE="Abbot;Costello;">
<PARAM NAME="TipStrings"
 VALUE="Click Me For Abbot's Info;Click me for Costello's Info;">
<PARAM NAME="Names" VALUE="Tab2;Tab1;">
<PARAM NAME="NewVersion" VALUE="-1">
<PARAM NAME="TabsAllocated" VALUE="2">
<PARAM NAME="Tags" VALUE=";;">
<PARAM NAME="TabData" VALUE="2">
<PARAM NAME="Accelerator" VALUE="A;C;">
<PARAM NAME="FontCharSet" VALUE="0">
<PARAM NAME="FontPitchAndFamily" VALUE="2">
<PARAM NAME="FontWeight" VALUE="0">
<PARAM NAME="TabState" VALUE="3;3">
</OBJECT>
<OBJECT ID="TextBox1" CLASSID="CLSID:8BD21D10-EC42-11CE-9E0D-00AA006002F3"
 STYLE="TOP:50pt;LEFT:33pt;WIDTH:248pt;
 HEIGHT:104pt;TABINDEX:0;DISPLAY:NONE;ZINDEX:1;">
<PARAM NAME="VariousPropertyBits" VALUE="2894088219">
<PARAM NAME="Size" VALUE="8731;3651">
<PARAM NAME="Value" VALUE="This is information about Costello.
 He likes to eat . . .  His phone number is 555-555-5555">
<PARAM NAME="FontHeight" VALUE="280">
<PARAM NAME="FontCharSet" VALUE="0">
<PARAM NAME="FontPitchAndFamily" VALUE="2">
<PARAM NAME="FontWeight" VALUE="0">
</OBJECT>
</DIV>
```

Working With Common Controls

Let's briefly look at a few common controls immediately available when you use Control Pad: Microsoft ActiveX HotSpot Control 1.0 and Microsoft ActiveX Image Control. Many more common and third-party controls can be programmed by using methods similar to those described in this chapter. I won't go into as much detail with these controls, however, because I've already addressed basic programming functionality.

Microsoft ActiveX HotSpot

The HotSpot is a useful tool for `Click` events. When users click within an area defined by the HotSpot control, the `Click` event is triggered.

Properties for the control are minimal: `CodeBase`, `Enabled`, `Height`, `ID`, `Left`, `MouseIcon`, `MousePointer`, `TabIndex`, `TabStop`, `Top`, `Visible`, and `Width`. Events for the control include `AfterUpdate`, `BeforeUpdate`, `Click`, `DblClick`, `Enter`, `Error`, `Exit`, `MouseDown`, `MouseEnter`, `MouseExit`, `MouseMove`, and `MouseUp`.

Try this sample exercise. Place a HotSpot control in a new HTML layout. Drag the boundaries to approximate a 3-inch-by-3-inch box. Then save the file as `spotit.alx`. Draw a CommandButton on top of the HotSpot control, making it about 1 1/2 inches square. Change the caption for the CommandButton to `Click NEAR Me`. Choose Format | Bring to Front while the CommandButton is selected.

Open the Script Wizard and program the HotSpot's `Click` event with two simple actions:

```
msgbox "You performed the perfect Hot Spot user action.
➥You clicked near me and not on me.", 16, "ActiveX Testing"
Layout1.BackColor=0
```

Now click the `MouseEnter` event and add these lines:

```
msgbox, "You're Getting Very Warm", 16 "ActiveX Testing"
Layout1.Backcolor=255
```

Click the `MouseExit` event and add these lines:

```
Layout1.BackColor=65280
msgbox "You just left the HotSpot area.", 16, "ActiveX Testing"
```

Click the CommandButton1 `Click` event and enter this line:

```
msgbox "You clicked on me. You are supposed
➥to click next to me.", 16, "ActiveX Testing"
```

Save your file again as `spotit.alx` and insert the HTML Layout control into a file called `spotit.htm`. Load the file in Internet Explorer and begin your mouse interaction.

As you move into the hidden area defined by the HotSpot control, an event is triggered. The background color changes to red and a message box appears. If you click the CommandButton, a message box informs you that you clicked the CommandButton. You also clicked within the HotSpot, so you'll get a confirmation message.

If you click *near* the CommandButton in the HotSpot control, you get a red background and message boxes indicating that you're warm and that you executed a perfect HotSpot action. If the mouse moves back out of the HotSpot area, a message box displays a warning that you've left the HotSpot's control area.

> **NOTE**
>
> If you have difficulty getting out of this routine because of the message boxes, simply move your mouse well out of the HotSpot area on your page, and then press Enter to clear any message boxes.

Figure 7.11 shows how your control appears in IE after moving into the control, moving back out of the control area, and then clearing all the message boxes. Listing 7.7 shows the code generated.

FIGURE 7.11.

The background color is green. This is how it looks after moving away from the HotSpot and clearing all message boxes.

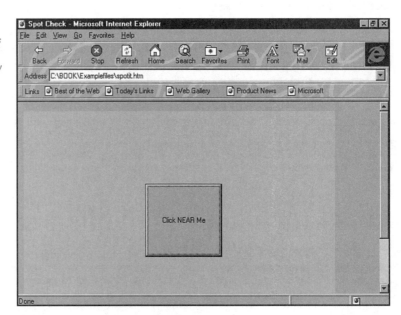

Listing 7.7. The code for `spotit.alx` generated in the exercise.

```
<SCRIPT LANGUAGE="VBScript">
<!--
Sub CommandButton1_Click()
msgbox "You clicked on me. You are supposed to
➥click next to me.", 16, "ActiveX Testing"
end sub
-->
</SCRIPT>
```

```
<SCRIPT LANGUAGE="VBScript">
<!--
Sub HotSpot1_MouseExit()
Layout1.BackColor=65280
msgbox "You just left the HotSpot area.", 16, "ActiveX Testing"
end sub
Sub HotSpot1_MouseEnter()
msgbox "You're Getting Very Warm", 16, "ActiveX Testing"
Layout1.Backcolor=255
end sub
Sub HotSpot1_Click()
msgbox "You performed the perfect Hot Spot
➥user action. You clicked near me and not
➥on me.", 16, "ActiveX Testing"
Layout1.BackColor=0
end sub
-->
</SCRIPT>
<DIV ID="Layout1" STYLE="LAYOUT:FIXED;WIDTH:400pt;HEIGHT:300pt;">
<OBJECT ID="HotSpot1" CLASSID="CLSID:2B32FBC2-A8F1-11CF-93EE-00AA00C08FDF"
 STYLE="TOP:58pt;LEFT:124pt;WIDTH:157pt; HEIGHT:157pt;ZINDEX:0;">
<PARAM NAME="VariousPropertyBits" VALUE="8388627">
<PARAM NAME="Size" VALUE="5529;5530">
</OBJECT>
<OBJECT ID="CommandButton1" CLASSID="CLSID:D7053240-CE69-11CD-A777-00DD01143C57"
 STYLE="TOP:91pt;LEFT:157pt;WIDTH:99pt; HEIGHT:91pt;TABINDEX:1;ZINDEX:1;">
<PARAM NAME="Caption" VALUE="Click NEAR Me">
<PARAM NAME="Size" VALUE="3492;3202">
<PARAM NAME="FontCharSet" VALUE="0">
<PARAM NAME="FontPitchAndFamily" VALUE="2">
<PARAM NAME="ParagraphAlign" VALUE="3">
<PARAM NAME="FontWeight" VALUE="0">
</OBJECT>
</DIV>
```

The ActiveX Image Control

The ActiveX Image Control is a common control very similar to the intrinsic Forms Image Control discussed earlier. This common control, however, doesn't include the same properties as the Forms Image Control when viewed in Control Pad—the MouseIcon and MousePointer properties are missing. The common control, which relies on the ISCTRLS.OCX file, also supports fewer events: BeforeDragOver, BeforeDropOrPaste, Click, DblClick, and Error are missing.

NOTE

Use this control for only a very basic display of an image. Use the intrinsic control for more functionality associated with the image.

Refer to the earlier section "The Image Control: Button, CheckBox and Combo" for details on programming a simple Image control. The ActiveX Image Control has an icon with an additional blue dot when added to Control Pad's toolbox.

Summary

In this chapter, you've explored intrinsic and common controls and how to design and program them by using ActiveX Control Pad. You manipulate the properties, events, and methods of each control with scripting and the visual interface provided by Control Pad.

In this chapter, you also explored the purpose and feel of many of the individual controls available in Control Pad's toolbox and learned some basic techniques to use to add interactivity to your controls.

Applying Existing Controls

by Dan Horsefield

IN THIS CHAPTER

CHAPTER

8

ActiveX technology offers you the ultimate in variety; several thousand unique ActiveX controls and applications were being offered commercially at the time this book was in development. In this chapter, you explore the use of one of these unique third-party controls. You also learn about other controls, how they're used, and how they're programmed.

You'll see that the control objects (controls) are somewhat similar in many respects, especially concerning the events associated with each control. You'll also learn that the controls are fairly easy to program with just a little bit of guidance. The control you'll explore is created in FutureSplash Animator, now know as Flash.

Using Macromedia Flash

Macromedia Flash was formerly known as FutureSplash Animator. In January 1997, Macromedia announced an agreement in which it would be acquiring FutureWave Software of San Diego. FutureWave had developed the FutureSplash Animator to create new, visually appealing animations and integrated controls. Meanwhile, Macromedia had developed Shockwave, which was gaining a considerable amount of interest on the Internet (to say the least).

I'm covering Flash (some call it Splash) because it has a great number of useful features—and because Macromedia is offering a 30-day trial evaluation copy of the software. Also, it comes with an excellent interactive tutorial. If you have a little trouble with one of the steps covered here, you can refer to the slow-moving tutorial, which provides step-by-step instructions.

Learning the Flash features can be of valuable assistance if you want to learn how programmers are introducing somewhat complex, customized, new animations on the Internet. When you've mastered a program like Flash (and that could take some time, considering the number of features), not many other tools will seem as intimidating. Learning new software packages such as Flash is something you'll have to devote some time to if you want to stay abreast of the mainstream programming efforts on the Web.

> **NOTE**
>
> One way to stay informed about new developments is to frequently visit Web sites intended for developers. One such site, at http://www.microsoft.com/workshop, contains links to various programming and authoring sites loaded with useful tools and programs.

Flash2 is available from Macromedia at http://www.macromedia.com/software. The Flash player, used to play animation files (movies) created in Flash, is integrated with Shockwave, a family of multimedia players offered by Macromedia. The player is automatically installed when the user views a Flash movie. The Flash trial version executable file is an installation program that places an OCX file called FSPLASH.OCX in the Windows/System/Occache directory. In ActiveX Control Pad, the additional controls box can access a Flash object or a Flash document.

After installing the program, open the Flash trial program and choose File | New. You'll see a full-featured, vector-based drawing and time-line motion editor onscreen. From this window you can view the lessons packaged with the program. Choose Library | Lessons from the menu and follow the tutorial steps offered.

With the Flash editor, you can draw new animation sequences, use existing symbols from the symbol palette included with the program, or import your own graphics. The drawing editor allows geometric straightening of crooked or wavy lines and offers easy-to-use tools for smoothing kinks in Bézier curves. The color features are very comprehensive, with flexible tools for filling contours, erasing the fills without erasing the contours, and many other features that you won't find in many drawing programs that sell today for several hundred dollars.

Flash can generate interesting effects with the program's built-in graphics or other user-owned graphics. For example, you can use built-in motion interpolation to program movement for any vector-based Adobe Illustrator encapsulated PostScript file (.eps). EPS is a commonly used vector graphics format that handles fonts as filled vector outlines.

These effects and the illustrations used in the lessons, although they might appear somewhat comical, can be very useful in real-life situations. The effects are simple to duplicate with your own existing graphics. By using the Flash editor's features, you easily can make visual improvements to graphics. With a little creativity, you can even create your own symbols to use in the program.

One lesson offered in the program's tutorial gives step-by-step instructions on how to drag a symbol of a car onscreen, create the first frame of a sequence with the car on one side of the screen, and then shrink the size of the car and place it on the opposite side of the screen.

The Flash motion interpolation features cause the car to appear to shrink as it travels across the page, giving the illusion that the car is moving away into 3D space. This is similar to morphing, which requires at least two images. In *morphing*, a computer program evaluates two images and generates all the images in between so that one image can morph to resemble the other. Flash's motion interpolation, however, is a unique kind of morphing that uses only two very small graphic files referred to as *symbols*. Computer scaling on the fly is used to create the images of different sizes, minimizing the file size of the animated movie. All the intermediate illustrations normally required in morphing aren't required for the illusion because of this computer scaling.

The size of the Flash movie player that's automatically installed on user machines when they reach the Web page sporting your Flash movie control is only about 100K. That's not bad for a Web program that supports animations on users' screens. The actual movie object, referred to as a Flash control object, is the integrated animation control that you'll place on a page for viewing in a Web browser.

The actual animation control's file size can be very small, if just a few of the symbols are used. The Flash player converts animations into an extremely compact file format and then streams the animation into the Web page. The animation can play as it's being downloaded. For users, playback is very fast, even with an analog modem connection below 28.8Kbps.

What's unique about a Flash control is that when an animation sequence is programmed and inserted into an application, *users* can be given control over how the animation runs. This feature can be useful in terms of educational value if it's handled correctly. It adds a new dimension to the interactivity of the control.

Look at a real-life business example for your introduction to Flash. A company's newest telemarketing customer gets verbal directions to the company's plant. The customer is excited about the product and needs to visit the plant to review his project with the plant's management team. The telemarketing salesperson he spoke with wasn't very familiar with the street names leading to the plant, and the customer is a bit concerned that he'll have problems finding it. So the customer, a bit too embarrassed to call the plant's receptionist for more verbal directions, decides to first check the company's Web pages to see whether there's a map or better directions regarding how to get to the plant.

On loading the company's home page in Internet Explorer, the customer finds a map link and clicks it. A Flash control pops up onscreen, showing a map with an airport, a plant, and highways and roads connecting the two locations. Buttons at the top of the page tempt the Web visitor to manipulate the animation for further instructions.

When the customer clicks the Play button, the animation begins with a little car following a route from a nearby airport to the plant. The customer tries the other buttons, labeled Rewind and Stop. Then he clicks the button labeled Instructions. A new Web page opens, explaining how to manipulate the map with the various controls and offering written directions to accompany the map. The customer learns that he can right-click the map and use the drop-down controls to zoom in or out, pan the drawing by dragging with his mouse, and stop or start the animation.

In this section, you'll build this control. Figure 8.1 shows what your finished control will look like and will help you draw the map and the controls as you go. The finished control, `flash.spl`, is an animated Flash movie file embedded in an HTML Web page called `flash.htm`.

Now the customer can use the controls to stop the animation, rewind it, click the Forward button to move one frame forward at a time, or simply pause the animation to take a phone call. He can view the map and instructions as long as necessary. He can also zoom in on the landmarks on the page to view small text and take a closer look at images on his screen, such as the illustrations of landmarks he will see on his trip.

The page can be as elaborate as your imagination. Considering that 19 events and 19 actions are available when a Flash object is inserted, it's easy to see that this tool can be useful.

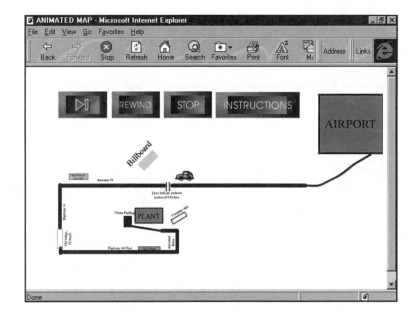

FIGURE 8.1.

The finished control loaded in Internet Explorer.

Programming Intuitive Actions

When programming this control, you don't even have to use any scripting to make it all happen. When users click the on-enter event, the available actions are automatically displayed. This button interactivity was created with point-and-click ease in the Flash drawing editor.

The CommandButtons are really programmed "button" images from the Flash editor. When a mouse pointer passes over a Flash "button," the image displayed on the button changes. When users click, the button's appearance changes again.

You've fulfilled your function by presenting visitors with a useful animated page containing interactive content that permits them to learn how to navigate to the plant. The bonus is that visitors aren't simply shown a written blow-by-blow sequence of highways and intersections to navigate. Instead, they can learn the directions at their own pace, unassisted, with visual content that will help them remember how to get to the destination.

Now comes the fun part—creating what was just described. You might want to review the animation lessons with Flash before proceeding, or you can try the steps and refer to the lessons if you hit a trouble spot. The lessons are accessible in Flash under the Library | Lessons menu.

In the Flash editor, draw a square to denote the location of the airport from which the visitor will depart. Follow these steps:

1. Click the pencil tool, and then click the stairstep icon (on the top). From the drop-down list, select the square box.

2. Click the color box below the square box icon and select red.

3. To change the line size, select the 1-point line denoted by `1.0-`.

4. Select the word `solid` from the last option box.

5. In the upper-right corner, click and drag until you have a half-inch square.

6. Click the paint bucket icon, click the color box, and then select a magenta color.

7. Click the square you drew. Flash fills the square with a magenta color.

8. Click the text tool (with the *A*), click the option that indicates point size, and then scroll up to select the 8-point type size.

TIP

If you want a point size that isn't listed, you can type that size in the text box.

---

9. Click the magenta box, type the word **AIRPORT**, and then click the arrow tool to end your text entry.

10. The text is now selected and a highlight line appears around the text. Use the arrow tool to drag the text into position over the box.

11. Click one of the box's boundaries to highlight the line segment and then press Delete. Do this for the other three boundary lines.

12. Choose Library | Lessons | Motion Interpolation from the menu, and then choose View | Symbol Palette.

13. Click the Page 4 tab at the right.

14. In the symbol palette, scroll down and select the word *car*. An image of a car appears at the top of the palette. Click the car image and drag it onto the page where the lesson instructions are located. Press Ctrl+C to copy the image to the Clipboard. From the Window menu, navigate back to your `Movie1:1` document.

15. To get the car into your movie, you want to make it a symbol that accompanies the movie. Simply paste it anywhere on the page by choosing Edit | Paste (or pressing Ctrl+V) and then choosing View | Symbol Palette. The car now appears in your symbol palette as an independent object.

16. Delete the car from the illustration. You'll add it from the symbol palette later on in a specific layer of the drawing.

Review Figure 8.1 to see how the drawing will appear in Internet Explorer after you complete the next series of steps. Notice that you now have an airport at the top right, a car (which you'll add later), and all the lines indicating highways and roads, as well as landmarks, to give visitors some help in getting to their destination.

17. Select the pencil tool and draw a highway from the airport to near the left edge of the screen. Make the highway two line segments, and place two vertical lines between the

two line segments to indicate that the scale of the drawing omits a section of the highway for illustration purposes.

The drawing can be as elaborate as you want to make it. You can add mile markers, billboards, buildings, side roads, and so on.

18. Use the rectangle tool and the paint bucket to draw the rectangle that represents the plant. Use the rectangle tool to draw the bridge in the lower-left corner. Use the circle tool under the pencil options to make a cul-de-sac near the plant's driveway entrance.

You wind up with an interesting challenge after drawing all the lines, color fills, the bridge, the rectangle indicating the name of the plant, and the text that names the highways and points out that the bridge is very old. You need to add color to the bridge, billboard, a highway sign, and a few other objects by using the ink bottle icon and the color selection option. Click the line segment after selecting the color to change the line color.

To color in the billboard sign and the highway sign near the first right-angle road intersection on the left of your screen, use the paint bucket icon again. If you want to make the highway lines look curved, you could use the arrow tool. As you move the mouse close to the center of a line segment, the mouse icon changes to an arc to indicate that when you click and drag the line, the line will change to a curve. Try it; if you want the line straight again, click undo.

Now you need to think about what and how you'll animate the illustration by using the Flash features. First, you need to make some adjustments regarding layers. The map illustration will reside on its own independent layer. To make this happen, follow these steps:

1. Make sure that you deleted the car from the illustration as mentioned earlier in Step 16, because it doesn't appear on this layer. Now all the elements except the car are in the window.

2. You may want to change the map elements to a symbol by choosing Edit | Select All and then Edit | Copy.

3. Choose View | Edit Symbols.

4. Open the symbol palette by selecting View | Symbol Palette. In the symbol palette, open the drop-down list and select New. Name the symbol map to correspond with the illustration you've created.

5. A blank screen with a crosshair appears. Choose Edit | Paste. Move the center of the map elements to the center of the crosshair.

6. Choose View | Edit Movie to return to the drawing. The page elements should still be selected. Delete them, because you now have a symbol.

7. Select the map symbol and drag it onto the page. Later, if you want to add elements to the map, use the View | Edit Symbols option to make the changes there and press Enter.

8. Click the Layer 1 icon, which currently looks like a pencil. (The pencil icon will always appear next to the current layer being edited.) The icon's Click event triggers

a drop-down menu; select Rename. At the prompt, enter the name **map** for Layer 1. Think of the current layer, map, as the current layer for editing purposes.

9. Click the square button just below the pencil icon button in the layers section of the editor. This is in the row directly below the map layer row. When you click, select New from the drop-down menu that appears. Rename this layer to car, using the same procedure you used to name the map layer.

10. To make this the current layer, click the hand icon for the car row and select Current from the top of the drop-down list of options. The icon should change from a hand to a pencil, indicating that this is now the current row with focus.

11. You need to add frames to your drawing so that you can animate the car symbol. The white portion of the rows to the right of the pencil and hand icons is where you add the frames. Above these white rows is a ruler with numbers that correspond to the number of frames in the animation. For this example, click the number 30 to place the frame insertion counter. Now click in the map row directly below the ruler and drag down through the car row. You should see a black highlight in both rows and a small gray box at the bottom-right portion of the highlighted column. The gray box is another drop-down menu. Click it and select Insert Frame (notice the shortcut, Ctrl+I).

   Your screen should have two rows of tick marks, indicating 30 frames in each row.

12. To program the animation, add a key frame. Make sure that the symbol palette is visible. Now click in the frames ruler at 30 to move the pointer to the 30 position. Select car from the scroll list and click and drag the car from the symbol palette to a position just below the airport rectangle. While the car is still selected, choose Tools | Scale and Rotate. Change the scale percentage to 45 and leave the rotation percentage at zero.

13. Drag the car down to a point just above the road under the airport. This is where the car will be in the first frame of the movie (even though the frame pointer is above 30). Before proceeding, be sure to click away from the car to deselect it. Now click in frame 30 of the car layer. The mouse icon will change to an I-beam with a gray box. Click in the gray box and select Make Key Frame. Now click in any other frame; you should see a blue dot in frame 30 of the car layer.

   To view the effect you just created and get a sense regarding why you made the key frame, choose Play | Rewind and then choose Play | Start. The animation bar moves from the first frame to the last, and the car doesn't move. You've effectively placed the car in each frame of the movie.

14. To animate the car, make sure that the frame pointer is still above frame 30. If it isn't, click in the frame ruler on 30 to move the pointer there. Select the car and drag it to a position just left of the plant. While it's still selected, choose Tools | Scale and Rotate, and change the scale to 125 percent.

15. Choose Play | Rewind to place the pointer back to the first frame. The car near the plant disappears, and the car near the airport reappears.

16. Choose Play | Start. The car remains near the airport until frame 30, and then appears near the plant at the end of the movie.

Although this isn't the effect you want, it demonstrates the effect of the steps you just completed. To make the motion smooth and stretch it over the 30 frames of the animation is easy, as you will see in the following section.

Creating a Smooth Animation

To create a smooth animation, click in the first frame of the car layer. When the mouse pointer changes to an I-beam, select the gray box next to the frame and then select Interpolation. Now select the motion option. In the dialog box that appears, select the Interpolate Scaling and Interpolate Motion checkboxes. The frames row of the car layer turns gray with a red arrow through it, indicating that motion interpolation has been added to the animation. Make sure that the frame pointer is above the first frame, and choose Play | Start. The car should move smoothly from a point just below the airport to the position just left of the plant. The car also gets larger as it moves, because you selected an option that suggested that the animation should interpolate scaling.

This still isn't the effect you want, but it demonstrates how motion interpolation works. The computer has calculated each position and size for the car for each frame between one and 30. To see what size and position has been calculated for any of the frames, simply place the frame pointer above the frame you want to see. Figure 8.2 shows how your illustration, time line, and layers should appear in the animation you've created to this point. Before proceeding, save the file as `splash.spa`.

FIGURE 8.2.

Notice the layer names and the small symbols in the time frames above the drawing.

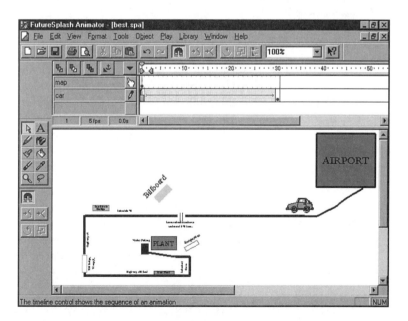

8

APPLYING
EXISTING
CONTROLS

Creating the Path

Now you'll create a path for the car to follow from the first frame to the last by following these steps:

1. The car layer is still the current layer, indicated by the pencil icon. Select the pencil icon and select Add Motion Guide from the drop-down list to place a third layer below the first two (the new layer gets the same name but has a blue icon just left of the word *car*). This new layer automatically becomes the current layer.

2. Select the toolbox pencil icon to draw the path. Below the tools are options for the pencil again. Select the smooth drawing tool from the square tool selection icon. You should see a new icon that looks like a snake. Select the color white from the color icon. Select 2.0 from the line size option and select solid (default). Make sure that the movie is in the rewind position with the pointer above the first frame.

3. This time, the path you want will follow the road map lines from the airport to the plant. The line can't be broken, so once you start, draw very slowly, curving around the vertical lines, curving around the square intersections, and then let go of the mouse when the path ends near the plant. To draw the path, click and drag the mouse from a point just in front of the car to a point left of the plant following the roadways. If you want, you can make a squiggle curve near the bridge to simulate a bumpy ride.

4. Now that you've drawn the "invisible" motion guide, you need to pay attention to where the endpoints are near the airport and the plant. Choose Edit | Select All and notice the location of the two endpoints. Place the frame pointer above the first frame; you'll see the car near the airport. Choose Tools | Snap unless a checkmark already is next to Snap.

5. Select the car near the airport and drag it toward where your invisible motion guide endpoint is. The center of the car will snap to the endpoint. Now place the frame pointer at 30. Select the car near the plant and drag it over the other end on the invisible motion guide. The car should snap to the endpoint. Select Play | Rewind and Play | Start. If the car doesn't follow the path next to the roadway, you need to repeat the last step, beginning with selecting all elements, so that you can see the ends of the motion guide. When the car is properly snapped to the endpoint in the first and last frames, the car will follow the path.

6. The car may remain in the same horizontal position throughout the animation, but that's not the desired effect. Click in the first frame of the car layer where the red dot appears, and from the gray box in the grid iron select Interpolation. Leave Motion selected and this time make sure that Rotate With Path is checked in the dialog box. Click OK. Now rewind and play the animation again. The car should rotate with the path and turn upside down when it travels along the line at the bottom of the window.

7. You're about to add some interactive buttons to the animation. Save your changes and go back to the Motion Interpolation lesson under the Window menu (if you left the

lesson open) or under the Library | Lessons menu. In the lesson, select View | Symbol palette. Select the VCR button at the bottom of the list of symbols, and a button symbol resembling a VCR's play button appears.

8. Drag the button onto the page in the lesson. If the page won't accept the button, the layers are locked. Go to page four of the lesson and try again, if this is the case. Now, with the button still selected, press Ctrl+C or choose Edit | Copy. You've placed the button on the Clipboard. Then choose Window | splash.spa. Select the map layer icon and then select Current. Press Ctrl+V or choose Edit | Paste to place the button in the drawing. Now delete it. It should now appear in your Symbol palette. Select VCR and the symbol will appear at the top of the Symbol palette. Click the icon near the symbol and select Rename. Change the name to BEGIN MAP.

Adding Other Meaningful Buttons

Now you need to get back to the Motion Interpolation lesson to copy another button. Choose Window | Motion Interpolation.spa. Scroll down to and select the Rewind symbol. You should see a similar button with the word Rewind in it. Drag the button onto the drawing and press Ctrl+C, or choose Edit | Copy. Now choose Window | splash.spa to get back to your drawing. Press Ctrl+V or choose Edit | Paste to add the button to your drawing. Now delete it. It should appear in your splash.spa Symbol palette.

Select the Rewind symbol in the Symbol palette, click the down-arrow icon, and select Duplicate. This way, you can make another identical symbol. A dialog box prompts you for the name of the new button. Enter **STOP** and click OK. The drawing window has changed and your drawing disappears. The Flash software has automatically placed you in the View | Edit Symbols window.

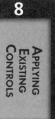

The Rewind button symbol appears here, but remember that you've given this new symbol the name STOP. You should notice something unusual at this point. The Stop button has four frames. Click in the frame counter ruler above the fourth frame. The symbol's text turns colors. This effect is characteristic of a button. Buttons are designed with four frames, each with different features. The first frame represents what the button will look like without the mouse pointer over it.

The second frame represents what the button will look like after the mouse pointer passes over the button. The third frame represents what the button will look like when users click the button. The fourth frame represents a rectangle that determines the size of the button's action area. Any mouse-over or click event within this area activates the button.

To modify the rewind button to make it a stop button, select the text in the middle of the button and make sure that the frame counter is over the first frame. (Remember, you're editing only one frame at a time.) To select just the text, choose Object | Ungroup to break the group of selected objects into separate elements, and then click the text. Select the zoom tool (magnifying glass) and click the center of the button.

Select the arrow tool in the toolbox, select the text, and then delete it. If the rewind text were text rather than individual letter objects, you could have selected another method to edit it. Next, click the text tool and select the color white from the color box. Select a font. Now click an open area on the page. A flashing cursor appears. Type the word **STOP**. Click the arrow tool and click where you placed the type. A highlight appears around the text. Drag the text over the button and center it.

Click above the second frame to place the frame counter pointer there. You should see the yellow word Rewind, which is the frame that will appear when the mouse pointer moves over the active button when it's placed in your drawing. Because you want it to appear different, make the text STOP yellow in this frame.

Click the word Rewind and press Delete. Click the text tool again, and the same options you used for the first word will appear. Change the color selection box to yellow. Now click the page and type **STOP**. Click the arrow tool to highlight the yellow word. Drag the text over the center of the button.

You've successfully updated the second frame. Now click the frame counter ruler above the third frame. The third and fourth frames are identical, so this is the last change you need to make.

Click the word Rewind and delete it. Select the text tool, change the color option to red, and click the page. Type the word **STOP**, click the arrow tool, and then drag the word to the center of the box. You now have successfully changed the Rewind button to a Stop button. To return to the page, choose View | Edit Movie. Select the BEGIN MAP button in the Symbol palette and drag the symbol onto the page. Place the button in the upper-left corner of the window. If the button won't move, choose Play | Buttons Active so you can work with the buttons in drawing mode.

Now, in the Symbol palette, select the REWIND symbol button and drag it onto the page, placing it just to the right of the BEGIN MAP button. If you want, you can edit the REWIND button and make the letters all capital letters so that it resembles the STOP button. You also may want to match the fonts.

In the Symbol palette, select the STOP button and then select the Duplicate option with the down arrow. Name this duplicated button INSTRUCTIONS. The symbol editor appears with a stop button. With the frame counter above the first frame, you'll again make modifications. This time, you already have the correct text colors for all three frames, so the changes will be easy.

Click the outer edge of the button to highlight the outer rectangle. Choose Tools | Scale (a different option from Scale and Rotate). Instead of a dialog box, you now have six control points around the rectangle. Click the left center control point and drag to the left, enlarging the button to almost twice its original size. Now pay attention to how wide the button is, because you must match this width when you select the second frame. Drag the button so that the center of the rectangle is over the crosshair. This is necessary so that all the button frames will appear in the same position.

You need to change the word STOP to the word INSTRUCTIONS. To do this, select just the text word STOP. If the outer rectangle is also highlighted, deselect it by clicking it. Now choose Object | Edit Object. Notice that a flashing cursor is placed to the right of where the word STOP is located. Backspace four times to erase the word and then type **INSTRUCTIONS**. If the word extends past your outer boundary, click the arrow tool and drag the word to the center of the button.

Figure 8.3 shows how your button should appear in the symbol editor window for the first frame.

FIGURE 8.3.

This is how the first frame of the button appears.

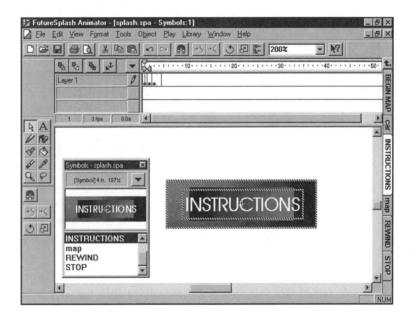

Choose Edit | Select All. The crosshair should be very close to the middle-left side of the letter C. Pay attention to this so that you can match it in the next frame. With the entire button selected, press Ctrl+C or choose Edit | Copy to copy the image to the Clipboard. Click the frame counter above the second frame. You should see a button image with the word STOP in yellow. Draw a window around the button image with the arrow tool and press Delete to erase it. Now press Ctrl+V or choose Edit | Paste to paste a copy of your Instructions image from the first frame on the page. Drag the button image until the left center of the letter C is over the crosshair, just like in the first frame.

If you want a dramatic effect when the mouse is moved over this button when your control is completed, you can scale the button larger in the vertical direction and drag the button slowly down and to the right. Later, this will make the button appear to move when the mouse icon travels over it. To change the color of the text, carefully select just the text. Now select the text tool and change the color selector below to the color yellow. Your text automatically changes to yellow.

You're ready for the third frame. Click above it in the frame counter ruler. You should see a button with the word STOP in red. This image looks slightly different than the other two; there's a small black border to the left and just above the button (you'll duplicate this later). Select the button with the arrow tool and delete this button. Now press Ctrl+V or choose Edit | Paste, and you'll see the Instructions image again. Drag it into place with the left center of the letter C over the crosshair. To change the text color to red, select only the text and click the text tool. Select the color red in the color options box.

To duplicate the black border you saw, simply draw a black rectangle slightly larger than the button and place it behind the button. Click the pencil tool, and in the options box select the Rectangle option. Click the line width option and select 2.0. Select black in the color option. Drawing just slightly outside the rectangle, drag a border around the button. The top and left sides of the rectangle need to touch the button image. Move the mouse pointer to a position close to the bottom of the new black rectangle. When the pointer changes to a curve shape, click to select the line segment and then press Delete to delete it. Do the same for the right line segment.

Choose View | Edit Movie, and your button is ready to be incorporated into the drawing. At this point, your button may not react the way you want it to when you drag it into the drawing. Follow these steps:

1. Click the down-arrow icon next to the illustration of the INSTRUCTIONS button. Make sure that the word BUTTON is selected. This lets the drawing editor know this is no ordinary symbol, but a group of frames. Now drag the button onto the page into position.

2. Choose Play | Buttons Active and move the mouse over each button in sequence. They should each turn colors. The BEGIN MAP button's triangle changes from blue to red. The text in the REWIND, STOP, and INSTRUCTION buttons changes from white to yellow. Now click each in turn. Each should have the appearance of motion, thanks to the unusual black borders. Each of the three buttons with text should have red text when the buttons are clicked.

3. If the letters seem to run together, you can quickly edit the buttons to remedy the situation. You won't have to move the buttons back into the drawing; the changes take effect automatically. Click INSTRUCTIONS in the Symbol palette. Click the down-arrow icon next to the image and select Edit. When the image appears, click the text once. Now right-click and select Font. A dialog box appears with the text specifications. Click the down-arrow to the right of the Letter space option and select .5. Click OK and then move the frame pointer to the second frame. Repeat this step for the third and fourth frame to change the letter spacing.

4. Don't leave the editor window; this time you'll take a shortcut. Click the tab at the right side of the screen that says REWIND. The button appears in the window. Repeat the right-click text step and change the letter spacing. Repeat it again for each frame in the button. Now select the tab at the right for the STOP button. Change the letter spacing for each frame and then choose View | Edit Movie. The change was automatic in the drawing window. Test each button to make sure that no steps were skipped in the exercise.

5. Programming the buttons is just a few clicks away. Choose Play | Buttons Active to uncheck this option. Now select the BEGIN MAP button. Choose Object | Properties. A dialog box appears, indicating that action for the button is set to None. Click the down-arrow icon, select Play, and click OK. Now click away from any objects to deselect the button. Select the REWIND button, choose Object | Properties, and then select Goto from the list. You see two more options:

   ■ *Page* refers to a numbered page, if your drawing contains more than one page. This example has just one page, and you can leave the box blank.

   ■ *Frame* refers to the frame counter in your animation. Select 1 so the movie will rewind to the first frame in the animation.

6. To program the stop button, click away from any objects in the drawing to deselect the REWIND button, select the stop button, choose Object | Properties, and from the list of actions select Stop. Click OK and click away from the button. Now click the INSTRUCTIONS button to select it, choose Object | Properties, and from the list select Get URL and type `instruct.htm` in the URL text box. Click OK. This URL is *relative*, which means that you don't have to specify a long path to the file. The file resides in the same directory with the HTML file that contains your animation file. Now the movie file is almost complete.

7. You've been drawing in a window that has scrollbars above and to the right. More working area is available in the drawing to the right and below the drawing. Scroll right and down in the scrollbars to view the empty illustration area. Now scroll back to the drawing. Choose View | Show Page to see all the open area. You need to increase the drawing to fill the horizontal space in the drawing. To do so, choose Edit | Select All or press Ctrl+A. All items should be highlighted. Now choose Tools | Scale and Rotate. Type **175** in the scale percentage input box and click OK. Drag the illustration into position, filling the horizontal space with some space remaining at the left edge where the car will travel along the Motion Guide line.

8. This scaling action has disrupted the key frame and last frame because the car has been moved from the endpoints of the Motion Guide. To fix it, click the frame counter above the first frame. Press Ctrl+A and view where the endpoint is near the airport. Click away from the elements to deselect everything. Now click the car to select it, and drag it to the endpoint. Place the frame counter above frame 30 and repeat the step to snap the car to the endpoint near the plant.

9. If your drawing is cropped off at the bottom, choose Format | Document. To increase the height of the drawing area, select 5.2 inches and check the bottom of your drawing to make sure that it fits. You also can increase or decrease the number of frames per second in the same dialog box to speed up or slow down the animation. Test the speed after each change by clicking the REWIND and BEGIN MAP buttons.

Figure 8.4 shows how your drawing now appears in Show Page view.

FIGURE 8.4.

Notice the alignment of the buttons. This can be achieved by choosing Format | Align while all buttons are selected.

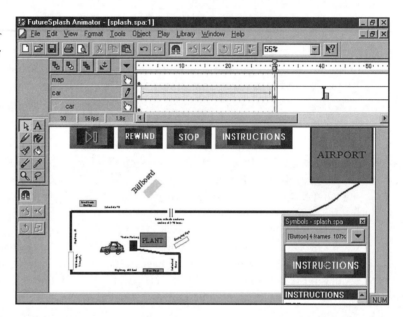

Save the file again as splash.spa. Don't test the INSTRUCTIONS button because you haven't created the HTML file it refers to yet. Test the first three buttons by choosing Play | Buttons Active and then clicking each button.

Now, to turn the drawing into an animation control, choose File | Export Movie. Check the boxes for Load Top Down and Generate Size Report. Move the quality pointer to the extreme right, to use the highest quality available for the graphics, and click OK. Use the file name splash.spl to keep things simple.

You also need to export the file as a GIF file so that if a browser can't load the movie, the GIF file will appear. Choose File | Export Image and select GIF from the supported formats option. Call the file splash.gif and save it in the same directory as the movie file and drawing file.

Embedding the Control in an HTML File

Now you need to place the control in an HTML file. You could use Control Pad, but that option isn't preferred because the HTML Layout editor doesn't work very well with the movie file. Instead, you'll open a sample HTML file that comes with Flash and view the file's lines of code. Then you can paste those lines into a new file and make a few modifications.

Open the sample HTML file by choosing Start | Programs | FutureWave Software. Now select the Sample HTML Index file. When the file opens, click the hammer next to Family Trip. In the browser, choose View | Source to see the text that's contained in the HTML file for the sample animation. Choose File | Save As and save the file as `splash.htm` in the same directory where the movie file is located. With the file still open, modify the file by changing the title text between the `<TITLE>` tags to read ANIMATED MAP. Delete the introductory paragraph text and accompanying formatting tags.

In the block defined by the `<OBJECT>` and `</OBJECT>` tags, you need to change a few things:

- Change the width to 600 and the height value to 355.
- Change the Movie Value text to `splash.spl`.
- Change the Play Value to `False` and the Quality Value to `Best`.
- Change the alternate image file to `splash.gif`.

You might want to experiment with the size values to get your animation as large as possible in the browser window without requiring scrolling by the user. This requires a little trial-and-error work. Listing 8.1 shows the code for the simple HTML page you've created that identifies the control.

Listing 8.1. `splash.htm`: The code for the simple HTML file you created, containing a single object, the Flash control animated movie file `splash.spl`.

```
<HTML>
<HEAD>
<TITLE>ANIMATED MAP</TITLE>
</HEAD>
<BODY BGCOLOR="#FFFFFF">
<center>
<!-- The OBJECT tag is used for ActiveX and Microsoft Internet Explorer 3.0 -->
<OBJECT
classid="clsid:D27CDB6E-AE6D-11cf-96B8-444553540000"
width=600 height=355>
<PARAM NAME="Movie" VALUE="splash.spl">
<PARAM NAME="Loop" Value="True">
<PARAM NAME="Play" Value="False">
<PARAM NAME="BGColor" Value="ffffff">
<PARAM NAME="Quality" Value="Best">
<PARAM NAME="Scale" Value="Showall">
<PARAM NAME="SAlign" Value="">
<!-- The EMBED tag is used for the Netscape Navigator Plug-in -->
```

8

continues

Listing 8.1. continued

```
<EMBED src="splash.spl" width=600 height=355
Loop="True" Play="True" BGColor="ffffff" Quality="Best" Scale="showall" SAlign=""
pluginspage="http://www.futurewave.com/downloadfs.htm">
<!-- The IMG tag is used for for all other browsers -->
<NOEMBED>
<IMG src="splash.gif" width=600 height=355>
</NOEMBED>
</OBJECT>
</center>
</BODY>
</HTML>
```

Now you need to create the HTML file on which to place the instructions. Follow these steps:

1. Open a new HTML file in Front Page Editor.

2. To use a background for the HTML file, choose File | New and then Normal. A white page appears.

3. Choose Format | Background and select the ClipArt tab from the dialog box. Animations is the default clipart selection. Change it to Backgrounds.

4. Double-click the `Blue` and `Pink.gif` sample. In the window, you should see a full pathname reference to the image called `Blue` and `Pink.gif`. Because you need a relative URL, erase the path but leave the filename. Click OK.

5. When you return to the editor window, the background hasn't changed. To fix this, copy the background image file from `C:\Program Files\Microsoft FrontPage\clipart\backgrounds` to your local directory where `splash.htm` resides.

6. In the Front Page Editor, save your file as `instruct.htm` to the same directory.

7. Choose View | Refresh. The image should appear as a background.

Adding Finishing Touches

You now are ready to proceed with an instruction page to assist visitors in using the animated map. Open a graphics editor, such as Corel Photopaint, Paintbrush, or a similar program, and open the `splash.gif` file you exported from the drawing. Select each button and copy an image of the button to a new `.gif` image file. In Photopaint, just draw a box around the button, choose Edit | Copy to File, and save the file to the same directory as a `.gif` file. Name your button image files `begin.gif`, `rewind.gif`, and `stop.gif`.

Now you can place references to these files into your HTML file, and they will appear on your Web page. In Front Page Editor, click in the window and type **INSTRUCTIONS FOR ANIMATED MAP**. Select the text by dragging over it, and click the large letter A in the horizontal toolbar. It has an up arrow next to it, indicating that this will increase the size of the text. Click it until the title is almost all the way across the page. Now select a brown color from the color palette.

Press Enter to move to the next line. Choose Insert | Image, and in the tab-strip dialog click the Other Location tab. Enter **begin.gif** in the text box and click OK. The BEGIN MAP button illustration should appear in the window. This will work only if you've saved your file as instruct.htm in the same directory with the begin.gif file. Now type some text below the button, indicating the button's purpose, and format it so that it's centered under the button.

Insert another image—the image of your REWIND button—by choosing Insert | Image, typing the filename **rewind.gif**, and clicking OK. Under this button image, place some more text describing the purpose of the button in the animated map. Repeat the step for the STOP button image stop.gif.

Now place some text explaining how to use the right-click tools in the Flash player in Internet Explorer. Explain how to zoom and pan. Then create a hyperlink that returns visitors to the animated map page by typing **Click here to RETURN TO ANIMATED MAP**. Select the words RETURN TO ANIMATED MAP and choose Insert | Hyperlink. Type **splash.htm** in the text box and make sure that the box above the text box indicates the type of link is "file."

Now you can continue the page with written directions to the plant from the airport. These may be helpful if visitors want to print the directions from the Web page. Figure 8.5 shows what the top of your HTML page should look like. See Listing 8.2 if you don't have an HTML editor and want to reproduce the page by using HTML tags and text.

FIGURE 8.5.

The instruct.htm *file in the Front Page Editor window. A bookmark is inserted at the top of the file, just left of the title for the page.*

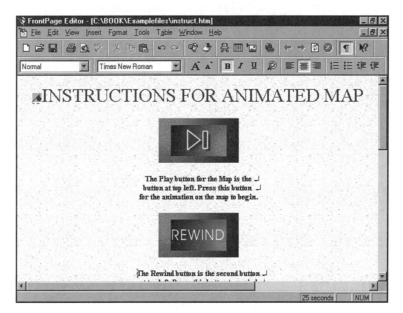

Listing 8.2. The code for the HTML file instruct.htm, created in Front Page Explorer.

```
<!DOCTYPE HTML PUBLIC "-//IETF//DTD HTML//EN">
<html>
<head>
<meta http-equiv="Content-Type"
```

continues

Listing 8.2. The code for the HTML file `instruct.htm`, created in Front Page Explorer.

```
content="text/html; charset=iso-8859-1">
<meta name="GENERATOR" content="Microsoft FrontPage 2.0">
<title>INSTRUCTIONS FOR MAP</title>
</head>
<body background="Blue%20and%20Pink.gif" bgcolor="#FFFFFF">
<p align="center"><a name="TOP"><font color="#804000" size="6"></font></a>
<font color="#804000" size="6">INSTRUCTIONS FOR ANIMATED MAP</font></p>
<p align="center"><img src="begin.gif" width="138" height="75"></p>
<p align="center"><font size="2"><strong>The Play button for the
Map is the<br>
button at top left. Press this button <br>
for the animation on the map to begin.</strong></font></p>
<p align="center"><img src="rewind.gif" width="138" height="75"></p>
<p align="center"><font size="2"><strong>The Rewind button is the
second button<br>
at top left. Press this button to rewind<br>
the animation to the beginning.</strong></font></p>
<p align="center"><font size="2"><strong></strong></font> </p>
<hr>
<p align="center"><font size="2"><strong>The Stop button suspends
the animation<br>
until you perform a play or rewind action.</strong></font></p>
<p>The following tools are accessible by clicking on the map with
the right button on your mouse. Right-click will open a drop-down
menu. Select one of the following:</p>
<p>ZOOM IN: Zooms in toward the center of the map. You will
notice now that the mouse icon has changed to a hand symbol.
Click and hold the mouse button down. Drag the map left, right,
up or down until the part of the map you wish to view is in view.</p>
<p align="center"><font size="4">Click here to </font><a
href="splash.htm"><font size="4">RETURN TO ANIMATED MAP</font></a></p>
<p> </p>
<p> </p>
<p>INSTRUCTIONS TO PLANT FROM AIRPORT:</p>
<p>Take I-70 West from the Airport and drive 11/2 hours until you
reach the Highway 19 exit. A winery billboard sign and a State
Historic Site sign are visible just before reaching the exit.
Travel south 14 miles and cross the old bridge over the Misssouri
River.</p>
<p>ETC., ETC. ETC.</p>
<p> </p>
</body>
</html>
```

Summary

In this chapter, you learned how to use a software vendor's ActiveX program to animate a Web page with ActiveX controls and no significant need for scripting. The visual interface provided by Flash from Macromedia eliminates writing code to create an animation. The Flash player permits Web-page visitors to install the player automatically and play the animated movie.

This should give you a good idea of what to expect from third-party controls and a basic understanding of what's involved to make the controls work when they are moved onto the Internet.

Creating ActiveX Scripts With VBScript

by Dan Horsefield

IN THIS CHAPTER

CHAPTER

9

The creation of Web scripting languages has redirected the work of processing data to the desktop PC. Web scripting was formerly confined to server-side processing. Common Gateway Interface (CGI) scripts, also sometimes referred to as CGI programs, were basic language text files launched and processed on a server.

CGI scripts are stored on the server, triggered when the browser file is loaded, and processed on the server. Output is ported back to the Web browser on the desktop, courtesy of the server.

The CGI method of processing data is still valuable. In many cases, a CGI script may be more appropriate because the designer of the interaction may require server processing. CGI scripts are no longer the only choice. The CGI language is losing ground to a new method of processing and a new language, *ActiveX scripting*. The new processing method requires embedding ActiveX scripting directly into the client-side HTML files. By using standard HTML tags (text commands), the browser locates a server's HTML Web page file and the client computer executes script written directly into the HTML file. The browser no longer has to locate and load the external CGI script or bind its output to the desktop PC where the browser is running. Instead, the browser merely loads the internal script as the page loads, binding the internal objects, and executes the user interaction (clicks, keystrokes, and mouse moves) with simple scripting calls.

The function calls aren't traditional. You don't place a line of code beginning with Go Sub. Instead, you write the HTML manually or with a scripting wizard utility. The resulting code includes a reference to the function or subroutine call.

Understanding Scripting

ActiveX scripting is based on a general language dataset that includes JavaScript programming language and Visual Basic Script (VBScript). JavaScript, based on an emerging new popular developer's language called Java, preceded the advent of the full ActiveX experience.

Microsoft knew that many programmers would embrace Visual Basic scripting because of the popularity of VB development programs it had sold and continued to support in the marketplace. But because Netscape's Navigator browser already supports client/server applications that use Java and JavaScript, Microsoft engineered Internet Explorer to accommodate both Java and VBScript. That way, Microsoft promoted Internet Explorer as a more compatible browser—one of the pivotal points that led users to scramble for compatibility. Everyone knew VBScript and Java would both be used on the Internet.

When Internet Explorer was introduced, an ActiveX layout control (.alx) would appear in the new browser's window, ready for user interaction. The file, embedded by reference in an HTML file, wouldn't appear in the browser window when viewed with Netscape Navigator. Netscape now supports ActiveX controls.

VBScript and JavaScript, when used to process ActiveX controls, are generally referred to as *ActiveX scripting languages*, even though ActiveX was a technology introduced by Microsoft.

Using Control Pad

ActiveX Control Pad and scripting are primarily used today for creating lightweight OLE-style controls on pages suitable for a PC or the Internet. Control Pad's features allow you to design an independent window (group of controls) by using its visual interface.

In this window, you place and program events for numerous ActiveX control objects. This programmed window (the window itself becomes an ActiveX control) is an *HTML Layout* control. A reference to each HTML Layout is typed in an HTML file (.htm or .html). When the HTML file is loaded in Internet Explorer, each HTML Layout referenced in the file appears as a rectangle with no borders within the Web page defined by the HTML code. With an HTML Layout, users can't view the code unless they have access to a stored copy of the .alx file.

ActiveX Control Pad features an HTML Layout tool, which is technically an ActiveX control container for other controls (the tool creates an HTML Layout window). The HTML Layout editing tool is launched by choosing File | New HTML Layout.

Control Pad isn't required to create ActiveX content in a Web page, but it makes it much easier. To insert a single control without an HTML file, you launch Control Pad, choose Edit | Insert ActiveX Control, and select the control from a list box. This method requires manual code scripting in the HTML editor window or in another HTML editor.

Programming in VBScript

VBScript, a subset of the Visual Basic language, is intended to make programming easier without permitting access to low-level Windows functions, including access to the user's API.

VBScript is designed to work within the Internet Explorer environment. This chapter provides some important points and examples. For a comprehensive listing reference for VBScript, go to http://www.microsoft.com/vbscript/us/download/vbsdoc.exe.

The default data type for VBScript is Variant. To convert the Variant data type to a type that matches your object's data type, use the following conversions:

- Use Asc(*string*) to return the ASCII code for the first letter of a string expression.
- Use CBool(*expression*) to return the value of a Boolean expression (True or False). If zero is the expression, False is returned. If other than zero, True is returned.
- Use CByte(*expression*) to force byte arithmetic in cases where currency, single-precision, double-precision, or integer arithmetic normally would occur.
- Use CCur(*expression*) to return the value of the expression converted into currency.
- Use CDate(*expression*) to return the value of the expression converted into a Date datatype. You can use time literals and numbers that fall within the range of

acceptable dates. When a number is converted to a date, the whole number portion is converted to a date. Any fractional part of the number is converted to a time of day, starting at midnight.

- Use CDbl(*expression*) to return a double datatype.

- Use Chr(*expression*) to return the character string equivalent to the ASCII value (0– 31) of a non-printable character. Chr(10) would return a linefeed, for example.

- Use CInt(*expression*) to return an integer value and force integer arithmetic where double-precision or other type arithmetic would otherwise be used.

- CLng(*expression*) converts the expression to the Long datatype.

- Use CSgn(*expression*) to return a Single number datatype.

- CStr(*expression*) converts a variant expression, such as a number, to a String datatype, which can be printed or displayed.

- The Hex(*expression*) function converts a number to the hexadecimal equivalent for the number. If a whole number isn't used, the number is rounded to the nearest whole number before evaluation.

- Use Oct(*expression*) to return the octal value of an expression.

For more information on the use or definitions of the various datatypes, download the VBSDOC.EXE file from http://www.microsoft.com/vbscript/. This self-extracting file includes a comprehensive collection of HTML files that will be installed on launching VBSDOC.EXE. Both 16-bit and 32-bit versions of the documentation are available at the Web site. Click the Free Downloads link and look for the VBScript Documentation icon.

Using Loops

Do...Loops are useful tools and similar to For...Next loops. You don't necessarily have to know how many loops are going to be needed. In the following example, the variable y is assigned to 32:

```
y=15
x=1
Do
x=x+1
ComboBox1.additem Cstr(x)
Loop Until x=y
```

To propagate a ComboBox with this script, create a ComboBox and then a CommandButton. Program the Click event for the CommandButton to execute this script.

If...Then...Else statements are used for conditional testing. In the following example, if CommandButton5 is clicked, you get a warning that tells you the y counter is at 5. The message appears two more times as the counter increments to 7.

```
</SCRIPT>
<SCRIPT LANGUAGE="VBScript">
<!--
```

```
Sub CommandButton5_Click()
y = 1
For i = 1 to 7
y = y + 1
If y > 5 then
msgbox "We're at 5", 16, "Warning"
End if
next
end sub
-->
</SCRIPT>
```

Elseif syntax allows two tests within the If loop. This reduces the code by one line each time it's used because Elseif doesn't have to be terminated with an End if each time the test is performed.

```
If y > 5 then
msgbox "We're at 5", 16, "Warning"
Elseif y > 7
msgbox "We're at 7", 16, "Warning"
End if
```

exit is a VBScript statement that forces a subroutine or function to terminate execution. It can be used with an If statement within a loop to terminate the loop before the count reaches the specified number of loops. In the following example, a loop is used to propagate a ComboBox, but the box goes only from 1 to 30 because of the exit statement:

```
For I = 1 to 99
y = I + 1
ComboBox1.additem Cstr(y)
If y = 30 then
exit sub
Next
```

Most programmers are familiar with For...Next loops. These loops can be nested. The syntax is very basic. The following example would increment the variable c 5,000 times.

```
c = 1
For x = 1 to 500
For y = 1 to 10
c = c + 1
Next
Next
```

To step the incrementation by units not equal to 1, use the following syntax:

```
For x = 1 to 500 Step .2
```

Select Case is used as an alternative structure for If...End If statements. It's used primarily when several options are available. ActiveX OptionButtons use this type of structure within their groups:

```
x = InputBox ("Enter a number between 1 and 4")
Select Case x
Case 1
msgbox "You selected 1."
```

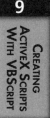

9

CREATING
ACTIVEX SCRIPTS
WITH VBSCRIPT

```
Case 2
msgbox "You selected 2."
Case 3
msgbox "You selected 3."
Case 4
msgbox "You selected 4."
End Select
```

> **CAUTION**
>
> The use of variables within the Select Case selection isn't supported. Use literals.

While...Wend is like the For...Next loops with an important distinction: The While...Wend (While End) structure keeps looping as long as a specified condition remains true. For example, if you want the loop to continue until a counter reaches 1,000, try this:

```
x = 1
While x < 1000
x = x + 1
msgbox x
Wend
```

Using Functions

Abs() is a rather rare function that returns a variable of the same type, but if the value was previously negative, it becomes positive. For example, if i equals –10, Abs(i) returns the value 10 and msgbox Abs(i) prints 10.

Alert() is a VBScript function similar to msgbox and can be substituted for msgbox in the code.

The Cos()function gives the cosine of an angle in radians:

```
x=Cos(.8)
returns 0.9999025240093
```

The DateSerial() function converts year, month, day, and time into a serial number.

The DateValue() function converts a String expression into a date/time serial number.

The Day() function extracts the day of the month from a serial number created by the previous functions or by the Now function, which gets the current computer date/time serial number.

Exp() is a mathematical function that calculates the exponential value of a variable or a literal number:

```
Exp (3)
```

Function is a type of statement used to return something to the location from which the function was called. In the following example, zero would be returned when the Validate()

function is called, if the input box called TextBox1 contains no data. This in turn would generate a message box informing users of the omission.

```
Sub CommandButton1_Click()
If Validate(TextBox1.Value) <> 0 then
Submit
exit sub
End If
msgbox "You forgot to enter data in TextBox1.", 16, "Warning"
End Sub

Function Validate(y)
Set MyForm = Document.MainForm
If MyForm.y.Value="" then
x = 0
End Function
```

Hex() is a function that returns the hexadecimal value of a numeric value, but the value returned is a text string data type. The following example would generate the hex equivalent, F, in a message box when run in Internet Explorer:

```
<SCRIPT LANGUAGE="VBScript">
<!--
Sub CommandButton3_Click()
n = Hex(15)
msgbox n, 16, "ActiveX Testing Hex 15"
end sub
-->
</SCRIPT>
```

The Hour() function tells users the hour based on a serial number that VBScript generates when functions such as Now are used. The hour is returned in military value, with 0 equivalent to 12 a.m. and 23 equivalent to 11 p.m. For example,

```
n = Hour(Cdbl(Now))
msgbox n, 16, "ActiveX Testing Hex 15"
```

InputBox() is a VBScript function that launches a pop-up box and pauses for user input to be assigned to a variable. The following example launches the box, prompts users for input with the text message, and waits for users to confirm that the input is complete. Then the input is stored in variable m.

```
m = InputBox ("Please enter your age.")
```

Instr() isolates a part of a string (parsing) and returns the number corresponding to the position where the first character of the string was encountered (if it's encountered). In the following examples, the returned value in the message box is 10. The first example begins with the default starting position, 1, because a starting position isn't specified. The second example starts at 3.

```
x = Instr("ABCDEFGHIJKLMNO", "J")
msgbox x, 16, "VBScript Testing"
OR
x = Instr(3, "ABCDEFGHIJKLMNO", "J")
msgbox x, 16, "VBScript Testing"
```

9

CREATING
ACTIVEX SCRIPTS
WITH VBSCRIPT

> **TIP**
>
> You might want to convert a character string to lowercase before using `InStr()` so that case matching won't deter your efforts. See the `Lcase()` function in the following paragraphs.

`Int()` rounds off a number that contains a fraction, deleting the fraction portion of the number. To round to the nearest whole number, use `Int(N+.5)`. Then if the fraction is .5 or higher, the next whole number is reached and the proper value is returned. If the fraction is less than .5, the fraction will be dropped.

The `IsArray()`, `IsDate()`, `IsEmpty()`, `IsError()`, `IsNumeric()`, and `IsObject()` functions are used to test the data type of a variable. Generally, these functions are used with `If...Then` statements:

```
y = InputBox ("Enter a Date")
If IsDate(y) then
msgbox Cstr(y) & "is the date."
End if
```

`LBound()` reveals the lower boundary of an array's index. Normal use of `LBound()` in VBScript returns zero because all arrays will begin with 0:

```
dim y(50)
x=LBound(y)
msgbox y
```

`Lcase()` forces lowercase character strings. The following example returns a lowercase string `Howdy Do...` in a message box:

```
x = "Howdy Do..."
y = Lcase(x)
msgbox y
```

`Left()` in VBScript strips the left side of the string beginning with the character identified by number in the `Left()` function statement. To strip the word *Howdy* from `Howdy Do...`, use this example:

```
x = "Howdy Do..."
y = Left(x,6)
msgbox y
```

`Len()` in VBScript measures the length of string. The following returns the number 17 and stores it in the x variable:

```
y="JUST ABOUT ENOUGH"
x = Len(y)
msgbox x
```

`Log()` is a math function that returns the natural logarithm of a number. In the following example, the result 3.0910245335832 is displayed in a message box:

```
x = Log(22)
msgbox x
```

Ltrim() removes leading spaces from a string being evaluated. The following example generates the string Howdy, howdy! in a message box:

```
x = "    Howdy, howdy!"
y = Ltrim(x)
msgbox y
```

Mid() extracts a portion of text from a string. You must specify the starting position from which to begin gathering data and enter the number corresponding to how many digits you want to extract, plus 1. In this example, I'm Howdy is extracted from the text string:

```
x="Howdy, I'm Howdy Do. How Do You Do"
y = Mid(x, 7, 10)
msgbox y
```

Minute() is used primarily to extract the current time in minutes, derived from using the Now function:

```
MsgBox Minute(Now)
```

Month() provides the month of the year and is generally used to provide an accurate date from Jan. 1, 100 to Dec. 31, 9999. It's used primarily with the Now function to return the current month identified by the PC's time/date clock:

```
MsgBox Month(Now)
```

Now is a function that translates an internal PC clock's serial number into a string expression equivalent to the current Month(), Day(), Year(), Hour(), Minute(), and Second(). See the discussions on these functions for examples of use.

Oct() is a math function that converts a numeral into a string representation of the octal value of the numeral. It's not used much today.

Right() strips (returns) a portion of text from the end of a string expression. This code displays bored in a message box:

```
x = "Labored"
y = Right(x, 5)
msgbox y
```

Rtrim() is used to remove trailing spaces from a string expression. See Ltrim() for syntax.

Second() is a function that returns the value in seconds for the current time when used with the Now statement:

```
x = Second(Now)
```

Sgn() evaluates a numeric variable to determine whether it's positive, negative, or zero. It returns the numeral 1 if the number is positive, 0 if it's zero, and −1 one if it's negative.

9

CREATING
ActiveX SCRIPTS
WITH VBScript

`Sin()` is a function that evaluates a numeric expression and returns the sine of an angle expressed in radians. Its syntax is similar to `Atn()`, `Cos()`, and `Tan()`. For example,

```
x = Sin(.8)
```

`Sqr()` is a function that provides the square root of any positive number:

```
x = 9
y = Sqr(9)
```

`StrComp()` is a function that compares string expressions to determine which is alphabetically lower (A <B <C <D, and so on). For example,

```
x=StrComp(Y,Z)
If x<0 then
msgbox "Y is less than Z"
If x=0 then
msgbox "Y is equal to Z"
If x>0 then
msgbox "Y is greater than Z"
```

`String()` is a simple function used to generate a number of instances of a specific character. Specify how many, and then the character enclosed in quotes:

```
x = String(35,"/")
msgbox x
```

`Tan()` returns the tangent of an angle expressed in radians:

```
x=5.2
y= Tan(x)
```

`Time()` is used to call the same information as the `time` command in DOS. You can assign the time to a variable as follows:

```
x = Time
```

`TimeSerial()` converts a time expressed in hours, minutes, and seconds to a unique serial number equivalent to one of 86,400 seconds in a day:

```
x=TimeSerial (11,30,59)
msgbox x
```

`TimeValue()` performs the same conversion as `TimeSerial`, but you input the time as a string value:

```
x = TimeValue("11:30:59")
msgbox x
```

`Trim()` is a function that removes any blank spaces from either end of a string. Refer to `Ltrim()` and `Rtrim()`.

`VarType()` is a function used to determine the variable subtype of a variable.

`Weekday()` is a function that returns a numeral in the range 1–7, which equates with a day of the week. Sunday is assigned 1 in the range; Saturday is 7.

```
x = Weekday(Now)
If x = 1
msgbox "Sunday"
end if
```

`Year()` is a function that reveals the year, based on a unique serial number for a specific point in time. `Year()` is commonly used with the `Now` function:

```
x = Year(Now)
msgbox Year
```

To try out some of the code examples and variations of these code examples in ActiveX Control Pad, you can load the `arrayit.alx` file and click the command buttons. Use the Script Wizard and compare the contents of the `Click` events programmed for the command buttons. The file isn't particularly a pretty one, but it was used to test many of the code samples in the text examples listed here.

Using Miscellaneous Statements

Arrays are variables clustered into theoretical rows and columns. In this dimension statement, x would equate to column one and 12 would create 12 rows within the column:

```
Dim x(12)
```

This creates 12 placeholders in the column to which data can be assigned. The same could be created by assigning the space with 12 lines of code that look like this:

```
x(1)=""
x(2)=""
```

`Clear` is a VBScript method that resets the `Err` object. Use `Err.Clear` to clear the error so debugging won't repeat the appropriate error message.

Concatenation is achieved by using the ampersand. To get the words *Jack And Jill,* use this code snippet:

```
j = "Jack " & "And" & "Jill"
msgbox j
```

`Erase` is a statement used to work one of two ways. The statement will reset all cells in a static array to zero, if they're numeric and blank for variables.

The `Erase` statement completely removes a dynamic array. Here's an example of how an `Erase` statement is used:

```
Dim x(2)
x(1) = 100
x(2) = 200
msgbox Cstr(x(1)) & " " & Cstr (x(2))
erase x
msgbox Cstr(x(1)) & " " & Cstr (x(2))
```

Place the code in a CommandButton's `Click` event and load it in Explorer. Click the CommandButton, and the first message box contains the `X(1)` and `X(2)` array values. The second message box displays nothing because the array was erased.

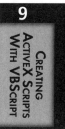

Err is a VBScript object that uses an error code system to help developers locate an error's origin at runtime. Err can report an internal scripting error or an OLE object's runtime error. Use of Err evaluates Err for a non-zero value. If the value is zero, no error was encountered in the code.

> **TIP**
>
> Use Err in an If statement to trap the error and assist users in resolving the problem.

In the following example, users are asked to input a number for the day of the week when they want you to call. The first If statement checks the value entered for the day of the week to make sure that it's not 8 or greater. The second If statement uses the cInt() function and Err to check to see whether a character other than a number was entered. The day of the week is represented by the InputBox variable q.

```
<SCRIPT LANGUAGE="VBScript">
<!--
Sub CommandButton8_Click()
On Error Resume Next
q = InputBox ("Please enter a number for the day of the week for us to call.")
If q => 8 then
msgbox "Please try again. The numeral you selected for day was " & q
exit sub
End if
If q <= 0 then
msgbox "Please try again. The value you selected for day was " & q
exit sub
End if
q = cInt(q)
If Err then
msgbox "Please try again. The value you selected for day was " & q
End if
end sub
-->
</SCRIPT>
```

Imp is a logical operator that compares two expressions to determine their relationship. Technically, the Imp operator performs a bitwise comparison of identically positioned bits in two numeric expressions and sets the corresponding bit. See the *VBScript Reference* documentation for tables that indicate the outcome of using this operator.

MsgBox *x* displays a pop-up box with a message designed by the programmer and waits for the user to click OK.

The TypeOf...Is statement evaluates the object to determine what action to perform on the object:

```
If TypeOf Object1 Is ComboBox then
Object1.additem "Next Item . . ."
End if
```

`Let` is a statement that historically has been used to assign a value to a variable. It has been retained to retain functionality with older code segments:

```
Let MyName = "Tex Reed"
```

`MOD` provides you with the remainder of a numeric division. This is useful in generating hexadecimal conversion programs and the like. This code example returns the number 4 in a message box:

```
x = 40 MOD 12
msgbox x
```

`Not` is a Boolean operator that lets you reverse the logic of a test. For example, `x = Not False` would return `True` to the x variable. With bit logic, 0 would become 1, or 1 would become 0.

`OnLoad` is a VBScript event that equates to when a file is loaded in a program. The `OnLoad` code runs in a subroutine during initial loading and without any user interaction.

`Option Explicit`, which forces dimensioning of variables, is a command used at the top of a script on a separate command line.

Parentheses are used to avoid confusion with the precedence of operators such as mathematical multiplication and addition. On a line that adds 3 to 5 and then multiplies by 10, the result would be 53 if no parentheses are used. The following example returns 35 to variable x. The items in the parentheses are evaluated first:

```
x = (5 + 3) * 10
```

You can invoke property changes with VBScript in connection with ActiveX controls. Many examples are used in the previous section of the chapter. ActiveX control properties are manipulated with event procedures. The following line changes the text in TextBox1 during runtime:

```
TextBox1.Value = "This is the new text."
```

Procedures are subroutines and functions. See the discussion on functions earlier in the section "Using Functions." Many functions are built into VBScript. They're addressed by their command names.

`Raise` is a method useful for simulating an error and testing the interaction when an error is encountered:

```
Err.Raise 35
```

`Randomize` is a statement used to allow the script to provide truly random numbers each time it runs. Each time the script is parsed (refreshed or loaded), a new and unique series of random numbers are available. Use `Randomize` on a separate line as the first command in the script.

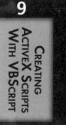

9

CREATING
ACTIVEX SCRIPTS
WITH VBSCRIPT

ReDim allocates space to temporarily hold an array during a procedure's executions. Use between Sub...End Sub or between Function...End Function.

Rem is used to create a remark on a line in the script. Everything on the current line following Rem will be ignored.

Rnd is used to generate random numbers. Specify the range 1 to 75 with the first code line; specify a range of 0 to 75 with the second code line:

```
x = Int(Rnd * 75 + 1)
y = Int(Rnd * 75)
```

The Set statement is used to assign an object a variable name. By using Dim to assign the variable and then Set, you can shorten the object name and reduce script typing. For example, you could continue to assign property changes with less typing in this code, which changes the CommandButton's BackColor property to red and displays a message box:

```
Dim x
Set x = CommandButton15
x.BackColor = 255
msgbox "Do you like red?"
```

UBound() returns the upper boundary value of an array's index. Refer to LBound() for syntax.

Ucase() forces all the characters of a string to be uppercase:

```
x="HOWDY, HOWDY"
y=UCase(x)
msgbox y
```

Xor is an operator used in encryption. You can use it with letters and numbers other than zeros:

```
Letter1 = "A"
Letter2 = "B"
Key1 = "N"
Key2 = "N"
x = Asc(Letter1) Xor Asc(Key1)
y = Asc(Letter2) Xor Asc(Key2)
x = chr (x)
y = chr (y)
msgbox x & y
```

To decrypt the example, substitute the values in the message box for A and B in the code example. Run the script again. The letters toggle back to their original values.

Summary

In this chapter, you learned how ActiveX scripting languages are different from CGI scripts, because the work is done on the client computer and doesn't rely on the bandwidth speed restrictions to process the interactive events being programmed. You also learned why VBScript was created and explored most of the commonly used loops, functions, and statements and their syntax. The simple examples can be easily programmed and tested in HTML files.

Organizing ActiveX Projects

by Dan Horsefield

IN THIS CHAPTER

CHAPTER 10

Visual Basic's use of project files for organizing an application is a very efficient way to prepare for packaging and distributing a final executable program, prototyping an Internet-enabled application, or creating a user control. Think of a project file as a collection of files that contain the data necessary to carry out the functionality of the executable program, control, or control group being programmed. Most file handling is done behind the scenes; you, as the programmer, don't have to pick apart the files themselves.

Using a Structured Project Approach

Start each new project, even if you're building a small ActiveX control, with a check list for creation. This will be your wish list, because all programmers who complete a project *wish* they had made more decisions *before* the programming rather than *during* the programming. This disciplined sort of planning saves literally hours of fighting a renegade program. Poorly planned programs lead to hours of debugging to remedy data type mismatches, invalid object references, calls to nonexistent methods, misspellings of variable names, reuse of the same common variable names, confusion regarding variables and constants, and so on.

Study the list before preparing the application for distribution to help determine whether the program should be optimized for performance or for file size. This optimization is occasionally necessary with programs that intensively use algorithms or are very large in terms of file size. Preparing this list as a first step also helps you focus on the consistent use of conventional name assignments for variables, constants, objects, forms, and so on. Consistency is achieved by using prefixes at the front of the name, as discussed later in the section "Using Naming Conventions."

All items on this wish list are factors you eventually have to study, analyze, or at least think about. In other words, you have to generate all the names on the list, write all the procedures, and so on. By first tackling the issues on paper (or, more conveniently, in a typed text file), you have a handy reference list to build from and a focused goal to achieve. This list doesn't need to be perfect; it requires only notation-style entries that you'll understand later in the process.

For example, an entry on the list might read *Input for company name,* `strCompName`, *check for null validation (*`NulChk`*), prompt Enter Company Name:.* In this example, you would have a line of code that uses an input box to gather company name data, assigns the value to a string variable named `strCompName`, and then calls a procedure that tests to make sure that something is entered in the input box when the user clicks OK.

> **NOTE**
>
> The phrase `NulChk` is simply the name of the validation procedure that performs this check for a null value. Validation routines are frequently required to make sure that the program segment can access all the data input required to perform its task.

It's difficult to imagine each instance of when you'll need a variable for counting, for example. By having a list, however, you can compare the new variable name you plan to use with other items on the list. This way, you can create a unique assignment for a variable name and compare the associated purpose of the variable with items on the list. The comparison can be helpful, because if the purpose of the item is similar to another purpose on the list, you probably can write the code snippet and reuse it in another part of the program (perhaps with a simple modification to the variable name and code comments, if necessary).

Your wish list should be designed to accommodate user needs. It's helpful to encourage users (or the supervisor of a group of users) to help define exactly what the program must do to achieve basic functionality before you start building. You should incorporate all functionality into your list so that subsequent embellishment of the program is limited to improving existing functionality and appearance. This can be done by using notes about what users want and placing a check mark next to items as they're added to your programming wish list.

When developing the visual interface and before proceeding with difficult parts of the code, you should get some feedback from a user, supervisor, or colleague regarding the appearance and planned events for the objects in the program that users will interact with.

If you didn't plan your last application from a check list, think of the last application you personally worked on and imagine how fast you could have completed the work if you had such a list. Also, think about the list in terms of group development. If everyone in a group developing an application has a similar list, a lot of initial confusion and wasted conversation about which party is doing what can be eliminated. The list will outline the appropriate responsibilities. Developers working on one part of the program can share code snippets that need only minor modifications for use by other programmers working on other parts of the project. The list will help programmers know who to coordinate with.

The following list is to be taken as a general guideline or template for creation of your wish list. Modify the list items to suit your unique application and personal programming style. If your project includes any of the items mentioned, make sure that you have them documented where you can easily find them:

1. A list of visual objects (user controls) that allow users to manipulate, organize, locate, and view the necessary data:

   - ■ Visual controls for the input of data.
   - ■ Visual controls for user interaction to manipulate the data.
   - ■ Visual controls for arranging data output.
   - ■ Visual controls for displaying data or images as output.
   - ■ Visual ActiveX controls—generally a *group of* visual controls—that can be reused in the program or other programs. (These are referred to as *user controls* in VB.)
   - ■ Visual messages to users containing output, instructions, message notifications, alerts, warnings, and so on.

10

ORGANIZING ACTIVEX PROJECTS

2. A simple flow chart showing the outcome of each step in the input-output cycle to be used in the program. This may require numerous pages of simple sketches. For example, each looping routine with a test (If...Then) would be shown on the chart as a box containing the name of the test and two arrows indicating whether the expression evaluates as true or false. At the end of the arrows are the next steps taken by the program, depending on the outcome of the test.

3. A hierarchy list of the classes of objects to be used in the project (thorough detail in the creation of classes reduces the length and complexity of a program):

   ■ Name and purpose of each class

   ■ Name and purpose of members of the classes

   ■ Subclasses of the class, if applicable

4. Identify actions that will be activated on input of data:

   ■ Dimensioning (declaring) of variables and data arrays. Keep notes regarding variable scope: Will they be global variables accessible from all modules, module-level public variables available to a specific module, or procedure-level variables that are created and terminated with each call to the procedure?

   ■ Declaration of array variables. Sometimes, especially with two-dimensional arrays (three dimensions and beyond are rarely used), making a simple sketch of rows and columns helps keep a visual representation in mind regarding how the data will be arranged. Some people have a knack for understanding rows and columns, but some might benefit from placing some sample data on an Excel worksheet page or a Microsoft Access table to mimic the use of the arrays to be used. If calculations based on data in specific locations in the array are required, this spreadsheet approach can be very helpful, especially if the logic to be used with the array isn't easily understood.

   ■ Assignment of data to named variables. Special attention to naming variables with respect to the scope and specific data types that will be used is required here. For example, use gstrCusName as a global variable name for the input from a textbox that will accept a user's name (gstr denotes the global scope and string data type associated with the variable). Use intCountA as the variable name for a counter in a procedure that uses integers to increment and decrement (int denotes that the data type Integer is associated with the variable, and the absence of a scope prefix indicates that the variable is procedure level). Use vntXsites as the variable name for an item that will be a string value containing numbers (vnt denotes the data type Variant). See the later section "Using Naming Conventions."

   ■ Purpose and name of all validation routines to be used to check the integrity or validity of the data. Use notes such as *Check for null characters in* strFirstName *field,* Private Sub CheckForNull() or *Check for alpha in numeric* strTelPhone *input field,* Private Sub CheckForNum().

5. A list of data types for each object or control variable to be used. This listing requires logical (conventional) naming to keep variable types organized, as noted earlier:

   ■ Property data types (Boolean, Integer, String, and so on)

   ■ Developer's hidden variable types (Integer, long, string, values used for comparisons, counters, control name condensations [name shortcuts], and so on)

6. A list of methods to be used for data manipulation:

   ■ Functions that return (pass) data values and calls that receive the data.

   ■ Subroutine procedures (branches) that manipulate data and return to the next line of code during program execution. These should be listed separately so that optimization considerations are easier to evaluate before distribution.

   ■ Counting routines.

   ■ Sorting routines.

   ■ Routines for creating concatenations or parsing of values.

7. A property value list:

   ■ Name, purpose, and scope of property value retrievals (`Property Get` statements)

   ■ Name, purpose, and scope of property value declarations (`Property Let` statements)

   ■ Name and purpose of property value groups (Property Bags and Property Pages to be created)

Using Containers in Your Program

You need a separate section of the wish list to top off the project with logical names for the major parts of the program (this part of the list can be created before or after the individual items listed in the previous section):

1. Project modules: The name, filename, and purpose of particular projects (`.vbp` files). Keep the projects concise in terms of function. Include the existing project modules you'll be reusing from a previous program at the top of the list. (If you're reusing a project, give it a unique name and filename immediately to prevent overwriting the existing project.) Evaluate the existing (reused) projects from the standpoint of removing extraneous portions first; then check for potential variable name conflicts by comparing with your planned list of variable names. The next step requires you to organize the modules as follows:

   ■ Assign unique names to your forms and MDI child window forms. Make sure that you give them unique filenames immediately to avoid overwriting your existing forms. Modify them for use in your project.

   ■ Assign unique names for your control modules. Give any existing control project a unique filename immediately after loading the project to avoid overwriting a control's file or installed registration data (OCX).

2. For project groups: Assign a unique group name to be used for the project group, if used. Use group or grp as part of the filename to avoid confusing groups with the individual projects.

When the list of notes about the programming to be performed is completed, review it for any confusing variable names that might be very similar. If there are any, give them more unique names. Review the list to see whether it appears to address all the predetermined needed user functionality.

Before starting Visual Basic, create a directory (or directories) to store the project files, forms, controls, and control groups. Usually, this is a single directory, unless a group of developers is working on the project. Multiple directories can be useful if the project is significant in size, because it might be desirable—on encountering significant problems—to start over with a new approach and delete an entire directory of files that are no longer needed.

Another reason for using subdirectories involves the naming of the forms, user controls, and project files. If you want to change a filename, you might need to change every name in the subdirectory. Deleting or renaming these files will be more difficult to achieve if several controls, projects, and forms all appear in a single directory. Remember, before testing and debugging the program, you can create a new comprehensive directory containing all files and place copies of all parts from the various subdirectories in the comprehensive directory. This creates original file backups during the debugging work. When a program change is made, save the changes to this comprehensive directory and also to the particular subdirectory where the repaired file should reside.

As you open existing projects in VB5, remember to save the project immediately under a new filename in a different subdirectory to avoid overwriting the existing file. The same goes for user controls. It's imperative that a user control doesn't have the same OCX file created twice, because duplication can lead to significant confusion. If the user control will be used as is with no modifications, there's no reason to re-create the OCX.

CAUTION

When creating an OCX file with the same filename as one previously used (overwriting an OCX), it's usually necessary to terminate Internet Explorer first because it can interfere with updating the OCX. Even though the current browser address and the current page loaded don't directly use the existing OCX, the browser apparently retains a link to the OCX. This access by IE prevents the old OCX with the same name from being overwritten and generates an error.

It's also a good idea to terminate ActiveX Control Pad before re-creating the OCX (if Control Pad's toolbox contains the custom user control associated with the OCX). The old tool in Control Pad must be removed and the new OCX custom tool must be added before the user control can be drawn in Control Pad. Any HTML layouts using the old (previous) OCX will no longer be valid. The script associated with the HTML layout is still valid, but the user control must be redrawn in the HTML Layout Editor.

At this juncture, you have all the tools needed to begin designing the application. The organization work is done. When you design a project, Visual Basic is so easy to use that it facilitates programming of very complex interfaces. To take advantage of the ease of the environment to speed development, follow this process:

1. Create your visual ActiveX user controls, which will contain the reusable groupings of objects including textboxes, labels, list boxes, combo boxes, command buttons, checkboxes, option buttons, images, and so forth. (Don't confuse these controls with ordinary form controls.)

   These user controls, unlike the form controls, must be placed precisely where they need to appear in the final application. Draw, resize, and assign properties to each control before adding the code. Again, try to use identical or very similar name and caption properties for each individual object, to speed up programming.

2. When all controls have their properties assigned and are sized and arranged properly in the control window, double-click them and add the procedures and methods that will allow messaging between application modules and the user control. A typical user control project will consist primarily of simple procedures and property assignments.

> **NOTE**
>
> When you're finished adding code, don't create the OCX yet. You'll need to see the control's code when you add the next project.

3. Add a project that contains at least one form on which the user control will later be drawn. This time, you don't have to be particular about object size and positioning. Place the objects vertically on the form and program each one, beginning at the top, to facilitate completing the code for each. Leave the layout of the objects on the form for later. It's very easy to move the objects without having any impact on the code; these objects can be resized and moved into position as a last step.

4. When you think you've finished adding code for the first procedure call that will perform messaging functions by using the user control (typically referenced by the name UserControl1 when you later draw it on the form), save the project under a unique filename and then remove it from the group.

5. With the user control project visible as the only project group, create your OCX. Choose File | Make *xxx*.OCX, where *xxx* is the name of your control.

6. Add the project with the form you just saved. Your toolbox now contains the new tool representing the OCX you just saved.

7. Click the new tool and draw your user control on your form.

8. Choose Run | Start to test the code for the first messaging function.

9. Debug as necessary before proceeding. There's a good chance that the code will need to be refined if this is the first user control you've tried to design and access by using the messaging method.

After the control methods and the first messaging function appear to be working properly, program the other objects on your form, one at a time. Test each before proceeding with the rest of the project group. Using message boxes after each important step in the project can assist with troubleshooting and speed up debugging. Although the debugging tools generally will highlight the offending code, sometimes it's helpful to know immediately how far the execution of logic has traveled before an error or unexpected event occurs. Unexpected events don't necessarily generate a debugging error, so use a message box to display the current value of the variables being used in the code segment; sometimes it will give a clue regarding the cause of the problem. You also can use message boxes to announce the state of the objects as the program proceeds.

> **NOTE**
>
> When designing a networked program (commonly referred to as a *client/server application*), be sure not to overburden the messaging between the client part of the application and an instance of the user control residing on the server. Try to keep all storage functions on the local client unless a central database or data object is used. If a central data access object is used, it most likely will reside on the server, and that's a special case.
>
> When you're using data access objects on a server, the data ordinarily must be manipulated or queried with Structured Query Language (SQL) statements. Try to achieve the processing of these queries on the server and temporarily store the results on the server. Refine the resulting set with additional queries by using messaging until only the required data remains, and then return only this data—the final output of all queries—to the client application. This technique isn't always available if the remote data object resides on a server that the developer can't maintain. In that scenario, depending on the workload created by the application, it might be appropriate to work with the people maintaining the server's data so that server-side programs can be installed to handle this work and reduce the amount of data being returned over the network.

Keeping Ergonomic Considerations in Mind

Most developers create fantastic programs without really noticing that some people might spend hours at a stretch looking at and using their application. Other developers will make the programs very ergonomic without even having to think about why they've designed a form the way they have.

Force yourself to think about the ergonomics that will have an impact on the individuals who will use the program. Assume that you have a command button that changes what's displayed in a list box. To improve the program, place the command button very close to the box to reduce the distance the user's eyes must travel when bouncing back and forth between the mouse pointer and the list box.

When possible, attempt to place the cursor at a ready position (selected state) in any text box that will be used routinely for keyboard input. If users will key in data every time a command button is activated, for example, design the procedure to resume focus to the box with a blinking cursor and a blank area to type the next segment of data. If users leave the text box and enter the next input in another text box, use the tab order properties. Likewise, if tabs and carriage returns aren't used in a specific text box to enter the data, program the "lost focus" event handler to activate any necessary procedure when a tab or carriage return is typed.

Try to avoid the need for scrolling when using an MDI form. If you're programming an HTML Web page, automatic scrolling jumps are handled by using links to bookmarks on the page to skip down to the area where the next task needs to be achieved.

If you're using Windows-style menus, be sure to use unique keyboard shortcuts for most or all menu selections, especially those that will be accessed frequently, by using the ampersand (&) symbol in the name of the menu selection. For example, use the menu name &Edit to make the E key the shortcut key for the Edit menu. Taking a little time to create these shortcuts might save users a significant amount of time when using the program. The best commercially available programs on the market accommodate users who prefer mouse moves as well as accomplished typists who prefer keyboard shortcuts.

Although gray forms aren't used much anymore, using background patterns and images creates a new set of challenges for programmers. When you use labels, for example, use colors that aren't too dark to display small text characters. Likewise, textures must have very small patterns so that they don't interfere with text displayed directly on the background. Remember that not all users will have total control over their monitor settings in a work environment. If the monitor is set to display the text very small, even if the resolution is set very high, dark colors with black text will blend together, making the text hard to read and causing undue eye strain.

Pay attention to tab order. When a textbox that's part of a group of textboxes being used for data entry is relocated on a form during design work, be sure to correct the tab order so that typists can tab sequentially across the page and down the page without using the mouse. Without this attention to detail, you can create a serious aversion to your program for accomplished typists.

Most Web page input boxes automatically feature a correct tab order as they're placed in the HTML code. With ActiveX Control Pad and VB5 forms, this tab order must be addressed in the properties dialog boxes. As the boxes are added, the next available tab number is assigned automatically. If you delete or move boxes, the tab ordering number values accompanying a box's tab property don't change automatically.

Don't place text too tightly in user controls such as labels and option buttons. Also avoid placing controls too close to each other. If your application will be used on the Internet, it won't necessarily be displayed the same way on every system, and you must accommodate for the difference by leaving room for larger display fonts and inaccuracies caused by differences in operating systems.

Distributing VB Controls on the Internet

Using Visual Basic to create a user control is very convenient, and so is the deployment of the application to a Web site. All you need to do is learn to use the Application Setup Wizard packaged with Visual Basic. For example, to package a user control contained in a project file named FirstUserControl.vbp, you merely launch the wizard to create a cabinet file. The cabinet file (.cab) will be the setup file that automatically installs the needed components on users' systems when the Web page is loaded.

Before you start with this chapter's project, you need to create a subdirectory named Distrib within the directory where the project file resides. (Each time you create a new project in a new directory, create a new subdirectory with the name Distrib to hold your distribution files.) The Setup Wizard automatically creates another subdirectory, Support, under Distrib to hold the uncompressed files used by the Setup Wizard to create the distribution files.

First, you'll work through an example of deploying this control on the Internet, and then I'll discuss some issues regarding your choices during the distribution process. To get started, launch the Application Setup Wizard, located in the same group as VB5's Control Creation Edition. The first screen, purely informational, describes the wizard's purpose: to create a setup program file and a dependency file, or just the program's dependency file. A checkbox allows you to turn off this dialog box on subsequent launches of the wizard. Click the Next button to continue.

The wizard now asks for the location of the VB project file you'll be packaging. You can select a template file with the extension .swt to give the browser all the information it needs to package the application or control. This template file is something you create so that you don't have to answer all the questions posed by the wizard on subsequent attempts to package the same application or a similar one.

For this project, click the Browse button and select the FirstUse.vbp file (copy the file from the CD-ROM first). This file contains a very basic user control with four command buttons and a simple combo box. Click the Create Internet Download Setup option. This will reveal an aqua-colored button to the left, inviting you to view the latest information about VB. This is a link to Microsoft's Visual Basic Web site. Simply click the Next button at the bottom of the dialog box to proceed.

The next dialog box permits you to browse to the appropriate directory where the files will be saved by the Application Setup Wizard. Select the Distrib subdirectory you just created, and then click Next.

Now you're at a fork in the road. You must decide whether to let the program connect to the Microsoft Web site to download the runtime components required for the control, or type your own URL and upload the runtime file to your Web site. For this project, leave the default button selected so your users' browsers will download the runtime module from Microsoft. This will help offload some of the work from your server.

The Safety button allows you to identify the status of the control with respect to Internet security and safety of the control when it runs on the client computer. Click the button, select Safe for Initialization and Safe for Scripting, and then click OK. This way, users can use the control without having to lower security in the IE's Options dialog box. Click Next to proceed.

Status messages will appear, telling you what's happening during the creation process. The next dialog box lists the two files required to be included as part of the setup kit: MSVBVM50.DLL, in the C:\Windows\System subdirectory on a Windows 95 system, and Firstuse.OCX, which you created to install your control initially on your own system. The MSVBVM50.DLL file is the Microsoft virtual machine, the runtime module. Figure 10.1 shows the dialog box with the files checked. Here, the OCX was created with the filename FirstUse2.OCX to avoid installing over the FirstUse.OCX file used earlier in the book.

FIGURE 10.1.

You can add files used by your control and check for summary details in this dialog box.

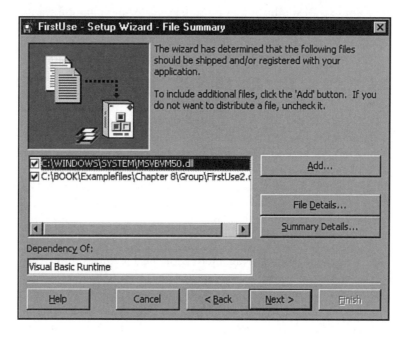

After you click Next in this dialog box, the final dialog box appears, indicating that the Setup Wizard has collected the information needed. Text onscreen also explains that you can create a template file to avoid having to navigate through each Setup Wizard dialog box the next time you use the wizard to package the same program or control. Click Finish to complete the process.

Now, if you navigate to the `Distrib` subdirectory in your project directory, you should see two files: the cabinet (`.cab`) file that will be uploaded to the Web site for automatic installation on the Web visitor's system, and a sample HTML file with the minimum code required to make a reference to the cabinet file. The `.cab` file was generated automatically by the wizard. Notice that the URL `codebase=FirstUse2.CAB` is local in the following example; you should change this to a full-path URL pointing to where the cabinet file will reside on the Web site.

```
<HTML>
<!-- If any of the controls on this page require licensing, you must create a
license package file. Run LPK_TOOL.EXE in the tools directory to create the
required LPK file.
<OBJECT CLASSID="clsid:5220cb21-c88d-11cf-b347-00aa00a28331">
<PARAM NAME="LPKPath" VALUE="LPKfilename.LPK">
</OBJECT>
-->
<OBJECT classid="clsid:BA42BD8E-5E5E-11C5-8AC3-444553540000"
id=FirstUserControl codebase="FirstUse2.CAB#version=1,0,0,0">
</OBJECT>
</HTML>
```

The Cabinet File

Microsoft has used cabinet files for some time for installing software on desktop PCs; Windows 95 installation floppy disks and CD-ROMs include numerous `.cab` files. `.cab` files are compressed and self-extracting (the extraction is actually handled by an information file packaged in the cabinet file). Creating the `.cab` file with the Internet Download Setup Wizard was easy. The ease of creation masks the real complexity of the `.cab` file. A cabinet file resource kit is available from Microsoft's Web site to assist with building distribution sets for new software.

The compression scheme MSZIP, used to create a `.cab` file, is similar to the PKZIP compression algorithm. PKZIP is a popular file-compression program that supports compressing a file or group of files spanning several floppy disks, when necessary. MSZIP is the program that actually compresses the files when using Microsoft's cabinet resources. A Microsoft software utility called Diamond is used to create the `.cab` file and it uses MSZIP. It launches MSZIP and compresses the necessary files to be installed, along with an information file. The Diamond software utility and the instructions for using it as a standalone program are available from Microsoft's Web site.

The Diamond utility creates an information file that directs the behavior of the `.cab` file when it's decompressed. If you've been participating in this exercise, you'll have a new file that's also created by the Application Setup Wizard in your `Support` directory. The so-called Diamond Directive File, named `FirstUse.ddf`, now resides in the directory called `Support` under your `Distrib` file directory. (Remember that `Distrib` resides under your project directory where you stored `FirstUse.vbp`.) Here are the contents of `FirstUse.ddf`:

```
.OPTION EXPLICIT
.Set Cabinet=on
.Set Compress=on
.Set MaxDiskSize=CDROM
```

```
.Set ReservePerCabinetSize=6144
.Set DiskDirectoryTemplate=
.Set CompressionType=MSZIP
.Set CompressionLevel=7
.Set CompressionMemory=21
.Set CabinetNameTemplate="FirstUse.CAB"
"FirstUse.INF"
"FirstUse.ocx"
```

This file contains the instructions for creating the .cab file in the language required by the .cab compression scheme. Its location in the Support directory doesn't mean it's included in the .cab file; the DDF file is used merely to create the compressed .cab file. Note that the lines that define settings begin with a period and that the names of the files to be compressed into the .cab file are enclosed in quotation marks. Understanding this file can be useful if you're manually creating the .cab file. It's read by the Diamond utility to establish what is to be incorporated into the .cab file.

Along with the DDF file in the Support directory is the actual OCX (binary) file to be included in the cabinet and the FirstUse.inf (text) file. The information (.inf) file includes the directions for installing the software on the Web site visitor's computer. It takes into account which operating system is running. Look at the following FirstUse.inf code lines:

```
;INF file for FirstUse.ocx
;DestDir can be 10 for Windows directory, 11 for
➥Windows\System(32) ;directory, or left blank for the Occache directory.
[version]
signature="$CHICAGO$"
AdvancedINF=2.0
[Add.Code]
FIRSTUSE.OCX=FIRSTUSE.OCX
MSVBVM50.DLL=MSVBVM50.DLL
[FIRSTUSE.OCX]
file-win32-x86=thiscab
RegisterServer=yes
clsid={BA42BD8E-5E5E-11C5-8AC3-444553540000}
DestDir=
FileVersion=1,0,0,0
[MSVBVM50.DLL]
hook=MSVBVMb5.cab_Installer
FileVersion=5,0,34,24
[MSVBVMb5.cab_Installer]
file-win32-x86=http://activex.microsoft.com/controls/vb5/MSVBVMb5.cab
InfFile=MSVBVMb5.inf
[Setup Hooks]
hook1=hook1
[hook1]
InfSection=DefaultInstall
[DefaultInstall]
AddReg=AddSafeToScript
[AddSafeToScript]
HKLM,"SOFTWARE\Classes\CLSID\{BA42BD8E-5E5E-11C5-8AC3-4445535400
➥00}\Implemented Categories\{7DD95801-9882-11CF-9FA9-00AA006C42C4}
HKLM,"SOFTWARE\Classes\CLSID\{BA42BD8E-5E5E-11C5-8AC3-4445535400
➥00}\Implemented Categories\{7DD95802-9882-11CF-9FA9-00AA006C42C4}
```

10

ORGANIZING ACTIVEX PROJECTS

> **NOTE**
>
> The Hypertext Transport Protocol Universal Resource Locator for the CAB installer is at `http://activex.microsoft.com` rather than at the usual `microsoft.com` domain. This server is considered reliable, but the only way you can make sure that the installation program can access these files is to place the files on your own Web site and change the URL to point to the `MSVBVM5.cab` file at your site.

If you used dynamic link libraries or referenced additional OCX files by placing specific control objects in your control, the filenames would appear under the `[Add.Code]` heading in the information file. The `[Add.Code]` section passes variables to the cabinet installer regarding the specific sections in the information file that contain additional information regarding how the files should be installed. For instance, the `FIRSTUSE.OCX=FIRSTUSE.OCX` entry directs the installer to locate the heading `[FIRSTUSE.OCX]` in the information file to determine where the file is located and how it should be installed.

> **NOTE**
>
> The filename now appears in all uppercase letters, indicating that the filenames aren't case-sensitive. This, of course, means that no duplicate filenames are allowed—for example, you shouldn't have a file called `FirstUse.ocx` and one called `FIRSTuse.ocx` in the same cabinet file. On UNIX machines, however, and even on Windows machines running UNIX-style server software, two identically named files could exist, with different capitalization of the letters.

The specific section for `FIRSTUSE.OCX` contains a line that indicates the file should be installed from the cabinet file if the client machine uses a Win32 operating system such as Windows 95 or Windows NT *and* uses an x86 processor platform. Any valid URL can be substituted for `thiscab` to pull the file from a remote server where the file resides. Don't use quotation marks around the URL.

The `DestDir=` setting, which was left blank by the Setup Wizard, permits Internet Explorer 3.0 to place the file in the default IE directory `\WINDOWS\OCCACHE`. If the number 10 is placed after the equal sign, as noted in the comments at the top of the file, the file is placed in the `\WINDOWS` subdirectory. If the number 11 is used as the value, the file is placed in the `SYSTEM` subdirectory or, on a Windows NT machine, in the `SYSTEM32` subdirectory.

If you've explored the files that were packaged with VB5's Control Creation Edition, you'll notice a file called `Diantz.exe` in the `\progra~1\VB5CCE\SETUPKIT\KITFIL32` subdirectory on your system. This file is the Diamond Cabinet Maker utility installed with the CCE. To use it, launch the MS-DOS prompt from Windows (or choose Start | Run, and then type **MS-DOS~1.pif**).

In the DOS window, enter **doskey** to start the doskey utility. Now type **cd \progra~1\vb5cce\setupkit\kitfil32**. (If you make a mistake, press the F8 function key, and the last line you typed reappears so you can fix it.) Then press Enter. Now you can type **dir** and see the Setup Wizard executable file (setupwiz.exe) and the diantz.exe file.

Suppose that you wanted to change the location from which the .cab file will pull your user control. First, copy your files from the Support subdirectory (created by the Setup Wizard) into this directory to use the utility manually. Edit the firstuse.ddf file's entry under the [FIRSTUSE.OCX] heading so that it reads file-win32-x86=http://www.*xxx*/firstuse.ocx, where *xxx* represents your domain and any appropriate subdirectory where the file resides at your Web site. For the exercise, you can just use the *xxx*.

Now type **diantz /f firstuse.ddf** to compress the file by using the Diamond directive file firstuse.ddf. As the cabinet file is built, the Diamond Cabinet Maker outputs status lines indicating the progress and other statistics, including the number of files in the cabinet, the combined file size before compression, the finished file size, the compression ratio (expressed as a percentage) achieved, the time to compress the files, and the throughput speed on which the time is based.

If you just type **diantz** on the command line and press Enter, you'll see the syntax definitions and additional switches, including one used to give the .cab file a different target filename. In the full versions of VB5, the diantz.exe file is replaced with a makecab.exe file that works the same way.

Safety

As noted earlier in this chapter, the Setup Wizard provides an option to establish safety parameters for the .cab file. Security and safety are significant issues in a distributed computing environment. They're even more significant in a distributed computing environment as diverse as the Internet.

Safety, in this context, refers only to safe computing for the user who will be automatically installing your control on the client operating system. The Safe for Initialization option should be checked only if the ActiveX control can't have any parameters set that would adversely affect a user's system. *Parameters*, in this context, refers to the parameter values users might assign in an HTML file's <OBJECT> tags where the control is defined. Because you can assign properties that accept these parameter values, you should test the control with a variety of "wrong" possible entries for those values to see whether it causes the browser to hang or return errors that make the control unusable. The control needs to be able to recover from such errors to be considered safe. It might be necessary to use error traps to prevent adverse effects on the client machine.

The Safe for Scripting option should be checked only if the ActiveX control can't be manipulated in a script to adversely affect the host or client machines. For example, if the control allows the script to overwrite a file with the same name on the host computer, the control wouldn't

10

ORGANIZING
ACTIVEX PROJECTS

be considered safe for scripting in some instances. For example, if you allow users to determine the filename, in theory the filename they select in a script could be set to overwrite an important system-related file on the client machine. Most system files are protected by the `System` attribute so they can't be overwritten, but suppose that an executable file name were selected. The damage could be significant and force users to reinstall the executable file.

If disk access or Windows API calls are included in the control, the testing of the control should be more intense, and special testing for allowed filename extensions might be important to make the control safe for use on the client system. Destructive computer users are sometimes very creative and will certainly continue to generate bad publicity in connection with the Internet. ActiveX controls in general are very safe, but creativity can overcome the safety precautions and pose serious threats to user systems and otherwise secure services provided on the Web.

Another way that destructive users sometimes attack systems is to cause the systems to overwork themselves. If your ActiveX control will receive input and write to disk, make sure that you have a test that will trigger an error message and error trap if the file size (the input variable's string length) isn't beyond a certain reasonable size. Also make sure that your control doesn't accommodate any endless loops or loop counts that users can set. Because you have the code for the control and users can't see it, you sometimes might have a false sense of security regarding the control's use. Just remember to keep in mind what users can and can't do, using the control's methods and parameters.

If your control will be distributed widely, consider hiring consultants who specialize in resolving Web site security and safety issues. Those consultants, if they possess sufficient scripting skills and understand ActiveX controls, can test your control for flaws that they might have encountered in their line of work. Microsoft's marketing program for ActiveX controls can also be useful. It might be appropriate to visit the ActiveX Web site and e-mail the people familiar with marketing the controls. They might offer pointers regarding safety and other issues you should consider before commercially distributing controls with global appeal.

Using Naming Conventions

Microsoft has suggested the use of naming conventions to assist developers with understanding and remembering the purpose of names used in the code and to help with understanding variable scope. Naming conventions are also helpful for keeping code flexible enough that future programmers can reuse the code without starting from scratch. Because such conventions are now listed in help files packaged with Visual Basic 5.0, using them should be considered somewhat universal. Trying to improve on the conventions might be seen by millions of other programmers as a departure from acceptable practices.

Some developers employed by corporations might even be evaluated to some degree regarding whether they're familiar with and use naming conventions. On large projects where more than one developer may be using a particular section of code, strict conformance to the naming convention might be a requirement. Using the naming conventions assists developers because all members of a particular group will be listed next to each other in Visual Basic's Properties window. This can make authoring more efficient.

The naming conventions are very easy to learn, especially for variables. Variable prefixes consist of three letters added to the beginning of your name for an item; these three letters indicate the variable's data type.

Object Naming Conventions

The prefix for objects is generally a three-letter condensation of the object's name. Table 10.1 lists the syntax for these prefixes and an example of each. Table 10.1's first entry, the prefix `cmd` for a command button, is added to the programmer's name for the command, `OpenTable`.

Table 10.1. Naming conventions for objects.

Prefix	Object Type	Sample Name Assignment
cmd	Command button	cmdOpenTable
pnl	3D panel	pnlFlightCtrls
ani	Animated button	aniPlayCtrls
chk	Checkbox	chkOn
cbo	Combo box	cboAllItems
cbo	Drop-down list box	cboOldItems
dlg	Common dialog	dlgSavAsFile
com	Communications	comNewFax
ctr	Control (type unknown)	ctrThisSub
dat	Data control	datPilots
dbcbo	Data-bound combo box	dbcboAirports
dbgrd	Data-bound grid	dbgrdRunwayOpts
dblst	Data-bound list box	dblstDestination
dir	Directory list box	dirScenarios
drv	Drive list box	drvSaveTo
fil	File list box	filSaveFrom
frm	Form	frmCheckList
fra	Frame	fraLeftView
gau	Gauge	gauFuelStatus
gra	Graph	graRadarSketch
grd	Grid	grdLandingOpts

continues

10

ORGANIZING
ACTIVEX PROJECTS

Table 10.1. continued

Prefix	Object Type	Sample Name Assignment
hsb	Horizontal scrollbar	hsbRadioVol
img	Image	imgRadarIcon
key	Key status	keyCaps
lbl	Label	lblAltimeter
lin	Line	linHDivider
lst	List box	lstWeapons
mpm	MAPI message	mpmRadarWarning
mps	MAPI session	mpsNextSession
mci	MCI movie	mciGetaMedal
mdi	MDI child form	mdiRearView
mnu	Menu	mnuCloseFile
msg	MS flex grid	msgFlexOctane
mst	MS tab	mstTabFour
ole	OLE object	oleMacrosheet
out	Outline	outAirTrafficSite
bed	Pen BEdit	bedLietName
hed	Pen HEdit	hedOfficrSig
ink	Pen ink	inkMountain
pic	Picture	picClouds
clp	Picture clip	clpBoatScene
rpt	Report	rptMissionStats
shp	Shape	shpRadarCircle
spn	Spin button	spnDates
txt	Text box	txtLastName
tmr	Timer	tmrDelay
upd	UpDown	updNameBuddy
vsb	Vertical scrollbar	vsbVerticalScroll
sld	Slider	sldBassSlide
ils	Image list	ilsAirportScenes
tre	Tree view	trePlaneHangars
tlb	Toolbar	tlbMaintUtils
tab	Tab strip	tabPlaneDescriptions

Prefix	Object Type	Sample Name Assignment
sta	Status bar	staStatusMarquee
lvw	List view	lvwWeatherConditions
prg	Progress bar	prgRadarClosing
rtf	Rich text box	rtfMissionReport

Variable Naming Conventions

The three- and four-letter prefixes for variables are similar to the three-letter conventions for objects, except that the prefix for a variable is used to indicate data type and scope. If the scope of a variable being used in the program is local (declared in a private sub or function), no special prefix is required and just the three-letter prefix is used. Most variables will be of this type in a well-written application.

If a variable's scope is module level—that is, if the variable is available as a private variable in the declarations section of a form (.frm) or a code module (.bas)—the prefix m is used, followed by the three-letter prefix, followed by the programmer's name for the variable. For example, if you have an integer variable that you want to call CookiesCount and it has module-level scope, the variable assignment would be mintCookiesCount As Integer. The first letter, m, refers to scope, the int refers to integer, and CookiesCount refers to the specific variable to hold the data.

If your program requires you to share a variable's data among forms and you have no efficient method for passing the variable data from form to form, you may need a variable of global scope. Variables of this type are generally used as a last resort because global scope variables tie up resources during runtime by allocating memory for the variable. Using a lot of public variables also tends to create a very complex set of virtual machine states.

Think of your application's variables as green LEDs. Every global variable requires the LED to stay on during the entire duration of the program. The module-level variable LEDs stay on during use of the form or module. The procedure-level variables flash on briefly as the procedure is run, and then blink back off. The idea is to keep as few LEDs lit as possible during your program's execution. You can create a simple program that makes icons representing LEDs appear and disappear as though they were being turned on and off as your program executes.

Using global variables also makes it more difficult to reuse code segments. The code segment has less value if it uses many global variables. Using a lot of global variables can weaken a program's stability and make it more prone to programming errors.

If the scope of your variable is global, the variable prefix to indicate that the scope is global is g. If the CountCookies data needs to be global in scope, for example, the variable assignment would be gintCountCookies As Integer, which normally would be found in the declarations section of a code module (.bas). If you use a public function or sub, all variables used in the procedure are also global in scope. It's a good idea to group all global variables in the same declarations section of a single module for various reasons.

Table 10.2 lists naming convention prefixes to be used with the scope prefix when assigning names to variables in a program written in Visual Basic.

Table 10.2 Naming conventions for variables.

Prefix	Variable Data Type	Sample Name
bln	Boolean	blnClosed
byt	Byte	bytBmpLocations
col	Collection Object	colOldTires
cur	Currency	curProfit
dtm	Date-Time	dtmTransaction
dbl	Double	dblRadius
err	Error	errEntryError
int	Integer	intNumofPlanes
lng	Long	lngScore
obj	Object	objNewImage
sng	Single	sngMedianVal
str	String	strZipCode
udt	User-Defined Type	udtWideReceiver
vnt	Variant	vntTextBoxVal

If you use more than two or three user-defined types in a program, it's a generally accepted practice to add the letter u to a programmer-defined prefix at the beginning of the object's name. For example, if you have six user-defined types for a client application and all of them have the same data in common (such as a basketball player's first name), you could give each variable the prefix ubal to indicate that it's a user-defined variable belonging to a logical group of user-defined variables.

Constant and Procedure Naming Conventions

The scope and data types of constants don't require a three- or four-letter prefix, but it's help-ful to use a one-letter prefix where appropriate to indicate scope and type. For example, a con-stant used as an integer with global scope would start with the prefix gi; a similar constant with procedure-level scope would require just the i for the prefix.

Constants and procedures should be mixed-case descriptions long enough to symbolize their use. If you abbreviate the descriptions, use the same abbreviation each time to reduce confusion. For example, `strTextName` shouldn't appear in the same program with `strTxtLastNam`. The second variable should be `strTextLastName`. Try to keep the name length to less than 32 characters for easy readability. This generally isn't very difficult.

Declaring All Variables

Declaring all variables is generally considered the professional way to build an application. In VB, you can save programming time by declaring all variables because it reduces the number of execution errors caused by typographical errors. It also makes any such errors easier to locate. For example, if you get an error that indicates the variable isn't found, you can bet that the variable where the execution halts contains a typographical error. You'll know this if you've developed the habit of declaring each variable as it's introduced.

On the Editor tab of the Options dialog box, select Require Variable Declaration to assign a declaration that reads `Option Explicit` to all your applications. This statement requires that you declare all the variables in your Visual Basic program. You also can enter the `Option Explicit` statement manually under the declarations section of your startup module.

Structured Coding Conventions

In addition to the standardization of the naming conventions, there are conventions for improving the code so that you can reuse and easily maintain it. This is referred to as *structured coding conventions*, which dictate that each procedure or function be preceded by a comment line. *Comment lines* aren't visible to the program execution; they exist merely to give programmers hints as to the purpose of the elements of the code. Each comment line begins with an apostrophe.

Listing 10.1 shows a sample overview comment for a search-and-replace subroutine. Here, the names of the variables have been changed to accommodate variable naming conventions.

Listing 10.1. A functional overview comment, demonstrating the use of structured coding conventions.

```
'********************************************************
' Purpose:  Acquires string input to search for all occurrences of a
'           specified string, acquires input for a replacement string and
'           calls function Replacer to perform the replacement
' Inputs:   strSearchString$: the string to be located.
'           strReplaceString$: the string to replace all occurrences
' Returns:  The integer value of replacements made, returned by Replacer,
'           is displayed in message box
'           Message box with warning and exit sub if null value
'           is encountered at the beginning of input for strSearchString
'********************************************************
Private Sub Replaceit_Click(Index As Integer)
 Dim strSearchString$, strReplaceString$
 strSearchString$ = InputBox("Enter string to be replaced (not spaces)")
```

continues

Listing 10.1. continued

```
MsgBox "Text to find is " & strSearchString
If strSearchString$ = "" Then     ' Tests for Null Value
    MsgBox "Sorry, can't replace a null value or spaces.", vbCritical,_
    "Replacer Error"
Exit Sub
strReplaceString = InputBox("Enter replacement string")
MsgBox "Text to replace with is " & strReplaceString
MsgBox Replacer(strSearchString, strReplaceString) & " replacements_
were made"
End Sub
```

The coding conventions require that the comments include headings for five categories:

- *Purpose.* Describe the generic purpose of the procedure or function, with no details regarding how it's implemented.

- *Assumptions.* List what wouldn't be obvious to other programmers. For example, list external variables, controls, an open file, and so on.

- *Inputs.* List each argument on a separate line and indicate the name of the input variable and the purpose. Tell what the input is being used for.

- *Effects.* Document what the procedure does to any external variable, control, or file. (Don't bother if the effect is obvious.)

- *Returns.* List any return values (or display output) that the code generates.

The coding conventions also require specific spacing for the lines of code, including the comments, with tabs and spaces. Use one space for the overview comment and one tab for the highest-level code lines, two tabs for the next level, and four tabs for code lines nested beyond that. This simply makes it easier for other programmers to follow the logic of the code because it establishes visual blocks.

Use an underscore character (_) to break up long strings of continuous code onto separate lines. This is very helpful for long strings that would be difficult to read on a VGA monitor. The file frmUnderScor.frm, shown in Listing 10.2, shows underscores being used. Paste the code into a form's OnLoad event to view the results, or see Figure 10.2 for onscreen results. A message box will appear with one long string of text at runtime.

Listing 10.2. Using underscores to break one line of code onto more than one line.

```
Private Sub Form_Load()
Dim strMsg As String
strMsg = "The line of text you will see in the" _
& " message box will not display the underscores" _
& " and will wrap normally in the message box." _
& " The use of the underscores in this example" _
& " simply makes it easier for the Visual Basic Developer" _
& " to read and debug the code."
MsgBox strMsg
End Sub
```

FIGURE 10.2.

The screen results of the frmUnderScore.frm *script show what happens when you use underscores to shorten long code lines.*

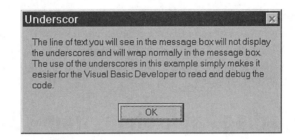

Dressing Up Your Application

If your file uses a lot of forms and takes a bit of time to load when it's first launched, you can make the application look more professional by creating what's sometimes referred to as a splash screen (not to be confused with Flash animations, which were called Splash movies when the software was formerly known as FutureSplash Animator). The *splash screen* is simply a separate form that loads when an application starts and displays simple graphics with information about the application (name, version, and purpose are typically illustrated). When you launch VB5, notice that Microsoft's splash screen displays information about Visual Basic while the various forms load in the background.

Here's the simple way to create a splash screen: Create a form called frmMySplash and set the StartupPosition property to 2 - Center Screen. You can select a bitmap for the Picture property or just add a text box with the text Picture Appears Here. Then add labels with the information about your program on this form. Size the form so that it doesn't cover the whole screen. Leave the BorderStyle property set to 1 - Fixed Single, or the code won't work. Change the property setting for ControlBox to False to make the bar at the top disappear.

Rather than have a startup form, you need to create a separate subroutine in a separate module. Choose Project | Add Module. The code window automatically opens. Call the subroutine Private Sub Main(). Assuming that you have an MDI parent form called MDIForm1, the first functioning form in your program is a child form called frmEnter, and your splash screen with the bitmap and information about your program is called frmMySplash, your code would look like this:

```
Private Sub Main()
' Load the splash screen form
frmMySplash.Show
MsgBox "Your splash screen should be centered here"
' Place your "on-load" loading code here so it_
' is achieved in the background while the splash screen has focus.
' Now load the child form frmEnter
frmEnter.Show
MsgBox "Loading frmEnter"
' Now unload the splash screen form
Unload frmMySplash
End Sub
```

Now in the Project Explorer, right-click the icon for your project and choose the option Project1 Properties. At the right, you'll see a drop-down box for the startup object. Click the down arrow and select Sub Main. This code will execute first when your program begins to load. Choose Start | Run to view how the forms load onscreen. Later, remove the msgbox entries and choose Start | Run to see how the code will manipulate the appearance of your application at runtime.

Distributing Applications from VBA

Although the bulk of this chapter to this point has focused on Visual Basic's Control Creation Edition, I can't ignore the diversity of applications that you can create in the Visual Basic Applications Edition. VBA has three primary functions that yield different styles of applications:

■ VBA 5.0 is an ActiveX (OLE) control container. The ActiveX controls are placed in VBA 5.0 forms in this scenario.

■ VBA 5.0 is an automation controller. Objects provided by the host (server) application, objects exposed by ActiveX controls, and objects exposed by other applications running on the client system can be accessed by VBA 5.0.

■ VBA 5.0 is an Automation server. You can use the VBA 5.0 object models for creating forms and a development environment. The bulk of this work will be done by using special software packages provided by Microsoft and VBA 5.0 licensees. For example, Microsoft Office 97 has a Developer's Edition that facilitates custom-designing applications that use the basic functionality of Microsoft Word, Access, PowerPoint, and Excel.

In general, you'll simply choose File | Make *xxx*.exe, where *xxx* is the name of your project to compile your code into an executable. To select options for how your program is optimized and compiled, right-click the project icon and select Project*xxx* properties, where *xxx* is the name for your project. Click the Compile tab, and then check the appropriate check boxes and option buttons to set your compiler preferences. Click OK. Use the Application Setup Wizard to make a distribution setup file.

VBA's Enterprise and Professional Editions contain a native code compiler, but the default method of compiling programs into executable programs uses interpreters (p-code). Using the interpreter option is generally required for all OCX-style controls that will be deployed on the Internet because the OCX must be interpreted by the particular client platform that will install the OCX and use its code.

For executables designed to run on the Windows platform (generally, Windows 95 and Windows NT), the native compiler can yield some reasonable improvements in speed, especially if lengthy algorithms are required. The binary compiled code executes faster when this number-crunching work is a significant part of a program. Testing by Microsoft has suggested that the bulk of most programs in use today don't require this kind of number crunching, so don't expect miracle gains in the performance of an application due to use of the native code compiler.

You might be able to recall that native code is what we started with when we began using computers. We used binary data for everything. If you take into account how the computing platforms have changed since the days of exclusive use of binary compiled machine language, you'll understand that these gains are really minimal for most programs.

It's with regret that I feel compelled to dispel the myth surrounding the market appeal of a native code compiler. Despite the hype, Microsoft estimates that typically only 5 percent of an application's time to execute is actually spent executing p-code. Most of the time is spent loading DLLs and forms. This means that even if the native compiler executed instantaneously, the highest performance gain for a typical program would be less than 5 percent. What this really means is that unless you're building a program such as a computer-aided drafting (CAD) application, a fractal generation program, or a function that transfers bits and bytes and heavily depends on number crunching and loops, don't expect more than a 3 percent to 4 percent performance gain.

This might be a shock to those who have read the Web claims about 5,000 percent performance gains that could be realized by using VB5 and a native code compiler. I believe it's unlikely that any *major* VB applications could realize anything exceeding a 100 percent performance gain unless the program is purely mathematical bits-and-bytes manipulation. That includes VB4 programs converted to VB5 and compiled with the native compiler.

Microsoft has indicated that the native code compiler still requires the distribution of the VB5 runtime dynamic link library. Loading this library alone may be a source of irritation to those who misunderstood the meaning of a native code compiler. Just because the code is compiled in the processor's native language doesn't mean the code can be implemented without the runtime library. The library file MSVBVM50.DLL, the virtual machine library used to run the programs, is still required for all Visual Basic projects.

Native commands understood by the processor chip can be included in the compiled application. These low-level instructions are in the chip's native machine language if you select the Compile to Native Code option. This might speed up loops and calls to services from the virtual machine DLL, but the impact may be less than dramatic. To set this option, right-click the Project1 icon in the Project Explorer and select Project1 Properties. Click the Compile tab and then the appropriate option button. Click OK.

Services provided by the virtual machine DLL file include startup and shutdown tasks, presentation of intrinsic controls, handling the functionality of forms, and initiating the execution of runtime functions.

Summary

This chapter showed how to organize an ActiveX project by using a structured approach to avoid common potential obstacles to smooth program development. You learned how to distribute your ActiveX control on the Internet by using a cabinet file. You also studied the

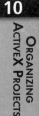

10

ORGANIZING
ACTIVEX PROJECTS

naming conventions that will help you and others in understanding your code, especially when reusing the work or debugging the program.

Finally, this chapter evaluated the final touches an application may require and explored some basic distribution issues so that your Visual Basic application can be deployed efficiently to users.

III

PART

Database Tools and Techniques

Creating Forms With the Data Form Wizard

by Mike McMillan

IN THIS CHAPTER

CHAPTER

11

One of the most time-consuming tasks in Visual Basic programming is designing forms. You need to consider so many things—from how to place controls on the form to programming the many possible events—that a project with several forms can overwhelm you. Visual Basic 5 provides the Data Form Wizard to automate many of the more routine tasks involved in designing a form that's bound to a database.

An Overview of the Data Form Wizard

The Data Form Wizard is used to generate Visual Basic forms that are made up of bound controls and the procedures necessary to work with data coming from database tables or queries that pull data from those database tables. The Data Form Wizard can design three different form types:

- A *single-record form*, based on a single database table or a query on a single database table
- A *grid (datasheet) form*, based on multiple selections from a single database table or query
- A *master/detail form*, based on a complex query joining two or more tables in a one-to-many data relationship

A single-record form displays on a form simply those fields you specify to the wizard, one record per screen. The grid form displays a group of data on the form at the same time in a spreadsheet view with the DBGrid control. The master/detail form displays the master record source in a single record format and the detail record source in a spreadsheet view, again with the DBGrid control.

The Data Form Wizard provides users with many other options to choose from as it designs the form. These options include

- Database type
- Database name
- Column to sort by
- Controls to appear on the form
- Name of the form

As you use the Data Form Wizard to create a form, you'll see just how flexible and time-saving this wizard can be in the initial prototyping of a Visual Basic application.

Installing the Data Form Wizard

The Data Form Wizard comes with Visual Basic 5 as one of the add-in options available from the Add-In Manager. This means that it has to be installed to be used. The good news is that installing the Data Form Wizard involves nothing more than checking it off in the options box in the Add-In Manager.

To install the Data Form Wizard, choose Add-Ins from the Visual Basic menu, and then select Add-In Manager. Figure 11.1 shows the Add-In Manager dialog box listing the available add-ins. To install the Data Form Wizard, check the box beside it, and then click OK to add the Data Form Wizard to the Add-Ins menu. Now when you want to use the Data Form Wizard, you can select it directly from that menu (see Figure 11.2).

FIGURE 11.1.
Selecting the Data Form Wizard add-in.

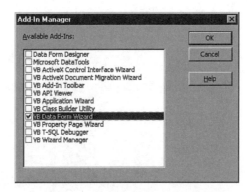

FIGURE 11.2.
The Data Form Wizard is added to the Add-Ins menu.

> **NOTE**
>
> If you want to uninstall the Data Form Wizard later on, just go through the same procedure, except remove the check mark for the wizard in the Available Add-Ins list and click OK.

Creating a Single-Record Form With the Data Form Wizard

The first type of form you can create with the Data Form Wizard is the *single-record form*. For many applications, such as a program to browse a database's contents, this type of form will be exactly what you need. As you'll see, selecting this form lets you place some or all of the fields from the database table you select on one form so that they can be viewed at the same time. You'll also be able to control what actions users can perform on the form, such as adding records to the database table, deleting records from the table, and so on. You'll also have control over where the fields and controls will be placed on the form.

First, select the Data Form Wizard from the Add-Ins menu. (If you can't find the wizard on the menu, return to the preceding section and follow the procedure to install it.)

The Data Form Wizard – Introduction Dialog Box

When you launch the Data Form Wizard, you'll first see the wizard's Introduction dialog box (see Figure 11.3).

FIGURE 11.3.

The Introduction dialog box of the Data Form Wizard.

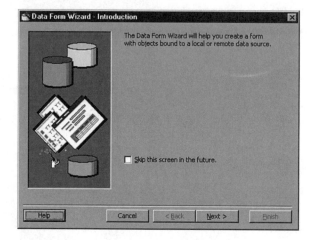

This dialog box merely points out that this wizard is used to create a form with controls that are bound to a local or remote database. There's also a checkbox that, when selected, prevents this Introduction dialog box from being displayed in subsequent sessions with the Data Form Wizard. At the bottom of the dialog box are five command buttons:

- *Help.* Opens the Help window for the Introduction step. Pressing F1 also displays the Help window.

- *Cancel.* Cancels all work done in this session and closes the Data Form Wizard.

- *Back.* Moves you back one dialog box. This button isn't available in this dialog box because it's the first step in the Data Form Wizard. In future dialog boxes, you can go back.

- *Next.* Moves to the next dialog box in the wizard.

- *Finish.* Accepts default selections for all remaining unchosen options and builds the data form. This button isn't available if you haven't made enough choices to build an appropriate data form.

The Data Form Wizard – Database Type Dialog Box

To continue with the Data Form Wizard, click the Next button. The Data Form Wizard – Database Type dialog box appears (see Figure 11.4).

FIGURE 11.4.
*The Data Form
Wizard – Database
Type dialog box,
showing available
database types.*

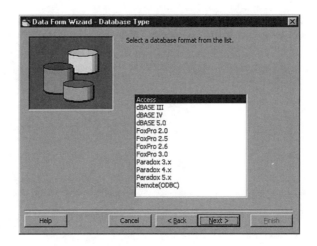

This dialog box lists five available database types that you can select from the list box:

- *Microsoft Access.* Any version of the Jet (.mdb) engine
- *dBASE.* dBASE III, dBASE IV, or dBASE 5.0
- *Microsoft FoxPro.* FoxPro versions 2.0, 2.5, 2.6, or 3.0
- *Borland Paradox.* Paradox versions 3.*x*, 4.*x*, or 5.*x*
- *Remote (ODBC).* Any ODBC-compliant database driver (for example, Microsoft SQL Server, Oracle, or Sybase)

Select the database type you want by highlighting it in the list box and clicking the Next button.

The Data Form Wizard – Database Dialog Box

If you don't select an ODBC database, the next dialog box you'll see is Data Form Wizard – Database. In this dialog box, you enter the database name you're connecting to and whether your record source will come from the tables associated with the database (or, if you're connecting to Microsoft Access, queries associated with the database).

To select a database, enter the full path to the database you're wanting to connect to in the text box. If you aren't sure of the full path, you can use the Browse button to find the database. If the database is an Access database, you can select tables and queries in the Record Sources group box; otherwise, you can select only tables. Figure 11.5 shows the full path to the `Biblio` database from Visual Basic 5, which is the database being used in this chapter.

After you enter the full path to the database and select the appropriate record sources, click Next to move to the next step.

FIGURE 11.5.
*The Database dialog
box after a database is
selected.*

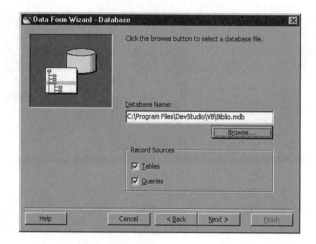

The Data Form Wizard – Form Dialog Box

The Data Form Wizard – Form dialog box allows you to select which layout type to use on the form:

- Single record
- Grid (datasheet)
- Master/detail

Figure 11.6 shows the Data Form Wizard – Form dialog box with the Single record form type selected. Notice also that in the upper-left portion of the dialog box is a representation of what a Single record form layout looks like. Figure 11.7 shows the Form dialog box with the Grid form type selected; Figure 11.8 shows the Form dialog box with the Master/Detail form type selected.

FIGURE 11.6.
*The Form dialog box
with a Single record
layout selected.*

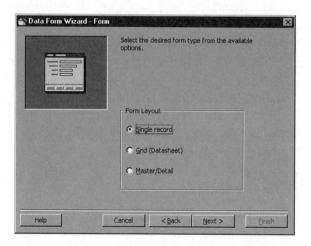

FIGURE 11.7.
*The Form dialog box
with Grid layout
selected.*

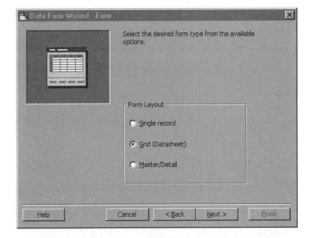

FIGURE 11.8.
*The Form dialog box
with Master/Detail
selected.*

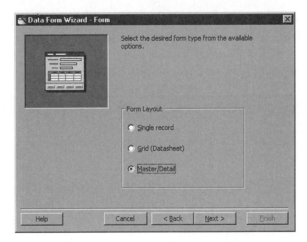

From this dialog box you can click Finish if you want to accept the defaults for the other dialog boxes. If you select Finish at this point, however, you won't be able to select the Record Source for your form, the controls that are placed onscreen, or the name the program gives to the form. So, to continue to the next dialog box, click Next.

The Data Form Wizard – Record Source Dialog Box

The Data Form Wizard – Record Source dialog box lets you select the record source for the data that will appear on the form and the fields that will be placed on the form (see Figure 11.9).

First, select the record source that will provide data to your form from the Record Source combo box. If the database is an Access database, the available tables and queries will appear in the combo box; otherwise, only table names will appear. You make a selection by clicking the highlighted table or query you want.

FIGURE 11.9.
*The Record Source
dialog box.*

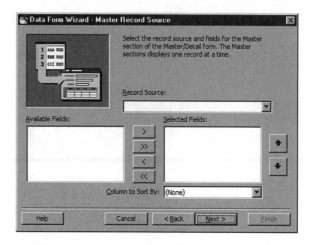

After a record source is selected, the available fields appear in the Available Fields list box. To select a field to add to the form, highlight it in the list box and click the > button to move it to the Selected Fields list box. Continue doing this until you have all the fields you want on the form listed in the Selected Fields list box.

> **TIP**
>
> To select all the fields at one time, click the >> button.

While selecting fields, or after you select them all, you can change the order in which the fields will appear on the form by highlighting a field in the Selected Fields box and clicking the up- or down-arrow button. Finally, if you want the data to be displayed in sorted order, select a field to sort on in the Column to Sort By combo box. This sort is a descending-order sort.

The Record Source dialog box shown in Figure 11.10 is configured with the Titles table from the `Biblio` database as the record source, and the selected fields are Title, ISBN, Description, Subject, and Comments. The Title field has been selected as the sort field.

Again, you can click the Finish button at this point to accept the defaults for the rest of the dialog boxes and complete the Data Form Wizard process. However, the next dialog box lets you decide which controls to place on the form, so click the Next button.

The Data Form Wizard – Control Selection Dialog Box

The Control Selection dialog box presents the different control buttons that you can place on the form. As shown in Figure 11.11, all control buttons are initially selected by default.

FIGURE 11.10.

The Record Source dialog box, completely configured.

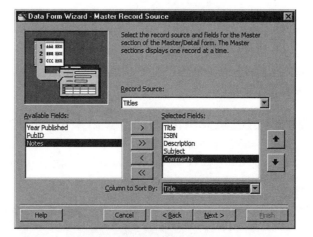

FIGURE 11.11.

The initial Control Selection dialog box.

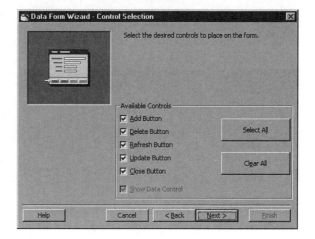

You can choose the following buttons from this dialog box:

- *Add.* Places an Add button on the form to allow adding new records to the database.
- *Delete.* Places a Delete button on the form to allow deleting records from the database.
- *Refresh.* Places a Refresh button on the form to refresh the displayed data from a database.
- *Update.* Places an Update button on the form to update a current record in the database.
- *Close.* Places a Close button on the form to close the form.
- *Show Data Control.* Makes the data control visible on the form (default).

You can choose any combination of controls. If you don't want any controls, click Clear All. If you change your mind and want all the controls, click Select All.

You can click Finish at this step and accept the defaults for the final dialog box. However, if you want to change the name of the form or save your selections for future uses of the Data Form Wizard, click Next to continue.

The Data Form Wizard – Finished! Dialog Box

The last step in the Data Form Wizard is the Finished! dialog box. As Figure 11.12 shows, a default title made from the table chosen earlier is displayed in the text box. If you don't like the default name, type over it.

FIGURE 11.12.

The Finished! dialog box, with the default form name displayed.

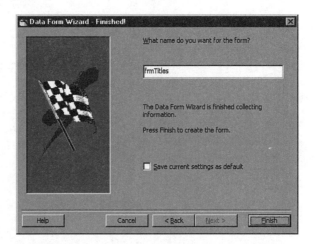

Below the text box is the Save Current Settings as Default checkbox, which you can select if you want to use the selections you made in this session of the Data Form Wizard in future sessions. For example, if you think you'll always choose a Grid style layout for your forms and you made that selection this time, select this checkbox to ensure that the wizard selects the Grid layout style as the default. If you don't select this checkbox, the wizard will display the system defaults as you go through the dialog boxes.

Finally, click the Finish button. (Notice that the Next button is now disabled because no more steps are left to create a data form.) A confirmation box appears to tell you that your form has been added to the current project (see Figure 11.13). If you don't want to see this confirmation box in future sessions with the Data Form Wizard, click the checkbox titled Don't Show This Dialog in the Future. Click OK to display your data form (see Figure 11.14).

At this point, the form is ready to be run. Of course, if you don't like the way the controls were placed on the form by the Data Form Wizard, you can change them around any way you like. You can change the properties of the controls to change the font size, the alignment of the

Creating Forms With the Data Form Wizard

CHAPTER 11

251

11

CREATING FORMS
WITH THE DATA
FORM WIZARD

control, and so on. However, if you change any of the properties that specify how the control is bound to the data control and the database, you might change what data, if any, is displayed in the control. So be careful when changing control properties!

FIGURE 11.13.
The Data Form Created confirmation box.

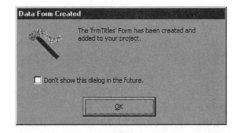

FIGURE 11.14.
The finished data form.

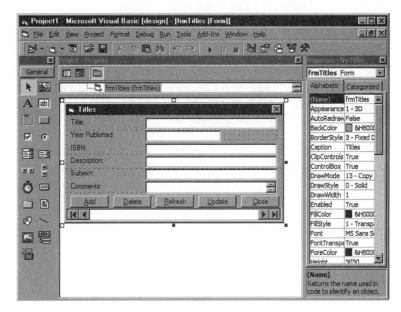

If you like the way everything is placed on the form, you can run the form to see how it works. Figure 11.15 shows the single-record form I created, displaying data from the Biblio database.

TIP

Make sure that the form created with the Data Form Wizard is the startup form; otherwise, add code to the startup form to make sure that it displays the new data form.

FIGURE 11.15.

A single-record form created with the Data Form Wizard.

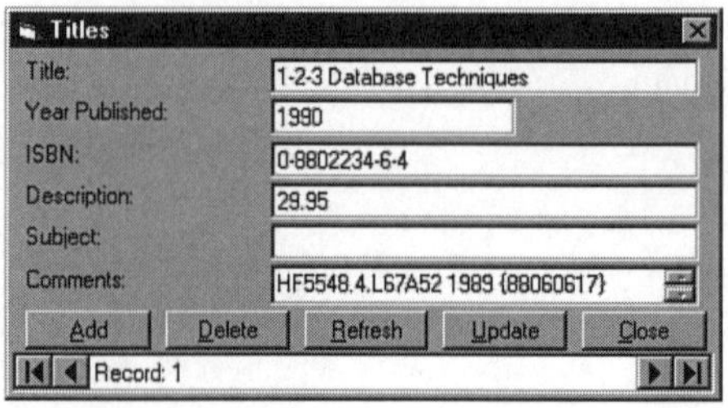

All the controls on the form are ones I chose in the Data Form Wizard except one, the data control, which is the bottom control on the form. The wizard adds this control automatically because Visual Basic requires it to be on the form before any bound controls can be placed on the form.

> **NOTE**
>
> In the Data Form Wizard – Control Selection dialog box, the data control is disabled because it can't be removed from the form if the controls placed on the form are to be bound to the database.

If you're not familiar with the data control, you should know that it performs two main functions on the data form. First, through some of its properties (discussed in Chapter 12, "Binding Controls to Your Database"), the data control connects the database to the tables or queries used as the record source.

The control's second function is to provide some basic navigational tools for moving around the database. On either side of the data control are a pair of buttons. Clicking the right-arrow button moves the display one record forward into the database table. Clicking the left-arrow button moves the display one record backward in the database table. The right arrow/bar button moves the display to the last record in the database table; the left arrow/bar button moves the display to the first record in the database table.

Creating a Grid Data Form

A second form type that you can create with the Data Form Wizard is the grid (datasheet) form. A *grid form* displays data from a database table in a spreadsheet-type layout by using the DBGrid control.

To create a grid data form, click the Grid radio button in the Data Form Wizard – Form dialog box. (The other dialog boxes and choices are the same as for the single-record form.) When you click the Finish button in the Finished! dialog box, the Data Form Wizard generates a grid form like the one in Figure 11.16.

Creating Forms With the Data Form Wizard

CHAPTER 11

253

11

CREATING FORMS
WITH THE DATA
FORM WIZARD

FIGURE 11.16.

A grid form generated by the Data Form Wizard.

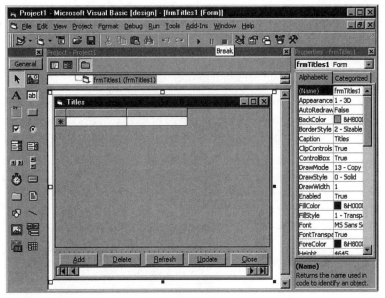

The grid form has the same control buttons that I placed on the single-record form, and the data control is also located at the bottom of the form. Instead of the text boxes and label controls I had on the single-record form, however, the grid form has an empty DBGrid control. To get a better view of how the data will be presented on this form, I need to run the program, which results in the form shown in Figure 11.17.

FIGURE 11.17.

The grid form, presenting data from the Biblio *database.*

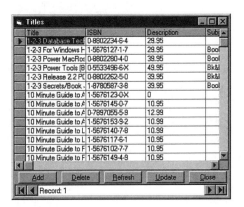

To make more of the form's columns visible, you can resize the form by dragging its corners or sides. To make more of the rows visible, drag the top or the bottom of the form.

Just like with the single-record form, you can add, delete, and update data on the table by using the command buttons at the bottom of the form. You can navigate through the table by using the arrow buttons on the data control.

Creating a Master/Detail Data Form

The third form type available with the Data Form Wizard is the *master/detail form*. This form allows you to create a form based on the data from more than one table, usually by joining two tables based on a field common to both tables.

For an example from the `Biblio` database, I want to create a form that lists all book titles published by a particular publisher. This type of form requires the creation of a master/detail form, with the Publisher table providing the master data and the Titles table providing the detail data.

To create the form, I click the Master/Detail radio button in the Data Form Wizard – Form dialog box and then click the Next button. Figure 11.18 shows the Data Form Wizard – Master Record Source dialog box.

FIGURE 11.18.

The Master Record Source dialog box.

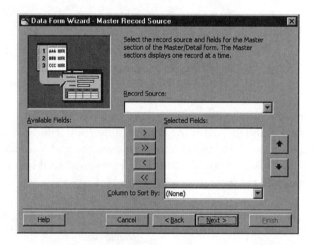

This dialog box asks which record source you want to use as the master record for the form. This data will display one record at a time on the form. For the Titles by Publisher example, I want the master record source to be the Publishers table.

Choosing Publishers in the Record Source combo box brings up a listing of fields from the Publishers table in the Available Fields list box. I can select as many of these fields as I need to display and add them to the Selected Fields list. Figure 11.19 shows the choices I made for this example.

One field in the Selected Fields list deserves special attention. Because I am linking book titles in the Titles table to publishers in the Publishers table, I need to create a link between the two tables. Often, a common field, called a *key field*, is used to create this link. For the Titles and Publishers tables, the key field is PubID, which is present in both tables. Although this field doesn't have to be one of the Selected Fields to appear on the form, it has been selected to appear in this example to illustrate its importance in providing a link between the two tables.

FIGURE 11.19.

*Making selections for
the master record
source.*

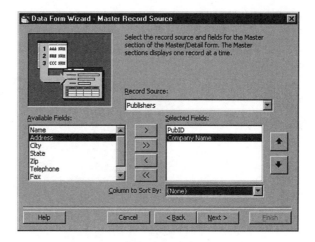

After all selections are made for the Master Record Source, click the Next button to move to
the next step: selecting a Detail record source. The Detail Record Source dialog box looks similar
to the Master Record Source dialog box. The table that will provide detail data for this master/
detail form is the Titles table. As with the Master Record Source dialog box, you select the
fields you want displayed in the detail section of the form from the available fields in the Titles
table. For this example, I want to see the book titles sorted in alphabetical order, so I select the
Title field in the Column to Sort By combo box. Figure 11.20 shows the final selections for
the Detail Record Source dialog box.

FIGURE 11.20.

*Making selections for
the Detail Record
Source dialog box.*

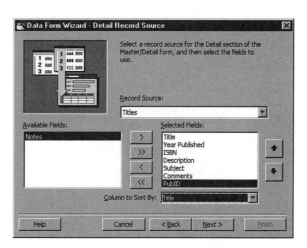

Click the Next button to move to the next step. Now you see a dialog box you haven't seen
before: the Data Form Wizard – Record Source Relation dialog box, which asks you to select
a field from both the master record source and the detail record source that links the two record

sources (the Titles and Publishers tables). As I've discussed, for this example the PubID field is the linking, or key, field. So I highlight the field in each list box (see Figure 11.21), and then click Next to move to the next step.

FIGURE 11.21.

Selecting the key field in the Record Source Relation dialog box.

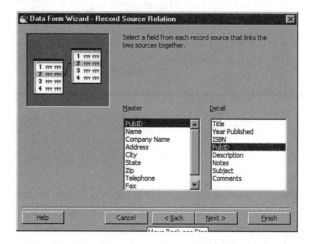

The rest of the steps to create a master/detail data form are just like the steps for creating the other two types of forms. I select the controls I want on the Control Selection dialog box and, finally, name the form in the Finished! dialog box. When you're finished, the Data Form Wizard generates a master/detail form like the one shown in Figure 11.22.

FIGURE 11.22.

The master/detail form generated by the Data Form Wizard.

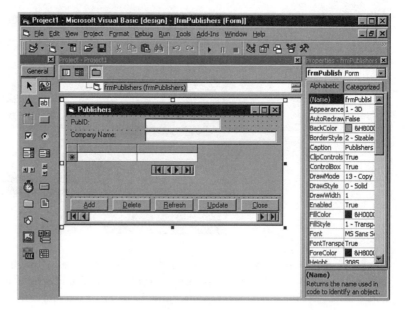

The top part of the form displays the labels PubID and Company Name, which make up the master section of the form. The detail section of the form contains an empty DBGrid control, which contains the detail data when the program is run. Notice that below the DBGrid control is a data control. A master/detail form needs two data controls to allow navigating through the master and detail sections. The data control below the DBGrid is for the detail section; the data control for the master section is at the bottom of the form. Figure 11.23 shows the master/detail form when the program is running.

FIGURE 11.23.

The master/detail form in the running program.

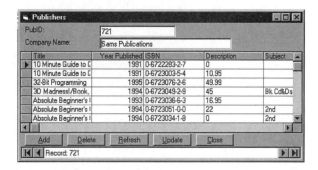

Each title associated with Sams Publications is shown in the Detail section. You can navigate through the grid with the up- and down-arrow keys to the right of the grid. To change publishers, click the left or right arrow on the data control at the bottom of the form.

Connecting to an ODBC Database

If you're accessing data from a database that doesn't reside on your PC, you'll probably connect to the database by using ODBC. I won't cover the details of setting up your PC to connect via ODBC (that comes in a later chapter), but I will show you the one different step the Data Form Wizard takes when you select a Remote (ODBC) database in the Data Form Wizard – Database Type dialog box.

When you select a remote database as the database type, the Data Form Wizard takes you to the Data Form Wizard – Connect Information dialog box, in which you provide some information concerning your ODBC setup. Again, I won't provide the details of setting up ODBC, but I will show you the Connect Information dialog box so you can see what information it wants (see Figure 11.24).

The first text box wants the DSN (Data Source Name) for your ODBC connection to the database. This information is located in the 32-bit ODBC program of your PC's Control Panel, if it has already been set up. If it hasn't been set up (or if you're not sure), have your system administrator check it for you. He or she can tell you how to set it up or, if it has been set up and you can't tell what the DSN is supposed to be, he or she can tell you what the correct DSN is for the database to which you want to connect.

FIGURE 11.24.
*The Data Wizard
Form – Connect
Information dialog box.*

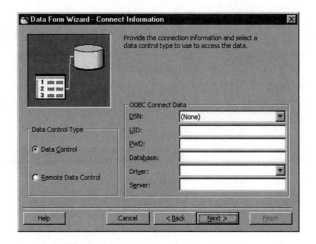

The second and third text boxes want a UID (user ID) and a PWD (password) for the data source. Again, your system administrator can tell you what these are.

The last text box wants the name of the database to which you're connecting. You can enter the database name here, or check with your system administrator to find out the proper name of the database.

Finally, on the left side of the dialog box are two radio buttons: Data Control and Remote Data Control. If you're not using the Enterprise Edition of Visual Basic, you don't have the Remote Data Control available to you and must select Data Control. If you're using the Enterprise Edition, you can select the Remote Data Control only if it has already been registered. (See Chapter 24, "Using the Remote Data Control (RDC).")

Summary

Using the Data Form Wizard to create forms bound to a database table or queries can be a time-saving tool in prototyping a new application. The Data Form Wizard can generate three types of forms:

- Single-record layout
- Grid (datasheet) layout
- Master/detail layout

This chapter has highlighted the flexibility the Data Form Wizard provides in selecting

- A database type
- The form type
- What tables or queries will be used to generate data
- The fields that will be displayed on the form and how they're displayed
- What controls will be displayed on the form
- A name for the form

Binding Controls to Your Database

by Mike McMillan

IN THIS CHAPTER

One of Visual Basic's most powerful features is its capability to access data from a database without requiring users to write code. The data control, one of Visual Basic's standard controls, provides all the back-end processing necessary to create powerful database front ends that can add, display, edit, and delete data from many different kinds of databases. You have to do nothing more than place some controls on a form and set the right properties to provide access to the database. This chapter provides detailed instructions on how to design and implement these powerful database front ends.

Using the Data Control

The single most important element for creating a database front end in Visual Basic is the data control, a standard Visual Basic control found in the toolbox. In Visual Basic 5.0, the data control is in the bottom-right corner of the standard controls found in the toolbox when Visual Basic first loads (see Figure 12.1).

FIGURE 12.1.

The data control in the toolbox.

The data control

The data control has a set of properties that lets you establish a connection with a database, a database table, and the fields on a table. Double-clicking the data control places it on the form (see Figure 12.2).

The data control provides four buttons for navigating through a database table:

- The right-arrow button moves one record forward in the table.
- The right-arrow/bar button moves to the last record of the table.
- The left-arrow button moves one record backward in the table.
- The left-arrow/bar button moves to the first record of the table.

FIGURE 12.2.
The data control on a form.

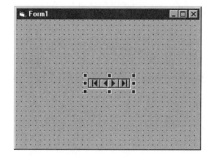

Like any other control, the data control can be resized after it's placed on a form. If you widen the control, you can see that between the two sets of navigational buttons is the control's caption (see Figure 12.3). This caption can have any descriptive title you want to give it, or you can leave it with its default caption. However, just as with other controls, giving the data control a logical name will help make your code easier to read, especially if you add other data controls to the form later.

FIGURE 12.3.
The caption of the data control.

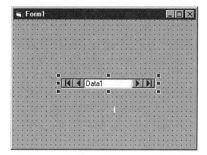

Setting the Data Access Properties of the Data Control

After you place the data control on a form, you need to connect it to a database. Connecting it to a database involves describing the database you're wanting to access at three levels:

- The database type, such as a Microsoft Access database
- The name of the database
- The name of the table that has the data you want to access

The data control uses three properties to set these access levels:

- `Connect`, to identify the type of database
- `DatabaseName`, to identify the database name
- `RecordSource`, to identify the database table

The first property to set is `Connect`, which tells Visual Basic what type of database you're connecting to. The standard data control allows connections to the following types of databases:

- Microsoft Access (all versions)
- dBASE III, IV, and 5.0
- Excel 3.0, 4.0, 5.0, and 8.0
- FoxPro 2.0, 2.5, 2.6, and 3.0
- Lotus WK1, WK3, and WK4
- Paradox 3.x, 4.x, and 5.x
- Text

Notice that three of the database types aren't databases at all; two are spreadsheets (Excel and Lotus), and one is plain text. As long as the data within these file types is organized in a row/column format, the data control can read them like a database table.

> **NOTE**
>
> Of the database types listed here, only the Microsoft products provide you with any access to the internal structure of the database, spreadsheet, or text file.

Figure 12.4 shows the properties associated with the data control I have placed on a form. The `Connect` property by default is set to Access. If you're connecting to this type of database, you don't have to do anything else with this property. If you want one of the other database types, however, click the `Connect` property and a drop-down button will appear at the right of the property. Clicking the drop-down button lists the other database types that you can connect to (see Figure 12.5). Simply select your choice to place the database type in the `Connect` property's box.

Figure 12.4.

The `Connect` *property in the Properties window of the data control.*

FIGURE 12.5.

A drop-down list of the database types for selection in the Connect *property.*

After you select the database type, you're ready to select the name of the database you're connecting to by setting the DatabaseName property, which is right below the Connect property. Clicking the DatabaseName property brings up a Browse button to the right of the property setting box (see Figure 12.6).

FIGURE 12.6.

Preparing to browse to select a database name.

When you click the Browse button, a dialog box appears to allow you to find the database that you want to connect to. Figure 12.7 shows the Biblio.mdb database being selected for the DatabaseName property. Clicking the Open button places the full path name to the database into the DatabaseName property box, as shown in Figure 12.8.

FIGURE 12.7.

Selecting the
Biblio.mdb *database.*

FIGURE 12.8.

The DatabaseName
property, set to access
a database.

With a database type and a database name selected, you're ready to select which table in the database you want to access by setting the RecordSource property. Clicking the RecordSource property displays a drop-down button like the one you saw with the Connect property. Clicking this button gives you a list of the different tables in the Biblio database that you can access (see Figure 12.9). Select the table you want by clicking it, and the table name will be added to the RecordSource property box (see Figure 12.10).

You're now ready to add controls to your form to display data from the database you're accessing.

Binding Controls to a Database

After the data control properties are properly set to connect to a database type, a particular database, and a specific database table, you next need to add controls to a form to display the data. Initially, you're going to create a form that displays data in text boxes, although later in the chapter you'll use some advanced Visual Basic data-bound controls that allow more complex views of database information.

FIGURE 12.9.

Viewing the list of tables in the Biblio *database.*

FIGURE 12.10.

Selecting a table name for the RecordSource *property.*

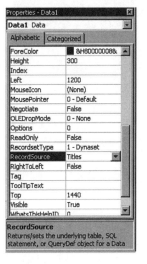

When the controls on a Visual Basic form are associated with a database table, the process of selecting the database, the table, and the record source is called *binding the control.* Visual Basic provides properties in each control to help with binding the control to a database table. After these properties are set, whenever the form is activated it displays data from the chosen database table and record source. This process is particularly useful because it doesn't involve writing any code, just setting the right properties.

Designing a Database Front-End Form

As in the design of any Visual Basic form, putting a little forethought into the design of the database front-end form helps make the form visually pleasing and more functional.

The information you'll display in the following example comes from the Titles table of the Biblio database that comes with Visual Basic. The Titles table has the following fields:

Title	Description
Year Published	Notes
ISBN	Subject
PubID	Comments

For this example, let's start with a very basic form design. Each field has a label to display the field name and a text box to hold the data associated with the field. Figure 12.11 shows the example form, frmTitles.

FIGURE 12.11.

The frmTitles *form will display data from the* Biblio *database table.*

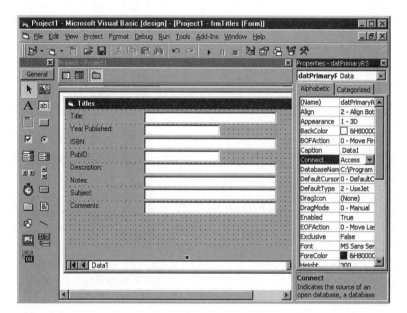

After you place the controls on the form, you're ready to bind them to the database. What you'll actually do is bind each control to its associated field in the Titles table. Notice in Figure 12.11 that the data control, Data1, is at the bottom of the form. Remember, you can't bind any controls on a form to a database until the data control is placed on the form and has its data access properties set. If you check the properties of the Data1 data control, you find the following properties and their settings:

- Connect, set to Access
- DatabaseName, set to c:\Program Files\DevStudio\VB\Biblio.mdb
- RecordSource, set to Titles

Now you're ready to bind your first field to the database. The top text box on the form is labeled Title. To bind the text box of Title to the Title field of the Titles table, you have to set two properties: DataField and DataSource.

You first need to set the DataSource property to the name of the data control on the form. In this example, the data control is named Data1, so that's what you enter for the DataSource property. When you click the DataSource property, a drop-down button appears. Clicking the button will pop up the name of the data control. Click the name, and the `DataSource` property will be set to `Data1`.

Next, set the `DataField` property, which associates a field on the table with a control on the form. Because the text box associated with the Title label will hold book titles, you want to associate it with the Title field on the Titles table. Click the `DataField` property, and a drop-down button appears. Click it, and all the fields from the Titles table pop up (see Figure 12.12). Click the Title name, and the `DataField` property will be set to `Title`.

FIGURE 12.12.

Listing the fields from the Titles table.

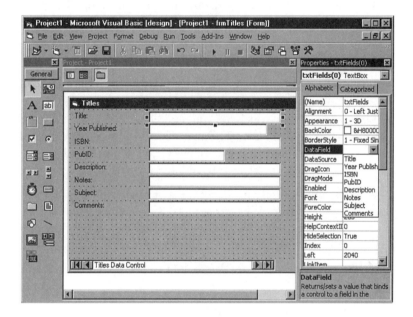

The other controls on the form are set in the same manner. When the `DataSource` and `DataField` properties are set for each text box, you're ready to run the project to display data from the Titles table. The first record in the table, with its data displayed in the newly created front end, is shown in Figure 12.13.

FIGURE 12.13.

The front end to the Titles table.

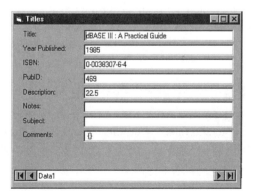

To move forward through the table, click the right-arrow button on the data control. To move to the last record, click the right-arrow/bar button. To move backward, click the left-arrow button. To move to the first record, click the left-arrow/bar button.

You now have a fully functional database front end that can be used to browse the Biblio table, and you created it without writing a single line of Visual Basic code. Of course, if you want to add any additional functionality to the program (such as adding new records, deleting records, or editing existing records), you'll have to write code to provide these functions. Still, you can create a functional database browser by doing nothing more than placing some controls on a form and setting a few properties.

Using the Data-Bound Controls

Although using text boxes to display data from a database table is adequate for simple database browsing, some applications require more complex views of the data in a database. One example is a *lookup table*, which lets you select a particular item and then displays all the other data associated with that item. The most direct way to implement a lookup table is to create a list box that's filled with table data. However, to do this by using a standard Visual Basic list box control requires writing code to add items to the list.

Another example is displaying data from a database table in a spreadsheet view so that users can edit a record while viewing other records in the table. The standard grid control can be made to do this, but only after writing lots of code to add the functionality not found in the grid control.

Visual Basic 5.0 provides three data-bound controls so you can create programs like the preceding examples:

- DBList for a data-bound list box
- DBCombo for a data-bound combo box
- DBGrid for a data-bound grid control

These controls have a set of properties that let you connect them to database tables through the data control to provide access to multiple records in the table. You can also use the data-bound list controls for a lookup table application, such as the one I just mentioned. For example, in the Biblio database, one DBList control can provide a list of publishers from the Publishers table that you can select from to access a list of the book titles in another DBList control on the same form.

Loading the Data-Bound Controls

The data-bound controls aren't part of the toolbox that's loaded when you first start Visual Basic; you have to add them to a project manually. To do this, select Components from the Project menu or press Ctrl+T. The Components dialog box appears (see Figure 12.14).

FIGURE 12.14.

The Components dialog box.

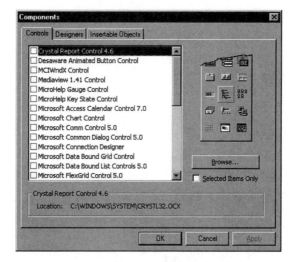

To add the data-bound controls to a project, simply click the checkboxes next to Microsoft Data Bound Grid Control and Microsoft Data Bound List Controls 5.0. Click OK to add these controls to the bottom of the toolbox (see Figure 12.15).

FIGURE 12.15.

The toolbox with the data-bound controls added.

Working with the Data-Bound List Box (DBList)

The DBList control acts like a standard list box control except in the way data is added to the list. With the standard list box, to add data to the list you have to write code by using the AddItem method. With the DBList control, the list is filled simply by setting the right properties to connect to a data control on the form with the DBList control. As with binding a text box, the

DBList control has a set of properties that you set to specify which data control to attach to and which field is its source of data.

The following properties must be set to bind the DBList control to a database table and a particular field:

- Set DataSource to the name of the data control.
- Set RowSource to the name of the data control used as a source of items for the DBList control.
- Set ListField to the name of the field in the table specified by RowSource that's used to fill the list.

After these properties are set, you can use the DBList control to pull data from a database table. The DBList control is filled with publisher names from the Publishers table in the Biblio database.

Creating a Lookup Table

In many programming applications, you'll want to present users with a list of choices to make and another list of alternatives based on the first set of choices. For example, by using the scenario briefly discussed in the preceding section, one list will include the list of book publishers, and the second list will include the book titles published by that publisher. By using just standard list boxes, creating a lookup table like this would require a lot of code to synchronize the lists. By using the DBList control, however, creating a lookup table involves nothing more than setting the right properties.

To create the lookup table of publishers and book titles, continue working with the DBList control that you've already set up. Recall that to fill the list with the names of the publishers, you had to set these properties: DataSource, RowSource, and ListField. To create a lookup table, you have to set some additional properties.

A lookup table works by having the DBList control with the "lookup" data (a term or phrase such as *Sams*) pass a key field to the second DBList control that has the data you're looking for. In the example, the Publishers and Titles tables are linked by the PubID field, which is common between both tables. Through this link, when you select a publisher, the DBList control passes the value of that publisher's PubID field to the second DBList control, which displays the Titles table data. The second DBList control takes the PubID value, passes it to its data control, matches it with a PubID field in its table, and displays the list of related book titles. If there isn't a match, nothing will happen.

Before you set the additional properties on the Publishers DBList control, you need to add another DBList control and another data control. The following properties are set for the Data2 data control (which is a DBList control):

Property	Value
Connect	Access
DatabaseName	c:\Program Files\DevStudio\VB\Biblio.mdb
RecordSource	Titles
DataSource	Data1
ListField	Title
RowSource	Data2

With these properties set, you can now use the Publishers table as a lookup table to find titles published by a certain publisher. Figure 12.16 shows two DBList controls and two data controls.

FIGURE 12.16.
The lookup table form.

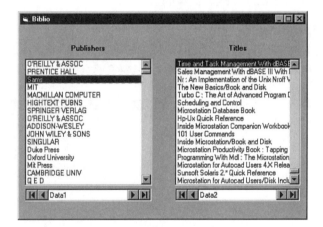

The DBList control on the left displays the names of book publishers from the Publishers table of the Biblio database. The DBList control on the right displays the list of book titles from the Titles table published by a publisher based on the value of the PubID field that's common between the record from the Publishers table and the record from the Titles table. The two DBList controls are linked so that as you move from one publisher to the next in the left DBList control, the list of book titles changes in the right DBList control.

Working with the Data-Bound Combo Box (DBCombo)

Another way to present a list of data bound to a database is with the DBCombo control. The main difference between the DBCombo control and the DBList control is that the DBList control presents the whole list, whereas the DBCombo control presents a text box with the selected item from the list in it and a drop-down list box containing the rest of the list.

The DBCombo control is bound to a database in the same way the DBList control is bound to a database. The following properties have to be set to bind the DBCombo control to a database table and a field:

- Set DataSource to the name of the data control.
- Set RowSource to the name of the data control used as a source of items for the DBCombo control.
- Set ListField to the name of the field in the table specified by RowSource that's used to fill the list.

Also, three styles are associated with the DBCombo control, just like with the standard Combo control. The style type determines what information will display in the selected text box and how the list of items bound to the control will be displayed. The styles are dbcDropDownCombo, dbcSimpleCombo, and dbcDropDownList.

dbcDropDownCombo

Figure 12.17 shows a DBCombo control bound to the Titles table in the Biblio database. This DBCombo control uses style 0: dbcDropDownCombo.

FIGURE 12.17.

The dbcDropDownCombo *style.*

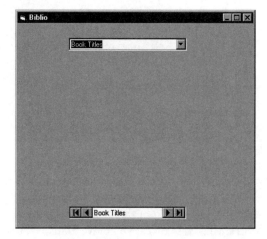

With this DBCombo style, the caption of the control appears in the selected text box. As with a standard Combo control, clicking the down arrow displays the list of items that can be selected from the list (see Figure 12.18).

You can now scroll through the list and select an item by clicking it; the selected item will be displayed in the text box. If you know the item you're looking for, you can type it into the text box, and the control will use a Soundex search to find the item in the list. Visual Basic performs a Soundex search by trying to perform a match as you type characters. Typing **Sa** is like searching for the pattern Sa*, with Visual Basic doing the searching while you type. Figure 12.19 shows a partial book title typed into the Selected text box.

FIGURE 12.18.
Using the
dbcDropDownCombo *style*
DBCombo control.

FIGURE 12.19.
Doing a Soundex search
in a DBCombo control.

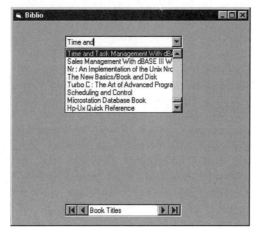

dbcSimpleCombo

Figure 12.20 shows a DBCombo control in the dbcSimpleCombo style. The control caption is displayed in the text box and the items in the list are shown one at a time, using the spin button to scroll through the list. When you click an item in the list, it's displayed in the text box. You also can type in the text box if you want to search for a specific item.

DbcDropDownList

The dbcDropDownList style displays an empty text box (see Figure 12.21). Clicking the drop-down button pops up the list of items to select. When you click an item, it's displayed in the text box. Unlike with the other two DBCombo styles, you can't do a Soundex search with this control.

FIGURE 12.20.

The dbcSimpleCombo *style.*

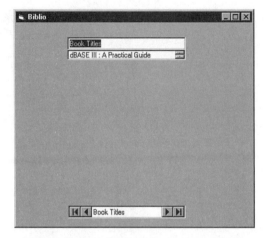

FIGURE 12.21.

The dbcDropDownList *style.*

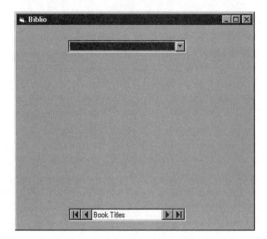

Working with the Data-Bound Grid Control (DBGrid)

The DBGrid control lets you present data from a database in a spreadsheet view, much like you can do with the standard grid control. Unlike the standard grid control, however, the DBGrid control automatically fills its rows and columns with data because it's linked to a data control. From the Recordset object of the data control, the DBGrid control can create and place column headers in the grid, as well as the data records themselves. These features make the DBGrid control highly preferable to the standard grid control for a spreadsheet view of data from a database.

Setting the Data Access Properties of the DBGrid Control

The following properties must be set on the DBGrid control to allow access to a database:

- ■ Set DataMode to Bound (to link to a data control).
- ■ Set DataSource to the name of the data control.

The DBGrid control is less flexible than the data-bound list controls. The DBGrid control is designed to display data from a database and not from a customized RowSource, such as a SQL statement. However, the DBGrid control does have some functionality not found in the data-bound list controls, which I discuss in the following section.

Using the DBGrid Control

The DBGrid control can be used to edit data as well as display it. Figure 12.22 shows a DBGrid control bound to the Titles table of the Biblio database. The DBGrid control, with data in its rows and columns, looks like the standard grid control. Because some of the column cells aren't wide enough to display all the data in the field, you can drag the right edge of a column cell in the column heading to make it wider (see Figure 12.23).

FIGURE 12.22.

The DBGrid control.

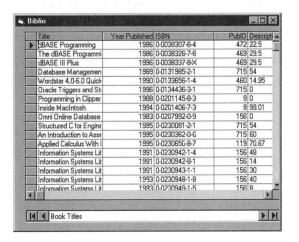

You can use the scrollbar at the bottom of the control to scroll across the fields on a row and the scrollbar at the right of the control to scroll through the rows. Of course, you also can scroll through the rows by using the arrow buttons on the data control.

FIGURE 12.23.

A widened column in the DBGrid control.

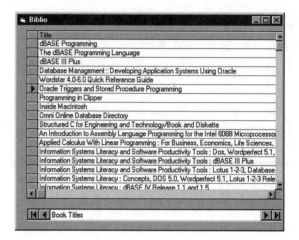

Summary

Binding controls to a database provides an easy yet powerful way to create database front-end browsing programs. By learning how to set the right properties, you can create controls on a form to display, add, edit, and delete data on a database without writing any code at all.

Visual Basic also provides a set of data-bound controls that provide views of multiple data records at one time. To create these views with the standard Visual Basic controls would take many lines of code.

Managing Your Databases With the Visual Data Manager

by Mike McMillan

IN THIS CHAPTER

One of Visual Basic 5's improvements over Visual Basic 4 is the Visual Data Manager (called the Data Manager in Visual Basic 4). The Data Manager in Visual Basic 4 was a database-access tool that let you perform very basic operations on a database. Data Manager's major capabilities included

- Creating a new database
- Opening an existing database
- Repairing a Jet database
- Compacting a Jet database
- Adding, editing, and deleting fields in a table
- Creating indexes on a table
- Attaching Access tables to SQL Server tables

As powerful as Visual Basic 4's Data Manager seemed to be, Visual Basic 5's new Visual Data Manager has many more powerful tools for managing databases within the Visual Basic environment.

This chapter covers using the Visual Data Manager to perform many aspects of database management from within Visual Basic 5:

- Creating a new database
- Editing an existing database
- Managing the database environment
- Building database queries with the Query Builder
- Creating and testing SQL statements

The Visual Data Manager, also called VisData, is an application that can help you manage your databases while working within the Visual Basic IDE. VisData is actually written in Visual Basic as an example of Visual Basic's powerful database-access features. It's installed as an add-in to the Visual Basic IDE and is loaded from the Add-Ins menu. If you have the Professional or Enterprise Edition of Visual Basic 5, you can find the source code for VisData in the \Samples directory.

VisData is a very powerful data manager. From VisData you can perform most of the operations on a database that you can from within the database's own development environment. This means that many administrative tasks that in the past forced you to leave the Visual Basic IDE can now be done in VisData. This is a major convenience because many times in the development of an application you'll need to make some sort of change to the database, such as changing a field name or adjusting a field length. Being able to do these types of database administration tasks in VisData saves a lot of time and doesn't require you to be an expert database administrator (not that anything is wrong with that).

Understanding the VisData Environment

When you select Visual Data Manager from the Add-Ins menu, you'll see the form shown in Figure 13.1.

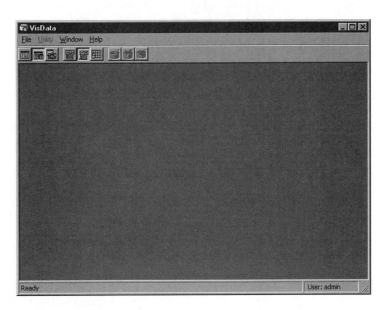

At this initial stage, the File menu has the following choices:

Open DataBase

New...

Workspace

Errors...

Compact MDB...

Repair MDB...

Exit

Figure 13.2 shows the File menu when first loading VisData.

To work with some data during this overview, open an existing database. Choose Open DataBase from the menu and then click Microsoft Access to open a database. In the dialog box that appears, double-click `Biblio.mdb` to load the `Biblio` database. You'll see two MDI forms: Database Window and SQL Statement (see Figure 13.3).

Figure 13.2.

The File menu in VisData.

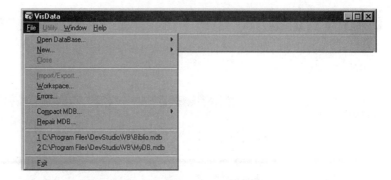

Figure 13.3.

The Database Window and SQL Statement forms.

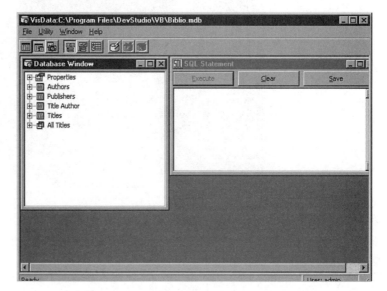

The Utility menu is enabled now that there's a database loaded that the utilities can work with. Table 13.1 shows the utilities VisData provides.

Table 13.1. VisData's utilities.

Utility	What It Does
Query Builder	Builds a search expression
Data Form Designer	Builds a database-access form
Global Replace	Builds a SQL statement to update a field for all records in a selected table
Attachments	Lists all attached tables and their connect strings
Groups/Users	Modifies groups, users, permissions, and owners

Utility	What It Does
System.MD?	Creates different System.mda files and sets up security for each one from the same application
Preferences	Sets a login time-out value, the last database loaded as the default, and a default query time-out value

The Database Window is an Explorer-like tree view that displays the structure of the tables of the database. The Properties setting in the Database Window holds the following settings for the Biblio database:

```
Name=
Connect=
Transactions=
Updatable=
CollatingOrder=
QueryTimeout=
Version=
RecordsAffected=
ReplicaID=
DesignMasterID=
Connection=
AccessVersion=
Build=
```

Of course, each property will have a value, if any, based on your particular installation of Microsoft Access. Figure 13.4 shows a partial view of the properties of my Biblio database.

FIGURE 13.4.

Partial view of author's
Biblio *properties.*

For each table in the database selected, you can view the following in the Database Window:

- ■ *Fields.* Each field in the table.
- ■ *Indexes.* Each index defined in the table.
- ■ *Properties.* Property settings for the table.

You can view the following properties for each table:

```
Name=
Updatable=
DateCreated=
LastUpdated=
Connect=
Attributes=
SourceTableName=
RecordCount=
ValidationRule=
ValidationText=
ConflictTable=
ReplicaFilter=
OrderByOn=
```

Again, the property settings for each table depend on your specific configuration. Figure 13.5 displays the property settings for the Authors table in the `Biblio` database based on my configuration.

FIGURE 13.5.

A partial view of the Authors table's properties.

Working with Tables in the Database Window Form

In addition to providing you with a view of the structure and properties of a database, the Database Window form lets you open a table and change a table design from within the form. By highlighting one of the tables in the Database Window and pressing the right mouse button, you can perform the following operations on the table:

- ■ *Open.* Opens a table for editing.
- ■ *Design.* Opens a table to change the table design.
- ■ *Rename.* Renames the table.
- ■ *Delete.* Deletes the table.
- ■ *Copy Structure.* Copies the structure of the table to another table.
- ■ *Refresh List.* Redisplays the table list.

- *New Table.* Creates a new table.
- *New Query.* Uses the Query Builder to create a new query.

Opening a Table in the Database Window

To open the Authors table, highlight it in the tree and press the right mouse button. Clicking Open brings up the Dynaset:Authors window (see Figure 13.6).

FIGURE 13.6.

The Dynaset:Authors window.

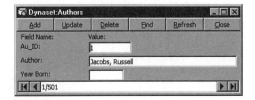

This window is called Dynaset:Authors because the type of `Recordset` I'm working with is a dynaset. I'm working with a dynaset because that's the type I chose from among the leftmost icons under the File menu. The other two choices you could make are Table-type and Snapshot-type. A *dynaset* is a dynamic set of records that contains the records from a database table or the results of a query. A dynaset is considered dynamic because you can add, edit, and delete records in a dynaset, which you can't do with a snapshot recordset.

> **NOTE**
>
> Remember that a Snapshot-type recordset is read-only and won't allow any changes to be made to the table.

Under the title bar of the Dynaset:Authors window are six buttons that provide functionality:

- *Add.* Adds a new record to the table.
- *Update.* Updates the table.
- *Delete.* Deletes a record from the table.
- *Find.* Finds a record in the table.
- *Refresh.* Regenerates the data in the table.
- *Close.* Closes the form.

Clicking Add brings up a new record with an autogenerated Au_ID field, a blank Author field, and a default Year Born date of `0`. Also, the Add button changes to Cancel so users can cancel adding the record if necessary (see Figure 13.7).

13

MANAGING YOUR
DATABASES

FIGURE 13.7.

Adding a new record.

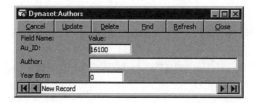

When you finish making changes to the table, click the Update button to commit the changes to the database. This simply means that you're satisfied with the changes you've made to the table and want to make them permanent. Clicking Update will bring up a confirmation box like the one shown in Figure 13.8. Click Yes to commit the changes or No to cancel the changes.

FIGURE 13.8.

The Commit Changes?
confirmation box.

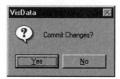

Clicking the Delete button brings up a confirmation box asking whether you want to delete the current record. Click Yes to delete the record or No to leave the record in the table.

Clicking Find brings up a dialog box asking you to enter a search expression, which can be any valid SQL WHERE clause for that table. Figure 13.9 shows a search expression entered into the text box. Click OK to have Visual Basic search for any records that match the expression. If a match is found, that record's data appears in the form. If a match isn't found, the form stays on the record it was on when you began the search. If for some reason your search expression has an error in it—perhaps because you misspelled a field name—a dialog box informs you of an error in the search expression.

FIGURE 13.9.

The Enter Search
Expression dialog box.

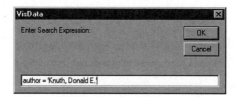

To see changes made in the table while you're using VisData, click the Refresh button. The table is regenerated to reflect any changes made to the table, and you're placed at the first record in the table.

Working with Table Designs

The commands on the Database Window's Design menu let you work with a table's structure. Right-click any entry in the Database Window for a pop-up menu with several choices. Choosing Design from the menu loads the Table Structure form, which has functions for

- Adding a field
- Removing a field
- Renaming a field
- Changing a field's ordinal position
- Allowing a field to be zero-length
- Designating a field as required
- Creating validation text for a field
- Creating a validation rule for a field
- Creating a default value for a field
- Adding an index
- Removing an index
- Renaming an index

Figure 13.10 shows the Table Structure form for the Authors table in the `Biblio` database.

FIGURE 13.10.

The Table Structure form, displaying the Authors table.

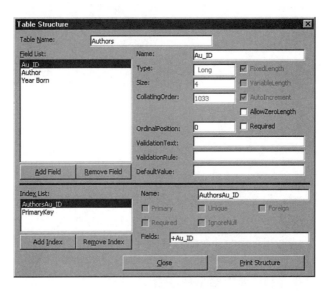

The information for the first field listed in the table is displayed when the form is first loaded. To display the structure of another field, click a field in the Field List. Figure 13.11 shows the structure of the Year Born field.

FIGURE 13.11.

The Year Born field selected in the Table Structure form.

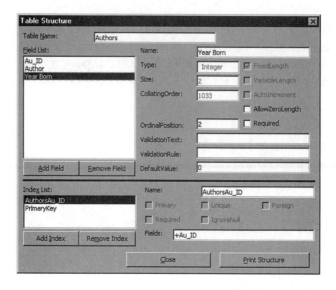

You can edit indexes the same way you edit fields. If you want to add an index to the table, click the Add Index button. The Add Index to Authors form will load, as shown in Figure 13.12.

FIGURE 13.12.

The Add Index to Authors form.

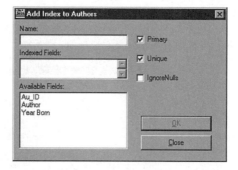

Enter a name, the fields to be indexed, whether the index is unique or primary, and whether the index should ignore null values. Click OK to add the index to the Index List. Click Close at any time if you decide not to create the new index.

When you finish editing the structure of the table, you can print the structure or close the form.

Using Query Builder

For most experienced Visual Basic programmers, building database queries is second nature. However, for newer programmers and for those Visual Basic programmers who haven't done a lot of database programming, creating database queries can be time-consuming. SQL, the non-procedural language that Query Builder is based on, is easy to use for simple queries but can become quite complex, especially when you're trying to pull information from more than one table.

Query Builder presents an interactive interface for you to create the equivalent of a SQL statement without actually writing SQL code. To do this, Query Builder provides prompts to fill in the necessary parameters for a query. Figure 13.13 shows the Query Builder form and its parameters.

FIGURE 13.13.

The Query Builder form.

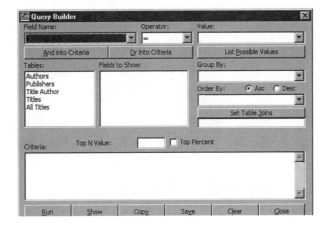

Building a Query in Query Builder

When the Query Builder form is first loaded, all the parameters are blank except the Operator parameter, which defaults to =. To build a query, the first thing you need to do is select a table to query. Selecting a table in the Tables List will fill in the first field from the table in the Field Name combo box. Also, all the fields from the table will be displayed in the Fields to Show list box (see Figure 13.14).

FIGURE 13.14.

Querying the Authors table.

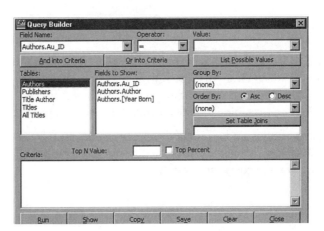

With the Field Name and Operator filled in, the only parameter missing to have a complete query is Value. In Figure 13.15, I have a query built to determine whether the famous algorithmist Donald Knuth is among the authors in the Authors table. Figure 13.15 shows the Query Builder form with the parameters entered.

FIGURE 13.15.

A complete Query Builder query.

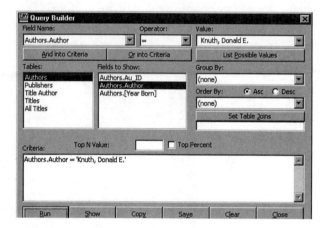

Running Query Builder Queries

To run the query, click the Run button at the bottom of the form. A dialog box appears, asking you whether this is a SQL *passthrough query* (a SQL-specific query that you use to send commands directly to a SQL database server). Click No, and a SQL Statement window will be displayed with the results of the query (see Figure 13.16).

FIGURE 13.16.

Results from the Query Builder query.

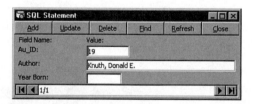

The Au_ID, Author, and Year Born fields are displayed. Also, the data control displays 1/1 as its caption, which means that the SQL Statement window is displaying number 1 of 1 records. Notice, too, that from this window you can perform Add, Update, Delete, Find, and Refresh operations on the table. To hide the SQL Statement window, click Close.

Another button at the bottom of the Query Builder form is Show. Clicking this button shows the SQL statement that was generated from Query Builder. Figure 13.17 displays the SQL statement for the query just created.

FIGURE 13.17.

The SQL statement generated from Query Builder.

> ### TIP
>
> The Show command is especially helpful if you're still learning SQL. I've known several people who became decent SQL programmers primarily from studying the SQL statements generated from an automated query builder.

Other Query Builder parameters are available that I can't cover in this section:

- Group By
- Order By
- Set Table Joins

Testing SQL Statements

Located next to the Database Window on the VisData form is the SQL Statement form, from which you can write and test SQL statements to see whether they return the value(s) you're looking for. This feature is one of the best improvements of VisData over the Visual Basic 4 Data Manager. Before Visual Basic 5, if you wanted to test a SQL statement before you added it to your code, you had to leave the Visual Basic IDE and run the SQL code from the database environment. Now you can write the SQL statement and test it without leaving Visual Basic.

The SQL Statement form couldn't be easier to use. Just click in the SQL Statement form, type your SQL statement, and click Execute. Figure 13.18 shows the SQL Statement form.

FIGURE 13.18.

The SQL Statement form.

The SQL Statement form has three buttons:

- *Execute*, which runs your SQL statement after you enter it into the form
- *Clear*, which erases any text that has been entered into the form
- *Save*, which saves the SQL statement as a `QueryDef` object that you can later reference in your code

Nothing is simpler than using the SQL Statement form—unless, of course, you don't know how to write SQL statements. To use the form, enter a SQL statement and click the Execute button. Figure 13.19 shows a SQL statement that again looks for Donald Knuth in the Authors table.

FIGURE 13.19.

A SQL statement ready to execute.

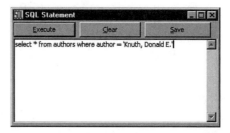

When you click Execute, a dialog box will ask whether the statement is a SQL passthrough query. Unless it is, click No, and the SQL code will execute. Figure 13.20 shows the results of executing the SQL statement. The results, as expected, are the same as with the Query Builder example.

FIGURE 13.20.

Results of SQL statement execution.

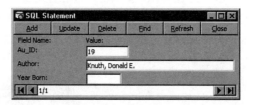

If you misspell something or use the wrong field name in the SQL statement, VisData will generate an error message. The error message will display an error number and an explanation of what VisData interprets as the cause of the error. Suppose that you type the following SQL statement into the form:

```
select * from author where author = 'Knuth, Donald E.'
```

When this statement is executed, the error message in Figure 13.21 is generated. The error message asks whether you want to display the Data Access Objects error collection. If you click Yes, the Errors form will display the error number, the object name, and an explanation of the error.

FIGURE 13.21.
*A VisData error
message.*

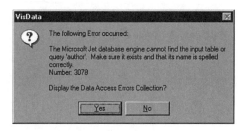

Finally, you can enter any legal SQL statement in the SQL Statement form. You've seen a simple
`select` query, but you can execute everything from inner and outer joins to crosstab queries in
the SQL Statement form.

Creating a New Database in VisData

You can use VisData to create a new database and the tables that make up the database. You
can create the following types of databases:

- Microsoft Access 2.0 and 7.0
- dBASE III, IV, and 5.0
- FoxPro 2.0, 2.5, 2.6, and 3.0
- Paradox 3.*x*, 4.*x*, and 5.*x*
- ODBC
- Text files

To create a new database, choose File | New | Microsoft Access | Version 7.0 MDB... from
the VisData menu. Here you'll use Access 7.0 because you're using 32-bit Visual Basic.

VisData displays a dialog box prompting you for the name of the database file. Enter **Clients**
and click the Save button. The Database Window and SQL Statement forms appear.

In the Database Window, right-click Properties. One selection that will appear is New Table.
Select New Table to display the Table Structure form (see Figure 13.22).

This form, which you've seen before when editing a table's structure, is used to create a table
and its structure. The first field to fill in is the Table field name. Here, you're creating a table
of client names and addresses, so type **Client Info** into the text box.

The next step is to create the fields that will make up the table. Click the Add Field button to
display the Add Field form (see Figure 13.23).

FIGURE 13.22.
The Table Structure form.

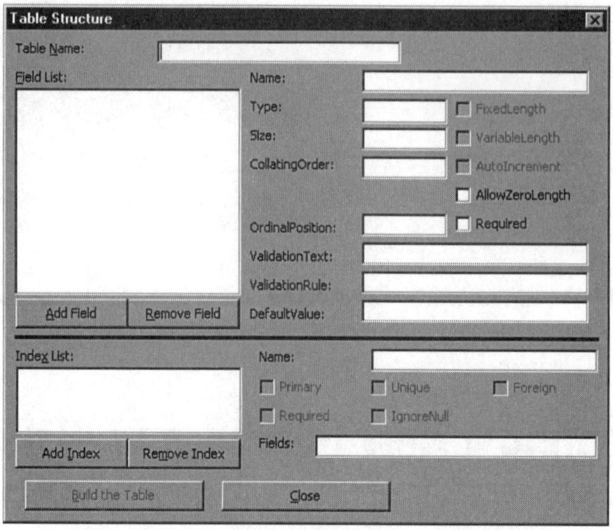

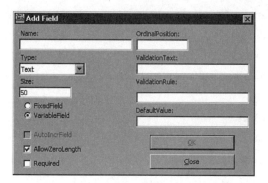

FIGURE 13.23.
The Add Field form.

Type a name into the text box and press Tab to go to the Type field. The following field types are allowed:

Boolean	Double
Byte	Date/Time
Integer	Text
Long	Binary
Currency	Memo
Single	

The next field is Size. Select a size that's long enough to hold the longest name, but not so long that you end up wasting a lot of space.

Next is a selection for whether you want the field to be fixed length or variable length. Because you don't know the exact size of each client name, select a variable field length.

The next selection is a grayed-out checkbox for AutoIncField. An AutoIncField is one that automatically increments its value by 1 every time a record is added. Because a text field can't do that, the field is disabled.

Following AutoIncField is AllowZeroLength. Many text fields need to be allowed to have a zero length because they might not always be storing any data. However, because you're entering the Name field, you don't want any blank names, so don't allow this to be a zero-length field.

Select the next checkbox, Required, if you want a field to be a required entry every time a new record is entered into the table. For this table, the name is definitely required, so select Required.

Following Required is OrdinalPosition. You can assign a position of each field in the table by putting values in this text box. You aren't really interested in OrdinalPosition for this example, so leave it blank.

Next you're prompted to enter information into the ValidationText text box. This text will appear if you enter a validation rule in the ValidationRule text box explained in the following paragraph. For example, if the validation rule says that the text can't be longer than 20 characters and users try to enter a field longer than 20 characters, the text in the ValidationText text box will be displayed.

If you want to limit what the user can enter for this field, enter a rule in the ValidationRule text box. An example might be that a number has to be within a range of numbers, as in `Between 10 and 20`.

Finally, the DefaultValue text box lets you enter a default value for the field. This value is placed in the field if users choose not to enter their own value.

After you fill out the information for a field, click Close. You'll be allowed to enter other fields and the values you've just discussed. When you've entered all the fields for the table, click Build Table. VisData will build the table, and then you can use it like any other Access database table.

Summary

This chapter has shown you how to use the VisData Visual Data Manager to create Visual Basic forms that are bound to databases and database tables. VisData can also be used to create new tables and to create, edit, and test SQL expressions.

Although you can use all VisData features without actually using VisData, you'll find that using VisData makes connecting your applications to databases easier and more efficient. Thus, VisData is a worthwhile addition to your Visual Basic toolkit.

Performing Reporting Magic With Crystal Reports

by Mike McMillan

IN THIS CHAPTER

Inputting, storing, and retrieving data are important functions for most computer applications, and Visual Basic provides lots of neat tools and utilities for working with these functions. Another function, reporting, is often the most important function of an application because communicating the data stored and manipulated in an application is always the end goal of application development. Many application designs begin with deciding on the content and layout of the reports the application will produce.

Beginning with Visual Basic 3.0, the Professional Edition (and the Enterprise Edition for Visual Basic 4) has provided the Crystal Reports report writer for an easy way to create professional-looking reports. As users of older versions of Visual Basic and BASIC will attest, designing reports was often the hardest and most-disliked part of application development. Crystal Reports makes report creation easy and, for the most part, fun.

This chapter discusses using Crystal Reports as a design tool for creating and managing high-level reports. In this chapter, you'll run Crystal Reports from inside the Visual Basic IDE, although you can run it standalone by choosing it from the Visual Basic 5 Program Manager group.

Designing Reports With Crystal Reports: An Overview

Crystal Reports provides you with the tools to completely design the look and grouping of a report. Designing the look of a report involves the following:

- Laying out the group headings
- Laying out the column headings
- Choosing font styles

Designing the grouping of a report involves deciding which group of data causes a break in a report. A good sample database you can use to design a report around is the `Biblio` database included with VB. This database includes several tables that present data on books, the authors of the books, and the publishers of the books. For example, by using `Biblio`'s Titles table, you might design a report that has a break in it every time a new publisher comes up in the report. This report might have a report title of "Titles by Publisher" and a group heading of "Titles by:", where the specific publisher is filled in after the colon.

You can add subtotals to these groupings, either for adding columns of numbers or for creating a count of the items of a group. By using the preceding example, you can create a row heading called "Number of Books Published:" that's printed for each publisher group, along with the number of books published. At the end of the report you can have another row heading, "Total Books Published:", for all the books published by all the publishers. These kinds of decisions go into creating a Crystal Reports report.

Using Crystal Reports

Crystal Reports is located on Visual Basic's Add-Ins menu. Selecting it brings up the Crystal Reports Pro form, as shown in Figure 14.1.

FIGURE 14.1.

The Crystal Reports Pro form.

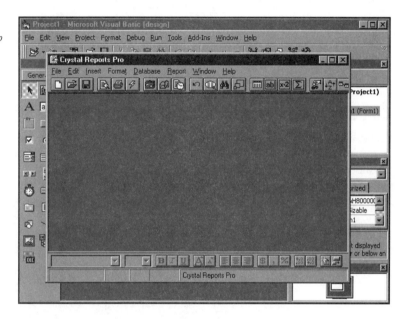

The Pro form has several different menu selections and a toolbar across the top. You examine the menu selections in more detail later; the toolbar consists of the following choices, in order from left to right:

- Create a new report
- Open an existing report
- Save the report
- Preview report in a window
- Print report to a printer
- Discard saved data and reprint report in previous window
- Export report to a file, to mail,…
- Mail a report
- Launch report to Crystal Reports Server
- Undo last change
- Select fields
- Search for a particular value in report

- Zoom report (fit to window, fit to width, full size)
- Insert a database field
- Insert a text field
- Insert a formula field
- Insert a summary (sum, maximum, count…) for selected field
- Select records to be used in report
- Set record or group sort order
- Visually link tables in report using expert

Creating a New Report

To create a new report, choose File | New or New from the toolbar. Crystal Reports has a set of *Experts*, report templates that you can pattern your report after. The different report Experts are shown in the Report Gallery in Figure 14.2.

FIGURE 14.2.

The Report Gallery.

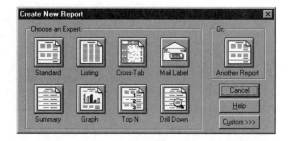

Besides the eight standard report Experts, if you've defined another type of Expert, you can select it with the Another Report button. You can create your own report Expert by clicking the Custom button.

The report Experts in the Report Gallery are used to create the following types of reports:

- *Standard.* A report that uses a tabular format and allows data groupings, subheadings, and subtotals.
- *Listing.* A tabular report that lists all data without any groupings, subheadings, or subtotals.
- *Cross-Tab.* A report that presents the data in a row-oriented format, like a spreadsheet.
- *Mail Label.* A report used to print mail labels or the data in a mail-label format.
- *Summary.* A report that prints only subtotal and total data.
- *Graph.* A report that prints data in a graphic format.
- *Top N.* A report that prints the top items based on user-selected criteria.
- *Drill Down.* A report that prints subheading data and the detail data that's part of the subheading.

For a standard report, click the Standard button. The Create Report Expert form is loaded (see Figure 14.3). This form presents tabbed pages, with each page representing one step in creating a report. The first page you see is Tables, which is discussed in the following section.

FIGURE 14.3.

The Create Report Expert form.

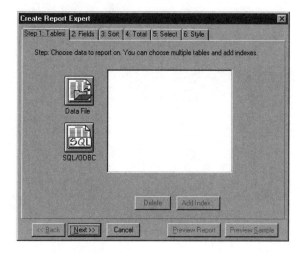

At the bottom of the Create Report Expert form are two navigation buttons (Back and Next), a Cancel button, a Preview Report button, and a Preview Sample button. The Back button returns you to previous steps in the Create Report Expert, and the Next button takes you to the next step. The Cancel button, of course, cancels the creation of the report. The Preview Report button prints a preview of the report based on how you've defined the layout (if you aren't far enough along in the creation process to print a preview, the button will be disabled). The Preview Sample button prints a sample report of the type you've selected (it's also disabled if you haven't entered enough information for Crystal Reports to generate a report).

The Tables Page

Step 1 is to select a data file that holds the data to base the report on. The two choices are Data File and SQL/ODBC. Choose Data File if you're building a report based on a desktop database file such as Microsoft Access, dBASE, Paradox, and so on. Choose SQL/ODBC if you're building a report based on a relational database system such as SQL Server, Oracle, and so on. For this example, choose Data File.

When you click Data File, a file directory dialog box appears. For this example, you're working with the `Biblio` database, so choose `biblio.mdb` from the File Name list box by double-clicking its name or by clicking it once and then clicking the Add button after you find the correct path to the database.

After you choose a database, a series of dialog boxes will appear, asking for an alias name for each table that makes up the database. Figure 14.4 shows an Alias Name dialog box.

FIGURE 14.4.

*The Alias Name
dialog box.*

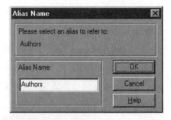

> **NOTE**
>
> An *alias* is used to have more than one name that refers to a database table. For different reasons, database administrators and others who control the design and maintenance of databases change table names. This doesn't present a problem unless there are specific formulas or references to the old table name. Then, of course, programs, queries, and so on won't work properly because the wrong table name will be used in the queries, formulas, and other references to the old table. The answer to this problem is to use an alias that points to the actual table, regardless of its name.

The original table name appears in the text box under Alias Name. If you want to use an alias, type it here; otherwise, leave it the same. Click OK if you're changing the name, or click Cancel if you're leaving it the same. An Alias Name dialog box will appear for each table in the database.

Click Done when you've gone through the series of Alias Name dialog boxes. You're then taken to Step 2.

The Links Page

Step 2, Links, presents the database schema that identifies the links between different tables. Figure 14.5 shows the partial schema diagram for the `Biblio` database presented in Step 2.

Figure 14.5 is a partial view of the schema only because the whole schema won't fit on the form. You can use the scrollbars along the right side and bottom of the page to view the parts of the diagram not shown.

If you like, you can rearrange the table boxes by dragging them to different positions on the form. Figure 14.6 shows all the table boxes brought into view by rearranging them.

Notice that the arrows indicating the links between tables are redrawn to follow the tables to their new locations. If, after trying to rearrange the schema, you find your arrangement more confusing than the system's original arrangement, you can click the Arrange button to have Visual Basic put the schema back in its original form.

FIGURE 14.5.

The Biblio *database schema.*

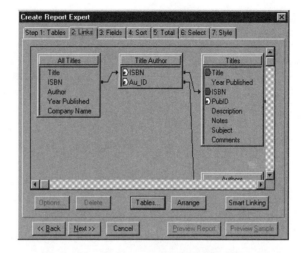

FIGURE 14.6.

The Biblio *database schema, rearranged.*

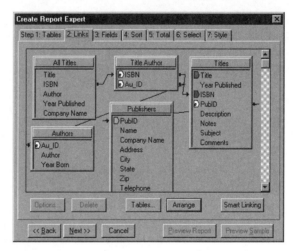

At the bottom of the Create Report Expert form during Step 2 are three enabled buttons: Tables, Arrange, and Smart Linking. These options, and others, are also available from a floating menu accessed by right-clicking a blank spot of the form. Figure 14.7 shows the Links floating menu.

The Links floating menu contains the commands for the buttons at the bottom of the form, plus several more menu commands:

- *Add Data File.* Adds a data file from a desktop database.
- *Add SQL/ODBC.* Adds a data file or a table view from a relational database.
- *Locate.* Finds a table in the schema and centers it on the form.
- *Cancel Menu.* Hides the floating menu from view.

14

PERFORMING REPORTING MAGIC

FIGURE 14.7.
The Links floating menu.

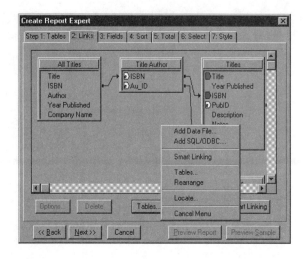

The links shown in the schema diagram are the links you or someone else set up when designing the database. You usually don't want to change them. If, for some reason, you want the report to be based on different links, you can change them during the Link step. Right-clicking a link brings up another floating menu, as shown in Figure 14.8.

FIGURE 14.8.
Floating-menu selections for changing a link.

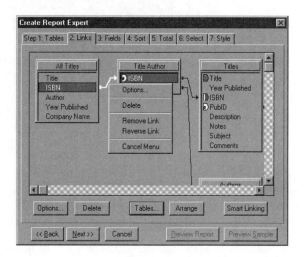

Choosing Options from the floating menu brings up the Link Options form (see Figure 14.9). From this form you can make the following changes:

- The order of the link (which table is the From table and which table is the To table)
- Which, if any, index to use
- The fields in the index

- Whether to allow partial matches
- What kind of link to use when linking to two files from one file
- The SQL join type to use (the default is =)

FIGURE 14.9.
*The Link Options
form.*

The other menu selections on the floating menu include the following:

- Delete and Remove Link both delete the link.
- Reverse Link makes the From table the To table and makes the To table the From table.
- Cancel Menu hides the floating menu.

For this example, don't change any of the links; move on to Step 3.

The Fields Page

Step 3, Fields, defines the database fields that will make up your report. The Fields page is shown in Figure 14.10. This page displays two list boxes (Database Fields on the left and Report Fields on the right), an Add button that allows you to move fields from the left list to the right list, a Remove button to move the fields back to the left column, and two All buttons to move all the fields either way.

Fields are moved in two ways:

- You can highlight a field with the mouse and click Add to move it to the right column.
- You also can double-click a field to move it from one column to the other, depending on where it starts from.

FIGURE 14.10.
The Fields page.

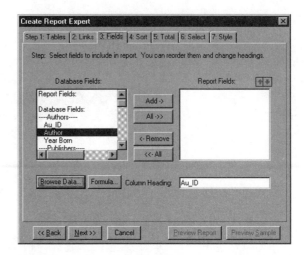

Below the two columns are the Browse Data and Formula buttons. If you highlight a field and click Browse Data, a list box appears showing the selected field's data. Figure 14.11 shows the Browse Data form displaying data from the Author field of the Authors table.

FIGURE 14.11.
The Author field's data.

For this example, you'll create a report listing book authors and their titles for the Macmillan Computer Publishing company, along with a description of each book. The fields you need for this report are Author from the Authors table, Title and Description from the Titles table, and Company Name from the Publishers table. Add them to the report by double-clicking them in the Database Fields list box.

Order is important, and although you can reorder the fields later, go ahead and put the fields in order as you add them to the report. To do this, simply select the field you want to go in the leftmost column of the report first, the field you want to go in the second column next, and so on. Figure 14.12 shows the finished Fields page.

FIGURE 14.12.
*The selected fields in
the Fields page.*

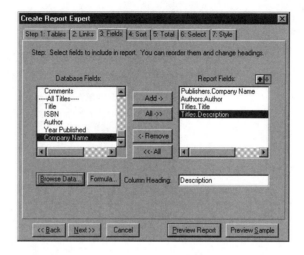

Another way to change the order of the fields is to use the up- and down-arrow buttons located above the upper-right corner of the Report Fields list box. To move a field up in the order, for example, highlight the field and click the up button; the field exchanges places with the field before it. To move a field down in the order, highlight a field and click the down button; the field exchanges places with the field after it.

After you have the fields in the order you want, you're ready to move to Step 4, Sort.

The Sort Page

This sample report is a list of all the titles, with author names and descriptions, of the books published by Macmillan Computer Publishing. Step 4 asks you to choose the fields you want to sort and group by, giving the report a logical ordering. For example, for this report, you probably want all the books written by the same author to be grouped together. So choose Author as the field to sort and group by (see Figure 14.13).

The order that the field is sorted in can also be specified. The Order combo box lists four order choices:

- Ascending order
- Descending order
- Specified order
- Original order

Below the Order combo box are two buttons: Browse Data and Group/Total Tip. The Browse Data button lets you look at the data for each field listed in the Report Fields list box. The Group/Total Tip button provides some online help for hints on creating the proper sorting and grouping for your data.

This example requires only one sort field, Author, so you're ready to move on to Step 5, Total.

14

REPORTING MAGIC
PERFORMING

FIGURE 14.13.

*The Sort page selection
with the Author field
selected.*

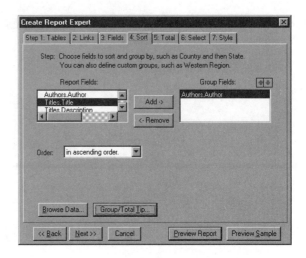

The Total Page

Step 5 allows you to add subtotals and counts to your fields. In the example, you want to know how many books are written by a particular author, so make the Author field a Total field (see Figure 14.14).

FIGURE 14.14.

*Choosing the Author
field to be subtotaled.*

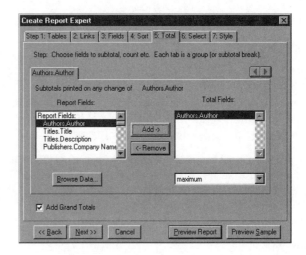

You can base the subtotal on one of four criteria listed in the combo box below the Total Fields list box:

■ Maximum identifies the highest value in the group.

■ Minimum identifies the lowest value in the group.

■ Count counts all the records in the group.

■ Distinct Count counts only distinct records in the group.

At the bottom of the page is the Add Grand Totals checkbox. If you check this box, each to-taled field will have a grand total at the end of the report.

Under the Report Fields list box is the Browse Data button, which allows you to look at the data in a field to help you choose the right fields for subtotaling.

You've selected the only field needed to subtotal on for this example, so you can move to Step 6, Select.

The Select Page

The Select step is used to create a filter for the records that will appear in the report. If you're familiar with SQL, this filter is like SQL's Where clause. In this example, you're reporting on book titles published by Macmillan Computer Publishing, so you need to create a filter that allows only records that match Macmillan Computer Publishing as the publisher to be part of the report.

To create the filter, select a field from the Report Fields list box. For this step, the list box is divided into two separate lists of fields: the fields that have been selected for the report and the fields that are part of the database tables. You aren't limited to using just the fields selected for the report in creating a filter; any field from the database you're working with will work. However, in this example, the field you want to create a filter on is in the list of fields on the report (Publishers).

To make the Publishers field the filtered field, highlight it in the Report Fields list box and click the Add button to move it to the Select Fields list box.

When a field is selected to be the filtered field, two combo boxes are loaded and displayed below the Report Fields list box. These combo boxes allow you to select the operator used to filter the field you've selected (see Figure 14.15).

The combo boxes are used together to create a logical operator for the filter. The first combo box presents only one choice: is. The second combo box presents a list of choices for creating the filter. By clicking the combo box, the following logical operators are presented:

```
any value              between

equal to               starting with

one of                 like

less than              formula:

greater than
```

FIGURE 14.15.

The Select page's operator combo boxes.

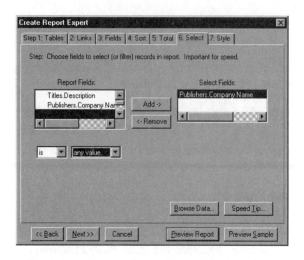

If you're a SQL programmer, you're very familiar with these choices. Even if you've never used SQL before, each choice is fairly self-descriptive. For example, between is used to select fields that are between one value and another value, as in the following SQL code:

```
Select * Where Publisher.Company Name between "Macmillan Computer Publishing" _
    and "Sams"
```

This code prints the data from all the fields where the company name of the publisher falls alphabetically between Macmillan Computer Publishing and Sams.

For the example, you want to filter out all the records except those that match SAMS Publishing, so you will select is and equal to from the two combo boxes.

A third combo box appears after you select the logical operator. This combo box lists data values from the field you've selected for your filter. Figure 14.16 shows the list of company names from the Publishers table that you can choose from to complete the filter.

Select SAMS by scrolling down the list until you find it. Click it, and SAMS will be highlighted in the combo box.

Toward the bottom of the page are two buttons, Browse Data and Speed Tip. The Browse Data button, as on the other pages, allows you to browse the data in the field highlighted in the Report Fields list box. The Speed Tip button provides some hints on how to make the filter you create select records faster.

You're finished with the Select page, so you can move to the final step, Style.

FIGURE 14.16.

The Publishers table's company names for the Select filter.

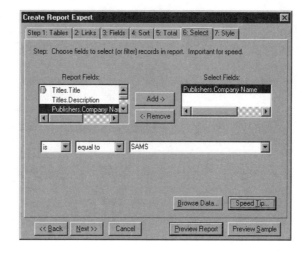

The Style Page

You use the Style page to give the report a title and to select a style for the report. The styles you can choose from include

Standard	Executive, Leading Break
Leading Break	Executive, Trailing Break
Trailing Break	Shading
Table	Red/Blue Border
Drop Table	Maroon/Teal Box

The styles are presented in a list box with a graphic representation of the style. Figure 14.17 shows the Table style selected and its graphic representation, as well as the title for the report you're creating in this example.

On the right side of the Style page is a button that you can click if you have a picture to add to the report. A dialog box will appear to help you browse to find the picture file you want to use. When you select the file, click OK to add the picture to your report.

Below the Add Picture button is the Preview Tip button. When clicked, this button provides some tips on how to use the Preview Report or Preview Sample buttons to make changes to your report after you complete these initial steps.

You're finished with the initial design of the report and can now preview it to see how it looks. To do this, click the Preview Sample button at the bottom of the Style page.

14

PERFORMING
REPORTING MAGIC

FIGURE 14.17.

The Style page selections.

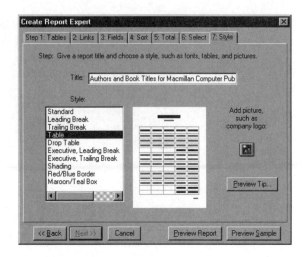

Previewing Your Report

When you click the Preview Sample button, a dialog box appears, asking whether you want to preview the report with all the records from the database or a specific number of records (the default is 100). Figure 14.18 shows this dialog box.

FIGURE 14.18.

The Preview Sample dialog box.

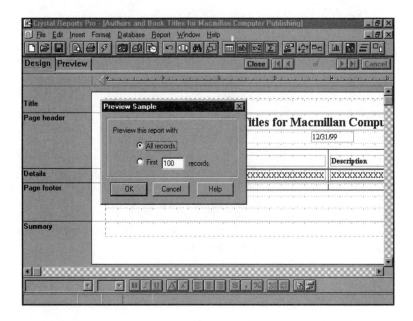

You probably won't want to select all the records for the Preview Sample, especially if you know that the report is going to select a lot of records. Instead, select the first x records, where x is the number you think will be enough to let you see the full layout of the report. In other words, the number selected needs to be enough to generate subgroups, subtotals, and so on if you've selected these options for your report. Because you've selected a table format for this sample report, you don't need to view too many records, so select 10 for the Preview Sample.

Click OK to have Crystal Reports generate the sample report. It can take a while for the sample to be created, depending on how many records are in the database (on my desktop system, it took about 4 minutes).

When Crystal Reports is finished generating the report, a preview screenshot of the report appears (see Figure 14.19). The report is displayed on a tabbed page labeled Preview.

FIGURE 14.19.

The Sample Preview report.

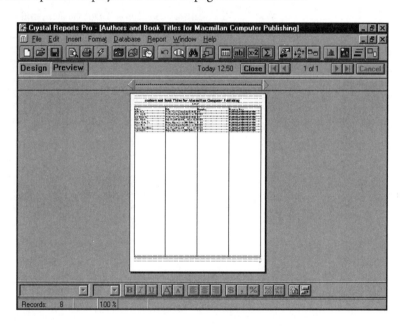

To get a better view of the data on the report, use the zoom button on the toolbar (the button with the three hollow boxes). Click it to have the report fill the whole screen (see Figure 14.20).

When the report is enlarged to full-screen size, you won't be able to see all the columns without scrolling. Use the scrollbar at the bottom of the form to scroll left or right. If the number of records chosen for the preview create more rows than will fit onscreen, use the scrollbar on the right for scrolling up or down.

Below the left/right scrollbar are two buttons on the right part of the Font toolbar. The button on the left, when clicked, displays the Report Style Expert to allow you to change the report style if you want to. The button to the right displays the Auto Arrange form, which asks whether you want to auto arrange the fields and lines in the report. If you've changed the style of the report by adding text boxes, line, or other elements, this form will arrange them into the style you've selected.

FIGURE 14.20.

The Sample Preview report, filling the screen.

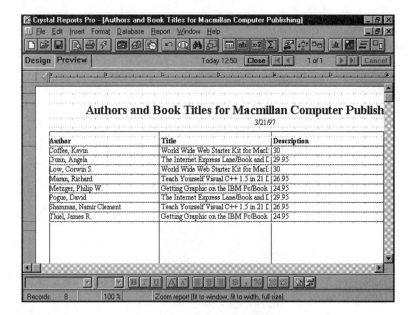

Right-clicking anywhere on the Preview Sample will bring up a floating menu (see Figure 14.21). Many of the items are checked because these are the default settings for Preview Sample. Besides the settings you can toggle on and off, you can change several other settings from this menu, including Page Margins, Set Report Title, and Set Print Date.

If you right-click inside one of the text boxes holding data, a different floating menu appears (see Figure 14.22). When you bring up this floating menu, all the records in the column are highlighted. The changes you make from this menu, then, affect all the records highlighted. To see an example of how this works, right-click one of the records in the Title column and choose Change Font. The familiar Font dialog box then appears. For this example, just change the font from regular to bold by selecting Bold in the Font style list box and clicking OK. Figure 14.23 shows the new Preview Sample.

FIGURE 14.21.
The Preview Sample floating menu.

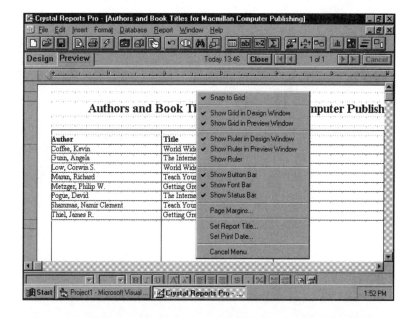

FIGURE 14.22.
The Field Data floating menu.

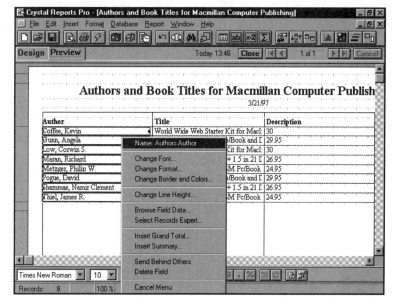

FIGURE 14.23.

*Changing the Title
column to a bold font.*

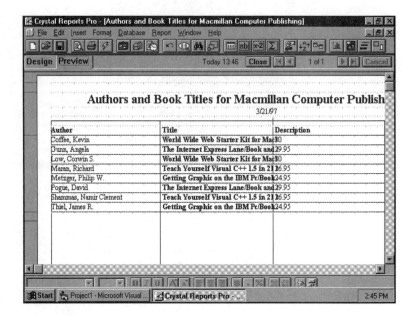

Saving Your Report

When you're finished generating your report, you need to save it. Click the disk icon on the toolbar; the File Save As dialog box appears. Crystal Report reports are saved with an .rpt extension. Type a name into the File Name text box and click OK to save the report. You can open this report later to make changes or to print it when you need to.

Summary

The report designer built into the Visual Basic IDE provides you with the full reporting capabilities of Crystal Reports Version 4.0. The report designer helps you attach to a database, lay out your report, choose the right fields, create groups and subtotals for the records of the report, filter out records you don't want in the report, and make changes to the report after the basic design is created.

Working With SQL and the T-SQL Debugger

by Anthony T. Mann

IN THIS CHAPTER

This chapter serves two distinct purposes. It begins with an overview of Structured Query Language (SQL), describing what it is and how it works from an ANSI perspective. The first section provides many tables and examples to illustrate the syntax used for communicating with a database engine, as well as a general discussion of the different ways you can handle the data you retrieve. The second half of the chapter deals with Microsoft's T-SQL Debugger, a tool for debugging stored procedures on SQL Server. You get a walk-through of the debugger, with examples and options pointed out to give you a thorough understanding of how it simplifies further communication with the server.

Working With Standard SQL

Structured Query Language (SQL) has quickly become the standard relational database language. SQL gives you a way to impose standards when you use a relational database. Some relational databases still don't support SQL, but the vast majority of them do. Here are some of the relational databases that support SQL:

SQL Server	Informix
Access	SQLBase
Sybase	Ingres
Oracle	

> **NOTE**
>
> This chapter covers some of the basics of the SQL language—that is, the American National Standards Institute (ANSI) SQL language. It's not database-specific, which means that certain database engines can have a slightly different syntax. This also means that some of the code presented might not work correctly for a given database engine. You must consult the documentation for your specific database engine to be sure.

You can use this SQL standard in a client/server environment or in a standalone environment. Either way, SQL is the language used to query the database engine. A *database engine* is the heart of the database; it's the way the database vendor decides how the database operates and functions, how data is stored, how syntax is used, and how processing occurs.

You can actually use SQL to do more than construct queries. Using SQL implies that you're querying the database to get data returned from it. In fact, there's much more to it than this. You use SQL to insert new data, update existing data, and even control the parameters of the database engine.

You can send SQL to a database engine by many means. The database engine comes with some sort of interactive tool for sending SQL statements to get some result. This is sometimes referred to as *Interactive Structured Query Language (ISQL)*.

This chapter deals with SQL as a whole. The subject of SQL can be, and has been, the subject of entire books. This chapter can't cover every aspect of SQL, but it covers the basics. It also doesn't get into specific database engines. Certain things are common in all SQL databases. These basic commonalties are the subject of the rest of this chapter. However, for the examples, the following sample data is used. The data is broken up into four tables, shown in Tables 15.1 through 15.4.

Table 15.1. The INVENTORY table.

Product ID	Description	Supplier ID	Quantity
MS001	Visual Basic	M001	45
MS002	Word For Windows	M001	100
MS003	Excel	M001	10
SO001	OCX-10 Home Automation/VB Interface	S002	145

Table 15.2. The SALES table.

Product ID	Staff ID	Date Sold	Quantity Sold
MS001	D001	8/26/96	5
SO001	M001	8/26/96	5

Table 15.3. The STAFF table.

Staff ID	Last Name	First Name
D001	Duck	Donald
M001	Mann	Anthony
M002	Mouse	Mickey

Table 15.4. The SUPPLIER table.

Supplier ID	Supplier
B001	Borland
I001	Intuit
M001	Microsoft
S001	Sams Publishing
S002	SoftHouse

The tables give you an idea of the structure of a database and how the fields relate to each other. Designing databases isn't the topic of this chapter; however, it's important to see how the data relates so that the examples presented later make sense.

By looking at Tables 15.1 through 15.4, you can see that the INVENTORY table contains a list of all items a company can stock. The table also contains a field for the quantity in stock and the product ID used to identify when a sale is made in the SALES table. Listing the description of the product every time a sale occurs is inefficient. Also, a supplier ID field identifies the company that supplies the product from the SUPPLIER table.

The SALES table relates to the tables discussed in the preceding paragraph, but also has a field for the staff ID (the person selling the item). The name of the person selling the item is looked up in the STAFF table, based on the staff ID.

That's how the four tables relate to each other. Each table contains very simple data. However, if the database is designed correctly, it makes no difference how much data is in the tables.

Retrieving Data

By far the most common SQL statement is the SELECT statement. This statement is used to retrieve rows of data from a table as well as for many other purposes (which are presented in the rest of this chapter). To use this statement, you must know the names of the columns in the table you're trying to receive, or you can use an asterisk to specify all columns. The statement has the following general syntax:

```
SELECT [ALL¦DISTINCT] [TOP xx [PERCENT]] select_list
FROM table_names
[WHERE {search_criteria¦join_criteria}
[{AND¦OR search_criteria}]]
[GROUP BY [ALL]aggregate_free_expression [,aggregate_free_expression...]]
[HAVING search_conditions]
[ORDER BY {field_list} [ASC¦DESC]]
```

where

- ALL specifies that every row is returned, including duplicates. (This is the default and doesn't need to be used.)

- DISTINCT specifies that only non-duplicate rows are to be returned.

- TOP specifies that you want only the top *xx* number of records returned. You can also specify the PERCENT keyword after the number *xx* to return only the top *xx* percentage of the total records to be returned. (See the later section "Limiting the Selection" for more information.)

- *select_list* is the list of column names in the tables to return, separated by commas.

- *table_names* is the list of tables that return data.

- *search_criteria* is the list of column names in the tables to return.

- *join_criteria* is the list of column names in one table that joins to other column names in a different table.
- *aggregate_free_expression* is an expression that doesn't include an aggregate. Refer to Table 15.6 later in this chapter for a list of aggregate functions that can't be included in this expression.
- *field_list* is a list of the columns the data is sorted on.
- ASC specifies that the sort order is ascending. (This is the default and doesn't need to be used.)
- DESC specifies that the sort order is descending.

If you're not intimately familiar with SQL, the preceding information can seem pretty confusing. Let me simplify it by providing examples from Tables 15.1 through 15.4.

Selecting Records

> **NOTE**
>
> The keywords throughout this chapter, such as SELECT, FROM, and so on, aren't case-sensitive. They're listed here in uppercase to set them apart from the regular text, but you can type them in lowercase.

To use the SELECT statement, you must know what you want to select and from what. In other words, you need to know the column names and the table names you're trying to select. If you don't know the column names, you must use an asterisk to select all columns in the tables. For example, if you want to select all values from the Supplier column in the SUPPLIER table, you use this statement:

```
SELECT Supplier
FROM SUPPLIER
```

Or you could use this:

```
SELECT *
FROM SUPPLIER
```

> **NOTE**
>
> Even though the keywords aren't case-sensitive, some databases have case-sensitive column names and table names. For this example, the table names have been designated in uppercase, whereas the column names have been designated in lowercase. Columns are sometimes referred to as *fields* and column names as *field names*. They're synonymous.

> **NOTE**
>
> Even though a SQL statement can consist of many lines of text, it's actually one statement. To help you understand this concept, as a general rule a statement consists of all lines of SQL text between two SELECT keywords.
>
> Also, even though these SQL text lines are shown on separate lines, they actually can be put on one line. They're generally constructed on multiple lines because they're easier to read. The SQL standard calls for the database engine (whichever one is used) to ignore the carriage return between SQL keywords in the statement.

The preceding SQL statement produces a complete list of the suppliers in the SUPPLIER table, but the order returned is the order in which they're entered into the table. If you want to sort the list alphabetically, you can use this statement:

```
SELECT Supplier
FROM SUPPLIER
ORDER BY Supplier
```

The ORDER BY keyword (sometimes referred to as the ORDER BY *clause*) needs a column name to know which column to sort on. This ensures that the data is ordered by the Supplier column. By default, the data is ordered in ascending order. To sort in descending order, use this statement:

```
SELECT Supplier
FROM SUPPLIER
ORDER BY Supplier DESC
```

If you want to select multiple columns, use the following statement:

```
SELECT Supplier,Supplier_ID
FROM SUPPLIER
ORDER BY Supplier
```

This statement selects the Supplier column first, followed by the Supplier_ID column. All values in the table are returned because you didn't limit the search. Two columns are selected in the preceding statement (which, coincidentally, is the total number of columns in the SUPPLIER table). However, if you have a table with 100 columns and you want to select all the columns, you don't have to type the names of all 100 columns. You can select all columns in a table with a statement like this:

```
SELECT *
FROM SUPPLIER
ORDER BY Supplier
```

The asterisk indicates that all columns are selected from the SUPPLIER table. The table is still sorted by the Supplier column in ascending order.

Limiting the Selection

You don't have to return all data from a table; you can limit the number of rows returned by using the WHERE keyword. Suppose that you want to find out what the supplier ID is for SoftHouse. You want to limit the number of rows in the SUPPLIER table to all rows where the supplier is equal to "SoftHouse". You can do this with the following code:

```
SELECT *
FROM SUPPLIER
WHERE Supplier = "SoftHouse"
ORDER BY Supplier
```

The data returned is only the data that matches the WHERE keyword (also referred to as the WHERE clause). If no supplier is named SoftHouse, no rows are returned.

> **NOTE**
>
> The string literal in the WHERE clause is case-sensitive. Therefore, "SoftHouse" isn't the same as "SOFTHOUSE".
>
> Also, some implementations of SQL require the use of single quotation marks (apostrophes) instead of double quotation marks.

The ORDER BY clause isn't necessary in the preceding statement, but it doesn't hurt it either. By design, each supplier appears in the SUPPLIER table only once. Because you're looking for only one supplier, the order is irrelevant. However, if you're looking for more than one supplier, it becomes relevant. Suppose that you're looking for "SoftHouse" or "Microsoft". Use this SQL statement:

```
SELECT *
FROM SUPPLIER
WHERE Supplier = "SoftHouse" OR Supplier = "Microsoft"
ORDER BY Supplier
```

In this case, two rows are returned: first the "Microsoft" row and then the "SoftHouse" row, thanks to the ORDER BY clause.

Another way to write the preceding statement is to use the IN keyword, which lets you list a range of values to test for. The values are separated by a comma. The preceding statement is rewritten as this:

```
SELECT *
FROM SUPPLIER
WHERE Supplier IN ("SoftHouse","Microsoft")
ORDER BY Supplier
```

Using the IN keyword can generally save a lot of typing because the column name doesn't have to be repeated. Table 15.5 lists additional keywords that you can use in the WHERE clause.

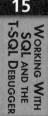

Table 15.5. Keywords that you can use in a WHERE clause.

Keyword	Purpose
IN	Tests for values in a specified range
NOT IN	Tests for values not in a specified range
LIKE	Tests for values that are like a specified value
NOT LIKE	Tests for values that aren't like a specified value
IS NULL	Tests for null values
IS NOT NULL	Tests for non-null values
AND	Tests for multiple conditions
OR	Tests for either specified condition
BETWEEN	Tests for values between a set of specified values
NOT BETWEEN	Tests for values not between a set of specified values
EXISTS	Tests for existing values
NOT EXISTS	Tests for non-existing values
ANY	Tests for any values
ALL	Tests for all values

A very common necessity is to return values that, for example, start with a certain letter, such as *S*. You can do this by using the LIKE keyword. If you want to return all rows from the SUPPLIER table for a supplier starting with an *S*, use this statement:

```
SELECT *
FROM SUPPLIER
WHERE Supplier LIKE "S%"
ORDER BY Supplier
```

This statement returns rows containing the suppliers "SAMS Publishing" and "SoftHouse". The following is the syntax for using the LIKE keyword, where you might have a percent sign before the constant, after the constant, or both:

```
LIKE "[%]constant[%]"
```

The constant is the value for which you're testing. The percent signs are wildcard symbols, just like asterisks in DOS. If you're looking for any supplier with an *S* in its name, use this statement:

```
SELECT *
FROM SUPPLIER
WHERE Supplier LIKE "%S%"
ORDER BY Supplier
```

NOTE

Microsoft Access uses an asterisk (*) wildcard symbol in place of the percent sign (%) when accessed through DAO. The percent sign applies to SQL Server and other client/server databases, as well as Access via ODBC. The rest of the syntax is the same. Also, the expression placed between wildcard symbols is case-sensitive.

NOTE

You must use at least one percent sign in a LIKE clause. If you don't, no rows are returned.

Because the SELECT keyword is used to return values, you can even go so far as to return a value that's not part of the database. This is referred to as a *calculated column*. For example, you can return a percentage of the quantity in the INVENTORY table. Instead of the following SQL statement, which returns the quantity that's actually in the database,

```
SELECT Quantity
FROM INVENTORY
```

you can use this SQL statement to return 10 percent of the quantities:

```
SELECT Quantity * .10
FROM INVENTORY
```

This works only for a numeric data type. You certainly can't do this if Quantity is a string.

Another way to limit the number of records returned is to use the TOP keyword. Suppose that you want to test a SQL statement to determine whether you've used the correct syntax. However, you don't want to return potentially millions of rows of data for a test. You can use the optional TOP keyword to limit the number of rows.

The TOP keyword without a following PERCENT keyword returns only the first *xx* number of records of the total recordset. For example, the following will return only the first 10 records from the SUPPLIER table:

```
SELECT TOP 10 *
FROM SUPPLIER
ORDER BY Supplier
```

If 250 records were in the table, only the first 10 would be returned. Likewise, this example will return the first 10 percent of the total records from the SUPPLIER table:

```
SELECT TOP 10 PERCENT *
FROM SUPPLIER
ORDER BY Supplier
```

Again, if 250 records were in the table, only the first 25 would be returned.

Setting Up Joins

A *join* is a way to return data from two tables. The key to doing this is that you must join or link the columns of data between the two tables so the database engine knows how to look it up. You create the join in the WHERE clause. If you want to select all items in the INVENTORY table but also with the company that supplied the item, you have to do a join between the INVENTORY and SUPPLIER tables. This is because a column (Supplier_ID) is common to both tables, and this column is what the join is based on. This is also called a *common key*, which is a "key" field used as a join. For the SUPPLIER table, it's the primary key, which means that this column is used to access a row in the table. It's not the primary key in the INVENTORY table because it isn't used to access a row in this table; the Product_ID column is the primary key in that table. Again, how to determine primary keys and database design isn't the purpose of this chapter.

To perform the join mentioned here, use this code:

```
SELECT Supplier, Description, Quantity
FROM SUPPLIER s, INVENTORY i
WHERE i.Supplier_ID = s.Supplier_ID
ORDER BY Supplier
```

This statement selects the Supplier, Description, and Quantity columns from the SUPPLIER and INVENTORY tables. For every occurrence of a supplier ID in the INVENTORY table, the supplier is looked up by using the same Supplier_ID column, and the values are assigned to be equal.

The individual letters s and i you see in the preceding code are *aliases*. You use these to identify a column in a table that has the same name in another table you're trying to access. If you don't specify this alias, you receive an error telling you that the column name is ambiguous. This alias gives the database engine a way to decipher which column you're referring to. The alias name goes after the table names in the FROM clause. The name can be any unique value (treated as a string without quotes) as long as it isn't the name of a table you're trying to access.

After the alias is established in the FROM clause, you can reference it by using this format, where *alias* is the name of the alias defined and *column* is the name of the column in the aliased table:

alias.column

For example, consider the WHERE clause in the previous statement:

```
WHERE i.Supplier_ID = s.Supplier_ID
```

It follows the syntax of *alias.column* on each side of the = sign. After the alias is established, you can use it in any of the SQL clauses that are part of that same statement.

If you're trying to select (return) columns in different tables, you must also reference the alias to avoid any ambiguity. Even if you aren't selecting columns with the same name, you may still use the alias. For example, the following isn't incorrect:

```
SELECT s.Supplier, i.Description, i.Quantity
FROM SUPPLIER s, INVENTORY i
WHERE i.Supplier_ID = s.Supplier_ID
ORDER BY s.Supplier
```

It performs the same function. However, it does introduce a possible element of error. At least one field in the ORDER BY clause needs to be in the SELECT clause. If you change the last line to the following, you receive an error because the Supplier column doesn't exist in the INVENTORY table:

```
ORDER BY i.Supplier
```

You can create even more complex joins. Suppose that you want to select the supplier, product description, and quantity, but return only the rows in the INVENTORY table where the supplier is "Microsoft". You have to do a join again to the SUPPLIER table because the only reference to SUPPLIER in the INVENTORY table is an ID, Supplier_ID, which is used as a lookup key in the SUPPLIER table. You can do the join with this statement:

```
SELECT s.Supplier, i.Description, i.Quantity
FROM SUPPLIER s, INVENTORY i
WHERE i.Supplier_ID = s.Supplier_ID
AND s.Supplier = "Microsoft"
ORDER BY s.Supplier
```

Again, the ORDER BY clause isn't absolutely necessary because only one row can be in the SUPPLIER table with the name "Microsoft".

You can use the techniques and topics discussed here to join many multiple tables in your application. However, remember that the more joins you do, the longer it takes the database engine to come back with the results.

Working With Aggregates

An *aggregate* is a mathematical SQL function. Table 15.6 lists the types of SQL aggregates available.

Table 15.6. SQL aggregates.

Aggregate	Purpose
COUNT()	Counts the number of rows returned
SUM()	Sums the number of rows returned
AVG()	Averages the number of rows returned
MAX()	Finds the maximum value in the rows returned
MIN()	Finds the minimum value in the rows returned

In each aggregate listed in Table 15.6, an expression (typically a column name) is expected in the parentheses. However, the expression can be any valid SQL expression.

15

WORKING WITH SQL AND THE T-SQL DEBUGGER

If you want to find out how many rows are returned from this statement,

```
SELECT s.Supplier, i.Description, i.Quantity
FROM SUPPLIER s, INVENTORY i
WHERE i.Supplier_ID = s.Supplier_ID
ORDER BY s.Supplier
```

you can use this statement instead:

```
SELECT COUNT(*), s.Supplier, i.Description, i.Quantity
FROM SUPPLIER s, INVENTORY i
WHERE i.Supplier_ID = s.Supplier_ID
ORDER BY s.Supplier
```

This statement returns four columns, the count of the number of rows returned, the supplier, the description, and the quantity. The joins in the statement were discussed earlier in the "Setting Up Joins" section.

When using an aggregate function, you can use a GROUP BY clause to tell the database engine how to do the calculation. For example, if you want to sum the number of items stocked for each supplier, you must use a GROUP BY clause. If you don't, how does the database engine know how to return the sum? Refer to Table 15.1 to follow this example. Would the database engine sum the quantities for each Product_ID, Description, Supplier_ID, or a combination of the three? That's where the GROUP BY clause comes in. In this scenario, you can perform the necessary function by using this statement:

```
SELECT SUM(Quantity)
FROM SUPPLIER s, INVENTORY i
WHERE i.Supplier_ID = s.Supplier_ID
GROUP BY s.Supplier
ORDER BY s.Supplier
```

This means that for every new supplier, the Quantity is summed. If the GROUP BY clause is omitted, only one row is returned, and it's the sum of all quantities.

Inserting Data

Without inserting data, there would never be the need to perform any UPDATE, DELETE, or SELECT statements. Inserting rows (or records) into a table requires an INSERT statement. The syntax of the INSERT statement is

```
INSERT [INTO] table[(column_list)]
VALUES{(insert_values)}¦sql_select_statement
```

where

- ■ *table* is the name of the table to insert into.

- ■ *column_list* is a listing of columns that have data inserted, separated by commas.

- ■ *insert_values* is the list of values to be inserted into the columns in *column_list*. The same number of values must be in the *insert_values* list as in the *column_list* list.

■ *sql_select_statement* is an alternative way to insert values into a table. You can select values of another table to be inserted. In this case, you don't use the VALUES keyword. You must make sure that the number of columns you're returning in your SQL statement is the same number as in the *column_list* list.

NOTE

Microsoft Access requires the INTO keyword; SQL Server doesn't.

To use the INSERT statement to insert a new supplier into the SUPPLIER table, you can use this statement:

```
INSERT SUPPLIER(Supplier_ID,Supplier)
VALUES ("C001","Crystal Services")
```

The row is simply inserted into the table. Here are some considerations, however:

■ Does the primary key field already exist?

■ Are you concerned about case sensitivity?

■ Are you inserting values with the correct data type?

These questions are very important. Except for the case-sensitivity question, the questions presented here can result in errors if they aren't addressed properly. For example, the following will result in error:

```
INSERT SUPPLIER(Supplier_ID,Supplier)
VALUES (1,"Crystal Services")
```

The Supplier_ID column doesn't expect a numeric data type; it expects a string data type. If you aren't going to include any characters, you must construct the SQL statement this way:

```
INSERT SUPPLIER(Supplier_ID,Supplier)
VALUES ("1","Crystal Services")
```

Rather than insert into a table by hard-coding the values, you can insert by selecting the values from another table. Suppose that you have a table, MASTER, which also has Supplier_ID and Supplier columns from which you'll select values. You can insert all items from the MASTER table like this:

```
INSERT SUPPLIER(Supplier_ID,Supplier)
SELECT Supplier_ID,Supplier
FROM MASTER
```

On the other hand, if you wanted to insert based only on a certain value from the MASTER table, you could construct your SQL SELECT statement based on any valid SQL rule. You could do this:

```
INSERT SUPPLIER(Supplier_ID,Supplier)
SELECT Supplier_ID,Supplier
FROM MASTER
WHERE Supplier="Crystal Services"
```

15

Working With SQL and the T-SQL Debugger

As presented in the "Retrieving Data" section earlier in the chapter, the WHERE clause limits the number of rows returned.

Deleting Data

Deleting rows (or records) from a table requires a DELETE statement. The syntax of the DELETE statement is

```
DELETE FROM table
[WHERE search_conditions]
```

where *table* is the name of the table to delete from, and *search_conditions* are any valid SQL expressions to limit the number of rows deleted.

The DELETE statement deletes an entire row or rows in the database. You can't delete only one column.

You can use the DELETE statement to delete all rows in the SUPPLIER table by using this statement:

```
DELETE FROM SUPPLIER
```

CAUTION

You don't receive a confirmation when you use the DELETE statement. If the statement is executed, the rows are deleted. It's that simple. Be very careful when you use the DELETE statement.

If you want to delete the rows only where the supplier is a certain value, you do it like this:

```
DELETE FROM SUPPLIER
WHERE Supplier = "Borland"
```

This statement deletes all values in the SUPPLIER table where the Supplier is "Borland".

NOTE

You must be careful when you delete (or update) a row in a table in case a value relates to a value in a different table. If it does, you might possibly orphan a row of data in the other table. Creating an *orphan* means that the value related to data in the table from which you deleted now has no way of being referenced, and that the row in the second table is just taking up space.

There are ways around this that aren't within the scope of this chapter, as stated earlier. When you design the database, you can place a trigger on the column so that orphaning doesn't happen inadvertently.

Updating Data

Updating rows (or records) in a table requires an UPDATE statement. The syntax of the UPDATE statement is

```
UPDATE table
SET assignment_list
[WHERE search_conditions]
```

where

- *table* is the name of the table to insert into.
- *assignment_list* is a listing of all updates that will take place.
- *search_conditions* are any valid SQL expressions to limit the number of rows updated.

If you want to update the Supplier_ID column of the SUPPLIER table, you can use the UPDATE statement:

```
UPDATE SUPPLIER
SET Supplier_ID="XXX"
```

All rows in the Supplier_ID column are updated to "XXX". To prevent the rows from being updated, you need to limit the search by using a WHERE clause with any valid SQL expression. You can limit the updating, as described earlier, to only where the Supplier is equal to "Borland". You do this as follows:

```
UPDATE SUPPLIER
SET Supplier_ID="XXX"
WHERE Supplier = "Borland"
```

> **CAUTION**
>
> You don't receive a confirmation when you use the UPDATE statement. If the statement is executed, the rows are updated. It's that simple. Be very careful when you use the UPDATE statement.

On the other hand, if you want to update based only on a certain value from the another table, you can use any valid SQL SELECT statement in place of *assignment_list* in the syntax presented earlier. Suppose that you have a table, MASTER, that also has Supplier_ID and Supplier columns out of which you'll select values. You can insert an item from the MASTER table to update a record in the SUPPLIER table like this:

```
UPDATE SUPPLIER
SET Supplier_ID = (SELECT Supplier_ID
FROM MASTER
WHERE Supplier = "SoftHouse")
WHERE Supplier = "SoftHouse"
```

The last two lines of the preceding statement look as though they're repeated, but they really aren't. The parentheses around the statement between the second and fourth lines indicate a query within a query. The inner query selects from the MASTER table the supplier ID where the supplier is "SoftHouse". The outer query, the UPDATE statement, updates the Supplier_ID column to the value returned from the inner query but limits the rows for which this applies to where the supplier is equal to "SoftHouse". If the last line isn't present, all rows in the Supplier_ID column are updated.

The query-within-a-query concept (called *nested queries*) opens up more possibilities for you when you use the SQL language. As you develop more advanced applications that retrieve data, you'll find that understanding SQL is vital.

Grouping SQL Statements into Transactions

A transaction is a very important part of proper database design. A *transaction* provides a way to group a series of critical SQL statements. This way, if something fails, you can revert the database to the state it was in before the statements were issued. The following three statements handle transactions:

- BEGINTRANS marks the beginning of a transaction.
- COMMITTRANS marks the end of a transaction.
- ROLLBACK rolls the transaction back to the state the database was in before BEGINTRANS was issued.

You indicate the beginning of the group of statements with the BEGINTRANS keyword. If there are no errors, the transaction ends with the COMMITTRANS keyword, which commits all statements executed since BEGINTRANS was issued. However, any errors must be handled in an error handler, which must tell the database not to issue any of the statements executed since the BEGINTRANS was issued. This is done with the ROLLBACK keyword.

The database can do this because it stores the data in a transaction log. The transaction log stores the data in a state that it was at the time the BEGINTRANS was issued. Therefore, the data can be rolled back by using the transaction log.

A good example of when you might use transactions is in an order entry/accounting application. In one transaction, with one order, you want to do the following things:

- Let the shipping department know about the items to be shipped
- Update the customer's record
- Decrease inventory

All these items need to be handled at once. If any of them fail, all need to fail. For example, if the SQL statement to decrease the inventory fails and you don't force the customer's record and the shipping department transactions to fail, there's no integrity between the sets of data. The customer's record would say that an item was ordered, the shipping department would ship the item, but the inventory wouldn't be decreased. As this situation continues, the inventory database would show a large number of items, but these items wouldn't actually exist because the shipping department keeps receiving orders to ship them out. The code fragment in Listing 15.1 illustrates how to use transactions with your SQL statements.

Listing 15.1. Multiple SQL statements wrapped in a transaction.

```
'Handle Error
On Error Goto SaveError
'Begin the transaction
BeginTrans
'Instruct the shipping department to ship the item
sCmd = "INSERT INTO Shipping(Cust_ID, Stock_Num, Qty) "
sCmd = sCmd + "VALUES (101, '119945A', 2) "
'issue statement
dbMain.Workspaces(0).Execute sCmd

'Update the customer's record
sCmd = "INSERT INTO Order(Cust_ID, Stock_Num, Qty, Price, Date) "
sCmd = sCmd + "VALUES (101, '19945A', 2, 19.95, '12/15/96') "
'issue statement
dbMain.Workspaces(0).Execute sCmd

'Update inventory
sCmd = "UPDATE Inventory "
sCmd = sCmd + "SET On_Hand = On_Hand - 2 "
sCmd = sCmd + "WHERE Stock_Num = '19945A' "
'issue statement
dbMain.Workspaces(0).Execute sCmd

'there were no errors, commit
CommitTrans
Exit Sub

'error handler
SaveError:
    MsgBox Error$
    Rollback
    Exit Sub
```

Altering the Database Structure With Data Definition Statements

You can use data definition statements to create or alter the database structure itself. You can use them to do the following:

- Create tables
- Add columns to tables
- Add indexes on tables
- Delete tables and indexes

These statements are issued from Visual Basic just as any other statement would be issued—by using the EXECUTE method of the database object.

Creating Tables

To create a table, you use the CREATE TABLE keywords, which use the syntax

```
CREATE TABLE table (field1 type [(size)] [index1] [, field2 type [(size)]
➥[index2] [, ...]][, multifieldindex [, ...]])
```

where

- *table* is the name of the table to be created.
- *field1*, *field2*... are the names of fields to be created in the new table. (At least one field must be created at this time.)
- *type* is the data type of the new field.
- *size* is the field size in characters for a text field.
- *index1*, *index2*... specifies a CONSTRAINT clause defining a single-field index.
- *multifieldindex* specifies a CONSTRAINT clause defining a multiple-field index.

Suppose that you wanted to create a table named Orders. This table would have five columns: Cust_ID, Stock_Num, Qty, Price, and OrderDate. Also, there would be a primary key index on the Cust_ID column:

```
CREATE TABLE Orders (Cust_ID Double CONSTRAINT PKey PRIMARY KEY, Stock_Num
➥TEXT(10), Qty Integer, Price CURRENCY, OrderDate DATE)
```

If you want to make the Cust_ID, Stock_Num, and OrderDate the primary key, you would do so like this:

```
CREATE TABLE Orders (Cust_ID Double, Stock_Num TEXT(10), Qty Integer,
➥Price CURRENCY, OrderDate DATE, CONSTRAINT PKey PRIMARY KEY(Cust_ID,
➥Stock_Num, OrderDate))
```

Adding or Deleting Columns and Indexes

To alter a table, use the ALTER TABLE keywords with the following syntax:

```
ALTER TABLE table {ADD {[COLUMN] field type[(size)] [CONSTRAINT index] I
CONSTRAINT multifieldindex} ¦
DROP {[COLUMN] field I CONSTRAINT indexname} }
```

where

- *table* is the name of the table to be altered.
- *field* is the name of the field to be added to or deleted from the table.
- *type* is the data type of the field.
- *size* is the field size in characters for text fields.
- *index* is the index for the field.
- *multifieldindex* is the definition of a multiple-field index to be added to table.
- *indexname* is the name of the multiple-field index to be removed.

Suppose that you wanted to add a Ship_Date column to the previous example. You could do that like this:

```
ALTER TABLE Orders
ADD COLUMN Ship_Date DATE
```

If you then wanted to delete a column, you could do that like this:

```
ALTER TABLE Orders
DROP COLUMN Ship_Date
```

You can use this same general syntax to add or delete indexes. The only difference is that you must follow the rules for the CONSTRAINT clause, which follows one of two basic syntaxes. The first is for a single field index, which follows this basic syntax:

```
CONSTRAINT name {PRIMARY KEY ¦ UNIQUE ¦
REFERENCES foreigntable [(foreignfield)]}
```

where

- *name* is the name of the index to be created.

- *foreigntable* is the name of the foreign table containing the field or fields specified by *foreignfield1*, *foreignfield2*, and so on.

- *foreignfield1*, *foreignfield2*... are the names of the fields in *foreigntable* specified by *ref1* and *ref2*. You can omit this field if the referenced field is the primary key of *foreigntable*.

The second is for a multiple field index, which follows this basic syntax:

```
CONSTRAINT name
{PRIMARY KEY (primary1[, primary2 [, ...]]) ¦
UNIQUE (unique1[, unique2 [, ...]]) ¦
FOREIGN KEY (ref1[, ref2 [, ...]]) REFERENCES foreigntable [(foreignfield1 [,
➥foreignfield2 [, ...]])]}
```

where

- *name* is the name of the index to be created.

- *primary1*, *primary2*... are the names of the fields to be designated as the primary key.

- *unique1*, *unique2*... are the names of the fields to be designated as a unique key.

- *ref1*, *ref2*... are the names of foreign key fields that refer to fields in another table.

- *foreigntable* is the name of the foreign table containing the field or fields specified by *foreignfield1*, *foreignfield2*, and so on.

- *foreignfield1*, *foreignfield2*... are the names of the fields in *foreigntable* specified by *ref1* and *ref2*. You can omit this field if the referenced field is the primary key of *foreigntable*.

Deleting Tables and Indexes

Deleting tables or indexes requires a very simple SQL statement that uses the DROP keyword. Of course, you know the name of the table to delete, but it can be difficult to know the name

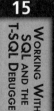

of an index. If you created it, you would know the naming conventions you've used. For example, a primary key index could be called Pkey. However, if you've used some other tool to create the tables and indexes, you might not know the name. One thing you could do is cycle through the Indexes collection to determine all index names.

The DROP keyword is used with this general syntax:

```
DROP {TABLE table ¦ INDEX index ON table}
```

where *table* is the name of the table to delete or the name of the index to delete that resides in a table, and *index* is the name of the index to delete.

If you wanted to delete the table Orders, you would do so like this:

```
DROP TABLE Orders
```

You'll receive no confirmation prompt before the table or index is deleted. Issuing the statement will perform the action.

> **NOTE**
>
> Client/server databases, such as SQL Server, also allow you to DROP databases, provided that you have the appropriate permissions to do so.

Using the T-SQL Debugger

Microsoft has included a new feature in the Enterprise Edition of Visual Basic 5.0 called the Transact-SQL Debugger (or T-SQL Debugger, for short). It isn't compatible with any other version of Visual Basic. Before the T-SQL Debugger existed, debugging stored procedures on SQL Server was very difficult. You had to raise errors under certain circumstances to know what was going on within the stored procedure. In other words, you had to devise a custom method of debugging stored procedures. The T-SQL Debugger changes all of that by providing a way to debug stored procedures from within Visual Basic.

Installing the T-SQL Debugger

To install the T-SQL Debugger, you need to know a few things. First, there are a client-side setup and a server-side setup. The client-side setup is installed automatically when you choose the Typical installation option. If you choose the Custom installation option, you must select the SQL Debugging option under Enterprise Features.

The server-side setup is a little more complicated:

1. Install Service Pack 2 for Windows NT 4.0, located on Visual Basic 5.0's CD-ROM in the \TOOLS\NT40.SP2 subdirectory. Reboot when prompted.

2. Make sure that SQL Server 6.5 or greater is installed, as well as SQL Server Service Pack 2. This service pack is located on Visual Basic 5.0's CD-ROM in the `\TOOLS\TSQL\SQL65.SP2` subdirectory. Reboot when prompted.

CAUTION

Make sure that no errors occur when you install SQL Server 6.5 Service Pack 2, because installing the service pack alters the database by issuing scripts that are necessary for you to continue. If any errors occur, your database won't be updated. Also, make sure that you reboot each time you're prompted. If you don't, this could affect the overall installation process.

---

3. Set up the actual T-SQL Debugger by running the `SDI_NT4.EXE` program on Visual Basic 5.0's CD-ROM in the `\TOOLS\TSQL\SRVSETUP` subdirectory.

Even though you're set up to debug your stored procedures, you should consider a few points before continuing:

■ Make sure that the MSSQLServer service is *not* set up to log on as a system account. Make sure that it's set to log on as a local account (see Figure 15.1).

FIGURE 15.1.
MSSQLServer service startup parameters.

■ If you're using TCP/IP as a protocol, make sure that the machines communicate with each other by typing **PING** at the server's command prompt, followed by the name of the computer you're trying to connect with. For example, Figure 15.2 shows the results of the **PING** command with a computer named NOTEBOOK.

■ Make sure that you have Remote Data Objects 2.0 or later installed on the client computer.

■ Make sure that the RPC Services (Remote Procedure Call and Remote Procedure Locator) are running on the Windows NT server.

15

WORKING WITH SQL AND THE T-SQL DEBUGGER

FIGURE 15.2.

Using the PING
command.

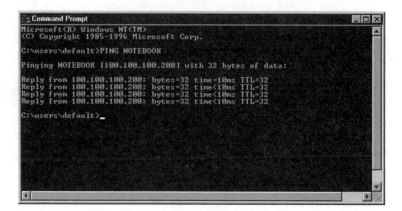

If you have problems, the system will tell you to look in the client and server logs but won't tell you where the logs are located. The server log is actually the Windows NT Application event log. The client log, AUTMGR32.LOG, is on the client machine in the \WINDOWS\SYSTEM subdirectory. This is a cumulative log, with the most recent entries at the bottom.

NOTE

If everything looks fine but you can't figure out why stored procedures aren't debugging, it's best to first reboot the client machine. If that doesn't work, try rebooting the server.

Using the T-SQL Debugger

As an add-in, the T-SQL Debugger must be selected for use. Choose Add-Ins | Add-In Manager from the Visual Basic menu. Make sure that a check mark is next to the VB T-SQL Debugger option (see Figure 15.3).

FIGURE 15.3.

*Selecting the T-SQL
Debugger for use.*

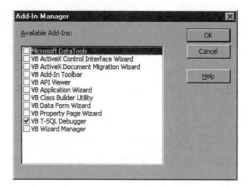

After you select it, notice that the Automation Manager is running. The Automation Manager runs because it's necessary to coordinate Remote Procedure Calls (RPC) with the server. Next, choose Add-Ins | T-SQL Debugger from the menu to start the debugger.

> **NOTE**
>
> You might notice that the T-SQL Debugger is actually offscreen. Apparently, Microsoft didn't take into account the resolution of the add-in. Simply move it to the center of the screen for use.

Creating Queries

When you invoke the T-SQL Debugger, notice a dialog box with three tabbed pages. You must fill in the first page, Settings, to establish an ODBC connection with SQL Server before you can continue. The following fields are required:

- DSN
- SQL Server
- UID
- Password (if any)

To begin, select a Data Source Name (DSN), a 32-bit data source registered with ODBC. If you don't have one on your machine, you can create one by clicking the Register DSN button and configuring a 32-bit DSN in the dialog box that appears.

Next, select or enter the name of the server where SQL Server is installed. For example, you might name your server SERVER-A. After you successfully log on, this server will be conveniently added to the drop-down list for future use.

Enter the database. If you leave the Database field blank, the default database (usually Master) is used. For example, type **pubs**.

UID is the user ID registered with SQL Server. Type a valid user ID, such as **sa** (the default administrator logon). Also type the password, if one exists.

Although they aren't necessary to change for you to continue, the following RDO (Remote Data Objects) options are available:

- Lock Type specifies the type of RDO locking that will occur. The possible values are rdConcurReadOnly, rdConcurValues, rdConcurLock, rdConcurRowver, and rdConcurBatch.
- Result Set specifies the type of RDO resultset that will be returned. The possible values are rdOpenKeyset, rdOpenForwardOnly, rdOpenStatic, and rdOpenDynamic.

15

WORKING WITH SQL AND THE T-SQL DEBUGGER

■ Options specifies miscellaneous options for how queries are executed. The possible values are `rdNone` and `rdExecDirect`.

Figure 15.4 shows how the Settings page looks when configured properly.

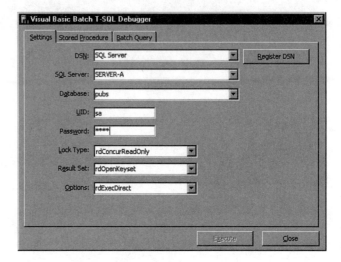

After the required fields are filled in, notice that the Stored Procedure and Batch Query tabs are enabled. Click the Stored Procedure tab to establish an RDO connection with the server. You'll see a list of stored procedures contained within the database (`pubs`) you selected in the earlier example. You'll see these possible stored procedures:

■ `byroyalty`

■ `reptq1`

■ `reptq2`

■ `reptq3`

Select a stored procedure to run (for example, the `byroyalty` stored procedure). Figure 15.5 shows what the Stored Procedure page now looks like.

Notice at the bottom of the dialog box that the Execute button becomes enabled. This is because the T-SQL Debugger is ready to debug the stored procedure.

Alternatively, you can traverse the list of parameters shown on the left and set values for them in the Value text box. This way, you can try different values to debug the stored procedures. However, as you'll see shortly, you can actually change the value in the debugger, just as you would in the Visual Basic debugger. As you change the values, notice that the Query text box changes to reflect the new values. This is the actual query that will be sent to the server.

FIGURE 15.5.

The Stored Procedure page of the T-SQL Debugger.

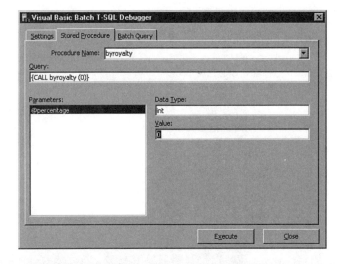

NOTE

Although you can actually change the value in the Query text box, it's not recommended because the Value text box doesn't reflect a change in this case.

If you want to execute the query at this time, see the next section, "Executing Queries."

You use the Batch Query page to place text that will be used in a batch query. A *batch query* is a series of SQL statements transmitted to the server, one after another, in a group. Figure 15.6 shows a sample batch query. Each item in the batch must be separated by the keyword GO.

FIGURE 15.6.

The Batch Query page of the T-SQL Debugger.

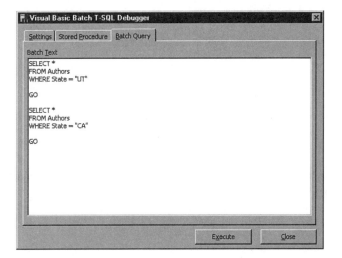

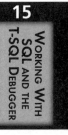

Executing Queries

To execute the query, simply click the Execute button. Doing so establishes another connection with the server and places the query in the debugger window (see Figure 15.7, showing the byroyalty stored procedure).

FIGURE 15.7.

The T-SQL Debugger with a stored procedure to execute.

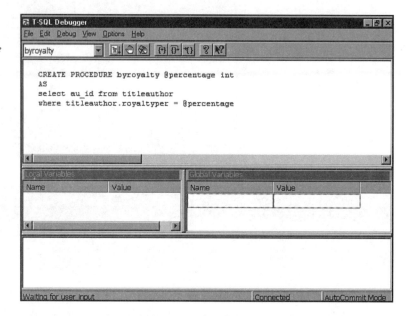

The debugger window has four panes:

- The top unlabeled pane contains the actual stored procedure text.
- The Local Variables pane lists the local variables in the stored procedure.
- The Global Variables pane lists global variables within SQL Server 6.5.
- The bottom unlabeled pane is the results window.

To execute the query, click the Go toolbar button, press the F5 key, or choose Debug | Go from the menu.

If you receive the error message shown in Figure 15.8, refer to the steps listed earlier in the "Installing the T-SQL Debugger" section or refer to the online help. If you don't receive an error, the stored procedure is executed (see Figure 15.9).

After you execute a query, notice that the Go toolbar button becomes disabled. To enable it, choose Debug | Restart from the menu or press Shift+F5. Now you can execute the query as before.

FIGURE 15.8.

A T-SQL Debugger server error.

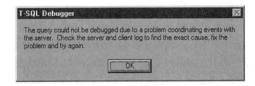

FIGURE 15.9.

The T-SQL Debugger after a stored procedure is executed.

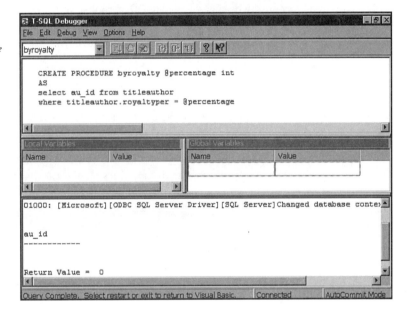

Debugging Queries

Debugging a query in T-SQL is very similar to the way you debug a query in Visual Basic. A *breakpoint* tells the debugger to pause execution when it reaches the code line containing the breakpoint. This way, you can check the values of variables at a specific point. You can set breakpoints by clicking a line of text in the query and then clicking the Set/Remove Breakpoint toolbar button, pressing the F9 key, or choosing Edit | Set Breakpoint from the menu. A red dot appears in the margin of the line containing the breakpoint.

After you set a breakpoint, you can step through the code as you would in Visual Basic. You have the following options:

- Step Into
- Step Over
- Run To Cursor

To activate the Step Into option, click the Step Into toolbar button, press the F8 key, or choose Debug | Step from the menu. Step Into executes every line of code. If the code calls a label or

15

WORKING WITH
SQL AND THE
T-SQL DEBUGGER

another procedure, Step Into steps through each line in that code as well. As each line is executed, the system pauses after each line of code. It's useful to set a breakpoint at a specific point in the code where you suspect a problem to be located, allowing the program to pause execution. Then stepping through the code to watch program execution helps find errors in code.

Activate the Step Over option by clicking the Step Over toolbar button (Step Over has no hotkey or menu option). The Step Over option executes each line in the current procedure, but not every line of code of a called procedure. The code is executed, but not every line is shown.

The Run To Cursor option lets you determine which line of code is executed next. To use it, place the cursor on the line you want to execute. Then click the Run To Cursor toolbar button or choose Debug | Run To Cursor from the menu (no hotkey is available). All lines of code between where the cursor was and where the cursor currently is will be skipped.

While you're debugging code (by setting breakpoints), you can query or set the values of variables to test different scenarios without having to rerun your query externally. Figure 15.10 shows the code stopped at a breakpoint, with the values of all local variables.

FIGURE 15.10.

The T-SQL Debugger stopped at a breakpoint.

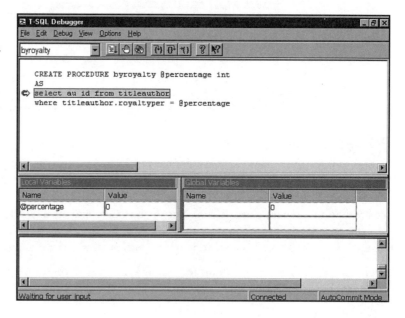

Notice in the Local Variables pane that the value of the @percentage variable is 0. Another way to tell the value of your variables is to place the mouse pointer over the variable to see the value in a tooltip.

To change the value, simply click the Value field in the Local Variables pane and manually change the value. After you change it, press Enter. Notice that placing the cursor over the variable changes it immediately. You then can step through the rest of the procedure and view the results. Change the percentage to 25 to view the results as shown in Figure 15.11. Two author IDs are returned at 25 percent.

FIGURE 15.11.

The T-SQL Debugger after a variable value is changed.

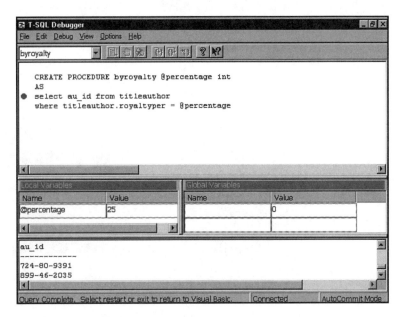

You use the Global Variables pane to query or set the values of global variables. These global variables, stored within SQL Server, are available to all stored procedures and queries. Again, only while debugging can you query or set the value of these options. For example, stop a query at a breakpoint and type the global variable **@@OPTIONS**, which stores different options within SQL Server. (All global variables begin with @@.) Press Enter to see the value of the global variable. This value might not be included in the stored procedure. Figure 15.12 shows what this pane looks like.

T-SQL Debugger Options

You can set two options while using the debugger. One is to view the call stack. If one stored procedure calls another, you'll have more than one query in the call stack. To view this stack, choose View | Call Stack from the menu. Figure 15.13 shows this window.

The other option is the mode that the debugger is in. You can choose between Auto Commit and Auto Rollback. With Auto Rollback, a query is automatically rolled back if it's not committed in code. With Auto Commit, every complete transaction is automatically committed when it's executed.

You can toggle between these two modes by choosing Options | Safe (Auto Rollback) Mode from the menu. If a check mark is next to this item, the debugger is in Auto Rollback mode; if there isn't a check mark, the debugger is in Auto Commit mode.

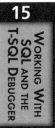

FIGURE 15.12.
*The T-SQL Debugger
after a global variable
is entered.*

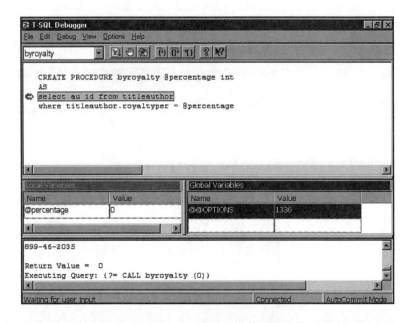

FIGURE 15.13.
*The T-SQL Debugger
call stack.*

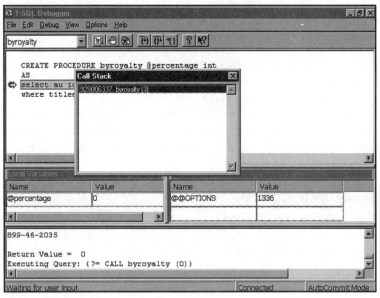

You can also add a watch to a global variable, just as you can add a watch in Visual Basic. A *watch* shows the value of specified variables. To add a watch, select Edit | Add Watch from the menu to place the watch in the Global Variables pane. To remove the watch, simply click it and press Delete.

Another nice feature is the ability to view the contents of a temporary table. To view the contents, simply choose View | Temp Table Dump from the menu. At the prompt, type the name of the temporary table. You then can view the results of the table.

You can view the results of your stored procedures or any messages in the Output Window. You can toggle the Output Window on and off by choosing View | Output Window. If a check mark is next to the option, the Output Window will be shown.

In addition to these stated options, you can choose your own colors for items in the debug window by choosing Options | Colors. The following items can have colors assigned:

Comment	Keyword
Constant	Number
Datatype	Operator
Function	String
Identifier	Execution Indicator

You can also choose the font for the text in the debugger by choosing Options | Font from the menu.

NOTE

You can also debug a stored procedure from within Visual Basic in break mode via the UserConnection object. You can right-click the object to see an option labeled Debug Stored Procedure. This will begin the debugging session listed throughout this chapter.

Summary

SQL is a very important topic because it has become the standard language of most databases. SQL varies slightly among different databases, but the core components discussed in this chapter are common to most databases, except where noted. This chapter gives a good insight into SQL and how it's used. Please use this chapter as an ongoing reference for your database projects.

Microsoft's introduction of the T-SQL Debugger into the Enterprise Edition of Visual Basic 5.0 is a tremendous improvement. Until now, debugging stored procedures was difficult, if not impossible: You had to devise your own schemes for returning values and error codes from stored procedures, a cumbersome task because the stored procedures had to be recompiled after these schemes were put in place.

The T-SQL Debugger makes it very easy to debug stored procedures. It allows you to step through your stored procedures, as well as query and set the value of variables. Using the T-SQL Debugger saves countless hours of tedious work. This chapter showed you how to use the T-SQL Debugger.

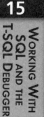

Getting Connected With the UserConnection Designer

by Ashton Hobbs

IN THIS CHAPTER

With the introduction of Visual Basic 5.0, you have a new tool with which to create sophisticated client/server applications. The UserConnection designer is a design-time tool and a runtime object that provides you with an easy way to manage all your database processing from one central location.

The UserConnection object allows you, as a database developer, to place all your database queries, whether they're simple SQL statements or complex stored procedures, in the UserConnection object at design time. You can then reference these queries and stored procedures much like you do methods of an object. This gives you the benefit of having the parameters to the queries and stored procedures displayed in the editor and also provides an easy way to encapsulate all your database logic in one central location.

In this chapter, you learn how to set up the UserConnection object, create a new UserConnection object, create queries for the UserConnection object, and then execute these queries from the Visual Basic Code Editor.

Setting Up the UserConnection Object

Although the UserConnection object is installed with Visual Basic, it's not automatically available to use in your applications. You have to turn on the UserConnection designer manually so that you can use it in your applications.

To set up the UserConnection designer for use in your applications, follow these steps:

1. Choose Project | Components from Visual Basic's menu bar.

2. In the Components dialog box, click the Designers tab to see the list of component designers available within Visual Basic.

3. Select the UserConnection designer by marking the checkbox beside the listing for the object. Your dialog box should look something like the one pictured in Figure 16.1.

FIGURE 16.1.

Selecting the UserConnection designer.

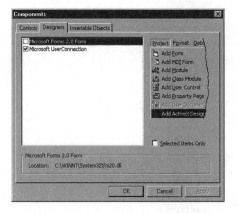

After you set up the UserConnection object designer, you can begin using the object in your applications. To add the object to your application, choose Project | Add ActiveX Designer | Microsoft UserConnection from the menu. This creates the UserConnection object and places it in the Designers group in the Project Explorer. It also displays the UserConnection Properties dialog box to allow you to set the initial properties for the object, such as how to connect to the database, the username and password, as well as which cursor library to use.

You can create multiple UserConnection objects to provide various functionality, including the capability to access multiple data sources, such as accessing a SQL database and an Access .mdb file. You can also add multiple objects to partition your application into various modules. You could have an object that contains the queries and stored procedures for each department or have one object for queries and one object for stored procedures.

The nice feature about the UserConnection object is that it lets you focus more on solving a business problem and not on solving a programming problem. The UserConnection object is a seamless way to simplify your database programming within Visual Basic.

Using the UserConnection Object

Now that you have the UserConnection object set up and ready to insert into your application, you can begin using the UserConnection object in your applications.

When you add the UserConnection object to your application by choosing the option from the menu, you're initially presented with the dialog box shown in Figure 16.2.

FIGURE 16.2.

The UserConnection *object's initial dialog box.*

As you can see, you can specify the connection information here in the object's Properties dialog box. The UserConnection object lets you connect to a data source by using an ODBC data source name or by using a DSN-less connection by specifying the ODBC driver that you'll be using and the database server to which you'll be connecting.

The Authentication page in the Properties dialog box lets you specify the authentication information for the object. You can specify a user name and a password that the object will use when it connects to the database specified on the Connection page of the Properties dialog box.

On the Authentication page, you also can specify whether to display an ODBC prompt to users. You can choose to always display the prompt, never display the prompt, or display only when needed. Depending on your situation, you may want to choose to always display the prompt if you're deploying a client/server application and want your users to validate themselves to the database.

> **TIP**
>
> I have found that, as a general rule for server applications, it's best to never display the prompt; for client applications, it's best to set the prompt to display only as needed.

The Miscellaneous page lets you specify various information for the object, such as the login timeout, query timeout, and the cursor library that should be used.

> **CAUTION**
>
> In my applications, I have discovered that Microsoft SQL Server stored procedures don't work well in a Server Cursor environment. They seem to return errors complaining about more than a `Select` statement being in the stored procedure. If you plan to use Microsoft SQL Server as your database and plan to use stored procedures, I recommend that you use a library other than Server Cursor.

Connecting to a Database

At design time, you can specify all the connection information needed to connect to a database. In your code, you need to call the `EstablishConnection` method to actually connect to the database by using the information in the `UserConnection` object. The syntax for the `EstablishConnection` object is as follows:

`object.EstablishConnection prompt, [readonly, ]options`

The `EstablishConnection` method can take three optional arguments:

- *prompt* lets you specify whether to display the ODBC prompt to users or use the information contained in the object to make a connection. The default is to not display the prompt unless to `DSN` is specified.
- The second argument is the read-only parameter, which lets you specify whether the connection will enable updates or be a read-only connection to the database.

> **TIP**
>
> A read-only connection is useful in reporting applications where you don't want users to be able to update the data they're reading.

■ You can use the *options* parameter to pass any options that you want the object to use. The only current available option is the `rdAsyncEnable` option, which lets you make query execution optional.

Listing 16.1 shows how to create a `UserConnection` object in code and then connect to the database by using the `EstablishConnection` method.

Listing 16.1. The `EstablishConnection` method.

```
Option Explicit
Private uConn as New UserConnection1

Private Sub DBConnect ()
    UConn.EstablishConnection
End Sub
```

Using `UserConnection` Object Events

The `UserConnection` object provides eight events that you can use to handle events generated by the object. These events are accessed directly from the `UserConnection` object designer window by clicking the View Code button in the designer's toolbar.

Table 16.1 lists the `UserConnection` object events and a short description of their purpose and how to use them.

Table 16.1. `UserConnection` object events.

Event	Description
BeforeConnect	Lets you process or display information directly before a call is made to connect to the database.
Connect	Fired after a connection is made to the database. You can use this event to check for any errors that occurred in connecting to the database.
Disconnect	Fired after the object disconnects from the database.
Initialize	Fired when an instance of the object is created.
QueryComplete	Occurs after a query is executed, allowing you to check whether the query was executed successfully.

continues

Table 16.1. continued

Event	Description
QueryTimeout	Fired when an executing query takes longer than the specified query timeout value. You can use this event to determine whether you'll continue waiting for the query to complete or terminate the running query.
Terminate	Fired if a connection to the database is terminated.
WillExecute	Occurs before a query is executed, allowing you to cancel execution of the query or perform special processing before the query is sent to the database to be executed.

Adding a New Query

The main purpose of the UserConnection object is to allow you to place all your database queries and stored procedures into a central location where they can be maintained and modified. In the following steps, you'll add a query to the UserConnection object and then write some code to execute the query and get the result set returned from the database.

This query will return a listing of all records from a table named Users. This very simple query is used only to illustrate how to use the UserConnection object; I hope your real-world queries are more involved than this SQL statement. Follow these steps to create a new query in the UserConnection object:

1. Open the UserConnection designer by double-clicking the object in the Project Explorer.
2. When the designer is open, you can add a new query by clicking the Insert Query toolbar button at the top of the designer.
3. When you click the Insert Query toolbar button, a Properties dialog box appears, allowing you to enter various information about the query. For this example, set the Query Name field to be TestQuery1.
4. Select the Based on User-Defined SQL option at the bottom of the dialog box and enter the following SQL statement:

   ```
   Select * from Users
   ```

5. After you enter all information, your dialog box should look like the one in Figure 16.3. When you've entered all information correctly, you can choose OK to return to the object designer.

FIGURE 16.3.

*The query properties
dialog box.*

You've now created a query method in the `UserConnection` object. To actually use that query, you need to write some code behind it. One nice thing about the `UserConnection` object is that the query you just created becomes a visible method of the object. You don't have to specify a query from a collection or select the query from a list; you can call the query directly as though it were a member of the object. Listing 16.2 shows how you execute the query and get the results returned from the query.

Listing 16.2. The execute query method.

```
Option Explicit
Private uConn as New UserConnection1

Private Sub Execute ()
    Dim rs as rdoResultSet

    uConn.EstablishConnection
    uConn.TestQuery1
    Set rs = uConn.LastQueryResults
End Sub
```

Notice that you call the `LastQueryResults` method of the `UserConnection` object. This method is what you use to get the resultset returned by the executed query. The resultset isn't returned by the query method as you might expect, but is stored internally in the `UserConnection` object until you call the `LastQueryResults` method to obtain the resultset.

Adding Parameterized Queries and Stored Procedures

In addition to executing standard queries, you can create queries and stored procedures that take arguments or parameters. For a stored procedure, the parameters are automatically given the correct names and data types. For your own parameterized queries, you need to specify the name of the argument, but the designer will usually assign the correct data type to your parameter, based on the column it's being compared against.

I'll forgo an example that uses stored procedures, because the object handles naming the parameters and setting the data types. Instead, let's modify the query used in the previous example to find records from the Users table that match a given parameter.

> **TIP**
>
> To get the return value from a stored procedure, get the return value of the stored procedure method. If the stored procedure returns a value of 10, the stored procedure method of the UserConnection object returns a value of 10.

You find records from the Users tables only where the LastName column is equal to a specified value. Follow these steps to create a parameterized query for execution in your code:

1. Create a new query as outlined in the previous example and name it TestQuery2.

2. In the SQL statement block, enter the following SQL statement:

   ```
   Select * From Users Where LastName = ?
   ```

3. Click the Parameters tab of the properties dialog box (see Figure 16.4). Change the Name to Lastname, the ODBC Binding Data Type to be a VarChar and the Visual Basic Data Type to be a String.

4. After you enter all information for the parameter, click OK and exit the UserConnection object designer.

FIGURE 16.4.

The Parameters page of the query properties dialog box.

Now execute the query, passing in the value of Smith as the parameter for LastName. Listing 16.3 shows how to execute the query, passing a parameter and then obtaining the resultset returned by the query.

Listing 16.3. Parameterized queries.

```
Option Explicit
Private uConn As New UserConnection1

Private Sub Method()
    Dim rs As rdoResultset

    uConn.EstablishConnection
    uConn.TestQuery2 'Smith'

    Set rs = uConn.LastQueryResults

End Sub
```

The UserConnection object is so useful because it lets you use Visual Basic's features to view information about the SQL query. Figure 16.5 displays the code window and what you see when writing code to execute the query. Notice that Visual Basic displays the name of the parameter and the data type required by the parameter.

FIGURE 16.5.

Coding parameterized queries.

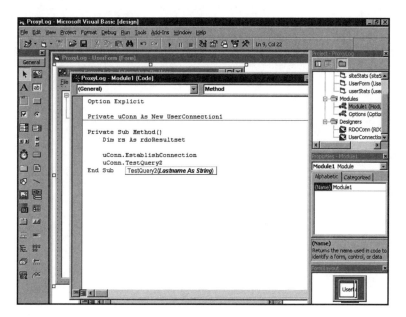

Summary

In this chapter, you've learned how to use the UserConnection object provided in Visual Basic to simplify the creation of database applications. Whether you're creating application servers or client/server applications, the UserConnection object can simplify your database development by providing a single location to place all database-related information and by also making query execution almost transparent.

Because of its ability to treat a database query as a method, the `UserConnection` object simplifies the coding of database applications. You no longer have to assign each parameter for a query or a stored procedure to a specific collection item. You can specify the parameters as arguments to a method, which means that you have more time for solving business problems and can spend less time on learning how to execute a query in Visual Basic.

Understanding ODBC Fundamentals

by Lowell Mauer

IN THIS CHAPTER

When you develop Visual Basic applications, you have two ways of accessing information stored in a database. Included in Visual Basic is a component called the Jet engine, which becomes a part of your database application. As you issue commands to retrieve information from the database, the commands are interpreted by the Jet engine, but the processing of these commands is done locally on your PC. This is true whether the database resides on your PC or is located on a file server somewhere else on the network.

In the client/server world, databases are usually too large to be located on a single PC. Also, many users probably require access to the information stored there. For these reasons, database servers are used to process any application request for data. Your application would issue a request for information, usually in the form of a SQL statement. This request is then passed to the database server, which processes it and returns a recordset containing the resulting data for the request. In this way, the actual processing of the recordsets is done by the server, not by your PC.

This chapter explores how to connect your database by using a method called ODBC, or Open Database Connectivity. Visual Basic and other PC-based data-access tools and programming languages use ODBC to communicate with most databases. This way, the application can reference an ODBC data source instead of the actual path and filename of the database. This really means that the database can reside anywhere on the network. ODBC is a component of Microsoft's Windows Open System Architecture (WOSA).

ODBC provides a set of application program interface (API) functions, which makes it easier for you to connect to a wide variety of database systems. Because of the use of ODBC standards, you can use the same set of functions and commands to access information in SQL Server, Oracle, or Interbase, even though the actual data-storage systems are quite different. Even a number of PC databases can be accessed with ODBC functions. Because of these standards, you don't have to learn different access languages for each database you want to use. The ODBC standard allows you to write standard SQL program code that's translated and then passed to the database in use.

Understanding ODBC Drivers

ODBC drivers are the DLL files containing the functions that connect to various databases. There are separate sets of drivers for each database system. For many standard databases, such as PC databases and SQL Server, these drivers are provided with Visual Basic. For other databases, you can obtain the ODBC driver from the manufacturer of that database.

ODBC drivers are divided into two types: single-tier or multiple-tier. A *single-tier* driver is used to connect to PC-based database systems that may reside on either the local machine or a file server. Multiple-tier drivers are used to connect to client/server databases where the SQL statement is processed by the server, not the local machine.

Each ODBC driver that you encounter must contain the following basic set of functions, known as the *core-level capabilities*:

- Provide database connections
- Prepare and execute SQL statements
- Process transactions
- Return result sets
- Notify the application of errors

To use an ODBC driver in your application, you need to install the ODBC driver on your PC and then create the ODBC definition for your database by using the ODBC Administrator.

Using the ODBC Administrator

Before you can use ODBC to connect to your database, you must have the ODBC drivers installed on your PC and set up the ODBC data source. You can do both by using the ODBC Administrator, an application that's installed when you install Visual Basic 5.0. Most ODBC suppliers also include the administrator application with their ODBC drivers.

> **NOTE**
>
> As with any software, several versions of the ODBC administrator are in use. This chapter discusses the version that comes with Visual Basic 5.0.

After you install the drivers on your PC, you can set up an ODBC data source reference for the related database that you want to use.

Accessing ODBC

To set up ODBC access on your system, you need to use the ODBC Administrator application. You'll find this in the Control Panel (see Figure 17.1), which is accessible by choosing Start | Settings | Control Panel.

When the ODBC Administrator is started, you'll see a Windows 95-style tabbed dialog box (see Figure 17.2). The initial tab is the User DSN definition page, which displays User or Local data source definitions.

FIGURE 17.1.

*The ODBC Adminis-
trator is located in the
Control Panel of
Windows 95.*

ODBC Administrator

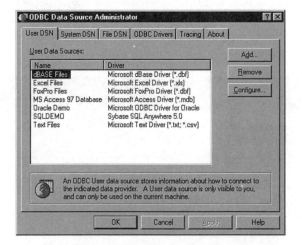

FIGURE 17.2.

*Local ODBC data
sources are displayed
and maintained on the
User DSN page.*

You can define three types of ODBC data sources with the ODBC Administrator:

- *User.* Data sources that are local to a computer for the current user.
- *System.* Data sources that any user can access on the computer.
- *File.* Definition file containing the ODBC connect information.

Each of these is used for specific reasons within a standalone or network environment. Generally, if you're developing a Visual Basic application that will be using an ODBC database, you define a User data source to access the database. Before you can add a data source definition, you need to make sure that the needed ODBC drivers are installed on your PC. To do this, click the ODBC Drivers tab (see Figure 17.3) for a list of the ODBC drivers already on your PC.

FIGURE 17.3.

With the ODBC Drivers page, you can obtain all the version information you might need about a driver.

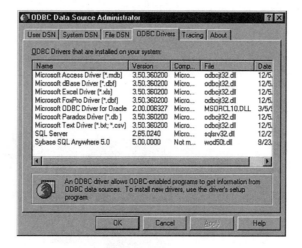

If you experience any problems when using an ODBC connection, first check to make sure that you're using the correct version of the driver. The ODBC Drivers page displays information about the current drivers installed on your PC. When checking versions, you should pay close attention to the company that supplied it and the date and time when it was created. The company becomes important when more than one ODBC driver is available for a database; the date and time can be useful if the company doesn't change the version number every time it makes a fix to the driver and redistributes it.

> **NOTE**
>
> ODBC drivers from different companies usually support different options for a particular database. Check to make sure that the driver you're using supports the functions you need on the database.

The Administrator application no longer controls the installation and deletion of ODBC drivers. These functions are now done by the setup program supplied with the drivers. After you determine that you have the ODBC drivers you need, you can define the data sources that your application will use to access the database.

Defining an ODBC Data Source

The first step in defining a data source for your application is to determine the type of data source you'll need. Each of the three data source types addresses specific application requirements for connecting to and accessing database information. For most single-use applications, the User DSN is the correct definition to use. However, using the System DSN definition is a good idea if you think the application might be used in a client/server environment. By using the System DSN definition, any user logged in to the PC can access the data source through this ODBC definition.

Defining a data source is the same for all the different types of DSN data sources. To add a new data source, click the Add button on the User DSN page (refer to Figure 17.2) to display the Create New Data Source dialog box (see Figure 17.4). This dialog box lists all the available ODBC drivers. Select the appropriate driver for the database you'll be using and click the Finish button.

FIGURE 17.4.

Selecting the ODBC driver is the first step to setting up a data source.

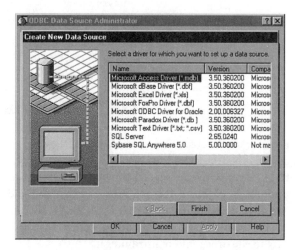

The next dialog box displayed depends on the database you're using. Each available database requires its own set of information to perform correctly. Figure 17.5 shows the dialog box for a Microsoft Access database.

FIGURE 17.5.

A Setup dialog box allows you to specify the information necessary to connect to an ODBC data source.

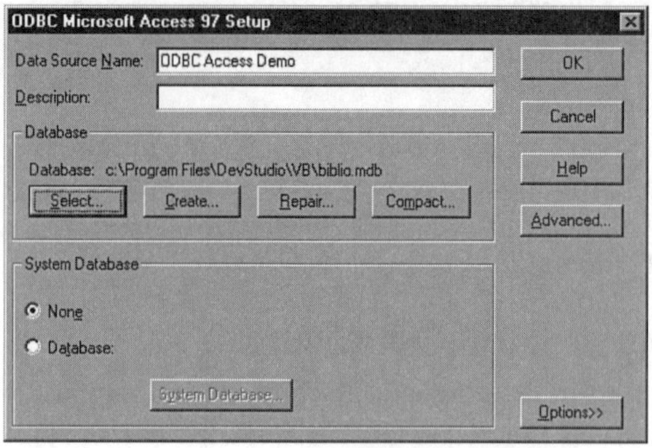

In the Data Source Name text box, enter the name that you'll use in your applications to refer to the data source. You also might want to include a Description of the data source. After entering the name, choose the actual database that you want to access with your program by clicking the Select button. An open-file dialog box appears. If this Access database is new, you can choose to create the database file from this dialog box. However, you still will need to add the table and column definitions to the file, using either Access or the Visual Data Manager. You also can perform maintenance on the Access database, such as repairing and compacting the file. After selecting your database and specifying a data source name, click OK to complete the definition process.

> **NOTE**
>
> You can define as many different data sources as you might need by using the same ODBC driver.

Although the dialog boxes for other databases are different from the one just described, you would specify both a data source name to be used by your applications and the connection information for the database that you'll access. Figures 17.6 and 17.7 show the dialog boxes for a server-based Oracle database and a PC-based SQL Anywhere database, respectively.

FIGURE 17.6.

The Oracle dialog box requires you to enter a database user ID, password, and network connection string, in addition to the data source name.

The DSN pages also allow you to modify or delete ODBC sources. To modify a data source, select the data source and click the Configure button, as shown earlier in Figure 17.2. This displays the same dialog box that you used to create the data source. To delete a data source, select it and click the Remove button. Now that you have the data source defined for your database, you're ready to start using it in a Visual Basic application.

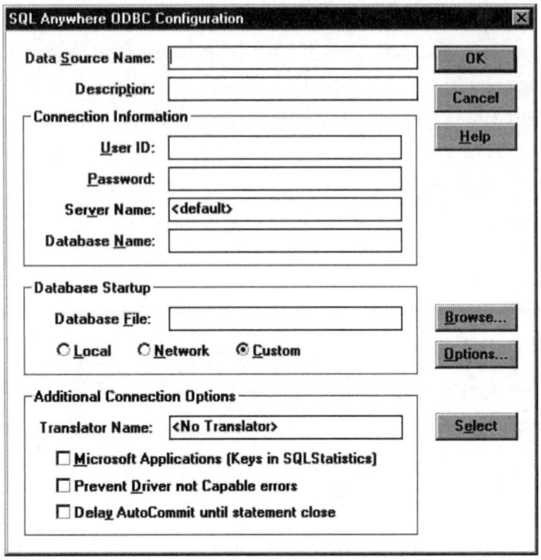

FIGURE 17.7.

The SQL Anywhere dialog box requires you to specify the database user ID, password, and full database name on the PC.

Referencing ODBC in a Visual Basic Application

Before the advent of remote data objects in Visual Basic, it was much more difficult to use ODBC databases in your programs. To use ODBC, you had to declare and make calls directly to the ODBC API functions in your program. Remote data objects have changed this by providing an interface to the ODBC API that uses the familiar Visual Basic Data control operations of setting properties and calling methods. Because properties and methods are used in all Visual Basic programs, accessing ODBC databases is now much easier for developers to understand and accomplish with minimal effort. As you'll see, except for the way you open the ODBC data source, everything else that you'll do in your application is done exactly as though you were using the standard Data controls.

Visual Basic has two methods of accessing databases:

- By using the Data controls to bind the data source directly to the controls on a Visual Basic form
- By programming the access directly in the application, using the Data Access Objects to connect to the data source

When you use ODBC data sources, Visual Basic provides a second set of tools instead of the standard Data controls and Data Access Objects. The Remote Data Control and Remote Data Objects are designed to be used with ODBC data sources.

Using the Remote Data Control

The fastest way to create applications with ODBC data sources is by using the Remote Data Control (RDC). The RDC lets you set a few properties of the control, and then handles all the tasks of making the connections to the ODBC data source for you. This way, the RDC automates the methods of the remote data objects in the same way that the data control automates the methods of the data access objects. To use the RDC, you must add the control to your application. By using the Components dialog box (see Figure 17.8), which you access from the Project menu, you can add the control.

FIGURE 17.8.

Using the Remote Data Control is easy after the control is added to your project.

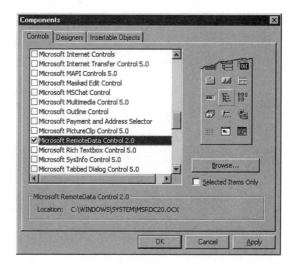

After you add the control to your project, notice a new control in the toolbox (see Figure 17.9). After you include the control in your project, you then add it to the forms that require access to the data source.

FIGURE 17.9.

The Remote Data Control uses a slightly different icon to distinguish itself from the standard Data control.

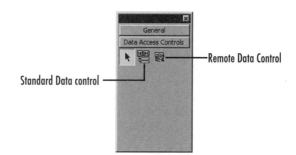

After putting the RDC on a form, you need to set the control's properties to identify which ODBC data source you want to access. The Property Pages for the control prompts you for the ODBC data source name (see Figure 17.10). Also, you need to enter a user name and password for the database. Finally, at the bottom of the dialog box, the Remote Data Control requires you to enter a SQL statement. As with the standard Data control, you can change this SQL statement in the form's load routine.

FIGURE 17.10.

Setting the properties for the Remote Data Control in the Property Pages.

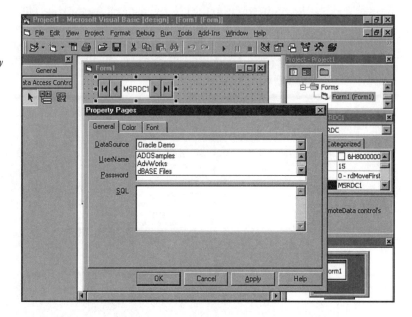

After setting up the Remote Data Control, you can use any bound control that you have to display and edit information in the resultset created by the data control. The bound controls are set up the same way they would be for use with the Data control, except that now the DataSource property of the bound controls points to a Remote Data Control. When set up, the bound controls are updated with new information each time a new row is accessed by the Remote Data Control.

Accessing a Database with RDO

If the Remote Data Control is too restrictive for what you need to do in your application, you can choose to access the data source through program code. The Remote Data Object (RDO) is designed to help you do just that. Again, the differences between the standard Data Access Object (DAO) and the Remote Data Object is with the way you'll connect to the data source and the command set that you'll use. To illustrate the similarities between the RDO and DAO models, Listings 17.1 and 17.2 both issue a SQL request to an Access database. The difference between the two listings is simply the objects and methods used to create the recordset to be used. When the recordset or resultset is established, all other statements are the same.

Listing 17.1. USINGRDO.TXT: Accessing information in an ODBC data source by using the RDO methods.

```
Dim WS As rdoEnvironment
Dim DB As rdoConnection
Dim RS As rdoResultset
Dim SQLSel As String
SQLSel = "Select * From Authors"
Set WS = rdoEngine.rdoEnvironments(0)
Set DB = WS.OpenConnection("ODBC Access Demo")
Set RS = DB.OpenResultset(SQLSel,rdOpenKeyset)
RS.MoveFirst
txtName.Text = RS("Author")
RS.Close
DB.Close
```

Listing 17.2. USINGDAO.TXT: Accessing the same information by using the DAO methods.

```
Dim WS As WorkSpace
Dim DB As Database
Dim RS As Recordset
Dim SQLSel As String
SQLSel = "Select * From Authors"
Set WS = DBEngine.Workspaces(0)
Set DB = WS.OpenDatabase("C:\Program Files\Devstudio\VB\Biblio.Mdb")
Set RS = DB.OpenRecordset(SQLSel,rdOpenDynaset)
RS.MoveFirst
txtName.Text = RS("Author")
RS.Close
DB.Close
```

Debugging ODBC Problems

When using ODBC to access your databases, sometimes you'll experience problems. When this happens, you need some information about the ODBC driver and what it's doing when a problem occurs. You can obtain this information from the ODBC Drivers page in the ODBC Administrator. The other information about what the driver is doing is a little more difficult to get. Two methods are available to you with Visual Basic and the ODBC Administrator that allow you to capture what's being done by the ODBC driver you're using. The ODBC Administrator provides a utility to trace all calls made to an ODBC driver from any program (see Figure 17.11).

The other way to capture information about the ODBC calls is to use a utility that comes with Visual Basic 5.0 called ODBC Spy (see Figure 17.12).

FIGURE 17.11.

Using the Trace utility provided with the ODBC Administrator.

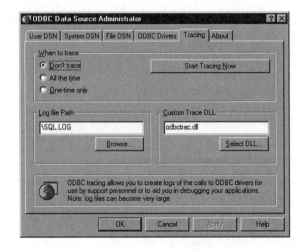

FIGURE 17.12.

Tracing ODBC calls by using the ODBC Spy utility.

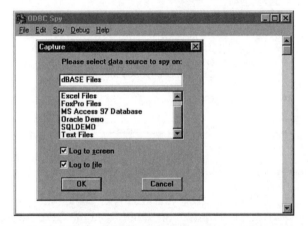

NOTE

The ODBC Spy utility isn't installed with Visual Basic 5. It can be found on Visual Basic's CD-ROM in the `\Tools\ODBCSPY` directory.

Each method will capture what the ODBC driver is doing; however, the level of detail varies. The ODBC Spy utility captures just enough of the calls to show what's happening and whether a call was successful or there was an error, as shown in the following:

```
SQLAllocEnv
    0x01000000
    SQL_SUCCESS
SQLAllocConnect
    0x01000000
    0x01010000
    SQL_SUCCESS
```

```
SQLGetInfo
    0x01010000
    SQL_DRIVER_ODBC_VER
    [5]02.50
    6
    5
    SQL_SUCCESS
SQLSetConnectOption
    0x01010000
    SQL_LOGIN_TIMEOUT
    0x0F000000
    SQL_ERROR
SQLDriverConnect
    0x01010000
    0x780C0000
    [36]DSN=Oracle Demo;UID=scott;PWD=tiger;
    SQL_NTS
    [53]DSN=Oracle Demo;UID=scott;PWD=tiger;ConnectString=2:;
    255
    53
    SQL_DRIVER_COMPLETE_REQUIRED
    SQL_SUCCESS
```

As you can tell from just this small section of the log, understanding what these entries mean can take some time. The ODBC log shows each individual call to the database and its resulting status code. If you remove all the internal notations, however, the log is a little easier to follow:

```
SQLAllocEnv
    SQL_SUCCESS
SQLAllocConnect
    SQL_SUCCESS
SQLGetInfo
    SQL_SUCCESS
SQLSetConnectOption
    SQL_ERROR
SQLDriverConnect
    SQL_DRIVER_COMPLETE_REQUIRED
    SQL_SUCCESS
```

The ODBC Administrator Trace utility captures a lot more detail for the same function. The section of the Trace log shown next is for the same ODBC calls as the ODBC Spy log shown previously. You can see that the Trace log contains not only what the call was, but also the program that made the call and other detailed information about the call:

```
VB5             fffa3dd9:fffaf711    ENTER SQLAllocEnv
        HENV *                  0x236a7a98

VB5             fffa3dd9:fffaf711    EXIT  SQLAllocEnv
➡  with return code 0 (SQL_SUCCESS)
        HENV *                  0x236a7a98 ( 0x0178255c)

VB5             fffa3dd9:fffaf711    ENTER SQLAllocConnect
        HENV                    0x0178255c
        HDBC *                  0x02460e60
```

```
VB5              fffa3dd9:fffaf711    EXIT  SQLAllocConnect
➤ with return code 0 (SQL_SUCCESS)
        HENV                0x0178255c
        HDBC *              0x02460e60 ( 0x017839a4)

VB5              fffa3dd9:fffaf711    ENTER SQLSetConnectOption
        HDBC               0x017839a4
        UWORD                      103
        UDWORD                      15

VB5              fffa3dd9:fffaf711    EXIT  SQLSetConnectOption
➤ with return code 0 (SQL_SUCCESS)
        HDBC               0x017839a4
        UWORD                      103
        UDWORD                      15

VB5              fffa3dd9:fffaf711    ENTER SQLSetConnectOption
        HDBC               0x017839a4
        UWORD                      110
        UDWORD                       0

VB5              fffa3dd9:fffaf711    EXIT  SQLSetConnectOption
➤ with return code 0 (SQL_SUCCESS)
        HDBC               0x017839a4
        UWORD                      110
        UDWORD                       0

VB5              fffa3dd9:fffaf711    ENTER SQLDriverConnectW
        HDBC               0x017839a4
        HWND               0x00000598
        WCHAR *            0x0178289c [      -3]
➤ "DSN=Oracle Demo;UID=scott;PWD=tiger;"
        SWORD                       -3
        WCHAR *            0x01783a70
        SWORD                      510
        SWORD *            0x007ff4ce
        UWORD                        3 <SQL_DRIVER_COMPLETE_REQUIRED>

VB5              fffa3dd9:fffaf711    EXIT  SQLDriverConnectW
➤ with return code 1 (SQL_SUCCESS_WITH_INFO)
        HDBC               0x017839a4
        HWND               0x00000598
        WCHAR *            0x0178289c [      -3]
➤ "DSN=Oracle Demo;UID=scott;PWD=tiger;"
        SWORD                       -3
        WCHAR *            0x01783a70 [     106]
➤ "DSN=Oracle Demo;UID=scott;PWD=tiger;ConnectString=2:;"
        SWORD                      510
        SWORD *            0x007ff4ce (106)
        UWORD                        3 <SQL_DRIVER_COMPLETE_REQUIRED>
```

It takes knowledge to understand the calls that the ODBC drivers make when you access a data source. However, if you spend the time learning how to read the logs, you can solve some of the problems that might crop up when using the ODBC drivers. For more information on ODBC drivers and database programming with VB, check out *Teach Yourself Database Programming with Visual Basic 5* or *Visual Basic 5 Database Developer's Guide*, both from Sams Publishing.

Summary

In this chapter, you took a quick look into what ODBC database connections really are and how they can be used within a Visual Basic application. As you've seen, in addition to the way you'll open the database connection, the rest of the program access for an ODBC database is the same as using the Visual Basic Jet engine to access the information. This chapter also explored how to use the ODBC Administrator to create and modify the ODBC data source definitions that you'll use. Finally, if you have a problem with the ODBC access, you learned how to trace the calls to the ODBC driver, using the ODBC Trace utility that comes with the Administrator.

17

UNDERSTANDING
ODBC
FUNDAMENTALS

Using Microsoft Visual Data Tools

by Ashton Hobbs

IN THIS CHAPTER

Visual Basic comes with some utilities not automatically installed with Visual Basic. You can install these utilities manually from the Visual Basic CD-ROM. The Microsoft Data Tools are great to install and use in creating and managing physical database objects. They provide features not offered by other database managers.

Installing the Visual Data Tools

Installing the Visual Data Tools is very straightforward. You can find the tools in the VB5.0\TOOLS\DATATOOL directory on the Visual Basic CD-ROM or on disk 1 of Microsoft Visual Studio. The Visual Data Tools are also available with the purchase of Microsoft Visual InterDev.

Looking at the Database Features

The Visual Data Tools, in addition to being great tools for developing Web applications, also are great for creating and managing databases.

One of the hardest parts about creating an application is getting the database portion correct. How many of you have had to recode because of a change to the database structure? Changes to the database probably cause more applications and components to require updating than any other source.

The Visual Data Tools don't replace good design techniques or database design tools such as ERwin or PowerDesigner, which help you better design a database. The Visual Data Tools allow you to create a database but provide only limited features for creating entity relationship models, as do the aforementioned database design tools. The Visual Data Tools database features also allow you to manage a database that's already created.

> **TIP**
>
> For more information about ERwin, visit the Logic Works Web site at http://www.
> logicworks.com/. For more information about PowerDesigner, visit Powersoft's site
> at http://www.powersoft.com/

The following sections cover some examples of how to use the database features provided by the Visual Data Tools with Microsoft SQL Server. Most features described here work with other databases, but some features are specific to Oracle and other features are specific only to Microsoft SQL Server.

Creating and Changing Database Tables

The Visual Data Tools provide a way to create new database tables and provide some advanced features when you're creating new tables and making changes to existing tables. By using these tools, you can create new tables within the database by using a data diagram. The Visual Data Tools let you add tables and columns, and specify advanced column properties such as column data type, user-defined data types, identity information, default values, and other properties.

The Visual Data Tools also offer a dream feature for database administrators. You can actually change the data type of a column within a table, and then have the Visual Data Tools make the change on the table, even if it already contains data. If you've ever had to make table changes while preserving data, you can tell this is a real time-saver. Previously, you would have had to back up the data within the table, drop the table, create the new table, and then move the data back into the new table.

The following steps show how to create a database table by using the database tools in the Visual Data Tools. You'll use the database diagrams available in the Visual Data Tools to create the table.

1. Make sure that you have an open database project. When you're in the project, right-click the Database Diagram and choose to create a new diagram.

> **TIP**
>
> To create a new database project, choose File | New and then select the Database Project Wizard from the Projects dialog box. The wizard then guides you through creating a project and connecting it to your database.

2. After the empty diagram is created, right-click anywhere in it and choose New Table. A dialog box appears, asking for the name of the new table.

3. After you specify the name of the table you want to create, you see a grid in which you can specify the columns you want in the table. Table 18.1 lists the properties that you can modify with the new table grid; Figure 18.1 shows the new table grid.

FIGURE 18.1.

Creating a new table.

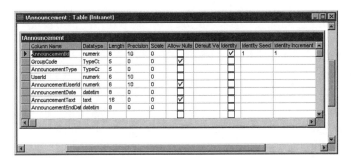

4. After you specify all the columns that you want in the table and the properties for all the columns, close the new table grid and save the structure of the database.

Table 18.1. Column properties for the example table.

Property	Description
Column Name	The name of the column and how it will be referenced from your queries and stored procedures.
Data Type	The data type that the column will use. You can use any standard data types provided by the database or any user-defined data types that you've created.
Length	Some data types let you specify a length that determines the amount of data allowed within the data type.
Precision	The precision of numeric columns. *Precision* indicates how many digits will be displayed for a number.
Scale	The scale of a numeric column. *Scale* is the number if digits allowed after the decimal point.
Allow Nulls	A selection box that determines whether the column will allow null values to be entered.
Default Value	The default value placed in the column if no value is specified when a new record is inserted.
Identity Column	A selection box that determines whether the column will be an identity key. An *identity key* is a column that's automatically populated with an increasing numeric value. Useful as a primary key of a table.
Identity Seed	The initial value for the identity column when a record is first inserted.
Identity Increment	The increment value added to new records that are defined as identity columns.

From the column grid, you can add a primary key to the table by highlighting the column or columns that you want to be the primary key for the table, and then clicking the Primary Key toolbar button (which has a key icon).

Viewing Data in Database Tables

By using the Visual Data Tools, you can add, delete, and modify data stored in the database table. You can edit the information in a grid, which is easier and quicker than using SQL Insert and Update statements, although the Visual Data Tools still allow you to create queries to manage data.

To view the data stored in a table, select the table that you want to view data for, and then double-click the table or right-click it and choose Open. The Visual Data Tools then display all the data for table in a grid format for you to view, modify, or insert new rows.

Creating Database Diagrams

One of the most useful features of the database tools provided by the Visual Data Tools is the capability to create database diagrams for tables in your table. Other products let you view tables in a diagram format, but the Visual Data Tools let you create multiple diagrams for your database, so you can have a database diagram for individual departments within your organization or for separate functions of your application.

The benefit of having separate diagrams is so that administrators and users can view tables related only to the work they're doing. This way, your administrators can work only on tables they're responsible for, thus making managing easier since they don't see the tables from other sections of the database.

Another benefit of using the Visual Data Tools database diagrams is that because they're saved in the database (in the dtProperties table), they can be modified by anyone with access to the Visual Data Tools and the database where the diagrams are stored. Unlike other tools that store the diagrams in proprietary files, the Visual Data Tools store the diagrams on the database for everyone to access.

To create a new diagram, all you need to do is to right-click the Database Diagrams option in Data Explorer and then choose New Diagram. When a blank diagram is presented to you, you can drag and drop tables from the Data Explorer to the new diagram. The diagram will display all the relationships between the tables contained on it. Figure 18.2 shows a database diagram with several tables on it. Notice the relationships pictured on the diagram between the various tables.

FIGURE 18.2.
The database diagram.

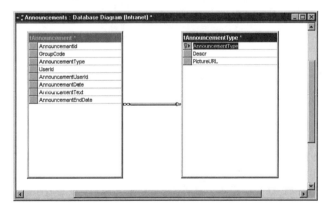

Creating Stored Procedures

The Visual Data Tools also provide you with tools for creating stored procedures and triggers.

> **NOTE**
>
> The ability to create stored procedures and triggers is available only on the Oracle and Microsoft SQL Server databases.

Creating stored procedures can sometimes be difficult, unless you have the database client tools installed. But why should you have to install database specific tools to create stored procedures? For all relational databases that I've worked with, the full text of the stored procedures is stored in the system tables for the database. The Visual Data Tools use the system tables to let you create new stored procedures or modify current stored procedures.

The Visual Data Tools also provide more information about your stored procedures than most other development tools. The tools let you view all the parameters and return values that your stored procedures use. Knowing the parameter names passed to the stored procedure is helpful when you want to pass only certain parameters and need to assign parameter values to parameter names. Figure 18.3 shows a sample stored procedure in the database editor window. Notice the parameters listed for the stored procedure on the left in the database explorer window.

FIGURE 18.3.

The stored procedure editor.

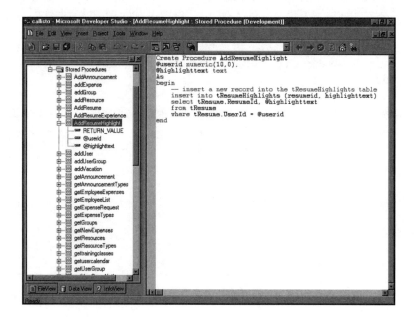

Summary

The Microsoft Visual Data Tools provide an easy and powerful way to create and manage your database. With the capability to add stored procedures, triggers, and views, the tools provide features above most of the other simple tools available.

The tools also provide you with detailed information about the stored procedures and tables, going as far as to provide a listing of the parameters that should be passed to a stored procedure. The Visual Data Tools also let you change a column's data type or length without requiring that you drop the constraints on the table, drop the table, create the new table, and then add the data back into the table. This in itself is worth the price of the tools. However, because the tools come as freebies with Visual Basic or Visual Studio, there's really no reason for you not to use them.

18

MICROSOFT
VISUAL DATA
TOOLS

IV
PART

Advanced Programming Topics and Techniques

Mail-Enabling
Your Applications
With MAPI

by Rob Thayer

IN THIS CHAPTER

As the use of intranets and the Internet becomes more commonplace, application programmers have to learn to tap into the power of this new technology. In the past, standalone programs were the norm, but the next generation of applications will require the capability to communicate on a global scale. For example, a few years ago it was sufficient to design a program to monitor machines in a factory and produce reports concerning their efficiency. Today, that same program might be expected to send those reports automatically to the factory foreman or to other management personnel thousands of miles away. The easiest way to do that is through electronic mail (e-mail). And that's where MAPI comes in.

In a nutshell, MAPI (Mail Application Programming Interface) is a specification that defines a complete messaging subsystem. Primarily, it defines common interfaces by which mail-related components can interact. These components include service providers such as *message store providers* that can create, submit, and store mail messages; *address book providers* that can maintain a database of message recipients; and *transport providers* that handle the actual transmission of messages. It may sound complicated, but it's not. The first few pages of this chapter provide you with a better understanding of what MAPI is and how it works. This chapter also shows how you can use MAPI to add electronic messaging functionality to your Visual Basic programs.

Understanding the MAPI Specification

Microsoft created MAPI to establish a common interface for various mail-related components, including those developed by other vendors. Primarily, it allows client applications (such as ones written in Visual Basic) to interact with service providers. In this context, *service providers* are programs that perform mail-related tasks. Three principal types of service providers are defined under MAPI: address book providers, message store providers, and transport providers. These provider types are discussed in more detail later, along with another important part of the MAPI system—the MAPI Spooler.

The MAPI specification uses a layered model (see Figure 19.1). At the top of the model are the client applications, which sometimes provide an interface that simplifies the use of e-mail messaging for end users. In other types of client applications, the messaging might be transparent to users.

The bottom layer of the model is the various service providers that furnish MAPI-compliant message services. It doesn't matter which programming language these components are written in as long as they "speak MAPI." Microsoft Exchange is a good example of a MAPI-compliant component because it acts as an address book provider and as a message store provider.

Tying together the top and bottom layers of the model is MAPI itself, which consists of the MAPI runtime system (DLLs) and the Message Spooler. MAPI provides interfaces to the client applications and the service providers, acting as a middleman or interpreter so that the two can "talk together."

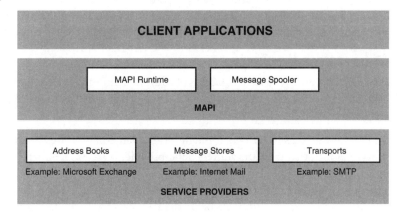

FIGURE 19.1.

The MAPI specification uses a layered model, with MAPI providing an interface between client applications and various service providers.

At a basic level, MAPI functions resemble the print spooler built into Windows 95 or Windows NT. When you're writing an application that prints a report, you don't have to worry about who manufactured the printer that will receive the report. That task is left to the Windows print spooler, which translates the report so that it will look fundamentally the same no matter what printer is being used. MAPI works the same way: It enables your application to send and receive electronic mail messages no matter what transport provider your system uses (as long as the transport provider is MAPI-compliant). It also enables you to use the services of MAPI-compliant address book and message store providers.

> **NOTE**
>
> As an experienced Visual Basic programmer, you might be a little confused that MAPI stands for *Mail Application Programming Interface*, because it doesn't function like the APIs you're used to. Under normal circumstances, an API consists of a related set of functions that can be called from within a VB program. Microsoft's first implementation of MAPI worked that way (that implementation is now referred to as *Simple MAPI*). Extended MAPI, which is used in VB5, doesn't work that way; instead, all MAPI services are accessed with two ActiveX controls (or COM objects). Like other ActiveX controls, they have events, methods, and properties. By responding to events, calling methods, and setting properties, much of MAPI's functionality is available to VB programmers.

MAPI Service Providers

MAPI service providers do the bulk of the work in the MAPI system. They also shield client application programmers from a great deal of additional coding, as you'll see later.

Although most programmers choose to use existing MAPI service providers such as Microsoft Exchange, it's possible to create your own custom service providers—doing so, though, can be difficult and requires a lower-level language such as C++. If you're interested in learning more about service provider creation, I recommend *Inside MAPI* by Microsoft Press.

Address Book Providers

Address book providers contain databases of addressing information for message recipients. These databases are organized into hierarchies, using *containers* that hold information for various recipients.

When a new message is created, it might be given an e-mail address such as jdoe@xyzco.com as its recipient. In that case, the address book provider is sidestepped, and the message is sent to its destination. If a literal name such as John Doe is given as the message's recipient, however, that name must be translated into a valid e-mail address. In that case, you use the address book provider to look up the literal name. If the name is found, the message is assigned an e-mail address, and it can continue on to the message store provider for delivery. If the name isn't found, a dialog box might appear that allows users to add the name (and a corresponding e-mail address) to their personal address book for later use.

Among other functions that improve the efficiency of e-mail messaging for end users, address books are also useful for creating distribution lists. A *distribution list* consists of one or more related e-mail addresses lumped together under a single name. When a message is addressed to that name, a copy is sent to each person in the distribution list. For example, business owners might want to send copies of their promotional newsletters to a hundred different subscribers each month. Rather than send 100 messages individually (a time-consuming chore), they can send the newsletter to a single address created as a distribution list. The address book provider does all the work and sends a copy of the message to each person on the list. By providing this kind of functionality, address book providers can be a very important part of the MAPI system.

Note that on any given computer, more than one address book provider might in use. MAPI merges all of them together, however, so that they appear as a single provider to the client application.

Message Store Providers

Message store providers maintain e-mail messages in some sort of database system, typically organized as a hierarchy that uses folders to group messages pertaining to a particular user or subject. Although the message store provider's code (in most cases, a DLL or OCX) is actually executed on the same machine as the client application that's using it, the message database itself can reside locally or on a network.

Message store providers also have another important function. They handle the transmission and receipt of e-mail messages, working closely with the system's transport provider. The following section discusses this in more detail, but keep in mind that it's through the message store provider that your client application will send outgoing messages and receive incoming messages.

Examples of message store providers include Microsoft Exchange, Lotus's cc:Mail, and Hewlett-Packard's OpenMAIL, although many more are available. Some message store providers, such as Exchange, can function as address book providers as well.

Transport Providers

Several underlying messaging protocols have become de facto standards, such as SMTP and X.400. Other protocols might be proprietary in nature. Regardless of which protocol is being used to send messages to and from the Internet or an intranet, it's the transport provider's job to translate those messages to work with the given protocol. Here's how it works:

1. Outbound messages (sent *from* the client application) are sent to the message store provider.
2. The message store provider hands the message over to the MAPI Spooler, which sends it to the transport provider.
3. The transport provider converts the message into a stream of bytes compatible with the messaging protocol being used.

Inbound messages work the same way, only in reverse:

1. The transport protocol receives a byte stream and converts it into a MAPI message.
2. The message is sent to the Spooler, which places it into a receive folder furnished by the message store provider.
3. The client application now has access to the new message and can retrieve it from the message store provider.

Because the message store providers and the MAPI Spooler handle transmission and receipt of messages, your client applications probably won't deal with transport providers at all. It helps, though, to know the role that these components play within the MAPI system.

The MAPI Spooler

Like transport providers, your client applications can't deal directly with the MAPI Spooler. But you should be aware of how the Spooler works.

The MAPI Spooler runs in a completely separate process from the client application, just as the Windows print spooler runs in its own process. Even if more than one client application is running, a single instance of the MAPI Spooler is used. When inbound messages are received, the Spooler must determine to which message store provider they should be delivered. Outgoing messages from different message store providers are sorted by submission order, placed into a common queue, and then sent to the appropriate transport providers one by one.

Using the MAPI Controls: MAPISession and MAPIMessages

All the MAPI functionality in Visual Basic 5 is provided by two very powerful ActiveX controls: MAPISession and MAPIMessages. The MAPISession control is the simplest of the two and is used only to begin and end MAPI sessions. The MAPIMessages control, on the other hand, provides all the message-related services available under MAPI. Both are invisible controls—they aren't displayed on the form when the program is in run mode.

The sequence of events for a typical MAPI application is as follows:

- Set properties for the MAPISession control that will affect the way in which a MAPI session will be started.
- Call the MAPISession control's SignOn method, which begins a new MAPI session.
- Use one or more MAPI services by setting properties or calling methods provided by the MAPIMessages control.
- Call the MAPISession control's SignOff method to terminate the MAPI session.

The MAPIMessages control allows you to retrieve messages from the mail server's inbox, perform operations on retrieved messages, and create new messages. It works closely with the mail server, which provides several dialog boxes related to many of the MAPI services. For example, when you create a new message with the MAPIMessages control's Compose and Send methods, a dialog box appears that facilitates the composition of a new message, saving you from an incredible amount of programming.

The way in which you use the MAPIMessages control might seem a little strange at first; I admit that it was a bit hard for me to get used to. But when you understand how the various properties and methods of the MAPIMessages control work together, you'll master MAPI programming very quickly. The two sample applications created later in this chapter give you a good introduction to how MAPI works in Visual Basic, so relax if you don't yet fully understand how the MAPI controls function. When you see them in action, they'll be a lot easier to comprehend.

Tables 19.1 and 19.2 list the unique methods and properties available for each control. Note that neither control has events and that "standard" properties, such as Name and Index, are excluded.

Table 19.1. Methods and properties for the MAPISession control.

Name	Description
Methods	
SignOff	Ends a MAPI session.
SignOn	Starts a MAPI session.

Name	Description
	Properties
Action	Starts or ends a MAPI session. This property should no longer be used but is included to provide backward compatibility with a previous version of MAPI.
DownloadMail	Specifies whether new mail should be downloaded from the mail server after beginning a MAPI session.
LogonUI	Specifies whether a dialog box should appear when a MAPI session is started.
NewSession	Specifies whether a new MAPI session should be started if a valid MAPI session already exists.
Password	Specifies the password for the account associated with the UserName property.
SessionID	Returns the handle for the current MAPI session. This value is set when the SignOn method is called.
UserName	Specifies the user or profile name to be used when starting a MAPI session.

Table 19.2. Methods and properties for the MAPIMessages control.

Name	Description
	Methods
Compose	Clears all components of the compose buffer.
Copy	Copies the currently indexed message to the compose buffer so that it can be edited.
Delete	Deletes a message, a recipient, or an attachment.
Fetch	Creates a message set from messages in the inbox. You can specify the type of messages included in the set by using the FetchMsgType and FetchUnreadOnly properties. The message set can also be sorted by first setting the FetchSorted property.
Forward	Copies the currently indexed message into the compose buffer so it can be sent (forwarded) to another e-mail address.
Reply	Copies the currently indexed message into the compose buffer so that a reply can be sent to the originator of the message.
ReplyAll	Sends copies of the reply to all recipients of the currently indexed message; it's similar to the Reply method.

19

MAIL-ENABLING
APPLICATIONS
WITH MAPI

continues

Table 19.2. continued

Name	Description
Methods	
ResolveName	Searches the address book for the currently indexed recipient of a message and returns an error if it's not found. If the AddressResolveUI property is True, a dialog box for address resolution is displayed rather than an error.
Save	Saves the message in the compose buffer.
Send	Sends the message in the compose buffer to the mail server for delivery.
Show	Displays the Address Book dialog box.
Properties	
Action	Performs a number of message-related functions. This property is no longer used but is included to provide backward compatibility with a previous version of MAPI.
AddressCaption	Specifies the caption that appears at the top of the Address Book dialog box.
AddressEditFieldCount	Specifies which editing controls are displayed in the Address Book dialog box.
AddressLabel	Specifies the caption on the To: button in the Address Book dialog box.
AddressModifiable	Specifies whether users can modify the address book.
AddressResolveUI	Specifies whether a dialog box should be displayed when the ResolveName method is called.
AttachmentCount	Returns the number of attachments for the currently indexed message.
AttachmentIndex	Sets or returns the pointer to the currently indexed attachment of a message.
AttachmentName	Specifies the filename of the currently indexed attachment.
AttachmentPathName	Specifies the full path to the currently indexed attachment.
AttachmentPosition	Specifies the position of the currently indexed attachment within the body of the message (in characters).
AttachmentType	Specifies the type of the currently indexed attachment (data file, embedded OLE object, or static OLE object).
FetchMsgType	Specifies the type of messages to be included in the message set when the Fetch method is called.
FetchSorted	Specifies the order in which the messages in the message set are sorted when the Fetch method is called.

Name	Description
	Properties
FetchUnreadOnly	Specifies that only unread messages should be retrieved from the inbox when the Fetch method is called.
MsgConversationID	Identifies that the currently indexed message is part of a message thread.
MsgCount	Returns the total number of messages included in the current message set.
MsgDateReceived	Returns the date on which the currently indexed message was received.
MsgID	Returns the ID number of the currently indexed message. This number is generated internally by the MAPI subsystem and should be unique for each message in the message set.
MsgIndex	Sets or returns the pointer to the currently indexed message.
MsgNoteText	Specifies the body of the currently indexed message.
MsgOrigAddress	Returns the address of the originator (sender) of the currently indexed message.
MsgOrigDisplayName	Returns the name of the originator (sender) of the currently indexed message.
MsgRead	Returns a value indicating whether the currently indexed message has been read.
MsgReceiptRequested	Specifies whether a return receipt has been requested for the currently indexed message.
MsgSent	Specifies a value indicating whether the currently indexed message has been sent to the mail server for delivery.
MsgSubject	Specifies the short subject description of the currently indexed message.
MsgType	Specifies the type of the currently indexed message.
RecipAddress	Specifies the e-mail address for the recipient of the currently indexed message.
RecipCount	Returns the total number of recipients for the currently indexed message.
RecipDisplayName	Specifies the name of the currently indexed message recipient.
RecipIndex	Sets or returns the pointer to the currently indexed message recipient.
RecipType	Specifies the type of the currently indexed message recipient.
SessionID	Returns the handle to the current MAPI session.

19

MAIL-ENABLING
APPLICATIONS
WITH MAPI

As you can see, there is quite a bit to these two controls, especially MAPIMessages. Don't worry; I'll go through just about all of it in this chapter.

Creating Simple MAPI Programs With Visual Basic

You're almost ready to start creating some sample MAPI programs with Visual Basic. Before you do, I'd like to briefly explain the three different types of MAPI applications: mail-enabled, electronic mail (e-mail), and mail-aware. Each provides a different level of electronic mail functionality:

- *Mail-enabled applications* are applications whose main function isn't specifically e-mail-related but contain some e-mail messaging services, often transparently to users. The example given earlier in this chapter of a program that monitors machines in a factory and e-mails information regarding their efficiency is a mail-enabled application. The first sample program that follows this section is also an example of a mail-enabled application.

- *Electronic mail, or e-mail applications,* provide electronic messaging services as their main function. These programs typically use a user interface that simplifies the creation and handling of e-mail messages by end users. Microsoft's Internet Mail is just one example of an electronic mail application.

- *Mail-aware applications* are similar to e-mail applications, but their main function might not be messaging-related. A word processor, for example, might allow you to compose a document and e-mail it to another person. In that way, it functions like an e-mail application. However, the capability to send the document is more a bonus than the main function of the program. Microsoft Word 97 allows you to e-mail its documents, so it's an example of a mail-aware application.

As time goes on, more and more programs will feature some degree of electronic messaging functionality. Most of these applications will be mail-enabled or mail-aware, incorporating e-mail services into their basic design as just another basic feature demanded by end users.

CAUTION

Before you begin creating MAPI client applications in Visual Basic, you must have a properly configured MAPI-compliant mail server on your system. A standalone or network computer running Windows 95 or Windows NT might use Microsoft Exchange, which is included with those operating systems. Not having the necessary components installed can result in unpredictable errors and the inability of the following sample applications to work properly. If you're unsure of whether your system has a mail server installed, consult the online help system or your network administrator.

Creating Mail-Enabled Applications

The first program you're going to create will be mail-enabled because such an application provides a good introduction to how MAPI works with Visual Basic without going into too much too soon. Later, you'll create a more robust program that covers many more of the services provided by MAPI.

This program is a very simple login/logout interface that might be used to track employee activity of some kind. Perhaps it could be a front end to another application. When employees begin to use the application, they log in with their user name and password. When finished, they log out, and someone else can use the application.

When three employees have logged in and out, an activity report with all six transactions (three logins and three logouts) is automatically generated and sent to a manager or supervisor for review. To make testing of the program a little bit easier, a button has been added so the activity report can be sent immediately rather than wait until all six transactions take place.

The program interface will look like the one shown in Figure 19.2. Notice that there are places for employees to enter their user name and password. There are also Log In and Log Out buttons, as well as a button to immediately generate and send the activity report.

FIGURE 19.2.

The interface for the employee login/logout program.

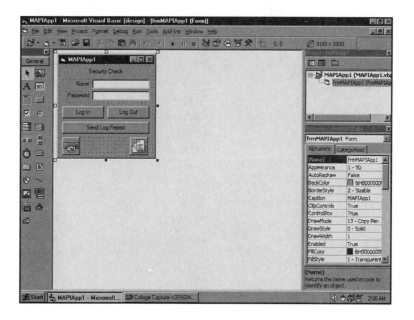

19

MAIL-ENABLING
APPLICATIONS
WITH MAPI

To create the program interface, add the various controls to the form; then use Table 19.3 to change the properties of the controls.

Table 19.3. Control properties for the employee login/logout program.

Control	Property	Setting
Form	Name	frmMAPIApp1
	Height	2895
	Left	60
	Top	345
	Width	3045
Label	Name	lblTitle
	Alignment	2 - Center
	Caption	Security Check
	Height	255
	Left	120
	Top	120
	Width	2775
Label	Name	lblName
	Alignment	1 - Right Justify
	Caption	Name
	Height	255
	Left	120
	Top	510
	Width	855
Label	Name	lblPassword
	Alignment	1 - Right Justify
	Caption	Password
	Height	255
	Left	120
	Top	870
	Width	855
TextBox	Name	txtName
	Height	285
	Left	1080
	Top	480
	Width	1815
TextBox	Name	txtPassword
	Height	285
	Left	1080
	PasswordChar	*
	Top	840
	Width	1815

Control	Property	Setting
CommandButton	Name	cmdLogIn
	Caption	Log In
	Height	375
	Left	120
	Top	1320
	Width	1335
CommandButton	Name	cmdLogOut
	Caption	Log Out
	Height	375
	Left	1560
	Top	1320
	Width	1335
CommandButton	Name	cmdSendLog
	Caption	Send Log Report
	Height	375
	Left	120
	Top	1800
	Width	2775
MAPISession	Name	mpsSession
	Left	120
	Top	2280
MAPIMessages	Name	mpmSendLog
	Left	2280
	Top	2280

19

MAIL-ENABLING
APPLICATIONS
WITH MAPI

NOTE

If the two MAPI ActiveX controls (MAPISession and MAPIMessages) aren't already in your toolbox, press Ctrl+T or choose Project | Components. In the Components dialog box, double-click Microsoft MAPI Controls 5.0 so that its box is checked; then click OK to add the two controls to your toolbox.

After you create the form, it's time to do some coding. This program uses only four subroutines, and only one actually uses the MAPI controls. I'll save that subroutine for last so I can discuss it in more detail.

Before you start coding these four subroutines, you need to add two module-level variables to the General Declarations section. These two variables will be used throughout the rest of the program:

```
Dim mintLogCount As Integer
Dim mstrLogActivity(6) As String
```

> **NOTE**
>
> When naming objects and variables in Visual Basic, I prefer using Microsoft's coding conventions. Notice that a three-character pneumonic precedes every object and variable name to indicate its type (frm for Forms, cmd for Command Buttons, int for integers, and so on). You also can precede variable names with a one-character scope indicator (g for global or m for module-level). I have found these coding conventions quite useful, and I advise you to consider adopting their use.

The first subroutine is for the Log In button's Click event (see Listing 19.1). When the event is triggered, the program verifies that users have typed something in the Name and Password text boxes. (Of course, the verification process would be much more involved if this were more than just a simple test program, with all names and passwords being looked up in an employee database. In the interest of keeping it simple, I'll ease up on the security a bit.)

Listing 19.1. Code for cmdLogIn's Click event.

```
Private Sub cmdLogIn_Click()

    ' Make sure that both a name and a password have been
    ' entered.
    If txtName.Text = "" Or txtPassword.Text = "" Then
        MsgBox "Please enter your name and password."
        Exit Sub
    End If

    ' If this was a real application, code for checking the
    ' user's login information would go here.

    cmdLogIn.Enabled = False     ' Disable LogIn button and...
    cmdLogOut.Enabled = True      ' ...enable LogOut button.

    txtName.Enabled = False
    txtPassword.Text = ""
    txtPassword.Enabled = False

    ' Add this login to the activity log.
    mintLogCount = mintLogCount + 1
    mstrLogActivity(mintLogCount) = "User " _
        & UCase$(txtName.Text) & " logged IN at " _
        & Time$ & " on " & Date$

End Sub
```

When an employee logs in, a transaction line with the username and the login date and time is added to the mstrLogActivity array. Later, this array is used to generate the activity report e-mailed to a supervisor.

The next section of code is for the Log Out button's `Click` event (see Listing 19.2). Like the routine in Listing 19.1, it adds a transaction line to the `mstrLogActivity` array. If the array has six transactions, the `SendActivityLog` subroutine is called. That's the subroutine that actually uses the two MAPI controls, which I'll get to in just a moment.

Listing 19.2. Code for `cmdLogOut`'s `Click` event.

```
Private Sub cmdLogOut_Click()

    ' Add this logout to the activity log.
    mintLogCount = mintLogCount + 1
    mstrLogActivity(mintLogCount) = "User " _
        & UCase$(txtName.Text) & " logged OUT at " _
        & Time$ & " on " & Date$

    ' If the activity log is "full", then send it out via
    ' e-mail.
    If mintLogCount = 6 Then
        SendActivityLog
    End If

    txtName.Text = ""
    txtName.Enabled = True
    txtPassword.Enabled = True

    cmdLogIn.Enabled = True
    cmdLogOut.Enabled = False

End Sub
```

Next, you have yet another `Click` event, this time for the Send Log Now button (see Listing 19.3). It also calls the `SendActivityLog` subroutine to e-mail the login/logout report.

Listing 19.3. Code for `cmdSendLogNow`'s `Click` event.

```
Private Sub cmdSendLog_Click()

' Check to see if there's actually anything in the activity
' log before sending it.
If mintLogCount = 0 Then
    MsgBox "Activity log empty - nothing to send!"
    Exit Sub
End If

SendActivityLog

End Sub
```

Now that you've taken care of the overhead, it's time to get down to business. Listing 19.4 shows the `SendActivityLog` subroutine.

Listing 19.4. The `SendActivityLog` subroutine, which handles all the MAPI services used by the login/logout program.

```
Public Sub SendActivityLog()

    Dim intMsgLoop As Integer
    Dim strMsgBuffer As String

    On Error GoTo SendActivityLogError

    ' Establish a MAPI session.
    mpsSession.UserName = "security"
    mpsSession.Password = "test"
    mpsSession.DownLoadMail = False
    mpsSession.LogonUI = False
    mpsSession.SignOn
    mpmSendLog.SessionID = mpsSession.SessionID

    ' Create the body of the message in a temporary buffer.
    strMsgBuffer = ""
    For intMsgLoop = 0 To mintLogCount
        strMsgBuffer = strMsgBuffer _
            & mstrLogActivity(intMsgLoop) & Chr$(13) & Chr$(10)
    Next intMsgLoop

    ' Compose and send the message.
    mpmSendLog.Compose
    mpmSendLog.RecipAddress = "schief@mapiland.com"
    mpmSendLog.RecipDisplayName = "Security Chief"

    mpmSendLog.MsgSubject = "Activity Log - " & Date$ _
        & "/" & Time$
    mpmSendLog.MsgNoteText = strMsgBuffer
    mpmSendLog.Send

    ' Set the activity log's index to zero, effectively
    ' "clearing out" the log.
    mintLogCount = 0

    mpsSession.SignOff

    Exit Sub

SendActivityLogError:
    MsgBox Error$, vbCritical, "Critical Error: " & Str(Err)
    End

End Sub
```

Because this routine does most of the work in the program and contains all the MAPI-related code, look at it in more detail.

To begin with, notice that an error handler has been implemented. Whenever you're working with the MAPI controls, it's always a good idea to set up some kind of error handling. A number of things can go wrong if you're not careful in your coding. In fact, the MAPI specification defines 36 different error conditions that can arise when using the MAPI controls. Under normal circumstances, you'll probably want to implement a much more robust error-handling routine that traps for specific errors or offers the users options when an error occurs. But in the interest of simplicity, you'll display only the error description and its value and then end the program. If you have the necessary 32-bit MAPI DLLs installed properly on your system, you won't run into any problems.

Because the subroutine in Listing 19.4 contains all the MAPI-related action in the program, I'll go through it section by section and discuss each part in more detail.

Establishing the MAPI Session

The following code segment establishes a MAPI session by using the MAPISession control (`mpsSession`):

```
' Establish a MAPI session.
mpsSession.UserName = "security"
mpsSession.Password = "test"
mpsSession.DownLoadMail = False
mpsSession.LogonUI = False
mpsSession.SignOn
mpmSendLog.SessionID = mpsSession.SessionID
```

The `UserName` and `Password` properties are changed to reflect the login information you want to use (in this case, a user name of `manager` and a password of `test`). If you want to run this program on your system, you'll have to change these two properties to something that works with your mail server—your own name and password, for example.

> **NOTE**
>
> You don't need to specify a password at all if you use a profile name instead of a user name. Most MAPI-compliant mail servers (including Microsoft Exchange) allow you to set up different profiles. A discussion of profiles and how Windows Messaging works is beyond the scope of this chapter. However, you can use the Windows help system to learn more on those topics.

The `DownLoadMail` property is set to `False`, specifying that any new messages shouldn't be retrieved when the user has signed on. Because this program's only function is to send an employee activity report to the appropriate party, it's not set up to receive mail.

The `LogonUI` property is also set to `False`. If it's set to `True`, a dialog box will appear that prompts for the user name and password to log on to the service provider. Because you don't want the dialog box to appear, you set this property to `False`, and no user intervention is required. If you use invalid values for the `UserName` and `Password` properties, the dialog box appears whether or not the `LogonUI` property is `True` or `False`. On the other hand, if you assign valid `UserName` and `Password` property values, the dialog box still won't appear, even if the `LogonUI` property is set to `True`.

After all the necessary properties are set, the MAPISession control's `SignOn` method is called. When a MAPI session is started, it's assigned a Session ID number. In the preceding code segment, that number is placed into `mpsSession`'s `SessionID` property. You must copy that value so that the MAPIMessages control knows which MAPI session to use when its own methods are called. Note that when a MAPI session has been initiated, the MAPISession control isn't used again until the MAPI session is to be terminated (using the `SignOff` method).

Adding Elements to a Temporary String Used to Hold the Message Body

The following code segment loops through the `mstrLogActivity` array and adds its elements to a temporary string (`strMsgBuffer`) used to hold the body of the e-mail message.

```
' Create the body of the message in a temporary buffer.
strMsgBuffer = ""
For intMsgLoop = 0 To mintLogCount
    strMsgBuffer = strMsgBuffer _
        & mstrLogActivity(intMsgLoop) & Chr$(13) & Chr$(10)
Next intMsgLoop
```

A carriage return and linefeed are added to the end of each element so the information doesn't get lumped into one long line of text.

Addressing and Sending the Message

Now you need to address and send the message. First, you call the MAPIMessages control's `Compose` method to clear all the components in the compose buffer, which is used to create new messages (or to edit and resend existing messages, as you'll see later):

```
' Compose and send the message.
mpmSendLog.Compose
mpmSendLog.RecipAddress = "manager@mapiland.com"
mpmSendLog.RecipDisplayName = "Mr. Manager"
mpmSendLog.MsgSubject = "Activity Log - " & Date$ _
    & "/" & Time$
mpmSendLog.MsgNoteText = strMsgBuffer
mpmSendLog.Send
```

The `RecipAddress` property is assigned the e-mail address of the person receiving the message, and the `RecipDisplayName` property gets the name of the recipient. In the example, I've used a fabricated e-mail address and name; you might want to change these two properties to a valid e-mail address that you can use to test the program.

Next, you give the message a subject, using the `MsgSubject` property, and assign the temporary string you created earlier to the message body (the `MsgNoteText` property). Now you're ready to send it. To do so, the MAPIMessages control's `Send` method is called. This sends the message to the mail server, which in turn relays it to the recipient specified by the `RecipAddress` property.

Resetting the Activity Log

After the activity log is sent, it should be reset or "cleared out" so that it can be used again. By setting the log's counter back to zero, you can record more employee activity in the log:

```
' Set the activity log's index to zero, effectively
' "clearing out" the log.
mintLogCount = 0
```

```
mpsSession.SignOff
```

Finally, you close your MAPI session by calling the MAPISession control's `SignOff` method. You don't have to tell the MAPIMessages control that the session is over, but you can no longer use that control's methods until a new session is started. Calling any of its methods without having a MAPI session in progress results in an error.

Saving the Project

Save the project as `vbu1901.vbp` and the form as `vbu1901.frm`; then compile and run the program. If you aren't on a network with an e-mail gateway or have to use dial-up networking to connect to the Internet, make sure that you've established a connection to the Internet first.

When the program runs, type a username and password—anything will do because you don't perform any validation on what's entered. Click the Log In button. The password will disappear, and text boxes are disabled until you click the Log Out button, so do that now. Then enter another name and password, if you want, and log in and out. Now click the Send Log Report button to send the activity log. All this work is transparent to the user, so it might not seem like anything has happened. But if you check the mailbox for the recipient assigned to the message, you'll see some new mail.

Before moving on to the next MAPI application, I'd like you to try a few things. Exit the program and change the line in the `SendActivityLog` subroutine from

```
mpmSendLog.Send
```

to

```
mpmSendLog.Send True
```

and run the program again. When you click the button to send the activity log, you'll see a window similar to the one shown in Figure 19.3.

The mail server displays this window, so it might look different on your system if you're not using Microsoft Exchange. You'll see a lot more of this window when you create the next application. For now, exit the program and remove the `True` argument from the line of code you just changed.

FIGURE 19.3.

The window displayed when the Send *method is called with a* True *argument.*

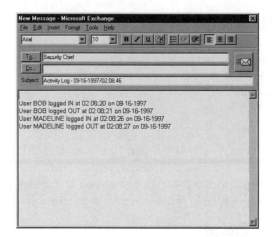

The last thing I'd like you to try before moving on to the next program is to add an attachment to the message sent by the login/logout application. Suppose that along with the employee activity log, you'd like to include another log file created by the application that the employees are using. This file is a simple ASCII text file named Use.log and is located in the C:\App directory (for testing purposes; feel free to change the filename and path to indicate a file that exists on your system). To add the attachment to the message, modify the section of code in the SendActivityLog subroutine so it looks like Listing 19.5.

Listing 19.5. The modified code segment in the SendActivityLog subroutine so that an attachment is added to the message being sent out.

```
' Compose and send the message.
mpmSendLog.Compose
mpmSendLog.RecipAddress = "manager@mapiland.com"
mpmSendLog.RecipDisplayName = "Mr. Manager"
mpmSendLog.MsgSubject = "Activity Log - " & Date$ _
    & "/" & Time$
mpmSendLog.MsgNoteText = strMsgBuffer
mpmSendLog.AttachmentType = mapData
mpmSendLog.AttachmentName = "Program Use Log"
mpmSendLog.AttachmentPathName = "C:\App\Use.log"
mpmSendLog.AttachmentPosition = Len(mpmSendLog.MsgNoteText)
mpmSendLog.Send
```

As you can see, four new lines have been added to SendActivityLog. All of them set properties of the mpmSendLog control:

- The AttachmentName property specifies a descriptive name for the attachment.

- The AttachmentPathName property specifies its full path and filename. To test the use of attachments, you have to change the AttachmentPathName property to reflect a file that exists somewhere on your system.

- The `AttachmentType` property indicates what kind of object the attachment is. It can be a data file (`mapData`), an embedded OLE object (`mapEOLE`), or a static OLE object (`mapSOLE`). In the example, the attachment is a regular data file, so the `mapData` constant is used.

- The `AttachmentPosition` property specifies where in the message body the attachment will be positioned. If you want it to appear after the third character, this property is set to 3. Often, attachments are placed at the end of the message. This is the case in the sample code, so the `AttachmentPosition` property is set to the length of the entire message body.

That just about wraps it up for the login/logout application. In the next section, you create a simple e-mail program that demonstrates how to use many more of the MAPI services in Visual Basic.

Creating E-Mail Applications

In the preceding section, you created an application that sends e-mail transparently—users weren't involved in the process of sending the messages. Now you'll create an application that relies totally on users: a simple e-mail program displaying messages read in from the mail server and allowing users to create and send new messages as well as perform various services on existing messages. Although it's a very primitive and simple program, it provides an example of an electronic mail application.

The program consists of three main sections. At the top is a ListBox containing the subjects of all messages read in from the mail server. In the middle is a Label displaying header information for the currently selected message. The last section is a TextBox displaying the body of the currently selected message.

When users click one of the message subjects in the ListBox, the name of the sender, the subject, and the date the message was received appear in the Label. The body of the message appears in the TextBox.

When a message is selected, users can click any of the following command buttons that perform message services: Reply, Reply All, Forward, Copy, and Delete. If users click the New button, they can compose and send a new message. Last but not least, users can view the address book by clicking the appropriately named Address Book button.

You might think that even a simple program like this would take quite a bit of coding. If so, you'll be pleasantly surprised. Because MAPI does most of the work for you, the amount of program code is minimal.

Begin by assembling the program's interface. By using Table 19.4 as a guide, add the various components and change their properties so that your form looks like the one shown in Figure 19.4.

Table 19.4. Control properties for the simple e-mail application.

Control	Property	Setting
Form	Name	frmMAPIApp2
	Caption	MAPIApp2
	Height	6465
	Left	60
	Top	345
	Width	6615
Label	Name	lblTitle
	Alignment	2 - Center
	Caption	Simple E-Mail Application
	Font	MS Sans Serif 12pt
	Height	375
	Left	1320
	Top	120
	Width	3975
CommandButton	Name	cmdMsgNew
	Caption	New
	Height	255
	Left	120
	Top	600
	Width	975
CommandButton	Name	cmdMsgReply
	Caption	Reply
	Height	255
	Left	1200
	Top	600
	Width	975
CommandButton	Name	cmdMsgReplyAll
	Caption	ReplyAll
	Height	255
	Left	2280
	Top	600
	Width	975
CommandButton	Name	cmdMsgForward
	Caption	Forward
	Height	255
	Left	3360

Control	Property	Setting
	Top	600
	Width	975
CommandButton	Name	cmdMsgCopy
	Caption	Copy
	Height	255
	Left	5520
	Top	600
	Width	975
CommandButton	Name	cmdMsgDelete
	Caption	Delete
	Height	255
	Left	5520
	Top	600
	Width	975
ListBox	Name	lstMessages
	Height	1035
	Left	120
	Top	1080
	Width	6375
Label	Name	lblMsgInfo
	BorderStyle	1 - Fixed Single
	Font	MS LineDraw 8pt
	Height	735
	Left	120
	Top	2280
	Width	6375
TextBox	Name	txtMsgBody
	Height	2775
	Left	120
	MultiLine	True
	ScrollBars	2 - Vertical
	Top	3000
	Width	6375
CommandButton	Name	cmdAddrBook
	Caption	Address Book
	Height	255

continues

Table 19.4. continued

Control	Property	Setting
	Left	3120
	Top	6120
	Width	1575
CommandButton	Name	cmdExit
	Caption	Exit Program
	Height	255
	Left	4800
	Top	6120
	Width	1695
MAPISession	Name	mpsSession
	Left	120
	Top	5880
MAPIMessages	Name	mpmMessages
	Left	720
	Top	5880

FIGURE 19.4.

The interface for the simple e-mail application.

When your form design is complete, you can begin adding the program's code. I'll take the sections one by one so I can explain each part in more detail.

Listing 19.6 shows the code for the form's Load event. There's really nothing new here. When the program starts, it first displays itself and then establishes a MAPI session. When a session is started, the FetchMessages subroutine is called. As you'll see in just a moment, that routine reads in the messages from the mail server and displays their subjects onscreen.

Listing 19.6. Code for the form's Load event.

```
Private Sub Form_Load()

    On Error GoTo ErrHandler

    ' Show the form so it shows up behind the login
    ' dialog box.
    Me.Show

    ' Start a new MAPI session.
    mpsSession.DownLoadMail = True
    mpsSession.LogonUI = True
    mpsSession.SignOn
    mpmMessages.SessionID = mpsSession.SessionID

    ' Read messages from the message server's InBox.
    FetchMessages

    ' If there are messages, display the first one.
    If lstMessages.ListCount > 0 Then
        lstMessages.ListIndex = 0
        lstMessages_Click
    End If

    Exit Sub

ErrHandler:
    CriticalError

End Sub
```

Note that I've added error handling to this code. In fact, I've done so in all the routines and events that perform some sort of MAPI function. Any error that arises will be handled by the `CriticalError` routine (see Listing 19.7). If an error does occur—and let's hope it doesn't—this routine displays a message box with the error number and description. It also terminates the MAPI session if it has already been started.

Listing 19.7. The CriticalError routine, which handles any errors that may occur throughout the program's various subroutines and events.

```
Public Sub CriticalError()

    ' An error has occurred. Inform the user and exit
    ' the program.
    MsgBox Error$, vbCritical, "Critical Error: " & Str(Err)
    If mpsSession.SessionID Then
        mpsSession.SignOff
    End If
    End

End Sub
```

The next code section (see Listing 19.8) is for the FetchMessages routine mentioned earlier. Its job is to retrieve all the messages in the mail server's inbox.

Listing 19.8. The FetchMessages routine, which retrieves messages from the mail server.

```
Public Sub FetchMessages()

    Dim intMsgIndex As Integer

    On Error GoTo ErrHandler

    ' Read all messages (read and unread) from the server,
    ' and sort as specified by the user's InBox.
    mpmMessages.FetchSorted = True
    mpmMessages.FetchUnreadOnly = False
    mpmMessages.Fetch

    ' Clear the List Box and add to it all of the
    ' messages just read.
    lstMessages.Clear
    intMsgIndex = 0
    If mpmMessages.MsgCount > 0 Then
        Do
            mpmMessages.MsgIndex = intMsgIndex
            lstMessages.AddItem mpmMessages.MsgSubject
            intMsgIndex = intMsgIndex + 1
        Loop Until (intMsgIndex = mpmMessages.MsgCount)
    End If
    Exit Sub

ErrHandler:
    CriticalError

End Sub
```

The first thing the routine in Listing 19.8 does is set some of the properties for the MAPIMessages control's Fetch method. The FetchSorted property is set to True, specifying that the messages should be retrieved in whichever order they are in the mail server's inbox. If the default value (False) were used, the messages would be retrieved in the same order in which they were received.

The FetchUnreadOnly property is also set here. By assigning it to False, it specifies that all messages should be retrieved, not just the unread ones. The default value for this property is True (retrieve unread messages only).

Next, the Fetch method is called. It sends all the messages in the mail server's inbox to your application and stores them in a message set. You can think of the *message set* as a kind of array because you can access messages in the set individually, just as you can access elements of an array individually. To index a message, you simply change the MAPIMessages control's MsgIndex property to point to the message you would like to access. You can then read other properties that apply to the message, such as MsgSubject, MsgNoteText, or MsgDateReceived. You also can call methods that perform some sort of function on the currently indexed message. For example, if you want to forward the current message, you would call the Forward method. It might sound a little strange, and it does take a little getting used to, but using the MAPI controls is really a snap.

Okay, back to the FetchMessages routine. Now that you have all the messages in the mail server's inbox stored in the message set, you need to list them onscreen somehow. This is where the ListBox control (lstMessages) comes in. The next piece of code adds all the message subjects in the message set to lstMessages (after clearing whatever was in there before).

First, you need to tell just how many messages had been read in when the Fetch method was called. This is stored in the MAPIMessages control's MsgCount property. If it's more than zero, you know that at least one message has been retrieved and is stored in the message set. In that case, you use a Do...Loop Until structure to loop through the message set and add each message subject to the ListBox. Note that you have to set msmMessages's MsgIndex property to point to a different message each time the loop is performed.

Listing 19.9 shows the Click event for the New button, which allows users to create a new mail message and send it to the mail server for delivery. Only two lines of this code actually perform that function, and they both call methods of mpmMessages, the MAPIMessages control. The Compose method is called first. It clears all components of the compose buffer. Next, the Send method is called. Use the True argument to indicate that a dialog box should be displayed so that users can add the various elements of the message (subject, body, and so on). The dialog box appears when the Send method is provided by the mail server, so it might be different from machine to machine.

Listing 19.9. Code for the new CommandButton's Click event.

```
Private Sub cmdMsgNew_Click()

    On Error GoTo ErrHandler

    ' Create a new message.
    mpmMessages.Compose
    mpmMessages.Send True

    lstMessages.SetFocus
    Exit Sub

ErrHandler:
    CriticalError

End Sub
```

If you're delighted to find out that it takes only two lines of code to create and send a new message with the MAPI controls, you'll be glad to know that all the other message services are just as easy.

> **NOTE**
>
> After the Send method is complete, the program focus is set to the lstMessages control. I added this line so that the focus would be taken off the New button—more of a cosmetic touch than anything else. I've also done the same in all the other CommandButton Click events, as you'll see.

Now start adding the code for the other buttons' Click events. They're all very similar. Listing 19.10 shows the first, cmdMsgReply_Click.

Listing 19.10. Code for the Reply button's Click event.

```
Private Sub cmdMsgReply_Click()

    On Error GoTo ErrHandler

    ' Reply to currently indexed message.
    mpmMessages.MsgIndex = lstMessages.ListIndex
    mpmMessages.Reply
    mpmMessages.Send True

    lstMessages.SetFocus
    Exit Sub

ErrHandler:
    CriticalError

End Sub
```

As promised, the code is short and simple. The MAPIMessages control's MsgIndex property is set to reflect the message number selected in the ListBox (lstMessages). This makes that message the currently indexed message. Next, mpmMessages's Reply method is called, which copies the current message to the compose buffer and adds RE: at the beginning of its Subject line. Finally, the Send method is called and the message dialog box is displayed.

As you can see, the code for the Reply All button's Click event (see Listing 19.11) is almost identical to Reply's Click event. The only difference is that rather than the Reply method be called, the ReplyAll method is used.

Listing 19.11. Code for the ReplyAll button's Click event.

```
Private Sub cmdMsgReplyAll_Click()

    On Error GoTo ErrHandler

    ' Reply to all recipients of the currently indexed
    ' message.
    mpmMessages.MsgIndex = lstMessages.ListIndex
```

```
    mpmMessages.ReplyAll
    mpmMessages.Send True

    lstMessages.SetFocus
    Exit Sub

ErrHandler:
    CriticalError

End Sub
```

These two buttons do have slightly different functions. The Reply button sends a reply message only to the originator (sender) of the message. The Reply All button, however, sends a copy of the reply message to all the recipients of the original message.

Moving on, you have the Forward button's Click event (see Listing 19.12). Again, it's very similar to the last two code listings. The Forward method copies the currently indexed message to the compose buffer. The message is then edited in the dialog box displayed when the Send method is called. The Subject line in the dialog box is prefixed with FW: when the Forward method is used.

Listing 19.12. Code for the Forward button's Click event.

```
Private Sub cmdMsgForward_Click()

    On Error GoTo ErrHandler

    ' Forward the currently indexed message.
    mpmMessages.MsgIndex = lstMessages.ListIndex
    mpmMessages.Forward
    mpmMessages.Send True

    lstMessages.SetFocus
    Exit Sub

ErrHandler:
    CriticalError

End Sub
```

Listing 19.13 shows the code for the Copy button's Click event. The Copy method simply copies the currently indexed message into the compose buffer. It doesn't alter the Subject line like some of the previously discussed methods.

Listing 19.13. Code for the Copy button's Click event.

```
Private Sub cmdMsgCopy_Click()

    On Error GoTo ErrHandler
```

19

MAIL-ENABLING
APPLICATIONS
WITH MAPI

continues

Listing 19.13. continued

```
     ' Copy the currently indexed message.
     mpmMessages.MsgIndex = lstMessages.ListIndex
     mpmMessages.Copy
     mpmMessages.Send True

     lstMessages.SetFocus
     Exit Sub

ErrHandler:
     CriticalError

End Sub
```

The last of the message services' code is for the Delete button (see Listing 19.14). It's a little different than the rest of the listings thus far because it doesn't call the `Send` method. After pointing to the current message, the `Delete` method is called and the message's subject is removed from the ListBox control.

Listing 19.14. Code for the Delete button's `Click` event.

```
Private Sub cmdMsgDelete_Click()

     On Error GoTo ErrHandler

     ' Delete the currently indexed message and remove its
     ' subject from the List Box.
     mpmMessages.MsgIndex = lstMessages.ListIndex
     mpmMessages.Delete
     lstMessages.RemoveItem lstMessages.ListIndex

     ' Some odds and ends to take care of.
     If lstMessages.ListCount > 0 Then
         lstMessages.ListIndex = 0
     Else
         lblMsgInfo = ""
         txtMsgBody = ""
     End If

     lstMessages.SetFocus
     Exit Sub

ErrHandler:
     CriticalError

End Sub
```

This routine also does a bit of housekeeping when a message is deleted. If no message subjects are left in the ListBox control, it blanks out any message currently onscreen. If some message subjects still remain in the ListBox control, it changes the ListBox pointer to highlight the first message in the list.

When users click one of the message subjects in the ListBox control, you want the corresponding message to be displayed. The code in Listing 19.15 displays the message's originator (sender), subject, and date received in the lblMsgInfo Label control and the body of the message in the txtMsgBody TextBox control.

Listing 19.15. lstMessages's Click event, displaying a message when users click a message subject.

```
Private Sub lstMessages_Click()

    ' When the user clicks on a message's subject, display
    ' the info (From, Subject, and Date) in the lblMsgInfo
    ' box and the message body in txtMsgBody.
    mpmMessages.MsgIndex = lstMessages.ListIndex
    lblMsgInfo = "From: " + mpmMessages.MsgOrigDisplayName + Chr$(13) _
        + "Subj: " + mpmMessages.MsgSubject + Chr$(13) _
        + "Date: " + mpmMessages.MsgDateReceived
    txtMsgBody = mpmMessages.MsgNoteText

End Sub
```

A single MAPIMessages method, Show, allows you to display an Address Book dialog box provided by the mail server. Listing 19.16 shows the code that displays the dialog box when the Address Book button is clicked.

Listing 19.16. Code for the Address Book button's Click event.

```
Private Sub cmdAddrBook_Click()

    On Error GoTo ErrHandler

    ' Show the Address Book dialog box.
    mpmMessages.Show

    lstMessages.SetFocus
    Exit Sub

ErrHandler:
    CriticalError

End Sub
```

You're almost done—only a few more subroutines to go! The Click event for the Exit button (see Listing 19.17) verifies that the users want to exit the program. It then terminates the current MAPI session and ends the program if users decide to proceed with the exit.

Listing 19.17. Code for the Exit button's Click event.

```
Private Sub cmdExit_Click()

    Dim intExit As Integer

    ' Make sure the user really wants to exit the
    ' program.
    intExit = MsgBox("Exit the program?", vbYesNo, _
        "Exit Program")
    If intExit = vbYes Then
        mpsSession.SignOff
        End
    End If

    lstMessages.SetFocus

End Sub
```

The last thing to add to the program is the bit of code shown in Listing 19.18. It prevents users from typing anything into the TextBox control (txtMsgBody) that contains the body of the currently selected message.

Listing 19.18. Code for txtMsgBody's KeyPress events, preventing users from typing anything into the text box used to display the message body.

```
Private Sub txtMsgBody_KeyPress(KeyAscii As Integer)

    ' Prevent users from typing into the text box that
    ' contains the message body.
    KeyAscii = 0

End Sub
```

Finally, you're ready to try out the program. Save the project as vbu1902.vbp and the form as vbu1902.frm; compile and run the program. The first thing you'll see is a dialog box similar to the one shown in Figure 19.5 (again, yours might look different if you're using a mail server other than Microsoft Exchange).

Figure 19.5.

When the program is run, the mail server requests a profile name.

After establishing a MAPI connection, the program receives messages from the mail server's Inbox. It might take a few moments after the MAPI session is established, but you'll then see a dialog box telling you that the program is checking for messages (see Figure 19.6).

FIGURE 19.6.

The program retrieves messages from the mail server's inbox.

When mail retrieval is completed, you'll see a list of the messages (if any) that were in the mail server's Inbox. Try sending a new message by clicking the New button. When you do, a window pops up like the one in Figure 19.7. (Again, yours might be different, based on the kind of mail server you're using.)

FIGURE 19.7.

When sending a new message, the mail server provides a window where you can compose and send the message.

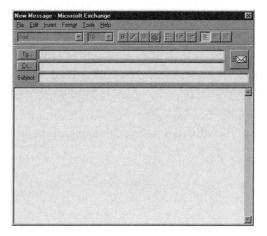

Don't forget to click the Send button when you're done composing your message. For the dialog box provided by Microsoft Exchange, the button to send the message is located to the right of the Subject line.

Try using some of the other message services in the program. Then click the Address Book button to display the Address Book dialog box (see Figure 19.8). In the Address Book dialog box, you can add new entries to your personal address book. You can also delete entries, create distribution lists, and perform several other operations.

That's it for the tour of the simple e-mail application. True to its name, it's very simple and does lack in some areas. For instance, it doesn't support message attachments, but it does show almost all the services supported under MAPI.

FIGURE 19.8.

The Address Book dialog box lets you change your personal address book.

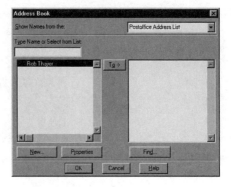

Summary

This chapter introduces the creation of MAPI applications with Visual Basic. It first discusses the MAPI specification and its various components. You learned that MAPI acts as a standard interface between electronic messaging client applications and service providers.

You also learned about the two powerful MAPI ActiveX controls, MAPISession and MAPIMessages. The MAPISession control is used to start and end MAPI sessions, and the MAPIMessages control provides all the MAPI message services.

The sample applications using the two ActiveX controls illustrate how easily you can implement MAPI in Visual Basic. These sample applications provide an introduction to MAPI programming.

Navigating the Registry

by Mike McMillan

IN THIS CHAPTER

CHAPTER 20

The *Registry* replaces the old Windows 3.*x* .INI files as the place where the operating system and application programs store system-specific information. When you install an application on your computer, the installation process puts information in the Registry that, in effect, tells your operating system about the application being installed.

The Registry, unlike the .INI files it replaces, is a hierarchical database that stores information in a proprietary format. .INI files, on the other hand, stored information in ASCII text files that anyone could read and change.

This chapter discusses the structure of the Registry, how to use the RegEdit utility program to view and edit the Registry, and—most importantly—how to access the Registry with Visual Basic to add information specific to the applications you've designed. In particular, you'll learn how to use three built-in VB functions for accessing, setting, and editing Registry values.

> **CAUTION**
>
> Making a mistake while editing the Registry can lead to serious—even fatal—problems with your operating system. Before you do any work with the Registry, back it up and store it in a very safe place. If you do make a mistake in the Registry, a backup could be the only way to save yourself the hassle and inconvenience of rebuilding your operating system.

Touring the Registry

I'll begin this tour of the Registry by first identifying the Windows tool I will use to conduct the tour: RegEdit. RegEdit is a Windows 95 program found in the c:\Windows subdirectory. Figure 20.1 shows the RegEdit icon on my desktop.

FIGURE 20.1.
The RegEdit icon.

You can use RegEdit from the c:\Windows subdirectory, or you can drag the icon onto your desktop to create a shortcut to the program. To use RegEdit, just double-click the icon to display the top level of the Registry.

As I mentioned in this chapter's introduction, the Registry is a hierarchical database. It's made up of six levels, called *keys*, that are broken down into subkeys and values. Each top-level key stores information about specific hardware or software settings. The top-level keys of the Registry are as follows:

- HKEY_CLASSES_ROOT stores information about OLE (object linking and embedding), DDE (dynamic data exchange), and shell integration.

- HKEY_CURRENT_USER contains information about the currently logged-in user, mostly software data pertaining to applications to which the user has access.

- HKEY_LOCAL_MACHINE stores information regarding hardware configuration on the user's PC, software installed on the user's PC, peripheral devices installed on the user's PC, and information about the Windows environment.

- HKEY_USERS contains information about all users with access to the computer system.

- HKEY_CURRENT_CONFIG stores information on multiple hardware configurations on the user's system.

- HKEY_DYN_DATA contains information about Plug and Play devices, performance statistics, and virtual device drivers for the user's computer system.

Figure 20.2 shows the top-level keys of the Registry as displayed by RegEdit.

FIGURE 20.2.

The Registry's top-level keys.

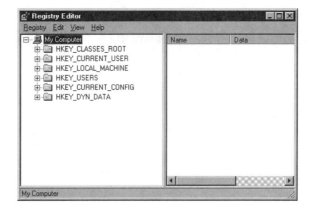

To look at the subkeys within a top-level Registry key, double-click the key's folder or click the key's + icon. Figure 20.3 shows the subkeys for HKEY_CURRENT_USER.

FIGURE 20.3.

The subkeys of HKEY_CURRENT_USER.

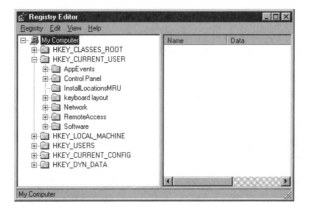

20

NAVIGATING THE REGISTRY

The Registry window is divided into two panes: on the left are the Registry's keys and subkeys, and on the right is the selected subkey's value name and data value. You can discover a subkey's value name and data value by double-clicking the subkey's folder just as you clicked the key's folder to get to the subkeys.

Before you can get to a subkey's value name and data, however, you might have to navigate more than one level of subkeys. Remember that the Registry is a hierarchical database, meaning that it has several layers of keys and subkeys. To get a better feel for how the Registry is organized, look at one of the HKEY_CURRENT_USER subkeys—SOFTWARE (see Figure 20.4). These subkeys reflect the software installed on my computer system and information about which of the software packages I've installed are storing information in this subkey. (I actually have more software installed than just Microsoft and Netscape packages; these two are the ones that use this subkey to store system information.)

Figure 20.4.

The Microsoft *and* Netscape *subkeys of* HKEY_CURRENT_USER\ Software.

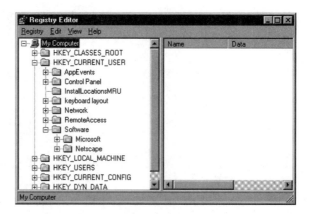

To continue this exploration of the Registry, expand the HKEY_CURRENT_USER\Software\Microsoft subkey to see what actual system information is being stored. Double-clicking the subkey displays more subkeys in RegEdit's left pane (see Figure 20.5).

To finally see some actual Registry data settings, double-click the Visual Basic line and the 5.0 line. In the right pane is a group of settings for Visual Basic 5.0 (Figure 20.6 shows RegEdit with the right pane pulled all the way to the left, hiding the left pane).

In the right pane are two columns: Name and Data. The Name column holds the name for the value setting; the Data column holds the value of the setting. For example, the BooksExePath setting in Figure 20.6 is the setting VB uses to find the Books OnLine application. The data value for this setting is C:\Program Files\DevStudio\VB\Vbonline\vbonline.exe. Whenever a user wants to load the Books OnLine application, Visual Basic knows to follow this path to find the program.

As you've probably noticed by looking at Figure 20.6, there appear to be two types of values that can be stored in Registry settings: strings and binary numbers. Although many more data types are possible, you run across these two types the most often.

FIGURE 20.5.

The subkeys of
HKEY_CURRENT_USER\
Software\Microsoft.

FIGURE 20.6.

Registry settings for
Visual Basic 5.0.

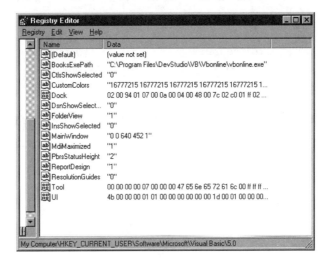

You can tell whether the Registry setting accepts string or binary data by looking at the icon displayed with the setting. The two icons in Figure 20.6 are a torn piece of paper with the letters ab on it (representing string data) and a torn piece of paper with 0's and 1's on it (representing binary data). Although you should always be able to determine the type of data stored in a Registry setting just by looking at it, you can use the icon as a guide.

You've now seen how to navigate through the Registry to get from the top-level keys to individual key values. Before you learn how to work with the Registry in Visual Basic, however, you need to understand how to set and change Registry settings.

20

NAVIGATING THE REGISTRY

Backing Up the Registry

The program that you've been using to examine Registry settings is also used to set and edit Registry values. But before you learn how to edit the Registry, you need to learn how to back it up in case of problems.

Because of the nature of the Registry's data, if you accidentally change or delete a piece of data in the Registry that's needed by the operating system, your whole system can become unusable. Therefore, it's necessary to always make a backup of the Registry before you make any changes to it.

You can back up the Registry in several ways:

■ Use a utility program called the Microsoft Configuration Backup (MCB), which is located on the Windows 95 CD-ROM. MCB allows you to back up the Registry up to nine times. The program keeps track of which backup is which, so you can tell MCB which backup copy you want to use to do it, should you ever need to restore your Registry.

■ Export it to an ASCII file. In RegEdit, choose Registry | Export Registry File. In the dialog box that appears (see Figure 20.7), enter a new name for the Registry file in the File Name text box and click OK. RegEdit creates an ASCII file with the filename you entered.

FIGURE 20.7.

Exporting the Registry file.

NOTE

When you export the Registry, make sure that you have the Registry at the top level, with none of the keys open. If one key is open when you export the Registry, only that key's information is exported.

Figure 20.8 shows part of the exported Registry file. You can examine this text file with any word processing program that can display ASCII text. If you export the whole Registry, however, you can't examine the exported file with Notepad; the file is too large for Notepad to display.

FIGURE 20.8.

A portion of the exported Registry.

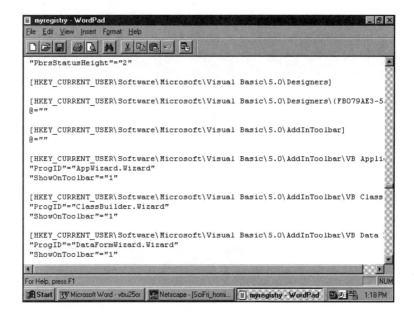

If you do somehow manage to damage your Registry during editing, you can import the exported file back into your system by choosing Registry | Import Registry File from the menu in RegEdit. In the dialog box that appears, enter the name of the export file, and the file's information is imported back into the Registry. The Registry then will be in the same state it was when you exported it.

Now that you know how to back up the Registry, you're ready to use RegEdit to change Registry settings.

Setting and Editing Registry Values With RegEdit

Editing a key is simple:

1. Double-click the Registry setting. A dialog box appears, asking you for a new value for the setting (see Figure 20.9).
2. To change the value of the key, simply delete the highlighted data and enter new data.

20

NAVIGATING THE REGISTRY

FIGURE 20.9.

Editing a Registry setting value.

CAUTION

Editing the Registry can create very serious system problems if you enter wrong information in a Registry setting. For example, if the data in Figure 20.9 is changed to a non-existent file path, the Books OnLine application will be unusable until the data is corrected.

To use RegEdit to add new settings to the Registry, follow these steps:

1. Right-click the Registry key under which you want to put the data, and choose New and then Key. A new subkey is created, titled Default (see Figure 20.10).

FIGURE 20.10.

Creating a new key with RegEdit.

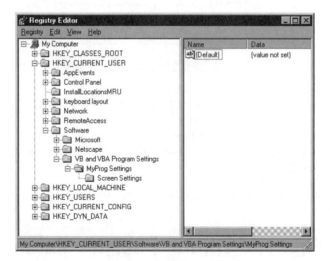

2. Type a name for the key. It appears in the tree in the place you created for it.
3. From here, you can create more subkeys and actually add data to them. To create a subkey data item and a value, move to the right pane after you create the subkey. In Figure 20.11, for example, a Registry setting for Screen Settings has been created under the MyProg Settings key. Right-click the Screen Settings key, click New, and then click String Value.

4. A new string value icon is created; at the prompt, enter a name for the setting. Figure 20.11 shows a new setting named Display Type.

FIGURE 20.11.

A new Registry setting for Display Type.

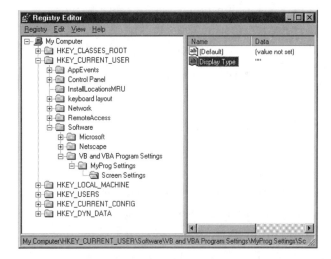

5. To add a value for the setting, double-click Display Type. A dialog box like the one you saw when you edited a setting will appear. Enter a value for the setting.

You now have a complete Registry setting (see Figure 20.12).

FIGURE 20.12.

Adding a value to the Display Type setting.

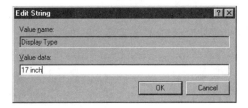

With this overview of the Registry complete, you're now ready to see how to use Visual Basic to change the Registry.

Changing the Registry With Visual Basic

Visual Basic provides a location in the Registry for storing information about applications created in VB:

HKEY_CURRENT_USER\Software\VB and VBA Program Settings\

In this location, you'll have to provide the name of your application, the section of the application (hardware, user information, and so on), and the key itself.

You can use two VB functions and two VB statements to create and edit your Registry settings:

- The SaveSetting statement creates or saves Registry settings.
- The GetSetting function retrieves Registry settings.
- The GetAllSettings function returns an array of Registry settings.
- The DeleteSetting statement deletes Registry settings.

The following sections describe how to use these functions and statements in your VB code to work with the Registry.

The SaveSetting Statement

To create a Registry setting, use the SaveSetting statement, which takes four arguments:

- *AppName* is the name of the application in the Registry.
- *Section* is the section of the setting under *AppName*.
- *Key* is the name of the key under which the setting will be saved.
- *Value* is the Registry value of the key.

Figure 20.13 shows a VB form that can set and change Registry settings. The following code for creating a Registry setting is found in the Create Registry Setting command button's Click event:

```
Private Sub Command2_Click()
    strAppName = Trim(Text1.Text)
    strSection = Trim(Text2.Text)
    strKey = Trim(Text3.Text)
    strRegValue = Trim(Text4.Text)
    SaveSetting strAppName, strSection, strKey, strRegValue
End Sub
```

FIGURE 20.13.

A VB form for creating and editing Registry settings.

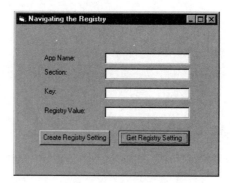

The code for the SaveSetting statement is very straightforward. The application name, section name, key name, and key value are entered in the text boxes. These strings are then given to the SaveSetting statement; when the statement is executed, the Registry setting is created.

You can also use the SaveSetting statement to change a Registry setting. Just change the value of the *Value* argument in the SaveSetting statement, and a new value is entered for the Registry setting. Figure 20.14 shows what will have to be entered to change the Display Type value from 17 inch to 21 inch.

FIGURE 20.14.

Changing a Registry setting with SaveSetting.

The GetSetting Function

To retrieve a Registry value, use the GetSetting function. The GetSetting function takes the following arguments:

- *AppName* is the name of the application in the Registry.
- *Section* is the section of the setting under *AppName*.
- *Key* is the name of the key under which the setting will be saved.
- *Default* is the default value to retrieve if there's no Registry value.

The code for using the GetSetting function is also very straightforward:

```
Private Sub Command1_Click()
    Dim strRegEntry As String
    strAppName = Trim(Text1.Text)
    strSection = Trim(Text2.Text)
    strKey = Trim(Text3.Text)
    strRegEntry = GetSetting(strAppName, strSection, strKey, "No value")
    Text4.Text = strRegEntry
End Sub
```

The first three arguments are entered in the text boxes, and the default setting value ("No value") is added to the end of the function. The last line of this code takes the value retrieved by the function and puts it into the Reg Value text box. Figure 20.15 shows the results of running the GetSetting function. If there hadn't been a value for this Registry setting, the last text box would have displayed the message No value.

20

NAVIGATING THE
REGISTRY

FIGURE 20.15.

Retrieving a Registry value with the `GetSetting` *function.*

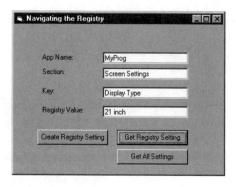

The `GetAllSettings` Function

To retrieve all the Registry settings for an application section, use the `GetAllSettings` function. This function takes just two arguments—the application name and the section name—and returns all the keys and their values in an array. To display the settings returned by `GetAllSettings`, use a control such as a list box.

Here's some code that returns all the Registry settings for the `Screen Settings` section of the `MyProg` application:

```
Private Sub Command3_Click()
    Dim varSettings As Variant
    strAppName = Trim(Text1.Text)
    strSection = Trim(Text2.Text)
    varSettings = GetAllSettings(strAppName, strSection)
    For x = 0 To UBound(varSettings, 1)
        List1.AddItem varSettings(x, 0) & " " & varSettings(x, 1)
    Next x
End Sub
```

As with the other examples seen in this section, this code is very straightforward. It resembles the other examples, except where the contents of the array are displayed in a list box by using a `For...Next` loop. Figure 20.16 shows the results of running this code with the `MyProg` example you've been using.

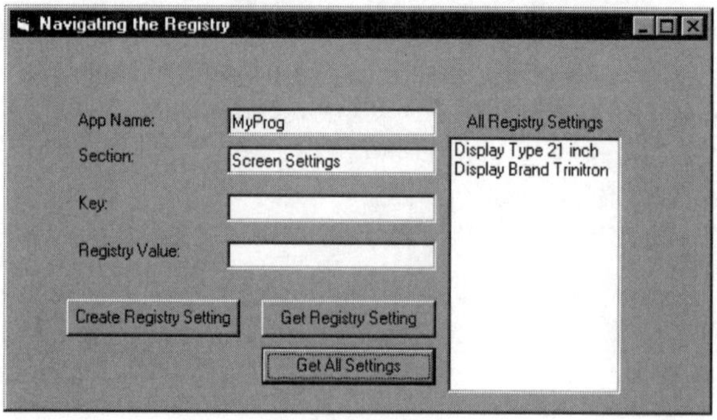

FIGURE 20.16.

Displaying all Registry settings in a list box.

The DeleteSettings Statement

To delete the value of a Registry key, use the DeleteSettings statement. This statement takes the regular arguments—application name, section name, and key name—and deletes the value that's associated with the key name. If you want to delete all the settings for the application, you just use the DeleteSettings statement with the application name; if you want to delete all the settings within a section of an application's Registry settings, use the DeleteSettings statement with the application name and the setting. For example, to delete the Display Type Registry setting, use the following line of code:

```
DeleteSetting "MyProg", "Screen Settings", "Display Type"
```

To delete the keys under the Screen Settings section, use this line of code:

```
DeleteSetting "MyProg", "Screen Settings"
```

Finally, to delete a whole application, use the following line of code:

```
DeleteSetting "MyProg"
```

Summary

The Registry provides a structured, hierarchical database for storing information about your applications and your user's computer systems. Unlike .INI files, which are used in previous versions of the Windows operating system, the Registry stores its information in a proprietary format and can't just be edited like a text file. This chapter explains how the Registry is structured, how to edit the Registry, and how to use Visual Basic functions and statements to store and retrieve information in the Registry.

Understanding the Extensibility Model

by John D. Conley III

IN THIS CHAPTER

CHAPTER 21

The key principle behind extensibility is that you can extend some object beyond its core base of behavior. You might say that one attribute of a good system is that its users can effectively extend it without jeopardizing the primary engine that drives it.

Visual Basic 5.0 is such a system. The core VB development environment is a very robust beast. But even this great system needs tweaking from time to time, especially where repetitious development chore patterns emerge. For instance, when you're building a huge SQL string, you must break up the string into repetitious lines of code, such as the following:

```
Dim sSQL As String
sSQL = sSQL & "SELECT SomeColumn FROM SomeTable "
sSQL = sSQL & "WHERE SomeIndex = '"  & SomeVariable
...
```

By implementing some clever extensible behavior to Visual Basic, you can automate the process of building large SQL strings so that all you need to do is add the column name(s), values, and WHERE clause constraints.

Assessing the Extensibility Object Model

To implement extensibility features, Visual Basic offers the powerful Extensibility Object Model (EOM). Through EOM, many core objects in Visual Basic itself are available to you at no extra charge (except for the cost of this book, perhaps). Of course, just because the EOM is a powerful interface into the rich world of the VB engine doesn't mean it's easy to learn, much less to implement. If it were that easy, you could probably just as easily develop your own Visual Basic compiler.

The EOM consists of six loosely coupled packages of objects with methods that implement key services of the Visual Basic development environment. (*Package* is an object-oriented term that refers to a group of related but distinct objects that carry out a common subsystem behavior.) These six object packages in the EOM are

- Core Objects
- Form Manipulation
- Event Response
- Add-in Management
- Project and Component Manipulation
- Code Manipulation

Understanding the Core Objects Package

The Core Objects package contains the bread and butter of Visual Basic extensibility. In a loose sense, it has the same importance as the MFC (Microsoft Foundation Classes) has in Visual C++. Its objects include the following:

Understanding the Extensibility Model

CHAPTER 21

435

21

UNDERSTANDING
THE EXTENSIBILITY
MODEL

- The root object
- The IDTExtensibility Interface object
- The Visual Basic instance variable

The Root Object

Just as CObject is the base class of the MFC in Visual C++, so is the VBE (Visual Basic Environment) object to the extensibility services of Visual Basic. The VBE object is also known as the root object of the extensibility model. It's the base object for every extensibility object and collection in Visual Basic. Each object and collection owns a reference to the VBE object via a VBE property. The collections owned by the VBE object include the following:

VBProjects

Windows

CodePanes

CommandBars

The VBProjects Collection

The VBProjects collection allows you to access a set of Visual Basic properties. This feature can be quite helpful if your development environment has an established process for developing software—that is, you could easily audit projects quickly to make sure that they're on track. You also could use this facility to rapidly and automatically add enterprise-wide classes or frameworks, or to complete subsystems into a set of projects before a developer adds the first line of new code.

Noteworthy Properties

The VBProjects collection has a few interesting properties to note:

- The Filename property returns the full pathname of the group project file.
- The StartProject property returns or sets the project that will start when users choose Start from the Run menu, click the Run arrow, or press the F5 key.

Noteworthy Methods

The VBProjects collection also has a set of useful methods, including these two:

- AddFromFile allows you to add or open a project or group project. Its only required argument is the string representing the path of the file you want to add. Also, an optional Boolean argument, if set to True when the file being added isn't a group project file, closes the existing group project; subsequently, the new project is created as the only open project. If it's set to True when the file being added is a group project file, the current group project is replaced by the one you're adding. If it's set to False when the file being added is a group project file, each project in the corresponding group project is inserted into the current group project. The AddFromFile method returns a reference to the VBNewProjects collection.

■ `AddFromTemplate` allows you to add project templates into the `VBProjects` collection. Its only required argument is the string representing the path of the file you want to use as a template. This method is quite similar to `AddFromFile`, except that you're dealing with project templates instead of project files.

The Windows Collection

With the `Windows` collection, you can access windows such as the Project and Properties windows. Also, this collection allows you to access a group of all currently open code windows and designer windows. VB adds a window to this collection each time you open a code or designer window. Similarly, each window you close is removed from this collection. With each window in the collection, for instance, you can show, hide, or position windows.

Invoking the `Close` method has different implementations for different types of windows. For instance, if you invoke `Close` on a code or designer window in the collection, that window is simply closed and removed from the collection. However, if you invoke it on a window that's a linked window frame, the window isn't closed, but rather unlinked from the other windows. If you invoke the `Close` method on a Project or Properties window, the object's `Visible` property is set to `False`, but it remains in the collection.

Noteworthy Properties

The `Windows` collection has one property I should briefly discuss: `LinkedWindowFrame`, a read-only property that returns the window object representing the frame that contains the window. With this property, you can access the object representing the linked window frame.

> **NOTE**
>
> A *linked window frame* is a window frame (a listview style area) containing links to more than one window. The Project and Properties windows in VB5 are examples of window frames.

The linked window frame has properties distinct from the window(s) it contains. If the window has no links with other windows in the frame, the `LinkedWindowFrame` property returns `Nothing`. An example of such a linked window frame would be the Project and Properties windows that are linked by default when you run Visual Basic 5.0.

Noteworthy Methods

You need to know about the `Windows` collection's `CreateToolWindow` method. Its syntax is as follows:

```
object.CreateToolWindow(AddInInst, ProgId, Caption, GuidPosition, DocObj) _
    As Window
```

This method creates a new Tool window containing a reference to the `DocObj` object you pass in as the fifth argument. The first argument, `AddInInst`, is an object instance of an add-in from the development environment you pass in. The *ProgId* argument is of the String data type and represents the program identifier of the ActiveX Document object. The *Caption* argument is also a String that contains text you want displayed as the caption for the window. The *GuidPosition* argument is a String that holds a unique identifier for the window.

The *DocObj* argument in the preceding code is an object that represents an ActiveX Document object. When you call this method, the *DocObj* argument you pass in will be set to an actual ActiveX Document object.

Noteworthy Collections

The Windows collection uses the CodePanes and CommandBars collections.

The CodePanes collection allows you to access the collection of code panes now open in your Visual Basic project.

The CommandBars collection allows you to access the collection of command bars. Each command bar object is a menu-style toolbar, combining the best of the menus and toolbars that users have come to expect. Each command bar object in the collection can itself contain other command bar objects, given the type of command bar you implement. The different types of command bars are

- Pop-up
- ComboBox
- Button

The VBE object has a CommandBarEvents property that, when accessed, returns the current CommandBarEvents object. Also, the user of your command bar can actually move to another area inside a menu or toolbar. Programmatically speaking, you shouldn't hard-code its actual position.

Referencing an object within the CommandBars collection can be pretty straightforward. To reference the Add-Ins menu object, you would declare a command bar object variable and instantiate it as follows:

```
Set cmdBar = VBInst.CommandBars("Add-Ins")
```

With this approach, you don't have to memorize the object's ordinal position.

TIP

Because some built-in attributes of the CommandBars collection and each command bar object might change with subsequent versions of Visual Basic, you might consider creating your own classes to encapsulate its methods and properties. That way, the other classes and modules in your system will refer to your class, which in turn delegates its methods and property assignments to the CommandBars collection, the command bar object, or both.

continues

continued

This is useful especially in those cases where the software manufacturer changes the name of a method or property in a new version of its software, yet you had already implemented the previous version in numerous systems across your enterprise. Then you can carefully implement the new version of that software with later versions of your own.

Suppose that you have a third-party component with a class BankAccount in it, and that class had an attribute (property) called AccountNum. That's the current version, and you use that component in 10 systems within your company (and each system, in turn, uses the component in 20 subsystems). When the new version comes out, the software company changed the attribute name to AccountNumber. You can see how much work that would be if you didn't encapsulate that component into a class (interface class). With an interface class, all enterprise systems would refer to it, and in turn this class would delegate its members to the component. When the component changes, only the interface class is affected; all other classes can stay in production.

You use the Events object to access properties that allow add-ins to connect to all events in Visual Basic for Applications. The properties of the Events object return objects of the same type as the property name. For example, the CommandBarEvents property returns the CommandBarEvents object.

You can use the SelectedVBComponent property to return the active component. (The *active component* is the component being tracked in the Project window.) If the selected item in the Project window isn't a component, SelectedVBComponent returns Nothing.

The IDTExtensibility Interface Object

The IDTExtensibility Interface object exposes the public methods and properties of the extensibility model. By *expose*, I mean that because you don't directly use the services (methods) and properties of the underlying extensibility model, you need to invoke the methods of the model's agent, so to speak. You can think of interfaces as public agents for the private implementation of an extensibility model object you instantiate.

Before you use the IDTExtensibility Interface object, you need to designate a class to implement it. To implement this interface, insert the following line in the General Declarations section of your class module:

```
Implements IDTExtensibility
```

This line causes a new entry to appear under the Class item in the left-hand drop-down box (object list) of your class module. You'll insert your implementation code in the methods and properties associated with IDTExtensibility.

Understanding the Extensibility Model

CHAPTER 21

439

21

UNDERSTANDING
THE EXTENSIBILITY
MODEL

The four methods for Add-In servicing (for managing your add-ins) are as follows:

`OnConnection`

`OnDisconnection`

`OnStartupComplete`

`OnAddInsUpdate`

If you noticed, these methods have names similar to those of events. When an actual event occurs, these methods (known as *Add-In event handlers*) are fired. The class in your code that implements `IDTExtensibility` must implement these four event-handling methods, even if that means you put a `Rem` comment command or a comment character (`'`) in the interface method.

The Visual Basic Instance Variable

The Visual Basic instance variable (also known as a *dynamic identification variable*) identifies a particular instance of your Visual Basic session. This instance identifier is what allows you to have separately identifiable running instances of Visual Basic in memory.

The instance variable is of the type `VBIDE.VBE`. To use this variable, declare it in a class module or general module (also known as a *class utility* in MS Visual Modeler, a software design tool now available for Visual Basic 5.0). Therefore, if you declared it in a class module as private, the declaration would look like the following:

`Private mVBInst As VBIDE.VBE`

The prefix `m` identifies the variable as a module-level variable.

Understanding the Form Manipulation Package

The objects and object collections within the Form Manipulation package offer methods (or services) to allow you to automate common development tasks that are particular to forms in your Visual Basic projects. That is, you can iterate through all the forms (each of type `VBForm`) in a project, much the way you're probably accustomed to doing by using the `Forms` collection. Along the same lines, you can manipulate all the controls on a `VBForm` object by using the `VBForm`'s public collection, `VBControls`.

Within the Form Manipulation package are several objects, including `CommandBar` and `CodePane`.

The CommandBar Object

The `CommandBar` object allows you to work with menus and toolbars, as discussed earlier in the section "Noteworthy Collections." Visual Basic lets you create and delete command bars as well as modify their attributes, such as size, location on the form, and their icons. You also can handle the events associated with command bars by using the `Events.CommandBarEvents` collection of the current instance of VB (`VBInst`).

The CodePane Object

The CodePane object allows you to display the lines of code you may have in a given object, as discussed earlier in the section "Noteworthy Collections." This object is a public member of the CodeModule object. You refer to a CodePane object by using a syntax similar to this:

```
Set MyCodePane = MyVBComponent.CodeModule.CodePane
```

Understanding the Event Response Package

Quite obviously, when you extend Visual Basic with the EOM, you require some mechanism for processing every action VB users carry out. The EOM provides the capability to respond to such events. The source of events can be an object or a collection of objects. Now, you can process events for the VBA object, as well as collections such as VBProjects, VBComponents, VBControls, and References. Typical events you might want to process could include

- Starting a new project
- Ending an existing project
- Adding a member to a project or deleting one (that is, forms, components, classes, and so on)
- Adding an object to a collection or removing one (that is, forms, components, classes, projects, and so on)
- Adding a reference to a project or deleting one

You can probably find many more uses for Event Response objects. The idea here is that you can better manage the methodology and process of developing Visual Basic software systems by using the ability to respond to events in the Visual Basic development environment.

Understanding the Add-In Management Package

Managing add-ins is essential to using the EOM. Visual Basic provides you with the AddIns collection and the AddIn object for working with add-ins. By using each AddIn object, you can connect and disconnect add-ins, as well as use objects exposed within them.

Understanding the Project and Component Manipulation Package

Visual Basic's Extensibility Object Model allows you to manipulate one or more projects and components within corresponding project or component collections. Remember that a project is the development environment entity containing all components that make up your current software-development effort. A component, in turn, is a member of that project and can be a form, a code module, a control, or whatever member is necessary to implement your project.

The object types for project objects are VBProject (a single object) and VBProjects (a collection of VBProject objects). The object types for component objects are VBComponent (a single object) and VBComponents (a collection of VBComponent objects). When you add a new VBProject to the VBProjects collection, the VBProjects collection returns a reference to the newly added VBProject object after it's finished adding the object to the collection. The same pattern applies to VBComponent and VBComponents as well.

Understanding the Code Manipulation Package

At the center of the Code Manipulation package is the CodeModule object. Unlike the CodePane object, which allows only read-only access to code, the CodeModule object allows you to alter code. In turn, unlike the CodePane object, the CodeModule object doesn't let you view the code. Therefore, if you want to view and alter code, you need the services of the CodePane object in the Form Manipulation package. This combined use of services would loosely couple the Code Manipulation and Form Manipulation packages.

In saying that you can alter the code, I mean that you can add, delete, or replace blocks of code. So if you decided to create your own version of Visual Modeler (Microsoft's object-oriented modeling tool for VB5), you could use the CodeModule object to automatically create the code from your models.

The CodeModule object is quite useful, particularly for software development managers, system architects, and the like. You can use the CodeModule object, for instance, to count the number of lines of code in a component's module. The CodeModule property for the line count is CountOfLines. CodeModule would be a public object within a VBComponent object.

With the CountOfLines property, you could use the CodeModule's Line property to refer to a particular line of code (represented as a string). Therefore, by using the CountOfLines and Lines properties, you could grab all the text in a module by using syntax similar to the following:

```
For CurrentLineNumber = 1 To MyVBComponent.CodeModule.CountOfLines
        AllCodeText = AllCodeText & _
        MyVBComponent.CodeModule.Lines(CurrentLineNumber, 1) & CRLF
Next CurrentLineNumber
```

where CurrentLineNumber is the number representing the current line of code, MyVBComponent is an arbitrary project component you specify (that is, form, class, and so on), and AllCodeText is the string value that represents all the lines of code you just accumulated.

Implementing the Extensibility Model in a Practical Way

Listing 21.1 shows a method (or function) called getCodeLineCount that demonstrates one way to reference the CodeModule object. With this method, I want to return the number of lines of code in a given code module.

Listing 21.1. Implementing code-manipulation objects in the extensibility model to return the number of lines of code in a code module.

```
' Returns the number of lines of code in module
Public Function getCodeLineCount()
    Dim MyVBProject As VBProject
    Dim MyVBComponent As VBComponent
    Dim sVBProject As String
    Dim sVBComponent As String

sVBProject = "SomeProject"
sVBComponent = "SomeComponent"

    Set MyVBComponent = _
    vbi.VBProjects.Item(sVBProject).VBComponents.Item(sVBComponent)
    getCodeLineCount = _ MyVBComponent.CodeModule.CountOfLines
End Function
```

Listing 21.2 shows how you can insert code from an external source into the current code module.

Listing 21.2. Implementing code-manipulation objects in the extensibility model to add additional code or comments in a code module.

```
' Add text to a given code module.
Public Sub addCodeText(argSomeCode As String)
    Dim MyVBProject As VBProject
    Dim MyVBComponent As VBComponent
    Dim sVBProject As String
    Dim sVBComponent As String

sVBProject = "SomeProject"
sVBComponent = "SomeComponent"

    If (sVBProject <> "") And (sVBComponent <> "") And (argSomeCode _
        <> "") Then
        Set MyVBComponent = _
        vbi.VBProjects.Item(sVBProject).VBComponents.Item(sVBComponent)
        MyVBComponent.CodeModule.AddFromString argSomeCode
    End If
End Sub
```

Summary

In this chapter, you've learned quite a bit about the Extensibility Object Model and its members. The EOM is really quite a useful service for extending Visual Basic's behavior. It facilitates a better way to manage the Visual Basic development process by allowing you to manage and manipulate each project programmatically.

This ability to extend Visual Basic more than compensates for its lack of pure inheritance capabilities (as some would argue) by allowing you to automate the software reuse process. System auditors can easily audit projects to ensure compliance with company policy (is this a benefit or a threat to ingenuity?). If you have a favorite application-design tool that doesn't generate code for Visual Basic, you can bridge this compatibility gap with the EOM. If your company has a motto that must be placed on every application's main form, and this motto changes every month for some new marketing campaign, you could automate the process of adding the latest motto to every main form by using the EOM.

Visual Basic's extensibility features make it a top contender for the favorite software-development tool of corporate America. After reading this chapter, you should have some sense of Visual Basic's new stature.

## CHAPTER 22

Creating Your Own Wizards With the Wizard Manager

by John D. Conley III

IN THIS CHAPTER

No other company has maximized the potential for user-friendly application wizards more than Microsoft. This software giant has pretty much spoiled users with its inviting wizards for Microsoft Office and development tools such as Visual C++ (Class Wizard) and Visual Basic (Application Wizard), among others. Although this approach has made Microsoft even more millions of dollars, the rest of us "one-person development shops" have had to scurry to play catch-up because more users are demanding similar wizardry in their custom applications. Most developers have found this to be one tough act to follow.

Starting with Visual Basic 5.0, you now have a stop-gap solution—the Wizard Manager, which helps you create custom wizards for your application. By using wizards, you can capture the various ways users will use your application step by step without intimidating them with a sizable learning curve. Each task (or use) that users will accomplish with your application is encapsulated within your wizard.

> **NOTE**
>
> You can use the Wizard Manager only with the Professional and Enterprise Editions of Visual Basic 5.0.

In short, the Wizard Manager manages your wizard's screens as you develop them. With the management facility comes the ability to add, modify, and remove screens from your wizard. In addition to screen management, you can also add new steps, manipulate the ordering of steps, and remove steps. The only caveat to using the Wizard Manager is that, as a first-time user, you may need a wizard to use it. It's not that intuitive to use because you have to right-click within the Wizard Manager main application container to access all its features. Also, despite its name, it doesn't create all the logic for your wizard; instead, it creates your wizard's skeleton or framework. (It probably should be called Wizard Framework Manager.)

Only you know how your application responds to the way your users will use it. The Wizard Manager simply helps you communicate between your wizard and your application in a step-by-step, orderly manner.

Understanding the Ways of the Wizard Manager

The Wizard Manager uses a single form, frmWizard, that houses each frame of your wizard. This form contains all the frames. All frames aren't visible at the same time, however; each becomes visible as its Left property is set to the Left property of the area in the form that's visible to the user. This might not sound like the most sophisticated way to handle this process of swapping frames in and out of the visible area, but it still gets the job done.

What does this all mean? Suppose that you're required to create an application that lets users download several different mainframe files from a host server, extract data based on certain criteria, and print reports based on these user-performed tasks. Rather than expect users to navigate menus or click a series of non-intuitive buttons that don't show relationships between them, your wizard could help users concentrate on what they're doing. So you might create a step that offers users a list of mainframe files to download, a subsequent step to allow users to specify the criteria for extracting data from these files, and a third step to actually print the report in the desired format to a default printer or a printer they specify.

To users, this is better than having to read an application guide to find out how to select and download a mainframe file, read about which button to click next to extract the data, and then read about another button to select a report format. The wizard-driven approach to graphical user interfaces is fast becoming the preferred visual application architecture for users.

Using the Wizard Manager for the First Time

The Wizard Manager has several features to help you create useful wizards. Despite all its usefulness, the Wizard Manager is rather small and isn't quite consistent with the rest of the Visual Basic development environment's look and feel. Figure 22.1 shows what the Wizard Manager looks like.

FIGURE 22.1.

The Wizard Manager, although rather small in appearance, is quite powerful.

To use the Wizard Manager add-in, you need to make sure that it's activated in the Add-Ins menu. Choose Add-Ins | Add-In Manager from the menu. The Add-In Manager dialog box should appear (see Figure 22.2).

FIGURE 22.2.

Use the Add-In Manager to activate the Wizard Manager add-in.

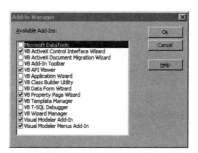

Click the checkbox labeled VB Wizard Manager, click OK, and then open the GeoFacts sample in the \Vb\Samples folder. Add a form and name it frmWizard. Now start the Wizard Manager by choosing Add-Ins | Wizard Manager from the menu. You'll see a window similar to the one shown in Figure 22.1.

When the Wizard Manager Add-In is up and running, you're ready to use its features to create your wizards.

If you right-click anywhere in the Wizard Manager window, you'll get a pop-up menu. Near the bottom of the menu is the New Wizard item. This isn't the most intuitive way to get started with the Wizard Manager because the buttons are meaningless if you haven't started a new wizard. When you choose this menu item, the Wizard Manager creates a wizard project (see Figure 22.3).

FIGURE 22.3.

Choosing New Wizard in the pop-up menu creates a default wizard project for you.

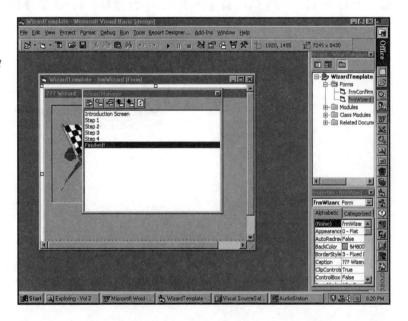

Each new wizard project comes with a step titled Introduction Screen, a default set of four steps, and a Finished! step. These are merely labels for each step, meaning that you can override them to display whatever caption you want.

The very first wizard step is the Introduction Screen. Here, you'll want to display a visually appealing graphic and some accompanying text to introduce your wizard and the application. The next four steps (or however many you actually need) encapsulate the major business uses of the system.

22

A USE-CASE SCENARIO

If you're familiar with the object-oriented analysis method for refining user requirements called *use-case analysis*, you'll understand that an application's architecture is built around each way users will use the application you're developing. Roughly speaking, each use is called a *use case*. For the most part, wizards are perfect complements to the use-case approach to evolving applications, because each frame in your wizard automates a particular use of the application.

The Finished! step is the last form users see. You're probably familiar with the checkered racing flag seen on most wizards; the Wizard Manager doesn't veer away from this tradition. Of course, you can change this image to whatever image you want—just make sure that it provides a visual cue to users that they've accomplished a sequence of tasks.

WATCH YOUR STEPS

In a sense, you might view each wizard step as objects of the class step. Each step object has a caption property (the ones you see in the Wizard Manager list) and is an aggregate of three types of controls: an Image control, a Label control, and a TextBox control. The Image control is an object that displays the image for the current step in your wizard. The Label control provides users with instructions for the current step instance. The TextBox control might be used to provide default information that can be used as values for the programming you do behind each step.

Using the Wizard Manager Buttons

The Wizard Manager has several buttons to help you better facilitate the process of creating wizards. Before you create a wizard, look at each button and menu in the Wizard Manager.

The Add New Step Button

The Add New Step button allows you to add a new step to your wizard. You add each subsequent step by using this button. When you click this button, a new step is inserted just before the Finished! step—and after the last step, if any—in the list of your wizard steps.

The Insert Step Button

The Insert Step button varies from the Add New Step button in that the Wizard Manager inserts a new step just before the currently selected step, regardless of the Finished! button. The Insert Step button works only if you've already selected a step, thereby making it current. For instance, if you click Step 1, Step 1 becomes current, and Wizard Manager prompts you to specify a name for the new step. It's then inserted ahead of Step 1, therefore making Step 1 the second step.

The Move All Off Screen/Move Step Button

You use this button to make sure that the first dialog box the users see is the one you want them to see. Wizard Manager makes the last step you worked on, by default, the first dialog box the user sees when your wizard starts up. You'll need to use this button as the last thing you do before ending your current Wizard Manager session.

The Move Step Down/Up One Position Button

These two buttons simply swap the currently selected step with the step below and above it. For instance, if you selected Step 1 and wanted to swap its position with the position of Step 2 in the step list, simply click the Move the Current Step Down button. If Step 2 were the currently selected step and you wanted to swap its position with that of Step 1, simply click the Move the Current Step Up button. If you hadn't selected a step and then clicked one of these buttons, the Wizard manager wouldn't know how to respond to your request and will therefore ignore it.

The Refresh Step List Button

Click this button to refresh the list of steps to show the changes you made to any of the steps. You probably won't use this button often because changes to step names are reflected immediately.

Creating Your First Wizard

If the Wizard Manager is still up and running, you can proceed to create a new wizard. If not, run Wizard Manager by choosing it from the Add-Ins menu. Right-click anywhere in the subsequent window and choose New Wizard. If you didn't add a form called `frmWizard` to the `GeoFacts` sample project, you'll get a message like the one shown in Figure 22.4. If you get this message dialog, click Yes and save the `MyWizard` project to the `GeoFacts` folder.

FIGURE 22.4.

A Wizard Manager alert dialog box.

> **CAUTION**
>
> If you're in the middle of developing a wizard and decide to right-click one of the steps in the step list to start over and create a new wizard, you'll probably encounter an unexpected error 380, and the Wizard Manager dialog will appear cross-hatched as if disabled (and it is). At this point, you may have to restart Visual Basic to display the Wizard Manager again (although your forms, modules, resource files, and classes will still be in your project).

You can also save the wizard at some preliminary stage in its creation, to build another version of it in a different direction, as it were. Use the Save File As dialog box, which prompts you to save your new wizard project file (.VBP) to a location you specify. The default project filename is MyWizard.vbp. Make sure the wizard has the name you want to give it and save it to \Vb\Projects.

Using Wizard Manager Project Files

You'll notice that the Wizard Manager created several Visual Basic project files by default, as listed in Table 22.1. Each component in Table 22.1 is discussed in more detail later in the chapter.

Table 22.1. Default VB project files generated by Wizard Manager.

Filename	Code Name	Form Description
Confirm.frm	frmConfirm	Ensures that users have a pretty good understanding of a task to be undertaken.
Wizard.frm	frmWizard	Displays every step (frame) to users. This is the main component of your wizard's graphical user interface (GUI).
wizard.bas	modWizard	Contains global functions and constants. Chiefly used for accessing .INI files, the Registry, and the Resource file.
wizard.cls	Wizard	Manages the frmWizard form, implements the IDTExtensibility interface, and manages interaction between your wizard and the menu.
wizard.res	none	Contains images and text strings.

> **NOTE**
>
> The IDTExtensibility interface contains methods that the Visual Basic engine invokes each time an add-in connects to it, as when Wizard Manager itself connects to the VB development environment. The IDTExtensibility interface also includes preconfigured procedures that you need to manage add-ins in Visual Basic.

Setting the Wizard Template Project Properties

The Wizard Manager lets you manage the project properties of your wizard just as you would with your regular Visual Basic projects. To access your wizard's project properties, choose Project | WizardTemplate Properties from the menu. You should see a dialog box that looks similar to the one shown in Figure 22.5.

FIGURE 22.5.

The Wizard Manager lets you manage the property settings of your wizard project.

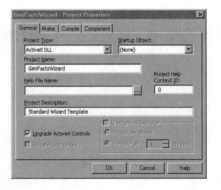

As you can see, your wizard's project type defaults to ActiveX DLL. Because you're incorporating the wizard into your sample application, set the project type to Standard EXE. Visual Basic won't like this because the wizard class is exposed to clients outside the project. Therefore, VB will warn you that it has reset the class instancing properties to have only project-wide scope. Accept this by clicking OK. You can specify a startup object of Sub Main if you have a global subroutine named Main in one of your code modules. If not, ignore the Startup Object combo box.

For your project name, enter **GeoFactsWizard**. For a description of your wizard project, enter **GeoFacts Wizard** in the Project Description textbox. Don't worry about a help filename or project help context ID. You can also ignore the Upgrade ActiveX Controls checkbox and the Make, Compile, and Component tabs. Click OK. Then choose Project | References from the menu to make sure that your project has a reference to the Microsoft Excel 5.0 Object Library (GeoFacts needs this).

In the Visual Basic IDE, change the `caption` property of `frmWizard` to GeoFacts Wizard. That's it for the properties. If `frmGeoFacts` and `Module1` haven't been added to the `GeoFactsWizard` project, add them at this time (they're located under `\Vb\Samples\Pguide\GeoFacts`).

Your wizard project will need a `Sub Main` defined in a code module. This `Main` method is the starting point for the compiler to communicate with your ActiveX DLL. You can add this method to your code module in one of three ways. The faster way, which requires little typing, is to choose Tools | Add Procedure from the menu. You should see the Add Procedure dialog box like the one shown in Figure 22.6.

FIGURE 22.6.

*Use the Add Procedure
dialog box to add
procedures to your
classes quickly.*

Type **Main** in the text box. Keep the default Type and Scope attributes. Click OK. Within the `Class_Initialize` method of the `Wizard` class, call the private `LoadMe` method. Your `Class_Initialize` method should resemble the following code:

```
Private Sub Class_Initialize()
    LoadMe
End Sub
```

In the General Declarations section of the `modWizard` module, enter the following:

```
Global theWizard As Wizard
```

This declaration specifies that the object `theWizard` is of the type `Wizard`. You won't instantiate it here because `Sub Main` is your startup method. This, in turn, means that you must add a line of code to `Sub Main` as follows:

```
Set theWizard = New Wizard
```

This line immediately calls `Class_Initialize`, which in turn calls `LoadMe` in the `Wizard` class. Listing 22.1 shows what `LoadMe` looks like.

Listing 22.1. The LoadMe method of the Wizard class.

```
Set mfrmWizard = New frmWizard
'pass the vb instance to the wizard module
Set mfrmWizard.VBInst = VBInstance
'load and show the form
mfrmWizard.Show vbModal
Set mfrmWizard = Nothing
```

The first line instantiates a private module-level object of the `frmWizard` form. (For you object-oriented fans, the `Wizard` class is a composite class because it's composed of a `frmWizard` object.)

The next line passes an instance of Visual Basic itself to the Wizard Manager to communicate with your wizard. The last line displays the wizard's form to users.

Before you show the form to users, however, you'll want to make the frames display some meaningful information. In the Wizard Manager window, right-click the Introduction Screen step. Choose Edit | Name from the menu to display the Edit Step Name dialog. Enter **Welcome to GeoFacts** and click OK. Delete Steps 2 through 4 by right-clicking each one and choosing Delete (the Wizard Manager will prompt you to confirm the deletion of each step; click Yes). In the `SetStep` sub that's a routine in `frmWizard`, delete the `Select Case` branches for these deleted steps. `SetStep` should now look like Listing 22.2.

Listing 22.2. frmWizard's SetStep method's Select Case statement

```
Select Case nStep
        Case STEP_INTRO

        Case STEP_1
            mbFinishOK = False

        Case STEP_FINISH
            mbFinishOK = True

End Select
```

Because the Finished! step name is fairly common, just leave that in.

The `wizard.res` file contains all the string resources `frmWizard` needs to display caption values for the form and its controls. This means that the caption of `frmWizard` by default will be Wizard Template. You can use the resource compiler to create a resource file of your own. For this chapter, just leave in the default values.

> **TIP**
>
> You can use the word processor of your choice to create your resource file from scratch. This would also require using the DOS-based resource compiler to compile the file into a resource file, which takes longer. To speed up the process, use the Application Wizard to create a resource file. You'll still need the resource compiler to modify the resulting .RC file, but at least you'll have a foundation on which to build.

In GeoFact's `Module1` code module is a method called `FillContinentsList`. This method populates the combo box on `frmGeoFacts` named `cboContinents` with a list of continents. You'll need to modify this method to accept an argument of type `ComboBox`, meaning that you'll pass in a reference to your combo box. Why? Because you also want to copy the cmbContinents (should actually be named cboContinents) combo box and paste it onto frmWizard in the Choose a Continent step.

If frmGeoFacts isn't already up, bring it up by double-clicking it in your project list to the right. Select the cmbContinents combo box. Choose Edit | Copy from the menu (or press Ctrl+C). Bring up the frmWizard form and click Choose a Continent in Wizard Manager. Choose Edit | Paste from the menu. Position the combo box so that its lower half is even with the lower half of the image control. frmWizard should look like the form shown in Figure 22.7.

FIGURE 22.7.

The enhanced frmWizard *after the* cmbContinents *combo box is added.*

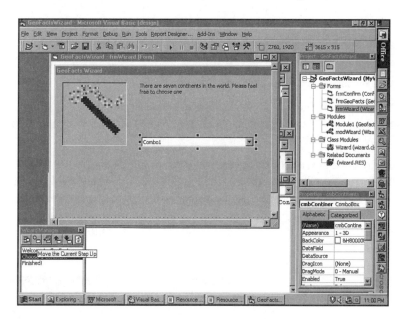

22

CREATING YOUR
OWN WIZARDS

Now you'll need to modify the global FillContinentsList sub. Bring up Module1 by double-clicking it in the project list. Go to FillContinentsList. In the empty argument list, add the following code:

```
argComboBox As ComboBox
```

Replace all occurrences of frmGeoFacts.cmbContinents with argComboBox. Your code for FillContinentsList should resemble Listing 22.3.

Listing 22.3. The new FillContinentsList method.

```
Sub FillContinentsList(argComboBox As ComboBox)
    Dim shtContinent As Excel.Worksheet

    ' Iterate through the collection of sheets and add
    ' the name of each sheet to the combo box.
```

continues

Listing 22.3. continued

```
For Each shtContinent In wbWorld.Sheets
    frmGeoFacts.cmbContinents.AddItem shtContinent.Name
Next
' Select the first item and display it in the combo box.
frmGeoFacts.cmbContinents.Text = frmGeoFacts.cmbContinents.List(0)

    Set shtContinent = Nothing
End Sub
```

Because `frmGeoWizard` referenced `FillContinentsList` in a tightly coupled manner (that is, the actual name of the combo box and its parent form were explicitly used in `FillContinentsList`), you'll need to modify the call to `FillContinentsList`. Bring up the `Form_Load` method of `frmGeoFacts`. Modify the call so that it looks like this:

`FillFeaturesList cmbContinents`

Do the same in the `Change` event of `cmbContinents` and the `Form_Load` event of `frmWizard`. Move the call to Setup from the `Form_Load` event of `frmGeoFacts` to that of `frmWizard`.

To keep things simple, hard code the Label controls in `frmWizard`'s `lblStep` array. As the last line of code in `frmWizard`'s `Form_Load` event, modify the caption of `lblStep(0)` to be some introductory text about `GeoFacts`. Change `lblStep(1)` to some wording that encourages users to select a continent from the list of continents in `cmbContinents`. (Feel free to use the wording in Figures 22.8, 22.9, and 22.10, respectively.) Finally, modify `lblStep(2)` to thank users again and explain that when they click Finish, the list of continents will default to the item they selected.

FIGURE 22.8.

Wording to introduce users to the wizard.

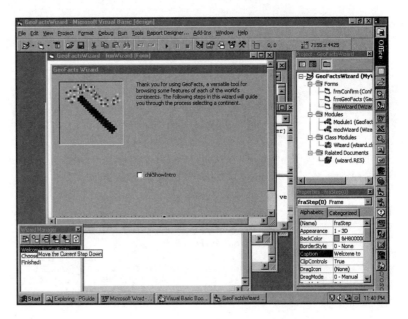

FIGURE 22.9.

Wording to invite users to select a continent.

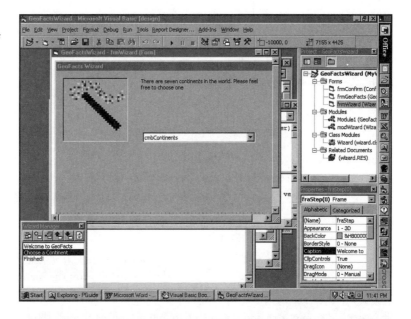

FIGURE 22.10.

Wording to inform users of what will happen next.

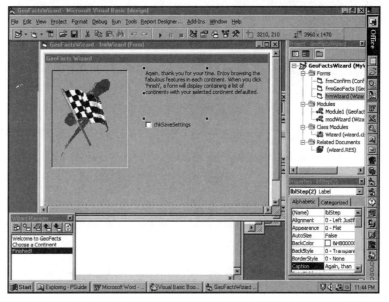

To further develop your code, you need to modify the `Select Case` statement again in the `SetStep` method of `frmWizard`. Add the following line to the branch of code under `STEP_FINISH`:

```
cmdNav(4).Enabled = True
```

If you omit this step, you won't be able to click the Finish button.

Now you can polish off your code for the Finish button. This button is actually part of a command button control array named cmdNav that's housed in frmWizard. Bring up the code for frmWizard and select cmdNav from the control list. Under the Click event, you'll notice a fairly sizable Select Case statement. Go down to the BTN_FINISH body of code, where you should see a call to unload frmWizard (Unload Me) as well as a conditional call to show the frmConfirm form. This form is used to let users know that the wizard chores are complete and the wizard is ready to turn over control to the application.

At this point, you can save settings gathered during the wizard steps to the Registry or an INI file. For simplicity's sake, just launch into the GeoFacts application. Insert a line just before the call to frmConfirm. Set frmConfirm's lblConfirm caption to something like You're finished. Now we'll process the info. As the last line, just before the End Select statement, add the following line:

```
frmGeoFacts.showForm msSelectedItem
```

Of course, you'll need to add a public method called showForm in frmGeoFacts. So bring up the code for frmGeoFacts and choose Tools | Add Procedure from the menu. Enter **showForm** and click OK.

showForm's purpose is to allow you to pass in an argument with the continent selection you allowed your users to make. The body of showForm should like Listing 22.4.

Listing 22.4. The showForm method.

```
Public Sub showForm(argSelection As String)
    Dim iItemCount As Integer
    cmbContinents.Text = argSelection
    Me.Show
End Sub
```

You'll need a module-level variable to hold the selected value of cmbContinents on the frmWizard form. In the General Declarations section, add the following line:

```
Private msSelectedItem As String
```

In the cmbContinents_Click event, add the following line:

```
msSelectedItem = cmbContinents.Text
```

Now you're ready to run your wizard. Go ahead and run the application, taking note of your instructions as entered in the labels. Be sure to select a continent other than North America so that you can see the selection in frmGeoFacts. Now you have a simple but useful wizard example that you can expand to more complex solutions.

NOTE

If you're having problems with the Boolean logic in frmWizard's SetNavBtns method, you're not alone. For the sake of this exercise, disable it by adding Exit Sub at the top of the sub. The Finish button may not become enabled properly.

Summary

In this chapter, you've learned the purpose and usefulness of the Wizard Manager in meeting rising user expectations for Windows applications. You've learned how to use the features offered by the Wizard Manager, as well as how it operates. You were taken step by step through the process of creating your first wizard and shown how to accommodate the Wizard Manager's weaknesses. This chapter has explained to you how to tweak Wizard Manager and the sample GeoFacts application to make them work together for you.

22

CREATING YOUR
OWN WIZARDS

Extending Visual Basic 5.0 With Enhanced Add-Ins

by Paul Kimmel

IN THIS CHAPTER

Visual Basic 5.0 lets you customize the development environment. The Add-In Manager makes it easy for you to extend the Visual Basic 5.0 IDE by adding ActiveX programs to the IDE. That add-ins are ActiveX programs or ActiveX dynamic link libraries makes extending Visual Basic as easy as using the Add-In Manager to incorporate ActiveX programs that you've acquired or developed.

Unleashing the power and flexibility of ActiveX add-ins allows you and your development team to extend Visual Basic in ways that will make your team more productive than ever before. Although Microsoft historically has proffered developers feature-rich tools, no longer will development teams have to wait for the next compiler release to add time-saving innovations. This chapter shows you how to develop and incorporate add-ins in the Visual Basic environment.

Working With Enhanced Add-Ins

Enhanced add-ins are ActiveX programs in the form of dynamic link libraries or executable programs. Add-ins extend the capabilities of Visual Basic 5.0 and help the development process. An example of a useful add-in is the API viewer, which makes it much easier to find Windows API references and incorporate them into your source code.

The two kinds of ActiveX add-ins are dynamic link libraries (DLLs) and executables (EXEs). Dynamic link libraries are referred to as *in-process controls*, which run in another process's address space. Executable controls are referred to as *out-of-process controls*, which run in their own address space.

Use the ActiveX EXE project type if the add-in must run as a standalone application as well as within another application's memory space. Microsoft suggests that you most likely will want to use the in-process DLL build when creating ActiveX controls for add-ins, because it offers a better performance return. But the better performance is gained only if you want the add-in to run only in the VB5 IDE, and if it contains references to properties only in Visual Basic.

TIP

To change the project type, choose Project | Properties from the menu and change the Project Type on the General page (see Figure 23.1).

Several available add-ins exemplify the DLL and EXE kind of ActiveX extensions to Visual Basic. APILoad.exe is the API Viewer, Crw32.exe (Crystal Reports) is the designer referred to in Visual Basic, and many others are included.

FIGURE 23.1.

Change the project type on the General page.

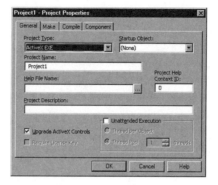

Creating an Add-In Project

You can follow the same steps for creating an add-in that you would for writing any other application. Depending on the add-in's complexity, you'll want to perform some analysis, design, programming, and testing. The Visual Basic 5.0 IDE automates much of the work required to create an add-in. This section covers those steps.

As mentioned earlier, the two types of ActiveX add-ins are DLL (referred to as in-process) and EXE (referred to as out-of-process). Microsoft includes both as project types (see Figure 23.2). For this example, because you'll be creating a more-preferred ActiveX DLL add-in, choose File | New and double-click the ActiveX DLL icon in the New Project dialog box to begin the process.

FIGURE 23.2.

Select the ActiveX DLL project type from the New Project dialog box.

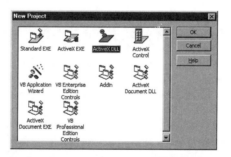

NOTE

The Addin project type is in the New Project dialog box too (refer to Figure 23.2). This project type performs a greater number of the preliminary steps for you automatically. After you understand the additional required steps for creating add-ins, consider using the Addin project type to expedite the process.

The following sections discuss the remaining steps in depth so that you can understand how each step completes the task of developing Visual Basic IDE add-ins. Following the sections, the steps are summarized in a numbered list for future reference. (Skip to the section "Basic Steps for Creating Every Add-In" if you just want the summarized version.)

Add-In Libraries

Your add-in will need to refer to two special libraries: the Microsoft Office 8.0 Object and Microsoft Visual Basic Extensibility libraries. These libraries provide the basic essential functionality and hooks into the Visual Basic IDE so that your add-in can be incorporated into and work within VB5.

The Microsoft Visual Basic 5.0 Extensibility reference lets you reference the `IDTExtensibility` object interface, which provides you with references necessary for add-ins. These references are `OnAddinsUpdate`, `OnConnection`, `OnDisconnection`, and `OnStartupComplete`. The `IDTExtensibility` interface methods are inserted into the Procedure combo box of the class module containing

```
Implements IDTExtensibility
```

You generate the procedures for these methods in the same way that you create event handlers for objects: In the class module, select the `IDTExtensibility` object. The four procedures appear in the Procedure combo box. Select each procedure in turn, adding a comment to keep the Visual Basic IDE from removing the empty function bodies from the code view. (Remember that Visual Basic removes empty functions.) Each of the four methods—`OnAddinsUpdate`, `OnConnection`, `OnDisconnection`, and `OnStartupComplete`—must be defined in the Add-In class module.

> **NOTE**
>
> The `IDTExtensibility` interface is new in Visual Basic 5.0. It was introduced in effort to reduce errors related to improperly defined `IDTExtensibility` methods.

The Microsoft Office 8.0 Object Library reference gives you access to the Visual Basic command bars. It unifies the concept of menus, toolbars, and buttons all in a command bar object. Although each item varies in appearance, they all roughly respond to click events and can display a text caption and a bitmap. You see how to use the command bar access later in the section "Using the Object Library to Add CommandBars to Visual Basic."

Add-In Project Files

You need at least three kinds of files for your VB add-in:

- The interface methods for the ActiveX control must be placed in a class file (`.cls`). When you created the ActiveX DLL project, one of these files was created for you. You must place the extensibility event handlers in the class file.

- By convention, the bulk of the rest of your code should be placed in a basic module—a `.bas` file.
- The entire project is logically wrapped up in a `.vbp` project file. This file lets you establish settings on a project-wide basis—for example, you can specify the inclusion of the Microsoft Visual Basic 5.0 Extensibility interface and the Microsoft Office 8.0 Object Library, which gives you access to the Visual Basic IDE command bar.

Special API Functions

Add-ins must to be registered in the Windows Registry and the `VBADDIN.INI` file. Compiling your add-in creates the necessary Registry entries automatically. `VBADDIN.INI` lists the add-ins available to Visual Basic 5.0. Listing 23.1 shows what my `VBADDIN.INI` looks like; a value of 1 indicates that the add-in is on the Add-Ins menu in the IDE.

Listing 23.1. My `VBADDIN.INI` add-ins for Visual Basic 5.

```
[Add-Ins32]
VBSDIAddIn.Connect=0
DataToolsAddIn.Connect=0
AppWizard.Wizard=0
WizMan.Connect=0
ClassBuilder.Wizard=0
AddInToolbar.Connect=0
ControlWiz.Wizard=0
DataFormWizard.Wizard=0
ActiveXDocumentWizard.Wizard=0
PropertyPageWizard.Wizard=0
APIDeclarationLoader.Connect=1
AddInProject.AddInClass=0
```

You can ensure that an add-in is entered properly into the `VBADDIN.INI` file in many ways:

- By entering it manually (which is cumbersome).
- By making an installation disk that adds the entry, if you're distributing the add-in.
- By using the API method `WritePrivateProfileString`. To add the declaration for `WritePrivateProfileString` to a Visual Basic module, use the APIDeclarationLoader add-in (referred to as the API Viewer in the Add-In Manager dialog box in Figure 23.3).

A technique for automating the inclusion of comments would be to define a function in the module that executes the API function, and run that function in Visual Basic's Immediate window. Listing 23.2 demonstrates the coordinated effort to use this technique.

FIGURE 23.3.

*Use the API Viewer
to add the*
WritePrivateProfileString
*declaration or any API
declaration to a module.*

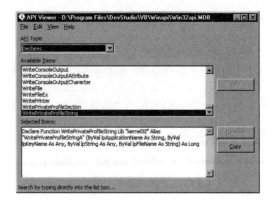

Listing 23.2. Defining functions for updating the VBADDINI.INI file.

```
 1: Private Declare Function WritePrivateProfileString Lib "kernel32" Alias _
 2: "WritePrivateProfileStringA" (ByVal lpApplicationName As String, _
 3: ByVal lpKeyName As Any, ByVal lpString As Any, _
 4: ByVal lpFileName As String) As Long
 5:
 6: Public Sub UpdateAddIn()
 7:    Dim Default, Result  As String
 8:    Default = "Project.AddInName"
 9:    Result = InputBox("Enter new AddIn name:", "Add-In Updater", Default)
10:    If Len(Result) > 0 Then
11:        If (WriteAddInProfileString(Result) = True) Then
12:            MsgBox "VBADDIN.INI Updated!"
13:        Else
14:            MsgBox "VBADDIN.INI Error!"
15:        End If
16:    End If
17: End Sub
18:
19: Private Function WriteAddInProfileString(ByVal ProfileString As String) _
20:    As Boolean
21:
22:    Dim rc As Long
23:    rc = WritePrivateProfileString("Add-Ins32", ProfileString, "0", _
24:        "VBADDIN.INI")
25:    WriteAddInProfileString = rc
26: End Function
```

Listing 23.2, which you can find on this book's CD-ROM in the AddInUpdateModule.bas file, demonstrates how you can simplify an API function indirectly through a Visual Basic function with fewer parameters. More importantly, you can use AddInUpdateModule.bas to update the VBADDIN.INI file. Any add-ins must be referred to in this file to show up in the Add-In Manager (see Figure 23.4). To test the functionality of the code, execute it in the Immediate Window (choose View | Immediate Window), which lets you run procedure and functions like command-line programs.

FIGURE 23.4.

The Add-In Manager shows all the add-ins available.

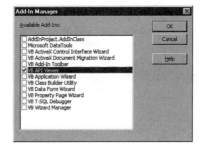

The code in Listing 23.2 uses the `WritePrivateProfileString` API method to modify the `VBADDIN.INI` file. Follow these steps to re-create the project and to test the code:

1. Load Visual Basic 5.0.
2. Start a new Standard EXE project.
3. Add a new module by choosing Project | Add Module from the menu.
4. Type the code in Listing 23.2, or load the code from this book's CD-ROM.
5. Choose View | Immediate from the menu to open the Immediate window.
6. In the Immediate window, type **UpdateAddIn** to execute that procedure. (You should see the Add-In Updater input box shown in Figure 23.5)

FIGURE 23.5.

Use the Immediate window to test code at the functional level.

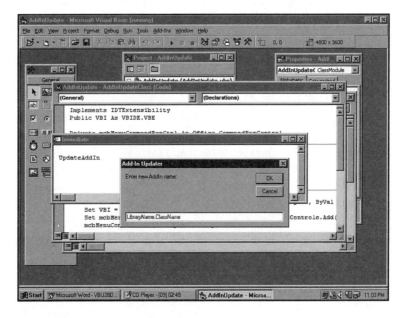

7. Type a practice add-in name, using the *LibraryName.ClassName* format.
8. Open `C:\Windows\VBADDIN.INI` (using the actual Windows directory from your system) to verify that the Add-In entry appears in `VBADDIN.INI`.

23

EXTENDING VB5 WITH ENHANCED ADD-INS

VB5's Add-In Manager displays add-ins listed in VBADDIN.INI. Your add-ins will need an appropriate entry in this .INI file for the Add-In Manager to display them. The next section explains all the steps into a single listing.

Basic Steps for Creating Every Add-In

Every add-in requires that you perform the steps outlined in the previous sections. For future reference, they're summarized here so you can use them as a quick reference after you understand the role of each step. Load Visual Basic 5.0 and follow these steps to create a new add-in project:

1. Press Ctrl+N to open the New Project dialog box.
2. Double-click the ActiveX DLL project type.
3. Choose Project | References from the menu.
4. In the References dialog box, click the checkbox next to the Microsoft Office 8.0 Object Library and the Microsoft Visual Basic 5.0 Extensibility references. (Make sure that these items are checked, as you will need them for the add-in to work properly.)
5. Click OK.
6. Choose Project | Add Module from the menu to add a new module to your project.
7. If the API Viewer is already listed in the Add-Ins menu, skip to step 8. Otherwise, choose Add-Ins | Add-In Manager and add the API Viewer.
8. Choose Add-Ins | API Viewer from the menu.
9. Find the following declaration and insert it into the module that you added in step 6:

```
Declare Function WritePrivateProfileString Lib "kernel32" Alias _
 "WritePrivateProfileStringA" (ByVal lpApplicationName As String, _
 ByVal lpKeyName As Any, ByVal lpString As Any, _
 ByVal lpFileName As String) As Long
```

This function will be used to update the VBADDIN.INI file.

10. In the class module (named class1.cls by default and created when you started the project), add **Implements IDTExtensibility** in the General (global) procedure area. This line adds a reference to the IDTExtensibility object, including event-handler definitions for OnConnection, OnDisconnection, OnStartupComplete, and OnAddinsUpdate.
11. Use the Procedure combo box in the code view to generate the empty event-handler procedures for the IDTExtensibility object: OnConnection, OnDisconnection, OnStartupComplete, and OnAddinsUpdate.
12. Add your code.
13. Remember to save your project frequently and especially after the last change. Proceed to the remaining sections on programming and testing to complete the creation of your add-in.

These steps create a shell project with all the right basic requirements incorporated. Creating an add-in requires you to create the basic add-in shell, add your code to solve the problem, compile the project, and test the add-in. When those steps are complete, you may use Add-Ins | Add-In Manager from the menu to add the add-in item to the Add-Ins menu. The remaining sections in this chapter help you complete a couple of add-ins.

Creating an Add-In Registration Add-In

This section applies all the steps thus far to begin a practical add-in project. The add-in you'll create uses the module code in Listing 23.2 to create an add-in registration ActiveX DLL. The add-in you'll create will allow you to register future add-ins from the Add-Ins menu in Visual Basic 5.0.

> **NOTE**
>
> The add-in completed in this chapter is on this book's CD-ROM as AddInUpdate.vbp. You can use it to verify the steps outlined in the chapter.

To begin the add-in project, follow steps 1 through 6, 10, and 11 from the preceding section. (Steps 7, 8, and 9 will be completed by reusing the code in Listing 23.2.) After you create the basic project, follow these steps to complete the AddInUpdate.dll:

1. Choose Project | Add Module and select the existing module (or, if you want to write the code from scratch—and you skipped the example in Listing 23.2—add a new module and enter the code in Listing 23.2).

2. Select the module from Listing 23.2 and press F4 to bring the Properties window in focus.

3. In the Properties window, change the Name property to AddInUpdateModule.

4. Repeat steps 2 and 3 for the class and the project, naming the class AddInUpdateClass and the project AddInUpdate.

5. Save the project, naming all the files AddInUpdate.

6. Open the Immediate window (choose View | Immediate from the menu) and execute the UpdateAddIn function to add this add-in to VBADDIN.INI. Enter **AddInUpdate.AddInUpdateClass** in the input box shown in Figure 23.5. (You can use steps 1 through 8 in "Special API Functions" as a refresher.)

These steps allow you to create the control. The ActiveX DLL will compile and execute correctly, but you'll need to provide developers with the means of activating the add-in. The next section discusses changes you need to make to extend the Visual Basic 5.0 user interface, giving developers access to your add-in. Doing so will require you to make use of the Microsoft Office 8.0 Object Library.

Programming an Add-In

Creating an add-in is like writing any other Visual Basic program. You may choose to use some number of forms, classes, and modules depending on the complexity of the task you're trying to automate. You've learned how to write Visual Basic programs. Writing code for event handlers, using controls, and writing reusable code in modules is something you learned to do in earlier chapters. An add-in exploits these skills you already have.

The example in this section demonstrates how to use the Microsoft Office 8.0 Object Library. To complete this example, you will continue to work with the add-in registration ActiveX DLL from the earlier sections.

Understanding the Microsoft Office 8.0 Object Library

Microsoft has redefined toolbars, menus, and buttons as command bars. Although toolbars, menus, and buttons have slightly different appearances, they're semantically the same thing. Each input graphical device displays text and graphics and generally responds to basic user inputs, such as a mouse click.

The Microsoft Office 8.0 Object Library provides developers with access to the library that can extend command bars in Visual Basic 5. You'll need this library to add a user interface to your add-in. You'll use object references from this library to add an item to the Visual Basic Add-Ins menu that provides access to the UpdateAddIn.dll file defined earlier (see Figure 23.6).

FIGURE 23.6.

The Microsoft Office 8.0 Object Library provides developers access to the command bars in the Visual Basic 5.0 IDE.

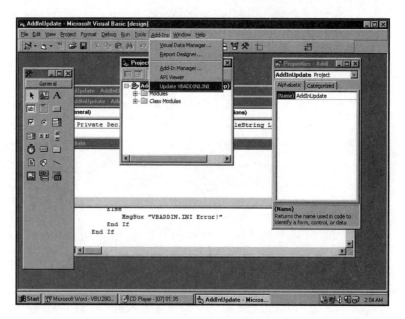

Using the Object Library to Add CommandBars to Visual Basic

The Microsoft Office 8.0 Object Library provides a user interface that allows you to extend the Visual Basic 5.0 IDE. Listing 23.3 contains the modifications that you can add to the ActiveX DLL add-in class to add command bar buttons. Listing 23.3 also demonstrates how to add a menu item to the Add-Ins menu. (Later, Listing 23.4 proffers replacement code that shows how to simply switch the code from adding a menu item to adding a button.)

Listing 23.3. AddInUpdateClass.cls: Defining an ActiveX DLL that updates the VBADDIN.INI file used by the Add-In Manager.

```
1:  Implements IDTExtensibility
2:  Public VBI As VBIDE.VBE
3:
4:  Private mcbMenuCommandBarCtrl As Office.CommandBarControl
5:  Private WithEvents MenuHandler As CommandBarEvents
6:
7:  Private Sub IDTExtensibility_OnAddInsUpdate(custom() As Variant)
8:      ' The comment keeps the code from being stripped out.
9:  End Sub
10:
11: Private Sub IDTExtensibility_OnConnection(ByVal VBInst As Object, ByVal _
12:     ConnectMode As VBIDE.vbext_ConnectMode, ByVal AddInInst As VBIDE.AddIn, _
13:     custom() As Variant)
14:     Set VBI = VBInst
15:     Set mcbMenuCommandBarCtrl = VBI.CommandBars("Add-Ins").Controls.Add()
16:     mcbMenuCommandBarCtrl.Caption = "Update VBADDINI.INI"
17:     Set MenuHandler = VBI.Events.CommandBarEvents(mcbMenuCommandBarCtrl)
18: End Sub
19:
20: Private Sub IDTExtensibility_OnDisconnection(ByVal RemoveMode _
21:     As VBIDE.vbext_DisconnectMode, custom() As Variant)
22:     mcbMenuCommandBarCtrl.Delete
23: End Sub
24:
25: Private Sub IDTExtensibility_OnStartupComplete(custom() As Variant)
26:     ' A comment to keep the function in place.
27: End Sub
28:
29: Private Sub MenuHandler_Click(ByVal CommandBarControl As Object, _
30:     Handled As Boolean, CancelDefault As Boolean)
31:     Call UpdateAddIn
32: End Sub
```

Listing 23.3 contains changes necessary to add-in classes to provide users with command bar access to the Add-Ins menu in Visual Basic 5.0. Line 1 implements the extensibility interface discussed in the earlier section "Add-In Libraries." Line 2 defines a reference to the Visual Basic for Applications object (VBE), named VBI. Line 4 defines a private reference mcbMenuCommandBarCtrl to a CommandBarControl, which is the base object for command bars. Line 5 uses the WithEvents keyword to define MenuHandler as an object variable that can respond to ActiveX events from CommandBarEvents.

When MenuHandler is defined, it appears in the Objects combo box in code view. Selecting MenuHandler from the Objects combo box gives you access to the list of available events. Command bars have a single Click event.

Line 14 sets the reference VBI to the current Visual Basic IDE running, referred to by VBInst. Line 15 adds a control to the command bar passed as the string argument; the recipient of the control is the Add-Ins menu, and the returned reference is assigned to the mcbMenuCommandBarCtrl reference. Line 16 sets a caption for the menu. Where the control is added determines what kind of control is added. For instance, if the CommandBars parameter were "Standard", the added control would be a CommandBarButton and Caption would be treated as the ToolTipHint. Line 17 returns a CommandBarEvents object for the CommandBarControl passed as the argument for the function. The events object is MenuHandler.

The OnConnection event handler for the add-in creates the CommandBarControl, and in the OnDisconnection handler in line 22 the button is deleted. This fairly simple add-in begins its real task when the click event is fired and the procedure in line 30 of Listing 23.3 is called. Listing 23.4 demonstrates how easy it is to create a button control for the Add-In versus a menu item.

To create a CommandBarButton for the add-in, you must revise the code in Listing 23.3 to how it appears in Listing 23.4. Replace the code in the OnConnection event handler as shown.

Listing 23.4. A modified OnConnection for Listing 23.3: Creating a CommandBarButton for the standard toolbar.

```
11: Private Sub IDTExtensibility_OnConnection(ByVal VBInst As Object, ByVal _
12:    ConnectMode As VBIDE.vbext_ConnectMode, ByVal AddInInst As VBIDE.AddIn, _
13:    custom() As Variant)
14:    Set VBI = VBInst
15:     Set mcbMenuCommandBarCtrl = VBI.CommandBars("Standard").Controls.Add()
16:    mcbMenuCommandBarCtrl.Caption = "Update VBADDIN.INI"
17:    Clipboard.SetData LoadPicture("c:\windows\Blue Rivets.bmp")
18:    mcbMenuCommandBarCtrl.PasteFace
19:    mcbMenuCommandBarCtrl.Caption = "Update VBADDINI.INI"
20:    Set MenuHandler = VBI.Events.CommandBarEvents(mcbMenuCommandBarCtrl)
21: End Sub
```

The changes in Listing 23.4 are intended to replace the OnConnection event handler for the original code in Listing 23.3.

> **CAUTION**
>
> Ensure that the bitmap resource loaded in line 17 is a valid filename. An error trying to load this resource may cause the entire ActiveX DLL to fail. Building discrete tools generally requires less code than building an entire application, but as is the case with add-ins, they typically perform more critical tasks requiring a greater degree of efficacy.

Testing Custom Add-Ins

You can test your add-ins in several ways. One way is to use the Immediate window to test discrete subprograms and functions independently of a particular application. If a function doesn't pass the Immediate window, it's clear that the algorithm can stand some further examination—it may mean that you may have too many dependencies or the function is doing too much. Consider breaking such functions up into discrete functions that perform smaller, more clearly defined tasks.

You also can use module files to test code that will ultimately go into an add-in. Developing code in modules in programs all by themselves and then incorporating them only after they pass rigorous testing is a type of development known as *scaffolding*. A scaffold provides you with an ideal place to test the efficiency and extensibility of individual modules. A scaffold also provides a disparate legacy of code that demonstrates how an individual code fragment can be used. Users may use your scaffold to learn how particular modules were intended to work and to experiment with their understanding of individual modules.

Listing 23.2 is a good example of scaffolding. If you'll recall from the earlier section "Special API Functions," you could test that functionality—modify the VBADDIN.INI file in any context, including the one for which the program was intended.

Often, dynamic link libraries are easier to build because they're smaller, forcing you to think about small problems at a time and not requiring you to concern yourself with too many integration problems. On the flip side, extensions to development tools typically are operating in the background and, if defined poorly, can cause the development tool or the operating system to behave badly. As an exercise, consider what you may do to prohibit errors related to a missing bitmap file in line 17 of Listing 23.4.

Registering Your Add-Ins

The process of making your add-in registers your project with the Windows 95 Registry. Figure 23.7 shows the AddInUpdate.AddInUpdateClass Registry entry in HKEY_CLASSES_ROOT viewed in the Registry Editor. You can compile your ActiveX add-in by choosing File | Make in Visual Basic from the menu. Compiling your application results in the necessary Registry entry.

NOTE

If you've compiled your add-in but need to rebuild it, remove the check mark next to your add-in in the Add-In Manager to unload the add-in from memory. You'll need to do this before you can recompile your add-in.

FIGURE 23.7.

Compiling your ActiveX add-in causes Visual Basic to update the Registry entry for you.

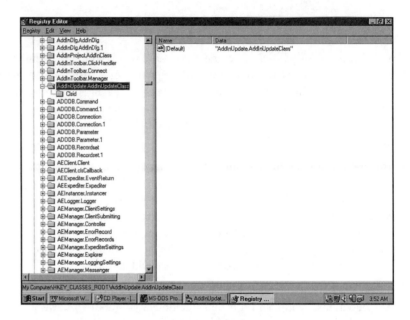

Now all you need to do is make an entry in the VBADDIN.INI file. The Add-In Manager uses VBADDIN.INI to list available add-ins. The entry can be made manually, but you can use the utility developed in this chapter to automate the process of registering add-ins.

Summary

This chapter demonstrated how the Extensibility Interface and the Microsoft Office 8.0 Object Library can help you extend Visual Basic itself. You can extend VB5 in ways as yet unimagined by every developer. The Visual Basic you've already learned is the biggest part of the hurdle; the steps outlined in this chapter will help you over the rest of the hurdle.

Creating an add-in is relatively easy. Using an ActiveX DLL project for the task is preferable. To that project you'll need to add project references to the Microsoft Extensibility Library and the Microsoft Office 8.0 Object Library. Roughly 30 lines of code later, and you're off and running. VB5's new Extensibility Interface will help keep you from making mistakes. The Add-In project type offers an added extra boost by performing a few of the basic steps for you automatically. Refer to this chapter anytime in the future for step-by-step instructions demonstrating how to create you own add-ins.

Using the Remote Data Control (RDC)

by Ashton Hobbs

IN THIS CHAPTER

In creating database applications, you sometimes have to link the data returned from a database to the editing controls located on a form. To this end, Visual Basic 5.0 provides the Remote Data Control to facilitate the development of database applications.

With the Remote Data Control (RDC), you can link a result set returned from a SQL `Select` statement or a stored procedure to various data-aware controls on a Visual Basic form. This way, you can control multiple controls with one object, because moving the record position in the Data Control displays new information in all the controls linked to the control.

Adding the Remote Data Control to Your Project

The Remote Data Control object isn't placed on the object list by default; you have to add the control manually. Follow these steps to place the control into the object list:

1. Choose Project | Components from the menu.
2. In the Components dialog box, select the Microsoft Remote Data Control from the list (see Figure 24.1).
3. Close the dialog box and then add the control to your project by dragging it from the object list to your form.

FIGURE 24.1.

The Components dialog box.

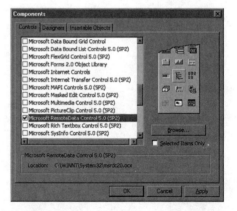

Using the Remote Data Control

After you add the RDC to your form, you need to specify the control's properties by using the Property Explorer or the control's custom property page. I generally recommend the property page, as it gives you a more well-defined view of the properties that you can edit. Figure 24.2 shows the custom property page for the Remote Data Control.

FIGURE 24.2.

The Custom property page for the RDC object.

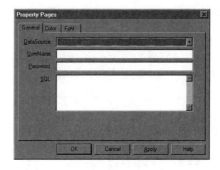

The most important properties that you can edit on the property page are the data source to use, the username and password to connect to the database, and the SQL statement to use to provide records to the control:

- The data source to use determines which database or database file is used to retrieve information. The data source can be any valid ODBC data source declared for the current computer.
- The username is the login name required to connect to the specified data source.
- The SQL statement for the RDC determines the resultset returned to the data control. You can specify any valid SQL Select statement or a stored procedure that returns a resultset to the data control.

Remote Data Control Properties

The Remote Data Control provides many properties similar to the ones provided by the rdoResultSet object. The following sections cover some of the more important properties provided by the RDC. Some properties, such as the fonts, aren't covered because they are self-explanatory.

The BOFAction and EOFAction Properties

The BOFAction property allows you to move to specified locations in the resultset. Use the rdMoveFirst constant to tell the control to move to the first record in the resultset. You also can use the rdBOF constant to move to a position before the first record in the resultset.

The EOFAction property lets you specify positions at the end of the file to move to. EOFAction provides three constants for positioning within the control:

- Use rdMoveLast to move to the last record.
- Use rdEOF to move to a position after the last record.
- Use rdAddNew to add a new record at the end of the current resultset and set it to be the current record.

The Connect Property

The Connect property lets you specify the connect string to use in connecting to a database. It generally specifies the data source name to use with the username, password, database, and other information needed to connect to the specified data source.

You can change the Connect property to be any string required by your applications. In many applications, it's common to save the connect information in the Registry or in an .ini file and then set the connect information to the values obtained in the Registry.

The CursorDriver Property

You can change the cursor driver used in retrieving information from the database. Table 24.1 lists the various cursor driver settings that you can use. The type of cursor driver that you use determines how the records are retrieved from the database.

Table 24.1. CursorDriver property settings.

Driver Setting	Description
rdUseIfNeeded	The control chooses an appropriate driver to use. If possible, a server-side cursor driver is chosen.
rdUseOdbc	The control uses the ODBC driver library.
rdUseServer	The control uses the server-side cursor driver.
rdUseClientBatch	The control uses an optimistic batch cursor driver library.
rdUseNone	The control doesn't use a cursor.

The various cursor drivers offer different options. Using some cursor drivers will prevent you from accessing the number of records in the resultset but will provide speed improvements over other drivers.

The Options Property

The Options property provides only two different options that can be specified but allows you to specify that a query is to be executed asynchronously. Executing a query in this manner allows execution to be returned to the application while the query is executing on the database. Asynchronous queries can benefit your applications by allowing you to cancel a query being executed or by giving control back to users while a long query is executing on the database server.

The following code line changes the execution method of the control to execution queries to execute asynchronously:

```
RemoteDataControl1.Options = rdAsyncEnable
```

The Prompt Property

The Prompt property allows you to determine what type of prompt users are presented with. A prompt is used to obtain connection information from users. For applications where users have separate login information, you probably want to show a prompt every time the application starts to obtain user-specific information. For other types of applications, you might want to never display the login prompt, such as an application that runs as a Windows NT service or an application that runs on a server such as an application server or an Internet component.

Table 24.2 lists the various constants that can be provided to the Prompt property.

Table 24.2. Prompt property settings.

Property	Description
rdDriverPrompt	The control displays the ODBC Data Sources dialog box to users.
rdDriverNoPrompt	The control uses information provided to it. If incorrect information is supplied, the control returns an error.
rdDriverComplete	The control uses the information provided to it. If incorrect information is supplied, the prompt is displayed as in the rdDriverPrompt setting.
rdDriverCompleteRequired	This setting behaves like rdDriverComplete but disables the control for information not required.

The ReadOnly Property

The ReadOnly property allows you to specify whether users should be allowed to edit the control's resultset. If the property is set to TRUE, users can't update the information contained in the control. If the value is set to FALSE, users can edit the information in the control normally.

> **NOTE**
>
> ReadOnly information is associated mostly with reporting.

The ResultSet Property

The ResultSet property of the Remote Data Control is where the information returned from the database is stored. This property is a standard rdoResultSet object and provides all the properties and method provided by the rdoResultSet object.

You can set the ResultSet property to the value of another rdoResultSet object. This way, you can use other methods to obtain a resultset and then use the RDC to provide the ability to link controls on the form with the data in the custom resultset. This feature is used commonly with the UserConnection object. By using the UserConnection object, you can create resultsets and then assign them to the Remote Data Control to provide linking capabilities to the edit controls on your forms. This way, you can centralize all database logic while still providing an easy way to populate edit controls on your forms.

Assigning a new rdoResultSet object is as easy as declaring a new object, opening a resultset from the database, and then setting the property value to the rdoResultSet object as in the following code:

```
Dim conn as new UserConnection1
Dim rs as rdoResultSet

' establish connection
conn.EstablishConnection

' Call method and get result set
conn.query1
Set rs = conn.LastQueryResult

' set remote data control result set
Set RemoteDataControl1.ResultSet = rs
```

Remote Data Control Events

The Remote Data Control provides several events over the standard mouse and drag events that you should be aware of. These events provide you with a means to handle errors and user responses, as well as provide you with the ability to perform some processing after an asynchronous query completes and returns from the server.

The following sections cover four events: Error, QueryCompleted, Reposition, and Validate. All these events are available from the code editor for the Remote Data Control object located on your form.

The Error Event

The Error event allows you to handle errors that occur in the Remote Data Control while none of your code is executing. Because the Remote Data Control automatically retrieves the resultset of a specified SQL statement after the Form_Load event, you have no code running to intercept any errors that occur during this process. The Error event lets you capture these errors and perform any processing required by your application.

The Error event provides many arguments that you can use to determine the nature of the error. It also provides a return argument that you can use to tell the control whether it should display the error message to users. The CancelDisplay argument allows you to stop the control from displaying the standard database error message and to display a custom message depending on your application's needs. You can set the value to TRUE or to the predefined constant of rdDataErrContinue to prevent the standard error message from being displayed. The default for the argument is FALSE or the constant rdDataErrDisplay, which will display the error message to users. You can return nothing or not code for the event if you want the control to generate the error message and display it to users.

The QueryCompleted Event

The QueryCompleted event is simply a blank method for you to perform any processing required after an asynchronous query finishes processing. When you set the control to execute queries asynchronously, the control executes the query on the database and then returns control back to the application while the query is executed. The QueryCompleted event provides you with a way to handle any special processing after the results return from the database for the query.

This event can be useful for queries that require large amounts of time to process. A useful feature is to execute a query and then allow users to continue with another process in the application. When the query is completed, you can display a message to tell users that the query is complete and that they can now view the results, or you can perform any other processing after query results are returned from the database.

The Reposition Event

The Reposition event occurs whenever the current row position changes in the control. If you use any of the Move methods or any other method that changes the current row position, this event is fired. In this event, you can provide custom processing such as updating the current form to represent the data now displayed in the new row.

The Validate Event

The Validate event allows you to handle any processing that you want to occur before a SQL statement is processed and sent to the database. This event occurs before a new row becomes the current row, before the Update method is invoked, and before the Delete, UnLoad, and Close actions occur. Validate allows you to stop the current action from happening or to change the action to a different action.

By using the Action argument, you can change the requested action to some other action by passing back the appropriate setting. Changing the action might be useful if users have edited information on the current row and are requesting to move to a different row. You might ask users if they want to save the information they just edited before moving and choose to cancel the action or invoke an edit or update action in place of their move action. Table 24.3 lists all the available action constants that can be used for the Action argument.

Table 24.3. Action argument settings.

Setting	Description
rdActionCancel	Cancels the requested operation
rdActionMoveFirst	Executes the MoveFirst action
rdMovePrevious	Executes the MovePrevious action

continues

24
USING THE
REMOTE DATA
CONTROL (RDC)

Table 24.3. continued

Setting	Description
rdActionMoveNext	Executes the MoveNext action
rdActionMoveLast	Executes the MoveLast action
rdActionAddNew	Executes the AddNew action
rdActionUpdate	Executes the Update action
rdActionDelete	Executes the Delete action
rdActionFind	Executes the Find action
rdActionBookmark	Executes the Bookmark action
rdActionClose	Executes the Close action
rdActionUnload	Executes the Unload action
rdActionUpdateAddNew	Inserts a new row into the control
rdActionUpdateModified	The current row is changed
rdActionRefresh	Executes the Refresh action
rdActionCancelUpdate	Cancels the Update action
rdActionBeginTransact	Begins a transaction in the control
rdActionCommitTransact	Commits a transaction in the control
rdActionRollbackTransact	Rolls back a transaction in the control
rdActionNewParameters	Informs the control that the parameters or columns for the result set have changed
rdActionNewSQL	Informs the control that the SQL statement for the control has changed

Remote Data Control Methods

The Remote Data Control provides many of the same methods provided by the rdoConnection object, but the following sections cover some of the more important methods. The RDC provides various methods for transaction handling, canceling execution of a query, and updating the contents of the control's resultset.

The BeginTrans Method

The BeginTrans method lets you start a new transaction within the control. This new transaction can later be committed or rolled back, depending on the error status of the query's execution.

If you don't begin a transaction before executing SQL statements, these SQL statements are executed automatically against the database and take effect immediately. By using the BeginTrans method, you can wait until all transactions are completed before applying them to the database.

To use the `BeginTrans` method for a Remote Data Control named `RDC1`, use the following syntax:

```
RDC1.BeginTrans
```

This code would begin a transaction on the database and proceed to log executed SQL statements until a `CommitTrans` or `RollBackTrans` method is called.

The `CommitTrans` Method

The `CommitTrans` method is the successful way to end a `BeginTrans` action. `CommitTrans` informs the database that no errors were encountered and that all query executions requested within the transaction can be applied to the database.

If you fail to commit a transaction, the transaction could remain open and keep database resources locked. This can lead to dead locking when others request resources that you've locked and you begin to request resources they have locked. You should keep your transactions together and not allow user response within a transaction.

The following code begins a transaction with a Remote Data Control object named `RDC1`, and then commits the transaction after several SQL statements by using the `CommitTrans` method:

```
RDC1.BeginTrans
...
'SQL Statements
...
RDC1.CommitTrans
```

This code commits the transaction to the database, thereby making any changes permanent.

The `RollBackTrans` Method

The `RollBackTrans` method is your way of telling the database that an error occurred somewhere within the transaction and that all queries executed within the transaction should be disregarded. This prevents the database from becoming out of whack with incomplete data in the database.

If you didn't use a transaction and were adding a user record with an accompanying user phone record and the user record insertion succeeded but the phone record insertion didn't, you would have a user in the database without a phone record. When someone looks at this user record, they would assume that the user has no phone number or that it's not known. Because users of your application shouldn't assume, it's better to have either none of the information or all the information.

The following code snippet begins a transaction, executes several SQL statements, and then rolls back the transaction, restoring the database to its state before the execution of the SQL statements:

24

USING THE REMOTE DATA CONTROL (RDC)

```
RDC1.BeginTrans
...
'SQL Statements
...
RDC1.RollbackTrans
```

The Cancel Method

The Cancel method is your way to stop the execution of a currently running asynchronous query. You can use this method to stop the processing of a query executed by the control.

To call the Cancel method, use the following syntax:

```
RDC1.Cancel
```

> **CAUTION**
>
> Stopping an executing query can have unpredictable results, and some queries can't be stopped once they're started. You should use the Cancel method carefully, as it can produce undesirable results.

The UpdateControls Method

The UpdateControls method allows you to, in essence, refresh the controls bound to the particular Remote Data Control. The RDC will redisplay in all bound controls the original data that was available, overwriting any modifications made to the data but not saved by users. This method can be helpful if users change their mind about new data and you want to revert to original data values.

The syntax for calling the UpdateControls method is as follows:

```
RDC1.UpdateControls
```

The UpdateRow Method

The UpdateRow method does just what it says—updates the current row and saves its data values to the database. Before allowing users to move to another row in the result set, you should prompt them to see whether they want to save their data. If they choose to save, you should call the UpdateRow method before moving to the new row.

The syntax for calling the UpdateRow method is as follows:

```
RDC1.UpdateRow
```

Summary

The Remote Data Control is fairly simple to use and provides more functionality and features than its cousin, the Data control. It allows you to use all the functionality of RDO without sacrificing the linking of the Data control.

You should use the Remote Data Control in any application where you're using RDO and want to display results returned from a database to the user to be edited. The Remote Data Control's real strength is its ability to make data available for editing. The rdoResultSet and rdoConnection objects offer the same database functionality that the Remote Data Control offers, but the RDC lets you make the database results visually presentable.

24

USING THE REMOTE DATA CONTROL (RDC)

Tuning and Optimizing Your Applications

by Mark Spenik

IN THIS CHAPTER

Visual Basic has evolved into an extremely powerful programming language. Visual Basic 5.0 has added many new language features as well as increased the performance of common tasks such as form displaying. Many tips and tricks required in earlier versions of Visual Basic are no longer required; however, with the many different application scenarios available to the Visual Basic 5.0 programmer, such as building ActiveX Internet components or distributed applications, optimizing and tuning is as important as ever.

In this chapter, you learn how to optimize and tune Visual Basic applications and components. This chapter shows you how to use several different utilities, such as the Visual Basic Code Profiler, to analyze existing applications. You also learn how to use various optimizing techniques and tricks and how to create and use a form template to perform simple code benchmarking.

Optimizing and Tuning with Visual Basic 5.0

Visual Basic 5.0 presents many new features and opportunities for optimizing and tuning applications and components. Visual Basic 5.0 is the first version of Visual Basic to exist only in a 32-bit form and include a native code compiler to speed up application execution times. Because Visual Basic 5.0 exists only in a 32-bit platform, you're dealing with an advanced 32-bit operating system such as Windows 95 or Windows NT, which offer improved performance and resource usage over Windows 3.x. This immediately raises the following questions:

- Do I still need to optimize and tune?
- Should I still worry about using up resources?

The answer to both questions is a resounding *yes*, and in this chapter you learn that optimizing and tuning Visual Basic 5.0 applications is more than telling end users to buy faster machines with more memory. Before getting into the finer points of optimizing and tuning Visual Basic applications, let's quickly review what optimizing and tuning is all about.

Understanding the Art of Optimizing and Tuning

Optimizing and tuning an application means one or more of the following:

- Increasing the execution speed of the application
- Effectively managing limited resources
- Decreasing the application size
- Increasing the display speed of an application
- Increasing the perceived speed of an application

You can tune an application for one or more of these definitions; however, it's difficult to tune an application for all of them, because several of these definitions work against each other. For example, optimizing for speed often increases the size of the program; likewise, optimizing for size often decreases the speed of the application.

I've read many different books and articles and listened to several speakers at Visual Basic conferences refer to optimizing and tuning as an art form. I don't think of optimizing and tuning as an art form used excessively by Visual Basic gurus; rather, I think of it as part of the software development cycle and obtainable by all programmers willing to put in a little extra time and effort. Consider some important optimizing and tuning points as you develop your application.

Using Proper Software Designs When Creating Applications

Back in the old days (that is, before Visual Basic), programming environments often required programmers and programming teams to use different methodologies to map out the application's functional and detail design specifications and data dictionaries before a line of code was even written. Today, many C++ programmers use more modern object-oriented methodologies to generate program specifications before they ever sit down and write a line of code. Unfortunately, my experience has been that when working with many different clients, programming teams, and programmers, the Visual Basic community doesn't follow the same design methodologies. All too often applications are prototyped and then quickly modified into the end product. These prototyped applications would benefit from a quick design session with object-oriented methodology or just some simple diagrams and brainstorming.

First, optimizing and tuning start in the design phase (for example, when you're selecting the proper algorithms and defining the data structures and objects used by your application). Select the faster, more efficient algorithms or plan on benchmarking a few. When defining your data structures, avoid slow and inefficient data types (such as variants) in favor of faster data types (such as integers and strings).

Testing on the Designated Platform or Environment

Too often developers test and develop on machines or in environments far superior to their application's actual production platform or environment. During the initial design phase, make sure that you take into account the production environment or platform in which your application will reside. For example, take into account platform parameters such as memory, disk space, and processor power. If the platform is a 486 with 8M of RAM, you don't want to deliver an application that uses Word 97 and Excel 97 via OLE Automation. The platform won't be able to support such functionality in a reasonable amount of time.

During the development phase, periodically test the application in the production environment to identify possible bottlenecks. By detecting bottlenecks early in the development cycle, you can resolve them before the application goes live and becomes critical.

Knowing What to Optimize

An important part of learning to tune and optimize Visual Basic applications is to understand what can be optimized, where to optimize, and what can't be optimized. You can optimize Visual Basic code, algorithms, and data access methods. You can't do anything to speed up your application if it's accessing files on a network, which is extremely slow.

A good example of knowing what to optimize and where is a client/server application that uses Microsoft SQL Server on the back end. The application is very fast except for one particular form that loads and displays very slowly. How should you approach optimizing and tuning for this application? There's no point tuning the forms that load quickly, because you're happy with their performance. Instead, you should focus on the one form that loads and displays very slowly. You can examine the data-access method used, although this probably isn't the problem because the other forms also use the same data-access method but run fine. You can optimize and tune the form display time by trying to limit the number of repaints, but after you optimize the form display, the form is still slow. What now?

You've already determined that the data-access methods are the same as on all the other forms and that you've done all you can to optimize the form display. At this point, it's time to stop trying to optimize the Visual Basic application and look more closely at the query used to populate the form. Is the query using indexes? Are the tables involved substantially larger than the tables used for the other forms?

It's the complexity of knowing what and where to optimize that has lead many to call optimizing and tuning an art. Optimize and tune things that you can change, such as Visual Basic code, algorithms, and display speed. Spend your time optimizing and tuning the poorly performing parts of your application, not the parts that are already running fast. Understand the big picture of your application's environment and any outside resources your application interacts with, such as the network, the database, and other components.

Testing Compiled Versions

When performing benchmark testing, test with complied versions of Visual Basic. After all, you'll be distributing compiled versions, and you take out the oddities and overhead of testing in the Visual Basic development environment.

Optimizing and Tuning During the Entire Life Cycle

As stated earlier, optimizing and tuning is part of the development life cycle, not something you do at the end. Tune and optimize your code throughout the development life cycle. Especially when completing an ActiveX component or a frequently used function, make optimizing and tuning part of the debugging and initial test phases.

Avoiding Over-Optimizing

Avoid spending several hours rewriting code that works fine and isn't a bottleneck. For instance, avoid writing the fast sort routine when your current bubble sort routine works fine and you call the routine only once to sort 20 items. It's an entirely different story, however, if you're sorting a large number of items, and the sort routine is called in a recursive routine and is now a bottleneck. Don't go crazy trying to optimize and tune each and every line. Write good, efficient code and spend your time fixing slow routines and bottlenecks.

Commenting Your Code Like a Maintenance Programmer

Too often, I have looked at well-written code from other consultants that performed well, but the consultants had failed to add a single line of comments! Comments *don't* increase the size of the applications or hinder your applications performance. *Comment your code!* Comments are used to help you, as well as other programmers, maintain and enhance your application in the future. Programmers forced to maintain and enhance existing systems (for example, maintenance programmers) know all too well the difficulty of working with poorly commented code, and they learn not to be part of the problem by adding lots of comments. Make sure that you comment your code so that you, as well as individuals who may inherit your applications in the future, can easily determine what the code is doing and why.

Creating and Using Templates to Perform Code Benchmarking

What if you're busy developing an application and reach a critical coding point? Maybe you're about to create several forms that populate combo boxes from a database, and you're wondering what will be the fastest database access method to use or what's the fastest recordset type. You want to begin using the proper methods from the start so that you don't have to go back later and change the code to take advantage of a faster method. What do you do? What else but write some code and perform some benchmark testing?

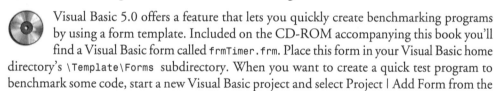 Visual Basic 5.0 offers a feature that lets you quickly create benchmarking programs by using a form template. Included on the CD-ROM accompanying this book you'll find a Visual Basic form called `frmTimer.frm`. Place this form in your Visual Basic home directory's `\Template\Forms` subdirectory. When you want to create a quick test program to benchmark some code, start a new Visual Basic project and select Project | Add Form from the main Visual Basic menu. The Add Form dialog box appears (see Figure 25.1).

FIGURE 25.1.
The Add Form dialog box.

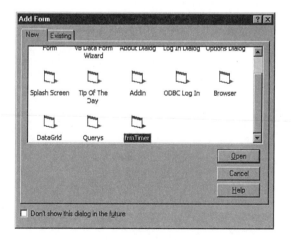

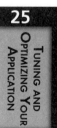

Select the frmTimer form shown in Figure 25.1. The frmTimer template includes skeleton code to quickly test two different coding algorithms and compare them. Add the code you want to test to the command button click event. Compile and execute the program by using the radio buttons to determine which algorithm you're testing. The amount of time required to execute each algorithm is displayed in a label control. Two label controls are used on the form, so after both tests are executed, you can easily compare the amount of time required to execute the algorithms. Listing 25.1 shows the code in frmTimer.

Listing 25.1. Benchmarking skeleton code.

```
Private Sub cmdTest_Click()
Dim Start, Finish, TotalTime

    If Option1.Value = True Then
        Start = Timer

        'Put the code you wish to time
        'here!

        'End of Code time test
        Finish = Timer
    Else
        'Option 2 selected
        Start = Timer

        'Put the code you wish to time
        'here!

        'End of Code time test
        Finish = Timer

    End If

    TotalTime = Finish - Start   ' Calculate total time.

    '
    'Set up display results
    '
    If Option1.Value = True Then
        'Option 1
        lblOpt1.Caption = "Total time to execute " & _
                          Option1.Caption & ": " & _
                          TotalTime
    Else
        'Option 2
        lblOpt2.Caption = "Total time to execute " & _
                          Option2.Caption & ": " & _
                          TotalTime

    End If

End Sub
```

The Visual Basic `Timer` function is used to perform benchmarking timing. Let's use the form template to benchmark a Visual Basic DAO performance tip. When you're modifying and adding database records with DAO, using the DAO object model methods (such as `Edit`, `AddNew`, and `Update`) is a common DAO programming practice. When you use these DAO methods to modify a large number of records, performance can become an issue. A faster way to modify records when working with DAO is to replace the DAO methods with SQL statements and the DAO `Execute` method (for example, `AddNew` is replaced with a SQL `Insert` statement, the `Update` method is replaced with a SQL `Update` statement, and the `Delete` method is replaced with a SQL `Delete` statement). You can further increase the performance by placing the entire operation within a transaction. The code in Listing 25.2 demonstrates this performance tip. The benchmarking form is shown in Figure 25.2.

Listing 25.2. DAO performance-timing code.

```
Private Sub cmdTest_Click()
Dim Start, Finish, TotalTime         'Timer Variables
Dim rstPublishers As DAO.Recordset 'Holds the recordset used by Option 2
Dim strSQL As String 'Update string for Option 2

    'With this timing example we just want to measure
    'the update time. All connections and recordsets
    'will be established prior to the timers starting.

    'Open the recordset for Option 1
    If Option1.Value = True Then
        'Open the Recordset object for the update
        'Only retrieve records from the state of CA
        '
        Set rstPublishers = _
                    gdbBiblio.OpenRecordset("SELECT * FROM Publishers", _
                    dbOpenDynaset)
    Else
        strSQL = "UPDATE Publishers Set Comments = "
        strSQL = strSQL & "'Buy VB Development Unleashed'"

    End If

    'Begin the timing operation
    If Option1.Value = True Then
        Start = Timer

        'DAO Update Timing Test - Note this is POOR
        'Performance - DO NOT UPDATE Several DATABASE
        'Records this way!
        With rstPublishers
            While Not .BOF And Not .EOF
                'Update the recordset comment field
                .Edit
                rstPublishers("Comments") = "Buy VB Development Unleashed"
                .Update
```

continues

Listing 25.2. continued

```
                    'Move to the next record
                    .MoveNext
            Wend
        End With

        'End of Code time test
        Finish = Timer

        'Clean up
        rstPublishers.Close
        Set rstPublishers = Nothing
    Else
        'Option 2 selected - SQL Updates and Transactions
        Start = Timer

        'Note: The following code performs much faster!
        'When updating, adding or deleting records using DAO
        'use transactions to speed up the operation.
        'When modifying or deleting a large number of records
        'use SQL statements
        gwksTest.BeginTrans
        gdbBiblio.Execute strSQL
        gwksTest.CommitTrans
        'End of Code time test
        Finish = Timer

    End If

    TotalTime = Finish - Start   ' Calculate total time.

    '
    'Set up display results
    '
    If Option1.Value = True Then
        'Option 1
        lblOpt1.Caption = "Total time to execute " & _
                          Option1.Caption & ": " & _
                          TotalTime
    Else
        'Option 2
        lblOpt2.Caption = "Total time to execute " & _
                          Option2.Caption & ": " & _
                          TotalTime
    End If

End Sub
```

> **NOTE**
>
> The code in Listing 25.2 uses the Visual Basic Microsoft Access database that ships with Visual Basic, Biblio.mdb. The code assumes that the database is in the same directory as the benchmarking application. Make the changes as necessary for your machine.

FIGURE 25.2.

The frmTimer
*benchmarking record
updating with DAO
methods rather than
SQL.*

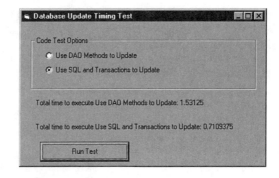

Reviewing Performance Tips and Tricks

Let's review some common Visual Basic 5.0 optimization and tuning tricks.

Using the Visual Basic Compiler to Tune and Optimize

Visual Basic 5.0 is the first version of Visual Basic to include a native compiler as well as the p-code compiler available in previous versions. P-code is compiled to pseudocode that's interpreted to machine code at runtime. Native compiled code is compiled to machine code, so no interpretation is required at runtime. Native compiled code is typically faster than p-code applications; however, p-code applications are smaller than the same native compiled program. Again, there's the paradox of tuning for speed versus size, and vice versa. The native code compiler included with Visual Basic includes advanced tuning options to further optimize your compiled application (for example, you can select options such as ignoring overflow checks with integers).

Keep in mind that native code isn't the final answer to optimizing your applications. Native code improves performance greatly with mathematical code, complex algorithms, and looping code (see Table 25.1). If your application relies on graphical displays or database access, you might not notice huge performance gains between the native compiled code and the applications generated by p-code. Table 25.1 shows the benchmarks obtained by an application compiled with p-code, native, and native with all the advanced options selected.

Table 25.1. Compiled application benchmark test (time in seconds).

Test	P-Code	Native	Native with Options
Graphics	3.84	3.84	4.01
Variant Counter	12.85	10.77	10.38
Long Counter	2.74	.44	.05
Double Counter	4.95	1.98	1.60
Splash Screen	1.32	1.27	1.26
String Copy	.28	.27	.27

25

TUNING AND OPTIMIZING YOUR APPLICATION

> **NOTE**
>
> The application used to obtain the various benchmark tests in Table 25.1 is the
> `optimize.vbp` project that ships with Visual Basic 5.0 in the `\Samples\PGuide\Optimize`
> subdirectory. The Optimizing application (see Figure 25.3) contains many good examples
> of common Visual Basic 5.0 performance and optimization tips.

FIGURE 25.3.

*The Visual Basic 5.0
Optimizing applica-
tion.*

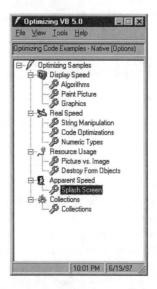

> **NOTE**
>
> The compiled versions of the Optimizing application used to generate Table 25.1 are
> slightly larger than the application generated by p-code. The sizes of each compiled
> application are as follows:
>
> - P-code: 481K
> - Native: 534K
> - Native with options: 532K

Sorting Strings With a List Box

If you need to sort some data quickly and don't have a sort routine already written, use a Visual
Basic list box control to sort the data. It makes no sense to spend time writing and optimizing
a sort routine to sort a couple of items when you can use a Visual Basic list box control to
perform the sort. Set the list box control's `Sorted` property to `True` and use the `AddItem` method

to add each item to the list box. You can then read the items from the list box in sorted order. This trick might not provide you with the fastest possible sort routine, but it's not slow and will help you meet your project deadlines.

Using the Windows API

For years, Visual Basic programmers have been taking advantage of the Windows API to improve application performance and add functionality that can't be accomplished by using Visual Basic alone. Entire books have been written about using the Windows API. You can use the API for simple speed-enhancing tricks, such as quickly finding a string in a list box, or for more complex tricks such as creating a thread from a Visual Basic application with the Windows API. The Windows API is a great way to increase your application's performance. Wrap your favorite API calls into a Visual Basic class module to make them easier to use and modify.

Using Data Controls to Conserve SQL Server User Connections

Using bound data controls to populate a combo box or fill text boxes in a form is a great way to rapidly put together fully functional data-entry forms. Sometimes, several data controls are used on a single form to retrieve data and fill combo boxes. In a Microsoft or Sybase SQL Server environment, each data control uses a database connection (referred to as a *user connection*). A connection for each data control surprises many programmers when they learn that their simple data-entry form uses five simultaneous connections, they have only a 10-user license, and seven users need to use the application. Of course, you could resort to writing code to query the database and populate the combo boxes or form; however, you lose the speed and ease of use provided by the data control.

When populating combo boxes and list boxes with static-type recordsets, use code methods so that you don't waste several user connections populating list and combo boxes. The code in Listing 25.3 shows how to use a data control to easily populate a data-bound grid or form while using only a single-connection global SQL Server connection.

Listing 25.3. Using a data control to populate a grid or form with only one global SQL Server connection.

```
Dim gTest As New RDO.rdoConnection 'Global RDO connection used by all the forms
Private Sub Form_Load()
Dim rsTest As RDO.rdoResultset 'Define a local RDO Resultset

'Set up the RDO connection parameters. These
'Will vary from one SQL Server to another.
With gTest
    .Connect = "uid=sa;pwd=;DSN=PubsDB;"
    .CursorDriver = rdUseOdbc
    .EstablishConnection rdDriverNoPrompt
End With

'Fill combo box
Set rsTest = gTest.OpenResultset("Select au_id from pubs..authors", rdOpenStatic)
```

continues

25

TUNING AND
OPTIMIZING YOUR
APPLICATION

Listing 25.3. continued

```
'Open the recordset using the global connection
Set rsTest = gTest.OpenResultset("Select * from pubs..authors", rdOpenStatic)

'Set the data control resultset
'This data control could be bound to a grid or
'other controls, however it will not use a new
'user connection. Instead it will use the global connection.
Set MSRDC1.Resultset = rsTest
```

> **NOTE**
>
> The code in Listing 25.3 uses RDO (Remote Data Objects), which is distributed only with the Enterprise Edition of Visual Basic and designed specifically for client/server databases such as Microsoft SQL Server and Oracle.

> **TIP**
>
> If the same set of static data is fetched from a remote database and is being used repeatedly throughout the application, you can boost performance by caching the recordset in a string array or other suitable data type. Subsequent access to the data is blazingly fast because the information is already in RAM and doesn't require a trip to the database to retrieve the resultset. As always, use caution when dealing with clients with low memory (8M–12M) and don't cache extremely large resultsets, as they will use up large amounts of memory.

Understanding Visual Basic Limitations

Not only is it important to know what tips and tricks can be used to help tune and optimize your code, but it's also important to know that Visual Basic has some limitations and what those limitations are before you create an application that exceeds those limitations. Some Visual Basic limitations are as follows:

- Only 254 control names can be used per form (control arrays count once).
- A line of Visual Basic code can't exceed 1,023 bytes.
- A Visual Basic form, class, or module can't load more than 65,534 lines of code.
- The code in a module can't exceed 64K.
- The maximum number of items a list box can store is 32K.

Reducing the Dots When Using Objects

I recently helped a programmer use the Microsoft Excel `WorkSheets` object to read information from a Lotus Notes database and an RDBMS (relational database management system) database into an Excel spreadsheet by using a Visual Basic application. The routine took more than five minutes to complete. I looked at the code to try to speed up the process, and the very first change I made to the code reduced the time to around 40 seconds. What was the change? I reduced the number of dots when referencing the Excel objects used in the code. For instance, Excel has a very complex object module, and often programmers write code that references several objects to get to the object they want to use. The following code illustrates this example:

```
oApplication.oWorkbooks(0).WorkSheets(0)
```

Each dot used requires multiple calls to the object and OLE services; by reducing the number of dots, you greatly reduce the number of calls. To reduce the number of dots, get a reference to the object you want to use; this technique, called *aliasing*, can be used with ActiveX Objects as well as objects created within your project.

The following example assigns the Excel `WorkSheet` object to a variable. The variable can then be used to execute the methods and properties of the worksheet object without the references to the Application or `Workbook` object, thus reducing the number of dots used:

```
Set oWorkSheet = oApplication.oWorkbooks(0).WorkSheets(0)
```

Using Method Parameters With Out-of-Process or Distributed Components

When calling out-of-process or distributed components, it's faster to pass parameters through a method call than to set several object properties and then invoke a method that uses the properties. Expensive cross-process calls are required for each property that's set, as well as for the method invoked. By using parameters with a method, the cross-process calls can be reduced to the method call. As an alternative, you can create a local object, set parameters on the local object, and then pass an object reference as a parameter to the remote object.

Increasing Perceived Speed With Splash Screens and Progress Indicators

If your application takes a long time to load, use a *splash screen* to give users something to look at during the load process. Splash screens improve the users' perception of the application's load time. If your application performs operations that take more than 5–7 seconds, display a progress indicator to aid the users' speed perception as well as indicate that the program is still functioning (users have a terrible habit of giving up and hitting Ctrl+Alt+Delete).

25

TUNING AND
OPTIMIZING YOUR
APPLICATION

Using Early Object Binding versus Late Binding

If you know the object type when using objects, use early binding. *Early binding* is when you declare the type of object that's to use the variable in your code. The following example declares a variable as an `Excel Application` object:

```
Dim oXl As Excel.Application
```

Early binding allows the compiler to check your code to make sure that the object actually supports the methods and properties you're using during compile time, as opposed to you finding out at runtime. Visual Basic lets you use early binding for objects by selecting a reference to the object through Visual Basic's main menu (choose Project | References). Early binding is also much faster than *late binding*, when you declare objects as follows:

```
Dim oXl as Object
```

Use late binding only when the type of object you'll be using is unknown at runtime.

Optimizing Display Speed

The key to optimizing display speed is to try to minimize the number of repaints and the amount of memory consumed by graphics. Some standard optimization and performance tips are as follows:

- If you don't use graphical methods, turn off the `ClipControls` property (forms and picture box control).
- For displaying images and bitmaps, use the image control instead of the picture box control. The image control uses substantially fewer resources than the picture box control.
- If you have many controls on a form, place them in a picture box control. When all the controls are set with the proper data, set the picture box control's `Visible` property to `False` while you load the controls on the form. Make the picture box visible to display the loaded form, thus reducing the number of repaints.

Optimizing Data Types

The following are useful tips when working with Visual Basic data types:

- Avoid variants.
- Use `long` integers or integers where possible.
- Never use floating-point data types (`single`, `double`, `currency`, and so on) for loop counters.

Optimizing File I/O Operations

To speed up file I/O, read file information into arrays. Also, rather than write a line at a time to a file, cache the information in a memory buffer (for example, a string variable) and then write the cache memory buffer to the file.

Optimizing Memory

Here are some useful tips to help you reduce the amount of memory used by your application:

- Avoid variants.
- Release memory used by objects (including forms) when you're done with them by setting them to Nothing.
- Unload unused forms.

Avoiding Calling Functions and Procedures in Different Modules

Visual Basic modules are loaded into memory on demand, not on application startup, which means that a module isn't loaded until a function or procedure in the module is called. During application startup, refrain from calling functions or procedures in many different modules. This slows application startup as each module is loaded into memory. Try to keep functions and procedures with similar functionality in the same module.

Selecting the Proper Component Type

Visual Basic 5.0 lets you create in-process (DLL) or out-of-process (EXE) ActiveX code components. Further complicating the type of component to create is the thread model you should select. Visual Basic 5.0 lets you mark components as thread safe and generate components that support multiple threads or single threads.

For your applications, should you create an in-process (DLL) or out-of-process (EXE)? That depends on the application or service you're providing. An in-process component is faster when it's used on the same machine, because it loads in the same address space as the application using the component. With DLLs, costly cross-process calls are avoided. In a distributed environment, however, out-of-process components deserve a second look because they provide asynchronous callback capabilities. By using asynchronous callbacks, a client can invoke a component method without *blocking* (that is, waiting for the component to finish). When the component completes the method, the client is notified. The Internet has been *the* hot technology area of the past year; take a closer look at creating components for Web-based applications.

Optimizing Web-Based Components

You can use Microsoft's Web browser, Internet Explorer, to download ActiveX components and use them on a client machine. When creating ActiveX components to execute in a browser, create in-process components (DLLs) for the best performance. ActiveX components can also be used on the Web server side by Microsoft's Internet Information Server (IIS) and the Active Server Page framework. When creating Web-based server ActiveX components, create the component as an in-process component (that is, an ActiveX DLL).

Generating an ActiveX DLL provides better performance than out-of-process components because an in-process component runs in the same process space as the application that uses the component (that is, Internet Information Server). As such, the application can reference the component's properties and methods without making the costly cross-process calls required in out-of-process components. Out-of-process components do have some positive features not available to in-process components that can be used in a distributed computing or client/server environment, such as asynchronous callbacks or asynchronous notification events. In a Web-based environment, stick to using ActiveX DLLs.

Multithreaded or Single-Threaded Components

You can't spawn a new thread with a Visual Basic application or component without using the Windows API from within your Visual Basic application to do so. However, multithreaded clients such as Internet Information Server can take advantage of multithreaded ActiveX components by spawning multiple threads of objects when creating objects from multithreaded components.

A *thread* is executing code; every application in a Windows environment has at least a single thread of execution. An application or component is said to be multithreaded if the application can create more than one thread of execution. Suppose that you have a financial database application and a computation that executes for a long time. If your application is multithreaded, you can start your computation by creating a thread to perform the computation and, while the computation thread is executing, begin to edit a database table by using another thread. Preemptive multitasking operating systems, such as Windows NT and Windows 95, allocate separate time slices for each thread that's to execute (that is, the computation thread and the edit table thread), giving the appearance of performing both tasks simultaneously.

When creating ActiveX components used in a Web or distributed environment, create multithread ActiveX components. Multithreaded ActiveX components are created at compile time by selecting the project option Unattended Execution. When the ActiveX DLL is compiled with the Unattended Execution checkbox selected, a DLL that supports multithreading is generated.

When creating multithreaded ActiveX components, keep in mind how Visual Basic DLLs use apartment-model threading. Remember also that ActiveX component automation uses serialization of request to prevent multiple threads from executing a new operation before previous operations have completed.

Keeping component serialization intact is important because Visual Basic ActiveX components aren't re-entrant. *Re-entrancy* is the code's capability to be executed by a thread. Before the thread completes, it yields control of the processor to another thread to process the same code. When the second thread yields processor control, the variables and stack pointer are restored to the exact state before the processor yielded control to another thread. Because Visual Basic ActiveX components aren't re-entrant, when you create ActiveX components, don't do any of the following in your component, which may cause the processor to yield to another thread before completing the current operation:

- Call DoEvents
- Raise an event handled by an object on another thread or process
- Invoke a method or property of an object in another thread or process

> **NOTE**
>
> Multithreaded applications don't always equate to a faster application. In many cases, multithreaded applications let you manage the perception that an application is executing faster by not locking up the user interface during a lengthy process. Multithreaded applications and components make more sense when developing for server-side processing. Also keep in mind that Visual Basic doesn't currently support debugging multithreaded applications.

Using the Visual Basic Code Profiler

Visual Basic ships with a code-analyzing tool called the Visual Basic Code Profiler to help you optimize and tune your applications. You can use the Code Profiler to determine how many times a code line or function has been executed. This form of profiling is called *code coverage* and is useful for finding *dead code* (code that's never executed) in your programs. By pointing out what code is executed the most, code coverage is helpful in determining which functions or lines of code you may want to re-examine and tune.

The Code Profiler also can be used for performance optimizing by timing how long each line of code or function takes to execute. Using the Code Profiler for optimizing application performance is useful in helping you determine which functions or lines of code are possible application bottlenecks, as well as what parts of your application you may need to optimize.

Installing the Visual Basic Code Profiler

The Visual Basic Code Profiler isn't part of the Visual Basic installation. You can find the profiler on the Visual Basic CD-ROM in the \Tools\Unsupprt\VBCP directory. To install the code profiler, follow these steps:

1. Copy the vbcp.dll file located on the Visual Basic 5.0 CD-ROM directory, \Tools\Unsupprt\VBCP, to a directory on your computer's hard drive (for example, the Visual Basic default directory).

2. To register the Code Profiler, use the Windows 95 or Windows NT 4.0 Explorer and the Registry utility, `RegSvr32.exe`. Start the Explorer and locate `RegSvr32.exe` on the Visual Basic CD-ROM in the `\Tools\RegUtils` directory.

3. Start another copy of Explorer. Locate the `vbcp.dll` file on you computer's hard drive. With the mouse, select `vbcp.dll`, drag the file onto `Regsrv32.exe`, and release. The Registry utility will register the Code Profiler DLL and display the successful Registry dialog box (see Figure 25.4).

FIGURE 25.4.

A successful Registry dialog box.

4. The following code is required in the Visual Basic Add-In initialization file, `VBADDIN.INI`, and is located in the Windows directory. Add the code if it doesn't exist:

```
[Add-Ins32]
VBCP.VBCPClass=0
```

5. From the Visual Basic Main Menu, select Add-Ins | Add-In Manager. The Add-In Manager dialog box appears (see Figure 25.5).

6. Check the VB Code Profiler and then click OK. The Visual Basic Code Profiler is now installed and ready to use.

FIGURE 25.5.

The Add-In Manager dialog box.

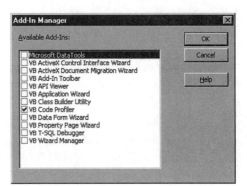

Using the Visual Basic Code Profiler

Using the Visual Basic Code Profiler is simple; before you open the project you want to profile, start the Code Profiler by selecting it from Visual Basic's Add-Ins menu. The Code Profiler dialog box appears (see Figure 25.6).

FIGURE 25.6.

The Visual Basic Code Profiler dialog box.

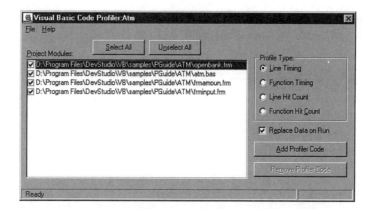

> **NOTE**
>
> The Code Profiler adds code to the project being analyzed and creates temporary files in you Visual Basic project. It's a good idea to back up your existing Visual Basic project before using the Code Profiler.

Follow these steps to profile your application:

1. In the Profile Type section, select the type of profile you want to run. The selections are as follows:

Line Timing	Amount of time required to execute each code line
Function Timing	Amount of time required to execute a function
Line Hit Count	Number of times a code line was executed during a run
Function Hit Count	Number of times a function was executed during a run

2. Mark the Replace Data on Run checkbox if you don't want to accumulate statistics from a previous test run. This cleans out the code profiler database and shows statistics for the current run.

   You should mark this checkbox if you want to select a different type of profile. Mixing statistical information from different profile runs isn't recommended because the old data may not be valid with the newly selected profile.

3. Click the Add Profiler Code button.

> **TIP**
>
> If you see an error message that says The Project or Component is dirty. Please save and try again, you need to save the current Visual Basic project and then reopen it.

This step adds lines of code to your application used by the profiler and creates temporary Visual Basic files. Listing 25.4 shows an example of code the profiler adds during this step.

Listing 25.4. Example of Visual Basic code with code profiler lines added.

```
Select Case DoFlag
       Case True
  VBCP_Update 1, "cmdStartStop_Click", 2
           cmdStartStop.Caption = "Start Demo"
  VBCP_Update 1, "cmdStartStop_Click", 3
           DoFlag = False
  VBCP_Update 1, "cmdStartStop_Click", 4
           mnuOption.Enabled = True
  VBCP_Update 1, "cmdStartStop_Click", 5
           If mnuCtlMoveDemo.Checked = True And _
              VBCP_UpdateIf(1, "cmdStartStop_Click", 6) Then
                ' Hide bouncing graphic again.
                picBall.Visible = False
  VBCP_Update 1, "cmdStartStop_Click", 7
           ElseIf mnuLineDemo.Checked = True And _
              VBCP_UpdateIf(1, "cmdStartStop_Click", 8) Then
                ' Remove lines from the form.
                Cls
```

> **NOTE**
>
> The profiler code is designated with VBCP_.

4. Run the Visual Basic project you're profiling. The Code Profiler collects statistics while you're using the application.

5. After you test all your application features, you can review the statistics collected by the Code Profiler by selecting one of the following menu options located under the Code Profiler's File menu:

   ■ *View Results.* Shows the results of the selected test profile.

   ■ *Export Results.* Exports the results to be used in other applications, such as Microsoft Excel.

   ■ *Project Statistics.* Provides statistical information on the project being profiled.

6. Select File | View Results, and the Analysis window appears (see Figure 25.7).

FIGURE 25.7.

The Visual Basic Code Profiler Analysis window.

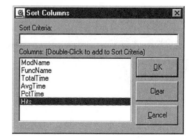

The title bar of the Analysis window reflects the test performed. For Figure 25.7, the Function Timing profile was selected. For the Function Timing profile, the Analysis window displays the module name, the name of the function called, the total time spent executing the function, the average time for each execution of the function, and the number of times the function was executed (that is, hits). If lines are being profiled instead of functions, the line number is displayed in the Analysis window as well as the line of text being profiled instead of the function name. You can perform other functions with the Analysis window, such as apply filters to the results, export the results, or sort the results, as shown in the Visual Basic Code Profiler Sort dialog box in Figure 25.8.

FIGURE 25.8.

The Visual Basic Code Profiler Sort dialog box.

The Sort dialog box lets you sort by a specific column. This feature is very useful when profiling a large project. For example, you can sort by the number of hits to quickly find the most used routines, or you could sort on the TotalTime, PctTime, or AvgTime to quickly locate possible bottlenecks.

NOTE

Setting the sort order requires double-clicking one of the columns to display another dialog box, which lets you sort the results in ascending or descending order.

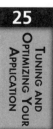

25

TUNING AND
OPTIMIZING YOUR
APPLICATION

Another feature of the Visual Basic Code Profiler is the project statistics information. Figure 25.9 shows a dialog box of project statistical information, such as the number of lines of code and functions in a project.

FIGURE 25.9.

The Visual Basic Code Profiler Statistics dialog box.

> **NOTE**
>
> When you're done profiling your project, don't forget to remove the profiling code that the Visual Basic Code Profiler adds. To remove the profiler code, click the Remove Profiler Code button shown in Figure 25.6.

Summary

In this chapter, you learned the many different factors and parameters you need to take into consideration to properly optimize and tune your Visual Basic applications. You learned some of the standard optimizing and tuning tricks, such as using long integers instead of variants whenever possible. Different tips and tricks were given to help you decide what to optimize and what not to optimize. The Visual Basic Code Profiler was discussed in detail as a tool to help you find dead code and to quickly locate functions and lines of code that require optimizing and tuning.

V
PART

Building and Distributing Your Applications

Using the Setup Wizard

by Lowell Mauer

IN THIS CHAPTER

CHAPTER 26

Installing a Windows application is always easy when the application has a setup or install program included with it. This chapter shows you how to create a setup program for your application.

After you finish developing your application and fully test it, you need to make it available to anyone who wants to use it. In the simpler days, this meant copying the finished program to a disk and giving it to users, who would then copy it onto their PCs. These days, Windows 95 and Windows NT make the process a little more difficult. You need to install more support files with your program than you might think.

To distribute your application, you'll need some type of installation program that copies your application files and any required Visual Basic files to the appropriate directories on the users' computers. Also, the installation program needs to check the version numbers of the system files that your application needs so that they're copied only if they're newer than the existing versions that might be installed on each computer.

Understanding the Setup Wizard

The Setup Wizard program helps you to create a professional-looking setup program for your application. In addition to setting up the standard install process, the Setup Wizard also includes the files and programs needed to allow users to uninstall your application if they want to. You also can modify your Setup program to let users select from a list of options to customize their installation of your application.

Visual Basic comes with the source code that's used to create the Setup program. You can use this Toolkit to add code that displays customized forms for users. Figure 26.1 shows an example of a custom form you might design for your users to see when installing Visual Basic 5 (see Figure 26.1).

FIGURE 26.1.

A sample Options form displayed during the Setup process.

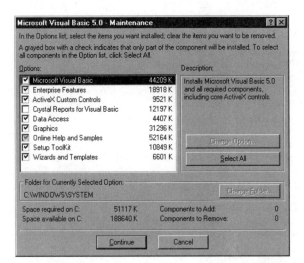

This chapter describes each step the Setup Wizard takes to create the finished application-setup program. It also takes a brief look at using the Setup Wizard to create an Internet download process. The Setup Wizard helps you create a professional installation program, taking you through several steps and prompting you for the information it needs to create the final setup program. The Setup Wizard takes these steps:

1. Creates a main Setup program.
2. Builds your application's executable file.
3. Creates an optional dependency file.
4. Compresses all files and assigns them to a disk layout.
5. Specifies the number of disks needed.
6. Copies distribution files to blank, formatted disks.
7. Notifies you when the process is completed.

Using the Setup Wizard to Create an Installation Program

When creating a production set of disks for your application, you have to follow several steps:

1. Select the project and options.
2. Choose the distribution method.
3. Specify the installation destination.
4. Add any ActiveX server components for remote automation.
5. Include any application-specific files.
6. Save the template and build the Setup program.

The Setup Wizard then compresses all the selected files. Then, depending on which installation setup you choose, either you'll be asked for disks or the wizard will simply copy the files to the specified hard drive directory.

Starting the Setup Wizard

To begin the creation process, start the Setup Wizard application from the Start menu by choosing Programs | Application Setup Wizard | Microsoft Visual Basic 5.0 (see Figure 26.2).

After the introduction form is displayed, click the Next button. You'll then be prompted to enter the path and filename for your application's project (.VBP) file (see Figure 26.3).

If you don't remember where your project is located, click the Browse button to locate your Visual Basic application project. If you want the Setup Wizard to rebuild the application, select the Rebuild the Project checkbox. If you don't select this checkbox and the executable doesn't exist in the same directory as the project, the wizard builds the executable. After you select the correct .VBP file, you need to select one of the displayed action options to choose the setup type. The default action, creating a setup program, is what you normally choose for a standard Visual Basic application.

FIGURE 26.2.

Choosing the Setup Wizard application from the Start menu.

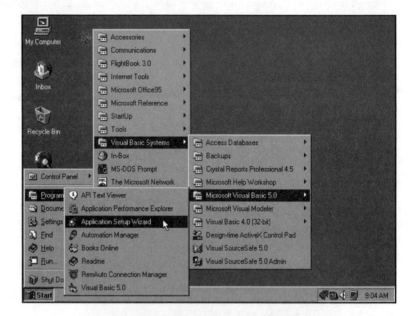

FIGURE 26.3.

Choosing your path and filename in the Setup Wizard's opening screen.

When creating ActiveX controls for use on the Internet, you select the second action option. Finally, you can choose to create a dependency file with the setup program or by itself.

NOTE

The Setup Wizard uses a *dependency file* to determine the files required by any object of an .ocx, .dll, or .exe file; an ActiveX component; or a project that can be used as a component in other projects.

If you're using components that you've created, you should run the Setup Wizard for those components to create a dependency file for each of them. Click Next to continue; Setup Wizard looks for these files and uses them to include any other files needed for these components to work. A list of components that the wizard couldn't find among the associated dependency files appears (see Figure 26.4).

FIGURE 26.4.

The list of components without an associated dependency file.

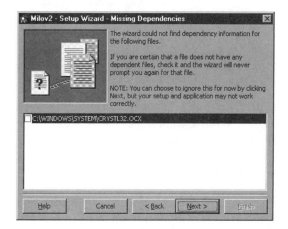

For any components listed, you should go back and create the needed dependency file before continuing the Setup Wizard process for your application. If the components listed don't have dependencies or you'll add the dependent files yourself, click Next to continue.

Choosing a Distribution Method

After you select the correct options, click Next to continue. The next step asks you how you want to distribute your application (see Figure 26.5). You can choose from the following:

■ By selecting the Floppy Disk option, you're telling the Setup Wizard that you'll be distributing the application on disk. At the end of the setup process, all the required files are copied to blank disks. Be sure to have enough blank disks ready for the copy process at the end of the wizard.

FIGURE 26.5.

*Selecting the distribu-
tion method for your
application.*

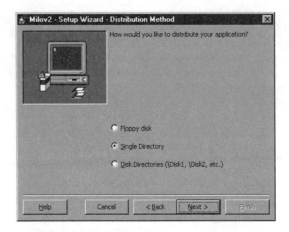

■ The Single Directory option copies all setup files for your application to a single
directory on a hard drive. This way, you can copy that directory to a network drive for
users to install your application from or to copy the files to a recordable CD-ROM for
distribution.

■ Using the Disk Directories option creates multiple subdirectories (that is, \Disk1,
\Disk2, and so on) and copies the files into the appropriate directories as though each
subdirectory represented a floppy disk. Your users can then run the setup program
directly from these directories or copy the files in each directory onto floppy disks to
create setup disks. (In this chapter, this option will be used.)

After you choose the distribution method, click Next to go on. Depending on the distribution
method you selected, one of three different dialog boxes appears. If you select the Floppy Disk
option, you see a dialog box that lets you specify the floppy drive and disk size that you'll be
using for the installation disks (see Figure 26.6).

FIGURE 26.6.

*The floppy disk
selection properties.*

If you select the Single Directory option, you see a dialog box that lets you select a hard drive and directory path into which you want to copy the installation files (see Figure 26.7).

FIGURE 26.7.

Selecting the directory path for the installation process.

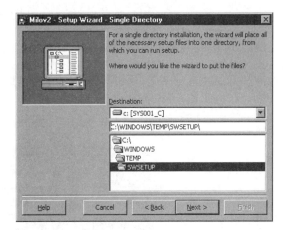

If you select the Disk Directories option, the dialog box that appears lets you specify the hard drive and directory path (see Figure 26.8). It also lets you specify the disk size to be used to calculate the space available for the disk image as it copies the installation files into the appropriate subdirectories.

FIGURE 26.8.

Specifying the disk image directory path and size.

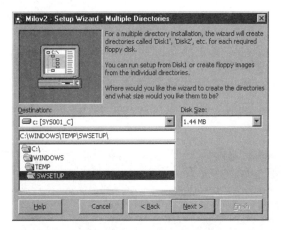

TIP

You should delete all subdirectories and files in the target directory or disks before continuing. The Setup Wizard won't do this for you.

Click Next to go to the next step in the process. If the directory path you specified doesn't exist, you'll be asked if it's okay to create it. Click Yes to create the directory path and continue. If your application uses Data Access Objects (DAO), Setup Wizard will let you select any ISAM database format(s) you might be using in your application. You can also specify the type of workspace you'll be using in the application—Jet or ODBCDirect (see Figure 26.9).

FIGURE 26.9.

Adding data access to your setup program.

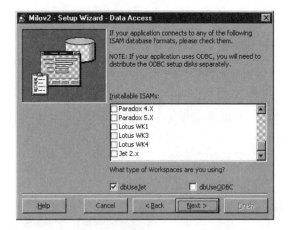

The differences between these workspaces are as follows:

- Jet (dbUseJet) includes the Jet database files with your setup.
- ODBCDirect (dbUseODBC) includes the Remote Data Objects (RDO) files with your setup.

Choose the correct options for the database you're using and click Next to continue. The next dialog box that appears (see Figure 26.10) lists any ActiveX server components that you application uses. If other ActiveX server components need to be installed with your application, you can add them here.

FIGURE 26.10.

*Working with ActiveX
server components for
your application.*

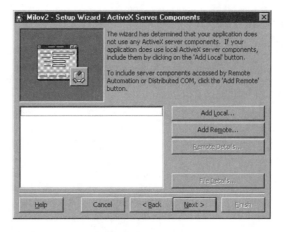

The Add Local button lets you select components from your PC's local hard drive. If your PC
is connected to a network, you'll see two more buttons—Add Remote and Remote Details—
which let you select components from the network or set the network installation information
for a component. Click Next to continue.

The Setup Wizard now lists all file dependencies it found for your application (see Figure 26.11)
and asks you to confirm the list.

FIGURE 26.11.

*The Setup Wizard,
displaying a list of all
files with dependencies.*

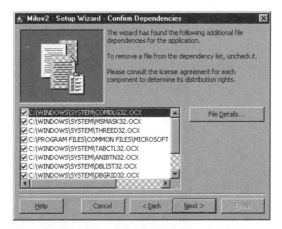

NOTE

You may want to clear the checkbox of any files that you know will already exist on the
user's machine. You must also clear the checkbox of any files for which you don't have
distribution rights. List in your release notes the files whose checkboxes you cleared so that
users can be sure that they have all necessary files.

Completing the Process

After checking the list of files, click Next to process the application setup. When the files are processed, you'll see a list of the files that the Setup Wizard will include on the setup disks (see Figure 26.12). If your application needs other files, such as a database file or .INI files, you can add them here by clicking the Add button, which displays a file selection dialog box from which to select them.

FIGURE 26.12.

*The File Summary list
of all files to be
installed.*

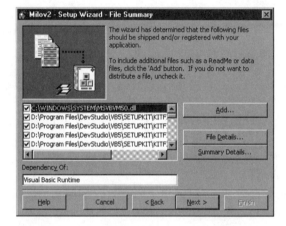

Also, for any file listed, you can check its details by clicking the File Details button, which displays the file version information and lets you specify where the file should be installed (see Figure 26.13).

FIGURE 26.13.

*The File Detail
information display.*

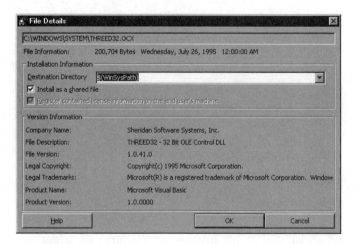

The Summary Details Button displays information about the application setup itself (see Figure 26.14).

FIGURE 26.14.

*The File Summary
information display.*

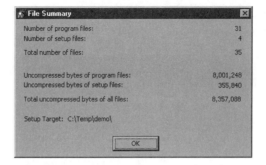

Click Next to complete the process. The final dialog box (see Figure 26.15) lets you save all the information you've entered for this setup as a template. This way, you can re-create the setup for your application by using the template instead of re-entering all the information again.

FIGURE 26.15.

*Click the button to save
the template before
completing the setup
creation.*

Click Finish to have the Setup Wizard compress the files and copy them to the specified target directories or disks. Remember, if you chose floppy disk as the distribution method, have enough blank disks ready to use.

Testing the Installation Disks

After you finish the creation process for the setup program, you should test it to ensure that all files required by your application are installed properly on the user's PC. Testing the setup program also prevents your users from getting frustrated when problems appear during the installation process.

Testing the setup program on your development PC won't result in an accurate test because all required files are already installed. Use a PC that doesn't have Visual Basic 5 or your application installed on it to perform the testing so that you can find any problems that may exist with the setup program. This will actually test your application and setup program to make sure that all the required files and setup parameters are installed properly by your setup program.

> **NOTE**
>
> Before retesting the setup program, you should run the uninstall process to remove all files that your application installed.

Making Manual Changes With the Setup Toolkit

The only time you would have to make changes to the setup project would be to add your own processing code to the program. You must create any forms to add to the installation process. Then you have to add the forms to the Setup1 project and re-create the .EXE file. The setup application actually consists of two programs—Setup and Setup1. Setup is created by Microsoft and is included with Visual Basic. This program calls Setup1, which is created by you and the Setup Wizard. Setup uses a file called SETUP.LST to know what files need to be copied onto the hard disk before installing your application. This file is also created by the Setup Wizard.

To have the setup program display a customized form, you would modify the Setup1.VBP project by creating the new form and then inserting a <FORM>.SHOW statement into the form_load routine of Setup1. You'll see a comment, as shown in the following code, that marks the exact location to add this command:

```
'This would be a good place to display an option dialog,
'allowing the user a chance to select installation options:
'samples, docs, help files, etc.
'Results of this dialog would be checked in the loop below
'
'ShowOptionsDialog (Function you could write with option
                    check boxes, etc.)
'
```

You would then have to add code later in the routine that would check to see which options were requested and then process them accordingly. You'll see another comment, as follows, that tells you where to insert this section of code:

```
' If you created an options dialog, you need to check results here to
' determine whether to copy the files in the particular section(s).
'
'If chkInstallSamples.Value = TRUE then
'    CopySection "Samples"
'End If
'
```

NOTE

After you make any modifications to the Setup1 code, remember to recompile the Setup1 application and compress it to commit these changes to the final Setup program. Also save the Setup Wizard Template to allow you to open it any time a change is needed.

For more information about customizing your setup program, see the *Visual Basic Programmer's Guide* on using the Setup toolkit.

Installing from the Internet

With Visual Basic 5, you now can create ActiveX controls as easily and quickly as you can create form-based applications. Because you can use these new ActiveX controls in an HTML Web application, the Setup Wizard can create a downloadable installation package that's used when users display the Web page that uses the ActiveX control.

When you create an installation process for an ActiveX control that is used on the Internet, four steps are involved in preparing your control for use on Web pages:

1. Package the component for Internet Component Download.
2. Digitally sign the component to be distributed.
3. Ensure that the component is safe for scripting and initialization.
4. Provide licensing of the components that require it.

Creating the Internet Component Download

On the Web, the browser is responsible for copying any files needed for a Web page to the user's hard disk if these files don't already exists there. Depending on the security settings of the user's browser, these files might not get copied at all. The Setup Wizard creates the Internet component download files needed by the browser to perform the install. The main file that's created is a cabinet (`.cab`) file, which contains all the information needed to download, install, and register the components required to run your control on an HTML page. The benefits of this architecture are as follows:

- The capability for file compression is available.
- The `.cab` file describes all files required for your `.ocx` and `.inf` files.
- Dependency files are downloaded only as necessary.
- It's easier to update when new versions of your component are created.
- The browser performs installation automatically.

The Setup Wizard takes you through the steps needed to create the files required for the Internet download. To create the installation files for your ActiveX component, start the Setup Wizard (see the earlier section "Using the Setup Wizard to Create an Installation Program"). In the Select Project and Options dialog box (refer to Figure 26.3), enter the location of your component's Visual Basic project and then select Create Internet Download Setup instead of the default Create a Setup Program option. Click Next to open the Internet Distribution Location dialog box.

CAUTION

This setup option should be used only to create the install files for an Internet Web page. If you're creating a setup program to distribute your control to developers for use at design time, be sure to select the Create a Setup Program option.

The Internet Distribution Location dialog box (see Figure 26.16) lets you specify where to put the `.cab`, `.htm`, and support files that the Setup Wizard creates. The `.cab` file is the software installation file, with the same format that Microsoft uses for the Windows 95 installation CD-ROM. Placing all your `.cab` files in one directory simplifies the administration and tracking of components that will be installed.

FIGURE 26.16.

Specifying the location for the installation files.

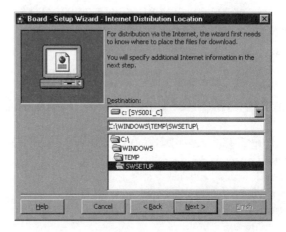

Select the drive and directory to which you want Setup Wizard to copy the files and then click Next to continue.

The Internet Package dialog box (see Figure 26.17) lets you specify the source for the common files that your component needs, if any. You can choose from the Microsoft Web site or your own server. It's recommended that you use the Microsoft Web site whenever possible to ensure that your users get the latest versions of Microsoft-supplied DLLs, and that customized versions of files are sent.

FIGURE 26.17.

Selecting the location for common files.

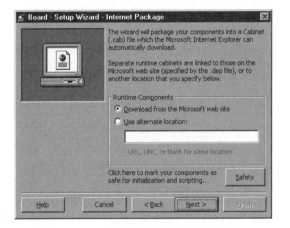

To mark your component as safe for initialization and scripting, click the Safety button to display the Safety dialog box (see Figure 26.18). Unless you design your component so that it's safe to interact with scripts and data passed to it during initialization, a malicious script or data can have harmful results on a user's computer. By default, Internet Explorer displays a warning and doesn't download a component that hasn't been marked as safe for scripting and initializing.

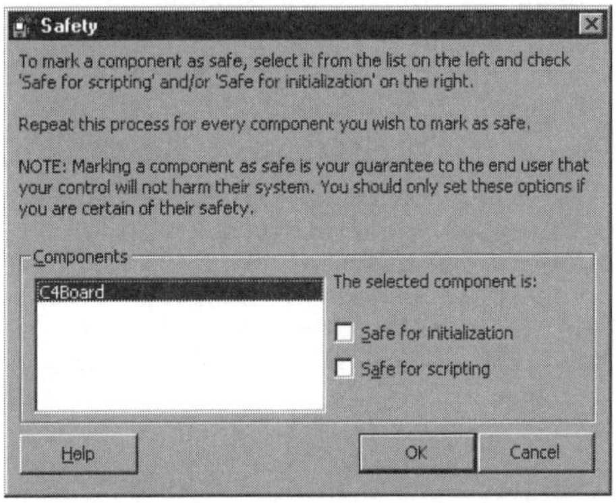

FIGURE 26.18.

Selecting the components that can be marked as safe for initialization or scripting.

NOTE

A component is said to be safe for scripting when it can't be scripted to harm the user's computer in any way. At the same time, a component is safe for initializing when its properties can't be passed data that could harm the user's computer in some way.

Click OK to return to the previous dialog box and then click Next to continue the creation process. The rest of the Setup program creation is the same as the standard setup process described earlier in this chapter. When it's finished, the wizard will have created five separate files, as shown in Table 26.1.

Table 26.1. The file types created by the Setup Wizard for an Internet download.

Extension	Description
.cab	The Windows setup or cabinet file that contains .ocx, .inf, and other dependent files
.htm	The HTML file that illustrates how to insert the ActiveX control into an HTML page with the CODEBASE attribute for automatic downloading and the license file definition
.ddf	The project file used for creating the .cab files
.inf	The Setup disk information file that includes information on how the control should be installed
.ocx	The ActiveX control component

The .htm file created in this example illustrates what the Setup Wizard produces. ActiveX controls are placed in an HTML page by using the Object tag. The actual download is controlled by the CODEBASE attribute:

```
<HTML>
<!--    If any of the controls on this page require licensing, you must
    create a license package file.  Run LPK_TOOL.EXE to create the
    required LPK file.  LPK_TOOL.EXE can be found on the ActiveX SDK,
    http://www.microsoft.com/intdev/sdk/sdk.htm.  If you have the Visual
    Basic 5.0 CD, it can also be found in the \Tools\LPK_TOOL directory.
    The following is an example of the Object tag:
<OBJECT CLASSID="clsid:5220cb21-c88d-11cf-b347-00aa00a28331">
    <PARAM NAME="LPKPath" VALUE="LPKfilename.LPK">
</OBJECT>
-->
<OBJECT ID="WebCal" WIDTH=210 HEIGHT=217
CLASSID="CLSID:271867CB-B8D5-11D0-9021-444553540000"
CODEBASE="webcal.CAB#version=1,0,0,0">
</OBJECT>
</HTML>
```

Examine the second <OBJECT> tag in this code. This tag contains the reference to the new control, WebCal. Each different ActiveX control you create will have a different CLSID, which is used to create an instance of the control on the HTML page. By using this information, the browser checks the Registry to see whether the control exists. When it doesn't exist, or when the version of the control is lower than the version specified in the CODEBASE attribute of the <OBJECT> tag, the browser downloads and installs the newer version of the control specified.

Digitally Signing Your Component

Code received via the Internet lacks a warranty and licensing information that would vouch for its reliability. This causes most users to be a little cautious about downloading components when asked if they want to. A *digital signature* provides an opportunity for you to sign your component so that users know where the component came from and who to call if there's a problem.

> **NOTE**
>
> For more information about digital signing, visit the ActiveX SDK Web site at www.microsoft.com/intdev/sdk/.

Providing Licensing for Your Components

If you're going to make a living creating ActiveX controls for the Internet, you should create controls that require a license for use in an HTML page. When using Visual Basic, the runtime license is supplied automatically to the controls. But this doesn't happen with an HTML page. The license manager that comes with Visual Basic supplies the license to the control from the .lpk file.

> **NOTE**
>
> For more information about creating a license file, see Chapter 28, "Using the License Packaging Authoring Tool."

Testing the Internet Component Download

Testing your download file is more complex than testing a standard setup program, because the software installs only if it's missing from the PC you're testing the setup on, or if an older version of the component exists. When testing the setup, you should test two unique things:

- Downloading or copying the files
- Verifying the safety levels of the components

When files are listed in the Confirm Dependencies dialog box, you should test the download on three platforms it could run on—Windows 95, Windows NT 3.51, and Windows NT 4.0—to make sure that the correct versions of these files get installed.

The easiest way to check your download is to remove the software registration from the Registry. You can do this by running Regsvr32, like this:

```
regsvr32 /u mycontrol.ocx
```

Then load the HTML page that uses your component; it should cause the software to be downloaded and reinstalled.

Next, you can check the safety levels of your control by creating additional HTML pages for testing each of these four safety options:

- No initialization or scripting
- Initialization with no scripting
- Scripting with no initialization
- Scripting and initialization

When you're finished testing your download setup, your component is ready to be distributed.

Summary

What you've seen in this chapter is how to put the finishing touches on your Visual Basic application or Internet component so that users will have a professional setup program to use when installing your application on their PCs. This setup process helps you ensure that all the needed files will be installed properly. By doing so, you're making sure that users can use your application without any problems.

Giving Your Users Help

by Lowell Mauer

IN THIS CHAPTER

CHAPTER 27

Every Windows application must provide users a way of getting help when faced with questions about the application. These days, Help systems are more than just having the manual available as a file on the PC. Help systems now consist of text, sound, video, and more. This chapter can't answer the question of what the content of your Help system should be, but it will show you what's available for you to use and how to create the Help system.

If you think that adding a complete Help system to your application is as difficult as creating your application, you're very wrong. Most applications make use of the built-in Windows Help application (`WinHelp.exe`) and provide only the Help system files (`.hlp`) that WinHelp uses to display the Help information. Deciding what the content of the Help system should be is the hardest part of the process.

This chapter shows you how to build, compile, and test the Help system files that you need to add to your Visual Basic application. You'll also see the different techniques you can use to include Help in your application.

Using the Help Workshop

Every version of Visual Basic has had a Help compiler included with it. The previous Help compiler allowed you to create a Windows Help file from Rich Text Format documents. To compile these files into a finished Help file, however, you needed to create a project file that contained all the information that the compiler needed to do its job. This project file was difficult to maintain, and the testing process for the Help file was cumbersome in the days of slower PCs. To develop a Help file, you needed to have several windows open and move between them. The compiler ran in a DOS window, and you needed to have your word processor open to make changes to the text files and Notepad to modify the project file. Finally, the finished Help file was also displayed so that you could test it. You needed four windows open. Also, if you were testing the calls from your Visual Basic application, you needed another window.

With Visual Basic 5, Microsoft has addressed many of the problems and complaints of using the Help provided compiler. The Help Workshop is a Windows 95 application tool that assists you in all phases of the creation process—except, of course, word processing. The Help Workshop comes with tools and information that you'll need to create a professional-looking Help system for a Windows 95 or Windows NT 4.0-based application. It's an easy-to-use interface that assists you in creating and maintaining the Help project files. The Workshop contains three tools to help you design and test your Help system:

- *Help Workshop.* You use this program to create the files needed for your Help project. It's also used to compile, test, and view your Help file. The Help Workshop replaces the Help compiler included with previous versions of Visual Basic.

- *HotSpot Editor.* You use this program to edit graphics to make part of them "hot," allowing users to click these spots to jump to a Help topic.

■ *Dialog Box Help Editor.* Working closely with Word 95 or Word 97, this program is used to create context-sensitive Help for programs designed for Windows 95 and later.

What's New in WinHelp 4.0

With every new release of the Windows operating system, the Help subsystem has been enhanced with new features. If you've used the WinHelp system before, you already have an understanding of what's involved in creating Help files. Also, your previous Help files will still work with the new system. However, there are many more features for you to learn. When using newer Help systems, you may have noticed that the initial Help Contents dialog box has changed. Before WinHelp 4.0, the Contents box for a Help file looked like the one shown in Figure 27.1.

FIGURE 27.1.

The familiar Contents display that most Windows users have come to love.

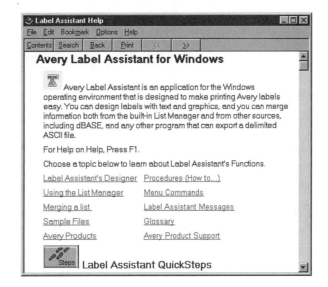

With Windows 95, the Help files have changed to show a more sophisticated look for the Contents display, called the Help Topics dialog box (see Figure 27.2). This change and many other new features and improvements have been added to the WinHelp system to enhance how the system is used. The Help Workshop lets you create Help files that take full advantage of all these new features.

The Help Topics Dialog Box

The new Help Topics dialog box is the gateway into your application's Help system. Three tabbed pages aid in finding the information needed: Contents, Index, and Find. The information displayed on these pages depends fully on how you build your Help files and the contents file. Later in this chapter, you'll see how to create the required files to make full use of the Help Topics dialog box. The following section discusses each page's unique features.

FIGURE 27.2.
*The Help Topics dialog
box gives users a new
look to the table of
contents.*

Contents Page

The Contents page displays the main Help topics as books within your Help system and jumps
to topics or macros that are displayed as pages. Each topic or book is displayed by title in categories you've set up. You can add jumps to topics in other Help files, as well as the capability
of running macros. You also can update automatically the topics of the Contents page when a
newer release of the application is installed on users' PCs.

Index Page

The old WinHelp 3.1 Search dialog box has been replaced by the new Index page. With the
Index page, users can look for topics based on keywords that you've added to your Help file
(see Figure 27.3).

Find Page

The Find page is used to search the Help file for topics that contain a word or phrase that users
specify in the top text box on the page (see Figure 27.4). The unique feature of the Find page
is that the word list required for the Find page to work can either be shipped with the application or created when users click the Find tab. This means that you don't need to build and
then ship large word-list files with your application for this feature to be available.

Other New Features

Besides the new interface for users, the WinHelp 4.0 application has many other features that
allow you to enhance the look and user interaction with the Help system. The following are
just some of these features:

- Improved text copying
- Enhanced secondary Windows support

- Working 3D buttons
- New menu options
- Additional macros
- Internet interaction
- Enhanced multimedia
- Help file testing tools

FIGURE 27.3.

Using the Index page has become easier with the new indented look.

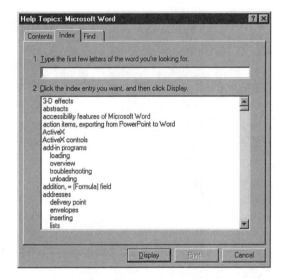

FIGURE 27.4.

The new three-step process on the Find page gives users exactly what they need.

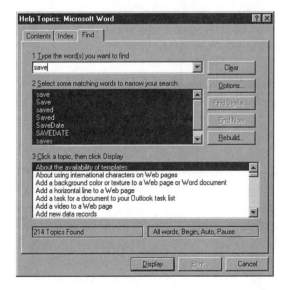

Help Workshop

The Help Workshop is a Windows-based tool that allows you to compile, test, and view your working Help files. It can be used to create the project file and is required to compile your Help file and the contents file, which is used to create the information displayed in the Contents page. The Microsoft Help Workshop has a user interface that enables an easy way of creating and compiling your Help files. When you're working with a Help file, the main display shows the project file for the Help system that you're creating (see Figure 27.5).

Figure 27.5.

An existing Help project file in the Help Workshop.

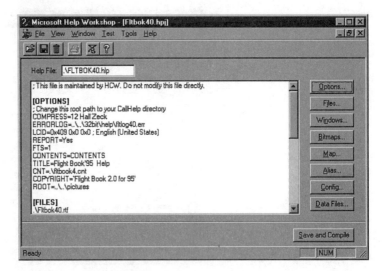

In addition to showing the project file, the buttons on the right side of the display allow you to modify any section of the project file. Each section of the project file is represented by one of the buttons listed in Table 27.1.

Table 27.1. The Help Workshop main command buttons.

Command Name	Description
Options	Displays a multitabbed dialog box that lets you modify any of the compile options for your Help system.
Files	Specifies the locations and names of all topics files used in the Help system.
Windows	Defines the size, location, and properties of all windows used by the Help system.
Bitmaps	Specifies the search path for any bitmaps used in the Help system. This option is included only to allow backward compatibility with older help file project files.

Command Name	Description
Map	Associates topic IDs with context numbers for context-sensitive help.
Alias	Allows you to link one set of topic IDs with another set of topic IDs.
Config	Defines one or more WinHelp macros that run when WinHelp opens the Help file.
Data Files	Defines the files stored in the Help file.

NOTE

You can't directly modify any of the text displayed in the main project file listing. You must select the appropriate command button to go to the respective dialog box to edit the information.

The Help Workshop assists you in creating the contents file needed to drive the Contents page. The Contents file editor (see Figure 27.6) helps you build the category headings with their related topic jumps and macros. For each line in this file, you can set the Title, Topic Id, the Help file to use if it's not the main Help file, and the window type to use when displaying the information.

FIGURE 27.6.

Using the Contents file editor makes it easy to create the Help contents file.

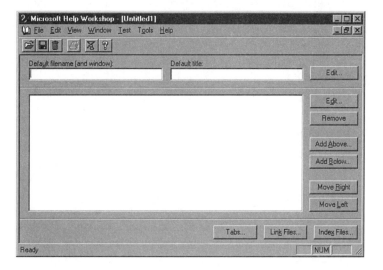

Using these tools is the best way to understand how they help you. In the following section, you'll see how to create a small topics file that will include jumps, pop-ups, and macros. You'll use the workshop to create the project file and the contents file. Then, when you're finished creating the Help system, you'll see how to use the workshop to test the completed Help files.

Building a Help System

A Help system is made up of one or more document files that you create. Some of these files will contain the text or graphics that appear in your finished Help topics. Other files will contain the information that controls how your Help windows will look and act. In the final compile process, the Help Workshop takes all these files and turns them into a finished Help system. The best part of this process is that if you don't like any part of the finished product, you can quickly change it and recompile.

By using the Help Contents page, users can select an item to view and then navigate from one topic to another, based on what they need to find out. In addition to topic jumping, application Help systems usually provide pop-up windows that give detailed information about a particular word, phrase, or picture without actually going to another Help page. Follow these steps to create your own custom Help system:

1. Create the Help topics files in an RTF file with any word processor that supports Rich Text Format.
2. Create the Project file for the application.
3. Create the contents file to display the Table of Contents.
4. Compile and test the Help files by using the Help Workshop.
5. Attach your finished Help system to your Visual Basic application when and where needed.

When finished, you need to distribute only two file types with your application: the actual Help files (.hlp) and the contents file (.cnt). Because WinHelp comes with Windows 95 and Windows NT, your users can open your Help file by double-clicking its icon or accessing it from the Help menu. If a contents file was created, the Help Topics dialog box is displayed; if not, the specified topic is displayed instead.

Help files can be as simple or as complex as you want them to be. To create the topics files, you need to know how to perform the following tasks in a word processor:

- Saving files in Rich Text Format (.rtf)
- Inserting and displaying footnotes
- Formatting text as hidden, underlined, and double-underlined
- Changing line spacing
- Inserting page breaks
- Inserting graphics into a text document

> **NOTE**
>
> All examples in this chapter were created with Microsoft Word as the word processor. If you're using WordPerfect, refer to its help documentation on how to perform these tasks.

The Help text or topics files contain topics linked together via hypertext "jump words" or special hypergraphics. Without linking, the topics in a Help file would be isolated islands of information; users couldn't move from one topic to another. They would have to return to the Table of Contents to go to another topic in the Help system. The easiest way to link topics is to create hypertext that allows users to jump between topics or display a pop-up window. These jumps serve the same purpose as cross-references in a book and consist of coded text or graphics that tell WinHelp to display another topic in the main Help window.

Building a Topics File

Topics files are nothing more than fancy word processing files, each file containing one or more topics. A completed Help file is a combination of these topics files that provides users with information they need. When designing and creating topics files, you want to decide what the flow will be from one topic to another. By looking at the Visual Basic 5 Help system, you can see how the Table of Contents and topics flow as users follow their thoughts from the first topic to the last topic for a particular question. Figure 27.7 shows the topics diagram for a subset of the Visual Basic 5 Help system.

FIGURE 27.7.

An example of how Visual Basic topics relate to each other.

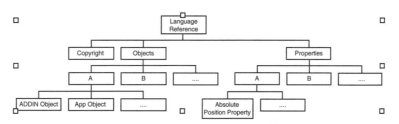

Each page in the document file separated by a hard-coded page break creates one topic in the Help system. Also, because Help is an online facility, each topic can be as long as needed. To create a Help text file, you'll work with the following formatting commands:

- Underline
- Double-underline
- Hidden text

> **TIP**
>
> It's helpful to reveal all formatting codes while you create your topics files.

A topics file contains the words, pictures, sounds, and videos that make up your Help system. To create most topics files, all you need to do is the following:

1. Enter the text for each topic.
2. Separate each topic with a page break.
3. Add footnotes to activate Help features.
4. Add any graphics or multimedia files.

> **TIP**
>
> When working with topics files, I find it easier to put the formatting command buttons on the toolbar. This way, the commands are easy to use—you don't have to look for them in the related options dialog boxes.

When entering text for a topics file, you create hypertext jumps by double-underlining the jump phrases; any pop-up phrases are formatted with single-underlining. Both have a context string formatted as hidden text that's used as the "tag" phrase or location for the jump or pop-up to go to.

> **CAUTION**
>
> When creating a jump to another topic, be careful not to have spaces between the double-underlined text and hidden text. This will prevent the jump from occurring.

Entering the Text

Open your favorite word processing program to start the text-entry process. For the examples in this chapter, small text files are used to demonstrate hyperlinks, pop-ups, and other Help system features. Figure 27.8 shows the Contents topics page for a completed Help file.

First notice the use of double-underlining in Figure 27.8. Double-underlined words or phrases will appear as green, single-underlined hypertext in your Help system. When users click these words or phrases, WinHelp automatically jumps to the page referenced by the jump tag, which is the hidden text immediately following the jump phrase.

Your demo Help file will contain three topics pages taken from this chapter: the Table of Contents page, one pop-up page, and one secondary topics page (see Figure 27.9). As the first page of your topics file, enter the text from Listing 27.1. Don't forget to save your work after entering each page.

FIGURE 27.8.

A completed Contents topics page shown in Microsoft Word.

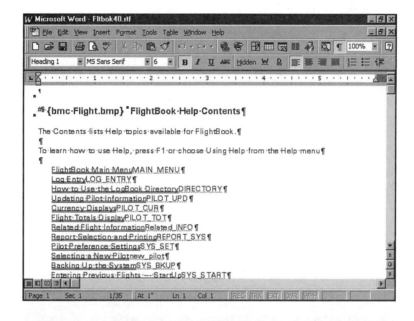

FIGURE 27.9.

The completed topics file using Listings 27.1 through 27.6 as input.

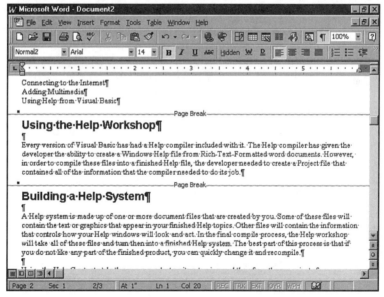

27

GIVING YOUR
USERS HELP

Listing 27.1. CH27TOC.TXT: Table of Contents text for the demo Help file.

```
Every Windows application must provide to the user a way of getting Help when faced
with questions about the application. These days Help systems are more than just
having the manual available as a file on the PC. Help systems now consist of text,
sound, video and more. While this chapter cannot answer the question of what the
content of your Help system should be, it will show you what is available for you
to use and how to create the Help system.

Using the Help Workshop
Building a Help System
Enhancing the Help System
Connecting to the Internet
Adding Multimedia
Using Help from Visual Basic
```

Now, press Ctrl+Enter to insert a page break and then enter the text shown in Listing 27.2. This will become the second page of your topics file.

Listing 27.2. CH27WSHP.TXT: Using the Help Workshop.

```
Every version of Visual Basic has had a Help compiler included with it. The Help
compiler has given the developer the ability to create a Windows Help file from
Rich-Text-Formatted word documents. However, in order to compile these files into a
finished Help file, the developer needed to create a Project file that contained
all of the information that the compiler needed to do its job.
```

Insert another page break into the file and then enter the text shown in Listing 27.3. Repeat this process for the remaining text in Listings 27.4, 27.5, and 27.6.

Listing 27.3. CH27HELP.TXT: Building a Help system.

```
A Help system is made up of one or more document files that are created by you.
Some of these files will contain the text or graphics that appear in your finished
Help topics. Other files will contain the information that controls how your Help
windows will look and act. In the final compile process, the Help Workshop will
take all of these files and turn then into a finished Help system. The best part of
this process is that if you do not like any part of the finished product, you can
quickly change it and recompile.
Using the Help Contents tab, the user can select an item to view and then from
there, navigate from one topic to another, based on what the user needs to find
out. In addition to 'topic jumping', application Help systems usually provide pop-
up windows that give detailed information about a particular word, phrase or
picture without actually going to another Help page.
```

Listing 27.4. CH27INET.TXT: Connecting to the Internet.

```
Many of the newer applications like Microsoft Office 97 use jumps in their Help
system to take the user to specific pages on the World Wide Web. When creating your
Help system, you can also provide the user with a way to locate you web site or any
```

other web site on the Internet. To make this happen, the macro ExecFile will be
used. This macro will run programs that will connect to the Internet using Internet
Explorer.

Listing 27.5. CH27NEW.TXT: What's new in WinHelp 4.0 pop-up topic.

With every new release of the Windows operating system, the Help subsystem has been
enhanced with new features. If you've used the WinHelp system before, then you
already have an understanding of what is involved in creating Help files. In
addition, your previous Help files will still work with the new system. However,
there are many more features for you to learn. When using newer Help systems, you
may have noticed that the initial Help Contents dialog box that is displayed has
been changed.

Listing 27.6. CH27TOCX.TXT: Introducing the new Topics dialog box.

The new Help Topics dialog box is the gateway into your application's Help system.
There are three tabs that aid in finding the information needed. The information
that is displayed on these tabs is fully dependent on how you build your Help topic
files and the Contents file. Later in this chapter, you will see how to create the
required files to make full use of the Help Topics dialog box.

Finally, for each topic that you have, you want to add a title in a bold, larger font size at the top
of the page.

Labeling the Topics

Now that you have some topics, you need to identify them by assigning a unique *topic ID* to
each one. This way, WinHelp knows the location of each topic in the Help system. Footnotes
are used to create these topic IDs. You'll use three symbols in the footnote area to set up the
important features of the Help system (see Table 27.2).

Table 27.2. Custom footnote symbols used in defining the Help text file.

Footnote Symbol	Description
#	Defines a topic ID for each topics page in the file
$	Sets the page title, which will appear in the Help system's Search list box
K	Defines one or more keywords that users can then search for on the Index page

In the footnote section, the # symbol is used to connect a topics page with its topic ID or jump
tag. This identifies each topic in the Help system. Each tag must be unique within the Help
system. Although the compiler can successfully compile topics that don't have jump tags, users
of the Help system won't be able to view these topics unless they contain keywords that can be
searched on.

NOTE

If a topic has no topic ID or keywords defined, users can't view it.

The $ symbol is used to define the title for each Help topic in the file. Titles usually appear at the beginning of the topic and in the Bookmark menu and Search list box, if the topic contains keywords.

The final symbol, K, is used to specify the topic keywords that may be used to search for related topics. The WinHelp system lists matching topics by their titles in the Search dialog box. This symbol is the only one of the three that allows multiple words or phrases to be listed. The following footnote example shows a keyword list for the topic titled aligning found in the Microsoft Word Help system:

```
K drawing object;graphics;tables;text
```

The custom footnote symbols must be the first items that appear on the jump page, followed by the Help topic title, if any, and then by any text that you want in the topic. To insert a footnote in Word, position the cursor at the beginning of the page and then choose Insert | Footnote from the menu to display the Footnote and Endnote dialog box (see Figure 27.10).

Figure 27.10.

Using the Footnote and Endnote dialog box makes inserting footnotes easy.

Click the Custom Mark option button and then enter one of the three symbols described in Table 27.2. When you click OK, the screen splits into two windows, one with the topics page and the other showing the footnotes (see Figure 27.11).

Set the topic IDs by adding the footnotes in Table 27.3 to each page of the topics file. The custom footnote symbol that you should use for now is #.

Table 27.3. Topic ID text for each page in the demo Help file.

Page	Footnote Text
1	Contents
2	HelpWorkshop

Page	Footnote Text
3	BuildingHelp
4	Internet
5	WhatsNew
6	TopicsDialog
7	Multimedia

FIGURE 27.11.

Footnotes added to a topic are displayed at the bottom of the Word window.

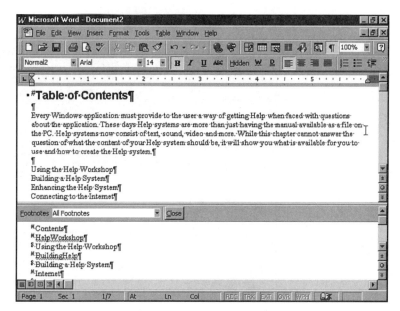

By setting these footnotes, you can now set the jump hyperlinks within each topic to allow users to jump between topics. To set a link for a topic, you need to format the word or phrases that you want as the links. On the first page of the Help topics file, place the cursor at the end of the sentence Using the Help Workshop and enter the topic ID **HelpWorkshop**. Now select the sentence Using the Help Workshop and double-underline it. Next, select the word HelpWorkshop and format it as hidden text. This will take users to the topic defined by the jump topic *Help Workshop*. You should notice that the hidden text that you entered matches the topic ID for the page to jump to.

Now, perform the same tasks for the remaining topic jumps listed on page 1, as shown in Figure 27.12. All three of these jumps should be double-underlined.

 The last thing to add to this initial demo is a picture. To keep it simple, use the flag.bmp file on the CD-ROM that comes with this book. The best way to insert a picture is by using the bitmap statement. The syntax of this statement is as follows:

```
{bmx[t] filename.ext}
```

For *x*, substitute a value from Table 27.4.

Table 27.4. Bitmap statement values.

Value	Description
c	Aligns the graphic as a text character in the same place in the paragraph where the statement occurs
L	Aligns the graphic along the left margin
R	Aligns the graphic along the right margin

FIGURE 27.12.

The topics file showing the hyperlinks and footnotes for each topic in the file.

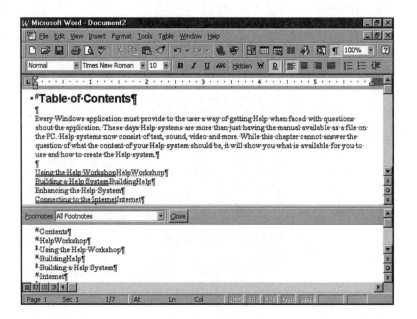

The optional [t] parameter makes the white background of the graphic transparent so that the background color of the Help topic is displayed.

Insert the name of your bitmap in place of *filename.ext*. You can also specify whether you want the graphic to be *transparent*, meaning that any white pixels in the graphic will be replaced with the background color of the topic.

Save your Help topics file in Rich Text Format and close your word processor. Congratulations—you've created your first Help topics file. You must now create the project file that will be used to compile the topics into a working Help system.

Building a Project File

The project file contains all the instructions for compiling your Help topics files into a working Help file that WinHelp can use. When you use the Help Workshop to create the project file, the minimum information you need to have is specified for you when you choose File | New from the menu. The remaining information that you can specify depends on the size and complexity of the Help file that you're creating, as well as your own creativity.

Follow these steps to build the project file:

1. Start the Help Workshop by choosing Microsoft Help Workshop and then Help Workshop from the Start Menu.
2. Choose File | New from Help Workshop's menu.
3. In the New dialog box, select Help Project and click OK.
4. The Project File Name selection dialog box appears. Enter **VBDemo** as the project name and click Save. (Don't worry about the Save as Type box; you can leave it blank.)

   The workshop screen should now display the default options for your project (see Figure 27.13).

FIGURE 27.13.

The default options for the new Help project are displayed, helping to create a project file.

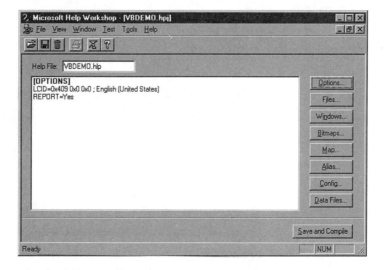

5. Specify where your topics files are located and their names. Click the Files button on the right to display the Topic Files dialog box, where you can add or remove file references from your Help project (see Figure 27.14).
6. Click the Add button to display the Open dialog box, locate the topics file you've already created, and select it. Click the Open button and then OK to add this file to the project.

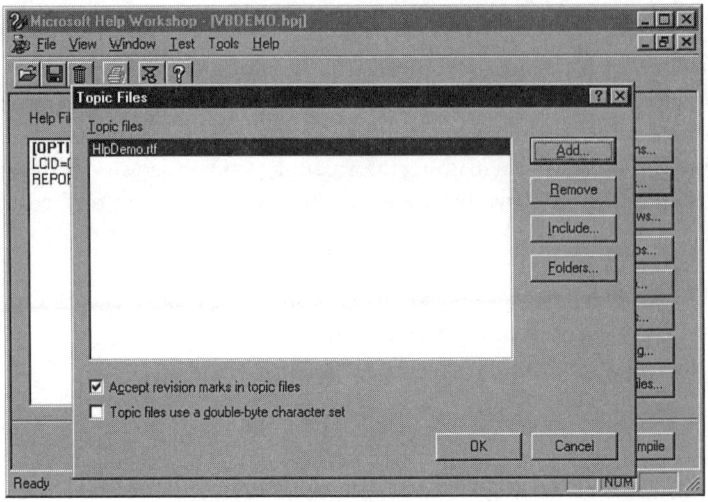

FIGURE 27.14.

Adding the topics files to your project by using the Workshop Dialog boxes.

7. To tell the project where to find the bitmap you added to the topics file, click the Bitmaps button. In the Bitmaps dialog box, locate the folder the bitmap is in and then click OK.

The project file now has enough information to compile your topics file into a working Help file (see Figure 27.15).

FIGURE 27.15.

The finished project file contains several parameter sections that were added.

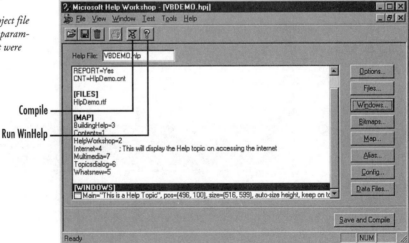

The workshop toolbar in Figure 27.15 contains two buttons that you'll be using to compile and then test your Help file. To compile your Help project, click the Compile button; the Compile to a Help File dialog box appears (see Figure 27.16). This dialog box lets you set the Help project filename to compile. Also, you can have the workshop windows minimized while the project is compiling and have WinHelp automatically display the Help file when the compile is completed.

FIGURE 27.16.

Compiling the Help project with the Help file compile dialog box.

If you don't want to watch the progress of the compile, you can have the window minimized during the compile; however, when you create the Help project for the first time, it can be useful to watch the process. Click the Compile button in the Compile a Help File dialog box to complete the process of compiling the topics files into a Help file. If you didn't select the option to have WinHelp automatically display the Help file when completed, you need to click the Run WinHelp button. This will display the View Help File dialog box (see Figure 27.17).

FIGURE 27.17.

Using the View Help File dialog allows you to test the Help file the way it would be used.

This dialog box displays the current help project file, the defined Help filename and path, and a list of any mapped topic IDs. By using this dialog, you can view your new Help file as though it were opened by a program, as though users double-clicked its file icon in Windows Explorer, or as a pop-up using a mapped topic ID to select a given topic. Select the A Double-Clicked File Icon option and click View Help to display the Table of Contents topic from the new Help file (see Figure 27.18).

FIGURE 27.18.

The compiled Table of Contents as users will see it.

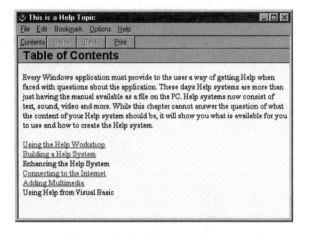

You may have noticed that the workshop fills in the names of the Help project and finished Help files for you in the appropriate boxes. When testing your new Help file, you'll find that there are no mapped topic IDs, because you haven't added any to the project yet. To add topic ID mapping, you should first close the Help file if it's still open, and then click the Map button in the workshop window to display the Map dialog box (see Figure 27.19). This dialog box lists the topic IDs that have been mapped and their related values. To add a new one to this list, click Add to display the Add dialog box.

FIGURE 27.19.

Mapped topic IDs are defined and listed in the Map dialog box.

Using numeric values to reference Help topics makes it easier to use the Help file when adding it to your Visual Basic application. The mapped numbers are used in the program calls to the WinHelp application. In the Add dialog box, you can enter only three values: the topic ID defined in the topics file, a numeric value, and an optional comment. To see how mapped topic IDs work, enter the topic ID `HelpWorkshop` and the numeric value `2`; if you want, you then can enter a comment describing this topic. When you're finished, click OK to add this topic to the mapped list. Then click OK again to return to the main workshop window. Your project file should now have a new section in it called MAP.

Recompile the Help file and then click the Run WinHelp button. You should now have the new mapped topic ID listed in the Mapped Topic IDs drop-down box (refer to figure 27.17). Select the mapped value, select A Pop-Up as the way to display the Help file, and click View Help. The topic that you selected displays as a pop-up immediately (see Figure 27.20).

FIGURE 27.20.

Displaying Help information as a pop-up.

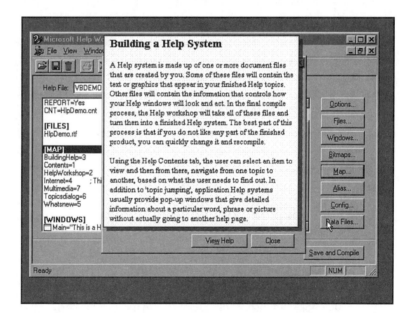

When adding mapped topic IDs, you should decide on an organized numbering scheme that lets you keep track of the topics you're using. You now have a completed Help system. It doesn't look any different than the old non-Windows 95 Help design, however, because you haven't created the new Help Topics dialog box yet. The next section shows you how and why the Help Topics dialog box is used.

Using the Help Topics Dialog Box

The easier it is for your users to find Help, the less frustrated they will be when looking for solutions and answers in your application. A complete Help system increases user satisfaction when they use the application. Users will access the Help system from several locations within your application as well as display it by double-clicking its icon in Windows Explorer. In the Help system that you've created, you can see that the Index button at the top of the Help dialog box is grayed out, because no keywords are defined in any of the topics files you created.

When the Help Topics dialog box appears, you can determine which of three default pages appear. You can also determine the information that appears on two of those pages. If you want a Contents page to appear, you must provide a contents file with the Help file you created. If you want the Index page to appear, you must define keywords in your topics. Finally, the Find page always appears, unless you specify that you don't want it displayed.

The items listed on the Contents page are defined in the contents file that you'll create by using the Help Workshop. Because the Contents page information is kept in a separate file, whatever appears on the Contents page is dynamic, meaning that you can add or remove items from the list independently of the Help system content. As your application is enhanced, you don't have to change the original Help file; you just add a second Help file to your application and include the topics in the contents file.

Creating a contents file is really easy when using the Help Workshop. As you create the contents file, the Help Workshop displays each item with a book or page icon, depending on the position of the item. This way, you can see the finished list as you create it.

Building the Contents File

In the Help Workshop, choose File | New from the menu; then select Help Contents from the new list and click OK. An empty Contents window appears in the Help Workshop (see Figure 27.21). This is where you'll create the contents file.

When the contents file is first created, you need to specify default information that WinHelp will use to locate the entries in the contents file, display the correct title at the top of the Help Topics dialog box, and display the Help information in the correct window type. To set this default information, click the Edit button located at the top-right of the window to display the Default Help Information dialog box (see Figure 27.22). In the Default Help Filename text box, enter the name of your Help file. Then, in the Default Window text box, enter the window type you want to use to display the topics in your Help file. Finally, in the Default Title text box, you can optionally enter the title you want displayed in the Help Topics dialog box. You can change any of these default settings when entering the actual items in the contents list.

FIGURE 27.21.

The contents file creation window displays the Contents list as you work.

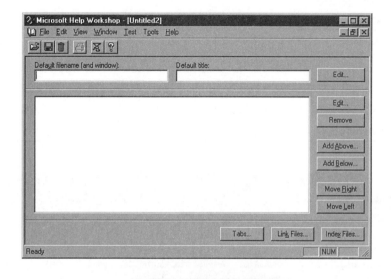

FIGURE 27.22.

The Default Help Information for the Help Topics dialog box.

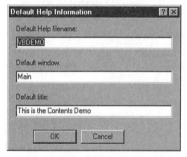

27

GIVING YOUR
USERS HELP

> **NOTE**
>
> Help window types are defined in the project file. The window type of Main is the default type generated in the project file for you.

Before going any further, save the contents file. The name that you give it doesn't have to be the same name as the Help file, as long as you set the contents file name parameter in the project file. You can add four types of entries to the contents file, each entry giving users the capability of performing a particular function (see Table 27.5).

Table 27.5. Contents file entry options.

Option	Description
Heading	Used to define a category level shown as a Book icon
Topic	Defines each main page of the Help system
Macro	Lets users launch a macro directly from the Topics dialog box
Include	Includes other contents files in the main contents file

NOTE

If a heading has no topic titles beneath it, it won't appear in the Topic dialog box.

When adding items, remember that headings are identified by book icons that can be double-clicked to display the subheadings or topics that they contain. To add the first entry to the list, you can click the Add Above or Add Below button—it doesn't matter. The Edit Contents Tab Entry dialog box appears (see Figure 27.23).

FIGURE 27.23.

Adding entries to the Contents page is done with the Edit Contents Tab Entry dialog.

This is where you can override the default settings for the contents file. For the first item, select the Heading option at the top of the form. Then enter `Giving Your Users Help` as the Title and click OK. You should see a book icon appear with the title you entered next to it. Next, add the remaining topics and headings, as listed in Table 27.6.

Table 27.6. Topics items added to the contents file.

Entry Type	Title	Topic ID
Topic	Using the Help Workshop	HelpWorkshop
Topic	Building the Help System	BuildingHelp

Entry Type	Title	Topic ID
Heading	Enhancing the Help System	(none)
Topic	Connecting to the Internet	Internet
Topic	Adding Multimedia	Multimedia

After you add these entries, the Contents dialog box should look like the one shown in Figure 27.24.

FIGURE 27.24.

The finished Contents page displayed in the Help Workshop.

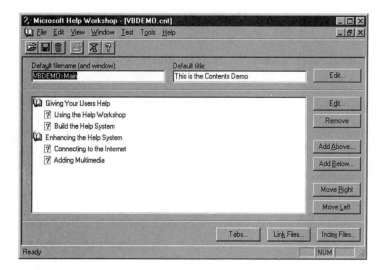

After saving the changes to the contents file, you can test it. One neat thing about the contents file is that if its name is the same as the name of the Help file, you don't have to recompile the Help file to test it. If you've named it differently, you must specify the contents filename on the File page of the Options dialog box in the Help Workshop for your project. To test the contents file, click the Run WinHelp button, select the Invoked by a Program option, and click View Help. The Help Topics dialog box appears, as shown in Figure 27.25. Try clicking the book icons and then the item icons to see what happens.

Adding Keywords to the Index Page

If you recall, the Index page appears only if you have keywords defined in your topics files. Then, by double-clicking a keyword displayed on the Index page, users can display the related topic. To add keywords to your Help topics, you add a K footnote to the topics to which you want to add keywords. For each K footnote, you can define as many keywords as you need for the topic page, each one separated by a semicolon (;). If you assign the same keyword to more than one topic, the keyword appears only once in the index. However, when users double-click that keyword, the Topics Found dialog box appears (see Figure 27.26).

FIGURE 27.25.

*The Finished Help
Topics dialog box
displayed to users.*

FIGURE 27.26.

*The Topics Found
dialog box displays
multiple topics for a
keyword.*

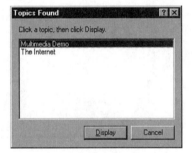

Add some keywords to the demo Help file, using the techniques and syntax described earlier in this chapter. Remember that the K footnote symbol must be uppercase, and each keyword is separated by a semicolon (;). Unlike the Contents page, you must recompile the Help file for the keywords to be included on the Help Topics dialog box. After recompiling, test your Help file again to see how the Index page works.

Because indexes can sometimes contain several levels of entries, just as the Contents page does, second-level entries are indented under their related first-level entry, listing the specific topics within that category. You can create the same effect in your Help Index by defining first- and second-level keywords. The Windows 95 Help Index is a good example of this technique (see Figure 27.27).

Creating first- and second-level keywords requires only a slight change in the way you define the keywords. To add a first-level keyword to your Help file, add a K footnote and type the keyword followed by a comma (,) and a semicolon (;), as follows:

```
K Workshop,;
```

Neither the comma nor the semicolon appears in the Index text. Next, immediately following the semicolon, type the first-level keyword again, followed by a comma, a space, the second-level keyword, and another semicolon, as follows:

```
K Workshop,; Workshop, Using the Help Workshop;
```

FIGURE 27.27.

The Windows 95 Help Index, with second-level indexes listing related keywords.

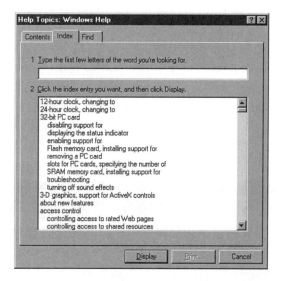

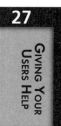

> **NOTE**
>
> To use the same first-level keyword in multiple topics, you need to specify it the same way in each topic.

Add a few first- and second-level keywords to your Help file, recompile it, and see what it looks like.

Setting Up the Find Page

The Find page allows users to perform a full-text search through every word in a Help file. For example, if users enter the word *open* on the Find page in the Windows 95 Help Topics dialog box, every topic that contains the word *open* is listed. When users click the Find tab for the first time, the Find Setup Wizard appears to help users set up the full-text search index. Users have to do this only once, unless they deleted the index file (.fts) that contains this information.

> **NOTE**
>
> The only topics included in the Find page search are the ones with Titles defined as $ footnotes.

If you want a full-text search index to be available to your users immediately, you can have it created when you create the Help file by specifying it on the FTS page of the Options dialog box. You then need to include this new file (.fts) with the contents file (.cnt) and the Help file (.hlp) when you distribute your application.

Understanding the Difference Between the Index and Find Pages

The Index page contains the keywords that you've defined in the Help file. They can be terms for beginners or for advanced users. The keywords can be synonyms for terms used in the topic or words that describe the topic. The index provides users with many ways of getting to the information. The more ways you give users, the easier it will be for them to find what they want.

The Find page lists only words that appear within the Help topics. To find a topic, users must use a word exactly as it appears in the text. By using the Find page, users can easily list every topic that contains a specific word.

> **TIP**
>
> If the name of a program element changes, you can use the Find tab to locate each occurrence of it in your Help file.

You now have a Windows 95 Help system that contains the new Help Topics dialog box and uses the full-text search capabilities of WinHelp. Next, you see how to add a few of the more advanced features to your Help system.

Enhancing the Help File

Although you can add many more features to the Help file, this section delves into only a few of the more common ones. The following are features that you can add:

Video and sound files	Training card Help
WinHelp macros	A customized Help display
Internet access	Secondary Help windows
Context-sensitive Help	Complex graphics with hotspots

You'll add several single-line topics to the Help system you've already created. These additions will be used as context-sensitive Help descriptions. You'll also change the appearance of the Help window. Finally, you'll see how to add a macro to the Help project to enhance the way the Help file can be used.

Adding Context-Sensitive Help

If you've been using Windows for any length of time, you're already familiar with the concept of context-sensitive help. Accessing context-sensitive help is as easy as selecting an object in a Windows application and pressing the F1 key. Of course, this doesn't happen automatically; the application must be designed to make use of this feature.

Besides pressing the F1 key, users have several other ways of accessing context-sensitive help in an application:

- Clicking the question-mark button on a dialog box and then clicking the object that they want help with
- Clicking a Help button in a dialog box
- Clicking a Help button in an error message box

Any of these methods uses context references that you must define in the Help project file. To create context-sensitive help, you use the mapped topic IDs in the program code to display the correct Help topic when users request it. For example, if users click the question-mark button and then click an item in a dialog box, the program sends the topic ID assigned to that item to WinHelp, which then displays the related topic.

The actual process of creating the context-sensitive Help topics is the same as any other topic in the Help file. You create new topics pages to be used by the application program. The second part of the process is to establish a set of context references so that WinHelp and your application can exchange the correct information between them. In Visual Basic applications, the *context reference* is a unique number placed in the `HelpContextID` property for a particular object. You can assign any number to a context ID, but remember that each context ID must be unique. (You already know how to relate the context IDs to the related topic IDs, using the Help Workshop's Map dialog box.)

In your topic file, enter two or three single-line topics and set the # footnote to an appropriate topic ID. Don't worry about the content of the text; it doesn't really matter at the moment. If you want, you can use a variation of the following text as a stub:

```
This is the context-sensitive help for topic 1
```

Next, by using the Help Workshop, assign each topic ID in the Help file to values 1 through 8 with the techniques you learned earlier in this chapter. Don't recompile the Help file yet. Because these context IDs are used by the Visual Basic program, you won't see any difference in your Help file now.

Using Secondary Window Formats

You can use two types of windows in your Help files: main and secondary. The main window has a menu bar and a button bar and can't be sized automatically. A Help file has only one of this type of window. The menu bar in the main window provides the Display History option, which allows users to display a list of topics that have been accessed during this session. The other option is the Bookmark menu, which allows users to mark a topic to return to later.

Although a secondary window doesn't have a menu bar, it can have a button bar and can be sized automatically. You can define up to 255 secondary windows in a Help file, with a maximum of nine displayed at any one time.

To see how all this works, define a main and a secondary window to your Help project by using the Windows button in the Help Workshop. In the Window Properties dialog box (see Figure 27.28), define new windows for your project. You also can customize the position, color, buttons, and macros that will appear in each window, as well as set the default title for the top of each window.

FIGURE 27.28.

Defining new window styles in the Window Properties dialog box.

To create a secondary window, all you need to do is name it. You can then use this name in your project, contents, and topics files to specify which window you want the topic displayed in.

In the Window Properties dialog box, click the Add button to display the Add a New Window Type dialog box. To create a main window, use Main as the new window name; otherwise, enter the name that you want to use, up to eight characters. As a starting point, select one of the three standard window types listed in the drop-down box:

- *Procedure.* This window type is normally used for displaying procedures. It's autosizing, contains three buttons on the button bar, and is positioned in the upper-right corner of the screen.

- *Reference.* This window type is normally used for displaying reference material. It's autosizing, contains three buttons on the button bar, is positioned on the left side of the screen, and takes up approximately two-thirds of the screen's width.

■ *Error message.* This window type is normally used for displaying error messages. It's autosizing, contains no buttons, and lets WinHelp determine the position (upper-right corner of the screen, unless users change the position).

These are the types used in Windows 95 Help. Think of them as templates to get you started; you can modify them as you see fit.

Select one of these types and click OK. Next, change a reference in a topic to use this new window. In the topic with the ID of Internet, change the hyperlink jump tag to

```
Internet>window2
```

where *window2* is the name of the secondary window that you just defined. Recompile the Help project and open the Help file. Navigate to the Contents Page and click Internet Jump. You'll see that rather than change the content of the main window, the Help system displays a new, secondary window (see Figure 27.29).

FIGURE 27.29.

Secondary windows allow you to give users information in separate windows.

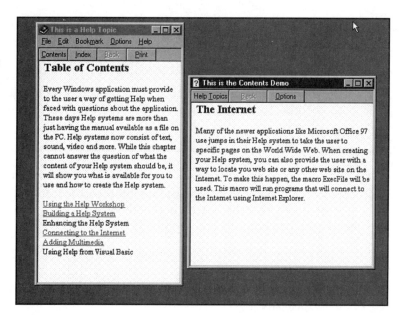

Adding Macros

Help macros allow you to add more functionality to your Help system, which then can be used to customize user interaction with your Help system. You can use more than 50 available macros. Help macros are routines built into the WinHelp program with which you can add and remove custom buttons and menus, change the function of buttons and menu items, and execute applications from within Help. In this example, you'll see how to add a macro that executes Notepad so that users can take notes about what they're reading.

The macro that you'll use is ExecFile, which launches a Windows-based application from within your custom Help system. The syntax of this macro is the following:

```
ExecProgram("CommandLine", DisplayState)
```

The "CommandLine" is the command line for the application that you want to execute. This command must appear in quotation marks. WinHelp will search for this application in the following paths:

- Current directory
- Windows directory
- The user's path
- The directory of the currently displayed Help file

The DisplayState parameter is a value that indicates how the application is to be displayed when it's executed. The values of this parameter are as follows:

0	Normal window
1	Minimized window
2	Maximized window

A second macro called CreateButton is used to add the ExecFile macro as a button in your Help system's button bar for each window where you want it displayed. The syntax of this macro is as follows:

```
CreateButton("ButtonId", "Caption", "Macro")
```

"ButtonId" is a name that WinHelp will use to identify the button. This string must be enclosed in quotation marks. This is also the value you would use in a DisableButton or DestroyButton macro to disable or remove the button.

The second parameter, "Caption", is the text that users will see on the button. To give users hotkey access, place an ampersand (&) before the correct letter in the string.

The last parameter, "Macro", is the macro that you want to execute when this button is clicked. This information must also be enclosed in quotation marks. Here is the final macro that you'll add to your Help windows:

```
CreateButton("Take_Note", "&Take Notes", "ExecFile('notepad.exe', 0)")
```

The single quotes in the ExecFile macro parameter distinguish between it and the quotes for the CreateButton and the ExecFile strings. Add this macro to the macro tab of each window that's defined in your Help project.

To complete the process, recompile the Help file and then open it. You should see a new button on the button bar (see Figure 27.30). When you click the Take Notes button, Windows Notepad should be displayed.

FIGURE 27.30.

*The demo Help system
with a button that
opens the Notepad
application.*

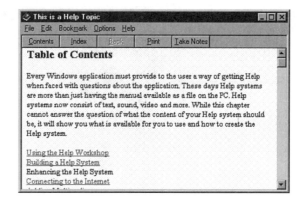

Linking to the Internet

Many of the newer applications, such as Microsoft Office 97, use jumps in their Help systems to take users to specific pages on the World Wide Web. When creating your Help system, you can also provide users with a way to locate your Web site or any other Internet Web site. To make this happen, the macro ExecFile will be used to connect to the Internet, using Internet Explorer.

The ExecFile macro works as though you were running a program from the command prompt. You specify the file or program and the arguments for the program you're running. As an example, if you wanted to use Internet Explorer to jump to the Sams Publishing home page, the jump text in the topics file would look like the following code:

```
Sams Publishing! ExecFile(start,http://www.mcp.com)
```

where everything from the exclamation point on is set as hidden text.

The program used in this example is start, which connects to the Internet and passes the Web address specified in the macro. (This program is included with Windows 95, so don't worry about whether you have it.)

Adding Multimedia

Another way to enhance your Help system is by adding video and sound clips to it. Video can be useful and fun to include in your Help system. Windows 95 uses it in its *Online User's Guide*. Several topics include animation to explain how to perform a particular function. You can include video in any topic window, including pop-ups. An embedded window is created for the multimedia file and is automatically resized to accommodate the image or controller (see Figure 27.31).

FIGURE 27.31.

Running a video in the Help system.

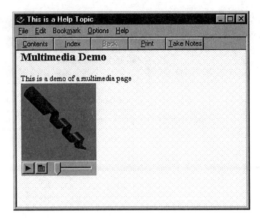

If the window isn't large enough to display the entire image, WinHelp crops the right and bottom edges. Users can then resize the image to display any part of the original image that wasn't displayed.

To add a video clip or clips to your Help file, you use the following syntax:

```
{mci [_left, _right] [[options,] filename.ext}
```

If you want to have the video clip aligned, you use the `_left` or `_right` parameters. The `options` parameter can be one of the several values listed in Table 27.7.

Table 27.7. Video display options.

Option	Description
External	Doesn't include the video file in the Help file itself
Noplaybar	Hides the playbar (use only for autoplay and repeat)
Nomenu	Hides the menu button on the playbar
Repeat	Repeats the file automatically
Play	Plays the file automatically when the MCI window is displayed

If you wanted to add a video clip to your Help system that will display the drill bit video included in the Visual Basic installation, you add the following line to your topics file:

```
{mci repeat, Drillrle.avi}
```

You also can add a video clip to a pop-up topic. Remember, though, that a pop-up disappears when users click anywhere onscreen. As a result, you must play the video clip automatically when the pop-up appears and hide the playbar. Then users won't try to click somewhere to start the video. This statement would look like the following:

```
{mci play noplaybar, drillrle.avi}
```

Accessing Help from a Visual Basic Application

Besides using the Help system independently, your users will probably need to access it from within the Visual Basic application. Visual Basic provides several methods to access the WinHelp system. To learn how to use these methods, you'll create a small Visual Basic application and then add the different methods to the program. This application includes a single form with several objects on it. On this one form, you add the different objects and program code to execute the various commands needed to display different topics from your Help file.

The Windows 95 Common Dialog Control

The Common Dialog control provides a standard set of dialog boxes for operations such as opening and saving files. One function that it provides is the capability of displaying Help by using WinHelp. To see how to use the Common Dialog control, start Visual Basic and create a new project. Add controls to the default form and set their properties as shown in Table 27.8.

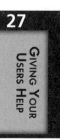

Table 27.8. Adding controls to the form.

Control	Property	Value
Command Button	Name	cmdClose
	Caption	Close
Command Button	Name	cmdHelp
	Caption	Help
Common Dialog	Name	CommonDialog
	HelpFile	*<path\filename>*

The Help Common Dialog properties can be changed by using the custom properties sheet (see Figure 27.32).

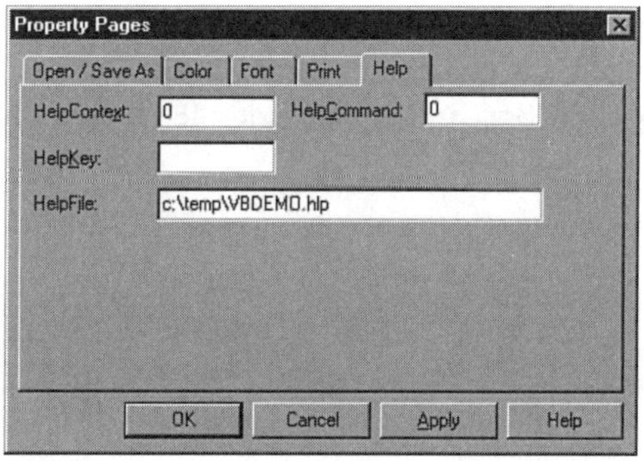

FIGURE 27.32.

The custom properties for the Help Common Dialog control.

![Property Pages dialog showing Help tab with HelpContext: 0, HelpCommand: 0, HelpKey: empty, HelpFile: c:\temp\VBDEMO.hlp]

The Common Dialog control itself isn't visible when the application is executing. Only when you access this control in your application will the control be seen. When you've added these controls, the next step is to add the code to be executed when the command buttons are clicked. Copy Listing 27.7 into the general area of the forms code window.

Listing 27.7. HLPCODE1 . TXT: Visual Basic code to access the Help system.

```
Const HelpFinder = &h00B
Private Sub cmdClose_Click()
End
End Sub

Private Sub cmdHelp_Click()
CommonDlg.HelpCommand = HelpFinder
CommonDlg.ShowHelp
End Sub
```

This code calls the Help system and displays the Help Topics dialog box. Execute your application and click the Help command button to see your Help file.

CAUTION

Applications that have used the HELP_CONTENTS and HELP_INDEX commands to display the Contents topic and keyword index of the Help file will no longer work properly. These commands are no longer recommended. Instead, you should use the HELP_FINDER command.

Visual Basic 5.0 doesn't provide a Common Dialog control constant for the HELP_FINDER command. To access the Contents topic in a Help file, declare the WinHelp command as a constant in your applications general area as follows:

```
Const HelpFinder = &h00B
```

You can use the same logic to display any topic by simply adding one line of code to the routine and changing the command. In the cmdHelp_Click routine, change the variable from Help_Finder to cdlHelpContext. Then add the following line of code to specify the topic you want to display:

```
CommandDlg.HelpContext = 3
```

NOTE

The above code line works only if you previously defined a Mapped Topic ID with the value of 3.

This code line references the mapped value that you've already defined in the Help file project. Now when you execute the program and click the Help button, the specified topic is displayed.

Help Menu Basics

Every Windows 95 application has a well-defined Help menu with several common options that most users know very well (see Figure 27.33). By using the Common Dialog control, you can add the same functionality to your application. The Help Common Dialog can perform many actions with WinHelp. The available commands are contained in the Visual Basic constants listed in Table 27.9.

Figure 27.33.

The standard windows Help Menu.

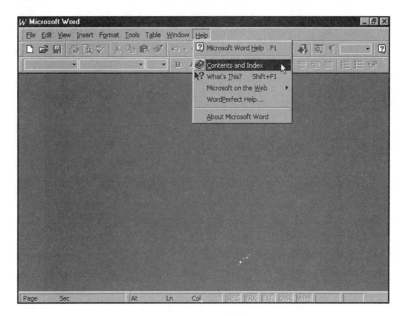

Table 27.9. Visual Basic constants for the Help Common Dialog control.

Constant	Value	Description
cdlHelpCommand	&H102&	Executes a Help macro.
cdlHelpContents	&H3&	Displays the Help Contents topic as defined by the Contents option in the project file.
cdlHelpContext	&H1&	Displays Help for a particular topic. You must also set a topic ID in the HelpContext property.
cdlHelpContextPopup	&H8&	Displays the Help topic identified by a context number in a pop-up window.

continues

Table 27.9. continued

Constant	Value	Description
cdlHelpForceFile	&H9&	Ensures that WinHelp displays the correct Help file.
cdlHelpHelpOnHelp	&H4&	Displays Help for using the Help application itself.
cdlHelpIndex	&H3&	Displays the index of the specified Help file.
cdlHelpKey	&H101&	Displays Help for specified keywords. You must also set a keyword in the HelpKey property for this to work.
cdlHelpPartialKey	&H105&	Displays the topic if only one match is found, or a list of topics. If no match is found, the Search Dialog box is displayed.
cdlHelpQuit	&H2&	Informs the Help application that the Help file is no longer being used.
cdlHelpSetContents	&H5&	Sets the contents topic that's displayed when the F1 key is pressed.
cdlHelpSetIndex	&H5&	If the Help file has more than one index, sets the topic specified in the HelpContext property as the current index for the specified Help file in the HelpFile property.

Add the menu items shown in Figure 27.34; then add the code shown in Listing 27.8 to your application. You'll see that the code accesses the different functions of the Help system simply by using the different commands available.

FIGURE 27.34.

The Demo Help menu in the Menu Editor.

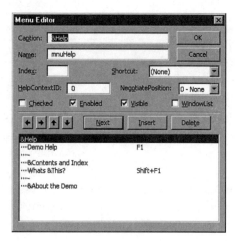

Listing 27.8. HLPCODE2.TXT: The Help Menu program code used to call the different Help functions.

```
Private Sub mnuContents_Click()
CommonDlg.HelpCommand = cdlHelpContents
CommonDlg.ShowHelp
End Sub

Private Sub mnuDemo_Click()
CommonDlg.HelpCommand = HelpFinder
CommonDlg.ShowHelp
End Sub
```

Context-Sensitive Help

After you understand how to use the Common Dialog, context-sensitive help is easy to implement. To see how it works, add a textbox to your form and name it `txtInput`. Each object that you can place on a form has two properties that allow you to set up context-sensitive help:

`HelpContextID`	When users press the F1 key, Visual Basic automatically calls Help and passes this value to display the specified Help topic.
`WhatsThisHelpID`	When users click the WhatsThis button and then clicks an object, this value is used to display the Help topic.

The WhatsThis button and the F1 key are mutually exclusive; only one can be active at one time on a form. To use this function, set `WhatsThisHelpID` to a topic value from your Help file. Then set the form's `WhatsThisButton` and `WhatsThisHelp` properties to True. The `WhatsThisHelp` property determines whether context-sensitive help uses the What's This pop-up provided by the Windows 95 Help system. This property must be used with the `WhatsThisButton` property.

> **NOTE**
>
> The `WhatsThisHelp` property must be `True` for the `WhatsThisButton` property to be `True`. For these buttons to be shown on the form, the following properties must also be set as shown:
>
> ```
> ControlBox property = True
> BorderStyle property = Fixed Single or Sizable
> MinButton and MaxButton = False
> ```
>
> or
>
> ```
> BorderStyle property = Fixed Dialog
> ```

Set these properties to `True` or set the forms border style to `Fixed Dialog`. Now when you run your application, you'll see a new button with a question mark in it at the top-right of the title bar. When you click this button, the mouse pointer changes (see Figure 27.35).

27

GIVING YOUR
USERS HELP

FIGURE 27.35.

*The main application
with the* WhatsThisHelp
property being used.

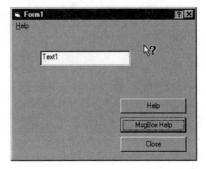

When you click an object that has WhatsThisHelpID set, the specified Help topic is displayed.

Message Box Help

Whenever a message box is displayed, it's a good idea to give users some way of displaying the Help topic associated with the message. It's really quite simple to add a Help button to a message box. The message box syntax has parameters that allow you to pass the Help file information to it:

```
MsgBox(prompt[, buttons] [, title] [, helpfile, context])
```

The *buttons* value determines which buttons and icons are displayed on the message box. Add the constant vbMsgBoxHelpButton to the other constants in the *buttons* parameter. Then you need to set the *helpfile* and *context* values. The following code displays a message box with a Help button that, when clicked, displays the Help topic that's mapped to the context ID of 4.

```
MsgBox "this is a help demo", vbCritical + vbMsgBoxHelpButton, _
"Demo", "c:\temp\usdemo.hlp", 4
```

Add a new command button to your form and place this code in its click-event routine. Run your application and click the command button you just added. The displayed message box will have a Help button on it (see Figure 27.36). Clicking this Help button displays the topic specified by the context ID.

FIGURE 27.36.

*A message box with
Help button included.*

Summary

In this chapter, you learned how to use the Help Workshop to create a Help system that will complement your Visual Basic application. Also, you've seen how to add several of the available features to your Help system to enhance the overall look and feel of it. You also learned how to access the Internet and add multimedia to your Help system. Finally, you explored how to connect the Help file to your Visual Basic applications by using properties and methods of several different controls and features included with Visual Basic 5.0.

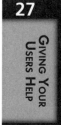

Using the License Package Authoring Tool

by Lowell Mauer

IN THIS CHAPTER

Whenever you spend large amounts of time and effort creating an application, you worry about people using it without paying for that privilege. This chapter discusses how to protect your hard work by adding a license or key to your application that must be present for the program to work.

Having your application or control code check for a licensing key is the best way to prevent illegal use. Licensing itself is a very sensitive issue. Without licensing, anybody can take a control that you've created, include it in a new control he's creating with a few minor changes, and then sell it as his own. Of course, this isn't good. Therefore, to protect your investment, you want to use Visual Basic 5.0's licensing capabilities.

In a Web application, any HTML page with licensed controls on it requires a single associated license package file that stores the runtime licenses for all controls on the page. The HTML page should point to a license package by using a relative URL. An *URL (Uniform Resource Locator)* identifies the full path of a document, graphic, or other file on the Internet.

As with almost every process on a PC, a tool is available to help the developer of ActiveX controls create the licensing package required for an Internet application. The License Package Authoring Tool comes with the Visual Basic 5.0 Control Creation Edition as well as the Professional and Enterprise Editions of Visual Basic 5.0. This tool is a very simple program that gathers information about the license requirements of the controls you select from a list and creates a package file that the client browser will use to verify the usage of your control in the Web application.

You can create the .1pk file and the associated HTML element tag that refers to it by using the License Package Authoring Tool. You can find this tool in the Tools directory of your Visual Basic CD-ROM.

Understanding How Licensing Works

When developers purchase your control component and run your setup program, the license key for your control is added to the Registry on their PCs. Then, whenever they put an instance of your control on a form, Visual Basic (or any other developer's tool) tells the control to create itself by using the Registry key. If developers have a copy of your control component but didn't install it from an original set of setup disks, the Registry key won't exist on that PC. When they try to use the control, they get an error because the control can't create instances of itself without the key.

> **NOTE**
>
> Simply copying your .ocx file to another computer and registering it doesn't transfer the license key, so the controls can't be used.

Adding a License

Adding licensing support to your application or control is quite easy. When creating your control, add licensing support by selecting Project | <MyProject> Properties from the menu to open the Project Properties dialog box. On the General page (see Figure 28.1), mark the Require License Key checkbox to enable licensing for this project and click OK to close the dialog box.

FIGURE 28.1.

Notifying your application or control that you want licensing to be included with the compiled file.

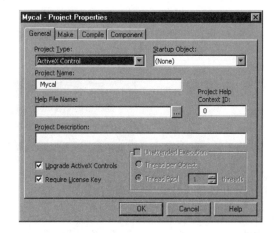

Now when you create the .ocx file for your control, Visual Basic creates a .vbl file containing the Registry key for licensing your control component. Finally, when you use the Setup Wizard to create the setup program for your .ocx, the .vbl file is included automatically in the setup procedure.

> **NOTE**
>
> For more information about using the Setup Wizard, see Chapter 26, "Using the Setup Wizard."

Distributing the Controls

When developers compile programs that use any of your controls, the license key for each component is compiled into that compiled program. When they create a setup program for that application, your .ocx is included. Users can then purchase the compiled program and run setup. Your control is installed with the rest of the files for that application, but your license key isn't added to the Registry.

Each time users run the program, the Visual Basic runtime DLL asks your control to create a runtime instance of itself, and passes it the key that was compiled into the program. Your control doesn't have to check the Registry for the key because Visual Basic passed it the key. This way, users can run a compiled application without having to have the license key in the Registry for every licensed control that the application uses.

If users of this application have development tools on their PCs, they might notice that your control is installed on the PC and that they can add your .ocx file to a new project. However, the first time they try to put an instance of your control on a form, Visual Basic tells the control to create itself by using the Registry key. The key doesn't exist in the Registry, so the control can't be used in the development environment and users will get an error message (see Figure 28.2).

FIGURE 28.2.

Visual Basic informs users when it can't load a control because of a licensing issue.

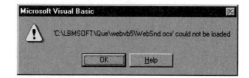

Licensing and the Internet

You can use licensed controls in any Internet application, with the client browsers that support control licensing. The control component and the license key must both be available to be downloaded from the application's Web server to the PC of the user accessing the application's Web page.

The downloaded license key isn't added to the Registry. Instead, the browser asks the control to create a runtime instance of itself and passes it the downloaded license key. The owner of the Web server that uses your control must have purchased and installed your control, just as a developer would, to supply the control and the license to anyone who accesses the Web application from his server. If the license isn't available from the server, the control creation will fail, and the browser will receive a standard control-creation error. Whether the browser passes this message to the person accessing the Web page or simply ignores it depends on who developed the browser.

When a component is used on an HTML page, the browser is considered the container for the control. The development environment can be any of the new Web programming tools available (that is, Microsoft FrontPage or Microsoft Visual InterDev) or any text-editing program, such as Notepad. Therefore, the method for arranging the component's runtime licensing must be different from the method used in an environment such as Visual Basic.

When using Visual Basic as the development environment, you buy a design-time license for controls you want to include in your application or for new controls. When you design an interface, Visual Basic uses the license to embed a free runtime license for the control with the design (for example, the form or User Control), allowing anyone to use the compiled application without paying separately for the control. However, when an HTML page is used for development, the complete code contents of the page (the HTML and other scripting) are available as readable text to anyone who wants to view them. Including runtime licensing information there would make your control available to anyone. To avoid this, the runtime license information for components reached through an HTML page should be included in a separate file that's stored on the Web server but not copied to the user's PC.

An Internet browser that supports licensing usually requires an HTML page with licensed components to include a reference to an associated license package that stores the runtime licensing information for all components an HTML page uses. Before a component that requires licensing information can be created through an HTML page, the Internet Explorer Licensing Manager must be invoked and directed at the .lpk file to verify licensing. The following code fragment shows how to include the .lpk file in an HTML page:

```
<OBJECT
CLASSID="clsid:5220cb21-c88d-11cf-b347-00aa00a28331">
<PARAM NAME="LPKPath" VALUE="MyCompnt.LPK">
</OBJECT>
```

Here, the <OBJECT> tag contains the CLASSID of the created .lpk file and two parameters. The first parameter, NAME, is the path the .lpk file is in on the Web server. The second parameter, VALUE, is the actual name of the .lpk file. At runtime, the browser extracts the necessary runtime licenses from the license package to create the licensed controls embedded in the HTML page.

28

USING THE LICENSE PACKAGE AUTHORING TOOL

TIP

When creating a reference to your license package, be sure to make the URL reference relative to the HTML page rather than fully qualified. Without their own copies of the .lpk file, users can't copy an HTML page with a relative URL and expect the licensing information to be available.

Someone might still be able to find and copy the .lpk file. To dissuade possible problems, you can include a legal copyright statement, which is stored in plain-text at the top of the .lpk file.

NOTE

A license package file exists to provide information for all the components that require runtime licenses for an entire HTML page. For this reason, you can't create an .lpk file at the Visual Basic project level. It can be created only after compilation of the project is completed.

The glue that ties all this together is the browsers that support the License Manager. The License Manager is what supplies the license information to the control from the .lpk file.

Creating the License Package for a Web Component

You use the License Package Authoring Tool to create the appropriate .lpk files required for your Web pages. To run this tool, locate it in the Tools directory on the Visual Basic CD-ROM and start the program. This tool presents a list of all installed controls that you can embed in the .lpk file (see Figure 28.3).

FIGURE 28.3.

*The License Package
Authoring Tool displays
only one dialog box.*

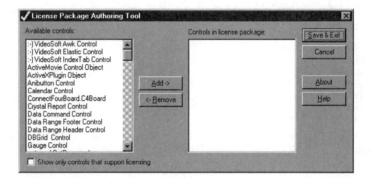

To list only those controls that support licensing, click the Show Only Controls That Support Licensing checkbox at the bottom of the dialog box. Select the controls to include in the Web page being created and click the Add button to move the selected controls into the list of controls that will be included in the license package. When you click the Save & Exit button to finish the process, the tool prompts you for the name and location of the .lpk file you're creating.

Following is an example of a created .lpk file:

```
LPK License Package
/////////////////////////////////////////////////////////////////////////////
//   WARNING:  The information in this file is protected by copyright law    //
//   and international treaty provisions. Unauthorized reproduction or        //
//   distribution of this file, or any portion of it, may result in severe   //
//   criminal and civil penalties, and will be prosecuted to the maximum     //
//   extent possible under the law.  Further, you may not reverse engineer,  //
//   decompile, or disassemble the file.                                     //
/////////////////////////////////////////////////////////////////////////////
{3d25aba1-caec-11cf-b34a-00aa00a28331}
wV/QuqbM0BGGQIURFU1QAAA=
AQAAAA=
5WpJvE6bzhGm1QAAwL6TlQwAAAA
0ADEAMAAzADIAMgAxADgAOAAwADMAMwA=
```

As you can see, this file contains a clear text warning cautioning users about copyright violations, the CLASSID of the .lpk file, and the actual key information for each control included in this package.

> **NOTE**
>
> The License Package Authoring Tool uses the License Manager components. You must make sure that the License Manager is installed on your system and registered before you use this tool.

The basics of the License Manager are as follows:

- Each HTML page that uses a licensed control requires a license file (.lpk).
- Only the first encountered .lpk file is used on any HTML page.
- The .lpk file must contain runtime licenses for all the licensed controls on the HTML page.
- The .lpk file must be on the same server as the HTML page.
- The .lpk file contains a plain-text copyright notice to warn against copying of .lpk files.

Summary

This chapter has attempted to provide a summary explanation of licensing and how to incorporate it into your application- and control-creation processes. It has shown you how to use the tool that comes with Visual Basic to create the required license package file that users' Internet browsers will need in order to use the controls you've created when browsing a Web application that uses them.

Visual SourceSafe: A Necessity for Serious Developers

by Lowell Mauer

IN THIS CHAPTER

Back when creating programs meant single files that contained all the necessary code for an application, you could easily keep track of any changes that you made to that program file. As applications became more complex, however, the need for tracking and controlling these changes increased. *Change control*, as it was known for many years in the large or mainframe computer world, was very quickly incorporated into the development process for any large application project.

When the personal computer came on the scene, the evolution of change control or source control started all over again. In the beginning of PC programming, it was usually done by one or two programmers in a very controlled environment. As PCs become larger and faster, and the applications that run on them have become large, multiple-file projects, source control is again an integral part of the development and maintenance process.

Microsoft Visual SourceSafe Version 5 is a product that lets you control any changes to your application source code. It's an easy-to-use tool that individual developers or a large development team can use to track and maintain changes made to their complex projects.

Understanding Source Control

Understanding the concept of source control is the first step toward knowing why you need to do source control if you are or plan to be a serious Windows application developer. If you've ever done any programming, you know the problems of protecting your source code. What would you do if you realized that the changes you just saved to the file are wrong and you have to go back to an earlier version of the code? Without source control, you would need to save or back up the files to several different locations so that you could always go back to a previous copy of a file.

With a tool such as Visual SourceSafe, you no longer need to worry about making multiple copies of your files. The tool also keeps track of your program changes. Source control allows you to create components that can be compiled into many different applications. This *sharing* of components keeps you from having to deal with the question, "Which version of the component am I using here?" If you don't know which version is which, you might compile an application that doesn't work correctly. Visual SourceSafe is the tool that lets you design and program your Windows application in Visual Basic without worrying about any of these problems.

Introducing Visual SourceSafe

Visual SourceSafe is a project-oriented version-control system for individual or team development of software applications, or any other work that benefits from using source control. It stores and tracks changes to files of any type—text or binary. Visual SourceSafe supports team application development by allowing team members to share files, modify them independently, and later merge the changes back into a single copy of the file. Team members can review a file's history and recover to an earlier version of a file. Visual SourceSafe is flexible enough to support any project size and any number of users.

Unlike other version-control programs, Visual SourceSafe provides these features in a project-oriented system that keeps track of relationships among files so that developers don't have to. Version 5 is a 32-bit compatible application that comes with Visual Basic 5.0 (Enterprise Edition only) or can be purchased separately. You can use Visual SourceSafe directly with any of the Microsoft Visual development tools, including Visual Basic 5.0. The most commonly used commands are available from within the Visual Basic 5.0 environment. The rest of the Visual SourceSafe command set is always available from the Visual SourceSafe Explorer interface.

Understanding What Visual SourceSafe Can Do for You

A typical software development team can include many programmers, writers, testers, and designers, or it can be a single programmer working in the comfort of his or her own home. Any development effort also should have the following functions performed to protect the application:

- Check files in and out, keep them where they belong, and store important documents
- Record all file activity
- Make sure that files go only to those with the proper security
- Keep track of utilities and keep things running smoothly

Rather than rely on programmers to keep track of the changes they make or worry about changes made by others, you can have Visual SourceSafe take control of these changes. This way, one programmer can be prevented from changing a section of code that another programmer is already modifying.

The most important feature of Visual SourceSafe is what the name says—keeping your source files safe. Using SourceSafe with your applications is like checking books in and out of a library; the only difference is that these "books" can't get lost. The advantages of using SourceSafe are as follows:

- The ability of two or more programmers to check out files at the same time
- Sharing common code files between projects without needing separate copies
- Checking files in and out easily and adding comments to describe the changes made
- Preventing program files from accidental deletion

Visual SourceSafe is a history service that keeps the records for your application project. By knowing the history of any given program file, you can tell what the changes were, who made them, and when they were made. This way, you can choose the correct version of the program file to use with your application. Also, by using passwords on the SourceSafe user definitions, you can prevent unwanted usage of any program file that's included in the SourceSafe project.

Installing Visual SourceSafe

The first step in installing Visual SourceSafe is the *Server Setup*, the Visual SourceSafe administrator that creates the SourceSafe database to which all users have access. Also, each user might want to take a second step and do a personal setup. The Server Setup step improves performance and reduces network traffic but—more importantly—registers Visual SourceSafe for direct integration into Visual Basic 5.0 Enterprise and Professional Editions. For single developers, the setup is done by using the standalone PC as the network server.

> **NOTE**
>
> Visual SourceSafe integration into the Visual Basic environment won't work until you've done a network or client setup.

When Visual SourceSafe is installed, an empty Visual SourceSafe database is created for you. The next step is to run the Visual SourceSafe Administrator's program and add all your users to the Visual SourceSafe user list.

> **NOTE**
>
> The number of users that you can legally add to this list is based on the number of Visual SourceSafe licenses you've purchased.

Administrating the Visual SourceSafe Environment

When you're the administrator of the SourceSafe environment, you're responsible for maintaining the user list and the associated working parameters for each user. Also, you keep the database working smoothly, backing it up and fixing any problems that may occur.

The Visual SourceSafe database is where all program file master copies, file history, and project structures are stored. A project is always contained within one database, but you can have multiple projects stored in one database or multiple projects stored in multiple databases.

When you start the Visual SourceSafe Administrator, you'll see the Administrator's visual interface, which lists the users defined in the SourceSafe database (see Figure 29.1).

The user list shows every user who has access rights to the Visual SourceSafe environment. Any user who doesn't appear in this list can't access the database. By default, when you install Visual SourceSafe, this list has only two entries: Admin and Guest. These users are defined as follows:

- There can be only one Admin user. This user can't be deleted or have its user name changed. The Admin user has full access rights and has the right to undo the checkout of a file that another user has checked. Finally, Admin is the only user who can run the Visual SourceSafe Administrator and modify the user list.

- The Guest user is a default template that you can use to create other users. It's also used to provide access to the Visual SourceSafe database for occasional or first-time users. You can delete the Guest user and can also change its access rights.

FIGURE 29.1.

The Visual SourceSafe Administrator displays users defined in the database.

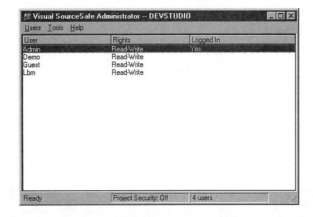

Selecting a user from the list and then choosing Tools | Options from the menu brings up the SourceSafe Options dialog box (see Figure 29.2).

FIGURE 29.2.

The SourceSafe Options dialog box for a user.

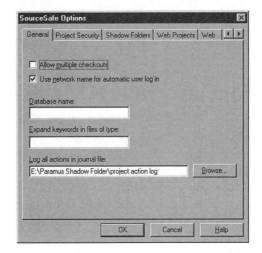

The pages in this dialog box cover several different areas of the Visual SourceSafe environment for each user:

- ■ The General page includes settings that affect all the users defined in the user list.
- ■ The Project Security page controls whether security is on or off for a project. If security is on, you can then set default access rights for the users.
- ■ The Shadow Folders page is used to set the shadow folder for a particular project. A *shadow folder* is a central folder that contains current versions of all files in a project.
- ■ The Web Projects page sets the information that applies to a single Web project.

29

VISUAL SOURCESAFE

- The Web tabbed page sets options for all Web projects at once rather than for an individual Web project.
- The File Types page sets the types of files users can store in Visual SourceSafe.

After you install Visual SourceSafe and set up the user list, it's advisable to back up your database. Then you should continue to back up the database on a regular basis. Make sure that these backups are *full* backups, not incremental or differential.

It's also recommended that you run the ANALYZE program to check your Visual SourceSafe database for corruption. If any corruption is found, the ANALYZE program can often be used to repair the problem.

> **TIP**
>
> Updates to the ANALYZE program are periodically posted to the Visual SourceSafe Web site at www.microsoft.com/ssafe. You should check this site every so often to keep this utility up-to-date.

With the administration setup completed, you can now work with Visual SourceSafe, including any projects for which you want to track the history and changes.

Understanding Project-Oriented Programming

Because you've been using a development tool such as Visual Basic 5.0, you're already familiar with the concepts of project-oriented programming, even though you may not realize it. When doing any type of program development, you're making changes to only a few of the modules in the application at a time. When the application contains many different files that are then compiled together to form it, it's easier to keep all these files together in a project. Visual SourceSafe gives you the tools to get the files you need from the project, make the changes needed, and then return the files to Visual SourceSafe for safekeeping.

Using Projects in Visual SourceSafe

Because Visual SourceSafe is a project-oriented tool, you must have a project to place the files in before you can do anything with them. When you begin working with Visual SourceSafe, then, the first thing to do is create a project for your application. The organization of projects is similar to the organization of folders on your PC. Projects contain subprojects in the same way that folders contain subfolders.

When you're designing projects, it's always a good idea to mirror the directory structure you created in your project in the project structure in Visual SourceSafe. For example, if your files are in one folder with four subfolders, you should create a project in Visual SourceSafe with four subprojects. The Visual SourceSafe Explorer provides the graphical representation of the relationships of projects and subprojects (see Figure 29.3).

FIGURE 29.3.

The Visual SourceSafe Explorer interface shows you the control project directory layout that should match the application's directory structure on the hard drive.

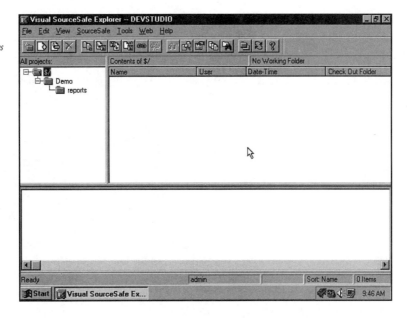

The Visual SourceSafe Explorer is the main user interface; you use it to navigate your project tree, select files, and execute the commands that act on those projects and files. The files in your project are stored in the Visual SourceSafe database. You'll never work with the master copy of any program file that's stored in Visual SourceSafe except occasionally to compare another copy to it. Visual SourceSafe provides each user with a copy of the file to read or change. Each time someone checks in a file, Visual SourceSafe stores not only the changed file, but the history of the changes as well.

NOTE

Changes you store in Visual SourceSafe are never lost.

When using Visual SourceSafe, you need to have several other folders defined on your PC. You use these folders to work with your application program files. You need shadow folders and working folders.

Visual SourceSafe uses shadow folders to hold the current versions of all the files in a single project. These folders don't contain the master copy of a file or the local copy of a file. They do, however, provide a central location from which to look at the overall structure of the project you're working with. They also serve as a good place to build or compile the project from.

When you use Visual SourceSafe to control your programming projects, you can't actually work with a file within Visual SourceSafe. When you want to work on a file, you must obtain a copy of the file from Visual SourceSafe and then have a place to put it. That place is your *working*

29

VISUAL SOURCESAFE

folder. Visual SourceSafe attaches a separate working folder on your PC for every project it controls. This working folder is your personal workspace for a given project.

Your working folder is a directory on your hard disk that you use to work on files you've obtained from Visual SourceSafe. You can use an existing folder on your hard disk drive as your working folder or create a new one from within Visual SourceSafe or by using the Windows 95 Explorer.

> **NOTE**
>
> You must set a working folder *before* you start working on any files that are stored in Visual SourceSafe projects.

To retrieve a file from Visual SourceSafe, you request to check out the file from the SourceSafe project. It's then copied into your working folder for that project, thus providing you with a local copy to work with. If you haven't yet specified a working folder for the project, Visual SourceSafe prompts you to do so. After you make changes to the file, you check the file into Visual SourceSafe, which copies it from your working folder into your current project.

> **NOTE**
>
> Working folders are associated with projects, not with individual files. You can't choose a different working folder for each file in a project. However, each individual user can, and should, have a separate working folder for each project.

Visual SourceSafe has made checking out a file from its associated project very easy. Start Visual SourceSafe and log in with the user name allowed to access the project you're working with. The file list for the project appears (see Figure 29.4).

Then, from the list of files available in the project, select the files you want to use and choose SourceSafe | Check Out from the menu to have the files copied to your working folder. You're now ready to work with these files.

Another Visual SourceSafe feature is its capability to mark a file or files as *shared*, thus allowing that file to be part of two or more projects at the same time. The master copy of the file resides in the Visual SourceSafe database, but the file is accessible from all projects that share it. When someone makes a change to a shared file in any project, the change is immediately made to all projects sharing the file. Sharing files saves time and resources by avoiding duplication of effort and storage.

FIGURE 29.4.

Opening Visual SourceSafe for a specific project lists all the available files in the project and also shows whether any are already checked out by a user.

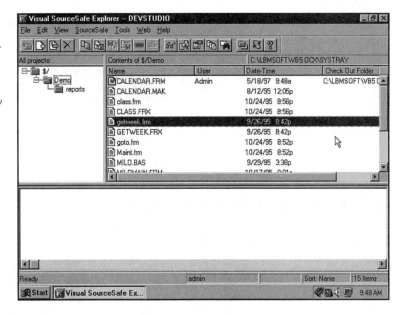

Checking the Files Back In to Visual SourceSafe

After you finish making the needed changes to a file in your working folder, you should return the file to the Visual SourceSafe project it came from. The Check In command on the SourceSafe menu is used to replace the file into the project. The Check In dialog box gives you several options when returning the file to the project (see Figure 29.5):

- Keep the file checked out to allow you to continue working on it after you check in your changes.

- Remove the copy of the file from your working folder after the check in is complete. By default, a read-only copy of the file is left in your working folder.

- Display differences between the version of the file you're checking in and the version you checked out.

- Browse folders in search of other files you've checked out that you would like to check in.

In addition to these settings, you also can enter a comment that describes the changes you've made to the file. When you're working in a team environment with shared files, you should make it a practice to list the differences and history of the file before checking it back into the SourceSafe project. This way, you can see whether anyone else worked with the file while you were working with it; if someone did, you can then check for differences. This list will let you see whether your changes will be affected by changes made by the other programmer.

FIGURE 29.5.

When checking a file into the project, you can choose between two actions.

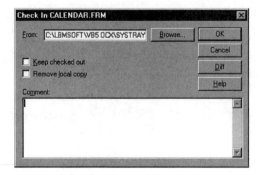

Adding Files to the SourceSafe Project

When you create a project in Visual SourceSafe, you need to add the files you want to track to the SourceSafe project. You can add these files to the project by using the Add File dialog box (see Figure 29.6) or by dragging and dropping from the Windows Explorer to the SourceSafe Explorer. If you have an entire folder that you want to put in the project, you can add it the same way you would add a single file to the project.

FIGURE 29.6.

Adding files or folders to the SourceSafe project is as easy as saving a file to your hard disk.

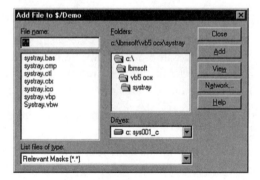

Tracking Different Versions of Your Project

If you're working with an application that will grow over time, as Microsoft Word has grown and changed from version to version, you need to use version tracking to keep the changes straight. You'll see version tracking in almost every application that runs on a PC. When an application goes from version 1 to version 2, someone must keep track of what changes were made for the new version. Also, the older version must still be kept around for users who don't upgrade to the newer version. Visual SourceSafe has three methods of tracking the different versions of files and projects you're working with:

■ *Version numbers.* These internal numbers are maintained by Visual SourceSafe. You have no control over these numbers. Every version of every file and project in Visual SourceSafe has a version number. The version number is always a whole number and always increases.

- *Labels.* You can apply to any version of a project or file. A label is a free-form string of up to 31 characters. The following are all valid labels: 1.0, 2.01b, and Field Test 3.

- *Date/time.* These strings tell when a file was last modified was checked in. Visual SourceSafe supports 12-hour format (with an a or p suffix) and 24-hour format.

The best of these methods is to allow Visual SourceSafe to control the versioning itself. Letting SourceSafe do the version numbering keeps you from forgetting to change the version label or mislabeling a file. To use this method, you do absolutely nothing, because version numbering is automatic.

Using Visual SourceSafe from Visual Basic 5.0

Now that you've seen what Visual SourceSafe is and what it can do, look at how Visual Basic works with it. When using Visual Basic 5.0 with Visual SourceSafe, you get all the features of SourceSafe, but they're fully integrated into the Visual Basic development environment. Whether you're working with an existing Visual Basic project or starting a new project, Visual SourceSafe is present to make sure that the project will be controlled, if you want it to be.

Using an Existing Visual Basic Project

When you start Visual Basic and open an existing project, the first thing that happens if Visual SourceSafe is installed on your PC is that SourceSafe recognizes that the project isn't in the SourceSafe database and asks whether you want to add the project. If you say that you want to add it, you're then prompted to log in to SourceSafe (see Figure 29.7).

FIGURE 29.7.

Logging into SourceSafe is required whenever interacting with SourceSafe.

Enter your SourceSafe user name and password (if any), and then click OK. Next, you're prompted to select the SourceSafe folder where you want to add this project (see Figure 29.8). The new project folder can be added to the root level of the database or created as a subfolder of an existing project folder.

If the folder you want to use doesn't exist, click the Create button to add the new folder to the database. When you have the folder you need, click OK to continue. Now that the project folder exists, you're shown a list of files that are in the Visual Basic project (see Figure 29.9). Select the files that you want to add to the SourceSafe project and click OK.

FIGURE 29.8.

Adding the project folder is the first step in protecting your work.

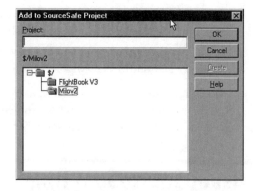

FIGURE 29.9.

Choose the files to include in the SourceSafe project.

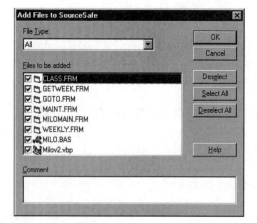

After you select the files, Visual SourceSafe finishes the process by actually adding these files to the project and copying them to the shadow folder that the administrator of SourceSafe created for you. While this is happening, a status box onscreen shows SourceSafe at work. Don't expect to be able to start programming yet. Display a form in Visual Basic, and you'll see something new in the title bar (see Figure 29.10).

The label (Read Only) means just that. You must check out a form or module file before you can make any changes to it. To work with Visual SourceSafe, choose Tools | SourceSafe from the menu to display the appropriate dialog box. If you chose to check out files, choose Check Out from the menu to get the Check Out dialog box (see Figure 29.11).

FIGURE 29.10.

The newly protected files in a project are read-only, preventing any changes from being made.

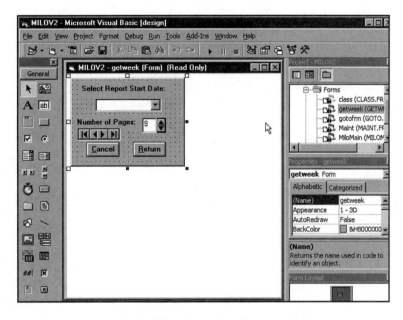

FIGURE 29.11.

Using the SourceSafe Check Out dialog box to select several files at the same time to work with.

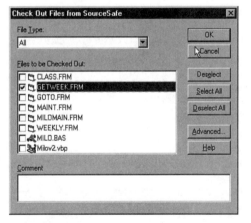

Select the files you need and click OK. If you need to check out only a single file, you can right-click the file in the project window to display a pop-up menu (see Figure 29.12) and select the Check Out option. All the other Visual SourceSafe functions are available from this menu.

29

VISUAL
SOURCESAFE

FIGURE 29.12.

*Using the SourceSafe
options from the Visual
Basic pop-up menu.*

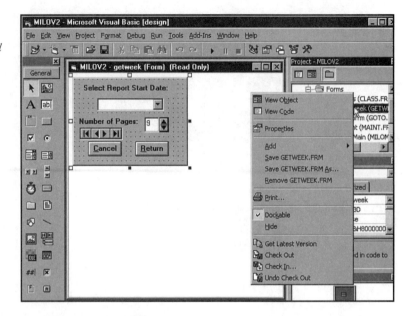

Creating New Visual Basic Projects

When you're creating a new Visual Basic application, you won't be prompted by SourceSafe until you're ready to save the project the first time. Visual SourceSafe prompts you for all required information to create the SourceSafe project from your new Visual Basic application.

If you're joining a project team that's already using SourceSafe, you'll have to create the working project on your PC. To do this, choose Tools | SourceSafe | Create Project from SourceSafe from the menu. This will display the project folders from the SourceSafe database. After you select a project folder, you're prompted for the local directory in which to create the project. When you click OK, this directory and the Visual Basic project are created on your PC.

> **NOTE**
>
> Remember, when you're finished making changes to a file, check it back in to the SourceSafe project to protect those changes.

Summary

This chapter shows you just the tip of the iceberg when it comes to source control and using Visual SourceSafe to perform these functions. By using Visual SourceSafe in a Visual Basic environment, you're making one of the best decisions of your programming career.

By having all your Windows application code protected and tracked, you can produce newer versions of your software without sacrificing the needs of users who still want to use the older versions. It also gives you an easy way to use common code files, allowing you to reuse already coded and tested routines in new applications.

I

INDEX

Symbols

V

MACMILLAN COMPUTER PUBLISHING USA

A VIACOM COMPANY

Technical ---- Support:

If you need assistance with the information in this book or with a CD/Disk accompanying the book, please access the Knowledge Base on our Web site at **http://www.superlibrary.com/general/support**. Our most Frequently Asked Questions are answered there. If you do not find the answer to your questions on our Web site, you may contact Macmillan Technical Support **(317) 581-3833** or e-mail us at **support@mcp.com**.

Visual Basic 5 Fundamentals Unleashed

Multiple authors

It's the ultimate introductory reference for all Visual Basic programmers. This must-have guide provides the most crucial entry-level topics in Visual Basic programming, including designing forms; implementing OLE; and working with arrays, data structures, and more. In no time, you will master the fundamentals of this robust language and be ready to take on the more advanced topics.

- Concentrates on topics essential for beginning developers, such as application wizard file I/O, standard controls, error handling, program flow, and more
- Offers a companion volume for users ready to tackle the more advanced features of Visual Basic—*Visual Basic 5 Development Unleashed*
- CD-ROM contains source code and author examples from the book, as well as third-party controls and two books fast-linked in electronic format

$29.99 US/$42.95 CDN
0-672-31073-2   *650 pp.*

Teach Yourself Database Programming with Visual Basic 5 in 21 Days, Second Edition

Michael Amundsen & Curtis Smith

Programmers use Visual Basic, the 32-bit programming language from Microsoft, to create Windows and Windows 95 applications. You also can use it to program applications for the Web. This book shows you how to design, develop, and deploy Visual Basic applications for the World Wide Web.

- Presented in a daily format, with each week focusing on a different area of database development
- Written by Microsoft Certified Visual Basic Professionals
- CD-ROM includes chapter examples, function libraries, Microsoft Access/Jet 2.5 compatibility layer, and the WHAT6 Help Authoring Tool

$45.00 US/$63.95 CDN   *New - Casual - Advanced*
0-672-31018-X   *1,080 pp.*

Visual Basic 5 Developer's Guide

Tony Mann

The *Visual Basic 5 Developer's Guide* takes the programmer with a basic knowledge of Visual Basic programming to a higher skill level. You learn how to exploit the new features of the latest version of Visual Basic, as well as implement Visual Basic in a network setting and with other technologies and software.

- Learn expert programming techniques and strategies to create better applications
- Contains a full section of real-world examples that you can incorporate in your own applications
- CD-ROM contains the complete source code for all the programs in the book

$49.99 US/$70.95 CDN   *Accomplished - Expert*
0-672-31048-1   *1,032 pp.*

Platinum Edition Using Visual Basic 5

Loren D. Eidahl

Platinum Edition Using Visual Basic 5's unique approach provides an unparalleled reference and tutorial by assuming basic knowledge at the start and then progressing rapidly into more challenging issues. The two hottest and least understood topics in Visual Basic today are COM programming and distributed computing. *Platinum Edition Using Visual Basic 5* covers both topics in exhaustive depth, using clear examples and concise writing. The CD-ROMs provide the finishing touches with thousands of additional pages of Visual Basic coverage, a vast array of prebuilt controls, a library of complete applications, and a comprehensive electronic index.

- Designed for developers who want in-depth coverage of core topics and new technologies and features
- Provides an unparalleled reference and tutorial by assuming basic knowledge at the start and then progressing rapidly into more challenging issues
- Covers COM programming and distributed computing in exhaustive depth, using clear examples and concise writing

$60.00 US/$84.95 CDN   *All User Levels*
0-7897-1412-4   *1,400 pp.*

Add to Your Sams Library Today with the Best Books for Programming, Operating Systems, and New Technologies

The easiest way to order is to pick up the phone and call
1-800-428-5331
between 9:00 a.m. and 5:00 p.m. EST.
For faster service please have your credit card available.

ISBN	Quantity	Description of Item	Unit Cost	Total Cost
0-672-31073-2		Visual Basic 5 Fundamentals Unleashed	$29.99	
0-672-31018-X		Teach Yourself Database Programming with Visual Basic 5	$45.00	
0-672-31048-1		Visual Basic 5 Developer's Guide	$49.99	
0-7897-1412-4		Platinum Edition Using Visual Basic 5	$60.00	
		Shipping and Handling: See information below.		
		TOTAL		

Shipping and Handling: $4.00 for the first book, and $1.75 for each additional book. Floppy disk: add $1.75 for shipping and handling. If you need to have it NOW, we can ship product to you in 24 hours for an additional charge of approximately $18.00, and you will receive your item overnight or in two days. Overseas shipping and handling adds $2.00 per book and $8.00 for up to three disks. Prices subject to change. Call for availability and pricing information on latest editions.

201 W. 103rd Street, Indianapolis, Indiana 46290

1-800-428-5331 — Orders   1-800-835-3202 — FAX   1-800-858-7674 — Customer Service

Book ISBN 0-672-31072-4

What's on the CD?

The companion CD-ROM contains the authors' source code and samples from the book and many third-party software products.

Windows 95 Installation Instructions

1. Insert the CD-ROM into your CD-ROM drive.
2. From the Windows 95 desktop, double-click the My Computer icon.
3. Double-click the icon representing your CD-ROM drive.
4. Double-click the icon titled SETUP.EXE to run the installation program.

Installation creates a program group named VB5 Development Unl, which contains icons to browse the CD-ROM.

NOTE

If Windows 95 is installed on your computer and you have the AutoPlay feature enabled, SETUP.EXE starts automatically whenever you insert the disc into your CD-ROM drive.

NOTE

This CD-ROM uses long and mixed-case filenames requiring the use of a protected-mode CD-ROM driver.